Logic and Specification

COMPUTER SCIENCE:
RESEARCH AND PRACTICE

Series Editors: Alan Brown, Carnegie Mellon University, Pittsburgh, USA

Norman Fenton, Centre for Software Reliability, City University, London, UK

The aim of this series is to provide a route for rapid publication of up-to-date industrial and academic research material in Computer Science, hence, academic studies, industrial techniques, and collaborative academic/industrial research work are all of potential interest to this series. A typical subject for a book in the series may be an analysis of a research topic, the results from analytical experiments, a discussion of an innovative industrial technique or material from an advanced tutorial or taught course. As a result, books in the series may take a number of forms – edited volumes, a write-up of a research project, a technical monograph or an advanced text book – but in all cases work will be placed in context to be of interest to as wide a computer science community as possible.

Titles in this series

Logic and Specification
Extending VDM-SL for advanced formal specification
C. Middelburg

Software Metrics
Understanding software
Edited by A. Melton

Speech Recogniser Assessment
M. Goldsmith

Logic and Specification

Extending VDM-SL for advanced formal specification

Cornelis A. Middelburg

Department of Computer Science
PTT Research
AK Leidschendam
The Netherlands

and

Department of Philosophy
Utrecht University
Utrecht
The Netherlands

CHAPMAN & HALL COMPUTING
London · Glasgow · New York · Tokyo · Melbourne · Madras

Published by Chapman & Hall, 2–6 Boundary Row, London SE1 8HN

Chapman & Hall, 2–6 Boundary Row, London SE1 8HN, UK

Blackie Academic & Professional, Wester Cleddens Road, Bishopbriggs, Glasgow G64 2NZ, UK

Chapman & Hall Inc., 29 West 35th Street, New York NY10001, USA

Chapman & Hall Japan, Thomson Publishing Japan, Hirakawacho Nemoto Building, 6F, 1-7-11 Hirakawa-cho, Chiyoda-ku, Tokyo 102, Japan

Chapman & Hall Australia, Thomas Nelson Australia, 102 Dodds Street, South Melbourne, Victoria 3205, Australia

Chapman & Hall India, R. Seshadri, 32 Second Main Road, CIT East, Madras 600 035, India

---

First edition 1993

Printed in Great Britain at the University Press, Cambridge

ISBN 0 412 48680 6

A catalogue record for this book is available from the British Library

Middelburg, Cornelis A.
Logic and specification : extending VDM-SL for advanced formal specification / Cornelis A. Middelburg. – 1st English language ed.
p. cm.
Includes index.
ISBN 0-412-48680-6
1. Programming languages (Electronic computers)–Semantics. 2. Software engineering. 3. Logic, Symbolic and mathematical.
I. Title.
QA76.7.M53 1993
005.1′2–dc20 92-38105
CIP

∞ Printed on permanent acid-free text paper, manufactured in accordance with the proposed ANSI/NISO Z 39.48-199X and ANSI Z 39.48-1984

Contents

Preface

This book is about formal specification of software systems and semantics of specification languages. The role of logic is striking. The notation employed in formal specification includes logical notation. The perception that the meaning of a specification can be taken to be a presentation of a logical theory underlies the approach to the semantics of specification languages which is applied in this book. Modularization mechanisms for building large structured specifications are regarded as operations for adapting and combining presentations of logical theories of a special kind. This book has been titled 'Logic and Specification' because logic turns out to play such a predominant part in various aspects of specification examined here.

A large software system often needs a precise specification of its intended behaviour. In order to achieve precision, specifications are written in a specification language with a well-defined syntax and formal semantics (a semantics by which the meaning of constructs in the language is precisely described using established concepts from mathematics). Formal specification refers to the use of such a specification language in writing specifications.

This book describes the outcome of a project which addressed the problem of giving a formal semantics for a specification language. This area is still in development. A main aim of this book is to illustrate a particular approach to tackle the problem of giving a formal semantics for a specification language. The language used for illustration, known as VVSL, extends VDM-SL (the specification language offered by the Vienna Development Method) with features for specifying interfering operations and for modular structuring of specifications. It is a specification language which is directly motivated by actual practices of software engineering.

The particular approach uses a mathematical framework for the semantics of specification languages consisting of the logic MPL_{ω}, the algebra DA (a model of modular specification based on this logic) and $\lambda\pi$-calculus (a variant of classical lambda calculus). It was first applied to the recently developed specification language COLD-K. This book contains a presentation of this mathematical framework and a presentation of a formal semantics of VVSL based on this framework. The latter presentation shows how MPL_ω, DA and $\lambda\pi$-calculus are used to give a formal semantics for a specification language. For that purpose, the approach could just as well be applied to another specification language. Indeed, it was applied to VVSL for another main purpose, viz. to provide VVSL with a formal semantics.

VVSL is an interesting specification language. It incorporates the version of VDM-SL used in *Systematic Software Development using VDM* by C.B. Jones – published by Prentice Hall International. The extensions of VDM-SL aim to meet actual needs of advanced formal specification tasks (VVSL was first used to produce a formal specification of the PCTE interfaces). Another aim of this book is to demonstrate the practical usefulness of the extensions concerned for realistic specification tasks. It contains two complete formal specifications in VVSL.

One specification describes the basic concepts of the relational data model and the operations which can be performed by a hypothetical relational database management system. The other specification describes the underlying concepts and operations of a hypothetical system for handling concurrent access to a relational database by multiple transactions. Both specifications show how large specifications can be modularly structured in VVSL. The latter specification also shows how operations which interfere through shared state components can be specified in VVSL. Each of these specifications describes an idealization of existing systems of a certain kind. Either provides a reference point against which the correctness of proposed solutions to common problems in systems of the kind concerned can be established.

This book provides research material intended for academic and industrial researchers in computer science interested in formal specification in general or semantics of specification languages in particular. The material concerning semantics of specification languages does not get round real problems which are often not dealt with in theoretical work. This material matters mostly to researchers working on foundational issues of the semantics of specification languages and developers of specification languages. It can also be used as illustration in theoretical courses. Some background in mathematical logic and set theory is assumed. The case study type material is mainly interesting to developers of software systems who are interested in formal specification. It can be used in software engineering courses on formal specification. The case studies are instances of advanced formal specification. They deal with examples of practical application which are not simplified. The case studies are expected to appeal to researchers working on databases as well.

This book is organized as follows. Chapter 1 pays attention to the role of formal specification in formal methods for the development of software. Among other things, the main features of VDM-SL are outlined. The remaining chapters concentrate on VVSL. Chapter 2 gives a general overview of the special features of VVSL. Chapters 3 to 9 are concerned with giving a formal semantics for VVSL. The approach applied in this book uses a mathematical framework which is presented in Chapters 3 and 6. The appropriate specializations and generalizations of this framework for the semantics of VVSL are described in Chapters 4 and 7. The semantics itself is presented in Chapters 5 and 8. Chapter 9 discusses some points raised by the material in Chapters 3 to 8, but for which space could not be found there. Chapters 10 to 13 are concerned with advanced case studies in VVSL. The case studies are related to relational databases. An introduction to them is given in Chapter 10. The underlying concepts of relational database management systems and the operations for data manipulation and data definition which can be performed by such systems are described in Chapters 11 and 12, respectively. Underlying concepts and operations of systems for handling concurrent access to a relational database by multiple transactions are described in Chapter 13. A glossary of the mathematical notation used in this book is provided in Appendix A and a glossary of VVSL notation is provided in Appendix B.

This book is a major revision of my Ph.D. thesis (Middelburg, 1990). It has been substantially rewritten and restructured so as to streamline the material. A number of technical changes have made it possible to simplify parts of the material that is concerned with giving a formal semantics for VVSL, including material on the mathematical framework which forms the basis of the semantics. The new Chapter 1 put the material into context.

Acknowledgements

The material in this book has grown out of my contribution to the ESPRIT project 1283: 'VDM for Interfaces of the PCTE'. I wish to thank the members of the project team for their critical feedback on my contribution. The work presented in this book has been carried out partly at PTT Research. I wish to express my appreciation to my department head, Jeroen Bruijning, for his support. I also wish to thank my colleagues Martin Kooij and Ben Lippolt for patiently solving most of the problems that I encountered with the computer network and several computer programs during the writing of this book. I am much indebted to Loe Feijs, Hans Jonkers, Karst Koymans and Gerard Renardel de Lavalette for their foundational work related to COLD-K. This book has been largely based on that work. I also wish to express special gratitude to them for their interests in the work presented in this book and their comments on preliminary versions of parts of it. Special thanks go to Jan Bergstra and Cliff Jones for providing inspiration and encouragement.

1

General Introduction

The aim of this chapter is to put the material presented in later chapters into context. Key themes of this book are (1) advanced formal specification, (2) extension of an existing specification language for advanced formal specification and (3) semantics for the extended specification language. Formal specification is a major aspect of formal methods for the development of software. The Vienna Development Method (VDM) (Jones, 1990) is a particular formal method for software development. This chapter illustrates with the help of VDM what formal methods have to offer. Thus, it gives an idea of what formal specifications are and what they can be used for.

VDM is used as an example because background on VDM is useful anyhow: this book addresses extensions of VDM-SL, the specification language offered by VDM. Furthermore, it is one of the most widely used formal methods and has achieved a level of maturity and acceptance. The International Standardization Organization (ISO) is working on a standard for VDM-SL. Besides VDM, Z currently rouses much interest. There are many similarities between VDM and Z, but they also have complementary merits. VDM and Z are briefly compared. However, this chapter does not contain a survey of formal methods. Both VDM and Z are *model-oriented* methods, where the approach is to specify a system by describing a model of it. This contrasts sharply with the property-oriented or *algebraic* approach to specification, where a system is described in terms of its desired properties. For completeness, this approach is broadly compared with the approach of VDM.

This chapter pays attention to the role of formal specification in formal methods for the development of software. The remaining chapters of this book concentrate on a new language for writing specifications that has come about by combining VDM-SL with languages for specifying interference and modular structuring. Those chapters pay attention to issues ranging from the mathematical basis for its semantics to the practical usefulness of its special features for their purposes. This chapter ends with glancing at the relevant extensions of VDM-SL. The next chapter offers an introduction to the new language itself.

In summary: this chapter gives an idea of what formal methods stand for, illustrates this using VDM, compares VDM with some other approaches, and touches upon extensions of VDM-SL. It also informs briefly on the development and exploitation of VDM and on computer-based support for VDM.

1.1 Formal methods

The need for precise specifications is accepted in most engineering disciplines. Software systems are in no less need of precise specifications. A precise specification of what is required of a software system that is to be developed provides a reference point against which the correctness of the ultimate system can be established and guided by which it can be constructed. For example, precise arguments can be given for design decisions. These aspects of precise specification are regarded as the most important aspects by professional developers.

Apart from that, there are other aspects of precise specification which can be very useful. For example, a precise specification also makes it possible to analyse a system before its development is undertaken. This opens up a way to increase the confidence that the specified system conforms to the requirements for it. If a change to an existing software system is contemplated – which is the rule rather than the exception – then its consequences have to be taken into account before the change is actually carried out. Without a precise specification, it is often difficult to grasp the consequences.

In order to achieve sufficient precision, a specification must be written in a specification language with a syntax and semantics which describe the form and meaning of its constructs in a fully precise way. For if there may be dispute about the form or intended meaning of constructs in the language concerned then there can be no question of a sufficiently precise specification.

Formal methods bring mathematical precision into software development. The major aspects of formal methods are *formal specification* and *verified design*. In the past, the accent was on formal specification. Currently, it shifts to verified design and supporting tools for verification in design. Formal specification languages without accompanying design and verification techniques are no longer considered to be formal methods.

Formal specifications employ mathematical notation extended to make it easier to specify software systems. These extensions are given a precisely defined meaning based on established concepts from mathematics. This makes it possible to settle disputes about the intended interpretation of any particular formal specification. It also opens up the possibility of formulating claims concerning specifications as mathematical theorems and constructing mathematical proofs to justify these claims.

Formal methods assume that first a formal specification can be made of what is required of a system to be developed and that next the design can be decomposed into manageable steps which can be separately justified.

Verified designs employ formal proofs to justify design steps. Each design step generates a number of proof obligations which must be discharged by formal proofs. There are several paradigms for verified design, each with specific kinds of proof obligations. Verified design in VDM is an example of the important paradigm of 'iterative specification, design and verification'. Other paradigms are 'program transformation' and 'constructive mathematics'.

In practice, verified design means that computer-based support is highly desirable for formal software development methods. Particularly, assistance is needed to find the proofs that the discharge of proof obligations takes. The proofs concerned are mostly unlike proofs in mathematics. The proofs in software development are basically long and tedious. They are mainly intended to cross-check that no details have been overlooked in a design. However, the amount of detail involved is usually large. For that very reason, formal proofs as well as computer-based support for it are essential. Note that computer-based support for verified design amounts to computer-aided design.

Existing development methods such as SDM (Turner, 1987) are mainly about the planning and organization of the development of computer-based systems. They suggest what phases are required within the development process, offer guidance on how to structure each phase in terms of mutually dependent activities and indicate how these activities should be approached and undertaken. Emphasis is on the management aspects of the development process and the quality assurance. Nothing is offered to specify the necessary programs in a sufficiently precise and unambiguous way and to construct these programs such that they fully agree with their specifications.

Formal methods for software development are exactly about these matters. However, they do not proscribe the use of ideas and heuristics from other methods. Therefore, formal methods may complement development methods such as SDM. They allow details of specification and construction of programs to be captured in a mathematically precise way. This is useful for programs which are large, complex or critical. Such programs occur in systems of different kinds. This includes administrative systems – the kind of systems which SDM is geared for.

The use of formal methods of developing software may contribute to a solution of certain problems that could not be tackled satisfactorily otherwise. More expectations and promises applying to the usefulness of formal methods can be given. Suffice it to quote Jones – one of the key people in this area – from (Jones, 1990, pp. 279–280). One quotation concerns formal specification:

> 'The mathematical notation can, when used with care, achieve conciseness of expression as well as precision. I believe that these ideas are important. But a major issue relating to specifications is whether they match the user's requirements.'

Another quotation concerns verified design:

> 'The material relating to design aims to provide developers with ways to increase their confidence that the systems they create satisfy the specifications. This must be part of a software engineer's training. With machine-checked proofs, an enormous increase in confidence would be justified, but it must be understood that nothing can ever provide absolute certainty of correctness.'

The latter quotation makes out a good case for (considering) the use of formal methods.

The next four sections outline a specific formal method, viz. VDM.

1.2 Development and exploitation of VDM

VDM is a formal method for the description and development of software which has emerged from a software development approach conceived around 1973–1975. VDM addresses all of the stages of development from specification through to code. Its language for writing formal specifications, called VDM-SL, is probably one of the most widely used formal specification languages for the description of complex systems. The method was developed in an industrial environment and has been used in a wide variety of applications. It has been used, amongst other things, for compilers (Pascal, CHILL, Ada, occam) and interpreters (Prolog), database management systems (PRTV, IMS, System 2000, System R), operating systems (IBM OS/360, operating system of System X partially), graphics systems (GKS), a formal development support system (*mural*), and the architecture of hypertext systems.

VDM is clearly explained in the book (Jones, 1990), which makes VDM accessible to the software engineer. Realistic case studies can be found in the companion book (Jones and Shaw, 1990). A knowledge of programming and some familiarity with logic and set theory should be sufficient to learn the method. Of course, experience is needed to tackle large or complex problems, but the usual myth about the necessity for high level training rests on nothing.

A draft ISO standard for VDM-SL is now available for comment. An important development in the area of supporting tools is the availability of the formal development support system *mural* (Jones, Jones, Lindsay and Moore, 1991), which is suited for VDM. Research dedicated to VDM currently pays attention to topics related to software development that are not yet or insufficiently covered by VDM – and other formal methods –

such as specification and design of parallel programs, specification in object-oriented style and modular structuring of specifications.

Formal specification and verified design in VDM are illustrated in Section 1.3 and Section 1.4, respectively.

1.3 Formal specification in VDM

A VDM specification describes what is required of a system to be developed in terms of the operations which can be performed by the system. The notion of *state* is central. Operations may yield results which depend on a state and may change that state. Generally, operations correspond to subprograms – such as procedures – of the final system. A *pre-condition* is used to bound the circumstances under which the system is required to perform an operation and a *post-condition* is used to delimit the possible effects of performing the operation. Pre- and post-conditions are logical expressions. The kinds of data (objects) manipulated by the operations are described in terms of abstract mathematical concepts such as (finite) sets and sequences.

The important ingredients of VDM-SL are the logical notation of a special logic of partial functions, LPF (Barringer, Cheng and Jones, 1984), notations for finite sets, maps, sequences and *composite objects*, the notation of implicit specifications of functions and operations – with pre- and post-conditions – and the notation of direct definitions of functions and operations. Belonging to each ingredient are proof rules.

Specifications give also rise to proof obligations in VDM. Pre- and post-conditions can be used to specify functions and operations which cannot be implemented. That is why it has to be shown for each function and operation specification that there exists an implementation of it.

Example: an employment agency

This example is about a system which keeps track of the state of an employment agency with respect to the persons seeking employment and the vacancies offered by companies. It also answers questions such as 'who are suitable candidates for this vacancy?' This means that the skills of a person seeking employment as well as the required skills for vacancies are recorded. Because a company may have several vacancies for which the same skills are required, vacancies are identified by vacancy numbers. The states of this system may be defined as follows:

$$\begin{array}{lll} \mathit{Agency} :: & \mathit{cands}: & \mathit{Person} \xrightarrow{m} \mathit{Skills} \\ & \mathit{vacs}: & \mathit{Vacno} \xrightarrow{m} \mathit{Vacdata} \end{array}$$

$$Skills = Skill\text{-}\mathsf{set}$$

$$Vacno = \mathbb{N}$$

$$\begin{array}{lll} Vacdata :: & comp: & Company \\ & skills: & Skills \end{array}$$

The states of this system are composed of two components: *cands* and *vacs*. The first component is used to keep track of information about the persons seeking employment (called candidates) and the second component is used to keep track of information about the vacancies offered by companies. Both components are finite maps. The range of the first component consists of finite sets (of skills) and the range of the second component consists of objects which are once again composed of two components (*comp* and *skills*). *Person*, *Skill* and *Company* need not be further defined at this point. They can be regarded as being given.

The operation to introduce a new candidate can now be specified:

$$\begin{array}{ll} \multicolumn{2}{l}{APPLY(p{:}\ Person,\ s{:}\ Skills)} \\ \mathsf{ext} & \mathsf{wr}\ cands{:}\ Person \xrightarrow{m} Skills \\ \mathsf{pre} & p \notin \mathsf{dom}\ cands \\ \mathsf{post} & cands = \overleftarrow{cands} \cup \{p \mapsto s\} \end{array}$$

In the pre-condition is expressed that $APPLY(p, s)$ must be executed successfully if person p is not already seeking employment. In the post-condition is expressed that p must be added to the persons seeking employment (with skills s). In the post-condition the names of the state components refer to the state prior to the execution of the operation if they have been decorated with a backward-pointing hook ($\leftharpoondown$) and to the state after execution otherwise. The post-condition appears to be rather like an assignment statement. It should be borne in mind that it is a logical expression which asserts a relationship between values.

The specification of an operation does not consist only of a pre-condition and a post-condition, but also of an *external clause* (starting with the keyword ext) in which is enumerated which state components may be interrogated and/or modified. wr indicates that the state component concerned may be interrogated and modified and rd indicates that it may only be interrogated. In the specification of the operation *APPLY*, the external clause means that only the state component *cands* may be interrogated and that this state component may also be modified.

The above operation specification gives rise to the following proof obligation for *implementibility*:

$$\begin{array}{l} \forall ag \in Agency, p \in Person, s \in Skills \cdot \\ \quad pre\text{-}APPLY(ag, p, s) \ \Rightarrow\ \exists ag' \in Agency \cdot post\text{-}APPLY(ag, p, s, ag') \end{array}$$

In other words, for each combination of initial state and arguments there has to be at least one possible final state. Note that the pre- and post-condition of the operation *APPLY* are quoted. This convention is part of VDM-SL. The proof of the above follows immediately from the definition of the operation $\cup$ on maps. It is often the case that proof obligations of this kind can be discharged with a minimum of work.

Note that the specified operation *APPLY* is deterministic. For each combination of initial state and arguments there is only one possible final state. This is not the case for the following operation to introduce a new vacancy:

$$
\begin{array}{ll}
\multicolumn{2}{l}{SUBSCR(c\colon Company, s\colon Skills)\ n\colon Vacno} \\
\mathsf{ext} & \mathsf{wr}\ vacs\colon Vacno \xrightarrow{m} Vacdata \\
\mathsf{pre} & \mathsf{true} \\
\mathsf{post} & n \notin \mathsf{dom}\ \overleftarrow{vacs} \wedge vacs = \overleftarrow{vacs} \cup \{n \mapsto mk\text{-}Vacdata(c, s)\}
\end{array}
$$

This operation has to assign a vacancy number to the new vacancy. The post-condition leaves open how this occurs. It only asserts that the assigned vacancy number should not be already in use. In the post-condition use is made of a special property of LPF, the underlying logic of VDM. $\overleftarrow{vacs} \cup \{n \mapsto mk\text{-}Vacdata(c, s)\}$ is undefined if $n \notin \mathsf{dom}\ \overleftarrow{vacs}$ is false. Now the question is what the truth value of $vacs = \overleftarrow{vacs} \cup \{n \mapsto mk\text{-}Vacdata(c, s)\}$ is. However, this does not cause any problem because the truth value of a formula of the form $A \wedge B$ is always false in LPF if one of the formulae A and B is false (likewise it is always true if both formulae are true, and undefined otherwise). The pre-condition true expresses that this operation must be executed successfully under all circumstances.

The specified operations *APPLY* and *SUBSCR* are both for keeping the state of the employment agency up to date. *APPLY* does not yield any result, but *SUBSCR* yields the number that has been assigned to the new vacancy. The following operation only interrogates the state to show the persons that are suitable candidates for a given vacancy, but it does not modify the state:

$$
\begin{array}{ll}
\multicolumn{2}{l}{SUITCAND(n\colon Vacno)\ ps\colon Person\text{-}\mathsf{set}} \\
\mathsf{ext} & \mathsf{rd}\ cands\colon Person \xrightarrow{m} Skills \\
 & \mathsf{rd}\ vacs\colon Vacno \xrightarrow{m} Vacdata \\
\mathsf{pre} & n \in \mathsf{dom}\ vacs \\
\mathsf{post} & ps = \{p \in Person \mid skills(vacs(n)) \subseteq cands(p)\}
\end{array}
$$

One can think of other useful operations, such as an operation *AVAILVAC* to inquire the numbers of the available vacancies for a given candidate, an operation *VACDATA* to inquire the information about the vacancy with a given number, and an operation *ASSIGN* to assign a given vacancy to a given candidate. These operations are only mentioned here, but we shall return to *VACDATA* in a later section.

1.4 Verified design in VDM

VDM distinguishes two kinds of steps in verified design, viz. data reification and operation decomposition. Design steps of both kinds give rise to proof obligations. The proof obligations associated with data reification have to do with the various aspects of it, such as data representation and modelling of functions and operations. For operation decomposition the proof obligation depends upon the kind of decomposition: sequential decomposition, decomposition into conditionals or loops, etc.

Given an abstract specification of a system, a design step might consist of the choice of representation for its states (which should reflect implementation considerations) and the modelling of its operations on the chosen representation. In VDM, this is called data reification. The relationship between the representation and the abstraction is expressed by a function which is called a *retrieve function.*

In the case of the example of the previous section, the following representation might be chosen:

$$\begin{array}{lll} Agency_c :: & cands\colon & Person \xrightarrow{m} Skills \\ & vacs\colon & Vacdata^* \\ & vacnos\colon & Vacno\text{-}\mathsf{set} \end{array}$$

An implementation consideration for this choice might be that usually all information about vacancies will be looked up sequentially. The component *vacnos* is meant to record the vacancy numbers that are in use. In this representation, these vacancy numbers also serve as indices to the sequence *vacs*. The retrieve function belonging to it is defined as follows:

$$\begin{array}{l} retr\colon Agency_c \to Agency \\ retr(ag_c) \triangleq \\ \quad mk\text{-}Agency(cands(ag_c), \{n \mapsto vacs(ag_c)(n) \mid n \in vacnos(ag_c)\}) \end{array}$$

One of the proof obligations associated with this design step is a proof obligation for *adequacy*:

$$\forall ag \in Agency \cdot \exists ag_c \in Agency_c \cdot retr(ag_c) = ag$$

In other words, for each abstract state there must be at least one representation. The proof of the above, using VDM's induction rule for finite maps, follows relatively easily from some elementary properties of finite sequences and maps. Proof obligations of this kind usually require inductive proofs.

Modelling of the operation *SUBSCR* might lead to the following:

$SUBSCR_c(c{:}\ Company, s{:}\ Skills)\ n{:}\ Vacno$

ext wr $vacs{:}\ Vacdata^*$
wr $vacnos{:}\ Vacno$-set

pre true

post $n \notin \overleftarrow{vacnos} \wedge vacnos = \overleftarrow{vacnos} \cup \{n\} \wedge$
$\forall n' \in \overleftarrow{vacnos} \cdot vacs(n') = \overleftarrow{vacs}(n') \wedge$
$vacs(n) = mk\text{-}Vacdata(c, s) \wedge$
$\forall m \notin \overleftarrow{vacnos} \cdot n \leq m$

In this case, the smallest unused index is assigned to the new vacancy. For a correct modelling, an arbitrary unused index is sufficient.

This operation modelling gives rise to the following proof obligation (which is known as a *result rule*):

$$\forall ag_c, ag_c' \in Agency_c, c \in Company, s \in Skills, n \in Vacno \cdot$$
$$post\text{-}SUBSCR_c(ag_c, c, s, ag_c', n) \Rightarrow$$
$$post\text{-}SUBSCR(retr(ag_c), c, s, retr(ag_c'), n)$$

In other words, when viewed via the retrieve function, the operation on the representation may have no other effects than those of the original abstract operation. The proof of the above follows, mainly by equational reasoning, from generally known properties of finite sequences and maps.

The next section gives an idea of the assistance which a specific support system for formal methods such as VDM provides for the discharge of proof obligations.

1.5 Computer-based support for VDM

Also in VDM, verified design means that computer-based support is desirable. Available is a formal development support system, called *mural*, its main components are a VDM support tool and a proof assistant. Together they provide support for the creation of VDM specifications and designs as well as for the discharge of the associated proof obligations. The main idea underlying the design of *mural* is that it must offer a more inviting environment than pencil and paper. For the most part, this is reached because the user, rather than the system, is leading in finding proofs.

The VDM support tool supports the creation of VDM specifications and designs (which can be grouped into developments). The proof obligations associated with the created specifications and designs can also be generated with the VDM support tool. These proof obligations can then be discharged with the help of the proof assistant. Frequently, the generated proof obligations are very illuminating. They are also useful in case no formal proofs are provided: although we may assume that design steps are based on insight, the proof obligations often bring out details which have been overlooked.

Important aspects of the proof assistant are: (1) the user guides the creation of a proof based on his insight and the system carries out routine work; (2) the system leaves the user free not to work out all the steps of a fully formal proof.

During the creation of a proof, the user continuously sees a presentation of the incomplete proof on the screen. What is not yet formally justified has been marked. If the user wants to work out the proof further by applying one of the proof rules in a specific way, then the system takes care of bringing its presentation on the screen up to date. Among the routine work meant under (1) is the search for potential next steps in a proof if the user cannot find them himself and the checking of the consequences of each of these steps for the course of the proof. All this means that the user does not need to plan the proof by hand.

The freedom as mentioned under (2) is important because it is not always useful to work out all the steps of a fully formal proof. As in mathematics, there are usually steps in the proofs which might be regarded as trivial steps. The proof of such steps does not increase the confidence that a product is being developed which will satisfy the requirements for it. However, it remains known what is not formally justified so that it can be returned to later in case of doubt.

1.6 VDM and other methods

In previous sections VDM was used to illustrate what formal methods have to offer. This section informs briefly on Z and the algebraic approach by comparison with VDM in respect of formal specification.

Z

The closest method to VDM is Z which has emerged from a style of specification and design conceived around 1980. The meaning of constructs in the Z notation in terms of mathematical concepts is treated extensively by Spivey (1988). Just as in VDM, the description of a system in Z consists of a definition of the states of the system followed by the specification of the operations which can be performed by the system.

For comparison, the example from Section 1.3 is partly repeated below in the Z notation. The states may be defined in Z as follows:

[*Person*, *Skill*, *Company*]

Agency

cands: *Person* ⇻ *Skills*
vacs: *Vacno* ⇻ *Vacdata*

$$Skills \mathrel{\widehat=} \mathbb{F}\, Skill$$

$$Vacno \mathrel{\widehat=} \mathbb{N}$$

```
┌─ Vacdata ──────────────────────────
│ comp: Company
│ skills: Skills
└────────────────────────────────────
```

The abstract mathematical concepts in terms of which the states are described here, do not differ from the ones used in Section 1.3. Apart from details on the level of concrete syntax, the only difference is that *Person*, *Skill* and *Company* are here explicitly regarded as being given.

When specifying operations in Z, in addition to the given formal semantics of the Z notation some informal conventions about the correspondence between specifications and operations are needed: (1) arguments have names which end with a question mark, (2) results have names which end with a exclamation mark, (3) the names of state components refer to the final state if they are followed by $'$ and refer to the initial state otherwise (the names with $'$ are introduced by Δ). Note that VDM does not have such informal conventions.

The operation to introduce a new candidate can be specified in Z as follows:

```
┌─ APPLY ────────────────────────────
│ ΔAgency
│ p?: Person
│ s?: Skills
├──────────────
│ p? ∉ dom cands
│ vacs' = vacs
│ cands' = cands ∪ {p? ↦ s?}
└────────────────────────────────────
```

The pre- and post-condition are not, as in VDM, separated. The expressiveness of Z is increased by this, but at the same time it is made difficult to associate suitable proof obligations with specifications and design steps. There is no special notation to indicate that a certain state component may only be interrogated. Therefore the condition $vacs' = vacs$ has been included above.

As in VDM, the specification of non-deterministic operations is no problem in Z. For example, the specification of the operation to introduce a new vacancy might be specified as follows:

$$
\begin{array}{|l}
\multicolumn{1}{l}{\_\,SUBSCR\,\_\_\_\_\_\_\_\_\_\_\_\_\_\_\_\_\_\_\_\_\_\_\_\_\_\_\_\_\_\_\_\_\_\_\_\_\_\_\_\_\_\_\_\_\_\_\_\_\_\_\_\_\_\_\_\_\_\_} \\
\Delta Agency \\
c?\colon Company \\
s?\colon Skills \\
n!\colon Vacno \\
\hline
cands' = cands \\
n! \notin \mathrm{dom}\ vacs \\
vacs' = vacs \cup \{n! \mapsto \mu\, Vacdata \mid comp = c? \wedge skills = s?\} \\
\hline
\end{array}
$$

Clearly, there are many similarities between the notations of VDM and Z. Due to the differences, VDM is better suited for software development from specification through to code and Z for the analysis phase preceding specification.

The algebraic approach

The algebraic approach embraces techniques for specification, design and verification which takes the line that a system is described in terms of its desired properties. Generally, these properties are described by giving (conditional) equations which relate the operations concerned to each other. Many algebraic specification languages have been developed. Among them are Clear (Burstall and Goguen, 1981), ACT ONE (Ehrig, Feys and Hansen, 1983), the Larch Shared Language (Guttag and Horning, 1986) and ASF (Bergstra, Heering and Klint, 1989). Although much work has been done on the mathematical foundations of algebraic formal methods for software development, little is known about such methods. A good overview of the algebraic approach is given by Wirsing (1990).

In order to be able to give an idea of algebraic specification with the help of the example from Section 1.3, the following is assumed: (1) partial functions (functions that do not always yield a result) are allowed and (2) all models that satisfy the given equations are taken into account. These assumptions exclude many existing algebraic specification languages. Accepting partial functions leads to the problem that either side of an equation may be undefined. In such cases, the equation will be considered to be false. By so doing, the meaning of equations, especially conditional ones, does not always agree with the intuition.

In the algebraic approach states are not directly defined. Furthermore, the initial state of each operation must explicitly be treated as an actual argument of the operation and the final state of each operation that modifies the state must explicitly be treated as an actual component of the result. Only in this way can the operations be related to each other by means of equations. The states are then implicitly specified by the equations concerned. A way to find the equations needed is as follows: (1) choose a collection of primitive interrogation operations (operations that interrogate the state) from which the required interrogation operations can be derived, (2) characterize each of the modification operations (operations that modify the state) by equations which sufficiently describe its effects on the results of all primitive interrogation operations, and (3) characterize each of the required interrogation operations by equations which sufficiently describe its result in terms of the primitive interrogation operations.

The operation *apply* (the operation names are now written in lower case letters) might be characterized by the following conditional equations:

$$\begin{array}{ll}
iscand(apply(a,p,s),p) = true & \text{if } iscand(a,p) = false \\
iscand(apply(a,p,s),p') = iscand(a,p') & \text{if } iscand(a,p) = false, \\
 & \quad p \neq p' \\
candata(apply(a,p,s),p) = s & \text{if } iscand(a,p) = false \\
candata(apply(a,p,s),p') = candata(a,p') & \text{if } iscand(a,p) = false, \\
 & \quad iscand(a,p') = true \\
isvac(apply(a,p,s),n) = isvac(a,n) & \text{if } iscand(a,p) = false \\
vacdata(apply(a,p,s),n) = vacdata(a,n) & \text{if } iscand(a,p) = false
\end{array}$$

The choice of primitive interrogation operations is as follows: an operation *iscand* to inquire whether or not a given person is a candidate (i.e. seeking employment), an operation *candata* to inquire the skills of a given candidate, an operation *isvac* to inquire whether or not a given number is in use as a vacancy number, and the operation *vacdata*. Note that the primitive interrogation operations *iscand* and *candata* together take over the role of the state component *cands* (Section 1.3). Likewise *isvac* and *vacdata* together take over the role of the state component *vacs*. This emphasizes one of the greatest differences compared to model-oriented specification as in VDM: states are not explicitly described. It seems that by doing so the intuitive clarity of the specification is lost. Furthermore each operation has to be regarded as a function. This complicates the specification of non-deterministic operations (e.g. the operation *subscr*) considerably.

The above suggests that algebraic specification of operations is rather difficult. This is not very surprising considering that the notation employed is very elementary and not at all adapted to make it easier to specify software systems. For example, there are no special provisions to describe systems in terms of operations which interrogate and/or modify a state such as in VDM-SL. Algebraic specification is, however, relatively easy for the data types which are used in VDM-SL to model the states of a system (natural, integer and rational numbers, finite sets, maps and sequences, etc.). This holds also for other data types which are useful or needed for some kinds of applications (e.g. finite relations). Such algebraic specifications, generally, lead to simplification of the proofs that the discharge of proof obligations takes. Therefore, algebraic specification techniques seem to show to full advantage in a specification language in which algebraic specification (of data types) can be combined with model-oriented specification (of state-based systems).

COLD-K

Such a specification language is COLD-K. COLD is an abbreviation of 'Common Object-oriented Language of Design' and K stands for 'Kernel'. This language can be regarded as an algebraic specification language extended with special provisions to describe state-based systems. COLD-K and the allied formal method were developed recently at the Philips Research Laboratories in Eindhoven (Jonkers, 1989b; Feijs and Jonkers, 1992).

VDM-SL can be viewed as a restricted version of COLD-K with a lot of syntactic sugar. Therefore, it is not useful to repeat the example from Section 1.3 once again in COLD-K. For the implicit specification of operations, formulae of dynamic logic are used in COLD-K. This is only one of the points where COLD-K is superior to VDM-SL in descriptive power. Proof obligations are, however, only associated with specifications and design steps making use of the restricted version of COLD-K corresponding to VDM-SL.

1.7 Extensions of VDM

When putting formal specification into practice, there is sometimes a need for specifying operations that are sensitive to interference by concurrently executed operations. It also happens that provisions for modular structuring of specifications are needed because of the size or complexity of the system being specified. The ESPRIT project 'VDM for Interfaces of the PCTE' (VIP) was faced with this. It had to deal with the absence of a language that could meet the needs of the most important task of the project: producing a formal specification of the PCTE interfaces (VIP, 1988a, 1988b). This led to the development of an extended version of VDM-SL, called VVSL, short for 'VIP VDM Specification Language'. The extensions of VDM-SL relate to the following special features of VVSL:

- operations that are sensitive to interference by concurrently executed operations through shared state components can be implicitly specified in a VDM-like style with the use of inter-conditions, which are formulae from a language of temporal logic, in addition to the usual pre- and post-conditions;
- large state-based specifications can be modularly structured by means of modularization and parametrization mechanisms which permit two modules to have state components in common, including hidden state components, and allow requirements to be put on the modules to which a parametrized module may be applied.

VVSL has been improved in the course of the work on the formal specification of the PCTE interfaces based on the feedback by the specifiers about their actual needs. This led to various preliminary versions of VVSL, which were also developed by the author.* The somewhat sketchy first paper (Middelburg, 1988) on VVSL applies to a preliminary version. The other papers on VVSL, such as (Middelburg, 1992a, 1992b), apply to the ultimate version.

Specifying interference

What matters to the users (persons, programs or whatever) of a software system are the operations that the system can execute and the observable effects of their execution. A software system may provide for concurrent execution of multiple operations in a multi-user environment. If the system provides for concurrent execution, then it may arise that some of its operations are intentionally made sensitive to interference by concurrently executed operations. Some operations of the PCTE interfaces are of this kind.

The execution of an operation that is sensitive to interference through shared state components terminates in a state and/or yields a result that depends on intermediate state changes effected by the concurrent execution of other operations. Its execution may even be suspended to wait for an appropriate state change (which may additionally lead to non-termination). If such an operation is specified by means of a pre- and post-condition only, then which interference is required for the occurrence of many final states and/or yielded results is not described. Describing this with inter-conditions can be done in a way that is similar to the way it is naturally discussed.

Modular structuring

The following goals of modular structuring of a formal specification are generally recognized: (1) to enhance the comprehensibility of the specification, (2) to improve the adaptability of the specification and (3) to make reuse of existing modules possible. As the size or complexity of the system being specified increases, it becomes more important to achieve these goals. Therefore, provisions for modular structuring of specifications especially supply a need in the case of large and complex systems such as the PCTE.

In the case of a good modular structure, the development of theories about the separate modules becomes possible. This can be of help to the

* It is worth mentioning that the preliminary version of VVSL described by the author in the report (VIP, 1987) and the language described under the name EVDM by Oliver (1988) are the same.

justification of design steps and the clarification of what is described in a module (to enhance its potential for reuse). One might want a modular structure that is suitable for subsequent development of the system being specified, but it is questionable whether this is generally obtainable.

In VVSL, modules can be adapted and combined by means of *renaming*, *importing*, and *exporting*. The basic modularization concepts of decomposition and information hiding are supported by importing and exporting, respectively. Renaming provides for control of name clashes in the composition of modules. The usual flat VDM specifications are used as the basic building blocks. Modules can also be parametrized over modules, by means of *abstraction*, and these parametrized modules can be instantiated for given modules, by means of *application*. The concept of reusability is primarily supported by abstraction and application.

Giving semantics for VVSL

VVSL can be regarded as a combination of VDM-SL and the language of a temporal logic together with a structuring language that is put on top of it. However, it was not sufficient to combine these languages syntactically. In order to achieve a formal specification, they had also to be combined semantically. This book describes, among other things, the outcome of a project which applied a particular approach of giving a semantics for a specification language to VVSL.

The logic MPL_ω, the algebra DA (a model for modularization of specifications) and $\lambda\pi$-calculus (a variant of classical lambda calculus for parametrization of specifications) are used in later chapters to give a formal semantics for VVSL.

MPL_ω is mainly obtained by additions to the language, the proof system and the interpretation of classical first-order logic. These additions make it more suitable as a semantic basis for specification languages which are intended for describing software systems. However, classical reasoning is not invalidated. The semantics presented describes the meaning of flat specifications, the building blocks of modularly structured specifications, as presentations of theories by sets of formulae of MPL_ω.

DA has some special features, which make it more suitable as the underlying model for modularizing model-oriented, state-based specifications than the models proposed for modularly structured algebraic specification. Nevertheless, many laws commonly holding in those models also hold in DA. In $\lambda\pi$-calculus, no essential deviations from classical typed lambda calculus are imposed: $\lambda\pi$-calculus has parameter restrictions in lambda abstractions and consequently a conditional version of the rule (β). This extension permits requirements to be put on the actual parameters to which parametrized modules may be applied. The semantics presented describes the meaning of modularly structured specifications as terms from an instance of $\lambda\pi$-calculus for a subalgebra of DA extended with higher-order generalizations of the operations of this algebra. The building blocks of these terms are the constants of the relevant subalgebra of DA. These constants are the above-mentioned presentations of theories by sets of formulae of MPL_ω.

The next chapter goes into the special features of VVSL. Subsequent chapters contain presentations of MPL_ω, DA, $\lambda\pi$-calculus and a formal semantics of VVSL based on this framework.

2

Introduction to VVSL

The purpose of this chapter is to make the reader familiar with the specification language which is the subject of the formal semantics presented in later chapters. It is not intended to be a tutorial on VVSL. It only gives a general overview of the special features of VVSL. These special features are connected with the following extensions of VDM-SL:

- the addition of an inter-condition to the implicit specification of operations (which includes a pre-condition and a post-condition), to support implicit specification of operations which interfere through shared state components;
- the provision of modularization and parametrization mechanisms which are adequate for writing large state-based specifications in VDM style and have a firm mathematical foundation.

The work on the formal specification of the PCTE interfaces in the VIP project (VIP, 1988a, 1988b) led to these extensions. They are based on the actual needs of the specifiers.

This chapter shows how interfering operations can be specified in VVSL with the use of inter-conditions and how specifications of systems can be modularly structured in VVSL. The other main features of VVSL are in common with VDM-SL. These were outlined in the previous chapter. There is, however, one important difference between VDM-SL and its variant as incorporated in VVSL: the type discipline of the latter is stronger. Therefore, the type discipline of VVSL is also sketched in this chapter. Quoting pre- and post-conditions is not supported by VVSL. Although it is a syntactic difference of minor importance, it is worth noticing further that in VVSL, unlike in VDM-SL, the headers used for explicit specification (i.e. direct definition) of functions are similar to the headers used for implicit specification.

VVSL without its modularization and parametrization constructs is referred to as *flat* VVSL. The *structuring sublanguage of* VVSL consists of the modularization and parametrization constructs complementing flat VVSL.

2.1 Specifying interference in VVSL

This section explains the specification of interfering operations with inter-conditions. This approach to specifying interference is broadly compared with alternative approaches. In order to motivate the addition of an inter-condition to the usual implicit specification of operations, the need for specifying interference is first illustrated by means of an example. The same example will later be used to illustrate the use of the inter-condition.

Example: wait and lock (first attempt)

This example is about an operation to lock a given object. Because the objects concerned can only be locked when they are not locked, execution of the operation is meant to be suspended to wait until the object is not locked. Waiting should be interruptable to prevent it lasting for ever. The state component *locked* is used to indicate which objects are currently locked. The state component *signal* is used for interruption. The following is an attempt to specify this operation in VDM-SL:

$WLOCK(obj\colon Object)$
ext rd $signal\colon \mathbb{B}$
    wr $locked\colon Object\text{-}set$
pre true
post $obj \in locked \vee signal$

The external clause allows the state components *locked* and *signal* to be interrogated by *WLOCK*, but it may only modify *locked*. The pre-condition means that *WLOCK*(*obj*) must be executed successfully under all circumstances. The post-condition requires that it must terminate in a state where *obj* is locked or *signal* is up. According to this specification it is sufficient that *WLOCK*(*obj*) just pretends to lock *obj* if *obj* is already locked. It cannot be expressed in the post-condition that it should wait until *obj* is not locked. Neither the synchronization required here nor other ways in which an operation might interfere with its environment can be specified with pre- and post-conditions. This problem can be solved by the addition of an inter-condition.

Specifying interference with inter-conditions

VVSL can be considered to be a variant of VDM-SL in which operations which interfere through shared state components can be specified while maintaining the VDM style of specification where possible. This is mainly accomplished by adding an inter-condition to the usual implicit specification of operations. The *inter-condition* is used to delimit the possible effects of performing the operation concerned which relates to interference through shared state components.

In case of sensitivity to interference, the pre-condition of an operation only bounds the circumstances under which the system is required to start execution of the operation, but it allows that the operation is only executed successfully if certain interference by concurrently executed operations occurs. Moreover, the post-condition will be rather weak in general, for initial states must often be related to many final states or results which should only occur due to certain interference by concurrently executed operations through shared state components. The inter-condition is mainly needed to describe which interference is required for successful execution and/or the occurrence of such final states or results.

An operation is called *atomic* if it is insensitive to interference by concurrently executed operations and it is called *non-atomic* otherwise. The inter-condition can be used to express that an operation is atomic, but this may also be indicated by leaving out the inter-condition. This means that atomic operations can be implicitly specified as in VDM-SL. For such operations, the new interpretation is equivalent to the original VDM interpretation. The inter-condition is normally used to specify the way in which a non-atomic operation interferes with its environment. For example, it can be used to specify the synchronization required by the operation *WLOCK*.

Example: wait and lock (second attempt)

The operation can now be specified as follows:

$WLOCK(obj\colon Object)$
ext rd $signal\colon \mathbb{B}$
  wr $locked\colon Object\text{-}set$
pre true
post $obj \in locked \lor signal$
inter is-E $\mathcal{U}$ $(obj \notin locked \land \text{is-I} \land \bigcirc(obj \in locked \land \neg \bigcirc \text{true})) \lor$
  is-E $\mathcal{U}$ $(signal \land \neg \bigcirc \text{true})$

The inter-condition means that one of the following occurs:

- Eventually *WLOCK*(*obj*) will lock *obj* at a point in time that *obj* is not locked and it will terminate immediately thereafter. Until then all changes have to be effected by its interfering environment.
- Eventually *WLOCK*(*obj*) will terminate at a point in time that *signal* is up. Until then all changes have to be effected by its interfering environment.

So the inter-condition excludes non-termination of *WLOCK*(*obj*): it normally waits until the object to be locked is not locked, but it can be interrupted if otherwise it would be waiting for ever.

The inter-condition is a formula from a temporal language which is outlined below. The outline includes an explanation of the temporal operators used above: is-I ('is internal'), is-E ('is external'), $\bigcirc$ ('next'), and $\mathcal{U}$ ('until').

The temporal language

An inter-condition defines the possible successions of state changes that can be generated by the operation concerned working interleaved with an interfering environment, distinguishing between state changes effected by the operation itself and state changes effected by its interfering environment. The state changes of the former kind are called *internal steps*, those of the latter kind are called *external steps* and the successions of state changes are called *computations*. Computations of atomic operations have at most one internal step and no external steps. Successful executions correspond to finite computations.

An inter-condition is a formula from a temporal language which has been inspired by a temporal logic that includes operators referring to the past (Lichtenstein, Pnueli and Zuck, 1985), a temporal logic that includes the 'chop' operator (Hale and Moszkowski, 1987), a temporal logic that includes 'transition propositions' (Barringer and Kuiper, 1985) and a temporal logic with models in which 'finite stuttering' cannot be recognized (Fisher, 1987). The operators referring to the past, the chop operator and the transition propositions obviate the need to introduce auxiliary state components acting as history variables, control variables and scheduling variables, respectively.

For a given computation and a given point in that computation, the evaluation of a temporal formula yields *true*, *false* or *neither-true-nor-false*. The meaning of the logical connectives and quantifiers is as in LPF (Barringer, Cheng and Jones, 1984), the underlying logic of VDM. They distinguish between false and neither-true-nor-false. The temporal operators identify false and neither-true-nor-false. So the three-valuedness can be safely ignored when only the temporal operators are considered. The meaning of the temporal operators is explained by the following informal evaluation rules:

is-I: Evaluation yields true if there is an internal step from the current point in the computation.

is-E: Evaluation yields true if there is an external step from the current point in the computation.

$\varphi_1 \, \mathcal{C} \, \varphi_2$: Evaluation yields true if it is possible to divide the computation at some future point into two subcomputations such that evaluation of φ_1 yields true at the current point in the first subcomputation and the evaluation of φ_2 yields true at the starting point of the second subcomputation, or the computation is infinite and evaluation of φ_1 yields true at the current point in the computation

$\bigcirc\varphi$: Evaluation yields true if there is a next point in the computation and evaluation of the temporal formula φ yields true at that point.

$\varphi_1 \,\mathcal{U}\, \varphi_2$: Evaluation yields true if evaluation of the temporal formula φ_2 yields true at the current or some future point in the computation and evaluation of the temporal formula φ_1 yields true at all points until that one.

$\ominus\varphi$: Evaluation yields true if there is a previous point in the computation and evaluation of the temporal formula φ yields true at that point.

$\varphi_1 \,\mathcal{S}\, \varphi_2$: Evaluation yields true if evaluation of the temporal formula φ_2 yields true at the current or some past point in the computation and evaluation of the temporal formula φ_1 yields true at all points since that one.

$\bigcirc\tau$: Evaluation yields the value that is yielded by evaluation of the temporal term τ at the next point in the computation. In case there is no next point, evaluation is undefined.

$\ominus\tau$: Evaluation yields the value that is yielded by evaluation of the temporal term τ at the previous point in the computation. In case there is no previous point, evaluation is undefined.

The notations $\Diamond\varphi$ (meaning 'eventually φ'), $\Box\varphi$ (meaning 'henceforth φ') and their counterparts for the past can be defined as abbreviations:

$$\begin{array}{llllll} \Diamond\varphi & := & \mathsf{true}\;\mathcal{U}\;\varphi, & \quad \diamondminus\varphi & := & \mathsf{true}\;\mathcal{S}\;\varphi, \\ \Box\varphi & := & \neg(\Diamond\neg\varphi), & \quad \boxminus\varphi & := & \neg(\diamondminus\neg\varphi). \end{array}$$

An inter-condition is a temporal formula that must yield true at the starting point of the computations of the operation concerned.

Dynamic constraints

Just as in VDM-SL, an invariant can be used to restrict the possible states of a system. In addition to this, a *dynamic constraint* can be used to restrict its possible computations as well. Its role is similar to that of a state invariant. A dynamic constraint is a temporal formula that must yield true at all points of the computations of any operation. This means that a dynamic constraint can be thought of as a kind of global inter-condition.

A dynamic constraint for a lock manager offering, amongst other things, the operation *WLOCK* specified before might be:

$$\mathsf{dyn}\ \mathit{signal} \;\Rightarrow\; \Diamond\neg\bigcirc\mathsf{true}$$

In this dynamic constraint is expressed that any operation of the lock manager must eventually terminate after the signal has gone up.

Alternative approaches to specifying interference

If an operation that is sensitive to interference is specified by means of a pre- and post-condition only, then its specification does not describe which interference is required for the occurrence of many final states and/or yielded results. For example, the earlier specification of *WLOCK* without the inter-condition permits that the operation just pretends to lock the given object if it is already locked, while it should wait until the object is not locked. Rely- and guarantee-condition pairs, as proposed by Jones (1983) for specifying interference, can be regarded as abbreviations of simple inter-conditions. Their main limitation is the inadequacy in case synchronization with concurrently executed operations is required. Synchronization is often needed (also for *WLOCK*). Stølen (1991) adds a wait-condition to the rely- and guarantee-condition pairs to make it possible to deal with synchronization. It appears that this recent addition allows many non-atomic operations to be adequately specified, but it is certain that auxiliary state components must be employed. Because internal steps and external steps can only be related via the auxiliary state components, the specifications concerned will fail to mirror the intuition behind the operations.

Specifying interference with inter-conditions can be done close to the way it is naturally discussed. Moreover, anything that can be specified with rely-, guarantee- and wait-conditions (with or without auxiliary state components) can also be specified with inter-conditions. It is argued by Stølen that it is less intricate to reason about shared-state interference with rely-, guarantee- and wait-conditions. The examples show that the intricacy is still present, but it has been disguised by relying on the judicious use of auxiliary state components.

2.2 Modular structuring of specifications in VVSL

Goals of modular structuring of specifications were given in Section 1.7. This section discusses the modular structuring of specifications with the modularization and parametrization constructs of VVSL. This approach to modular structuring is also broadly compared with alternative approaches. The modularization and parametrization constructs of VVSL are informally explained and their use is illustrated by means of an example.

The goals of modular structuring lead to the use of the following main criteria for the choice of modular structure: (1) the intuitive clarity of the modular structure, (2) the simplicity of the separate modules and (3) the suitability of the separate modules for reuse. Of course, provisions for modular structuring should make it easy to meet these criteria. A larger and more complex example is required to illustrate this. Such examples are given in Chapters 11 to 13.

The language for modularization and parametrization

VVSL can be considered to be a variant of VDM-SL for flat specifications together with a language for modularization and parametrization that is put on top of it, both syntactically and semantically. The usual flat VDM specifications can be adapted and combined by means of *renaming*, *importing*, and *exporting*. Flat specifications are the basic modules. Like all modules, they are essentially interpreted as presentations of logical theories. The models of their logical theory coincide with the models according to the original interpretation. Modules can also be parametrized over modules, by means of *abstraction*, and these parametrized modules can be instantiated for given modules, by means of *application*.

The modularization and parametrization constructs of VVSL are like those of COLD-K (Jonkers, 1989b) and have the same semantic basis. Description Algebra, an algebraic model of modular specification introduced by Jonkers (1989a), is used as the semantic foundation of modularization. $\lambda\pi$-calculus, a variant of classical lambda calculus introduced by Feijs (1989), is used as the semantic foundation of parametrization. The modularization and parametrization constructs of VVSL can be informally explained in terms of:

visible names: a collection of names for types, state components, functions and operations which may be used externally;

formulae: a collection of formulae representing the properties characterizing the types, state components, functions and operations denoted by the visible names (hidden names may also occur in these formulae as symbols).

Together, these collections constitute a theory presentation.

Due to the possibility of 'identifier overloading', the names mentioned above must be 'typed names' and not just the identifiers which are used as names in VVSL (except in signatures and renamings, see below). A typed name has one of the following forms:

t	for types,
$v\colon t$	for state components,
$f\colon t_1 \times \cdots \times t_n \rightarrow t_{n+1}$	for functions,
$op\colon t_1 \times \cdots \times t_n \Rightarrow t'_1 \times \cdots \times t'_m$	for operations.

In VVSL, the constructs for denoting sets of typed names are called *signatures*. A signature is usually an enumeration of the typed names concerned:

$$u_1, \ldots, u_n,$$

where u_j $(1 \leq j \leq n)$ is a typed name. Related to signatures are *renamings*. They correspond to mappings from typed names to typed names and are used to replace the visible names of a module by new ones. A renaming is of the following form:

$$u_1 \mapsto i_1, \ldots, u_n \mapsto i_n,$$

where u_j $(1 \leq j \leq n)$ is a typed name and i_j is the new untyped name for it. The translation of the new untyped name to the appropriately typed one is straightforward.

The modularization and parametrization constructs of VVSL are the following:

module $\mathcal{D}$ end: The basic module construct. Its visible names are the names introduced by the definitions $\mathcal{D}$. Its formulae represent the properties characterizing the types, state components, functions and operations which may be associated with these names according to the definitions. If this construct occurs as an importing module, then the visible names from the imported module, that are used but not introduced in it, are treated as if they are introduced.

rename R in M: The renaming module construct has the same meaning as the module M, except that the names have been changed according to the renaming R.

import M_1 into M_2: The import module construct combines the two modules M_1 and M_2. Its visible names are the visible names of both modules. The formulae representing the properties characterizing what is denoted by these names (as well as hidden ones, if present) are also combined.

export S from M: The export module construct restricts the visible names of module M to those which are also in the signature S, leaving all other names hidden. The formulae remain the same.

abstract $m_1 \colon M_1, \ldots, m_n \colon M_n$ of M: The module abstraction construct parametrizes the module M. Usually, the module names $m_1, \ldots, m_n$ occur in M. The visible names and formulae of the abstraction module depend upon what these module names stand for. That is, $m_1, \ldots, m_n$ act as formal parameters. What the actual parameters may be is restricted by the parameter restriction modules $M_1, \ldots, M_n$. The visible names of the actual parameter corresponding to m_i must include the visible names of the parameter restriction module M_i. Likewise the properties represented by its formulae must include those represented by the formulae of M_i.

apply M to $M_1, \ldots, M_n$: The module application construct instantiates the parametrized module M. The modules $M_1, \ldots, M_n$ act as actual parameters. Its meaning is the meaning of M when its formal parameters stand for $M_1, \ldots, M_n$. If some actual parameter does not satisfy the parameter restriction associated with the corresponding formal parameter, then the meaning is undefined.

let $m \triangleq M_1$ in M_2: The local module definition construct introduces locally a name for a module. Its meaning is the meaning of M_2 when the module name m stands for M_1.

The definitions of the basic module construct may be free. A free definition is a definition in which the keyword free occurs following its header. A free definition introduces a free name and a non-free definition introduces a defined name. A free name is a name which is supposed to be defined elsewhere. This means that, in case of a free name, the body of the definition must be considered to describe assumptions about what is denoted by the name.

In case of name clashes, the union of the formulae of the imported module and the importing module of the import construct may lead to undesirable changes in the properties represented by the formulae. Therefore, a restriction applies to visible names. Visible names are allowed to clash, provided that the name can always be traced back to at most one non-free definition. Name clashes of hidden names can be regarded as being avoided by automatic renamings, in case the name can be traced back to more than one non-free definition. Otherwise they are not avoided. This makes it possible for two modules to have hidden state components in common.

Actually, all constituent modules of modularization constructs may be parametrized modules. However, the meaning of the modularization constructs is here only explained for the non-parametrized case. For the import construct and the export construct, the generalization is straightforward. For the rename construct, it involves the renaming of renamings. This is not always possible. The parametrization constructs support higher-order parametrized modules.

Example: an access handler

This example is about an access handler for relational databases, i.e. a system which handles concurrent access to stored relations by multiple transactions. A complete modularly structured specification of such a system is given later in Chapter 13. The most important module is outlined in this section. The operations which constitute the interface of the access handler are specified in this module.

Most of these operations can be regarded as requests on behalf of some transaction to perform an action on a subset of a stored relation. Transactions are introduced as the units of consistency. It is assumed that each action which is performed on behalf of a transaction may violate database consistency, but that each transaction, when executed alone, preserves database consistency. The access handler provides for the interleaved performance of actions requested by several transactions in such a manner that each transaction sees a consistent database and produces a consistent database.

```
ACCESS_HANDLING is
  abstract
    X: REL_NM,
    Y: ATTRIBUTE,
    Z: VALUE,
    U: TRANS_NM
  of

  abstract
    V: apply VAL_CONST to Z
  of

  export
    START: ⇒ Trans_nm,
    COMMIT: Trans_nm ⇒,
    ABORT: Trans_nm ⇒,
    SELECT:
      Trans_nm × Rel_nm × Simple_wff ⇒ Relation × Status,
    INSERT: Trans_nm × Rel_nm × Simple_wff ⇒ Status,
    DELETE: Trans_nm × Rel_nm × Simple_wff ⇒ Status,
    CREATE: Trans_nm × Rel_nm ⇒ Status,
    DESTROY: Trans_nm × Rel_nm ⇒ Status
  from

  import
    X
    U
    apply RELATION to Y, Z
    apply apply SIMPLE_WFF to Y, Z to V
    apply apply AH_STATE to X, Y, Z, U to V
  into

  module
    types
      Status = {GRANTED, REJECTED}
    operations
      START()tnm: Trans_nm
        ...
      COMMIT(tnm: Trans_nm)
        ...
      ⋮
  end
```

The module **ACCESS_HANDLING** is based on assumptions with respect to relation names, attributes, values, transaction names and value constants. In order to formalize this, the module is parametrized by means of abstraction (the assumptions are expressed in the parameter restriction modules).

The interface of the access handler comprises operations for starting and stopping a transaction (by successful termination or abortion), operations for accessing a subset of one of the stored relations to interrogate it (by selection) or to modify it (by insertion or deletion), and operations for creating and destroying stored relations. These operations reflect roughly what is offered in the access handlers of existing RDBMSs. Only these access handling operations are exported. The idea is that interrogating or modifying the various state components should only be done by means of the operations made available by the access handler.*

The definitions of the access handling operations are based on definitions regarding relations, simple formulae and states of the access handler. In order to formalize this, the modules concerned are imported. The states of the access handler provide all the details of the active transactions that can be used to grant their waiting and coming requests in a consistency preserving order. They also provide all the details that are required to abort any of the active transactions. More explanation of what the imported modules are about is given in Chapters 11 and 13.

Alternative approaches to modular structuring

There are various approaches to modular structuring of specifications. The approach of COLD-K has been adopted for VVSL. This approach to modular structuring deviates somewhat from established approaches. Firstly, the meaning of a module is a theory presentation. It has this in common with the approach of the Larch Shared Language (Guttag and Horning, 1986). In other approaches, their meaning is usually more abstract (viz. a theory or a model class). Secondly, the origins of names are taken into account in the treatment of name clashes in the composition of modules. It has this in common with the approach of Clear (Burstall and Goguen, 1980). In other approaches, name clashes are usually treated in an ad hoc way. Together, these two deviations from established approaches to modular structuring make it possible for two modules to have hidden state components in common.

This is considered important. Effective separation of concerns often motivates the hiding of state components from a module. In case a suitable modular structuring requires that the same state components are accessed from several modules, it is indispensable for the adequacy of a modular-

* State components are actually called state variables in VVSL.

ization mechanism that it permits two or more modules to have hidden state components in common. It is usually wanted if loosely connected operations interrogate and/or modify the same state component(s). This occurs in many large software systems. Chapter 12 provides an example. Operations for querying and updating a database are not specified in the same module as operations for changing the schema of the database. Only operations are exported from the modules concerned, but the operations of both kinds interrogate or modify the current database as well as the current database schema. This means that these modules have two hidden state components in common.

2.3 Types in VVSL

Types play a predominant role in the well-formedness of expressions in VVSL. Subtypes and overloading of function names, which are both supported by VVSL, complicate the typing of expressions. This section discusses the type discipline of VVSL, which is related to the typing approach for subtypes and generic operators described by Reynolds (1985) and their treatment by Goguen and Meseguer (1987). This type discipline is briefly compared with the usual type disciplines of strongly typed languages and the weak type discipline of VDM-SL and its main consequences are illustrated by means of small examples.

Subtypes

The type discipline of VVSL aims to classify exactly the expressions that possibly make sense as well-typed expressions. This means that the well-typed expressions also include the expressions for which it is not possible to decide whether the meaning is defined or not. Such expressions are reminiscent of expressions in programming languages that need dynamic type checking. This means that the type discipline of VVSL is not truly strong.

In strongly typed languages without subtyping, every well-formed expression has a unique *type*. A type determines a set of values which are called the elements of the type. The value of an expression is always an element of its type.

In strongly typed languages with subtyping, there is a *subtype* ordering on types and every well-formed expression has a unique minimal type with respect to this ordering. If a type T is a subtype of a type T' then the set determined by the type T is always a subset of the set determined by the type T'. The usefulness of such an order relation on types lies in the fact that an element of a type T that is a subtype of a type T' can be allowed in any situation where an element of the type T' is expected: the required conversion is simply an inclusion function. Consequently, every expression having type T can be used as an expression having type T'. This means that the requirement that expressions have unique types is not applicable to languages with subtyping, but uniqueness of minimal types is. It is useful to assume that the subtype ordering is a pre-ordering. The effect of a subtype ordering on the possible types of expressions remains unchanged if it is replaced by the least pre-ordering extending it. Furthermore, the existence of minimal types for every set of types is guaranteed by a subtype ordering that is a pre-ordering. Their uniqueness, needed to describe the meaning of expressions unambiguously, is not guaranteed by this property.

It is typical of the type discipline suggested above that it is too rigid and too inexpressive. In VVSL, a type is frequently defined as a subtype of another type. With this type discipline, it becomes practically impossible to define functions on the former type recursively in terms of functions on the latter type. Therefore, the type discipline has been weakened for VVSL: every expression having type T can also be used as an expression having a type T' that is a subtype of the type T provided that this lowering of the type does not lead to non-uniqueness of its minimal type. The implied conversion is a retraction function, i.e. a partial function which maps the elements of the subtype to themselves and which is undefined otherwise – which corresponds to dynamic type checking. With this weakened type discipline, the value of an expression is not necessarily an element of its minimal type. However, the value of the expression is possibly an element of its minimal type in the sense that it is always an element of a type of which this minimal type is a subtype. Moreover, its minimal type is the least type with this property. This is about the best that can be done without relying on proofs. Note also that – owing to the restriction on the lowering of types – an expression having type T cannot be used as an expression of type T' if T and T' are incomparable, i.e. T is not a subtype of T', nor is T' a subtype of T.

For example, with types A, B and C defined by

$$A = \mathbb{N}^*$$

$$B = \mathbb{N} \xrightarrow{m} \mathbb{B}$$

$$C = A|B,$$

an expression of the form $c(1)$, where c is an expression having type C, is ill-typed in VVSL. Lowering the type of c would lead to non-uniqueness of its minimal type. Therefore, the minimal type of c is just the union type C. Consequently, $c(1)$ is definitively ill-typed. Note that lowering the type of c, which is required for $c(1)$ to make sense, would require conversion to a type which may be incomparable with the type of which the actual value of c is an element.

The ability to lower the type of an expression to a certain extent is one of the main differences between this and the type discipline of strongly typed languages with subtyping. Another main difference is a restraint imposed on the subtype ordering.

In VVSL, a type can be defined as a subtype of another type or as a union of other types which are thereby subtypes of the defined types. The subtype ordering includes only what arises straight from the prevalent type definitions, from reflexivity and from transitivity. Properties based on the underlying sets such as monotonicity of type constructors are not taken into account. In a model-oriented specification, one describes the types of interest in terms of basic types and type constructors. In case two such types are described in the same way, e.g. by using the same type constructor, automatic conversion between the two constructed types, just because the underlying set allows it, is considered to be useless. This is, however, the case in VDM-SL.

For example, with types D and E defined by

$$D = \mathbb{N}\text{-set}$$

$$E = \mathbb{Z}\text{-set},$$

D is not a subtype of E, since monotonicity of the set type constructor is not taken into account in VVSL.

A type discipline where every expression having type T can also be used as an expression having type T' provided that T and T' are subtypes of a common type, which is even weaker than the type discipline of VVSL, is considered to be unacceptable. Even when there cannot be a single value that is an element of more than one of the types concerned (as for the types $\mathbb{B}$ and $\mathbb{Z}$), this condition can be met in VVSL (by defining another type as the union of the types). Roughly speaking, this lowering of types is allowed by the weak type discipline of VDM-SL.

Minimal typing rules

In Section 5.8, a minimal typing predicate is defined by a set of inductive rules. These rules can be viewed as type inference rules that prescribe how to establish the minimal type of an expression from the minimal types of its immediate subexpressions. There is one rule for each kind of expression. Just as the value of an expression depends upon the meanings assigned to the names occurring free in it, so its minimal type depends upon the minimal types assigned to the names occurring free in it. Contexts are used to record names and their types (contexts are further explained in Section 5.1). We say that expression e is *well-typed* in a context N if there is a type T such that expression e has minimal type T in context N. For any expression well-typedness is a prerequisite for well-formedness.

Overloading of function names

Overloading of function names is allowed. Consequently, the meaning of the function name f in an application expression of the form $f(e_1, \ldots, e_n)$ and the type of the application expression generally depend on the types of the argument expressions $e_1, \ldots, e_n$. In other words, overloading of function names leads to generic function names. There is a complication due to subtyping. The complication arises if the function name f is introduced for two functions of n arguments where the i-th argument type of the one function is a subtype of the i-th argument type of the other function (for $1 \leq i \leq n$). To describe the meaning of $f(e_1, \ldots, e_n)$ unambiguously, the former function needs to be a restriction of the latter function. This condition is met by the various pre-defined function names for which the above-mentioned situation occurs. For user-defined function names, this cannot be guaranteed in advance. Because well-typedness should stand for an unambiguous meaning, the situation is only allowed for pre-defined function names. In other words, an application expression $f(e_1, \ldots, e_n)$ is deemed to be ill-typed, if there is not a unique f (in its context) that fits the minimal types of the argument expressions $e_1, \ldots, e_n$, unless f is a pre-defined function name. In the case of a pre-defined function name, the function with the greatest argument types is chosen.

Types and modules

Defining types in VVSL introduces subtype relationships with accompanying implicit conversions. If types are defined as subtypes of basic types (boolean type, natural type, etc.) or constructed types (sequence types, set types, etc.) constructed from basic types and/or other defined types, then the introduced subtype relationships are pragmatically relationships between 'abstract data types' and their 'representations'. A modularization mechanism for model-oriented specifications that does not hide such representations is not very useful. Therefore, the modularization mechanism provided by VVSL hides such representations. This means that the subtype relationships concerned contribute only to the subtype ordering inside the defining module. Besides, all pre-defined type and function names associated with the types used for representation are not visible outside the defining module.

Owing to its hiding of representations, the modularization mechanism provides naturally for the prevention of the inadvertent introduction of needless restrictions on the well-formedness of expressions due to multiple use of the same basic or constructed type for representation. Note that exporting only provides for hiding of user-defined names. Therefore, explicit hiding of representations by means of exporting is not possible.

Subtype relationships between defined types do contribute to the subtype ordering outside the defining module whenever the types concerned are visible. The practical usefulness of union types would be severely diminished without this provision. It would, for example, be impossible to apply functions on union types outside the defining module. Moreover, inheritance is supported: a module about a type T is inherited in a module about a type T' by importing the former module into the latter and defining the type T' as a subtype of T.

3

Foundations of Flat VVSL

The main aim of this chapter is to introduce the logic which is used as the basis for the semantics of flat VVSL presented in Chapter 5. This logic, called MPL$_\omega$ (Many-sorted Partial infinitary Logic), is a many-sorted infinitary first-order logic of partial functions. MPL$_\omega$ has some features in addition to those of classical first-order logic, which make it suitable as the basis for a semantics of flat VVSL. These features are mainly obtained by additions to the language, proof system and interpretation of classical first-order logic. In this way, no essential deviations from classical reasoning are imposed. The language, proof system and interpretation of MPL$_\omega$ were first presented by Koymans and Renardel de Lavalette (1989).

The first section gives an overview of the special features of MPL$_\omega$ and discusses its suitability as a semantic basis for flat VVSL. The language, proof system and interpretation of this logic are precisely defined in subsequent sections. The presentation of MPL$_\omega$ in this chapter is for the greater part the result of a major rewrite of the one in (Koymans and Renardel de Lavalette, 1989). A number of technical changes have made it possible to simplify the treatment. Properties that are relevant to the use of this logic for a semantics of VVSL are also presented. For the proofs, the reader is referred to (Koymans and Renardel de Lavalette, 1989; Renardel de Lavalette, 1989). The last section shows how a large class of inductive definitions of predicates and functions can be treated as abbreviations of formulae of MPL$_\omega$. This was first sketched in (Koymans and Renardel de Lavalette, 1989, Section 4) and later worked out in detail by (Renardel de Lavalette, 1989, Appendix D). The last section of this chapter streamlines and expands the latter treatment.

3.1 Introduction to MPL$_\omega$

This section gives an idea of what MPL$_\omega$ is and connects this with its role in a semantics of VVSL. Subsequent sections go into the details of MPL$_\omega$.

Overview of MPL$_\omega$

In MPL$_\omega$, sort symbols are used in addition to function and predicate symbols. Sort symbols are interpreted as non-empty domains of values. There is a standard equality predicate symbol $=_S$ (used in infix notation) for every sort symbol S. Every function symbol has a type $S_1 \times \cdots \times S_n \to S_{n+1}$ and every predicate symbol has a type $S_1 \times \cdots \times S_n$, where $S_1, \ldots, S_{n+1}$ are sort symbols. We write $f\colon S_1 \times \cdots \times S_n \to S_{n+1}$ and $P\colon S_1 \times \cdots \times S_n$ to indicate this. S_i $(1 \leq i \leq n)$ corresponds to the i-th argument domain and S_{n+1} corresponds to the result domain.

Functions are generally partial functions. Hence, not every term will refer to an object in the intended domain. In other words, partial functions give rise to non-denoting terms (alternatively called undefined terms). The potential occurrence of non-denoting terms in formulae makes reasoning about partial functions problematic in classical first-order logic. MPL$_\omega$ adopts an approach to solve the problem with non-denoting terms in formulae, which stays within the realm of classical two-valued logics. Atomic formulae that contain non-denoting terms are logically false. In this way, the assumption of the excluded middle does not have to be given up. When a formula cannot be classified as true, it is inexorably classified as false. No further distinction is made. However, denoting terms and non-denoting terms can be distinguished. $t =_S t$ means that t is denoting (for terms t of sort S), which is also written $t{\downarrow_S}$. There is a standard undefined constant symbol $\uparrow_S$ for every sort symbol S. $\uparrow_S$ is a non-denoting term of sort S.

If $A_0, A_1, A_2, \ldots$ are countably many formulae, then the formula $\bigwedge_n A_n$ can be formed. This allows a large class of recursive and inductive definitions of functions and predicates to be expressed as formulae of MPL$_\omega$.

If A is a formula, then the term $\iota x\colon S\,(A)$ can be formed which is called a description. Its intended meaning is the unique value x of sort S that satisfies A if such a unique value exists and is undefined otherwise. This means that not every description will be denoting. Descriptions can be eliminated: it is possible to translate formulae containing descriptions into logically equivalent formulae without descriptions.

Free variables may be non-denoting, but in $\iota x\colon S\,(A)$, $\forall x\colon S\,(A)$, $\exists x\colon S\,(A)$, x is always denoting. So we have $t{\downarrow_S} \leftrightarrow \exists x\colon S\,(x =_S t)$. Owing to the different treatment of free variables and bound variables, frequent reasoning about non-denoting terms can be avoided.

The formation rules for MPL$_\omega$ are the usual formation rules with an additional rule for descriptions and with the rule for binary conjunctions replaced by the rule for countably infinite conjunctions from L$_\omega$ (Karp, 1964; Keisler, 1971), classical first-order logic with countably infinite conjunctions. The proof system of MPL$_\omega$ presented in a later section is a Gentzen-type sequent calculus that resembles one for L$_\omega$. Obviously, there are additional axioms for equality, undefined, and description.

A set of sort, function and predicate symbols that contains all sort symbols occurring in the types of the function and predicate symbols from the set is called a signature. The formulae that contain only symbols from a signature Σ constitute the language of MPL_ω over Σ. The language of MPL_ω over Σ is interpreted in structures which consist of an interpretation of every symbol in Σ as well as an interpretation of each of the equality symbols associated with the sort symbols in Σ. These interpretations have to be in accordance with the treatment of non-denoting terms outlined above. The classical interpretation of the connectives and quantifiers is used. Unlike bound variables, free variables may be non-denoting.

Suitability of MPL_ω

VVSL is close to a strongly typed language. It is more convenient to interpret VVSL in a many-sorted logic than to interpret it in a logic without sorts (akin to having only one sort available), because the types map naturally to sorts.

MPL, the finitary fragment of MPL_ω (obtained by replacing countably infinite conjunctions and disjunctions by binary conjunctions and disjunctions), is suitable for the semantics of the expression sublanguage of VVSL. Functions used in VVSL are generally partial functions, but MPL handles partial functions. Moreover, it does so without imposing essential deviations from classical reasoning.

In the definition sublanguage of VVSL, a function can be defined directly in terms of a defining expression in which the function being defined may be recursively used. Such recursively defined functions require an additional non-standard feature of the logic used for the semantics. An obvious choice is to add a least fixpoint operator to MPL, but to add countably infinite conjunctions also allows a large class of recursive definitions to be expressed as formulae. In contrast to adding a least fixpoint operator, adding countably infinite conjunctions to MPL does not invalidate the interpolation property (see Section 3.6). The interpolation property is a prerequisite for appropriate properties of the modularization mechanisms of full VVSL.

Connections with LPF

MPL_ω is a two-valued logic of partial functions. Several logics of partial functions have been developed in a three-valued setting. In particular, the logical expressions of VDM-SL are considered to be formulae of the language of the three-valued logic of partial functions, called LPF (Barringer, Cheng and Jones, 1984).

In this logic, non-denoting terms make atomic formulae that are logically neither-true-nor-false. Thus, the assumption of the excluded middle is given up. The classical connectives and quantifiers have counterparts in

LPF. Each behaves according to its classical truth-condition and falsehood-condition; only if neither of them meets it will yield neither-true-nor-false. This is Kleene's strong way of extending the classical connectives and quantifiers to the three-valued case (Kleene, 1952). Classical reasoning cannot be used out of the positive fragment of LPF. In particular, the deduction theorem does not hold in LPF. The departures from classical reasoning are mainly consequences of the fact that, unlike formulae of MPL_ω, formulae of LPF inherit the possibility of being non-denoting.

The logical expressions of VVSL and the ones of VDM-SL are the very same. Like the other parts of flat VVSL, this part is provided with a semantics by interpretation in the language of MPL_ω. The approach to this interpretation, which is actually an interpretation of the language of LPF in the language of MPL_ω, is connected with the layered approach to handle partial functions adopted in the logic PPλ (Gordon, Milner and Wadsworth, 1979). It is proved in (Middelburg and Renardel de Lavalette, 1992) that LPF can be reduced to MPL_ω in the following sense: formulae of LPF can be translated into formulae of MPL_ω and what can be proved remains the same after translation. As a corollary we have that reasoning in LPF can be taken for being derived from reasoning in MPL_ω.

The next four sections describe MPL_ω precisely. The first of these sections gives the assumptions which are made about sort, function and predicate symbols and introduces the notion of signature.

3.2 Signatures for MPL_ω

A language of MPL_ω is constructed with sort, function and predicate symbols that belong to a certain set, called a signature. For a given signature, say Σ, the language concerned is called the language of MPL_ω over signature Σ or the language of $\text{MPL}_\omega(\Sigma)$. The corresponding proof system and interpretation are analogously called the proof system of $\text{MPL}_\omega(\Sigma)$ and the interpretation of $\text{MPL}_\omega(\Sigma)$, respectively.

We assume a set *SORT* of *sort symbols*, a set *FUNC* of *function symbols*, and a set *PRED* of *predicate symbols*. Every $f \in \mathit{FUNC}$ has a *function type* $S_1 \times \cdots \times S_n \to S_{n+1}$ and every $P \in \mathit{PRED}$ has a *predicate type* $S_1 \times \cdots \times S_n$ ($S_1, \ldots, S_{n+1} \in \mathit{SORT}$). To indicate this, we use the notation $f\colon S_1 \times \cdots \times S_n \to S_{n+1}$ and $P\colon S_1 \times \cdots \times S_n$. For every $S \in \mathit{SORT}$, there is a standard function symbol $\uparrow_S\colon \to S$, called *undefined*, and a standard predicate symbol $=_S\colon S \times S$, called *equality*. Function symbols of function type $\to S$ are also called *constant symbols* of sort S.

Definition. A *signature* Σ is a finite subset of $\mathit{SORT} \cup \mathit{FUNC} \cup \mathit{PRED}$ such that

$$\textit{for all } f \in \Sigma, f\colon S_1 \times \cdots \times S_n \to S_{n+1} \;\Rightarrow\; S_1, \ldots, S_{n+1} \in \Sigma;$$
$$\textit{for all } P \in \Sigma, P\colon S_1 \times \cdots \times S_n \;\Rightarrow\; S_1, \ldots, S_n \in \Sigma.$$

We write $\mathrm{S}(\Sigma)$ for $\Sigma \cap SORT$, $\mathrm{F}(\Sigma)$ for $\Sigma \cap FUNC$, $\mathrm{P}(\Sigma)$ for $\Sigma \cap PRED$, $\mathrm{SF}(\Sigma)$ for $\{\uparrow_S \mid S \in \mathrm{S}(\Sigma)\}$, $\mathrm{SP}(\Sigma)$ for $\{=_S \mid S \in \mathrm{S}(\Sigma)\}$. *SIGN* denotes the set of all signatures for MPL$_\omega$.

We also assume a set *VAR* of *variable symbols*. Every $x \in VAR$ has a *sort* S ($S \in SORT$). Furthermore, it is assumed that *SORT*, *FUNC*, *PRED*, *VAR*, $\{\uparrow_S \mid S \in SORT\}$, and $\{=_S \mid S \in SORT\}$ are mutually disjoint sets. We write *SYMB* for $SORT \cup FUNC \cup PRED \cup VAR$. We write $w \equiv w'$, where $w, w' \in SYMB$, to indicate that w and w' are identical symbols.

The language, proof system and interpretation of MPL$_\omega(\Sigma)$ are defined in Section 3.3, Section 3.4 and Section 3.5, respectively.

3.3 Language of MPL$_\omega(\mathbf{\Sigma})$

The language of MPL$_\omega(\Sigma)$ contains terms and formulae. They are constructed according to the formation rules which are given below.

Definition. The *terms* and *formulae* of MPL$_\omega(\Sigma)$ are simultaneously and inductively defined by the following formation rules:

1. variable symbols of sort S are terms of sort S, for any $S \in \mathrm{S}(\Sigma)$;
2. if $f \in \mathrm{F}(\Sigma) \cup \mathrm{SF}(\Sigma)$, $f\colon S_1 \times \cdots \times S_n \to S_{n+1}$ and $t_1, \ldots, t_n$ are terms of sorts $S_1, \ldots, S_n$, respectively, then $f(t_1, \ldots, t_n)$ is a term of sort S_{n+1};
3. if A is a formula and x is a variable of sort S, $S \in \mathrm{S}(\Sigma)$, then $\iota x\colon S\,(A)$ is a term of sort S;
4. $\top$ and $\bot$ are formulae;
5. if $P \in \mathrm{P}(\Sigma) \cup \mathrm{SP}(\Sigma)$, $P\colon S_1 \times \cdots \times S_n$ and $t_1, \ldots, t_n$ are terms of sorts $S_1, \ldots, S_n$, respectively, then $P(t_1, \ldots, t_n)$ is a formula;
6. if A is formula, then $\neg A$ is a formula;
7. if $\langle A_n \rangle_{n<\omega} = \langle A_0, A_1, \ldots \rangle$ are formulae, then $\bigwedge_n A_n$ is a formula;
8. if A is a formula and x is a variable of sort S, $S \in \mathrm{S}(\Sigma)$, then $\forall x\colon S\,(A)$ is a formula.

We write $sort(t)$, where t is a term, for the sort of t.

The string representation of formulae as suggested by the formation rules above can lead to syntactic ambiguities. Parentheses are used to avoid such ambiguities.

Definition. For every countable set Γ of formulae of MPL$_\omega(\Sigma)$, $sig(\Gamma)$, the *signature* of Γ, is the smallest signature such that for every formula $A \in \Gamma$, A is a formula of MPL$_\omega(sig(\Gamma))$. We write $sig(A)$, where A is a formula, for $sig(\{A\})$.

We shall henceforth use (with or without subscripts):

S and S' to stand for arbitrary sort symbols in $\mathrm{S}(\Sigma)$,
f and g to stand for arbitrary function symbols in $\mathrm{F}(\Sigma)$,

P and Q to stand for arbitrary predicate symbols in $\mathrm{P}(\Sigma)$,
x, y and z to stand for arbitrary variable symbols (of appropriate sorts),
t and t' to stand for arbitrary terms of $\mathrm{MPL}_\omega(\Sigma)$,
A and A' to stand for arbitrary formulae of $\mathrm{MPL}_\omega(\Sigma)$.

Notational conventions and abbreviations

Constant symbols may be used as terms: in terms of the form $f(t_1, \ldots, t_n)$ the parentheses may be omitted whenever $n = 0$. The undefined symbols ($\uparrow_S$) are used without subscript when this causes no ambiguity. The equality symbols ($=_S$) are used in infix notation. They are also used without subscript when this causes no ambiguity. Sometimes $\forall x_1 \colon S_1 \, (\cdots \forall x_n \colon S_n \, (A) \cdots)$ is simply written as $\forall x_1 \colon S_1, \ldots, x_n \colon S_n \, (A)$.

Definitions. Disjunction, existential quantification, etc. are introduced as abbreviations:

$$
\begin{array}{lcl}
A_1 \wedge A_2 & := & \bigwedge_n A'_n, \text{where } A'_0 = A_1, A'_n = A_2 \text{ for } 0 < n < \omega, \\
A_1 \vee A_2 & := & \neg(\neg A_1 \wedge \neg A_2), \\
A_1 \rightarrow A_2 & := & \neg A_1 \vee A_2, \\
A_1 \leftrightarrow A_2 & := & (A_1 \rightarrow A_2) \wedge (A_2 \rightarrow A_1), \\
\bigvee_n A_n & := & \neg \bigwedge_n \neg A_n, \\
\exists x \colon S\,(A) & := & \neg \forall x \colon S\,(\neg A), \\
t{\downarrow_S} & := & t =_S t, \\
t_1 \simeq_S t_2 & := & (t_1{\downarrow_S} \vee t_2{\downarrow_S}) \rightarrow t_1 =_S t_2, \\
t_1 \neq_S t_2 & := & \neg(t_1 =_S t_2).
\end{array}
$$

The need to use parentheses in the string representation of formulae is reduced by ranking the precedence of the logical symbols $\neg$, $\wedge$, $\vee$, $\rightarrow$, $\leftrightarrow$. The enumeration presents this order from the highest precedence to the lowest precedence.

The definedness symbols ($\downarrow_S$), non-existential equality symbols ($\simeq_S$), and non-equality symbols ($\neq_S$) are also used without subscript when this causes no ambiguity.

The atomic formula $t_1 =_S t_2$ is false whenever t_1 or t_2 is non-denoting. So $=_S$ does not satisfy $\uparrow_S =_S \uparrow_S$. $t_1 \simeq_S t_2$ is true whenever both t_1 and t_2 are non-denoting. So $\simeq_S$ satisfies $t \simeq_S t$ for all terms t of sort S.

Free variables and well-formedness

The terms and formulae of $\mathrm{MPL}_\omega(\Sigma)$ that can be constructed from the signature Σ according to the formation rules which are given above include ill-formed terms and formulae. Only terms and formulae with a finite number of free variables are well-formed.

Definition. The free variables of terms and formulae are given by the function *free*, which is inductively defined by

$$\begin{array}{ll}
\mathit{free}(x) & = \{x\}, \\
\mathit{free}(f(t_1, \ldots, t_n)) & = \mathit{free}(t_1) \cup \ldots \cup \mathit{free}(t_n), \\
\mathit{free}(\uparrow s) & = \{\,\}, \\
\mathit{free}(\iota x\colon S\,(A)) & = \mathit{free}(A) - \{x\}, \\
\mathit{free}(\top) & = \{\,\}, \\
\mathit{free}(\bot) & = \{\,\}, \\
\mathit{free}(P(t_1, \ldots, t_n)) & = \mathit{free}(t_1) \cup \ldots \cup \mathit{free}(t_n), \\
\mathit{free}(t_1 = t_2) & = \mathit{free}(t_1) \cup \mathit{free}(t_2), \\
\mathit{free}(\neg A) & = \mathit{free}(A), \\
\mathit{free}(\bigwedge_n A_n) & = \bigcup\{\mathit{free}(A_n) \mid n < \omega\}, \\
\mathit{free}(\forall x\colon S\,(A)) & = \mathit{free}(A) - \{x\}.
\end{array}$$

So $\mathit{free}(E)$ is the set of variable symbols occurring free in the term or formula E. We write $\mathit{free}(\Gamma)$, where Γ is a set of formulae, for $\bigcup\{\mathit{free}(A) \mid A \in \Gamma\}$. A variable symbol x is called *free in* Γ if $x \in \mathit{free}(\Gamma)$. A formula A of MPL$_\omega(\Sigma)$ is a *closed* formula iff $\mathit{free}(A) = \{\,\}$.

Definition. A term or formula E of MPL$_\omega(\Sigma)$ is *well-formed* iff $\mathit{free}(E)$ is finite. In what follows, terms and formulae are always assumed to be well-formed.

The notion of a free occurrence of a variable in a term or formula is also used in connection with substitution and proofs.

Substitution

Substitution is basic for proofs in MPL$_\omega$. It is also used in the definition of abbreviations. For the latter purpose, it is sometimes convenient to use simultaneous substitution of several variables.

Definition. Let $x_1, \ldots, x_n$ be distinct variable symbols and let $t_1, \ldots, t_n$ be terms such that x_i and t_i are of the same sort (for $i = 1, \ldots, n$). Then $[x_1 := t_1, \ldots, x_n := t_n]$ is a *substitution* for variables. A substitution $\theta = [x_1 := t_1, \ldots, x_n := t_n]$ denotes a function on terms and formulae that is inductively defined by

$$\begin{array}{lcll}
\theta(x) & = & t_i \quad \text{if } x \equiv x_i \ (1 \le i \le n), & \\
 & & x \quad \text{if } x \not\equiv x_1, \ldots, x \not\equiv x_n, & \\
\theta(f(t'_1, \ldots, t'_m)) & = & f(\theta(t'_1), \ldots, \theta(t'_m)), & \\
\theta(\uparrow s) & = & \uparrow s & \\
\theta(\iota x\colon S\,(A)) & = & \iota y\colon S\,([x := y](\theta_x(A))) & \text{if } x \text{ free in } t_1, \ldots, t_n \\
 & & & \quad (y \text{ not in } \theta_x(A)), \\
 & & \iota x\colon S\,(\theta_x(A)) & \text{otherwise,}
\end{array}$$

$$
\begin{array}{lll}
\theta(\top) & = \top, & \\
\theta(\bot) & = \bot, & \\
\theta(P(t'_1,\ldots,t'_m)) & = P(\theta(t'_1),\ldots,\theta(t'_m)), & \\
\theta(t'_1 = t'_2) & = \theta(t'_1) = \theta(t'_2), & \\
\theta(\neg A) & = \neg\,\theta(A), & \\
\theta(\bigwedge_m A_m) & = \bigwedge_m \theta(A_m), & \\
\theta(\forall x{:}\,S\,(A)) & = \forall y{:}\,S\,([x := y](\theta_x(A))) & \text{if } x \text{ free in } t_1,\ldots,t_n \\
 & & (y \text{ not in } \theta_x(A)), \\
 & \ \forall x{:}\,S\,(\theta_x(A)) & \text{otherwise,}
\end{array}
$$

where θ_x stands for:

$$
\begin{array}{ll}
[x_1 := t_1,\ldots,x_{i-1} := t_{i-1}, x_{i+1} := t_{i+1},\ldots,x_n := t_n] & \text{if } x \equiv x_i\ (1 \le i \le n), \\
\theta & \text{if } x \not\equiv x_1,\ldots,x \not\equiv x_n.
\end{array}
$$

So $\theta(E)$ is the result of simultaneous replacement of the terms $t_1,\ldots,t_n$ for the free occurrences of the variable symbols $x_1,\ldots,x_n$ in E, avoiding free variables in $t_1,\ldots,t_n$ becoming bound by means of renaming bound variables.

The proof system presented in the next section only requires understanding of the substitution of a single variable. Simultaneous substitution of several variables is needed in Section 3.7.

3.4 Proof system of $\mathbf{MPL}_\omega(\mathbf{\Sigma})$

The proof system of $\mathrm{MPL}_\omega(\Sigma)$ is formulated as a Gentzen-type sequent calculus.

Definition. A *sequent* is an expression of the form $\Gamma \vdash \Delta$, where Γ and Δ are countable sets of formulae of $\mathrm{MPL}_\omega(\Sigma)$ with only finitely many different free variables, i.e. *free*(Γ) and *free*(Δ) are finite. Instead of $\{\,\} \vdash \Delta$ we write $\vdash \Delta$, and instead of $\Gamma \vdash \{\,\}$ we write $\Gamma \vdash$. Furthermore, we write Γ, Δ for $\Gamma \cup \Delta$ and A for $\{A\}$.

The intended meaning of the sequent $\Gamma \vdash \Delta$ is that the conjunction of the formulae in Γ entails the disjunction of the formulae in Δ. A sequent is proved by a derivation obtained by using the axiom schemas and rules of inference given below.

We shall use Γ, Δ, Γ' and Δ' to stand for arbitrary countable sets of formulae of $\mathrm{MPL}_\omega(\Sigma)$ with only finitely many different free variables.

Definition. The *proof system* of $\mathrm{MPL}_\omega(\Sigma)$ is defined by the following axiom schemas and rules of inference:

Logical Axioms.

$(\top)\quad \vdash \top$

$(\bot)\quad \bot \vdash$

(taut) $\quad A \vdash A$

Non-logical Axioms.

(eqv) $\quad \vdash \forall x\colon S\,(x = x) \land \forall x\colon S, y\colon S, z\colon S\,(x = y \land x = z \to y = z)$

(sub) $\quad t_1 = t_2, [x := t_1]A \vdash [x := t_2]A$

$(f{\downarrow})\quad \vdash f(t_1, \ldots, t_n){\downarrow} \to t_1{\downarrow} \land \ldots \land t_n{\downarrow}$

$(\uparrow\downarrow)\quad \vdash \neg(\uparrow_S{\downarrow})$

$(P{\downarrow})\quad \vdash P(t_1, \ldots, t_n) \to t_1{\downarrow} \land \ldots \land t_n{\downarrow}$

$(={\downarrow})\quad \vdash t_1 = t_2 \to t_1{\downarrow} \land t_2{\downarrow}$

$(\iota)\quad \vdash \forall y\colon S\,(y = \iota x\colon S\,(A) \leftrightarrow \forall x\colon S\,(A \leftrightarrow x = y))$

Rules of Inference.

$$(\neg L)\ \frac{\Gamma \vdash \Delta, A}{\Gamma, \neg A \vdash \Delta} \qquad (\neg R)\ \frac{\Gamma, A \vdash \Delta}{\Gamma \vdash \Delta, \neg A}$$

$$(\textstyle\bigwedge L)\ \frac{\Gamma, A_i \vdash \Delta}{\Gamma, \bigwedge_n A_n \vdash \Delta}\ \text{for all } i \qquad (\textstyle\bigwedge R)\ \frac{\langle \Gamma \vdash \Delta, A_n \rangle_{n<\omega}}{\Gamma \vdash \Delta, \bigwedge_n A_n}$$

$$(\forall L)\ \frac{\Gamma \vdash \Delta, t{\downarrow}_S \quad \Gamma, [x := t]A \vdash \Delta}{\Gamma, \forall x\colon S\,(A) \vdash \Delta} \qquad (\forall R)\ \frac{\Gamma, x{\downarrow}_S \vdash \Delta, A}{\Gamma \vdash \Delta, \forall x\colon S\,(A)}$$

$$(\text{cut})\ \frac{\Gamma \vdash \Delta, A \quad \Gamma', A \vdash \Delta'}{\Gamma, \Gamma' \vdash \Delta, \Delta'} \qquad (\text{weak})\ \frac{\Gamma \vdash \Delta}{\Gamma, \Gamma' \vdash \Delta, \Delta'}$$

Restriction on the axiom schema (ι): $\quad y$ not free in A.
Restriction on the rule $(\forall R)$: $\quad x$ not free in $\Gamma \cup \Delta$.

Multiple instances of axiom schema (eqv) for the same sort symbol are superfluous.

Definition. A *derivation* (or *proof*) is a possibly infinitely branching tree with branches of finite length, where the nodes are labelled with sequents in such a way that the labels of terminal nodes are instances of axiom schemas and the label of any non-terminal node is obtained from the labels of its immediate descendants by applying an inference rule. A sequent $\Gamma \vdash \Delta$ is *derivable* if there exists a derivation with its root labelled by $\Gamma \vdash \Delta$. We write $\mathrm{MPL}_\omega(\Sigma)\colon \Gamma \vdash \Delta$ (and sometimes just $\Gamma \vdash \Delta$ without more ado) to indicate that $\Gamma \vdash \Delta$ is derivable.

This sequent calculus resembles a Gentzen-type sequent calculus for infinitary classical first-order logic with equality. There are additional non-logical axiom schemas concerning definedness for the function and predicate symbols (including the undefined and equality symbols). There is also an axiom schema for descriptions. The slightly adapted rules for the universal quantifier are due to the treatment of free and bound variables: free variables may not denote but bound variables always do.

The interpretation presented in the next section can be viewed as a justification of the axioms and rules of inference given above: the axioms are all valid under the interpretation and the rules of inference preserve validity.

3.5 Interpretation of $\mathbf{MPL}_\omega(\mathbf{\Sigma})$

Terms and formulae of $\mathrm{MPL}_\omega(\Sigma)$ are interpreted in structures which consist of an interpretation of every symbol in the signature Σ as well as an interpretation of the equality symbols. The interpretations of sort symbols must be sets containing a special element $\bot$. When a term is non-denoting, $\bot$ is used as its interpretation. The interpretation of every symbol concerned is in accordance with the following treatment of non-denoting terms: atomic formulae that contain non-denoting terms are logically false.

Definition. A *structure* $\mathbf{A}$ with signature Σ consists of:

1. for every $S \in \mathrm{S}(\Sigma)$, a non-empty set $S^\mathbf{A}$ such that $\bot \in S^\mathbf{A}$;
2. for every $f \in \mathrm{F}(\Sigma)$, $f\colon S_1 \times \cdots \times S_n \to S_{n+1}$,
   a total map $f^\mathbf{A}\colon S_1^\mathbf{A} \times \cdots \times S_n^\mathbf{A} \to S_{n+1}^\mathbf{A}$ such that

   $$\begin{array}{l} \textit{for all } d_1 \in S_1^\mathbf{A}, \ldots, d_n \in S_n^\mathbf{A}, \\ \quad d_1 = \bot \textit{ or } \ldots \textit{ or } d_n = \bot \Rightarrow f^\mathbf{A}(d_1, \ldots, d_n) = \bot; \end{array}$$

3. for every $P \in \mathrm{P}(\Sigma)$, $P\colon S_1 \times \cdots \times S_n$,
   a total map $P^\mathbf{A}\colon S_1^\mathbf{A} \times \cdots \times S_n^\mathbf{A} \to \{\mathsf{T}, \mathsf{F}\}$ such that

   $$\begin{array}{l} \textit{for all } d_1 \in S_1^\mathbf{A}, \ldots, d_n \in S_n^\mathbf{A}, \\ \quad d_1 = \bot \textit{ or } \ldots \textit{ or } d_n = \bot \Rightarrow P^\mathbf{A}(d_1, \ldots, d_n) = \mathsf{F}; \end{array}$$

4. for every $S \in \mathrm{S}(\Sigma)$,
   a total map $=_S^\mathbf{A}\colon S^\mathbf{A} \times S^\mathbf{A} \to \{\mathsf{T}, \mathsf{F}\}$ such that

   $$\begin{array}{l} \textit{for all } d, d' \in S^\mathbf{A}, \\ \quad =_S^\mathbf{A}(d, d') = \begin{array}{ll} \mathsf{T} & \text{if } d \neq \bot \textit{ and } d' \neq \bot \textit{ and } d = d', \\ \mathsf{F} & \text{if } d = \bot \textit{ or } d' = \bot \textit{ or } d \neq d'. \end{array} \end{array}$$

Instead of $w^{\mathbf{A}}$ we write w when it is clear from the context that the interpretation of symbol w in structure $\mathbf{A}$ is meant.

The interpretation of terms and formulae of $\mathrm{MPL}_\omega(\Sigma)$ in a structure $\mathbf{A}$ is furthermore defined with respect to an assignment in $\mathbf{A}$, which is a function that assigns to variables of sorts in Σ elements of the corresponding domains in $\mathbf{A}$.

Definition. Let $\mathbf{A}$ be a structure with signature Σ. Then an *assignment* in $\mathbf{A}$ is a mapping $\alpha\colon VAR \to \bigcup\{S^{\mathbf{A}} \mid S \in \mathrm{S}(\Sigma)\}$ such that $\alpha(x) \in S^{\mathbf{A}}$ if x is a variable of sort S. For every assignment α in $\mathbf{A}$, variable symbol x of sort $S \in \mathrm{S}(\Sigma)$ and element $d \in S^{\mathbf{A}}$, we write $\alpha(x \to d)$ for the assignment α' such that $\alpha'(y) = \alpha(y)$ if $y \not\equiv x$ and $\alpha'(x) = d$.

The interpretation of terms is given by a function mapping term t of sort S, structure $\mathbf{A}$ and assignment α in $\mathbf{A}$ to the element of $S^{\mathbf{A}}$ that is the value of t in $\mathbf{A}$ under assignment α. Similarly, the interpretation of formulae is given by a function mapping formula A, structure $\mathbf{A}$ and assignment α in $\mathbf{A}$ to the element of $\{\mathsf{T},\mathsf{F}\}$ that is the truth value of A in $\mathbf{A}$ under assignment α. We write $[\![t]\!]^{\mathbf{A}}_\alpha$ and $[\![A]\!]^{\mathbf{A}}_\alpha$ for these interpretations. The superscripts are omitted when it is clear from the context which structure is meant.

Definition. The *interpretation* functions for terms and formulae are inductively defined by

$$
\begin{array}{lcll}
[\![x]\!]_\alpha & = & \alpha(x), & \\
[\![f(t_1,\ldots,t_n)]\!]_\alpha & = & f([\![t_1]\!]_\alpha,\ldots,[\![t_n]\!]_\alpha), & \\
[\![\uparrow s]\!]_\alpha & = & \bot, & \\
[\![\iota x\colon S\,(A)]\!]_\alpha & = & \textit{the unique } d \in S - \{\bot\} & \\
 & & \textit{such that } [\![A]\!]_{\alpha(x\to d)} = \mathsf{T} & \text{if it exists,} \\
 & & \bot & \text{otherwise,}
\end{array}
$$

$$
\begin{array}{lcl}
[\![\top]\!]_\alpha & = & \mathsf{T}, \\
[\![\bot]\!]_\alpha & = & \mathsf{F}, \\
[\![P(t_1,\ldots,t_n)]\!]_\alpha & = & P([\![t_1]\!]_\alpha,\ldots,[\![t_n]\!]_\alpha), \\
[\![t_1 = t_2]\!]_\alpha & = & =_S([\![t_1]\!]_\alpha,[\![t_2]\!]_\alpha),
\end{array}
$$

$$
\begin{array}{lcll}
[\![\neg A]\!]_\alpha & = & \mathsf{T} & \text{if } [\![A]\!]_\alpha = \mathsf{F}, \\
 & & \mathsf{F} & \text{if } [\![A]\!]_\alpha = \mathsf{T}, \\
[\![\bigwedge_n A_n]\!]_\alpha & = & \mathsf{T} & \text{if } [\![A_n]\!]_\alpha = \mathsf{T} \textit{ for all } n < \omega, \\
 & & \mathsf{F} & \text{if } [\![A_n]\!]_\alpha = \mathsf{F} \textit{ for some } n < \omega, \\
[\![\forall x\colon S\,(A)]\!]_\alpha & = & \mathsf{T} & \text{if } \textit{for all } d \in S - \{\bot\},\ [\![A]\!]_{\alpha(x\to d)} = \mathsf{T}, \\
 & & \mathsf{F} & \text{if } \textit{for some } d \in S - \{\bot\},\ [\![A]\!]_{\alpha(x\to d)} = \mathsf{F}.
\end{array}
$$

We write $\mathbf{A} \models A[\alpha]$ for $[\![A]\!]^{\mathbf{A}}_\alpha = \mathsf{T}$.

The notion of consequence is useful to characterize the relation between the interpretation of $\mathrm{MPL}_\omega(\Sigma)$ and the proof system of $\mathrm{MPL}_\omega(\Sigma)$.

Definition. For countable sets Γ and Δ of formulae of $\mathrm{MPL}_\omega(\Sigma)$, Δ is a *consequence* of Γ, written $\Gamma \models \Delta$, iff for all structures $\mathbf{A}$ with signature Σ, for all assignments α in $\mathbf{A}$, if $\mathbf{A} \models A[\alpha]$ for all $A \in \Gamma$ then $\mathbf{A} \models A'[\alpha]$ for some $A' \in \Delta$.

Theorem. MPL_ω has the following soundness and completeness properties:

soundness: if $\Gamma \vdash \Delta$, then $\Gamma \models \Delta$;
completeness: if $\Gamma \models \Delta$, then $\Gamma \vdash \Delta$.

Proof: See (Koymans and Renardel de Lavalette, 1989, Section 3.2). □

3.6 Properties of MPL_ω

Some other properties are presented here without proofs. They are relevant to the use of this logic as the underlying logic for a semantics of VVSL.

The splitting interpolation property is needed for appropriate properties of the modularization mechanisms of VVSL. Informally, this interpolation property can be described as follows: if a conjunction of formulae entails a formula A, then a part of the conjunction, say Γ, can always be replaced by a formula that is entailed by that part of the conjunction. In order to exclude trivial cases, each symbol that occurs in the replacing formula must also occur in Γ and either A or the remaining part of the conjunction (variable symbols occurring free included).

Theorem. MPL_ω has the following splitting interpolation property:
Let Γ and Δ be countable sets of formulae of $\mathrm{MPL}_\omega(\Sigma)$ with only finitely many different free variables and let A be a formula of $\mathrm{MPL}_\omega(\Sigma)$. Then

if $\mathrm{MPL}_\omega(\Sigma)\colon \Gamma, \Delta \vdash A$,
then $\mathrm{MPL}_\omega(\Sigma)\colon \Gamma \vdash I$ and $\mathrm{MPL}_\omega(\Sigma)\colon \Delta, I \vdash A$

for some formula I such that
$\mathit{par}(\{I\}) \subseteq \mathit{par}(\Gamma) \cap (\mathit{par}(\Delta) \cup \mathit{par}(\{A\}))$,

where $\mathit{par}(\Gamma) = \mathit{sig}(\Gamma) \cup \mathit{free}(\Gamma) \cup \{\mathit{sort}(x) \mid x \in \mathit{free}(\Gamma)\}$.
Proof: The normal interpolation property (obtained by taking $\Delta = \{\,\}$) is proved for MPL_ω in (Koymans and Renardel de Lavalette, 1989, Section 3.3) using splitting interpolation as the induction hypothesis. For MPL_ω, the normal interpolation property is equivalent to the splitting interpolation property. □

At the level of theories (i.e. sets of formulae that are closed under entailment), this is equivalent to saying that exporting (restriction of the theory to a subsignature) distributes over importing (closed union of two theories) provided that the exported signature is a common subsignature of the signatures of both theories.

The proof of the following result in (Renardel de Lavalette, 1989, Appendices B,C) shows that MPL_ω is well related to classical first-order logic with countably infinite conjunctions.

Theorem. MPL_ω can be reduced to $\mathrm{L}^=_\omega$, classical first-order logic with equality and countably infinite conjunctions:

$$\mathrm{MPL}_\omega(\Sigma){:}\quad \vdash A \text{ iff } \mathrm{L}^=_\omega(\Sigma^*){:}\ \mathrm{Ax}(\Sigma) \vdash A^*$$

for appropriate mappings $\bullet^*$ (for signatures and formulae) and an appropriate mapping Ax (mapping signatures of MPL_ω to sets of formulae of $\mathrm{L}^=_\omega$).

Proof: By the construction of appropriate mappings. These mappings are straightforward to construct, see (Renardel de Lavalette, 1989, Theorem C.1.2). □

MPL, the finitary fragment of MPL_ω, is obtained from MPL_ω by replacing countable conjunctions by binary conjunctions. This is done as follows:

replace formation rule 7 (Section 3.3) by the rule:

If A_1 and A_2 are formulae, then $A_1 \wedge A_2$ is a formula;

replace rules of inference ($\bigwedge L$) and ($\bigwedge R$) (Section 3.4) by the rules:

$$(\wedge\ L)\ \ \frac{\Gamma, A_1, A_2 \vdash \Delta}{\Gamma, A_1 \wedge A_2 \vdash \Delta} \qquad (\wedge\ R)\ \ \frac{\Gamma \vdash \Delta, A_1 \quad \Gamma \vdash \Delta, A_2}{\Gamma \vdash \Delta, A_1 \wedge A_2};$$

replace the interpretation rule for countable conjunctions (Section 3.5) by the following rule:

$$[\![A_1 \wedge A_2]\!]_\alpha \;=\; \begin{array}{ll} \mathsf{T} & \text{if } [\![A_1]\!]_\alpha = \mathsf{T} \textit{ and } [\![A_2]\!]_\alpha = \mathsf{T} \\ \mathsf{F} & \text{if } [\![A_1]\!]_\alpha = \mathsf{F} \textit{ or } [\![A_2]\!]_\alpha = \mathsf{F}. \end{array}$$

Furthermore, sets of formulae in sequents must be finite and derivations must be finitely branching trees.

The following result shows that the step from binary conjunctions to countably infinite conjunctions is only a minor step; it does not change anything in an essential way.

Theorem. MPL_ω is a conservative extension of MPL, i.e.

for every formula A of $\mathrm{MPL}(\Sigma)$, $\mathrm{MPL}_\omega(\Sigma)$: $\vdash A$ iff $\mathrm{MPL}(\Sigma)$: $\vdash A$.

Proof: See (Renardel de Lavalette, 1989, Theorem C.1.1). □

The soundness, completeness and interpolation results of MPL_ω carry over to its finitary fragment. Besides, MPL can be reduced to $\mathrm{L}^=$, classical (finitary) first-order logic with equality. This demonstrates the lack of interference between countably infinite conjunctions and the other special features of MPL_ω.

3.7 Inductive definitions in MPL$_\omega$

A large class of inductive definitions of predicates and functions can be regarded as mere abbreviations of formulae of MPL$_\omega$. In this section, inductive predicate definitions $P \overset{\mathrm{I}}{:=} A$ and inductive function definitions $f \overset{\mathrm{I}}{:=} A$ (the symbol $\overset{\mathrm{I}}{:=}$ is read as 'is inductively defined by') are defined as abbreviations of formulae using additional abbreviations. The additional abbreviations introduce notation from set theory (e.g. set comprehension) and notation from λ-calculus (e.g. lambda abstraction) for explicit definition of predicates and functions. Set comprehension for explicit definition of predicates, lambda abstraction for explicit definition of functions and predicate operators (which map predicates to predicates) can also be treated as definitional extensions of MPL$_\omega$, see (Renardel de Lavalette, 1989, Section D.1.7).

Firstly, the intuition of defined predicates as predicates which are explicitly defined by set comprehension is made precise.

Defined predicates

Definition. A *defined predicate* of MPL$_\omega(\Sigma)$ is an expression of the form

$$\{x_1: S_1, \ldots, x_n: S_n \mid A\},$$

where $x_1, \ldots, x_n$ are distinct variable symbols of sorts $S_1, \ldots, S_n$, respectively.
The *type* of a defined predicate $\{x_1: S_1, \ldots, x_n: S_n \mid A\}$ is $S_1 \times \cdots \times S_n$.
For terms $t_1, \ldots, t_n$ of sorts $S_1, \ldots, S_n$, $\{x_1: S_1, \ldots, x_n: S_n \mid A\}(t_1, \ldots, t_n)$ is defined as an abbreviation of a formula of MPL$_\omega(\Sigma)$ by

$$\{x_1: S_1, \ldots, x_n: S_n \mid A\}(t_1, \ldots, t_n) := [x_1 := t_1, \ldots, x_n := t_n]A \wedge t_1{\downarrow} \wedge \ldots \wedge t_n{\downarrow}\,.$$

$t_1{\downarrow} \wedge \ldots \wedge t_n{\downarrow}$ is added in order to guarantee that all defined predicates are strict, i.e. yield false if some argument is undefined.
Each predicate symbol $P \in \mathrm{P}(\Sigma)$, $P: S_1 \times \cdots \times S_n$, is identified with the defined predicate $\{x_1: S_1, \ldots, x_n: S_n \mid P(x_1, \ldots, x_n)\}$.

We shall henceforth use D, D' and D'' (with or without subscripts) to stand for arbitrary defined predicates of MPL$_\omega(\Sigma)$.

Definition. The following abbreviations of defined predicates are used:

$$\emptyset_{S_1 \times \cdots \times S_n} := \{x_1: S_1, \ldots, x_n: S_n \mid \bot\},$$
$$(x_1: S_1, \ldots, x_n: S_n)^{\mathbf{C}} := \{y_1: S_1, \ldots, y_n: S_n \mid y_1 \neq x_1 \vee \ldots \vee y_n \neq x_n\},$$
$$\bigcup\{\{x_1: S_1, \ldots, x_n: S_n \mid A_m\} \mid m \in \omega\} := \{x_1: S_1, \ldots, x_n: S_n \mid \textstyle\bigvee_m A_m\}.$$

Definition. *Inclusion* and extensional *equality* between defined predicates are defined as abbreviations of formulae of MPL$_\omega(\Sigma)$ by

$$\{x_1\colon S_1,\ldots,x_n\colon S_n \mid A_1\} \subseteq \{x_1\colon S_1,\ldots,x_n\colon S_n \mid A_2\} := \forall x_1\colon S_1,\ldots,x_n\colon S_n\,(A_1 \to A_2),$$
$$\{x_1\colon S_1,\ldots,x_n\colon S_n \mid A_1\} = \{x_1\colon S_1,\ldots,x_n\colon S_n \mid A_2\} := \forall x_1\colon S_1,\ldots,x_n\colon S_n\,(A_1 \leftrightarrow A_2).$$

Definition. *Functionality* of $D = \{x_1\colon S_1,\ldots,x_n\colon S_n, y\colon S \mid A\}$ is defined as an abbreviation of a formula of MPL$_\omega(\Sigma)$ by

$$\mathrm{Func}(D) := \forall x_1\colon S_1,\ldots,x_n\colon S_n, y\colon S, z\colon S\,(D(x_1,\ldots,x_n,y) \wedge D(x_1,\ldots,x_n,z) \to y = z).$$

Having introduced defined predicates, we may consider the (simultaneous) replacement of defined predicates for the occurrences of predicate symbols in terms and formulae.

Definition. Let $P_1,\ldots,P_n$ $(n \geq 0)$ be distinct predicate symbols and let $D_1,\ldots,D_n$ be defined predicates such that P_i and D_i are of the same type $(i = 1,\ldots,n)$. Then $[P_1 := D_1,\ldots,P_n := D_n]$ is called a *predicate substitution.* A predicate substitution $\rho = [P_1 := D_1,\ldots,P_n := D_n]$ denotes a function on terms and formulae that is defined analogously to variable substitution, with the following rule for predicate application:

$$\begin{array}{rcll} \rho(P(t_1,\ldots,t_m)) & = & D_i(\rho(t_1),\ldots,\rho(t_m)) & \text{if } P \equiv P_i\ (1 \leq i \leq n), \\ & & P(\rho(t_1),\ldots,\rho(t_m)) & \text{if } P \not\equiv P_1,\ldots,P \not\equiv P_n. \end{array}$$

The main difference with positive predicate substitution (defined below) is that the rule for negation is analogous to the one for variable substitution, i.e. it is simply $\rho(\neg A) = \neg\rho(A)$.

Definition. If ρ is a predicate substitution, then ρ^+ is called a *positive predicate substitution* and ρ^- is called a *negative predicate substitution.* A positive predicate substitution $\rho^+ = [P_1 := D_1,\ldots,P_n := D_n]^+$ and a negative predicate substitution $\rho^- = [P_1 := D_1,\ldots,P_n := D_n]^-$ denote functions on formulae not containing descriptions (i.e. terms of the form $\iota x\colon S\,(A)$) that are defined analogously to predicate substitution, with the rule for predicate application replaced by the rules:

$$\begin{array}{rcll} \rho^+(P(t_1,\ldots,t_m)) & = & D_i(t_1,\ldots,t_m) & \text{if } P \equiv P_i\ (1 \leq i \leq n), \\ & & P(t_1,\ldots,t_m) & \text{if } P \not\equiv P_1,\ldots,P \not\equiv P_n, \\ \rho^-(P(t_1,\ldots,t_m)) & = & P(t_1,\ldots,t_m), & \end{array}$$

and with the rule for negation replaced by the rules:

$$\begin{array}{ll} \rho^+(\neg A) & = \neg\rho^-(A), \\ \rho^-(\neg A) & = \neg\rho^+(A). \end{array}$$

Positive predicate substitution is used below for turning a formula which inductively defines a predicate into a corresponding predicate operator. The restriction to formulae not containing descriptions is not very important, since descriptions can be eliminated from any formula – by applying the mapping $\bullet^*$ defined in (Koymans and Renardel de Lavalette, 1989, Section 3.1.2). The reason for the restriction is that occurrences of predicate symbols in a description are at the same time 'positive' and 'negative'.

Defined predicates are now used to introduce predicate operators.

Predicate operators and their fixpoints

If a predicate is explicitly defined by means of a recursive definition, then the definition determines a mapping from predicates to predicates, called a predicate operator in this section. The least fixpoint of this predicate operator is considered to be the predicate being defined. Abbreviations are introduced below which are in accordance with this intuition.

Definition. A *predicate operator* of $\mathrm{MPL}_\omega(\Sigma)$ is an expression of the form

$$\Lambda P.D.$$

If $P\colon S'_1 \times \cdots \times S'_m$ and $D = \{x_1\colon S_1, \ldots, x_n\colon S_n \mid A\}$, then the *type* of a predicate operator $\Lambda P.D$ is $S'_1 \times \cdots \times S'_m \to S_1 \times \cdots \times S_n$.
For a defined predicate D' of type $S'_1 \times \cdots \times S'_m$, $(\Lambda P.D)D'$ is defined as an abbreviation of a defined predicate of $\mathrm{MPL}_\omega(\Sigma)$ by

$$(\Lambda P.D)D' \;:=\; \{x_1\colon S_1, \ldots, x_n\colon S_n \mid [P := D']A\}.$$

Definition. For a predicate operator Φ of type $S_1 \times \cdots \times S_n \to S_1 \times \cdots \times S_n$, $\mathrm{Fix}(\Phi)$, the *fixpoint* of Φ, is defined as an abbreviation of a defined predicate of $\mathrm{MPL}_\omega(\Sigma)$ by

$$\mathrm{Fix}(\Phi) \;:=\; \bigcup\{\Phi^m(\emptyset_{S_1 \times \cdots \times S_n}) \mid m \in \omega\},$$

$$\text{where } \Phi^0(D) \;:=\; D \text{ and } \Phi^{m+1}(D) \;:=\; \Phi(\Phi^m(D)).$$

If Φ is a continuous predicate operator, then one can prove that $\mathrm{Fix}(\Phi)$ is indeed the least fixpoint of Φ.

Definition. For a predicate symbol P, $P\colon S_1 \times \cdots \times S_n$, and a defined predicate $D = \{x_1\colon S_1, \ldots, x_n\colon S_n \mid A\}$, the predicate operator $\Lambda P.D$ is called *continuous* iff

$$\begin{array}{l} \{\forall y_1\colon S_1, \ldots, y_n\colon S_n\,(A_m \to A_{m+1}) \mid m \in \omega\} \vdash \\ \forall x_1\colon S_1, \ldots, x_n\colon S_n([P := \{y_1\colon S_1, \ldots, y_n\colon S_n \mid \bigvee_m A_m\}]A \leftrightarrow \\ \qquad\qquad\qquad \bigvee_m [P := \{y_1\colon S_1, \ldots, y_n\colon S_n \mid A_m\}]A) \end{array}$$

is derivable for all countably infinite sets $\{A_0, A_1, A_2, \ldots\}$ of formulae of $\mathrm{MPL}_\omega(\Sigma)$.
We also write $A \in \mathrm{Cts}(P, x_1\colon S_1, \ldots, x_n\colon S_n)$ for $\Lambda P.\{x_1\colon S_1, \ldots, x_n\colon S_n \mid A\}$ is continuous.

Fact. Let $\Phi = \Lambda P.D$ be a predicate operator of type $S_1 \times \cdots \times S_n \rightarrow S_1 \times \cdots \times S_n$. If Φ is continuous, then $\mathrm{Fix}(\Phi)$ is the least fixpoint of Φ, i.e.

$$\vdash \Phi(\mathrm{Fix}(\Phi)) = \mathrm{Fix}(\Phi),$$
$$\vdash \Phi(P) \subseteq P \rightarrow \mathrm{Fix}(\Phi) \subseteq P.$$

Proof: $\mathrm{Fix}(\Phi)$ is Kleene's least fixpoint construction (which stops at ω for a continuous operator), expressed in MPL_ω. □

So we have introduced a least fixpoint operator in MPL_ω by means of abbreviations. This means that explicit recursive definitions of predicates can be expressed as formulae in MPL_ω. Inductive definitions can also be expressed as formulae in MPL_ω if they can be translated into corresponding explicit recursive definitions. This is possible for a large class of inductive definitions.

Inductive predicate definitions as formulae

If a predicate P is implicitly defined by means of an inductive definition A, then we can usually obtain a corresponding defined predicate D such that

$$\vdash [P := D]A,$$
$$\vdash A \rightarrow D \subseteq P.$$

For example, the predicate P inductively defined by

$$P(0) \wedge \forall y{:}\, N\, (P(y) \rightarrow P(s(y)))$$

can also be defined as the least fixpoint of the predicate operator

$$\Lambda P.\{x{:}\, N \mid x = 0 \vee \exists y{:}\, N\, (P(y) \wedge x = s(y))\}.$$

A formula equivalent to $x = 0 \vee \exists y{:}\, N\, (P(y) \wedge x = s(y))$ can be obtained from the inductive definition as follows:

1. replace the positive occurrences of P by $\{z{:}\, N \mid z \neq x\}$ in the formula that inductively defines P:

$$\{z{:}\, N \mid z \neq x\}(0) \wedge \forall y{:}\, N\, (P(y) \rightarrow \{z{:}\, N \mid z \neq x\}(s(y)));$$

2. take the negation of the resulting formula:

$$\neg\, (0 \neq x \wedge \forall y{:}\, N\, (P(y) \rightarrow s(y) \neq x)).$$

It appears that this transformation can also be applied to other formulae. This is now worked out in detail, mainly by introduction of appropriate abbreviations.

Definition. Let $P{:}\, S_1 \times \cdots \times S_n$. Then $\delta P.A$, the predicate P which is inductively defined by A, is defined as an abbreviation of a defined predicate of $\mathrm{MPL}_\omega(\Sigma)$ by

$$\delta P.A :=$$
$$\mathrm{Fix}(\Lambda P.\{x_1{:}\, S_1, \ldots, x_n{:}\, S_n \mid \neg[P := (x_1{:}\, S_1, \ldots, x_n{:}\, S_n)^{\mathbf{C}}]^+ A\}).$$

If the recursive definition obtained from the inductive definition A determines a continuous predicate operator and A is moreover 'complement preserving', then $\delta P.A$ is indeed the predicate inductively defined by A.

Definition. Let $P\colon S_1 \times \ldots \times S_n$. Then a formula A is called *complement preserving* for P, written $A \in \mathrm{Pres}(P)$, iff

$$\vdash [P := \{x_1\colon S_1, \ldots, x_n\colon S_n \mid \neg[P := (x_1\colon S_1, \ldots, x_n\colon S_n)^{\mathbf{C}}]A\}]A;$$

A is called *admissible* for P, written $A \in \mathrm{Adm}(P)$, iff

$$\begin{array}{ll} \neg[P := (x_1\colon S_1, \ldots, x_n\colon S_n)^{\mathbf{C}}]^{+} A & \in \mathrm{Cts}(P, x_1\colon S_1, \ldots, x_n\colon S_n) \text{ and} \\ {[P := Q]^{-} A} & \in \mathrm{Pres}(P), \end{array}$$

where Q is a predicate symbol of the same type as P such that $Q \notin sig(A)$.

Fact. Let $A \in \mathrm{Adm}(P)$. Then $\delta P.A$ is the (defined) predicate P which is inductively defined by A, i.e.

$$\begin{array}{l} \vdash [P := \delta P.A]A, \\ \vdash A \to \delta P.A \subseteq P. \end{array}$$

Proof: See (Renardel de Lavalette, 1989, Theorem D.2.5). □

A sufficient syntactic condition for admissibility is now given. If A is a formula without descriptions of the form

$$\bigwedge_m (\forall x_1\colon S_1, \ldots, x_l\colon S_l \\ (\bigwedge_{i=1}^{k_m} (A_{mi}) \wedge t_{m1}{\downarrow} \wedge \ldots \wedge t_{mn}{\downarrow} \to P(t_{m1}, \ldots, t_{mn})))$$

where every formula A_{mi} is of the form $P(t_1, \ldots, t_n)$ or does not contain P, then $A \in \mathrm{Adm}(P)$. See also (Renardel de Lavalette, 1989, Section D.3). If $A_1 \in \mathrm{Adm}(P)$ and $\vdash [P := Q]^{+} A_1 \leftrightarrow [P := Q]^{+} A_2$ for some predicate symbol Q of the same type as P such that $Q \notin sig(\{A_1, A_2\})$, then also $A_2 \in \mathrm{Adm}(P)$.

Finally, inductive definitions of predicates can be defined as abbreviations of formulae of MPL_ω.

Definition. Let $P\colon S_1 \times \cdots \times S_n$. Then the *inductive predicate definition* $P :\stackrel{\mathrm{I}}{=} A$ is defined as an abbreviation of a formula of $\mathrm{MPL}_\omega(\Sigma)$ by

$$P :\stackrel{\mathrm{I}}{=} A \ := \ \forall x_1\colon S_1, \ldots, x_n\colon S_n\, (P(x_1, \ldots, x_n) \leftrightarrow (\delta P.A)(x_1, \ldots, x_n)).$$

If A is not admissible for P, then the meaning of this abbreviation possibly does not correspond to the intended one (viz. the one reflected in the fact above).

Inductive definitions of functions can be treated by translating them to inductive definitions of equivalent predicates.

Defined functions

Firstly, the intuition of defined functions as functions which are explicitly defined by function abstraction is made precise below.

Definition. A *defined function* of $\text{MPL}_\omega(\Sigma)$ is an expression of the form

$$\lambda x_1\colon S_1, \ldots, x_n\colon S_n.t,$$

where $x_1, \ldots, x_n$ are variable symbols of sorts $S_1, \ldots, S_n$, respectively.
The *type* of a defined function $\lambda x_1\colon S_1, \ldots, x_n\colon S_n.t$ is $S_1 \times \cdots \times S_n \to \mathit{sort}(t)$.
For terms $t_1, \ldots, t_n$ of sorts $S_1, \ldots, S_n$, $(\lambda x_1\colon S_1, \ldots, x_n\colon S_n.t)(t_1, \ldots, t_n)$ is defined as an abbreviation of a term of $\text{MPL}_\omega(\Sigma)$ by

$$(\lambda x_1\colon S_1, \ldots, x_n\colon S_n.t)(t_1, \ldots, t_n) := \iota y\colon S\,(y = [x_1 := t_1, \ldots, x_n := t_n]t \wedge t_1\downarrow \wedge \ldots \wedge t_n\downarrow) \quad (y \text{ not free in } t).$$

Note that it is not simply defined by

$$(\lambda x_1\colon S_1, \ldots, x_n\colon S_n.t)(t_1, \ldots, t_n) := [x_1 := t_1, \ldots, x_n := t_n]t,$$

since this would not guarantee that all defined functions are strict. In (Renardel de Lavalette, 1989), it was only defined as an abbreviation for terms t of the form $\iota x\colon S\,(A)$.
Each function symbol $f \in \text{F}(\Sigma)$, $f\colon S_1 \times \cdots \times S_n \to S$, is identified with the defined function $\lambda x_1\colon S_1, \ldots, x_n\colon S_n.f(x_1, \ldots, x_n)$.

Definition. *Inclusion* and extensional *equality* between defined functions are also defined as abbreviations of formulae of $\text{MPL}_\omega(\Sigma)$ by

$$\lambda x_1\colon S_1, \ldots, x_n\colon S_n.t_1 \subseteq \lambda x_1\colon S_1, \ldots, x_n\colon S_n.t_2 := \forall x_1\colon S_1, \ldots, x_n\colon S_n\,(t_1\downarrow \to t_1 = t_2),$$
$$\lambda x_1\colon S_1, \ldots, x_n\colon S_n.t_1 = \lambda x_1\colon S_1, \ldots, x_n\colon S_n.t_2 := \forall x_1\colon S_1, \ldots, x_n\colon S_n\,(t_1 \simeq t_2).$$

Inductive function definitions as formulae

A defined function $f\colon S_1 \times \cdots \times S_n \to S$, which is described by an inductive definition, can be obtained by translating the inductive definition of the function f into an inductive definition of a corresponding predicate $P_f\colon S_1 \times \cdots \times S_n \times S$, i.e. a predicate P_f such that

$$\vdash \forall x_1\colon S_1, \ldots, x_n\colon S_n, y\colon S\,(f(x_1, \ldots, x_n) = y \leftrightarrow P_f(x_1, \ldots, x_n, y)).$$

Definition. For a function symbol $f\colon S_1 \times \cdots \times S_n \to S$ and predicate symbol $P_f\colon S_1 \times \cdots \times S_n \times S$, the translation of the formula which inductively defines function f into a formula which inductively defines the corresponding predicate P_f is given by a mapping $\sigma_{f\sim P_f}$ defined on terms and formulae. This mapping and an auxiliary mapping $\epsilon_{f\sim P_f}$ defined on terms are simultaneously defined by the rules below. To enhance readability we use σ, ϵ without subscripts. It is assumed that, in a formula containing f, every occurrence of f is provided with a unique index. For each index i, x_i denotes a distinct variable symbol of sort S not free in the translated term or formula.

$$
\begin{array}{lcll}
\epsilon(t) & = & \top & \text{if } f \text{ not in } t, \\
\epsilon(g(t_1,\ldots,t_m)) & = & P_f(\sigma(t_1),\ldots,\sigma(t_m),x_i) & \text{if } g \equiv f \text{ and } i \text{ is index of the occurrence of } f, \\
 & & \epsilon(t_1) \wedge \ldots \wedge \epsilon(t_m) & \text{if } g \not\equiv f,
\end{array}
$$

$$
\begin{array}{lcll}
\sigma(t) & = & t & \text{if } f \text{ not in } t, \\
\sigma(g(t_1,\ldots,t_m)) & = & x_i & \text{if } g \equiv f \text{ and } i \text{ is index of the occurrence of } f, \\
 & & g(\sigma(t_1),\ldots,\sigma(t_m)) & \text{if } g \not\equiv f,
\end{array}
$$

$$
\begin{array}{lcll}
\sigma(P(t_1,\ldots,t_m)) & = & P(t_1,\ldots,t_m) & \text{if } f \text{ not in } t_1,\ldots,t_m, \\
 & & \exists x_1{:}\, S,\ldots,x_l{:}\, S\ (\epsilon(t_1) \wedge \ldots \wedge \epsilon(t_m) \wedge P(\sigma(t_1),\ldots,\sigma(t_m))) & \text{otherwise,}
\end{array}
$$

where $x_1,\ldots,x_l$ are the variables x_i occurring in $\epsilon(t_1) \wedge \ldots \wedge \epsilon(t_m)$,

σ commutes with $\neg$, $\bigwedge$ and $\forall$.

Definition. Let $f{:}\, S_1 \times \cdots \times S_n \to S$. Then $\delta f.A$, the function f which is inductively defined by A, is defined as an abbreviation of a defined function of $\mathrm{MPL}_\omega(\Sigma)$ by

$$\delta f.A \ := \ \lambda x_1{:}\, S_1,\ldots,x_n{:}\, S_n.\iota y{:}\, S\ ((\delta P_f.\sigma(A))(x_1,\ldots,x_n,y)),$$

where P_f is a predicate symbol of type $S_1 \times \cdots \times S_n \times S$ such that $P_f \notin sig(A)$.

If the translation of the inductive definition A for the corresponding predicate is admissible, then $\delta f.A$ is indeed the function inductively defined by A under the condition that this corresponding predicate is functional.

Definition. For $f \in \mathrm{F}(\Sigma)$, $f{:}\, S_1 \times \ldots \times S_n \to S$, a formula A of $\mathrm{MPL}_\omega(\Sigma)$ is called *admissible* for f, written $A \in \mathrm{Adm}(f)$, iff

$$\sigma(A) \in \mathrm{Adm}(P_f).$$

A is called *functionality preserving* for f iff

$$\vdash \mathrm{Func}(\delta P_f.\sigma(A)).$$

Fact. Let $A \in \text{Adm}(f)$. Then $\delta f.A$ is the (defined) function f which is inductively defined by A provided that A is functionality preserving for f, i.e.

$$\vdash \text{Func}(\delta P_f.\sigma(A)) \rightarrow [f := \delta f.A]A,$$
$$\vdash \text{Func}(\delta P_f.\sigma(A)) \rightarrow (A \rightarrow \delta f.A \subseteq f).$$

Proof: See (Renardel de Lavalette, 1989, Theorem D.4.4). □

A sufficient syntactic condition for admissibility is now given. If A is a formula without descriptions of the form

$$\bigwedge_m \forall x_1{:}\, S_1, \ldots, x_l{:}\, S_l(\bigwedge_{i=1}^{k_m}(A_{mi}) \wedge t_{m1}{\downarrow} \wedge \ldots \wedge t_{mn}{\downarrow} \rightarrow \forall x{:}\, S\,(t = x \rightarrow f(t_{m1}, \ldots, t_{mn}) = x))$$

where every formula A_{mi} is of the form $P(t_1, \ldots, t_n)$ or does not contain f and every term t_{mi} does not contain f, then $A \in \text{Adm}(f)$.

Finally, inductive definitions of functions can be defined as abbreviations of formulae of MPL_ω.

Definition. Let $f{:}\, S_1 \times \cdots \times S_n \rightarrow S$. Then the *inductive function definition* $f :\overset{\text{I}}{=} A$ is defined as an abbreviation of a formula of $\text{MPL}_\omega(\Sigma)$ by

$$f :\overset{\text{I}}{=} A \;:=\; \forall x_1{:}\, S_1, \ldots, x_n{:}\, S_n\,(f(x_1, \ldots, x_n) \simeq (\delta f.A)(x_1, \ldots, x_n)).$$

If A is not admissible for f or not functionality preserving for f, then the meaning of this abbreviation possibly does not correspond to the intended one.

The main definitions of the preceding subsections can now be generalized to simultaneous inductive definitions in the usual way, i.e. by regarding the simultaneous definition of several predicates or functions as the definition of a tuple of predicates or functions.

Simultaneous inductive definitions

Definition. A *tuple of predicate symbols* and a *tuple of defined predicates* are expressions of the form $\langle X_1, \ldots, X_n \rangle$, where the X_i are predicate symbols and the X_i are defined predicates, respectively.

We shall use (with or without subscripts):

$\boldsymbol{P}$ to stand for arbitrary tuples of predicate symbols of $\text{MPL}_\omega(\Sigma)$.
$\boldsymbol{D}$, $\boldsymbol{D}'$, $\boldsymbol{D}''$ to stand for arbitrary tuples of defined predicates of $\text{MPL}_\omega(\Sigma)$.

Definition. For predicate types $T_1, \ldots, T_n$, $\emptyset_{\langle T_1, \ldots, T_n \rangle}$ is defined as an abbreviation of a tuple of defined predicates by

$$\emptyset_{\langle T_1, \ldots, T_n \rangle} := \langle \emptyset_{T_1}, \ldots, \emptyset_{T_n} \rangle.$$

$\bigcup\{\boldsymbol{D}_m \mid m \in \omega\}$, where $\boldsymbol{D}_m = \langle D_{m1}, \ldots, D_{mn}\rangle$, is also defined component-wise:

$$\bigcup\{\boldsymbol{D}_m \mid m \in \omega\} \;:=\; \langle \bigcup\{D_{m1} \mid m \in \omega\}, \ldots, \bigcup\{D_{mn} \mid m \in \omega\}\rangle.$$

Definition. A *tuple-of-predicates operator* is of the form $\Lambda\boldsymbol{P}.\boldsymbol{D}$. Let $\boldsymbol{P} = \langle P_1, \ldots, P_{n'}\rangle$, $\boldsymbol{D} = \langle D_1, \ldots, D_n\rangle$, $D_i = \{x_{i1}\colon S_{i1}, \ldots, x_{in_i}\colon S_{in_i} \mid A_i\}$. For a tuple of defined predicates $\boldsymbol{D}' = \langle D'_1, \ldots, D'_{n'}\rangle$ such that $\boldsymbol{P}$ and $\boldsymbol{D}'$ are component-wise of the same type, $(\Lambda\boldsymbol{P}.\boldsymbol{D})\boldsymbol{D}'$ is defined as an abbreviation of a tuple of defined predicates by

$$(\Lambda\boldsymbol{P}.\boldsymbol{D})\boldsymbol{D}' \;:=\; \langle D''_1, \ldots, D''_n\rangle$$
$$\text{where } D''_i = \{x_{i1}\colon S_{i1}, \ldots, x_{in_i}\colon S_{in_i} \mid [P_1 := D'_1, \ldots, P_{n'} := D'_{n'}]A_i\}.$$

Definition. For a tuple-of-predicates operator $\boldsymbol{\Phi} = \Lambda\boldsymbol{P}.\boldsymbol{D}$ with $\boldsymbol{P}$ and $\boldsymbol{D}$ of the same length, say n, and component-wise of the same type, say T_i, $\mathrm{Fix}(\boldsymbol{\Phi})$, the fixpoint of $\boldsymbol{\Phi}$, is defined as an abbreviation of a tuple of defined predicates by

$$\mathrm{Fix}(\boldsymbol{\Phi}) \;:=\; \bigcup\{\boldsymbol{\Phi}^m(\emptyset_{\langle T_1, \ldots, T_n\rangle}) \mid m \in \omega\},$$
$$\text{where } \boldsymbol{\Phi}^0(\boldsymbol{D}) \;:=\; \boldsymbol{D} \text{ and } \boldsymbol{\Phi}^{m+1}(\boldsymbol{D}) \;:=\; \boldsymbol{\Phi}(\boldsymbol{\Phi}^m(\boldsymbol{D})).$$

Definition. Let $\boldsymbol{P} = \langle P_1, \ldots, P_n\rangle$, where $P_i\colon S_{i1} \times \cdots \times S_{in_i}$. Then $\delta\boldsymbol{P}.A$, the tuple of predicates $\boldsymbol{P}$ which are inductively defined by A, is defined as an abbreviation of a tuple of defined predicates by

$$\delta\boldsymbol{P}.A \;:=\; \mathrm{Fix}(\Lambda\boldsymbol{P}.\langle D_1, \ldots, D_n\rangle)$$
$$\text{where } D_i = \{x_{i1}\colon S_{i1}, \ldots, x_{in_i}\colon S_{in_i} \mid$$
$$\neg[P_i := (x_{i1}\colon S_{i1}, \ldots, x_{in_i}\colon S_{in_i})^{\mathrm{C}}]^+ A\}.$$

We write $(\delta\boldsymbol{P}.A)_i$ for the i-th component of $\delta\boldsymbol{P}.A$.

If A is admissible for P_i (for all i), then $\delta\boldsymbol{P}.A$ is indeed the tuple of predicates inductively defined by A.

Fact. Let $\boldsymbol{P} = \langle P_1, \ldots, P_n\rangle$ be a tuple of predicate symbols such that A is admissible for $P_1, \ldots, P_n$. Then $\delta\boldsymbol{P}.A$ is the tuple of (defined) predicates $\boldsymbol{P}$ which are inductively defined by A, i.e.

$$\vdash [P_1 := (\delta\boldsymbol{P}.A)_1, \ldots, P_n := (\delta\boldsymbol{P}.A)_n]A,$$

$$\vdash A \to \bigwedge_{i=1}^{n} (\delta\boldsymbol{P}.A)_i \subseteq P_i.$$

Proof: Analogously to the case of non-simultaneous inductive definitions, see (Renardel de Lavalette, 1989, Theorem D.2.5). □

Simultaneous inductive definitions of predicates can now be defined as abbreviations of sets of formulae of MPL_ω.

Definition. Let $\boldsymbol{P} = \langle P_1, \ldots, P_n\rangle$ with $P_i\colon S_{i1} \times \cdots \times S_{in_i}$. Then the *simultaneous inductive predicate definition* $\boldsymbol{P} :\overset{\mathrm{I}}{=} A$ is defined as an abbreviation of a set of formulae by

$$\begin{aligned}&\boldsymbol{P} :\overset{\mathrm{I}}{=} A \ := \{A_1, \ldots, A_n\}\\ &\text{where } A_i = \forall x_{i1}\colon S_{i1}, \ldots, x_{in_i}\colon S_{in_i}\\ &\qquad (P_i(x_{i1}, \ldots, x_{in_i}) \leftrightarrow (\delta \boldsymbol{P}.A)_i(x_{i1}, \ldots, x_{in_i})).\end{aligned}$$

If A is not admissible for P_i (for some i), then the meaning of this abbreviation possibly does not correspond to the intended one.

Definition. A *tuple of function symbols* and a *tuple of defined functions* are expressions of the form $\langle X_1, \ldots, X_n\rangle$, where the X_i are function symbols and the X_i are defined functions, respectively.

We shall use $\boldsymbol{f}$ (with or without subscripts) to stand for arbitrary tuples of predicate symbols of MPL$_\omega(\Sigma)$.

Definition. Let $\boldsymbol{f} = \langle f_1, \ldots, f_n\rangle$, where $f_i\colon S_{i1} \times \cdots \times S_{in_i} \to S_i$. Then $\delta \boldsymbol{f}.A$, the tuple of functions $\boldsymbol{f}$ which are inductively defined by A, is defined as an abbreviation of a tuple of defined functions by

$$\begin{aligned}&\delta \boldsymbol{f}.A \ := \langle M_1, \ldots, M_n\rangle\\ &\text{where } M_i = \lambda x_{i1}\colon S_{i1}, \ldots, x_{in_i}\colon S_{in_i}.\\ &\qquad \iota y_i\colon S_i\,((\delta \boldsymbol{P}_{\boldsymbol{f}}.\sigma(A))_i(x_{i1}, \ldots, x_{in_i}, y_i)),\end{aligned}$$

where the P_{f_i} are different predicate symbols, $P_{f_i}\colon S_{j1} \times \cdots \times S_{in_i} \times S_i$, such that $P_{f_i} \notin sig(A)$, and σ is a composition of the mappings $\sigma_{f_i \sim P_{f_i}}$ (the order of composition does not matter).

Simultaneous inductive definitions of functions can now be defined as abbreviations of sets of formulae of MPL$_\omega$.

Definition. Let $\boldsymbol{f} = \langle f_1, \ldots, f_n\rangle$, where $f_i\colon S_{i1} \times \cdots \times S_{in_i} \to S_i$. Then the *simultaneous inductive function definition* $\boldsymbol{f} :\overset{\mathrm{I}}{=} A$ is defined as an abbreviation of a set of formulae by

$$\begin{aligned}&\boldsymbol{f} :\overset{\mathrm{I}}{=} A \ := \{A_1, \ldots, A_n\}\\ &\text{where } A_i = \forall x_{i1}\colon S_{i1}, \ldots, x_{in_i}\colon S_{in_i}\\ &\qquad (f_i(x_{i1}, \ldots, x_{in_i}) \simeq (\delta \boldsymbol{f}.A)_i(x_{i1}, \ldots, x_{in_i})).\end{aligned}$$

If A_i is not admissible or functionality preserving for f_i (for some i), then the meaning of this abbreviation possibly does not correspond to the intended one.

4

Specialization for Flat VVSL

In Chapter 3, the logic MPL_ω was introduced. The semantics of flat VVSL presented in Chapter 5 describes the meaning of constructs in flat VVSL in terms of formulae from this logic. The specific symbols, signatures and formulae used for this semantics are presented in this chapter.

In the definition of the language, proof system and interpretation of MPL_ω, only a few assumptions about symbols are made. First, it is explained how the symbols are actualized for the use of this logic for a semantics of flat VVSL (this is made more precise in Chapters 6 and 7) and the main domain for the semantics of flat VVSL, a domain of formulae, is defined. Thereafter, abbreviations of formulae concerning states, computations and implicit conversions are introduced. Finally, it is explained how the symbols are constructed that correspond to pre-defined names and types associated with basic types (boolean, natural, etc.) and constructed types (sequence types, set types, etc.) and what kinds of formulae occur in the axioms associated with each of the basic and constructed types (all this is made more precise in Appendix D).

4.1 Symbols and signatures for VVSL

This section introduces the kind of symbol that is used for the semantics of VVSL given in later chapters and explains how this kind of symbol is precisely used. This includes a description of the sets of symbols that underlie the domain of signatures and the domain of formulae for the semantics of flat VVSL, which are defined in the next section. This section is an abridged version of Sections 6.2 and 7.1, which are more precise. Moreover, this section leaves out anything that is irrelevant to an understanding of the logic-based semantics of flat VVSL.

Symbols with origins

In the definition of MPL_ω, only a few assumptions about symbols were made. Thus, symbols may be actualized in many ways. For the use of MPL_ω in the formal definition of flat VVSL, this is done in a way which also takes into account the semantic foundations of the modularization and parametrization constructs complementing flat VVSL, which are presented in Chapter 6. Symbols are actualized using identifiers, origins and symbol types. The symbol types are in turn built from indicators for the different kinds of types (sort, obj, func and pred) and sort symbols.

In full VVSL, name clashes may occur in the composition of modules. In order to solve this name clash problem in a satisfactory way, the origin of each occurrence of a name should be available. This is explained in detail in Section 6.1. Mainly due to parametrization, origins cannot simply be viewed as pointers to the definitions of the names. A name defined in a parametrized module should have different origins for different instantiations of the parametrized module. This means that in addition to origin constants, origin variables, which can later be instantiated with fixed origins, and compound origins are needed.

We assume three disjoint countably infinite sets OCon, OVar and Ident of *origin constants*, *origin variables* and *identifiers*, respectively.

The set Orig of *origins* is the smallest set including OCon and OVar and closed under construction of finite sequences.

Symbols are actualized according to the following rules:

- each sort symbol S is a triple $\langle i, a, \mathsf{sort}\rangle$,
- each function symbol $f\colon S_1 \times \cdots \times S_n \to S_{n+1}$ is a triple $\langle i, a, \langle \mathsf{func}, S_1, \ldots, S_{n+1}\rangle\rangle$,
- each predicate symbol $P\colon S_1 \times \cdots \times S_n$ is a triple $\langle i, a, \langle \mathsf{pred}, S_1, \ldots, S_n\rangle\rangle$,
- each variable symbol x of sort S is a triple $\langle i, a, \langle \mathsf{obj}, S\rangle\rangle$,

for some $i \in \mathsf{Ident}$ and $a \in \mathsf{Orig}$. Sym denotes the set of all symbols that are actualized in this way. SType denotes the set of all symbol types (i.e. possible third components of symbols). We write $\iota(w)$, $\omega(w)$ and $\tau(w)$, where $w = \langle i, a, t\rangle \in \mathsf{Sym}$, for i, a and t, respectively.

This actualization of symbols for MPL_ω is implicit in the remainder of this chapter. It originates from DA (Description Algebra), which is introduced in Chapter 6 and used, together with $\lambda\pi$-calculus, as the basis for the semantics of the structuring sublanguage of VVSL presented in Chapter 8.

A *symbol signature* is a signature that consists of sort symbols, function symbols and predicate symbols from Sym.

Symbols are *name equivalent* if they have the same identifier, the same kind of type, the same number of sort symbols occurring in the type and corresponding sort symbols that are name equivalent. An equivalence class of the name equivalence relation on Sym is called a *name*. We write $\overline{w}$, where $w \in$ Sym, for the name with representative w and we write $\overline{W}$, where $W \subseteq$ Sym, for the set of names with representatives in W.

The names introduced here are very similar to the typed names of VVSL. If only flat VVSL is considered, then the origins of symbols can be safely ignored except in the treatment of modification rights of operations, which is too closely coupled with the modularization and parametrization mechanisms of full VVSL.

Specialization for VVSL

Not all symbols of the kind described above can be freely used in the semantics of VVSL. Besides symbols corresponding to user-defined names, symbols corresponding to pre-defined names and symbols corresponding to constructed types, there are also symbols used which do not correspond to either user-defined names, pre-defined names or constructed types. In some respects, these different categories of symbols must be distinguished. This gives rise to VVSL specific restrictions on the ways in which symbols may be built from identifiers, origins and symbol types. The specifics of these symbols, called module symbols, are described below.

We assume three disjoint countably infinite subsets of Ident: the set UIdent, the set PIdent and the set CIdent. Symbols with an identifier from UIdent and PIdent correspond to user-defined names and pre-defined names, respectively, in VVSL. Symbols with an identifier from CIdent correspond to types in VVSL. Sometimes a user-defined name has to be constructed from another user-defined name. Therefore, we also assume an injective mapping mk: UIdent $\rightarrow$ UIdent that is an identity mapping on its range. In a concrete representation $mk(c)$ will usually be obtained by prefixing the string *mk*- to the string that constitutes the identifier c provided that it is not already so prefixed. A symbol w is called a *special* symbol if $\iota(w) \notin$ UIdent $\cup$ PIdent $\cup$ CIdent.

The symbols corresponding to user-defined or pre-defined names of types and functions are now described.

A *type symbol* is a sort symbol S that is no special symbol. MType denotes the set of all type symbols.

A *proper function symbol* is a function symbol $f\colon S_1 \times \cdots \times S_n \rightarrow S_{n+1}$ with an identifier from UIdent $\cup$ PIdent, such that the sort symbols $S_1, \ldots, S_{n+1}$ are type symbols. MFunc denotes the set of all proper function symbols.

The indication proper is used to distinguish function symbols that correspond to user-defined or pre-defined names of functions.

Sort symbols for the state space and the computation space allow function symbols and predicate symbols which correspond to names of state components, called state variables in VVSL, and names of operations, respectively. The sort symbols for the state space and the computation space as well as various associated function and predicate symbols are special symbols. The origin of all these symbols is $\langle\rangle$.

The *state sort symbol* State and the *computation sort symbol* Comp are special sort symbols with different identifiers. The *initial state symbol* $\mathsf{s0}\colon \to \mathsf{State}$ is a special function symbol. The *state selection function symbols* $\mathsf{st}_n\colon \mathsf{Comp} \to \mathsf{State}$ (for all $n < \omega$) are special function symbols with different identifiers. The *internal transition predicate symbols* $\mathsf{int}_n\colon \mathsf{Comp}$ and the *external transition predicate symbols* $\mathsf{ext}_n\colon \mathsf{Comp}$ (for all $n < \omega$) are special predicate symbols with different identifiers. Σ_{Comp} denotes the set of all these basic symbols associated with the state space and the computation space.

Having introduced symbols for the state space and the computation space, the symbols corresponding to user-defined names of state variables and operations can also be described.

A *state variable symbol* is a function symbol $v\colon \mathsf{State} \to S$ with an identifier from UIdent, such that the sort symbol S is a type symbol. MVar denotes the set of all state variable symbols.

An *operation symbol* is a predicate symbol $op\colon S_1 \times \ldots \times S_n \times \mathsf{Comp} \times S'_1 \times \ldots \times S'_m$ with an identifier from UIdent, such that the sort symbols $S_1, \ldots, S_n, S'_1, \ldots, S'_m$ are type symbols. MOp denotes the set of all operation symbols.

Variable symbols ranging over all values of a type (for every type), variable symbols ranging over all states and variable symbols ranging over all computations are also needed.

A *value symbol* is an object symbol x such that the sort of x is a type symbol. MVal denotes the set of all value symbols.

A *state symbol* is an object symbol s such that the sort of s is State, and a *computation symbol* is an object symbol c such that the sort of c is Comp. The origin of all state and computation symbols is $\langle\rangle$. MState denotes the set of all state symbols and MComp denotes the set of all computation symbols.

The write variables specified for an operation, indicate that the operation leaves all state variables other than the ones mentioned as write variables unmodified. In the semantics, it has to be made explicit what exactly is left unmodified. In full VVSL, this may expand by module composition. Because of this it turns out to be convenient to have modification predicate symbols for every collection of write variables. Losing the identity of state variables by explicit renaming is prevented by using origins instead of names.

The *modification predicate symbols* $\mathsf{mod}_l\colon \mathsf{State} \times \mathsf{State}$ (for all $l \in \mathsf{Orig}^*$) are special predicate symbols with different identifiers. The origin of mod_l is l. Mod denotes the set of all modification predicate symbols.

Any element of a type can be generated in a certain way. This gives an induction principle for the type, which has also to be made explicit. Hence, it is necessary to have generation predicate symbols for every type.

The *generation predicate symbols* $\mathit{gen}^S\colon S$ (for all $S \in \mathsf{MType}$) are special predicate symbols with the same identifier. The origin of gen^S is $\omega(S)$, the origin of S. Gen denotes the set of all generation predicate symbols.

A number of pairs of conversion function symbols is associated with the basic types $\mathbb{Z}$ and $\mathbb{Q}$, every basic type that is an 'enumerated type' (see Section 5.7), and every defined type. They are special function symbols which are used for implicit conversion from subtype to type and vice versa.

The *conversion function symbols* are inclusion function symbols and retraction function symbols. The inclusion function symbols $\imath_{S \to S'}\colon S \to S'$ (for $S, S' \in \mathsf{MType}$) are special function symbols with the same identifier. The corresponding retraction function symbols $\imath^{-1}_{S' \to S}\colon S' \to S$ (for $S', S \in \mathsf{MType}$) are also special function symbols with the same identifier. However, the identifiers concerned are different. The origin of $\imath_{S \to S'}$ is $\langle \omega(S), \omega(S') \rangle$ and the origin of $\imath^{-1}_{S' \to S}$ is $\langle \omega(S), \omega(S') \rangle$. Conv denotes the set of all conversion function symbols.

Definition. MSym, the set of all *module symbols*, is defined by

$$\begin{aligned}\mathsf{MSym} := \; & \mathsf{MType} \cup \mathsf{MFunc} \cup \mathsf{MVar} \cup \mathsf{MOp} \cup \\ & \Sigma_{\mathsf{Comp}} \cup \mathsf{Mod} \cup \mathsf{Gen} \cup \mathsf{Conv} \cup \mathsf{MVal} \cup \mathsf{MState} \cup \mathsf{MComp}\,.\end{aligned}$$

A *module symbol signature* is a symbol signature Σ such that

$$\Sigma \neq \{\} \;\Rightarrow\; \{\underline{\mathrm{B}}, \mathit{tt}, \mathit{ff}\} \cup \Sigma_{\mathsf{Comp}} \cup \mathsf{Mod} \subseteq \Sigma \subseteq \mathsf{MSym}\,.$$

MSSig, the set of all module symbol signatures, is defined by

$$\mathsf{MSSig} := \{\Sigma \mid \Sigma \text{ is a module symbol signature}\}.$$

$\underline{\mathrm{B}}, \mathit{tt}, \mathit{ff}$ are used to denote the symbols which are associated with the basic type $\mathbb{B}$, i.e. the type denoting the set of boolean values (see also Appendix D).

4.2 Semantic domains for flat VVSL

Having introduced module symbols and module symbol signatures, the semantic domains for the semantics of flat VVSL can be introduced.

Definition. The domain Form of module symbol formulae is defined by

$$\mathsf{Form} := \{A \mid A \text{ is a formula of } \mathrm{MPL}_\omega(\Sigma), \text{ for some } \Sigma \in \mathsf{MSSig}\}.$$

The auxiliary domain Term of module symbol terms is defined by

$$\mathsf{Term} := \{t \mid t \text{ is a term of } \mathrm{MPL}_\omega(\Sigma), \text{ for some } \Sigma \in \mathsf{MSSig}\}.$$

In the semantics of flat VVSL presented in Chapter 5, the abbreviations of formulae introduced in Sections 3.3 and 3.7 are used instead of the abbreviated formulae.

Definition. The auxiliary domain EForm of module symbol formulae and simultaneous inductive function definition rules is defined by

$$\mathsf{EForm} := \mathsf{Form} \cup \{f \overset{\mathrm{SI}}{:=} A \mid f \in \mathsf{MFunc}, A \in \mathsf{Form}\}.$$

The simultaneous inductive function definition rules can be eliminated by replacing them by formulae.

Definition. The elimination of the simultaneous inductive definition rules from a subset of EForm is given by the mapping $\boldsymbol{\mu}: \mathcal{P}(\mathsf{EForm}) \to \mathcal{P}(\mathsf{Form})$, which is inductively defined by:

$$\Gamma' \subseteq \mathsf{Form} \wedge \Gamma = \Gamma' \cup \{f_j \overset{\mathrm{SI}}{:=} A_j \mid 1 \leq j \leq n\} \Rightarrow$$
$$\boldsymbol{\mu}(\Gamma) = \Gamma' \cup \langle f_1, \ldots, f_n \rangle \overset{\mathrm{I}}{:=} A_1 \wedge \ldots \wedge A_n.$$

4.3 States and computations

The special sort symbols State and Comp are used to represent the state space and computation space, respectively. A computation can be viewed as a non-empty finite or countably infinite sequence of states and connecting transitions which are labelled to distinguish between internal and external transitions:

- The special function symbol st_n $(n < \omega)$ is used for the partial function which maps each computation to its $(n + 1)$-th state (if it exists).
- The special predicate symbol int_n $(n < \omega)$ is used for the predicate which holds for a computation if there exists a $(n + 1)$-th state transition and it is moreover an internal transition.
- The special predicate symbol ext_n $(n < \omega)$ is used for the predicate which holds for a computation if there exists a $(n + 1)$-th state transition and it is moreover an external transition.

This intuition is captured by the formula Compax of MPL_ω, which relates the sorts State and Comp with the functions and predicates st_n, int_n and ext_n $(n < \omega)$. This formula states that the n-th state of computation c exists if the $(n + 1)$-th state of c exists, that the n-th transition of c exists iff the $(n + 1)$-th state of c exists and that the n-th transition of c is not both internal and external. Furthermore, it states that if, for each n, the n-th state of computation c_1 and the n-th state of computation c_2 are the same (in case it exists for either one) and moreover the n-th transition of c_1 and the n-th transition of c_2 are both internal or both external, then c_1 and c_2 are the same.

Definition. The formula Compax is defined as follows:

$$
\begin{array}{l}
\text{Compax} := \\
\quad \forall c\colon \mathsf{Comp} \\
\quad\quad (\mathsf{st}_0(c){\downarrow} \wedge \bigwedge_n (\mathsf{st}_{n+1}(c){\downarrow} \rightarrow \mathsf{st}_n(c){\downarrow}) \wedge \\
\quad\quad\; \bigwedge_n ((\mathsf{st}_{n+1}(c){\downarrow} \leftrightarrow \mathsf{int}_n(c) \vee \mathsf{ext}_n(c)) \wedge \neg(\mathsf{int}_n(c) \wedge \mathsf{ext}_n(c)))) \wedge \\
\quad \forall c_1\colon \mathsf{Comp},\, c_2\colon \mathsf{Comp} \\
\quad\quad (\bigwedge_n (\mathsf{st}_n(c_1) \simeq \mathsf{st}_n(c_2) \wedge \\
\quad\quad\quad\quad (\mathsf{int}_n(c_1) \leftrightarrow \mathsf{int}_n(c_2)) \wedge (\mathsf{ext}_n(c_1) \leftrightarrow \mathsf{ext}_n(c_2))) \rightarrow c_1 = c_2).
\end{array}
$$

Let $S \in \mathsf{MType}$ be the sort symbol that is used for the set of values determined by the type T. Then for each state variable of (VVSL) type T, a corresponding function symbol of (MPL_ω) type $\mathsf{State} \rightarrow S$ is used for the function which maps each state to the value taken by the state variable in that state. States that are not distinguishable by means of the state variables are not required to be really equal. Equality of states is not considered important; the values taken by the state variables is what matters.

Let $S_i \in \mathsf{MType}$ be the sort symbol that is used for the set of values determined by the type T_i, for $1 \leq i \leq n$, and let $S'_i \in \mathsf{MType}$ be the sort symbol that is used for the set of values determined by the type T'_i, for $1 \leq i \leq m$. Then for each operation with argument types $T_1, \ldots, T_n$ and result types $T'_1, \ldots, T'_m$, a corresponding predicate symbol of type $S_1 \times \cdots \times S_n \times \mathsf{Comp} \times S'_1 \times \cdots \times S'_m$ is used for the predicate which holds for values $x_1, \ldots, x_n$, computation c and values $y_1, \ldots, y_m$ if c is a computation of the operation for arguments $x_1, \ldots, x_n$ that yields results $y_1, \ldots, y_m$.

Each operation definition mentions a set of write variables. This indicates that all state variables other than the variables mentioned as write variables are left unmodified by the operation. In full VVSL, what is left unmodified may expand by module composition. To accommodate this, a binary predicate mod_l on states is introduced for every finite sequence l of origins (in Section 4.1). $\mathsf{mod}_l(s_1, s_2)$ is intended to express that state s_1 may only be transformed into state s_2 by modifying state variables with origins in l. On the definition of a state variable v, a formula is associated with v. This formula states that, for l with the origin of v not in l, the state variable v is left unmodified in the transition from state s_1 to state s_2 if $\mathsf{mod}_l(s_1, s_2)$ holds. Varmod(v) is defined as an abbreviation of this formula.

Definition. For a state variable symbol v, i.e. a function symbol v of type $\mathsf{State} \rightarrow S$ for some sort S, the formula Varmod(v) is defined by

$$
\begin{array}{l}
\text{Varmod}(v) := \\
\quad \displaystyle\bigwedge_{l \in (\mathsf{Orig} - \{\omega(v)\})^*} (\forall s_1\colon \mathsf{State},\, s_2\colon \mathsf{State}(\mathsf{mod}_l(s_1, s_2) \rightarrow v(s_1) \simeq v(s_2))).
\end{array}
$$

Varmod(v) is used to guarantee that state variable v can only be modified with appropriate modification rights.

For the computations of an operation, the set of write variables leads to the restriction that in internal transitions all state variables other than the write variables must be left unmodified. Each operation definition also mentions a set of read variables. Only state variables mentioned as read variable or write variable are of concern to the behaviour of the operation. For the computations of an operation, this leads to the additional restriction that in every transition at least some state variable from the read variables or the write variables must be modified, unless the transition is followed by infinitely many transitions where this does not happen. Modcomp(R, W, c) is defined as an abbreviation of the formula expressing these two restrictions.

Definition. For sets R and W of state variable symbols, and computation symbol c, the formula Modcomp(R, W, c) is defined by

$$
\begin{aligned}
&\mathrm{Modcomp}(R, W, c) := \\
&\quad \textstyle\bigwedge_n (\mathsf{int}_n(c) \to \mathsf{mod}_l(\mathsf{st}_n(c), \mathsf{st}_{n+1}(c))) \wedge \\
&\quad \textstyle\bigwedge_n (\bigwedge_{v \in R \cup W} (v(\mathsf{st}_n(c)) \simeq v(\mathsf{st}_{n+1}(c))) \to \\
&\qquad \textstyle\bigwedge_m (\bigwedge_{v \in R \cup W} (v(\mathsf{st}_{n+m}(c)) \simeq v(\mathsf{st}_{n+m+1}(c))))),
\end{aligned}
$$

where l is defined as follows: let $\{\omega(v) \mid v \in W\} = \{a_1, \ldots, a_k\}$, where $a_1, \ldots, a_k$ are ordered according to some fixed linear order on Orig, then $l = \langle a_1, \ldots, a_k \rangle$.

So Modcomp(R, W, c) expresses that internal transitions in computation c leave state variables other than the state variables W unmodified, and no two consecutive states in computation c are the same after projection to the state variables $R \cup W$, unless c is infinite and all following states are the same.

The formulae, that are abbreviated by expressions of the form Varmod(v) and Modcomp(R, W, c), capture the main aspects of the mechanism of interrogation and modification rights provided in VVSL by means of the external clause in operation definitions.

The following abbreviations of formulae are used in the interpretation of temporal formulae.

Definition. For computation symbols c, c', the formulae $\mathrm{Prefix}_k(c, c')$ and $\mathrm{Suffix}_k(c, c')$ $(k < \omega)$ are defined by

$$\begin{array}{l}\mathrm{Prefix}_k(c, c') \;:= \\ \quad \bigwedge_{m=0}^{k} (\,\mathsf{st}_m(c) \simeq \mathsf{st}_m(c') \wedge \\ \qquad (\mathsf{int}_m(c) \leftrightarrow \mathsf{int}_m(c')) \wedge (\mathsf{ext}_m(c) \leftrightarrow \mathsf{ext}_m(c'))) \wedge \\ \quad \neg(\mathsf{st}_{k+1}(c')\downarrow),\end{array}$$

$$\begin{array}{l}\mathrm{Suffix}_k(c, c') \;:= \\ \quad \bigwedge_n (\,\mathsf{st}_{k+n}(c) \simeq \mathsf{st}_n(c') \wedge \\ \qquad (\mathsf{int}_{k+n}(c) \leftrightarrow \mathsf{int}_n(c')) \wedge (\mathsf{ext}_{k+n}(c) \leftrightarrow \mathsf{ext}_n(c'))).\end{array}$$

$\mathrm{Prefix}_k(c, c')$ is a formula stating that computation c' is the prefix of computation c ending at the $(k + 1)$-th state of c. $\mathrm{Suffix}_k(c, c')$ is a formula stating that computation c' is the suffix of computation c starting at the $(k + 1)$-th state of c.

That the intuitions of prefix and suffix are captured by these formulae, follows from the last conjunct of the axiom characterizing computations (i.e. the formula abbreviated by Compax). Because no constructor functions for the (possibly infinite) computations are available, there are no simpler equivalent formulae.

The abbreviations $\mathrm{Prefix}_k(c, c')$ and $\mathrm{Suffix}_k(c, c')$ are used for 'chopping' computations.

4.4 Implicit conversions

VVSL is a typed specification language with subtyping. If T is a subtype of T' or vice versa, then an element of the type T can be allowed in many situations where an element of the type T' is expected. This requires the implicit application of conversion functions.

Let $S, S' \in \mathsf{MType}$ be the sort symbols that are used for the sets of values determined by the types T and T', respectively. Then, if T is declared to be a subtype of T', the two special function symbols $\imath_{S \to S'}$ and $\imath^{-1}_{S' \to S}$ are used for the conversion from T to T' and vice versa. These functions can be viewed as an inclusion mapping and its inverse (a retraction mapping), respectively.

If T is declared to be a subtype of T'' and T'' is declared to be a subtype of T', then T is a subtype of T'. Roughly, the composition of the function for conversion from T to T'' with the function for conversion from T'' to T' is used for the conversion from T to T' and similarly for the inverse conversion.

The situation is in fact somewhat more complicated, because there may also be a type T''' different from T'' for which it holds that T is declared to be a subtype of T''' and T''' is declared to be a subtype of T'. However, the compositions of conversion functions via different intermediate types yield the same result. The formula $\text{Convax}^{\leq}$ of MPL_ω states this commutability property of compositions of implicit conversions.

Definition. For a relation $\leq \subseteq \mathsf{MType} \times \mathsf{MType}$, the formula $\text{Convax}^{\leq}$ is defined by

$$\text{Convax}^{\leq} :=$$

$$\bigwedge_{\langle S,S' \rangle \in \mathsf{MType} \times \mathsf{MType}} (\forall x\colon S(\exists x'\colon S'$$

$$(\bigwedge_{\{S_1,\ldots,S_n\} \in ch(S,S')} (\imath_{S_{n-1} \to S_n}(\cdots \imath_{S_1 \to S_2}(x) \cdots) = x')))),$$

where $\{S_1, \ldots, S_n\} \in ch(S, S')$ iff $S = S_1$, $S' = S_n$, $S_i \leq S_{i+1}$ for $0 < i < n$.

Let $S, S' \in \mathsf{MType}$ be the sort symbols that are used for the sets of values determined by the types T and T', respectively, where T is a subtype of T' or vice versa. Then for each term t of sort S, the term $\text{Conv}^{\leq}_{S \to S'}(t)$ of MPL_ω is a term of sort S', which denotes the result of converting the element of type T that is denoted by t to an element of type T'.

Definition. For a relation $\leq \subseteq \mathsf{MType} \times \mathsf{MType}$, type symbols $S, S' \in \mathsf{MType}$ and term $t \in \mathsf{Term}$ of sort S, the term $\text{Conv}^{\leq}_{S \to S'}(t)$ is defined by

$$\text{Conv}^{\leq}_{S \to S'}(t) :=$$

$$\begin{cases} \iota x'\colon S' \big(\bigwedge_{\{S_1,\ldots,S_n\} \in ch(S,S')} (\imath_{S_{n-1} \to S_n}(\cdots \imath_{S_1 \to S_2}(t) \cdots) = x')\big) & \text{if } S \leq S' \wedge S \neq S', \\ \iota x'\colon S' \big(\bigwedge_{\{S_1,\ldots,S_n\} \in ch(S',S)} (\imath^{-1}_{S_2 \to S_1}(\cdots \imath^{-1}_{S_n \to S_{n-1}}(t) \cdots) = x')\big) & \text{if } S' \leq S \wedge S \neq S', \\ t & \text{if } S = S', \end{cases}$$

where $\{S_1, \ldots, S_n\} \in ch(S, S')$ iff $S = S_1$, $S' = S_n$, $S_i \leq S_{i+1}$ for $0 < i < n$.

The terms, that are abbreviated by expressions of the form $\text{Conv}^{\leq}_{S \to S'}(t)$, provide for the required type conversions in the interpretation of expressions of VVSL.

4.5 Basic and constructed types

The types of VVSL correspond to sort symbols of MPL_ω representing sets of values, characterized by associated defining axioms of these sort symbols, in accordance with the intended meaning of the types. Subtypes and identifier overloading, which are both supported by VVSL, have no such direct counterparts in MPL_ω.

In the scope of a definition that defines a type as a subtype of a basic or constructed type, pre-defined type and function names associated with the basic or constructed type may be used. This gives rise to additional symbols of MPL_ω with associated defining axioms. There are also symbols associated with a basic or constructed type for which there are no corresponding pre-defined names. This includes a sort symbol for the basic or constructed type itself and sort symbols for other basic or constructed types associated with it. For these symbols there are corresponding types instead of names. It also includes symbols for which there are no corresponding types either: generation predicate symbols connected with structural induction rules (for basic and constructed types) and implicit conversions function symbols (for basic types only). These symbols were introduced in Section 4.1. The symbols with an identifier that is available to the specifier, either directly as a pre-defined name or indirectly by a type, are called the *available* symbols associated with the basic or constructed type concerned. In Appendix D, the available symbols associated with a basic or constructed type and the defining axioms of all symbols associated with it are defined by mappings

$$asymbols\colon \mathsf{MType} \to \mathcal{P}(\mathsf{MSym}),$$
$$axioms\colon \mathsf{MType} \to \mathcal{P}(\mathsf{Form}),$$

respectively.*

For each basic or constructed type, the axioms include a defining axiom of an auxiliary unary generation predicate symbol, which holds for values that can be constructed by means of certain functions associated with the type, and an axiom stating that all values of the type can be constructed by means of these constructor functions. Furthermore, a defining axiom is included for each of the remaining functions associated with the type. If the type concerned has pre-defined subtype(s), then there are also the defining axioms of the accompanying pair(s) of conversion function symbols. There is also always an axiom that defines equality.

The origin and the symbol type of all symbols associated with the basic and constructed types are uniquely characterized. This is not the case for the identifier, for which only a restriction to a certain subset of Ident is given. In this way, the pre-defined names are not fixed. Roughly speaking, the origin of each symbol is composed of the origins of the symbols for all types on which its meaning depends. Thus, symbols associated with basic types (including enumerated types) have an empty origin. For each symbol, the set of symbols which must be name equivalent to the symbol is also uniquely characterized. This gives rise to more global restrictions on the identifiers of the symbols. For example, type symbols corresponding to set types must be name equivalent iff the symbols corresponding to the

* The nil constant symbol corresponding to the pre-defined constant name for the option value of a type defined as a union with option value is also given in this appendix.

element types of the set types are name equivalent and they must be name inequivalent to all type symbols not corresponding to set types.

The notations used in the following chapter to denote the symbols associated with the basic and constructed types, are presented in Appendix D.

5

Definition of Flat VVSL

This chapter contains a logic-based formal semantics for flat VVSL. The semantics presented describes the meaning of constructs in the language in terms of formulae from the language of MPL_ω, the logic that was introduced in Chapter 3. This presentation illustrates an approach to give a formal semantics for a model-oriented, state-based specification language without provisions for modular structuring of specifications. The presented logic-based semantics describes the meaning of flat VVSL specifications as sets of formulae characterizing what is described in them.

It is worth noticing again that MPL_ω, the logic used as the basis for this semantics, is mainly obtained by additions to the language, the proof system and the interpretation of classical first-order logic. These additions make it more suitable as a semantic basis for specification languages which are intended for describing software systems. However, no essential deviations from classical reasoning are imposed.

The illustrated approach is applicable to any model-oriented specification language. Generally, formal semantics for such specification languages are not logic-based. For example, the formal semantics of VDM-SL presented in the draft ISO standard describes the meaning of specifications in terms of the models which satisfy them. That is the traditional approach for model-oriented specification languages. However, a logic-based approach may be more appropriate for them. It provides a better starting-point for the development of a proof theory for the specification language concerned. Furthermore, most current models and theories of modular specification assume that flat specifications, which are used as the basic building blocks of modular specifications, correspond to presentations of theories in some logic.

One of the sections of Chapter 9 is concerned with proof rules for VVSL. The principal proof rules are presented and their connection with the semantics presented for VVSL is described informally and in broad outline. They include proof rules for a typed version of LPF, proof rules for a typed first-order temporal logic extending LPF and proof rules which are needed to construct proofs of facts about modules. In another section of that chapter, the logic-based approach is applied to another language to demonstrate the generality of the approach. The constructs of that language are common control constructs of imperative programming languages. It is a simplified version of an extension of VVSL which is needed to be able to specify operations, which possibly interfere, explicitly by a defining program.

VDM-SL is largely incorporated in VVSL. The semantics presented for this part is mostly equivalent to the originally intended semantics in (Jones, 1990). Both differ slightly from the semantics which is agreed for the standard, but it remains interesting to compare the semantics presented in this chapter with the one presented in the draft ISO standard with respect to the applied approaches.

The meaning of constructs in flat VVSL is only defined for well-formed constructs. The well-formedness of constructs is also described. Both the well-formedness and meaning of a construct generally depend on the definitions in the scope in which it occurs. Therefore the presentation of the syntax and semantics begins with a description of the *contexts* which are used for modelling the scope. In later sections, the well-formedness and meaning of constructs in flat VVSL is described with respect to a context. The syntax of flat VVSL is described by means of production rules in the form of a BNF grammar. These rules suggest a concrete syntax, but the intention is still that they describe the abstract syntax of VVSL. This intention is also explained.

Subsequently, there are sections which deal with the syntax and semantics of the sublanguages of flat VVSL. Each section starts with an overview of the sublanguage concerned, a presentation of its syntax and some general remarks regarding the well-formedness, syntactic properties and meaning of constructs in the sublanguage. Following this introduction, there are separate subsections on the constructs of the various forms that are distinguished by the production rules given in the syntax presentation for the sublanguage concerned. In fact, only a kernel of flat VVSL is defined in this chapter: the remainder is introduced as abbreviations in Appendix E.

The notations used in this chapter to denote the symbols corresponding to pre-defined names and types associated with the basic types and constructed types are presented in Appendix D.

5.1 Contexts

This section introduces two closely related notions of context. Some predicates and mappings, which are basic to the context dependent aspects of well-formedness and meaning of constructs, are also defined. The predicates and mappings, which are used to describe the typing of expressions, are defined in the next section.

In VVSL, a definition introduces a name for a type, a function from certain argument types to a certain result type, a state variable* of a certain type, an operation from certain argument types to certain result types or a value of a certain type; the constructs within which this name is visible, constitute the scope of the definition. For this name, there must be a corresponding symbol in MPL_ω. The corresponding symbol is obtained by combining the name with the type information concerned and an origin (representing the identity of the definition that introduces the name). Both the well-formedness and meaning of a construct depend on the symbols corresponding to the names that occur in the construct. A prerequisite for well-formedness is that these names have been introduced by definitions in the scope in which the construct occurs.

Definition. The set NSym of *normal symbols* is defined by

$$\begin{aligned}&\mathsf{NSym} := \\ &\quad \mathsf{MType} \cup \mathsf{MFunc} \cup \mathsf{MVar} \cup \mathsf{MOp} \cup \{x \in \mathsf{MVal} \mid \iota(x) \in \mathsf{UIdent}\}.\end{aligned}$$

Normal symbols are symbols corresponding to names that are user-defined or pre-defined.

A type definition also implicitly declares subtype relationships between the introduced type name and other types. The well-formedness and meaning of a construct also depend on the subtype relationships being in force. Pairs of type symbols are used to record the subtype relationships declared in type definitions.

Definition. The set SDcl of *subtype declarations* is defined by

$$\mathsf{SDcl} := \mathsf{MType} \times \mathsf{MType}.$$

A subtype declaration $\langle S_1, S_2 \rangle$ indicates that the type corresponding to S_1 is a subtype of the type corresponding to S_2.

The context of a construct consists of all symbols corresponding to names introduced by definitions in the scope in which the construct occurs and additionally the subtype declarations associated with the introduced type names. This provides all details about the names occurring in the construct on which its well-formedness and meaning depends.

Before contexts are defined, first an auxiliary predicate is introduced. It is used to check whether or not a type appears in another type.

Definition. The auxiliary predicate dep: $\mathsf{MType} \times \mathsf{MType}$ is inductively

* State variable is the name used in VVSL for state components.

defined by

$$\begin{array}{ll} dep(S,S), & \\ dep(S,\underline{\mathrm{L}}(S)), & \\ dep(S,\underline{\mathrm{F}}(S)), & \\ dep(S_1,\underline{\mathrm{M}}(S_1,S_2)), & \\ dep(S_2,\underline{\mathrm{M}}(S_1,S_2)), & \\ dep(S_i,\underline{\mathrm{C}}_c(S_1,\ldots,S_n)) & \text{(for } 1 \le i \le n). \end{array}$$

$dep(S_1, S_2)$ indicates that the type corresponding to S_1 appears in the type corresponding to S_2.

Contexts are defined in an indirect way. First, proto-contexts are defined. Thereafter, contexts are defined as proto-contexts of a special kind. Proto-contexts are needed in Chapter 8 to describe the meaning of constructs in the structuring language.

Definition. A *proto-context* C is a finite subset of $\mathsf{NSym} \cup \mathsf{SDcl}$ such that

$$\begin{array}{l} \forall \langle i, a, t(S_1,\ldots,S_n)\rangle \in C \cap \mathsf{NSym} \\ \quad (\bigwedge_{k=1}^{n} (\exists S \in C \cap \mathsf{NSym}(\overline{S} = \overline{S_k}) \Rightarrow S_k \in C), \\ \forall \langle S_1, S_2\rangle \in C \cap \mathsf{SDcl} \\ \quad (\forall S \in \mathsf{MType} \\ \qquad (\iota(S) \in \mathsf{UIdent} \wedge (dep(S,S_1) \vee dep(S,S_2)) \Rightarrow S \in C)). \end{array}$$

A *symbol context* is a proto-context C such that

$$\forall w_1, w_2 \in C \cap \mathsf{NSym}\ (\overline{w_1} = \overline{w_2} \Rightarrow w_1 = w_2).$$

The set Cxt of all symbol contexts is defined by

$$\mathsf{Cxt} := \{C \subseteq \mathsf{NSym} \cup \mathsf{SDcl} \mid C \text{ is a symbol context}\}.$$

We write $symbols(C)$ for $C \cap \mathsf{NSym}$ and $sdcls(C)$ for $C \cap \mathsf{SDcl}$.

The requirements on proto-contexts guarantee that they can be regarded as representations of symbol signatures if value symbols are ignored. The first requirement on proto-contexts is a condition akin to the closure condition that applies to signatures. The second requirement on proto-contexts is a closure condition concerning subtype declarations, which is needed because subtype declarations correspond to pairs of conversion function symbols. The additional requirement on symbol contexts ensures that there are no two distinct symbols in a context that are the same except for the origins occurring in them. This means in essence that there has to be a one-to-one correspondence between typed names and symbols. This strong origin uniqueness requirement is basic to the suitability of symbol contexts for their purpose in describing the meaning of constructs in flat VVSL.

Because the origins are not relevant to well-formedness, a simpler kind of context is more appropriate for well-formedness. It abstracts from the origins occurring in the symbols. This abstraction turns symbols essentially into typed names. Properly speaking, subtype declarations become couched in terms of types.

Definition. We write $\overline{C}$ for $\overline{symbols(C)} \cup \{\langle\overline{S_1}, \overline{S_2}\rangle \mid \langle S_1, S_2\rangle \in sdcls(C)\}$. The set NCxt of *name contexts* is defined by

$$\mathsf{NCxt} := \{\overline{C} \mid C \in \mathsf{Cxt}\}.$$

We write $names(N)$ for $N \cap \overline{\mathsf{NSym}}$ and $sdcls(N)$ for $N \cap \overline{\mathsf{SDcl}}$.

Note that the requirements on symbol contexts guarantee that no two symbols from a symbol context are identified in the corresponding name context.

The following auxiliary mapping allows us to introduce apposite notation to denote elements of name context. It maps types to their corresponding names (i.e. name equivalence classes of symbols). In Section 5.7, types are defined as constructs of various forms. Type denotes the set of all types.

Definition. The auxiliary mapping $name$: Type $\to \overline{\mathsf{MType}}$ is inductively defined by

$$
\begin{aligned}
&name(\mathbb{B}) = \overline{\underline{\mathrm{B}}},\\
&name(\mathbb{N}) = \overline{\underline{\mathrm{N}}},\\
&name(\mathbb{Z}) = \overline{\underline{\mathrm{Z}}},\\
&name(\mathbb{Q}) = \overline{\underline{\mathrm{Q}}},\\
&name(\{\, a_1, \ldots, a_n \,\}) = \overline{\underline{\mathrm{E}}(\{a_1, \ldots, a_n\})},\\
&name(t) = \overline{S} \;\Rightarrow\; name(t^*) = \overline{\underline{\mathrm{L}}(S)},\\
&name(t) = \overline{S} \;\Rightarrow\; name(t\text{-}\mathsf{set}) = \overline{\underline{\mathrm{F}}(S)},\\
&name(t_1) = \overline{S_1} \wedge name(t_2) = \overline{S_2} \;\Rightarrow\; name(t_1 \xrightarrow{m} t_2) = \overline{\underline{\mathrm{M}}(S_1, S_2)},\\
&\bigwedge_{k=1}^{n} name(t_k) = \overline{S_k} \;\Rightarrow\\
&\qquad\qquad name(\mathsf{compose}\ c\ \mathsf{of}\ s_1 \colon t_1 \ \ldots\ s_n \colon t_n) = \overline{\underline{\mathrm{C}}_c(S_1, \ldots, S_n)},\\
&t = \iota(S) \wedge \mathsf{sort} = \tau(S) \;\Rightarrow\; name(t) = \overline{S}.
\end{aligned}
$$

Notation. We write for $\overline{w} \in \overline{\mathsf{NSym}}$:

[type T] if $\tau(w) = \mathsf{sort}, \overline{w} = name(T)$;

[func $f \colon T_1 \times \cdots \times T_n \to T_{n+1}$]
  if $\iota(w) = f$,
    $\exists S_1, \ldots, S_{n+1}$

$$(\tau(w) = \langle \mathsf{func}, S_1, \ldots, S_{n+1}\rangle \wedge \bigwedge_{k=1}^{n+1} (\overline{S_k} = name(T_k)));$$

[var $v \colon T$] if $\iota(w) = v, \exists S\ (\tau(w) = \langle \mathsf{func}, \mathsf{State}, S\rangle \wedge \overline{S} = name(T))$;

$$[\mathsf{op}\ op\colon T_1 \times \cdots \times T_n \Rightarrow T'_1 \times \cdots \times T'_m]$$
$$\text{if } \iota(w) = op,$$
$$\exists S_1, \ldots, S_n, S'_1, \ldots, S'_m$$
$$(\tau(w) = \langle \mathsf{pred}, S_1, \ldots, S_n, \mathsf{Comp}, S'_1, \ldots, S'_m \rangle \wedge \bigwedge_{k=1}^{n} (\overline{S_k} = name(T_k)) \wedge \bigwedge_{k=1}^{m} (\overline{S'_k} = name(T'_k)));$$

$$[\mathsf{val}\ x\colon T] \text{ if } \iota(w) = x, \exists S\ (\tau(w) = \langle \mathsf{obj}, S \rangle \wedge \overline{S} = name(T)).$$

We write for $\langle \overline{S_1}, \overline{S_2} \rangle \in \overline{\mathsf{SDcl}}$:

$$[T_1 \leq T_2]$$
$$\text{if } \tau(S_1) = \mathsf{sort}, \tau(S_2) = \mathsf{sort}, \overline{S_1} = name(T_1), \overline{S_2} = name(T_2).$$

These notations are extensively used to describe the name context of constructs.

For restriction of the scope of state variable definitions, the following mapping is introduced.

Definition. The mapping $nonvars\colon \mathsf{NCxt} \to \mathsf{NCxt}$ is defined by

$$nonvars(N) \ := \ N - \{[\mathsf{var}\ v\colon T] \mid v \in \mathsf{UIdent}, T \in \mathsf{Type}\}.$$

$nonvars(N)$ is the name context N without the state variable names.

The name context of a construct provides all details about the names occurring in it on which its well-formedness depends. A property of identifiers, which is generally required for the well-formedness of a construct in which they appear, is the property of being defined in the context of the construct as a name of a certain kind. This property of identifiers makes precise what is informally described as occurring in the scope of its definition. However, this description is far from accurate in the presence of pre-defined names. An identifier that is a pre-defined type or function name associated with a basic or constructed type is considered to be defined as a type or function name in a context, provided that the basic or constructed type is used for type definition. The condition ensures that pre-defined names are not inadvertently used. This makes most sense in combination with the modularization and parametrization constructs of full VVSL. It is tantamount to letting the use of a basic or constructed type bring about the import of a module (corresponding to the type).

The property of an identifier to be defined in a context as a name of a certain kind is defined below. First several auxiliary mappings are introduced. Some of them are also used in Section 8.1.

The following mapping is used to find out which basic and constructed types contribute pre-defined names in a given context.

Definition. The auxiliary mapping $bctypes\colon \mathsf{Cxt} \to \mathcal{P}(\mathsf{MType})$ is defined by

$$\begin{array}{l} bctypes(C) \ := \\ \quad \{S \in \mathsf{MType} \mid \\ \quad\; \iota(S) \notin \mathsf{UIdent} \wedge \\ \quad\; \exists S', S'' \in \mathsf{MType}\ (dep(S, S'') \wedge \langle S', S'' \rangle \in sdcls(C))\}. \end{array}$$

$bctypes(C)$ is the set of all type symbols corresponding to basic and constructed types used for type definition in the context C. Note that this set is fixed by the subtype declarations from C. The predicate *dep* is used because the basic types $\mathbb{B}$, $\mathbb{N}$, $\mathbb{Z}$ and $\mathbb{Q}$ may appear as type names in constructed types.

The following mapping is used to find out which (mini-)context corresponds to the pre-defined type and function names that are associated with a given basic or constructed type.

Definition. The auxiliary mapping $predefs\colon \mathsf{MType} \to \mathsf{Cxt}$ is inductively defined by

$$\begin{array}{l} \iota(w) = \mathsf{PIdent} \wedge w \in asymbols(S) \ \Rightarrow \ w \in predefs(S), \\ dep(\underline{\mathrm{Z}}, S) \ \Rightarrow \ \langle \underline{\mathrm{N}}, \underline{\mathrm{Z}} \rangle \in predefs(S), \\ dep(\underline{\mathrm{Q}}, S) \ \Rightarrow \ \langle \underline{\mathrm{N}}, \underline{\mathrm{Z}} \rangle, \langle \underline{\mathrm{Z}}, \underline{\mathrm{Q}} \rangle \in predefs(S), \\ A' \subseteq A \ \Rightarrow \ \langle \underline{\mathrm{E}}(A'), \underline{\mathrm{E}}(A) \rangle \in predefs(\underline{\mathrm{E}}(A)). \end{array}$$

$asymbols(S)$ includes the symbols for all pre-defined names associated with the basic or constructed type corresponding to the type symbol S (the mapping $asymbols\colon \mathsf{MType} \to \mathcal{P}(\mathsf{MSym})$ is defined in Appendix D).
$predefs(S)$ is the set of symbols for all pre-defined names associated with the basic or constructed type corresponding to S and additionally all subtype declarations relevant to that type (in case $\mathbb{Z}$, $\mathbb{Q}$ or an enumerated type).

The following mapping is used to find out which context corresponds to the pre-defined type and function names considered to be defined in a given context.

Definition. The auxiliary mapping $predefs\colon \mathsf{Cxt} \to \mathsf{Cxt}$ is defined by

$$predefs(C) \ := \ \bigcup\{predefs(S) \mid S \in bctypes(C)\}.$$

$predefs(C)$ is the set of symbols for all pre-defined type and function names that are considered to be defined in the context C and all subtype declarations relevant to the pre-defined types concerned.

The property of an identifier to be defined in a context as a name of a certain kind is now defined. The predicates concerned are extensively used to describe the well-formedness of constructs.

Definition. The predicates *deftype*, *deffunc*, *defvar*, *defop* and *defval*:

$\mathsf{NIdent} \times \mathsf{NCxt}$ are defined by

$$\begin{array}{ll} \mathit{deftype}(t, \overline{C}) & :\Leftrightarrow \exists w \in (C \cup \mathit{predefs}(C)) \cap \mathsf{MType}\ (\iota(w) = t), \\ \mathit{deffunc}(f, \overline{C}) & :\Leftrightarrow \exists w \in (C \cup \mathit{predefs}(C)) \cap \mathsf{MFunc}\ (\iota(w) = f), \\ \mathit{defvar}(v, \overline{C}) & :\Leftrightarrow \exists w \in C \cap \mathsf{MVar}\ (\iota(w) = v), \\ \mathit{defop}(op, \overline{C}) & :\Leftrightarrow \exists w \in C \cap \mathsf{MOp}\ (\iota(w) = op), \\ \mathit{defval}(x, \overline{C}) & :\Leftrightarrow \exists w \in C \cap \mathsf{MVal}\ (\iota(w) = x). \end{array}$$

In the description of the well-formedness of constructs, we write 'i is defined as a type name in N' instead of $\mathit{deftype}(i, N)$, etc.

The subtype ordering being in force depends on the context. The property of a type to be a subtype of another type in a context is now defined. This predicate is basic to the typing of expressions.

Definition. The predicate sub: $\mathsf{Type} \times \mathsf{Type} \times \mathsf{NCxt}$ is inductively defined by

$$\begin{array}{l} [\mathsf{type}\ T] \in \overline{C \cup \mathit{predefs}(C)} \Rightarrow \mathit{sub}(T, T, \overline{C}), \\ [T_1 \leq T_2] \in \overline{C \cup \mathit{predefs}(C)} \Rightarrow \mathit{sub}(T_1, T_2, \overline{C}), \\ \mathit{sub}(T_1, T_2, N) \wedge \mathit{sub}(T_2, T_3, N) \Rightarrow \mathit{sub}(T_1, T_3, N). \end{array}$$

Instead of $\mathit{sub}(T_1, T_2, N)$, we write $T_1 \leq^N T_2$. In the description of the well-formedness of constructs, we just write 'T_1 is a subtype of T_2'.

For each N, $\leq^N$ is a pre-ordering on the set of all types that are defined in N, used for defining types in N or pre-defined as subtypes of the latter types.

A partial mapping, which gives the symbol with a certain symbol type corresponding to an identifier in a context, is defined below. A partial mapping, which gives the sort symbol corresponding to a type in a context, is also defined. A necessary condition for definedness is that the identifier itself and each identifier occurring in the type, respectively, is defined (as a name of the appropriate kind) in the context. This condition is met by all well-formed constructs. These mappings are extensively used to describe the meaning of well-formed constructs with respect to a context.

Definition. The two mappings sym: $\mathsf{MIdent} \times \mathsf{SType} \times \mathsf{Cxt} \to \mathsf{MSym}$ and sym: $\mathsf{Type} \times \mathsf{Cxt} \to \mathsf{MType}$ are inductively defined by

$$i = \iota(w) \wedge t = \tau(w) \wedge w \in \mathit{symbols}(C \cup \mathit{predefs}(C)) \Rightarrow \mathit{sym}(i, t, C) = w,$$

$$\mathit{name}(T) = \overline{w} \wedge w \in \mathit{symbols}(C \cup \mathit{predefs}(C)) \Rightarrow \mathit{sym}(T, C) = w.$$

We write:
T^C for $\mathit{sym}(T, C)$,
t^C for $\mathit{sym}(t, \mathsf{sort}, C)$,
$f^C_{T_1 \times \cdots \times T_n \to T}$ for $\mathit{sym}(f, \langle \mathsf{func}, T_1^C, \ldots, T_n^C, T^C \rangle, C)$,

v^C_T for $sym(v, \langle \mathsf{func}, \mathsf{State}, T^C\rangle, C)$,
$op^C_{T_1\times\cdots\times T_n \Rightarrow T'_1\times\cdots\times T'_m}$ for
$sym(op, \langle \mathsf{pred}, T^C_1, \ldots, T^C_n, \mathsf{Comp}, T'^C_1, \ldots, T'^C_m\rangle, C)$,
x^C_T for $sym(x, \langle \mathsf{obj}, T^C\rangle, C)$.

Semantically, implicit (type) conversion of expressions of VVSL corresponds to explicit (sort) conversion of terms of MPL_ω. The conversion of terms involved in the interpretation of an expression generally depends on the symbol context of the expression. This context determines the conversion function symbols to be used. Conversion of terms of MPL_ω is given by the following mapping.

Definition. The mapping cnv: $\mathsf{Term} \times \mathsf{MType} \times \mathsf{MType} \times \mathsf{Cxt} \to \mathsf{Term}$ is defined by

$$cnv(t, S_1, S_2, C) := \mathrm{Conv}^{\leq}_{S_1 \to S_2}(t),$$
$$\text{where } \leq\ = sdcls(C \cup predefs(C)).$$

Instead of $cnv(t, S_1, S_2, C)$, we write $cnv^C_{S_1\to S_2}(t)$.
$cnv^C_{S_1\to S_2}(t)$ is the conversion of term t from sort S_1 to sort S_2 in the symbol context C.

The abbreviations $\mathrm{Conv}^{\leq}_{S_1\to S_2}(t)$ (used above) and $\mathrm{Convax}^{\leq}$ (used below) were introduced in Section 4.4.

Depending upon the symbol context of an expression, the conversion of terms involved in the interpretation of the expression can sometimes be carried out in different ways. In these cases, the particular choice is irrelevant. The formula given by the following mapping states this.

Definition. The mapping $cnvax$: $\mathsf{Cxt} \to \mathsf{Form}$ is defined by

$$cnvax(C) := \mathrm{Convax}^{\leq},$$
$$\text{where } \leq\ = sdcls(C \cup predefs(C)).$$

$cnvax(C)$ is a formula stating that compositions of implicit conversions via different intermediate sorts must yield the same result, for the implicit conversions allowed in the symbol context C.

5.2 Contexts and typing

The typing of expressions is context dependent. In this section, the predicates and mappings which are used in Section 5.8 to describe the typing of expressions and further typing related properties are defined.

The least upper bound of a finite set of types with respect to the subtype ordering is now introduced. Because the subtype ordering in force depends on the context, least upper bounds with respect to the subtype ordering also depend on the context. Least upper bounds do not always exist. In order to deal with the potential non-existence in a comfortable way, a predicate is used. This predicate is used to describe the typing of expressions.

Definition. The predicate lub: $\mathcal{P}(\mathsf{Type}) \times \mathsf{Type} \times \mathsf{NCxt}$ is defined as follows:

$$lub(\{T_1, \ldots, T_n\}, T, N) :\Leftrightarrow$$
$$T \text{ is the least upper bound of } \{T_1, \ldots, T_n\} \text{ with respect to } \leq^N.$$

$lub(\{T_1, \ldots, T_n\}, T, N)$ indicates that T is the least type with $T_1, \ldots, T_n$ as subtypes in the name context N.

The lowering of a type is now defined. It is defined such that it is the least subtype of the type if that is uniquely defined and its least 'uniquely defined approximation' otherwise. This is used to lower the type of an expression to the least type such that, according to the subtype ordering being in force, the value of the expression is always an element of some type of which this type is a subtype. Thus, the expression becomes well-typed if it can make sense.

Definition. The mapping $lower$: $\mathsf{Type} \times \mathsf{NCxt} \to \mathsf{Type}$ is defined as follows:

$$lower(T, N) :=$$
$$\text{the least type } T', \text{ with respect to } \leq^N, \text{ such that}$$
$$T' \leq^N T \wedge \forall T'' \in \mathsf{Type}\,(T'' \leq^N T \;\Rightarrow\; (T' \leq^N T'' \vee T'' \leq^N T'))$$

$lower(T, N)$ is the least subtype of T that is comparable with all subtypes of T, in the name context N.

The raising of a type is now defined similarly. It is used to fix the greatest common type for the operands of an equality expression. In order to exclude unintended undefinedness, the operand values are implicitly converted (if necessary) to this type before being compared.

Definition. The mapping $raise$: $\mathsf{Type} \times \mathsf{NCxt} \to \mathsf{Type}$ is defined as follows:

$$raise(T, N) :=$$
$$\text{the greatest type } T', \text{ with respect to } \leq^N, \text{ such that}$$
$$T \leq^N T' \wedge \forall T'' \in \mathsf{Type}\,(T \leq^N T'' \;\Rightarrow\; (T' \leq^N T'' \vee T'' \leq^N T'))$$

$raise(T, N)$ is the greatest type with T as subtype that is comparable with all types with T as subtype, in the name context N.

In Section 5.8, the notation $N \vdash_{\mathrm{m}} e \,⦂\, T$ is introduced to indicate that, in context N, expression e has minimal type T. Generally, minimal typings of expressions can be inferred from minimal typings of immediate subexpressions. Minimal typings of value names and state variable names are basic ones. They are given by the following predicate.

Definition. The predicate $mtyping$: $\mathsf{UIdent} \times \mathsf{Type} \times \mathsf{NCxt}$ is inductively defined by

$$T =$$
$$\text{the unique type } T' \text{ such that } [\mathsf{val}\ i{:}\ T'] \in N \vee [\mathsf{var}\ i{:}\ T'] \in N \;\Rightarrow$$
$$mtyping(i, lower(T, N), N).$$

In the description of well-formedness of constructs, we write 'the minimal type of i in N is T' instead of $mtyping(i, T, N)$.

According to this definition, a value or state variable name has no minimal typing if it is introduced several times as the name of a value or state variable. This kind of ambiguity is not allowed.

The minimal type of application expressions of the form $f(e_1, \ldots, e_n)$ where the argument expressions $e_1, \ldots, e_n$ have minimal types $T_1, \ldots, T_n$, respectively, is regarded as the minimal typing of the function name f with respect to $T_1, \ldots, T_n$. Thus, minimal typings of function names can be given in roughly the same way as for value names and state variable names. A predicate giving minimal typings of function names is defined below. A function name has no minimal typing, if there is not a unique name that fits the supplied minimal types of the argument expressions, unless it is a pre-defined function name – because in that case it is guaranteed that the ambiguity has no semantic consequences. For pre-defined function names, the function with the greatest argument types is chosen in order to exclude unintended undefinedness.

The predicate giving minimal typings of function names is defined in terms of a predicate indicating the expected types of the arguments of the function corresponding to a given function name that fits supplied minimal types of the argument expressions. The latter predicate is defined first. It is also used to describe the meaning of application expressions.

Definition. The predicate *ftypes*: $\mathsf{NIdent} \times \mathsf{Type}^* \times \mathsf{Type}^* \times \mathsf{NCxt}$ is inductively defined by

$$\begin{array}{l}\langle T'_1, \ldots, T'_n\rangle = \\ \text{the unique sequence of types } \langle T''_1, \ldots, T''_n\rangle \text{ such that} \\ \bigwedge_{k=1}^{n} (T_k \leq^{\overline{C}} T''_k) \wedge \\ \exists T'' \in \mathsf{Type}\,([\mathsf{func}\ f\colon T''_1 \times \cdots \times T''_n \to T''] \in \overline{C}) \;\Rightarrow \\ \mathit{ftypes}(f, \langle T_1, \ldots, T_n\rangle, \langle T'_1, \ldots, T'_n\rangle, \overline{C}),\end{array}$$

$$\begin{array}{l}\langle T'_1, \ldots, T'_n\rangle = \\ \text{the greatest sequence of types } \langle T''_1, \ldots, T''_n\rangle, \\ \text{w.r.t. the component-wise extension of } \leq^{\overline{C}}, \text{ such that} \\ \bigwedge_{k=1}^{n} (T_k \leq^{\overline{C}} T''_k) \wedge \\ \exists T'' \in \mathsf{Type}\,([\mathsf{func}\ f\colon T''_1 \times \cdots \times T''_n \to T''] \in \overline{\mathit{predefs}(C)}) \;\Rightarrow \\ \mathit{ftypes}(f, \langle T_1, \ldots, T_n\rangle, \langle T'_1, \ldots, T'_n\rangle, \overline{C}).\end{array}$$

$\mathit{ftypes}(f, \langle T_1, \ldots, T_n\rangle, \langle T'_1, \ldots, T'_n\rangle, N)$ indicates that, in the name context N, $T'_1, \ldots, T'_n$ are the expected types of the arguments of the function corresponding to the function name f that fits minimal types $T_1, \ldots, T_n$ for the argument expressions.

Definition. The predicate *mtyping*: $\mathsf{NIdent} \times \mathsf{Type}^* \times \mathsf{Type} \times \mathsf{NCxt}$ is inductively defined by

$$\begin{array}{l} \mathit{ftypes}(f, \langle T_1, \ldots, T_n\rangle, \langle T_1', \ldots, T_n'\rangle, N) \wedge \\ [\mathsf{func}\ f\colon T_1' \times \cdots \times T_n' \to T'] \in N \ \Rightarrow \\ \mathit{mtyping}(f, \langle T_1, \ldots, T_n\rangle, \mathit{lower}(T', N), N). \end{array}$$

$\mathit{mtyping}(f, \langle T_1, \ldots, T_n\rangle, T, N)$ indicates that, in the name context N, T is the minimal type of the application expressions of the form $f(e_1, \ldots, e_n)$ where the argument expressions $e_1, \ldots, e_n$ have minimal types $T_1, \ldots, T_n$, respectively.

A well-formed expression or temporal term must be well-typed. An expression or temporal term is well-typed in a context if it has a minimal type in that context. The well-typedness of expressions and temporal terms is given by the following predicates.

Definition. The predicates $\mathit{wt}\colon \mathsf{Expression} \times \mathsf{NCxt}$ and $\mathit{wt}\colon \mathsf{TTerm} \times \mathsf{NCxt}$ are defined by

$$\begin{array}{l} \mathit{wt}(e, N) \ :\Leftrightarrow\ \exists T \in \mathsf{Type}\ (N \vdash_{\mathrm{m}} e \mathbin{⁝} T), \\ \mathit{wt}(\tau, N) \ :\Leftrightarrow\ \exists T \in \mathsf{Type}\ (N \vdash_{\mathrm{m}} \tau \mathbin{⁝} T). \end{array}$$

In the description of well-formedness, we write 'e is well-typed in N' and 'τ is well-typed in N' instead of $\mathit{wt}(e, N)$ and $\mathit{wt}(\tau, N)$, respectively.

In a well-formed equality expression or equality temporal formula the left-hand side and the right-hand side must be compatible. Two expressions or temporal terms are compatible in a context if their minimal types have a least upper bound in that context. The compatibility of two expressions and two temporal terms is given by the following predicates.

Definition. The predicates $\mathit{compatible}\colon \mathsf{Expression} \times \mathsf{Expression} \times \mathsf{NCxt}$ and $\mathit{compatible}\colon \mathsf{TTerm} \times \mathsf{TTerm} \times \mathsf{NCxt}$ are defined by

$$\begin{array}{l} \mathit{compatible}(e_1, e_2, N) \ :\Leftrightarrow \\ \exists T_1, T_2 \in \mathsf{Type} \\ \quad (N \vdash_{\mathrm{m}} e_1 \mathbin{⁝} T_1 \ \wedge\ N \vdash_{\mathrm{m}} e_2 \mathbin{⁝} T_2 \ \wedge\ \exists T \in \mathsf{Type}\ (\mathit{lub}(\{T_1, T_2\}, T, N))), \\ \mathit{compatible}(\tau_1, \tau_2, N) \ :\Leftrightarrow \\ \exists T_1, T_2 \in \mathsf{Type} \\ \quad (N \vdash_{\mathrm{m}} \tau_1 \mathbin{⁝} T_1 \ \wedge\ N \vdash_{\mathrm{m}} \tau_2 \mathbin{⁝} T_2 \ \wedge\ \exists T \in \mathsf{Type}\ (\mathit{lub}(\{T_1, T_2\}, T, N))). \end{array}$$

In the description of well-formedness, we write 'e_1 and e_2 are type compatible in N' instead of $\mathit{compatible}(e_1, e_2, N)$ and 'τ_1 and τ_2 are type compatible in N' instead of $\mathit{compatible}(\tau_1, \tau_2, N)$.

A well-formed expression or temporal term has a unique minimal type. This type is given by the (partial) mappings defined below. These mappings are used in Sections 5.8 and 5.9 for the definition of well-formedness.

Definition. The mappings $\mathit{mtype}\colon \mathsf{Expression} \times \mathsf{NCxt} \to \mathsf{Type}$ and *mtype*: $\mathsf{TTerm} \times \mathsf{NCxt} \rightarrow \mathsf{Type}$ are inductively defined by

$$N \vdash_{\mathrm{m}} e \mathrel{\overset{\circ}{\circ}} T \;\Rightarrow\; \mathit{mtype}(e, N) = T,$$
$$N \vdash_{\mathrm{m}} \tau \mathrel{\overset{\circ}{\circ}} T \;\Rightarrow\; \mathit{mtype}(\tau, N) = T.$$

In the description of well-formedness, we write 'the minimal type of e in N' and 'the minimal type of τ in N' instead of $\mathit{mtype}(e, N)$ and $\mathit{mtype}(\tau, N)$, respectively.

The mappings and predicates *lub*, *lower*, *raise*, *mtyping* and *ftypes* have a name context as last argument. In the remainder of this chapter, such arguments are always given as superscripts of the names concerned. In other words, we write $\mathit{lub}^N(\{t_1, \ldots, t_n\}, t)$ instead of $\mathit{lub}(\{t_1, \ldots, t_n\}, t, N)$, etc.

5.3 Syntax notation

The syntax of VVSL is described by means of production rules in the form of a BNF grammar. The intention is that the production rules describe abstract language constructs. The right-hand side of a production rule is considered to describe the production of abstract constructs which are objects composed of abstract constructs produced by the nonterminals occurring in the right-hand side of the rule and generated by a unique constructor function for the rule concerned. The rule also describes how applications of the constructor function – which yield constructs produced by the nonterminal occurring in the left-hand side – are written in the definitions of well-formedness and semantics. Thus, the intended concrete syntax is mimicked. This helps to make the definitions more readable.

If the syntax description was regarded as a context-free grammar, the resulting language would be ambiguous. Notwithstanding, the string representation as suggested by the syntax description is the intended concrete syntax. It is assumed that parentheses are generally used to avoid syntactic ambiguities with semantic consequences. Some of them cannot be avoided in this way. The intended resolution of these ambiguities is informally described following the production rules concerned.

The nonterminal *<empty>* has one production rule:

<empty> ::=

This means that *<empty>* produces only a construct without constituents. This construct is intended as a special construct that should be represented by an empty string.

There are nonterminals for which production rules are given in the presented syntax of VVSL, but which are not interesting from a semantic point of view. They are of an auxiliary nature.

5.4 Organization of the definition

Each section that deals with the syntax and semantics of a sublanguage of VVSL starts with an overview of the sublanguage concerned, a presentation of its syntax and some general remarks regarding the well-formedness, syntactic properties and meaning of constructs in the sublanguage.

Following this introduction, there are separate subsections on the constructs of the various forms that are distinguished by the production rules given in the syntax presentation for the sublanguage concerned. These subsections are subdivided into at least four parts: there are always parts for informal explanation, structure, well-formedness and meaning, but there is generally also a part for syntactic properties. The structure is a representation of the constructs of the form concerned as a production with variables for subconstructs. These variables range over the terminal productions of fixed nonterminals as follows (subscripts and primes are not shown):

B	*<basic-module>*
D^t	*<type-definition>*
D^v	*<variable-definition>*
D^f	*<function-definition>*
D^o	*<operation-definition>*
T	*<type>*
e	*<expression>*
E	*<logical-expression>*
φ	*<temporal-formula>*
τ	*<temporal-term>*
t	*<type-name>*
x	*<value-name>*
f, a, s	*<function-name>*
v	*<variable-name>*
op	*<operation-name>*
c	*<type-constructor-name>*
n	*<number>*

There are no production rules given for the nonterminals of the form <x-*name*>. They are supposed to produce *identifiers*, which are considered to be terminals. There are no production rules given for the nonterminal *<number>* either; (representations of) numbers are also considered to be terminals.

5.5 Basic modules

Basic modules are the building blocks of modularly structured specifications in full VVSL. They are considered to be complete specifications in flat VVSL. This language can be viewed as being composed of four sublanguages: one for *definitions*, one for *types*, one for *expressions* and *logical expressions*, and one for *temporal formulae*. Their hierarchical structure is indicated by the following:

- Basic modules are constructed mainly from definitions.
- Definitions (Section 5.6) are constructed from types, expressions and logical expressions, temporal formulae, and *names*.
- Types (Section 5.7) are constructed from names only.
- Expressions (Section 5.8) are constructed from logical expressions, names and *numbers*, and logical expressions (also Section 5.8) are constructed from expressions and names.
- Temporal formulae (Section 5.9) are also constructed from expressions and names.

The remainder of this section deals with the syntax and semantics of basic modules. It begins by introducing basic modules in broad outline.

Overview

In VVSL, one can define types, functions working on values of these types, state variables which can take values of these types, and operations which may interrogate and modify the state variables. State variable is the name used in VVSL for state components. A collection of definitions can be brought together in a basic module of the following form:

$$\mathsf{module\ types}\ \mathcal{D}^t\ \mathsf{state}\ \mathcal{D}^v\ \mathsf{functions}\ \mathcal{D}^f\ \mathsf{operations}\ \mathcal{D}^o\ \mathsf{end},$$

where $\mathcal{D}^t$, $\mathcal{D}^v$, $\mathcal{D}^f$ and $\mathcal{D}^o$ are the type definitions, the state variable definitions, the function definitions and the operation definitions, respectively. How one can define types, functions, state variables and operations, is described in Section 5.6.

Example. This example is about tuples. They are defined as maps from attributes to values. It is assumed that attributes and values are defined elsewhere. Tuples can be thought of as records, with the attributes corresponding to fields. Functions to construct tuples (*singleton* and *merge*), a function to select the value associated with a given attribute from tuples (*value*) and a function to check upon the truth or falsity of a given predicate for tuples (*holds*) are defined. Tuple predicates are defined as maps from tuples to truth values. A tuple predicate holds for a tuple if this map associates with the tuple the truth value true. Tuple predicates can be thought of as properties that tuples can have.

module
  types
    $Attribute$ free
    $Value$ free
    $Tuple = Attribute \xrightarrow{m} Value$ where $\mathsf{inv}(t) \triangleq \mathsf{dom}\, t \neq \{\,\}$
    $Tuple\_predicate = Tuple \xrightarrow{m} \mathbb{B}$
  functions
    $singleton(a\colon Attribute, v\colon Value)\, Tuple$
      $\triangleq \{a \mapsto v\}$
    $merge(t_1\colon Tuple, t_2\colon Tuple)\, Tuple$
      $\triangleq t_1 \cup t_2$
    $value(t\colon Tuple, a\colon Attribute)\, Value$
      $\triangleq t(a)$
    $holds(tp\colon Tuple\_predicate, t\colon Tuple)\mathbb{B}$
      pre $t \in \mathsf{dom}\, tp$
      $\triangleq tp(t)$
end

This basic module only contains definitions of types and functions. Such basic modules (as well as basic modules that only contain definitions of state variables and operations) are usual in modularly structured specifications. In this way state independent aspects and state dependent aspects are clearly separated in modularly structured specifications. This isolated simple basic module is not meant to illustrate a good choice to achieve the goals of modular structuring. Such examples are given in Chapters 11 to 13.

Syntax

Basic modules are the terminal productions of *<basic-module>*. Regarding flat VVSL as a language on its own, basic modules must be considered to be the sentences of flat VVSL, i.e. *<basic-module>* is the start symbol of the grammar for flat VVSL.

<basic-module> ::=
    module *<types>* *<state>* *<functions>* *<operations>* end

<types> ::=
    <empty>
  | types *<type-definitions>*

<type-definitions> ::=
<type-definition>
| *<type-definition>* *<type-definitions>*

<state> ::=
<empty>
| state *<variable-definition-option>*
inv *<logical-expression>* init *<logical-expression>*
dyn *<temporal-formula>*

<variable-definition-option> ::=
<empty>
| *<variable-definitions>*

<variable-definitions> ::=
<variable-definition>
| *<variable-definition>* *<variable-definitions>*

<functions> ::=
<empty>
| functions *<function-definitions>*

<function-definitions> ::=
<function-definition>
| *<function-definition>* *<function-definitions>*

<operations> ::=
<empty>
| operations *<operation-definitions>*

<operation-definitions> ::=
<operation-definition>
| *<operation-definition>* *<operation-definitions>*

In Section 5.6, the production rules for the nonterminals *<type-definition>*, *<variable-definition>*, *<function-definition>* and *<operation-definition>* are presented. For *<logical-expression>* and *<temporal-formula>*, the production rules are presented in Section 5.8 and Section 5.9, respectively.

The set BasicModule of syntactically correct basic module constructs is defined by

BasicModule := $\{B \mid B$ is a terminal production of *<basic-module>*$\}$.

Well-formedness. The well-formedness of syntactically correct basic module constructs is defined by a predicate

$$wf : \mathsf{BasicModule} \times \mathsf{NCxt}\,.$$

$wf(B, N)$ indicates that B is well-formed in the name context N. Instead of $wf(B, N)$, we write 'B is well-formed in N'. The well-formedness of basic modules is defined in terms of the well-formedness of definitions, logical expressions and temporal formulae (defined in Sections 5.6, 5.8 and 5.9), and the syntactic properties of definitions (defined in Section 5.6).

Syntactic properties. The name context associated with basic modules is defined by a mapping

$$\{\!\![\bullet]\!\!\} : \mathsf{BasicModule} \to \mathsf{NCxt}\,.$$

$\{\!\![B]\!\!\}$ consists of the names and the subtype declarations introduced by the definitions of basic module B.

If the keyword free occurs in a definition, then it introduces a free name. Roughly speaking, a free name is a name which is supposed to be defined elsewhere. This makes most sense in full VVSL, where it can be defined in another module. The free name context associated with basic modules is defined by a mapping

$$\{\!\![\bullet]\!\!\}_{\mathsf{free}} : \mathsf{BasicModule} \to \mathsf{NCxt}\,.$$

$\{\!\![B]\!\!\}_{\mathsf{free}}$ consists of the free names introduced by the definitions of basic module B. $\{\!\![B]\!\!\}_{\mathsf{free}}$ is a subset of $\{\!\![B]\!\!\}$. These syntactic properties are defined in terms of the syntactic properties of definitions (defined in Section 5.6).

Meaning. The meaning of basic modules is defined by a mapping

$$[\![\bullet]\!]^{\bullet} : \mathsf{BasicModule} \times \mathsf{Cxt} \to \mathcal{P}(\mathsf{Form})\,.$$

$[\![B]\!]^{C}$ is the set of formulae corresponding to the basic module B in a symbol context C. $[\![B]\!]^{C}$ is only defined if $\{\!\![B]\!\!\} \subseteq \overline{C}$ and B is well-formed in $\overline{C}$. The condition $\{\!\![B]\!\!\} \subseteq \overline{C}$ enforces that C supplies symbols for all names defined in B. This allows the meaning of basic modules in flat VVSL to be described without anticipating their role in modularly structured specifications. In flat VVSL, basic modules are regarded as merely collections of definitions together with some general assumptions about states and state changes. Information hiding is not covered by the meaning of basic modules in flat VVSL. The meaning of basic modules in flat VVSL is defined in terms of the meaning of definitions, logical expressions and temporal formulae (defined in Sections 5.6, 5.8 and 5.9).

In Chapter 8, the modularization and parametrization constructs which complement flat VVSL are provided with a well-defined semantics that is built on top of the logic-based semantics presented in this chapter. There, the meaning of a basic module as a modularization construct is described in terms of its well-formedness, syntactic properties and meaning according to the definition of flat VVSL presented in this chapter. The latter (context dependent) meaning, say $[\![B]\!]^C$, is just a subset of the set Form of formulae. The signature corresponding to the basic module in the context concerned is $sig([\![B]\!]^C)$. This aspect of the meaning of basic modules is not defined by a separate mapping.

Below basic modules are precisely described.

Basic module

$$\begin{array}{l}\textsf{module}\\ \quad \textsf{types}\ D_1^t\ \ldots\ D_{n_t}^t\ \ \textsf{state}\ D_1^v\ \ldots\ D_{n_v}^v\ \ \textsf{inv}\ E_1\ \ \textsf{init}\ E_2\ \ \textsf{dyn}\ \varphi\\ \quad \textsf{functions}\ D_1^f\ \ldots\ D_{n_f}^f\ \ \textsf{operations}\ D_1^o\ \ldots\ D_{n_o}^o\\ \textsf{end}\end{array}$$

is a basic module, where the definitions $D_1^t, \ldots, D_{n_t}^t$ introduce names for types, $D_1^v, \ldots, D_{n_v}^v$ introduce names for state variables which can take values of these types, $D_1^f, \ldots, D_{n_f}^f$ introduce names for functions working on values of these types, $D_1^o, \ldots, D_{n_o}^o$ introduce names for operations which may interrogate and modify the state variables. The types may be introduced by definitions in which the types are recursively used. The functions that are explicitly defined may also be introduced by definitions in which the functions are recursively used. The logical expression E_1 and E_2 state assumptions about what values the state variables can take in any state and initially, respectively. Either of these conditions gives rise to a proof obligation for its preservation by the operations. Similarly, the temporal formula φ states an assumption about what histories of values taken by the state variables can occur in any computation. This condition also gives rise to a proof obligation for its preservation by the (non-atomic) operations.

Structure:

$$\begin{array}{l}\textsf{module}\\ \quad \textsf{types}\ D_1^t\ \ldots\ D_{n_t}^t\ \ \textsf{state}\ D_1^v\ \ldots\ D_{n_v}^v\ \ \textsf{inv}\ E_1\ \ \textsf{init}\ E_2\ \ \textsf{dyn}\ \varphi\\ \quad \textsf{functions}\ D_1^f\ \ldots\ D_{n_f}^f\ \ \textsf{operations}\ D_1^o\ \ldots\ D_{n_o}^o\\ \textsf{end}\end{array}$$

Well-formedness in N:

$names(\{\![D_1^t]\!\}), \ldots, names(\{\![D_{n_t}^t]\!\})$ are disjoint sets,
$\{\![D_1^v]\!\}, \ldots, \{\![D_{n_v}^v]\!\}$ are disjoint sets,
$\{\![D_1^f]\!\}, \ldots, \{\![D_{n_f}^f]\!\}$ are disjoint sets,
$\{\![D_1^o]\!\}, \ldots, \{\![D_{n_o}^o]\!\}$ are disjoint sets,

$D_1^t, \ldots, D_{n_t}^t, D_1^v, \ldots, D_{n_v}^v, D_1^f, \ldots, D_{n_f}^f, D_1^o, \ldots, D_{n_o}^o$ are well-formed in N',

E_1, E_2 are well-formed in $\langle N', 1\rangle$,

φ is well-formed in N',

where

$N' = N \cup \bigcup_{i=1}^{n_t} \{\!\!\{D_i^t\}\!\!\} \cup \bigcup_{i=1}^{n_v} \{\!\!\{D_i^v\}\!\!\} \cup \bigcup_{i=1}^{n_f} \{\!\!\{D_i^f\}\!\!\} \cup \bigcup_{i=1}^{n_o} \{\!\!\{D_i^o\}\!\!\}$.

Names and subtype declarations:

$$\begin{array}{l}\{\!\!\{\mathsf{module} \\ \quad \mathsf{types}\ D_1^t\ \ldots\ D_{n_t}^t\ \ \mathsf{state}\ D_1^v\ \ldots\ D_{n_v}^v\ \ \mathsf{inv}\ E_1\ \ \mathsf{init}\ E_2\ \ \mathsf{dyn}\ \varphi \\ \quad \mathsf{functions}\ D_1^f\ \ldots\ D_{n_f}^f\ \ \mathsf{operations}\ D_1^o\ \ldots\ D_{n_o}^o \\ \mathsf{end}\}\!\!\}\ := \\ \qquad \bigcup_{i=1}^{n_t} \{\!\!\{D_i^t\}\!\!\} \cup \bigcup_{i=1}^{n_v} \{\!\!\{D_i^v\}\!\!\} \cup \bigcup_{i=1}^{n_f} \{\!\!\{D_i^f\}\!\!\} \cup \bigcup_{i=1}^{n_o} \{\!\!\{D_i^o\}\!\!\},\end{array}$$

$$\begin{array}{l}\{\!\!\{\mathsf{module} \\ \quad \mathsf{types}\ D_1^t\ \ldots\ D_{n_t}^t\ \ \mathsf{state}\ D_1^v\ \ldots\ D_{n_v}^v\ \ \mathsf{inv}\ E_1\ \ \mathsf{init}\ E_2\ \ \mathsf{dyn}\ \varphi \\ \quad \mathsf{functions}\ D_1^f\ \ldots\ D_{n_f}^f\ \ \mathsf{operations}\ D_1^o\ \ldots\ D_{n_o}^o \\ \mathsf{end}\}\!\!\}_{\mathsf{free}}\ := \\ \qquad \bigcup_{i=1}^{n_t} \{\overline{w} \in \overline{\mathsf{NSym}} \mid \overline{w} \in \{\!\!\{D_i^t\}\!\!\}, \mathsf{free}\text{ occurs in } D_i^t\} \cup \\ \qquad \bigcup_{i=1}^{n_v} \{\overline{w} \in \overline{\mathsf{NSym}} \mid \overline{w} \in \{\!\!\{D_i^v\}\!\!\}, \mathsf{free}\text{ occurs in } D_i^v\} \cup \\ \qquad \bigcup_{i=1}^{n_f} \{\overline{w} \in \overline{\mathsf{NSym}} \mid \overline{w} \in \{\!\!\{D_i^f\}\!\!\}, \mathsf{free}\text{ occurs in } D_i^f\} \cup \\ \qquad \bigcup_{i=1}^{n_o} \{\overline{w} \in \overline{\mathsf{NSym}} \mid \overline{w} \in \{\!\!\{D_i^o\}\!\!\}, \mathsf{free}\text{ occurs in } D_i^o\}.\end{array}$$

Meaning:

$$\begin{array}{l}[\![\mathsf{module} \\ \quad \mathsf{types}\ D_1^t\ \ldots\ D_{n_t}^t\ \ \mathsf{state}\ D_1^v\ \ldots\ D_{n_v}^v\ \ \mathsf{inv}\ E_1\ \ \mathsf{init}\ E_2\ \ \mathsf{dyn}\ \varphi \\ \quad \mathsf{functions}\ D_1^f\ \ldots\ D_{n_f}^f\ \ \mathsf{operations}\ D_1^o\ \ldots\ D_{n_o}^o \\ \mathsf{end}]\!]^C\ := \\ \qquad \mathit{axioms}(\underline{\mathrm{B}}) \cup \{\mathrm{s0}\downarrow, \mathrm{Compax}\} \cup \{\mathit{cnvax}^C\} \cup \\ \qquad \bigcup_{i=1}^{n_t} [\![D_i^t]\!]^C \cup \bigcup_{i=1}^{n_v} [\![D_i^v]\!]^C \cup \boldsymbol{\mu}(\bigcup_{i=1}^{n_f} [\![D_i^f]\!]^C) \cup \bigcup_{i=1}^{n_o} [\![D_i^o]\!]^C \cup \\ \qquad \{\varphi_1, \varphi_2, \varphi_3\},\end{array}$$

where:

$$\begin{array}{rl}\varphi_1 = & \exists s\colon \mathsf{State}(\mathrm{s0} = s \wedge [\![E_1]\!]^C_{\langle s\rangle, tt}) \wedge \\ & \forall s'\colon \mathsf{State} \\ & \quad ([\![E_1]\!]^C_{\langle s'\rangle, tt} \to \\ & \qquad \forall s''\colon \mathsf{State}(\bigvee_{v \in C \cap \mathsf{MVar}} (\neg\, v(s') \simeq v(s'')) \to [\![E_1]\!]^C_{\langle s''\rangle, tt})), \\ \varphi_2 = & \exists s\colon \mathsf{State}(\mathrm{s0} = s \wedge [\![E_2]\!]^C_{\langle s\rangle, tt}), \\ \varphi_3 = & \forall c\colon \mathsf{Comp}(\bigwedge_k (\mathrm{st}_k(c)\downarrow \to [\![\varphi]\!]^C_{c,k,tt})),\end{array}$$

and

s, s', s'' are fresh state symbols, c is a fresh computation symbol.

5.6 The definition sublanguage

The previous section dealt with the syntax and semantics of basic modules. Basic modules are constructed mainly from definitions. This section deals with the syntax and semantics of definitions. It begins by introducing the different kinds of definitions in broad outline.

Overview

The following kinds of definitions are distinguished: type definitions, function definitions, state variable definitions and operation definitions.

Type definitions

A type is defined by a type definition of one of the following forms:

$$\begin{aligned} t &= T \,\mathsf{where\ inv}(x) \triangleq E \\ t &= t_1 | \cdots | t_n \\ t &= [t_1 | \cdots | t_n]. \end{aligned}$$

A definition of the first form defines the type as a subtype of a basic type (boolean, natural, etc.) or constructed type (sequence type, set type, etc.) constructed from basic types and/or other defined types. The *invariant* is a restriction on the basic or constructed type that uniquely characterizes the subtype. The invariant may be absent, in which case there is no restriction on the type (i.e. it is equivalent to the invariant true). A definition of the second or third form defines the type as the union of a number of defined types.† For the last form there is an implicit union with a type whose only element is a special nil value which is often used to model an 'absent value'. Recursive type definitions are allowed.

Example. Relations can be defined as finite sets of tuples with the same attributes:

$$\begin{aligned} &\mathit{Relation} = \mathit{Tuple}\text{-}\mathsf{set} \\ &\mathsf{where\ inv}(r) \triangleq \\ &\quad \forall t_1 \in \mathit{Tuple}, t_2 \in \mathit{Tuple} \cdot t_1 \in r \wedge t_2 \in r \Rightarrow \mathsf{dom}\, t_1 = \mathsf{dom}\, t_2. \end{aligned}$$

Formulae for stating properties of tuples can be defined as the union of formulae of several forms:

$$\mathit{Selection\_wff} = \mathit{Eq} \mid \mathit{Less} \mid \mathit{Greater} \mid \mathit{Negation} \mid \mathit{Disjunction}.$$

† It is characteristic for a type constructor that it has associated constructor functions for generating values of the type. We take the view that inclusion functions are not constructor functions and consequently that the union of types does not correspond to a type constructor. Therefore the term 'constructed type' is not used for a union of types.

Function definitions

A function is *explicitly* specified by a function definition of the following form:

$$f(x_1\colon t_1,\ldots,x_n\colon t_n)\; t_{n+1}$$
$$\textsf{pre}\quad E$$
$$\triangleq\quad e$$

or it is *implicitly* specified by a function definition of the following form:

$$f(x_1\colon t_1,\ldots,x_n\colon t_n)\; x_{n+1}\colon t_{n+1}$$
$$\textsf{pre}\quad E_1$$
$$\textsf{post}\quad E_2.$$

The 'header' introduces a name for the specified function and defines the types of its arguments and result. The header also introduces names for the argument values and result value to be used within the 'body'. The body consists of a pre-condition and either a defining expression or a post-condition. The *pre-condition* defines the combinations of argument values for which the function should yield a result value. A *defining* expression always defines a specific result value from each of these combinations of argument values, while a *post-condition* defines generally a range of acceptable result values (i.e. the result value is not uniquely characterized). The pre-condition may be absent, in which case the function is total over the defined argument types (i.e. it is equivalent to the pre-condition true).

Example. The product of two relations can be explicitly specified as follows:

$$\mathit{product}(r_1\colon \mathit{Relation}, r_2\colon \mathit{Relation})\mathit{Relation}$$
$$\textsf{pre}\quad r_1 \neq \{\,\} \wedge r_2 \neq \{\,\} \;\Rightarrow\; \mathit{attrs}(r_1) \cap \mathit{attrs}(r_2) = \{\,\}$$
$$\triangleq\quad \{\mathit{merge}(t_1,t_2) \mid t_1 \in \mathit{Tuple}, t_2 \in \mathit{Tuple}\;;\; t_1 \in r_1 \wedge t_2 \in r_2\}.$$

The function $\mathit{attrs}\colon \mathit{Relation} \to \mathit{Attr\_set}$ can be implicitly specified as follows:

$$\mathit{attrs}(r\colon \mathit{Relation})\mathit{as}\colon \mathit{Attr\_set}$$
$$\textsf{pre}\quad r \neq \{\,\}$$
$$\textsf{post}\quad \exists t \in \mathit{Tuple} \cdot t \in r \wedge \textsf{dom}\, t = \mathit{as}.$$

In flat VVSL, just as in VDM-SL, operation is a general name for imperative programs and meaningful parts thereof (e.g. procedures). Unlike functions, operations may yield results which depend on a *state* and may change that state. The states concerned have a fixed number of named components, called state variables, attached to them. In all states, a value is associated with each of these state variables. Operations change states by modifying the value of state variables. Each state variable can only take values of a fixed type. State variables correspond to programming variables of imperative programs. In VDM-SL, one composite type is designated as the state space. The components of this composite type are treated as state variables. The approach taken in VVSL differs, because it would otherwise become needlessly hard to explain what it means when two or more modules have some state variables in common (particular hidden ones).

State variable definitions

A state variable is declared by a state variable definition of the following form:

$$v\colon t.$$

It introduces a name for the state variable and defines the type from which the state variable can take values. A *state invariant* and an *initial condition*, of the form

$$\mathsf{inv}\quad E_1$$

and

$$\mathsf{init}\quad E_2,$$

respectively, can be associated with a collection of state variable definitions. The state invariant is a restriction on what values the state variables can take in any state. The initial condition is a restriction on what values the state variables can take initially, i.e. before any modification by operations.

In VVSL, a *dynamic constraint*, of the form

$$\mathsf{dyn}\quad \varphi$$

can also be associated with a collection of state variable definitions. It is a restriction on what successions of state changes can occur during the execution of any operation in an interfering environment.

Example. If databases and database schemas have been defined, then state variables that take at any point in time the *current database* value and the *current database schema* value, respectively, can be declared as follows:

$$\begin{array}{ll} curr\_dbschema & : Db\_schema \\ curr\_database & : Database. \end{array}$$

Together these state variables constitute the changing state of a database management system. If the appropriate functions on databases and database schemas have been defined, then the condition that the current database schema must always apply to the current database and the condition that the current database schema and the current database must initially be empty, can be described by a state invariant and an initial condition, respectively, as follows:

inv $\quad is\_valid\_instance(curr\_database, curr\_dbschema)$
init $\quad curr\_dbschema = empty\_schema \wedge$
$\quad curr\_database = empty\_database.$

A simple example of the use of dynamic constraints was given in Section 2.1. A more complex example of the use of dynamic constraints is given in Chapter 13.

Operation definitions

An operation is implicitly specified by an operation definition of the following form:

$op(x_1 \colon t_1, \ldots, x_n \colon t_n)\ y_1 \colon t'_1, \ldots, y_m \colon t'_m$
ext $\quad$ rd $v_1 \colon t''_1, \ldots,$ rd $v_k \colon t''_k,$ wr $v'_1 \colon t'''_1, \ldots,$ wr $v'_l \colon t'''_l$
pre $\quad E_1$
post $\quad E_2$
inter $\quad \varphi.$

The header introduces a name for the specified operation and defines the types of its arguments and results. The header also introduces names for the argument values and result values to be used within the body. The body consists of an external clause, a pre-condition, a post-condition and an inter-condition. The *external clause* indicates which state variables may be interrogated and/or modified by the operation. The *pre-condition* defines the inputs, i.e. combinations of initial state and argument values, for which the operation should terminate, and the *post-condition* defines the possible outputs, i.e. combinations of final state and result values, from each of these inputs. Operations are potentially non-deterministic: the post-condition may permit more than one output from the same input. The pre-condition may be absent, in which case the operation should terminate for all inputs (i.e. it is equivalent to the pre-condition true). In the post-condition, one refers to the value of a state variable v in the initial state by $\overleftarrow{v}$ and to its value in the final state by v.

An initial state may lead to a final state via some intermediate states. However, one cannot refer to these intermediate states in the pre- and post-conditions of operation definitions. This is not appropriate for operations which are intended to be sensitive to interference by concurrently executed operations through shared state variables. For such operations, called *non-atomic* operations, intermediate states are relevant to their observable effects. In VVSL, an *inter-condition* can be used to define the possible successions of state changes that can be generated by the operation working interleaved with an interfering environment, distinguishing between state changes effected by the operation itself, called internal steps, and state changes effected by its interfering environment, called external steps. The inter-condition may be absent, in which case the operation is atomic, i.e. there is at most one internal step and no external steps. This is equivalent to the inter-condition $\bigcirc\mathsf{true} \Rightarrow (\mathsf{is\text{-}I} \wedge \bigcirc\neg\bigcirc\mathsf{true})$.

Example. If database queries and their well-formedness and evaluation have been defined, then an operation to add the tuples characterized by a given query to a relation stored in the database can be defined as follows:

$$
\begin{array}{ll}
\multicolumn{2}{l}{INSERT(rnm\colon Rel\_nm,\ q\colon Query)} \\
\mathsf{ext} & \mathsf{rd}\ curr\_dbschema\colon Db\_schema, \\
 & \mathsf{wr}\ curr\_database\colon Database \\
\mathsf{pre} & is\_wf(mk\text{-}Union(mk\text{-}Ref(rnm), q), curr\_dbschema) \\
\mathsf{post} & \mathsf{let} \\
 & dbsch\colon Db\_schema \triangleq \overleftarrow{curr\_dbschema}, \\
 & db\colon Database \triangleq \overleftarrow{curr\_database}, \\
 & r\colon Relation \triangleq \\
 & \quad eval(mk\text{-}Union(mk\text{-}Ref(rnm), q), dbsch, db), \\
 & db'\colon Database \triangleq update(db, rnm, r) \\
 & \mathsf{in} \\
 & curr\_database \\
 & \quad = \mathsf{if}\ is\_valid\_instance(db', dbsch)\ \mathsf{then}\ db'\ \mathsf{else}\ db.
\end{array}
$$

A simple example of the use of inter-conditions in specifying operations was given in Section 2.1. A more complex example of the use of inter-conditions is given in Chapter 13.

Free definitions

The definitions treated so far introduce defined names; the body defines what is denoted by the name introduced. Definitions may also introduce *free* names. In that case, the body does not define what is denoted by the introduced name. So definition is not really the right term. It is mainly used in situations where one wants to use a name which is supposed to be defined elsewhere. For example, one might want to use *Symbol* as a name of a type (of symbols) in the definitions of a type *String* and associated functions, without making a particular choice of symbols.

Definitions introducing free names are called free definitions. A free type definition is of the form $t\ \mathsf{free}$, and a free state variable definition is of the form $v\colon t\ \mathsf{free}$. A free function or operation definition is obtained by adding the keyword free at the end of the header. In a definition that introduces the same name as a defined name, the pre-condition from the free definition may be *weakened* and its post- and inter-condition may be *strengthened*.

In other words, the pre-, post- and inter-condition in a free definition must be considered to be assumptions about a function or operation 'not yet defined'. In case of a free operation name, the external clause may be made more restrictive in the definition that introduces the same name as a defined name. This means that some state variables may be removed from the external clause and some write variables (indicated by the keyword wr) may be changed to read variables (indicated by the keyword rd).

Example. This example is about typed relations. They are defined as relations that are valid instances of a given relation schema. In other words, typed relation is a generic concept with an instance for each relation schema. The valid instances of a given relation schema can be viewed as relations of the same type. If relation schemas and their valid instances have been defined, then typed relations can be defined as follows:

$$Typed\_relation \;=\; Relation \text{ where inv}(r)\ is\_valid\_instance(r, rsch)$$

where $rsch\colon\to Rel\_schema$ is defined as follows:

$rsch()Rel\_schema$ free
post true.

Syntax

Definitions are the terminal productions of *<definition>*. The different kinds of definitions must be distinguishable. For that reason, the nonterminals *<type-definition>*, *<variable-definition>*, *<function-definition>* and *<operation-definition>* are introduced.

<definition> ::=
    <type-definition>
  | *<function-definition>*
  | *<variable-definition>*
  | *<operation-definition>*

<type-definition> ::=
    <type-name> = *<type>*
    where inv (*<value-name>*) $\triangleq$ *<logical-expression>*
  | *<type-name>* = *<type-union>*
  | *<type-name>* = [*<type-union>*]
  | *<type-name>* free

<function-definition> ::=
    <function-name> (*<parameter-list>*) *<parameter>*
    <free-option>
    pre *<logical-expression>* $\triangleq$ *<expression>*
  | *<function-name>* (*<parameter-list>*) *<parameter>*
    <free-option>
    pre *<logical-expression>* post *<logical-expression>*

```
<variable-definition> ::=
    <variable-name> : <type-name> <free-option>

<operation-definition> ::=
    <operation-name> ( <parameter-list> ) <parameter-list>
    <free-option>
    ext <read-variable-list> <write-variable-list>
    pre <logical-expression> post <logical-expression>
    inter <temporal-formula>


<type-union> ::=
    <type-name>
  | <type-name> | <type-union>


<parameter-list> ::=
    <empty>
  | <nonempty-parameter-list>

<nonempty-parameter-list> ::=
    <parameter>
  | <parameter> , <nonempty-parameter-list>

<parameter> ::=
    <type-name>
  | <value-name> : <type-name>

<free-option> ::=
    <empty>
  | free

<read-variable-list> ::=
    <empty>
  | <nonempty-read-variable-list>

<nonempty-read-variable-list> ::=
    <read-variable>
  | <read-variable> , <non-empty-read-variable-list>

<read-variable> ::=
    rd <variable-name> : <type-name>

<write-variable-list> ::=
    <empty>
  | <nonempty-write-variable-list>
```

<nonempty-write-variable-list> ::=
  <write-variable>
  | *<write-variable>* , *<nonempty-write-variable-list>*

<write-variable> ::=
  wr *<variable-name>* : *<type-name>*
inter *<temporal-formula>*

The production rules of *<type>* are presented in Section 5.7, the production rules of *<expression>* and *<logical-expression>* in Section 5.8, and those of *<temporal-formula>* in Section 5.9.

The set Definition of syntactically correct definition constructs is defined by

$$\mathsf{Definition} := \{D \mid D \text{ is a terminal production of } \textit{<definition>}\}.$$

Well-formedness. The well-formedness of syntactically correct definition constructs is defined by a predicate

$$wf\colon \mathsf{Definition} \times \mathsf{NCxt}.$$

$wf(D, N)$ indicates that D is well-formed in the name context N. Instead of $wf(D, N)$, we write 'D is well-formed in N'. The well-formedness predicate for definitions is defined in terms of the well-formedness for types, expressions, logical expressions and temporal formulae (defined in Sections 5.7, 5.8 and 5.9).

Syntactic properties. The name context associated with definitions is defined by a mapping

$$\{\!\!\{\bullet\}\!\!\}\colon \mathsf{Definition} \to \mathsf{NCxt}.$$

$\{\!\!\{D\}\!\!\}$ consists of the names corresponding to the names introduced by the definition D and, if D is a type definition, the subtype declarations corresponding to the subtype relationships introduced by the definition D. Only type definitions that define a type in terms of an enumerated type or a composite type introduce more than one name. These syntactic properties are defined in terms of the syntactic properties of types (defined in Section 5.7).

Meaning. The meaning of definitions is defined by a mapping

$$[\![\bullet]\!]^{\bullet}\colon \mathsf{Definition} \times \mathsf{Cxt} \to \mathcal{P}(\mathsf{EForm}).$$

$[\![D]\!]^C$ is the set of formulae corresponding to the definition D in the symbol context C. $[\![D]\!]^C$ is only defined if D is well-formed in $\overline{C}$. The meaning of definitions is defined in terms of the meaning of types, expressions, logical expressions and temporal formulae (defined in Sections 5.7, 5.8 and 5.9).

The definitions of the different forms are now treated separately. Definitions introducing free names (by the occurrence of the optional keyword free) are treated combined at the end.

Type definition of subtype

A type definition $t = T$ where $\mathsf{inv}(x) \triangleq E$ introduces the name t for a type. It defines t as the subtype of the type T such that a value is an element of type t iff it is an element of type T and evaluation of the logical expression E yields true when value name x is assigned that value. The type T can be a user-defined type, a basic type, or a sequence type, set type, map type or composite type which is constructed from other user-defined or basic types. The possibility to define t as a subtype of a union type is ruled out syntactically.

In case T is not a user-defined type, there are pre-defined function names associated with T. These function names are implicitly introduced and defined.

Structure:

$t = T$ where $\mathsf{inv}(x) \triangleq E$

Well-formedness in N:

x is not defined as a state variable name in N,

T is well-formed in N,

E is well-formed in $\langle N \cup \{[\mathsf{val}\ x\colon T]\}, 0\rangle$.

Names and subtype declarations:

$\{\!\{t = T \text{ where inv}(x) \triangleq E\}\!\} := \{[\mathsf{type}\ t], [t \leq T]\} \cup \{\!\{T\}\!\}.$

Meaning:

$[\![t = T \text{ where inv}(x) \triangleq E]\!]^C := \{\varphi_1, \varphi_2, \varphi_3\} \cup [\![T]\!]^C,$

where:

$$\varphi_1 = \mathit{gen}^{t^C} :\overset{\mathrm{I}}{=} \forall x'\colon T^C([\![E]\!]^{C\cup\{x'\}}_{\langle\rangle,\mathit{tt}} \to \mathit{gen}^{t^C}(\imath^{-1}_{T^C\to t^C}(x'))),$$

$$\varphi_2 = \forall y\colon t^C(\mathit{gen}^{t^C}(y)),$$

$$\varphi_3 = \forall z\colon T^C(\mathit{gen}^{t^C}(\imath^{-1}_{T^C\to t^C}(z)) \to \imath_{t^C\to T^C}(\imath^{-1}_{T^C\to t^C}(z)) = z),$$

and

x' is a fresh value symbol such that $\iota(x') = x$ and $\tau(x') = \langle \mathsf{obj}, T^C\rangle$,
y is a fresh value symbol such that $\tau(y) = \langle \mathsf{obj}, t^C\rangle$,
z is a fresh value symbol such that $\tau(z) = \langle \mathsf{obj}, T^C\rangle$.

Type definition of union type

A type definition $t = t_1 | \cdots | t_n$ introduces the name t for a type. It defines t as the union of the user-defined and basic types $t_1, \ldots, t_n$, i.e. a value is an element of type t iff it is an element of one of the types $t_1, \ldots, t_n$. This means that each of the types $t_1, \ldots, t_n$ is a subtype of the type t. Each of the types $t_1, \ldots, t_n$ can be a user-defined type or a basic type.

There are pre-defined function names associated with each of the types $t_1, \ldots, t_n$ that are basic types. These function names are implicitly introduced and defined.

Structure:

$t = t_1 | \cdots | t_n$

Well-formedness in N:

$t_1, \ldots, t_n$ are defined as type names in N.

Names and subtype declarations:

$\{\!\!\{ t = t_1 | \cdots | t_n \}\!\!\} := \{[\mathsf{type}\ t], [t_1 \leq t], \ldots, [t_n \leq t]\} \cup \{\!\!\{t_1\}\!\!\} \cup \ldots \cup \{\!\!\{t_n\}\!\!\}.$

Meaning:

$[\![t = t_1 | \cdots | t_n]\!]^C := \{\varphi_1, \varphi_2, \varphi_3\} \cup [\![t_1]\!]^C \cup \ldots \cup [\![t_n]\!]^C,$

where:

$$\varphi_1 = \mathit{gen}^{t^C} :\stackrel{\mathrm{I}}{=} \bigwedge_{i=1}^{n} (\forall x_i : t_i^C(\mathit{gen}^{t^C}(\imath_{t_i^C \to t^C}(x_i)))),$$

$$\varphi_2 = \forall y : t^C(\mathit{gen}^{t^C}(y)),$$

$$\varphi_3 = \bigwedge_{i=1}^{n} (\forall x_i : t_i^C(\imath^{-1}_{t^C \to t_i^C}(\imath_{t_i^C \to t^C}(x_i)) = x_i)),$$

and

$x_1, \ldots, x_n$ are fresh value symbols such that for all $i = 1, \ldots, n$: $\tau(x_i) = \langle \mathsf{obj}, t_i^C \rangle$,
y is a fresh value symbol such that $\tau(y) = \langle \mathsf{obj}, t^C \rangle$.

Type definition of union type with nil

A type definition $t = [\, t_1 | \cdots | t_n \,]$ introduces the name t for a type. It defines t as the union of the user-defined and basic types $t_1, \ldots, t_n$ extended with an 'option' value nil, i.e. a value is an element of type t iff it is an element of one of the types $t_1, \ldots, t_n$ or it is the value nil. This means that each of the types $t_1, \ldots, t_n$ is a subtype of the type t. Each of the types $t_1, \ldots, t_n$ can be a user-defined type or a basic type.

There are pre-defined function names associated with each of the types $t_1, \ldots, t_n$ that are basic types. These function names are implicitly introduced and defined. nil is also implicitly introduced and defined.

Structure:

$t = [\, t_1 | \cdots | t_n \,]$

Well-formedness in N:

$t_1, \ldots, t_n$ are defined as type names in N.

Names and subtype declarations:

$\{\![t = [\,t_1|\cdots|t_n\,]]\!\} :=$

$\{[\mathsf{type}\ t], [t_1 \leq t], \ldots, [t_n \leq t], [\mathsf{func\ nil}\colon \to t]\} \cup \{\![t_1]\!\} \cup \ldots \cup \{\![t_n]\!\}.$

Meaning:

$[\![t = [\,t_1|\cdots|t_n\,]]\!]^C := \{\varphi_1, \varphi_2, \varphi_3\} \cup [\![t_1]\!]^C \cup \ldots \cup [\![t_n]\!]^C,$

where:

$$\varphi_1 = \mathit{gen}^{t^C} :\overset{\mathrm{I}}{=} \mathit{gen}^{t^C}(\mathit{nil}^{t^C}) \wedge \bigwedge_{i=1}^{n} (\forall x_i\colon t_i^C(\mathit{gen}^{t^C}(\imath_{t_i^C \to t^C}(x_i)))),$$

$$\varphi_2 = \forall y\colon t^C(\mathit{gen}^{t^C}(y)),$$

$$\varphi_3 = \bigwedge_{i=1}^{n} (\forall x_i\colon t_i^C(\imath^{-1}_{t^C \to t_i^C}(\imath_{t_i^C \to t^C}(x_i)) = x_i)),$$

and

$x_1, \ldots, x_n$ are fresh value symbols such that for all $i = 1, \ldots, n$:
$\tau(x_i) = \langle \mathsf{obj}, t_i^C \rangle$,
y is a fresh value symbol such that $\tau(y) = \langle \mathsf{obj}, t^C \rangle$.

Explicit function definition

An explicit function definition $f(x_1\colon t_1, \ldots, x_n\colon t_n)\ t_{n+1}$ $\mathsf{pre}\ E\ \triangleq\ e$ introduces the name f for a function from argument types $t_1, \ldots, t_n$ to result type t_{n+1}. It defines f directly in terms of a defining expression e in which the function being defined may be recursively used. If f is not recursively used in *inadmissible* ways, then it defines f as the least defined (strict) function such that, for all values $x_1, \ldots, x_n$ that are elements of the types $t_1, \ldots, t_n$, respectively, the value of that function for arguments $x_1, \ldots, x_n$ is the value that is yielded by evaluation of the expression e when f denotes that function.

The recursive use of f in e may be inadmissible in (set or map) comprehension, non-deterministic expressions of boolean type ($\mathbb{B}$) used as logical expressions, and equations containing non-deterministic expressions.

A non-deterministic expression is an expression in which a choice expression occurs (see Section 5.8 for choice expressions). Such expressions may yield more than one value. In case the expression e can yield more than one value for certain arguments $x_1, \ldots, x_n$, the function is just undefined for those arguments.

The logical expression E states an assumption about the function being defined by the expression e as follows: for all values $x_1, \ldots, x_n$ that are elements of the types $t_1, \ldots, t_n$, respectively, if evaluation of the logical expression E yields true, then the function being defined by the expression e is defined for arguments $x_1, \ldots, x_n$. This gives rise to a proof obligation for definedness.

Structure:

$f(x_1 \colon t_1, \ldots, x_n \colon t_n)\ t_{n+1}$ pre $E \triangleq e$

Well-formedness in N:

$x_1, \ldots, x_n$ are distinct identifiers,

$x_1, \ldots, x_n$ are not defined as state variable names N,

$t_1, \ldots, t_{n+1}$ are defined as type names in N,

E, e are well-formed in $\langle N \cup \{[\mathsf{val}\ x_1 \colon t_1], \ldots, [\mathsf{val}\ x_n \colon t_n]\}, 0\rangle$,

the minimal type of e in N is a subtype of t_{n+1}.

Names and subtype declarations:

$$\{\!\![f(x_1 \colon t_1, \ldots, x_n \colon t_n)\ t_{n+1}\ \mathsf{pre}\ E \triangleq e]\!\!\} := \{[\mathsf{func}\ f \colon t_1 \times \cdots \times t_n \to t_{n+1}]\}.$$

Meaning:

$$[\![f(x_1 \colon t_1, \ldots, x_n \colon t_n)\ t_{n+1}\ \mathsf{pre}\ E \triangleq e]\!]^C := \{\varphi_1, \varphi_2\},$$

where:

$$\begin{aligned}
\varphi_1 = {} & \forall x'_1 \colon t_1^C, \ldots, x'_n \colon t_n^C \\
& \quad ([\![E]\!]^{C \cup \{x'_1, \ldots, x'_n\}}_{\langle\rangle, tt} \to f^C_{t_1 \times \cdots \times t_n \to t_{n+1}}(x'_1, \ldots, x'_n){\downarrow}), \\
\varphi_2 = {} & f^C_{t_1 \times \cdots \times t_n \to t_{n+1}} :\stackrel{\mathbf{SI}}{=} \\
& \quad \forall x'_1 \colon t_1^C, \ldots, x'_n \colon t_n^C, y \colon t_{n+1}^C \\
& \quad ([\![e]\!]^{C \cup \{x'_1, \ldots, x'_n\}}_{\langle\rangle, y} \to f^C_{t_1 \times \cdots \times t_n \to t_{n+1}}(x'_1, \ldots, x'_n) = y),
\end{aligned}$$

and

$x'_1, \ldots, x'_n$ are fresh value symbols such that for all $i = 1, \ldots, n$:
$\iota(x'_i) = x_i$ and $\tau(x'_i) = \langle \mathsf{obj}, t_i^C \rangle$,
y is a fresh value symbol such that $\tau(y) = \langle \mathsf{obj}, t_{n+1}^C \rangle$.

Implicit function definition

An implicit function definition $f(x_1 \colon t_1, \ldots, x_n \colon t_n)\ x_{n+1} \colon t_{n+1}$ pre E_1 post E_2 introduces the name f for a function from argument types $t_1, \ldots, t_n$ to result type t_{n+1}. It defines f indirectly in terms of a pre-condition E_1 and a post-condition E_2 that must be satisfied. More precisely, it defines f as a function such that, for all values $x_1, \ldots, x_{n+1}$ that are elements of the types $t_1, \ldots, t_{n+1}$, respectively:

- if evaluation of the logical expression E_1 yields true, then the function f is defined for $x_1, \ldots, x_n$;
- if evaluation of the logical expression E_1 yields true and the value of the function f for arguments $x_1, \ldots, x_n$ is x_{n+1}, then evaluation of the logical expression E_2 yields true.

Structure:

$f(x_1\colon t_1, \ldots, x_n\colon t_n)\ x_{n+1}\colon t_{n+1}$ pre E_1 post E_2

Well-formedness in N:

$x_1, \ldots, x_{n+1}$ are distinct identifiers,

$x_1, \ldots, x_{n+1}$ are not defined as state variable names N,

$t_1, \ldots, t_{n+1}$ are defined as type names in N,

E_1 is well-formed in $\langle N \cup \{[\mathsf{val}\ x_1\colon t_1], \ldots, [\mathsf{val}\ x_n\colon t_n]\}, 0\rangle$,

E_2 is well-formed in $\langle N \cup \{[\mathsf{val}\ x_1\colon t_1], \ldots, [\mathsf{val}\ x_{n+1}\colon t_{n+1}]\}, 0\rangle$.

Names and subtype declarations:

$$\{\!\![f(x_1\colon t_1, \ldots, x_n\colon t_n)\ x_{n+1}\colon t_{n+1}\ \mathsf{pre}\ E_1\ \mathsf{post}\ E_2]\!\!\} := \{[\mathsf{func}\ f\colon t_1 \times \cdots \times t_n \to t_{n+1}]\}.$$

Meaning:

$$[\![f(x_1\colon t_1, \ldots, x_n\colon t_n)\ x_{n+1}\colon t_{n+1}\ \mathsf{pre}\ E_1\ \mathsf{post}\ E_2]\!]^C := \{\varphi_1, \varphi_2\},$$

where:

$$\varphi_1 = \forall x_1'\colon t_1^C, \ldots, x_n'\colon t_n^C\ ([\![E_1]\!]^{C\cup\{x_1',\ldots,x_n'\}}_{\langle\rangle,tt} \to f^C_{t_1\times\cdots\times t_n\to t_{n+1}}(x_1', \ldots, x_n')\downarrow),$$

$$\varphi_2 = \forall x_1'\colon t_1^C, \ldots, x_n'\colon t_n^C, x_{n+1}'\colon t_{n+1}^C\ ([\![E_1]\!]^{C\cup\{x_1',\ldots,x_n'\}}_{\langle\rangle,tt} \wedge f^C_{t_1\times\cdots\times t_n\to t_{n+1}}(x_1', \ldots, x_n') = x_{n+1}' \to [\![E_2]\!]^{C\cup\{x_1',\ldots,x_n',x_{n+1}'\}}_{\langle\rangle,tt}),$$

and

$x_1', \ldots, x_{n+1}'$ are fresh value symbols such that for all $i = 1, \ldots, n+1$: $\iota(x_i') = x_i$ and $\tau(x_i') = \langle \mathsf{obj}, t_i^C\rangle$.

State variable definition

A state variable definition $v\colon t$ introduces the name v for a state variable of type t. It defines v as a state variable that can take values which are elements of type t, but which can only be modified with appropriate modification rights.

Structure:

$v\colon t$

Well-formedness in N:

v is not defined as a state variable name in $N - \{[\mathsf{var}\ v\colon t]\}$,

t is defined as a type name in N.

Names and subtype declarations:

$$\{\!\![v\colon t]\!\!\} := \{[\mathsf{var}\ v\colon t]\}.$$

Meaning:

$[\![v\colon t]\!]^C \ := \ \text{Varmod}(v_t^C)$.

Operation definition

An operation definition

$$\begin{array}{l} op(x_1\colon t_1,\ldots,x_n\colon t_n)\ y_1\colon t'_1,\ldots,y_m\colon t'_m \\ \quad \mathsf{ext}\ \mathsf{rd}\ v_1\colon t''_1\ ,\ldots,\mathsf{rd}\ v_k\colon t''_k\ ,\ \mathsf{wr}\ v'_1\colon t'''_1\ ,\ldots,\mathsf{wr}\ v'_l\colon t'''_l \\ \quad \mathsf{pre}\ E_1\ \ \mathsf{post}\ E_2\ \ \mathsf{inter}\ \varphi \end{array}$$

introduces the name *op* for an operation from argument types $t_1,\ldots,t_n$ to result types $t'_1,\ldots,t'_m$. It defines *op* indirectly in terms of interrogation and modification rights on state variables, a pre-condition E_1, a post-condition E_2 and an inter-condition φ that must be satisfied. More precisely, it defines *op* as an operation such that, for all values $x_1,\ldots,x_n,y_1,\ldots,y_m$ that are elements of the types $t_1,\ldots,t_n,t'_1,\ldots,t'_m$, respectively:

- if c is a computation of the operation *op* for arguments $x_1,\ldots,x_n$ that yields results $y_1,\ldots,y_m$, then no step of c leaves all of the state variables $v_1,\ldots,v_k,v'_1,\ldots,v'_l$ unmodified, but internal steps leave state variables other than $v'_1,\ldots,v'_l$ unmodified;
- if evaluation of the logical expression E_1 yields true in some state s, then the operation *op* has a terminating computation with initial state s for the arguments $x_1,\ldots,x_n$;
- if evaluation of the logical expression E_1 yields true in some state s, c is a terminating computation with initial state s of the operation *op* for arguments $x_1,\ldots,x_n$ that yields results $y_1,\ldots,y_m$, and t is the final state of computation c, then evaluation of the logical expression E_2 yields true in the states $\langle s,t\rangle$;
- if evaluation of the logical expression E_1 yields true in some state s and c is a computation with initial state s of the operation *op* for arguments $x_1,\ldots,x_n$ that yields results $y_1,\ldots,y_m$, then evaluation of the temporal formula φ yields true at the starting-point of computation c.

In the case of atomic operations, the meaning of operation definitions is equivalent to the much simpler one that is usually adopted for atomic operations (based on the initial and final state of the computations, instead of the complete computations).

Structure:

$$\begin{array}{l} op(x_1\colon t_1,\ldots,x_n\colon t_n)\ y_1\colon t'_1,\ldots,y_m\colon t'_m \\ \quad \mathsf{ext}\ \mathsf{rd}\ v_1\colon t''_1\ ,\ldots,\mathsf{rd}\ v_k\colon t''_k\ ,\ \mathsf{wr}\ v'_1\colon t'''_1\ ,\ldots,\mathsf{wr}\ v'_l\colon t'''_l \\ \quad \mathsf{pre}\ E_1\ \ \mathsf{post}\ E_2\ \ \mathsf{inter}\ \varphi \end{array}$$

Well-formedness in N:

$x_1, \ldots, x_n, y_1, \ldots, y_m$ are distinct identifiers,

$x_1, \ldots, x_n, y_1, \ldots, y_m$ are not defined as state variable names in N,

$t_1, \ldots, t_n, t'_1, \ldots, t'_m$ are defined as type names in N,

$\{v_1, \ldots, v_k\}$ and $\{v'_1, \ldots, v'_l\}$ are disjoint sets,

N_S is a subset of N,

E_1 is well-formed in $\langle nonvars(N) \cup N_A \cup N_S, 1\rangle$,

E_2 is well-formed in $\langle nonvars(N) \cup N_A \cup N_R \cup N_S, 2\rangle$,

φ is well-formed in $nonvars(N) \cup N_A \cup N_R \cup N_S$,

where:

$$
\begin{aligned}
N_A &= \{[\mathsf{val}\ x_1 : t_1], \ldots, [\mathsf{val}\ x_n : t_n]\},\\
N_R &= \{[\mathsf{val}\ y_1 : t'_1], \ldots, [\mathsf{val}\ y_m : t'_m]\},\\
N_S &= \{[\mathsf{var}\ v_1 : t''_1], \ldots, [\mathsf{var}\ v_k : t''_k], [\mathsf{var}\ v'_1 : t'''_1], \ldots, [\mathsf{var}\ v'_l : t'''_l]\},
\end{aligned}
$$

Names and subtype declarations:

$$
\begin{aligned}
&\{\!\!\{ op(x_1 : t_1, \ldots, x_n : t_n)\ y_1 : t'_1, \ldots, y_m : t'_m\\
&\quad \mathsf{ext\ rd}\ v_1 : t''_1\ , \ldots, \mathsf{rd}\ v_k : t''_k\ ,\ \mathsf{wr}\ v'_1 : t'''_1\ , \ldots, \mathsf{wr}\ v'_l : t'''_l\\
&\quad \mathsf{pre}\ E_1\ \ \mathsf{post}\ E_2\ \ \mathsf{inter}\ \varphi \}\!\!\}\ :=\\
&\qquad \{[\mathsf{op}\ \ op : t_1 \times \cdots \times t_n \Rightarrow t'_1 \times \cdots \times t'_m]\}.
\end{aligned}
$$

Meaning:

$$
\begin{aligned}
&[\![op(x_1 : t_1, \ldots, x_n : t_n)\ y_1 : t'_1, \ldots, y_m : t'_m\\
&\quad \mathsf{ext\ rd}\ v_1 : t''_1\ , \ldots, \mathsf{rd}\ v_k : t''_k\ ,\ \mathsf{wr}\ v'_1 : t'''_1\ , \ldots, \mathsf{wr}\ v'_l : t'''_l\\
&\quad \mathsf{pre}\ E_1\ \ \mathsf{post}\ E_2\ \ \mathsf{inter}\ \varphi]\!]^C\ :=\\
&\qquad \{\varphi_1, \ldots, \varphi_4\},
\end{aligned}
$$

where:

$$
\begin{aligned}
\varphi_1 = \ & \forall x'_1 : t_1^C, \ldots, x'_n : t_n^C, c : \mathsf{Comp}, y'_1 : t_1'^C, \ldots, y'_m : t_m'^C\\
& \ (op^C_{t_1 \times \cdots \times t_n \Rightarrow t'_1 \times \cdots \times t'_m}(x'_1, \ldots, x'_n, c, y'_1, \ldots, y'_m) \rightarrow\\
& \ \ \mathrm{Modcomp}(\{v_1{}^C_{t''_1}, \ldots, v_k{}^C_{t''_k}\}, \{v'_1{}^C_{t'''_1}, \ldots, v'_l{}^C_{t'''_l}\}, c)),
\end{aligned}
$$

$$
\begin{aligned}
\varphi_2 = \ & \forall s : \mathsf{State}, x'_1 : t_1^C, \ldots, x'_n : t_n^C\\
& \ ([\![E_1]\!]^{C \cup \{x'_1, \ldots, x'_n\}}_{\langle s\rangle, tt} \rightarrow\\
& \ \exists c : \mathsf{Comp}, y'_1 : t_1'^C, \ldots, y'_m : t_m'^C\\
& \ \ (\mathsf{st}_0(c) = s \wedge \neg(\textstyle\bigwedge_k(\mathsf{st}_k(c)\downarrow)) \wedge\\
& \ \ \ op^C_{t_1 \times \cdots \times t_n \Rightarrow t'_1 \times \cdots \times t'_m}(x'_1, \ldots, x'_n, c, y'_1, \ldots, y'_m))),
\end{aligned}
$$

$$\begin{array}{rl}
\varphi_3 = & \forall s\colon \mathsf{State}, x_1'\colon t_1^C, \ldots, x_n'\colon t_n^C \\
& ([\![E_1]\!]^{C\cup\{x_1',\ldots,x_n'\}}_{\langle s\rangle,\mathit{tt}} \rightarrow \\
& \quad \forall c\colon \mathsf{Comp}, y_1'\colon t_1'^C, \ldots, y_m'\colon t_m'^C \\
& \quad (\mathsf{st}_0(c) = s \wedge \neg(\bigwedge_k(\mathsf{st}_k(c){\downarrow})) \wedge \\
& \quad\; op^C_{t_1\times\cdots\times t_n\Rightarrow t_1'\times\cdots\times t_m'}(x_1',\ldots,x_n',c,y_1',\ldots,y_m') \rightarrow \\
& \quad\; \exists t\colon \mathsf{State} \\
& \quad\;\; (\bigvee_k(\mathsf{st}_k(c) = t \wedge \neg(\mathsf{st}_{k+1}(c){\downarrow})) \wedge \\
& \quad\;\; [\![E_2]\!]^{C\cup\{x_1',\ldots,x_n',y_1',\ldots,y_m'\}}_{\langle s,t\rangle,\mathit{tt}}))), \\
\varphi_4 = & \forall s\colon \mathsf{State}, x_1'\colon t_1^C, \ldots, x_n'\colon t_n^C \\
& ([\![E_1]\!]^{C\cup\{x_1',\ldots,x_n'\}}_{\langle s\rangle,\mathit{tt}} \rightarrow \\
& \quad \forall c\colon \mathsf{Comp}, y_1'\colon t_1'^C, \ldots, y_m'\colon t_m'^C \\
& \quad\; (\mathsf{st}_0(c) = s \wedge \\
& \quad\; op^C_{t_1\times\cdots\times t_n\Rightarrow t_1'\times\cdots\times t_m'}(x_1',\ldots,x_n',c,y_1',\ldots,y_m') \rightarrow \\
& \quad\; [\![\varphi]\!]^{C\cup\{x_1',\ldots,x_n',y_1',\ldots,y_m'\}}_{c,0,\mathit{tt}})),
\end{array}$$

and

$x_1', \ldots, x_m'$ are fresh value symbols such that for all $i = 1, \ldots, n$:
$\iota(x_i') = x_i$ and $\tau(x_i') = \langle \mathsf{obj}, t_i^C \rangle$,
$y_1', \ldots, y_m'$ are fresh value symbols such that for all $i = 1, \ldots, m$:
$\iota(y_i') = y_i$ and $\tau(y_i') = \langle \mathsf{obj}, t_i'^C \rangle$,
s, t are fresh state symbols and c is a fresh computation symbol.

Definitions introducing free names

Definitions in which the optional keyword free occurs introduce free names. Except for type definitions, their well-formedness, their syntactic properties and their meaning in flat VVSL are the same as for the corresponding definitions without the keyword free. Because of this, they are not treated separately.

A definition in which the keyword free occurs introduces a free name instead of a defined name. This means that the body of the definition (empty in case of a free type name or a free state variable name) does not define the type, function, state variable or operation denoted by the name, but makes assumptions about it. This difference is not reflected by the meaning described here. Indeed, it is only useful if basic modules can be combined. Therefore, it is only reflected in the meaning of basic modules as modularization constructs, by a special treatment of free names (described in Chapter 8).

Structure:

t free

Well-formedness in N:

True.

Names and subtype declarations:

$\{\![t \;\mathsf{free}]\!\} := \{[\mathsf{type}\; t]\}$.

Meaning:

$[\![t \;\mathsf{free}]\!]^C := \{\}$.

Structure:

$f(x_1{:}\, t_1, \ldots, x_n{:}\, t_n)\; x_{n+1}{:}\, t_{n+1}\;\; \mathsf{free}\;\; \mathsf{pre}\; E_1\;\; \mathsf{post}\; E_2$

Well-formedness in N:

$f(x_1{:}\, t_1, \ldots, x_n{:}\, t_n)\; x_{n+1}{:}\, t_{n+1}\;\; \mathsf{pre}\; E_1\;\; \mathsf{post}\; E_2$ is well-formed.

Names and subtype declarations:

$$\{\![f(x_1{:}\, t_1, \ldots, x_n{:}\, t_n)\; x_{n+1}{:}\, t_{n+1}\;\; \mathsf{free}\;\; \mathsf{pre}\; E_1\;\; \mathsf{post}\; E_2]\!\} := \\ \{\![f(x_1{:}\, t_1, \ldots, x_n{:}\, t_n)\; x_{n+1}{:}\, t_{n+1}\;\; \mathsf{pre}\; E_1\;\; \mathsf{post}\; E_2]\!\}.$$

Meaning:

$$[\![f(x_1{:}\, t_1, \ldots, x_n{:}\, t_n)\; x_{n+1}{:}\, t_{n+1}\;\; \mathsf{free}\;\; \mathsf{pre}\; E_1\;\; \mathsf{post}\; E_2]\!]^C := \\ [\![f(x_1{:}\, t_1, \ldots, x_n{:}\, t_n)\; x_{n+1}{:}\, t_{n+1}\;\; \mathsf{pre}\; E_1\;\; \mathsf{post}\; E_2]\!]^C.$$

Structure:

$v{:}\, t\;\; \mathsf{free}$

Well-formedness in N:

$v{:}\, t$ is well-formed in N.

Names and subtype declarations:

$\{\![v{:}\, t\;\; \mathsf{free}]\!\} := \{\![v{:}\, t]\!\}$.

Meaning:

$[\![v{:}\, t\;\; \mathsf{free}]\!]^C := [\![v{:}\, t]\!]^C$.

Structure:

$$op(x_1{:}\, t_1, \ldots, x_n{:}\, t_n)\; y_1{:}\, t'_1, \ldots, y_m{:}\, t'_m\;\; \mathsf{free} \\ \mathsf{ext\ rd}\; v_1{:}\, t''_1, \ldots, \mathsf{rd}\; v_k{:}\, t''_k,\; \mathsf{wr}\; v'_1{:}\, t'''_1, \ldots, \mathsf{wr}\; v'_l{:}\, t'''_l \\ \mathsf{pre}\; E_1\;\; \mathsf{post}\; E_2\;\; \mathsf{inter}\; \varphi$$

Well-formedness in N:

$$op(x_1{:}\, t_1, \ldots, x_n{:}\, t_n)\; y_1{:}\, t'_1, \ldots, y_m{:}\, t'_m \\ \mathsf{ext\ rd}\; v_1{:}\, t''_1, \ldots, \mathsf{rd}\; v_k{:}\, t''_k,\; \mathsf{wr}\; v'_1{:}\, t'''_1, \ldots, \mathsf{wr}\; v'_l{:}\, t'''_l \\ \mathsf{pre}\; E_1\;\; \mathsf{post}\; E_2\;\; \mathsf{inter}\; \varphi$$

is well-formed in N.

Names and subtype declarations:

$$\{\!\![op(x_1\colon t_1,\ldots,x_n\colon t_n)\ y_1\colon t'_1,\ldots,y_m\colon t'_m\ \mathsf{free}$$
$$\mathsf{ext\ rd}\ v_1\colon t''_1\ ,\ldots,\mathsf{rd}\ v_k\colon t''_k\ ,\ \mathsf{wr}\ v'_1\colon t'''_1\ ,\ldots,\mathsf{wr}\ v'_l\colon t'''_l$$
$$\mathsf{pre}\ E_1\ \ \mathsf{post}\ E_2\ \ \mathsf{inter}\ \varphi]\!\!\}\ :=$$
$$\{\!\![op(x_1\colon t_1,\ldots,x_n\colon t_n)\ y_1\colon t'_1,\ldots,y_m\colon t'_m$$
$$\mathsf{ext\ rd}\ v_1\colon t''_1\ ,\ldots,\mathsf{rd}\ v_k\colon t''_k\ ,\ \mathsf{wr}\ v'_1\colon t'''_1\ ,\ldots,\mathsf{wr}\ v'_l\colon t'''_l$$
$$\mathsf{pre}\ E_1\ \ \mathsf{post}\ E_2\ \ \mathsf{inter}\ \varphi]\!\!\}.$$

Meaning:

$$[\![op(x_1\colon t_1,\ldots,x_n\colon t_n)\ y_1\colon t'_1,\ldots,y_m\colon t'_m\ \mathsf{free}$$
$$\mathsf{ext\ rd}\ v_1\colon t''_1\ ,\ldots,\mathsf{rd}\ v_k\colon t''_k\ ,\ \mathsf{wr}\ v'_1\colon t'''_1\ ,\ldots,\mathsf{wr}\ v'_l\colon t'''_l$$
$$\mathsf{pre}\ E_1\ \ \mathsf{post}\ E_2\ \ \mathsf{inter}\ \varphi]\!]^{C}\ :=$$
$$[\![op(x_1\colon t_1,\ldots,x_n\colon t_n)\ y_1\colon t'_1,\ldots,y_m\colon t'_m$$
$$\mathsf{ext\ rd}\ v_1\colon t''_1\ ,\ldots,\mathsf{rd}\ v_k\colon t''_k\ ,\ \mathsf{wr}\ v'_1\colon t'''_1\ ,\ldots,\mathsf{wr}\ v'_l\colon t'''_l$$
$$\mathsf{pre}\ E_1\ \ \mathsf{post}\ E_2\ \ \mathsf{inter}\ \varphi]\!]^{C}.$$

5.7 The type sublanguage

The previous section dealt with the syntax and semantics of definitions, including type definitions. Type definitions are constructed mainly from types. This section deals with the syntax and semantics of types. It begins by introducing types in broad outline.

Overview

In flat VVSL, one can build new types from basic types by type construction.

Basic types

The main basic types are the following:

- the *boolean* type $\mathbb{B}$, whose elements are the truth values;
- the *natural* type $\mathbb{N}$, whose elements are the natural numbers;
- the *integer* type $\mathbb{Z}$, whose elements are the integers;
- the *rational* type $\mathbb{Q}$, whose elements are the rational numbers.

More basic types can be introduced by enumeration of their elements which is denoted by an *enumerated* type $\{a_1,\ldots,a_n\}$, where the a_i are constants denoting the values concerned. All enumerated types have a finite number of elements. No operators are available on elements of an enumerated type.

Example. In a system which handles concurrent access to stored relations by multiple transaction, it is useful to have access modes to distinguish between read access, write access, etc. A corresponding basic type can be expressed as follows:

$$\{\mathsf{READ},\mathsf{WRITE},\mathsf{CREATE},\mathsf{DESTROY}\}.$$

Type construction

The constructed types are the following:

- a *sequence* type t^* for any basic or defined type t; its elements are the finite sequences of elements of type t;
- a *set* type t-set for any basic or defined type t; its elements are the finite sets of elements of type t;
- a *map* type $t \xrightarrow{m} t'$ for any basic or defined types t, t'; its elements are the finite maps from elements of type t to elements of type t' (the notation $t \xleftrightarrow{m} t'$ is for one-to-one maps);
- a *composite* type compose c of $s_1 \colon t_1 \ \ldots \ s_n \colon t_n$ for any user-definable name c and any basic or defined types $t_1, \ldots, t_n$; its elements are the composite values with n components, the i-th component of which is an element of type t_i $(1 \leq i \leq n)$, which are generated with *mk-c*,‡ the unique constructor function for generating elements of this type.

A composite type compose c of $s_1 \colon t_1 \ \ldots \ s_n \colon t_n$ introduces the function names s_i $(1 \leq i \leq n)$, which are implicitly defined as the selector functions for selecting the components of a value of the composite type (s_i for the i-th component). The type constructor name c marks the composite type off from other ones that do not differ in their component types.

Example. Databases can be defined as a subtype of the constructed type

$$Rel\_nm \xrightarrow{m} Relation.$$

Both queries that have the form of union queries and queries that have the form of product queries are built from two queries. They can be distinguished by using the following types:

compose *Union* of $q1$: *Query* $q2$: *Query*,

compose *Product* of $q1$: *Query* $q2$: *Query*.

Elements of the former type can only be constructed with the function *mk-Union* and elements of the latter type can only be constructed with the function *mk-Product*. The sub-queries can be selected by means of functions $q1$ and $q2$.

The notation

$$t :: \ s_1 \colon t_1 \ \ldots \ s_n \colon t_n \ \text{where inv}(x) \triangleq E$$

is used as an abbreviation of

$$t = \text{compose } t \text{ of } s_1 \colon t_1 \ \ldots \ s_n \colon t_n \ \text{where inv}(x) \triangleq E.$$

‡ *mk-c* is the name that is obtained by prefixing the string *mk-* to the type constructor name denoted by the meta-variable *c*.

Here the same name is used as a type name and as a type constructor name. For example, the type definition

Union = compose *Union* of *q*1: *Query q*2: *Query*

may also be written:

Union :: *q*1: *Query q*2: *Query*.

The symbol :: is read as 'is composed of'.

Syntax

Types are the terminal productions of *<type>*.

<type> ::=
  $\mathbb{B}$
  | $\mathbb{N}$
  | $\mathbb{Z}$
  | $\mathbb{Q}$
  | { *<atoms>* }
  | *<type-name>**
  | *<type-name>*-set
  | *<type-name>* $\xrightarrow{m}$ *<type-name>*
  | compose *<type-constructor-name>* of *<components>*
  | *<type-name>*

<atoms> ::=
  <function-name>
  | *<function-name>* , *<atoms>*

<components> ::=
  <component>
  | *<component>* *<components>*

<component> ::=
  <function-name> : *<type-name>*

The set Type of syntactically correct type constructs is defined by

Type := { T | T is a terminal production of *<type>*}.

Well-formedness. The well-formedness of syntactically correct type constructs is defined by a predicate

wf: Type × NCxt .

$wf(T, N)$ indicates that T is well-formed in the name context N. Instead of $wf(T, N)$, we write 'T is well-formed in N'.

Syntactic properties. The name context associated with types is defined by a mapping

$$\{\!\![\bullet]\!\!\}: \mathsf{Type} \to \mathsf{NCxt}\,.$$

$\{\!\![T]\!\!\}$ consists of the names corresponding to the names introduced by the type T. Only enumerated types and composite types introduce names.

Meaning. The meaning of types is defined by a mapping

$$[\![\bullet]\!]^\bullet: \mathsf{Type} \times \mathsf{Cxt} \to \mathcal{P}(\mathsf{Form}).$$

$[\![T]\!]^C$ is the set of formulae corresponding to the type T in the symbol context C. $[\![T]\!]^C$ is only defined if T is well-formed in $\overline{C}$.

The types of the different forms are now treated separately.

Boolean type

$\mathbb{B}$ is a basic type with two elements, called *boolean values* or *truth values*. Except for the constant names true and false, there are no pre-defined function names associated with $\mathbb{B}$. However, expressions that have type $\mathbb{B}$ can be used as operands of the logical connectives and quantifiers in logical expressions. Moreover, logical expressions can be used everywhere as expressions that have type $\mathbb{B}$.

Structure:

$\mathbb{B}$

Well-formedness in N:

True.

Names and subtype declarations:

$\{\!\![\mathbb{B}]\!\!\} \;:=\; \{\,\}.$

Meaning:

$[\![\mathbb{B}]\!]^C \;:=\; axioms(\underline{\mathrm{B}}).$

Natural type

$\mathbb{N}$ is a basic type. The elements of $\mathbb{N}$ are the *natural numbers*. There are pre-defined function names associated with $\mathbb{N}$. The usual arithmetic operators on natural numbers are available, such as $+$ (*addition*), $-$ (*substraction*) and $\leq$ (*less than or equal*).

Structure:

$\mathbb{N}$

Well-formedness in N:

True.

Names and subtype declarations:

$\{\!\{\mathbb{N}\}\!\} := \{\}$.

Meaning:

$[\![\mathbb{N}]\!]^C \;:=\; axioms(\underline{\mathbb{N}})$.

Integer type

$\mathbb{Z}$ is a basic type. The elements of $\mathbb{Z}$ are the *integers*. $\mathbb{N}$ is considered to be a subtype of $\mathbb{Z}$. There are pre-defined function names associated with $\mathbb{Z}$. The usual arithmetic operators on integers are available, including the unary $-$ (*negation*).

Structure:

$\mathbb{Z}$

Well-formedness in N:

True.

Names and subtype declarations:

$\{\!\{\mathbb{Z}\}\!\} := \{\}$.

Meaning:

$[\![\mathbb{Z}]\!]^C \;:=\; axioms(\underline{\mathbb{Z}})$.

Rational type

$\mathbb{Q}$ is a basic type. The elements of $\mathbb{Q}$ are the *rational numbers*. $\mathbb{Z}$ is considered to be a subtype of $\mathbb{Q}$. There are pre-defined function names associated with $\mathbb{Q}$. The usual arithmetic operators are available, including the unary $^{-1}$ (*reciprocal*).

Structure:

$\mathbb{Q}$

Well-formedness in N:

True.

Names and subtype declarations:

$\{\!\{\mathbb{Q}\}\!\} := \{\}$.

Meaning:

$[\![\mathbb{Q}]\!]^C \;:=\; axioms(\underline{\mathbb{Q}})$.

Enumerated type

$\{a_1, \ldots, a_n\}$ is a basic type with n elements. These elements are denoted by the names $a_1, \ldots, a_n$. The set of these n values can be viewed as a finite subset of some countably infinite set of *atoms*. One enumerated type is considered to be a subtype of another one if each name occurring in the former also occurs in the latter. There are no pre-defined function names associated with the type $\{a_1, \ldots, a_n\}$. The atom names $a_1, \ldots, a_n$ are considered to be user-defined. Expressions that have type $\{a_1, \ldots, a_n\}$ can be used as operands of the equality operator in logical expressions.

Enumerated types are basic types. The set of all atoms does not correspond to a type. The names a_i denote the same atoms in whatever enumerated type they occur.

Structure:

$\{a_1, \ldots, a_n\}$

Well-formedness in N:

$a_1, \ldots, a_n$ are distinct identifiers.

Names and subtype declarations:

$$\{\!\![\{a_1, \ldots, a_n\}]\!\!\} := \{[\mathsf{func}\ a_1{:} \to \{a_1, \ldots, a_n\}], \ldots, [\mathsf{func}\ a_n{:} \to \{a_1, \ldots, a_n\}]\}.$$

Meaning:

$$[\![\{a_1, \ldots, a_n\}]\!]^C := \mathit{axioms}(\underline{\mathrm{E}}(\{a_1, \ldots, a_n\})).$$

Sequence type

t^* is a constructed type. The elements of t^* are the finite sequences of elements of the basic or defined type t. There are pre-defined function names associated with t^*. The usual operators on sequences are available, such as hd (*head*), tl (*tail*), $\frown$ (*concatenation*) and len (*length*). Indexing a sequence $\mathcal{L}$ with index i is written $\mathcal{L}(i)$.

Structure:

t^*

Well-formedness in N:

t is defined as a type name in N.

Names and subtype declarations:

$\{\!\![t^*]\!\!\} := \{\}$.

Meaning:

$[\![t^*]\!]^C := \mathit{axioms}(\underline{\mathrm{L}}(t^C))$.

Set type

t-set is a constructed type. The elements of t-set are the finite sets of elements of the basic or defined type t. There are pre-defined function names associated with t-set. The usual operators on sets are available, such as $\cup$ (*union*), $\cap$ (*intersection*), $\in$ (*membership*) and card (*cardinality*).

Structure:

t-set

Well-formedness in N:

t is defined as a type name in N.

Names and subtype declarations:

$\{\![t\text{-set}]\!\} := \{\,\}$.

Meaning:

$[\![t\text{-set}]\!]^C := \mathit{axioms}(\underline{\mathrm{F}}(t^C))$.

Map type

$t \xrightarrow{m} t'$ is a constructed type. The elements of $t \xrightarrow{m} t'$ are the finite maps from elements of the basic or defined type t to elements of the basic or defined type t'. There are pre-defined function names associated with $t \xrightarrow{m} t'$. The map operators are perhaps not so wellknown, but are very useful. Two maps whose domains are disjoint can be combined using the operator $\cup$ (*merge*). One map can also be combined with another one (the domains do not have to be disjoint) using the operator $\dagger$ (*overwrite*), in which case the latter takes precedence over the former where there are domain elements in common. The domain of a map can be restricted using the operator $\lhd$ (*domain restriction*) or the operator $⩤$ (*domain deletion*). In an expression of the form $\mathcal{S} \lhd \mathcal{M}$, $\mathcal{S}$ is interpreted as a set of values which are allowed in the restricted domain. In an expression of the form $\mathcal{S} ⩤ \mathcal{M}$, $\mathcal{S}$ is interpreted as a set of values which are not allowed in the restricted domain. The domain and the range of a map can be obtained using the operators dom and rng, respectively. Applying a map $\mathcal{M}$ to a value d is written $\mathcal{M}(d)$.

Structure:

$t \xrightarrow{m} t'$

Well-formedness in N:

t, t' are defined as type names in N.

Names and subtype declarations:

$\{\![t \xrightarrow{m} t']\!\} := \{\,\}$.

Meaning:

$$[\![t \xrightarrow{m} t']\!]^C \;:=\; axioms(\underline{\mathrm{M}}(t^C, t'^C)).$$

Composite type

compose c of $s_1\colon t_1 \;\ldots\; s_n\colon t_n$ is a constructed type. The elements of this type are composite values with n components, the i-th component of which is an element of the basic or defined type t_i (for $i = 1, \ldots, n$). The type constructor name c distinguishes this composite type from other ones that do not differ in their component types. It determines the name of the unique constructor function for generating the elements of this type. This *constructor* function name is considered to be user-defined. It is constructed from the name c in a fixed manner, viz. by prefixing the string *mk-* to the string that constitutes the identifier c. The *selector* function names $s_1, \ldots, s_n$ may be absent, but if they are present then they are also considered to be user-defined (s_i selects the i-th component). Selecting the i-th component of a composite value $\mathcal{C}$ can also be written $\mathcal{C}(i)$.

Structure:

compose c of $s_1\colon t_1 \;\ldots\; s_n\colon t_n$

Well-formedness in N:

$t_1, \ldots, t_n$ are defined as type names in N,

$[\text{func } s_1\colon \text{compose } c \text{ of } s_1\colon t_1 \;\ldots\; s_n\colon t_n \to t_1]$,

$\vdots$

$[\text{func } s_n\colon \text{compose } c \text{ of } s_1\colon t_1 \;\ldots\; s_n\colon t_n \to t_n]$ are distinct names.

Names and subtype declarations:

$$\{\![\text{compose } c \text{ of } s_1\colon t_1 \;\ldots\; s_n\colon t_n]\!\} \;:=$$
$$\{[\text{func } mk(c)\colon t_1 \times \cdots \times t_n \to \text{compose } c \text{ of } s_1\colon t_1 \;\ldots\; s_n\colon t_n]\} \cup$$
$$\{[\text{func } s_i\colon \text{compose } c \text{ of } s_1\colon t_1 \;\ldots\; s_n\colon t_n \to t_i] \mid 1 \le i \le n\}.$$

Meaning:

$$[\![\text{compose } c \text{ of } s_1\colon t_1 \;\ldots\; s_n\colon t_n]\!]^C \;:=$$
$$axioms(\underline{\mathrm{C}}_c(t_1^C, \ldots, t_n^C)) \cup \{\varphi_i \mid 1 \le i \le n\},$$

where:

$$\varphi_i = \;\; \forall y\colon \underline{\mathrm{C}}_c(t_1^C, \ldots, t_n^C)(s_{i\,\text{compose } c \text{ of } s_1:t_1 \ldots s_n:t_n \to t_i}^{\;C}(y) \simeq \mathit{sel}_i(y)),$$

and

y is a fresh value symbol such that $\tau(y) = \langle \text{obj}, \underline{\mathrm{C}}_c(t_1^C, \ldots, t_n^C)\rangle$.

Type name

t is a user-defined type. The elements of a user-defined type are determined by the type definition concerned.

Structure:

t

Well-formedness in N:

t is defined as a type name in N.

Names and subtype declarations:

$\{\![t]\!\} := \{\}$.

Meaning:

$[\![t]\!]^C := \{\}$.

5.8 The expression sublanguage

Section 5.6 dealt with the syntax and semantics of definitions. The defining expressions and conditions occurring in definitions are expressions and logical expressions, respectively. This section deals with the syntax and semantics of expressions and logical expressions. It begins by introducing the different kinds of expressions in broad outline.

Overview

In this overview, the notation used in defining expressions and conditions in definitions, i.e. the expression sublanguage, is divided into general notation, logical notation and special notation for sequences, sets and maps.

General notation

The general notation is what can be used to denote values of any kind. It includes the following basic notation:

$f(e_1, \ldots, e_n)$	for function application,
$\mathsf{if}\ E\ \mathsf{then}\ e\ \mathsf{else}\ e'$	for conditional evaluation,
$\mathsf{let}\ x{:}\ t \triangleq e\ \mathsf{in}\ e'$	for local value definition.

Prefix notation (in case of unary function symbols), infix notation (in case of binary function symbols) and sometimes even mixfix notation are freely used for function application to enhance readability.

Example. Only the above-mentioned general notation is used in the following expression.

$\mathsf{let}\ db'{:}\ Database \triangleq update(db, rnm, r)\ \mathsf{in}$
$\mathsf{if}\ is\_valid\_instance(db', dbsch)\ \mathsf{then}\ db'\ \mathsf{else}\ db.$

The intended meaning is the database resulting from updating the relation *rnm* in *db* to *r*, if this database is a valid instance of *dbsch*, and *db* otherwise.

The above-mentioned general notation is wellknown. The following notation is perhaps not so wellknown. It is for an arbitrary choice of values which obey a selection condition: let $x_1\colon t_1, \cdots, x_n\colon t_n$ be s.t. E in e. For $n = 1$, this is similar to a local value definition, but a range of acceptable values instead of a specific value is defined.

Example. In the subexpression dom t of the following choice expression, t stands for an arbitrary tuple from a relation r:

let t: *Tuple* be s.t. $t \in r$ in dom t.

The intended meaning is the common attribute set of all tuples of r. Because all tuples in a relation have the same attributes, the choice of a tuple does not matter. However, it is easy to write choice expressions that can yield more than one value.

The following notation is for local definition and decomposition:

let $mk\text{-}c(x_1, \ldots, x_n) \triangleq e$ in e'.

The names $x_1, \ldots, x_n$ are introduced to refer in the expression e' to the components of the composite value denoted by e. It is actually defined as an abbreviation of

let $x_1\colon t_1, \ldots, x_n\colon t_n$ be s.t. $mk\text{-}c(x_1, \ldots, x_n) = e$ in e'.

This notation shows that composite value can be decomposed without using selector functions.

Example. If relation schemas have been defined as composite values with a tuple structure and a set of keys as components and tuple structures have been defined as finite maps from attributes to domains, then the domain of attribute a according to relation schema *rsch* can be expressed as follows:

let $mk\text{-}Rel\_schema(tstr, keys) \triangleq rsch$ in $tstr(a)$.

The following notation is for case distinction, local definition and decomposition:

$$
\begin{array}{l}
\mathsf{cases}\ e\ \mathsf{of} \\
\quad mk\text{-}t_1(x_{1_1}, \ldots, x_{1_{m_1}}) \quad \rightarrow e_1 \\
\quad \vdots \\
\quad mk\text{-}t_n(x_{n_1}, \ldots, x_{n_{m_n}}) \quad \rightarrow e_n \\
\mathsf{end}.
\end{array}
$$

If the type of e is t_i, then its value is the value denoted by the expression e_i (in case there is more than one matching type, the expression corresponding to the first one is selected). If e_i is selected, the names $x_{i_1}, \ldots, x_{i_{m_i}}$ are

introduced to be used in the expression e_i to refer to the components of the composite value denoted by e.
This notation can also be explained as an abbreviation.* It involves the general conditional notation in addition to the local definition and decomposition notation above.

Example. The case distinction notation is used in the following expression, which might be the defining expression of a function *sat* which checks whether tuple t has the property expressed by selection formula *sf* or not.

$$
\begin{array}{ll}
\textsf{cases } sf \textsf{ of} & \\
\quad \textit{mk-Eq}(a, ve) & \rightarrow t(a) = val(t, ve) \\
\quad \textit{mk-Less}(a, ve) & \rightarrow lt(t(a), val(t, ve)) \\
\quad \textit{mk-Greater}(a, ve) & \rightarrow lt(val(t, ve), t(a)) \\
\quad \textit{mk-Negation}(sf) & \rightarrow \neg\ sat(t, sf) \\
\quad \textit{mk-Disjunction}(sf_1, sf_2) & \rightarrow sat(t, sf_1) \vee sat(t, sf_2) \\
\textsf{end}. &
\end{array}
$$

Logical notation

Logical notation is what is used to express assertions. Logical notation is basic to implicit specification of functions and operations in VVSL. The logical expressions of the expression sublanguage constitute the logical notation. Expressions in VVSL commonly involve applications of functions that do not always yield a result, that is, partial functions. Such function applications give rise to expressions that do not refer to objects in the intended domain. These expressions are called non-denoting expressions or undefined expressions.

To deal with non-denoting expressions, the intended domain is extended with an object $\perp$ (undefined) to which the non-denoting expressions refer. Because the possibility of undefinedness includes logical expressions, the definition of the logical connectives and quantifiers is also extended. This is done, as in LPF (Cheng, 1986; Jones, 1990), by taking the definitions obtained by extending the classical truth-conditions and falsity-conditions with a clause yielding $\perp$ for the other cases:

$$
\begin{array}{lll}
\neg E & \text{is true} & \text{if } E \text{ is false}, \\
 & \text{is false} & \text{if } E \text{ is true}, \\
 & \text{is } \perp & \text{otherwise}, \\
 & & \\
E \vee E' & \text{is true} & \text{if } E \text{ is true or } E' \text{ is true}, \\
 & \text{is false} & \text{if } E \text{ is false and } E' \text{ is false}, \\
 & \text{is } \perp & \text{otherwise},
\end{array}
$$

* In Appendix E, this notation is precisely defined as an abbreviation.

$\exists x \in t \cdot E$	is true	if for some element c of type t, E is true when x is interpreted as c,
	is false	if for each element c of type t, E is false when x is interpreted as c,
	is $\perp$	otherwise.

This means that $\perp$ is treated as a third truth value which is interpreted as neither-true-nor-false. In the same vein, an equation $t_1 = t_2$ yields $\perp$ exactly when t_1 or t_2 is non-denoting. In case only logical expressions are involved that cannot be undefined, the logical connectives and quantifiers are just the classical ones. The other logical connectives and quantifiers are expressible by $\neg$, $\vee$ and $\exists$ in the classical way.

Example. The following logical expression states that the merge of two tuples is also a tuple if the attribute sets of the two tuples are disjoint.

$$\forall t_1 \in \mathit{Tuple}, t_2 \in \mathit{Tuple} \cdot \\ \quad \mathsf{dom}\, t_1 \cap \mathsf{dom}\, t_2 = \{\,\} \;\Rightarrow\; \exists t \in \mathit{Tuple} \;\cdot\; t = t_1 \cup t_2.$$

$t_1 \cup t_2$ is undefined if $\mathsf{dom}\, t_1 \cap \mathsf{dom}\, t_2 = \{\,\}$ is false. This does not cause any problem because the truth value of a formula of the form $A \Rightarrow B$ is always true if either A is false or B is true (likewise it is always false if A is true and B is false, and undefined otherwise).

Special notation

What remains is the special notation for sequences, sets and maps. The notations

$$[e_1, \ldots, e_n]$$
$$\{e_1, \ldots, e_n\}$$
$$\{e_1 \mapsto e'_1, \ldots, e_n \mapsto e'_n\}$$

are available to construct sequences, sets and maps, respectively, by enumeration of their elements (or pairs consisting of a domain element and a corresponding range element for maps). The notations

$$\{e \mid x_1 \in t_1, \ldots, x_n \in t_n \,;\, E\}$$
$$\{e \mapsto e' \mid x_1 \in t_1, \ldots, x_n \in t_n \,;\, E\}$$

are available to construct sets and maps, respectively, by comprehension, i.e. by formation according to a property being characteristic of their elements (or pairs consisting of a domain element and a corresponding range element for maps). It binds the value names $x_1, \ldots, x_n$ both in the 'element' expression(s) and the 'characterizing' logical expression. The implied quantification of the value names from $x_1, \ldots, x_n$ that do not occur free in the element expression(s) is existential quantification. The map comprehension expressions must be written so as to generate only maps: only one range element may be associated with each domain element.

Example. The tuple with a single attribute a and associated value v can be denoted by a very simple map enumeration:

$$\{a \mapsto v\}.$$

The set comprehension notation is used in the following expression, which is the defining expression of the function *product* of which the complete function definition was given in Section 5.6.

$$\{merge(t_1, t_2) \mid t_1 \in Tuple, t_2 \in Tuple \ ; \ t_1 \in r_1 \wedge t_2 \in r_2\}.$$

Syntax

Expressions are the terminal productions of *<expression>*. Because logical expressions must be distinguishable, the nonterminal *<logical-expression>* is introduced as well. *Logical expressions* are the terminal productions of *<logical-expression>*.

<expression> ::=
    <function-name> (*<expression-list>*)
  | if *<logical-expression>* then *<expression>* else *<expression>*
  | let *<value-binding>* in *<expression>*
  | let *<value-description>* in *<expression>*
  | [*<expression-list>*]
  | { *<expression-list>* }
  | { *<maplet-list>* }
  | { *<expression>* | *<domain-bindings>* ; *<logical-expression>* }
  | { *<maplet>* | *<domain-bindings>* ; *<logical-expression>* }
  | *<variable-name>*
  | *<variable-name>*
  | *<value-name>*
  | *<number>*
  | *<logical-expression>*

<logical-expression> ::=
    <expression>
  | *<expression>* = *<expression>*
  | ¬ *<logical-expression>*
  | *<logical-expression>* ∨ *<logical-expression>*
  | ∃ *<domain-binding>* · *<logical-expression>*

<value-binding> ::=
    <value-name> : *<type-name>* ≜ *<expression>*

<value-description> ::=
    <selected-values> be s.t. *<logical-expression>*

<selected-values> ::=
    <selected-value>
  | *<selected-value>*, *<selected-values>*

<selected-value> ::=
    <value-name> : *<type-name>*

<expression-list> ::=
    <empty>
  | *<nonempty-expression-list>*

<nonempty-expression-list> ::=
    <expression>
  | *<expression>* , *<nonempty-expression-list>*

<maplet-list> ::=
    <empty>
  | *<nonempty-maplet-list>*

<nonempty-maplet-list> ::=
    <maplet>
  | *<maplet>* , *<nonempty-maplet-list>*

<maplet> ::=
    <expression> $\mapsto$ *<expression>*

<domain-bindings> ::=
    <domain-binding>
  | *<domain-binding>* , *<domain-bindings>*

<domain-binding> ::=
    <value-name> $\in$ *<type-name>*

The logical expressions produced according to the first production rule of *<logical-expression>* are excluded from the production of expressions according to the last production rule of *<expression>*.

The sets Expression and LogicalExpr of syntactically correct expression constructs and logical expression constructs are defined by

$$\begin{aligned}&\mathsf{Expression} :=\\ &\quad \{e \mid e \text{ is a terminal production of } \textit{<expression>}\},\\ &\mathsf{LogicalExpr} :=\\ &\quad \{E \mid E \text{ is a terminal production of } \textit{<logical-expression>}\}.\end{aligned}$$

An expression e is *deterministic* iff no subexpression of e is produced according to the fourth production rule of *<expression>*.

Deterministic expressions are expressions of which it can be determined syntactically that they cannot yield more than one value.

Well-formedness. The well-formedness of syntactically correct expression constructs and logical expression constructs, respectively, are defined by predicates

$$\begin{aligned}&\mathit{wf}\colon \mathsf{Expression} \times \mathsf{NCxt} \times \mathcal{N},\\ &\mathit{wf}\colon \mathsf{LogicalExpr} \times \mathsf{NCxt} \times \mathcal{N}.\end{aligned}$$

$\mathit{wf}(e, N, k)$ indicates that the expression e is well-formed in the name context N and k ($k \in \{0, 1, 2\}$) states to refer to: a contents expression v may only be used if $k \in \{1, 2\}$, and an old contents expression $\overleftarrow{v}$ may only be used if $k \in \{2\}$. $\mathit{wf}(E, N, k)$ is used similarly for the logical expression E. Instead of $\mathit{wf}(e, N, k)$ and $\mathit{wf}(E, N, k)$, we write 'e is well-formed in $\langle N, k\rangle$' and 'E is well-formed in $\langle N, k\rangle$', respectively. The well-formedness of expressions is defined in terms of the well-formedness of logical expressions and vice versa.

Syntactic properties. The typing of expressions is described by means of typing rules which inductively define a predicate

$$\mathit{mtyping}\colon \mathsf{Expression} \times \mathsf{Type} \times \mathsf{NCxt}.$$

Instead of $\mathit{mtyping}(e, T, N)$, we write '$N \vdash_{\mathrm{m}} e \mathbin{⦂} T$'. It indicates that, in the name context N, e has minimal type T. Instead of inductive rules of the form

$$\mathit{mtyping}(e_1, T_1, N_1) \wedge \ldots \wedge \mathit{mtyping}(e_n, T_n, N_n) \wedge \psi \Rightarrow \mathit{mtyping}(e_{n+1}, T_{n+1}, N_{n+1}),$$

rules of the form

$$\frac{N_1 \vdash_{\mathrm{m}} e_1 \mathbin{⦂} T_1, \ldots, N_n \vdash_{\mathrm{m}} e_n \mathbin{⦂} T_n}{N_{n+1} \vdash_{\mathrm{m}} e_{n+1} \mathbin{⦂} T_{n+1}} \text{ if } \psi$$

are used to define the predicate *mtyping*. The expressions $e_1, \ldots, e_n$ are immediate subexpressions of e_{n+1} and ψ is an (optional) condition that is not of the form $N \vdash_{\mathrm{m}} e \mathbin{⦂} T$. These rules can also be viewed as type inference rules that prescribe how to establish the minimal type of an expression from the minimal types of its immediate subexpressions; in which case they read as 'from $N_1 \models_{\mathrm{m}} e_1 \mathbin{⨾} T_1, \ldots, N_n \models_{\mathrm{m}} e_n \mathbin{⨾} T_n$ infer $N_{n+1} \models_{\mathrm{m}} e_{n+1} \mathbin{⨾} T_{n+1}$, provided ψ'. There is exactly one rule for each form of expression given by the production rules of *<expression>*.

Meaning. The meaning of expressions and logical expressions are defined by mappings

$$[\![\bullet]\!]^{\bullet}_{\bullet,\bullet} \colon \mathsf{Expression} \times \mathsf{Cxt} \times \mathsf{MState}^{*} \times \mathsf{Term} \to \mathsf{Form},$$

$$[\![\bullet]\!]^{\bullet}_{\bullet,\bullet} \colon \mathsf{LogicalExpr} \times \mathsf{Cxt} \times \mathsf{MState}^{*} \times \mathsf{Term} \to \mathsf{Form}\,.$$

$[\![e]\!]^{C}_{\vec{s},y}$ expresses the fact that, in the symbol context C, the evaluation of the expression e in state(s) $\vec{s}$ yields value y. $[\![E]\!]^{C}_{\vec{s},y}$ is used similarly for the logical expression E (which yields a truth value y). The meaning of expressions is defined in terms of the meaning of logical expressions and vice versa. $[\![e]\!]^{C}_{\vec{s},y}$, where $\vec{s} = \langle s_1, \ldots, s_n \rangle$, is only defined if $n \leq 2$, e is well-formed in $\langle \overline{C}, n \rangle$, and $\mathit{sort}(y) = T^{C}$, for some type T such that $\mathit{type}(e, \overline{C}) \leq^{\overline{C}} T$ or $T \leq^{\overline{C}} \mathit{type}(e, \overline{C})$. Similarly, $[\![E]\!]^{C}_{\vec{s},y}$, is only defined if $n \leq 2$, E is well-formed in $\langle \overline{C}, n \rangle$ and $\mathit{sort}(y) = \underline{\mathrm{B}}$. For expressions, the type of the yielded value need not be the expected type, but it must be comparable with the expected type. In any situation where the type of the yielded value is a subtype of the type that is expected, there is an implicit conversion to that type. In the reverse case, there is an implicit conversion to the subtype. This gives rise to a proof obligation for definedness of the conversion.

The expressions and logical expressions of the different forms are now treated separately.

Application expression

The evaluation of the application expression $f(e_1, \ldots, e_n)$ can yield any value that is the value of the function denoted by f for arguments $x_1, \ldots, x_n$ which are values that can be yielded by evaluation of the expressions $e_1, \ldots, e_n$, respectively. Generally, the function denoted by f depends on the types of the argument expressions.

It is worth noticing here that expressions, logical expressions excluded, in which choice expressions occur, may yield more than one value.

Structure:

$f(e_1, \ldots, e_n)$

Well-formedness in $\langle N, k \rangle$:

f is defined as a function name in N,

$e_1, \ldots, e_n$ are well-formed in $\langle N, k \rangle$,

$f(e_1, \ldots, e_n)$ is well-typed in N.

Typing:

$$\frac{N \vdash_{\mathrm{m}} e_1 \mathbin{⨾} T_1, \ldots, N \vdash_{\mathrm{m}} e_n \mathbin{⨾} T_n}{N \vdash_{\mathrm{m}} f(e_1, \ldots, e_n) \mathbin{⨾} T} \text{ if } mtyping^N(f, \langle T_1, \ldots, T_n \rangle, T).$$

Meaning:

Let $\overline{C} \vdash_{\mathrm{m}} e_1 \mathbin{⨾} T_1, \ldots, \overline{C} \vdash_{\mathrm{m}} e_n \mathbin{⨾} T_n$,
$ftypes^{\overline{C}}(f, \langle T_1, \ldots, T_n \rangle, \langle T_1', \ldots, T_n' \rangle)$,
$[\mathsf{func}\ f \colon T_1' \times \cdots \times T_n' \to T'] \in \overline{C}$, $sort(y) = S$, then:

$$[\![f(e_1, \ldots, e_n)]\!]^C_{\vec{s},y} :=$$
$$\exists x_1 \colon T_1'^C, \ldots, x_n \colon T_n'^C$$
$$(\bigwedge_{i=1}^{n} ([\![e_i]\!]^C_{\vec{s},x_i}) \wedge cnv^C_{T'^C \to S}(f^C_{T_1' \times \cdots \times T_n' \to T'}(x_1, \ldots, x_n)) = y),$$

where

$x_1, \ldots, x_n$ are fresh value symbols such that for all $i = 1, \ldots, n$:
$\tau(x_i) = \langle \mathsf{obj}, T_i'^C \rangle$.

Conditional expression

The evaluation of the conditional expression $\mathsf{if}\ E\ \mathsf{then}\ e_1\ \mathsf{else}\ e_2$ can yield:

- any value that can be yielded by evaluation of the expression e_1, if evaluation of the logical expression E yields true;
- any value that can be yielded by evaluation of the expression e_2, if evaluation of the logical expression E yields false;
- no value, otherwise.

It is worth noticing here again that logical expressions cannot yield more than one value, even the ones in which choice expressions occur.

Structure:

$\mathsf{if}\ E\ \mathsf{then}\ e_1\ \mathsf{else}\ e_2$

Well-formedness in $\langle N, k \rangle$:

E, e_1, e_2 are well-formed in $\langle N, k \rangle$,

$\mathsf{if}\ E\ \mathsf{then}\ e_1\ \mathsf{else}\ e_2$ is well-typed in N.

Typing:

$$\frac{N \vdash_{\mathrm{m}} E \mathbin{⨾} \mathbb{B}, N \vdash_{\mathrm{m}} e_1 \mathbin{⨾} T_1, N \vdash_{\mathrm{m}} e_2 \mathbin{⨾} T_2}{N \vdash_{\mathrm{m}} \mathsf{if}\ E\ \mathsf{then}\ e_1\ \mathsf{else}\ e_2 \mathbin{⨾} T} \text{ if } lub^N(\{T_1, T_2\}, T).$$

Meaning:

$$[\![\mathsf{if}\ E\ \mathsf{then}\ e_1\ \mathsf{else}\ e_2]\!]^C_{\vec{s},y} := ([\![E]\!]^C_{\vec{s},tt} \wedge [\![e_1]\!]^C_{\vec{s},y}) \vee ([\![E]\!]^C_{\vec{s},ff} \wedge [\![e_2]\!]^C_{\vec{s},y}).$$

Local definition expression

The evaluation of the local definition expression $\mathsf{let}\ x{:}\, t \triangleq e_1\ \mathsf{in}\ e_2$ can yield any value that can be yielded by evaluation of the expression e_2 when value name x is assigned a value that can be yielded by evaluation of the expression e_1.

Structure:

$\mathsf{let}\ x{:}\, t \triangleq e_1\ \mathsf{in}\ e_2$

Well-formedness in $\langle N, k \rangle$:

x is not defined as a value or state variable name in N,

t is defined as a type name in N,

e_1 is well-formed in $\langle N, k \rangle$ and e_2 is well-formed in $\langle N \cup \{[\mathsf{val}\ x{:}\, t]\}, k \rangle$,

$\mathsf{let}\ x{:}\, t \triangleq e_1\ \mathsf{in}\ e_2$ is well-typed in N.

Typing:

$$\frac{N \vdash_{\mathrm{m}} e_1 \mathbin{⨾} T_1,\ N' \vdash_{\mathrm{m}} e_2 \mathbin{⨾} T_2}{N \vdash_{\mathrm{m}} \mathsf{let}\ x{:}\, t \triangleq e_1\ \mathsf{in}\ e_2 \mathbin{⨾} T_2}\ \text{if } T_1 \leq^N t,$$

where $N' = N \cup \{[\mathsf{val}\ x{:}\, t]\}$.

Meaning:

$$[\![\mathsf{let}\ x{:}\, t \triangleq e_1\ \mathsf{in}\ e_2]\!]^C_{\vec{s},y} \;:=\; \exists x'{:}\, t^C([\![e_1]\!]^C_{\vec{s},x'} \wedge [\![e_2]\!]^{C \cup \{x'\}}_{\vec{s},y}),$$

where

x' is a fresh value symbol such that $\iota(x') = x$ and $\tau(x') = \langle \mathsf{obj}, t^C \rangle$.

Choice expression

The evaluation of the choice expression

$\mathsf{let}\ x_1{:}\, t_1, \ldots, x_n{:}\, t_n\ \mathsf{be\ s.t.}\ E\ \mathsf{in}\ e$

can yield any value that can be yielded by evaluation of the expression e when value names $x_1, \ldots, x_n$ are assigned values for which evaluation of the logical expression E yields true. The use of choice expressions leads to expressions that can yield more than one value. In some situations this does not make sense: for element expressions in set and map comprehension and for expressions of boolean type used as logical expressions. In these situations, it is guaranteed that the expression concerned does not yield more than one value.

Structure:

$\mathsf{let}\ x_1{:}\, t_1, \ldots, x_n{:}\, t_n\ \mathsf{be\ s.t.}\ E\ \mathsf{in}\ e$

Well-formedness in $\langle N, k \rangle$:

$x_1, \ldots, x_n$ are distinct identifiers,

$x_1, \ldots, x_n$ are not defined as value or state variable names in N,

$t_1, \ldots, t_n$ are defined as type names in N,

E, e are well-formed in $\langle N \cup \{[\mathsf{val}\ x_1 \colon t_1], \ldots, [\mathsf{val}\ x_n \colon t_n]\}, k\rangle$,

$\mathsf{let}\ x_1 \colon t_1, \ldots, x_n \colon t_n\ \mathsf{be\ s.t.}\ E\ \mathsf{in}\ e$ is well-typed in N.

Typing:

$$\frac{N' \vDash_{\mathrm{m}} E \mathbin{⦂} \mathbb{B}, N' \vDash_{\mathrm{m}} e \mathbin{⦂} T}{N \vDash_{\mathrm{m}} \mathsf{let}\ x_1 \colon t_1, \ldots, x_n \colon t_n\ \mathsf{be\ s.t.}\ E\ \mathsf{in}\ e \mathbin{⦂} T},$$

where $N' = N \cup \{[\mathsf{val}\ x_1 \colon t_1], \ldots, [\mathsf{val}\ x_n \colon t_n]\}$.

Meaning:

$$[\![\mathsf{let}\ x_1 \colon t_1, \ldots, x_n \colon t_n\ \mathsf{be\ s.t.}\ E\ \mathsf{in}\ e]\!]^{C}_{\vec{s},y} :=$$

$$\exists x_1' \colon t_1^C, \ldots, x_n' \colon t_n^C ([\![E]\!]^{C \cup \{x_1', \ldots, x_n'\}}_{\vec{s},tt} \wedge [\![e]\!]^{C \cup \{x_1', \ldots, x_n'\}}_{\vec{s},y}),$$

where

$x_1', \ldots, x_n'$ are fresh value symbols such that for all $i = 1, \ldots, n$: $\iota(x_i') = x_i$ and $\tau(x_i') = \langle \mathsf{obj}, t_i^C \rangle$.

Sequence enumeration expression

The evaluation of the sequence enumeration expression $[e_1\ , \ldots,\ e_n]$ can yield any value that is a sequence of values $x_1, \ldots, x_n$ that can be yielded by evaluation of the expressions $e_1, \ldots, e_n$, respectively.

Structure:

$[e_1\ , \ldots,\ e_n]$

Well-formedness in $\langle N, k \rangle$:

$e_1, \ldots, e_n$ are well-formed in $\langle N, k \rangle$,

$[e_1\ , \ldots,\ e_n]$ is well-typed in N.

Typing:

$$\frac{N \vDash_{\mathrm{m}} e_1 \mathbin{⦂} T_1, \ldots, N \vDash_{\mathrm{m}} e_n \mathbin{⦂} T_n}{N \vDash_{\mathrm{m}} [e_1\ , \ldots,\ e_n] \mathbin{⦂} T'}$$

if for some T: $lub^N(\{T_1, \ldots, T_n\}, T)$, $lower^N(T^*) = T'$.

Meaning:

Let $\overline{C} \vDash_{\mathrm{m}} e_1 \mathbin{⦂} T_1, \ldots, \overline{C} \vDash_{\mathrm{m}} e_n \mathbin{⦂} T_n$, $lub^{\overline{C}}(\{T_1, \ldots, T_n\}, T)$, $sort(y) = S$, then:

$$[\![[e_1\ , \ldots,\ e_n]]\!]^{C}_{\vec{s},y} :=$$

$$\exists x_1 \colon T^C, \ldots, x_n \colon T^C$$

$$(\bigwedge_{i=1}^{n} ([\![e_i]\!]^{C}_{\vec{s},x_i}) \wedge cnv^{C}_{\underline{\mathrm{L}}(T^C) \to S}(x_1 \oplus (\cdots \oplus (x_n \oplus \emptyset) \cdots)) = y),$$

where

$x_1, \ldots, x_n$ are fresh value symbols such that for all $i = 1, \ldots, n$:
$\tau(x_i) = \langle \mathsf{obj}, T^C \rangle$.

Set enumeration expression

The evaluation of the set enumeration expression $\{e_1 , \ldots , e_n\}$ can yield any value that is a set whose elements are values $x_1, \ldots, x_n$ that can be yielded by evaluation of the expressions $e_1, \ldots, e_n$, respectively. The cardinality of the yielded set can be less than n, since there may be element expressions yielding the same value. In case the element expressions can yield more than one value, the cardinalities of the sets that can be yielded are not necessarily the same.

Structure:

$\{e_1 , \ldots , e_n\}$

Well-formedness in $\langle N, k \rangle$:

$e_1, \ldots, e_n$ are well-formed in $\langle N, k \rangle$,
$\{e_1 , \ldots , e_n\}$ is well-typed in N.

Typing:

$$\frac{N \models_{\mathrm{m}} e_1 \mathbin{⸬} T_1, \ldots, N \models_{\mathrm{m}} e_n \mathbin{⸬} T_n}{N \models_{\mathrm{m}} \{e_1 , \ldots , e_n\} \mathbin{⸬} T'}$$

if for some T: $\mathit{lub}^N(\{T_1, \ldots, T_n\}, T)$, $\mathit{lower}^N(T\text{-}\mathsf{set}) = T'$.

Meaning:

Let $\overline{C} \models_{\mathrm{m}} e_1 \mathbin{⸬} T_1, \ldots, \overline{C} \models_{\mathrm{m}} e_n \mathbin{⸬} T_n$, $\mathit{lub}^{\overline{C}}(\{T_1, \ldots, T_n\}, T)$,
$\mathit{sort}(y) = S$, then:

$$[\![\{e_1 , \ldots , e_n\}]\!]^C_{\overline{s},y} :=$$
$$\exists x_1 \colon T^C, \ldots, x_n \colon T^C$$
$$(\bigwedge_{i=1}^{n}([\![e_i]\!]^C_{\overline{s},x_i}) \wedge \mathit{cnv}^C_{\underline{\mathrm{F}}(T^C) \to S}(x_n \oplus (\cdots \oplus (x_1 \oplus \emptyset) \cdots)) = y),$$

where

$x_1, \ldots, x_n$ are fresh value symbols such that for all $i = 1, \ldots, n$:
$\tau(x_i) = \langle \mathsf{obj}, T^C \rangle$.

Map enumeration expression

The evaluation of the map enumeration expression $\{e_1 \mapsto e'_1 , \ldots , e_n \mapsto e'_n\}$ can yield any value that is a map whose domain elements are values $x_1, \ldots, x_n$ that can be yielded by evaluation of the expressions $e_1, \ldots, e_n$, respectively, and which maps the domain elements as follows: x_i maps to x'_j, for the greatest j such that $i \leq j \leq n$ and $x_i = x_j$, where $x'_1, \ldots, x'_n$ are values that can be yielded by evaluation of the expressions $e'_1, \ldots, e'_n$, respectively. The cardinality of the domain of the yielded map can be less than n, since there may be domain element expressions yielding the same value. In case the domain element expressions can yield more than one value, the cardinalities of the domains of the maps that can be yielded are not necessarily the same.

Structure:

$\{e_1 \mapsto e'_1, \ldots, e_n \mapsto e'_n\}$

Well-formedness in $\langle N, k\rangle$:

$e_1, e'_1, \ldots, e_n, e'_n$ are well-formed in $\langle N, k\rangle$,

$\{e_1 \mapsto e'_1, \ldots, e_n \mapsto e'_n\}$ is well-typed in N.

Typing:

$$\frac{N \vdash_{\mathrm{m}} e_1 \mathbin{⨾} T_1, N \vdash_{\mathrm{m}} e'_1 \mathbin{⨾} T'_1, \ldots, N \vdash_{\mathrm{m}} e_n \mathbin{⨾} T_n, N \vdash_{\mathrm{m}} e'_n \mathbin{⨾} T'_n}{N \vdash_{\mathrm{m}} \{e_1 \mapsto e'_1, \ldots, e_n \mapsto e'_n\} \mathbin{⨾} T''}$$

if for some T, T': $lub^N(\{T_1, \ldots, T_n\}, T)$, $lub^N(\{T'_1, \ldots, T'_n\}, T')$, $lower^N(T \xrightarrow{m} T') = T''$.

Meaning:

Let $\overline{C} \vdash_{\mathrm{m}} e_1 \mathbin{⨾} T_1, \overline{C} \vdash_{\mathrm{m}} e_1 \mathbin{⨾} T'_1, \ldots, \overline{C} \vdash_{\mathrm{m}} e_n \mathbin{⨾} T_n, \overline{C} \vdash_{\mathrm{m}} e_n \mathbin{⨾} T'_n$, $lub^{\overline{C}}(\{T_1, \ldots, T_n\}, T)$, $lub^{\overline{C}}(\{T'_1, \ldots, T'_n\}, T')$, $sort(y) = S$, then:

$$[\![\{e_1 \mapsto e'_1, \ldots, e_n \mapsto e'_n\}]\!]^C_{\bar{s},y} :=$$
$$\exists x_1 \colon T^C, x'_1 \colon T'^C, \ldots, x_n \colon T^C, x'_n \colon T'^C$$
$$(\bigwedge_{i=1}^{n} ([\![e_i]\!]^C_{\bar{s},x_i} \wedge [\![e'_i]\!]^C_{\bar{s},x'_i}) \wedge$$
$$cnv^C_{\underline{\mathrm{M}}(T^C,T'^C)\to S}(\{x_n \mapsto x'_n\} \oplus (\cdots \oplus (\{x_1 \mapsto x'_1\} \oplus \emptyset) \cdots)) = y),$$

where

$x_1, \ldots, x_n$ and $x'_1, \ldots, x'_n$ are fresh value symbols such that for all $i = 1, \ldots, n$: $\tau(x_i) = \langle \mathsf{obj}, T^C\rangle$ and $\tau(x'_i) = \langle \mathsf{obj}, T'^C\rangle$.

Set comprehension expression

The evaluation of the set comprehension expression

$\{e \mid x_1 \in t_1, \ldots, x_n \in t_n;\ E\}$

yields the set whose elements are the values that are yielded by evaluation of the expression e under the different assignments of values to the value names $x_1, \ldots, x_n$ for which evaluation of the logical expression E yields true. Assignments for which the expression e can yield more than one value do not contribute any element! In this way, it is guaranteed that (assuming that e has type t)

$$\{e \mid x_1 \in t_1 , \ldots , x_n \in t_n ;\ E\}$$

is semantically equivalent to

$$\{x \mid x \in t;\ \exists x_1 \in t_1, \ldots, x_n \in t_n \ .\ E \land x = e\}.$$

Structure:

$$\{e \mid x_1 \in t_1 , \ldots , x_n \in t_n ;\ E\}$$

Well-formedness in $\langle N, k\rangle$:

$x_1, \ldots, x_n$ are distinct identifiers,

$x_1, \ldots, x_n$ are not defined as value or state variable names in N,

$t_1, \ldots, t_n$ are defined as type names in N,

e, E are well-formed in $\langle N \cup \{[\mathsf{val}\ x_1 : t_1], \ldots, [\mathsf{val}\ x_n : t_n]\}, k\rangle$,

$\{e \mid x_1 \in t_1 , \ldots , x_n \in t_n ;\ E\}$ is well-typed in N.

Typing:

$$\frac{N' \vdash_{\mathrm{m}} E \mathbin{⁞} \mathbb{B},\ N' \vdash_{\mathrm{m}} e \mathbin{⁞} T}{N \vdash_{\mathrm{m}} \{e \mid x_1 \in t_1 , \ldots , x_n \in t_n ;\ E\} \mathbin{⁞} T'} \quad \text{if } lower^N(T\text{-}\mathsf{set}) = T',$$

where $N' = N \cup \{[\mathsf{val}\ x_1 : t_1], \ldots, [\mathsf{val}\ x_n : t_n]\}$.

Meaning:

Let $\overline{C} \vdash_{\mathrm{m}} e \mathbin{⁞} T$, $sort(y) = S$, then:

$$[\![\{e \mid x_1 \in t_1 , \ldots , x_n \in t_n ;\ E\}]\!]^C_{\vec{s},y} :=$$
$$\exists y' : \underline{\mathrm{F}}(T^C)$$
$$(\forall x : T^C$$
$$(\exists x'_1 : t_1^C, \ldots, x'_n : t_n^C$$
$$([\![E]\!]^{C \cup \{x'_1, \ldots, x'_n\}}_{\vec{s},tt} \land \forall x' : T^C([\![e]\!]^{C \cup \{x'_1, \ldots, x'_n\}}_{\vec{s},x'} \leftrightarrow x = x')) \leftrightarrow$$
$$x \in y' = tt) \land cnv^C_{\underline{\mathrm{F}}(T^C) \to S}(y') = y),$$

where

$x'_1, \ldots, x'_n$ are fresh value symbols such that for all $i = 1, \ldots, n$: $\iota(x'_i) = x_i$ and $\tau(x'_i) = \langle \mathsf{obj}, t_i^C\rangle$,
x, x' are fresh value symbols such that $\tau(x) = \tau(x') = \langle \mathsf{obj}, T^C\rangle$,
y' is a fresh value symbol such that $\tau(y') = \langle \mathsf{obj}, \underline{\mathrm{F}}(T^C)\rangle$.

Map comprehension expression

The evaluation of the map comprehension expression

$$\{e \mapsto e' \mid x_1 \in t_1 , \ldots , x_n \in t_n ;\ E\}$$

yields the map whose domain elements are the values that are yielded by evaluation of the expression e under the different assignments of values to the value names $x_1, \ldots, x_n$ for which evaluation of the logical expression E

yields true and which maps the domain elements as follows: the value that is yielded by evaluation of the expression e under a certain assignment maps to the value that is yielded by evaluation of the expression e' under the same assignment. Assignments for which the expression e or the expression e' can yield more than one value do not contribute any argument-value pair! In this way, it is guaranteed that (assuming that e has type t and e' has type t')

$$\{e \mapsto e' \mid x_1 \in t_1 \;, \ldots ,\; x_n \in t_n ;\; E\}$$

is semantically equivalent to

$$\{x \mapsto x' \mid x \in t \;, x' \in t';\; \exists x_1 \in t_1, \ldots , x_n \in t_n \;.\; E \wedge x = e \wedge x' = e'\}.$$

The evaluation will yield no value, if there are two assignments for which evaluation of E yields true, evaluation of e yields identical values and evaluation of e' yields different values.

Structure:

$\{e \mapsto e' \mid x_1 \in t_1 \;, \ldots ,\; x_n \in t_n ;\; E\}$

Well-formedness in $\langle N, k\rangle$:

$x_1, \ldots, x_n$ are distinct identifiers,

$x_1, \ldots, x_n$ are not defined as value or state variable names in N,

$t_1, \ldots, t_n$ are defined as type names in N,

e, e', E are well-formed in $\langle N \cup \{[\mathsf{val}\ x_1 : t_1], \ldots, [\mathsf{val}\ x_n : t_n]\}, k\rangle$,

$\{e \mapsto e' \mid x_1 \in t_1 \;, \ldots ,\; x_n \in t_n ;\; E\}$ is well-typed in N.

Typing:

$$\frac{N' \models_{\mathrm{m}} E \mathbin{⁏} \mathbb{B}, N' \models_{\mathrm{m}} e \mathbin{⁏} T, N' \models_{\mathrm{m}} e' \mathbin{⁏} T'}{N \models_{\mathrm{m}} \{e \mapsto e' \mid x_1 \in t_1 \;, \ldots ,\; x_n \in t_n ;\; E\} \mathbin{⁏} T''}$$

if $\mathit{lower}^N(T \xrightarrow{m} T') = T''$,

where $N' = N \cup \{[\mathsf{val}\ x_1 : t_1], \ldots, [\mathsf{val}\ x_n : t_n]\}$.

Meaning:

Let $\overline{C} \models_{\mathrm{m}} e \mathbin{⁏} T, \overline{C} \models_{\mathrm{m}} e' \mathbin{⁏} T'$, $\mathit{sort}(y) = S$, then:

$$
\begin{array}{l}
[\![\{e \mapsto e' \mid x_1 \in t_1 \;, \ldots ,\; x_n \in t_n ;\; E\}]\!]^{C}_{\vec{s},y} \;:= \\
\quad \exists y' : \underline{\mathrm{M}}(T^C, T'^C) \\
\quad\; (\forall u : T^C, v : T'^C \\
\quad\;\; (\exists x'_1 : t_1^C, \ldots, x'_n : t_n^C \\
\quad\;\;\; ([\![E]\!]^{C \cup \{x'_1, \ldots, x'_n\}}_{\vec{s},\mathit{tt}} \wedge \\
\quad\;\;\;\; \forall u' : T^C([\![e]\!]^{C \cup \{x'_1, \ldots, x'_n\}}_{\vec{s},u'} \leftrightarrow u = u') \wedge \\
\quad\;\;\;\; \forall v' : T'^C([\![e']\!]^{C \cup \{x'_1, \ldots, x'_n\}}_{\vec{s},v'} \leftrightarrow v = v')) \leftrightarrow \\
\qquad\qquad u \in \mathsf{dom}\, y' = \mathit{tt} \wedge y'(u) = v) \wedge \mathit{cnv}^C_{\underline{\mathrm{M}}(T^C, T'^C) \to S}(y') = y),
\end{array}
$$

where
$x'_1, \ldots, x'_n$ are fresh value symbols such that for all $i = 1, \ldots, n$:
$\iota(x'_i) = x_i$ and $\tau(x'_i) = \langle \mathsf{obj}, t_i^C \rangle$,
u, u' are fresh value symbols such that $\tau(u) = \tau(u') = \langle \mathsf{obj}, T^C \rangle$,
v, v' are fresh value symbols such that $\tau(v) = \tau(v') = \langle \mathsf{obj}, T'^C \rangle$,
y' is a fresh value symbol such that $\tau(y') = \langle \mathsf{obj}, \underline{\mathrm{M}}(T^C, T'^C) \rangle$.

Contents expression

The evaluation of the contents expression v yields the value taken by the state variable v in the current state. Contents expressions can only be used in initial conditions, state invariants, dynamic constraints, and the pre-, post- and inter-conditions of operation definitions.

Structure:

v

Well-formedness in $\langle N, k \rangle$:

$k > 0$,

v is defined as a state variable name in N,

v is well-typed in N.

Typing:

$$\frac{}{N \vdash_{\mathrm{m}} v \,\mathbin{\circ\!\!\!\circ}\, T} \text{ if } mtyping^N(v, T).$$

Meaning:

Let $[\mathsf{var}\ v\colon T'] \in \overline{C}$, $\vec{s} = \langle s_1, \ldots, s_n \rangle$, $sort(y) = S$, then:

$[\![v]\!]^C_{\vec{s},y} \;:=\; cnv^C_{T'^C \to S}(v^C_{T'}(s_n)) = y.$

Old contents expression

The evaluation of the old contents expression $\overleftarrow{v}$ yields the value taken by the state variable v in the previous state. Old contents expressions can only be used in the post-conditions of operation definitions.

Structure:

$\overleftarrow{v}$

Well-formedness in $\langle N, k \rangle$:

$k > 1$,

v is defined as a state variable name in N,

$\overleftarrow{v}$ is well-typed in N.

Typing:

$$\frac{}{N \vdash_{\mathrm{m}} \overleftarrow{v} \mathbin{\circ\!\!\!\circ} T} \text{ if } \mathit{mtyping}^N(v, T).$$

Meaning:

Let $[\mathsf{var}\ v{:}\ T'] \in \overline{C}$, $\vec{s} = \langle s_1, \ldots, s_n \rangle$, $\mathit{sort}(y) = S$, then:

$[\![\overleftarrow{v}]\!]^C_{\vec{s},y} \;:=\; \mathit{cnv}^C_{T'^C \to S}(v^C_{T'}(s_1)) = y.$

Reference expression

The evaluation of the reference expression x yields the value assigned to the value name x.

Structure:

x

Well-formedness in $\langle N, k \rangle$:

x is defined as a value name in N,

x is well-typed in N.

Typing:

$$\frac{}{N \vdash_{\mathrm{m}} x \mathbin{\circ\!\!\!\circ} T} \text{ if } \mathit{mtyping}^N(x, T).$$

Meaning:

Let $[\mathsf{val}\ x{:}\ T'] \in \overline{C}$, $\mathit{sort}(y) = S$, then:

$[\![x]\!]^C_{\vec{s},y} \;:=\; \mathit{cnv}^C_{T'^C \to S}(x^C_{T'}) = y.$

Numeral expression

The evaluation of the numeral expression n yields the natural number corresponding to the numeral n.

Structure:

n

Well-formedness in $\langle N, k \rangle$:

True.

Typing:

$$\frac{}{N \vdash_{\mathrm{m}} n \mathbin{\circ\!\!\!\circ} T} \text{ if } \mathit{lower}^N(\mathbb{N}) = T.$$

Meaning:

Let $\mathit{sort}(y) = S$, then:

$[\![n]\!]^C_{\vec{s},y} \;:=\; \mathit{cnv}^C_{\underline{\mathrm{N}} \to S}(\underbrace{\mathit{succ}(\cdots \mathit{succ}}_{n \text{ times}}(0)\cdots)) = y.$

Logical expression

The evaluation of the logical expression E as an expression yields the value that is yielded by evaluation of E as a logical expression.

Structure:

E

Well-formedness in $\langle N, k\rangle$:

E is well-formed in $\langle N, k\rangle$.

Typing:

$$\frac{}{N \vdash_{\mathrm{m}} E \mathbin{\raisebox{0.5ex}{$\circ$}\!\!\!\circ} T} \text{ if } \mathit{lower}^N(\mathbb{B}) = T.$$

Meaning:

Let $\mathit{sort}(y) = S$, then:

$[\![E]\!]^C_{\vec{s},y} := \exists y' : \underline{\mathrm{B}}([\![E]\!]^C_{\vec{s},y'} \wedge \mathit{cnv}^C_{\underline{\mathrm{B}} \to S}(y') = y),$

where

y' is a fresh value symbol such that $\tau(y') = \langle \mathsf{obj}, \underline{\mathrm{B}}\rangle$.

Truth-valued expression

The evaluation of the truth-valued expression e, which is an expression of type $\mathbb{B}$, as a logical expression yields:

- the truth value that is yielded by the evaluation of e as an expression, if the evaluation of e as an expression can only yield one value;
- no value, otherwise.

If the expression e can yield both true and false, then its evaluation as a logical expression is undefined. In that case, the truth of e when interpreted as a logical expression cannot be established.

Structure:

e

Well-formedness in $\langle N, k\rangle$:

e is well-formed in $\langle N, k\rangle$,

the minimal type of e in N is $\mathbb{B}$.

Meaning:

$$[\![e]\!]^C_{\vec{s},y} := \begin{cases} [\![e]\!]^C_{\vec{s},y} & \text{if e is deterministic} \\ \forall y' : \underline{\mathrm{B}}([\![e]\!]^C_{\vec{s},y'} \leftrightarrow y' = y) & \text{otherwise,} \end{cases}$$

where

y' is a fresh value symbol such that $\tau(y') = \langle \mathsf{obj}, \underline{\mathrm{B}}\rangle$.

Equality expression

The evaluation of the equality expression $e_1 = e_2$ yields:

- true, if the evaluations of the expressions e_1 and e_2 can only yield identical values;
- false, if the evaluations of the expressions e_1 and e_2 can only yield different values;
- no value, otherwise.

Consequently, the evaluation cannot yield true if either e_1 or e_2 can yield more than one value. If e_1 and e_2 can yield more than one common value, then its evaluation is not even defined. In that case, the truth of $e_1 = e_2$ is meaningless.

Structure:

$e_1 = e_2$

Well-formedness in $\langle N, k\rangle$:

e_1, e_2 are well-formed in $\langle N, k\rangle$,

e_1 and e_2 are type compatible in N.

Meaning:

Let $\overline{C} \models_{\mathrm{m}} e_1 \between T_1, \overline{C} \models_{\mathrm{m}} e_2 \between T_2$, $lub^{\overline{C}}(T_1, T_2, T')$, $raise^{\overline{C}}(T') = T$, then:

$$
\begin{array}{l}
[\![e_1 = e_2]\!]^C_{\vec{s},y} := \\
\quad \exists x_1\colon T^C, x_2\colon T^C \\
\quad\quad (([\![e_1]\!]^C_{\vec{s},x_1} \wedge [\![e_2]\!]^C_{\vec{s},x_2}) \wedge \\
\quad\quad\quad ((x_1 = x_2 \wedge y = tt) \vee (x_1 \neq x_2 \wedge y = f\!f))) \\
\qquad\qquad\qquad\qquad\qquad\qquad \text{if } e_1 \text{ and } e_2 \text{ are deterministic} \\
\quad \forall y'\colon \underline{\mathrm{B}} \\
\quad\quad (\exists x_1\colon T^C, x_2\colon T^C \\
\quad\quad\quad (([\![e_1]\!]^C_{\vec{s},x_1} \wedge [\![e_2]\!]^C_{\vec{s},x_2}) \wedge \\
\quad\quad\quad\quad ((x_1 = x_2 \wedge y' = tt) \vee (x_1 \neq x_2 \wedge y' = f\!f))) \leftrightarrow y' = y) \\
\qquad\qquad\qquad\qquad\qquad\qquad \text{otherwise,}
\end{array}
$$

where

x_1, x_2 are fresh value symbols such that for $i = 1, 2$: $\tau(x_i) = \langle \mathsf{obj}, T^C\rangle$,
y' is a fresh value symbol such that $\tau(y') = \langle \mathsf{obj}, \underline{\mathrm{B}}\rangle$.

Negation expression

The evaluation of the negation expression $\neg\, E$ yields:

- true, if evaluation of the logical expression E yields false;
- false, if evaluation of the logical expression E yields true;
- no value, otherwise.

Structure:

$\neg E$

Well-formedness in $\langle N, k\rangle$:

E is well-formed in $\langle N, k\rangle$.

Meaning:

$[\![\neg E]\!]^C_{\vec{s},y} := ([\![E]\!]^C_{\vec{s},tt} \wedge y = \mathit{ff}) \vee ([\![E]\!]^C_{\vec{s},\mathit{ff}} \wedge y = tt)$.

Disjunction expression

The evaluation of the disjunction expression $E_1 \vee E_2$ yields:

- true, if evaluation of the logical expression E_1 yields true or evaluation of the logical expression E_2 yields true;
- false, if evaluation of the logical expression E_1 yields false and evaluation of the logical expression E_2 yields false;
- no value, otherwise.

Structure:

$E_1 \vee E_2$

Well-formedness in $\langle N, k\rangle$:

E_1, E_2 are well-formed in $\langle N, k\rangle$.

Meaning:

$[\![E_1 \vee E_2]\!]^C_{\vec{s},y} :=$
$(([\![E_1]\!]^C_{\vec{s},tt} \vee [\![E_2]\!]^C_{\vec{s},tt}) \wedge y = tt) \vee (([\![E_1]\!]^C_{\vec{s},\mathit{ff}} \wedge [\![E_2]\!]^C_{\vec{s},\mathit{ff}}) \wedge y = \mathit{ff})$.

Exists expression

The evaluation of the exists expression $\exists\, x \in t \cdot E$ yields:

- true, if evaluation of the logical expressions E yields true under some assignment of a value to the value name x;
- false, if evaluation of the logical expressions E yields false under each assignment of a value to the value name x;
- no value, otherwise.

Structure:

$\exists\, x \in t \cdot E$

Well-formedness in $\langle N, k\rangle$:

x is not defined as a value or state variable name in N,

t is defined as a type name in N,

E is well-formed in $\langle N \cup \{[\mathsf{val}\ x{:}\ t]\}, k\rangle$.

Meaning:

$[\![\exists\, x \in t \,\cdot\, E]\!]^{C}_{\bar{s},y} :=$

$$(\exists x' \colon t^{C}([\![E]\!]^{C\cup\{x'\}}_{\bar{s},tt}) \wedge y = tt) \vee (\forall x' \colon t^{C}([\![E]\!]^{C\cup\{x'\}}_{\bar{s},ff}) \wedge y = ff),$$

where

x' is a fresh value symbol such that $\iota(x') = x$ and $\tau(x') = \langle \mathsf{obj}, t^{C}\rangle$.

5.9 The temporal formula sublanguage

Section 5.6 dealt with the syntax and semantics of definitions, which includes operation definitions. Definitions of operations which are sensitive to interference by concurrently executed operations through shared state variables contain a temporal formula. This section deals with the syntax and semantics of temporal formulae. It begins by introducing temporal formulae in broad outline.

Overview

The temporal notation extends the logical notation of VVSL. In the temporal notation, the usual temporal connectives are available, such as the monadic connectives $\bigcirc$ (*next*) and $\ominus$ (*previous*) and the dyadic connectives $\mathcal{U}$ (*until*) and $\mathcal{S}$ (*since*), in addition to the logical connectives. The temporal formulae characterize successions of state changes, distinguishing between internal state changes and external state changes. There are also two built-in nullary transition predicates, is-I and is-E, to indicate this. $\bigcirc$ and $\ominus$ may also be used to construct temporal terms which refer to values in future or past states.

Example. In a system which handles concurrent access to stored relations by multiple transaction, it is useful to have an operation for accessing a subset of one of the stored relations for reading it. The operation will normally produce a relation and a status as results and change the state. If it terminates, it yields GRANTED as status iff the appropriate access is granted to the transaction concerned. The operation is non-atomic. During execution, the following occurs if the read access requested by the transaction concerned is not liable for deadlock in the initial state:

1. Eventually the read access (*acc*) requested by the transaction concerned (*tnm*) will not conflict with the granted and waiting accesses of other transactions (according to *curr_acctable* and *curr_dbschema*). The next state is the final state ($\neg \bigcirc$true) and is reached by an internal step which changes the state by adding the requested access to the granted accesses of the transaction. GRANTED will be the status.
2. Until then all steps were external, except the initial step ($\neg \ominus$true) which only changes (if it is not also the final step) the current state by adding the requested access to the waiting accesses of the transaction.

In the inter-condition for the operation, this corresponds to the following temporal formula (the second argument of the temporal connective $\mathcal{U}$ corresponds to 1 and the first one corresponds to 2):

$$
\begin{array}{l}
((\neg \ominus \mathsf{true} \Rightarrow \\
\quad \mathsf{is\text{-}I} \wedge \\
\quad \bigcirc(curr\_acctable = add\_to\_waits(\ominus curr\_acctable, tnm, acc))) \wedge \\
\;(\ominus \mathsf{true} \Rightarrow \mathsf{is\text{-}E}))\ \mathcal{U} \\
(\neg\, conflicts(tnm, acc, curr\_acctable, curr\_dbschema) \wedge \\
\;\mathsf{is\text{-}I} \wedge \\
\;\bigcirc(\ curr\_acctable = add\_to\_grants(\ominus curr\_acctable, tnm, acc) \wedge \\
\qquad st = \mathsf{GRANTED} \wedge \neg \bigcirc \mathsf{true}))
\end{array}
$$

Syntax

Temporal formulae and *temporal terms* are the terminal productions of *<temporal-formula>* and *<temporal-term>*, respectively.

<temporal-formula> ::=
    is-I
  | is-E
  | *<temporal-term>*
  | *<temporal-term>* = *<temporal-term>*
  | *<temporal-formula>* $\mathcal{C}$ *<temporal-formula>*
  | $\bigcirc$ *<temporal-formula>*
  | *<temporal-formula>* $\mathcal{U}$ *<temporal-formula>*
  | $\ominus$ *<temporal-formula>*
  | *<temporal-formula>* $\mathcal{S}$ *<temporal-formula>*
  | $\neg$ *<temporal-formula>*
  | *<temporal-formula>* $\vee$ *<temporal-formula>*
  | $\exists$ *<domain-binding>* $\cdot$ *<temporal-formula>*
  | let *<temporal-value-binding>* in *<temporal-formula>*

<temporal-term> ::=
    <function-name> (*<temporal-term-list>*)
  | $\bigcirc$ *<temporal-term>*
  | $\ominus$ *<temporal-term>*
  | *<expression>*

<temporal-value-binding> ::=
    <value-name> : *<type-name>* $\triangleq$ *<temporal-term>*

<*temporal-term-list*> ::=
<*empty*>
| <*nonempty-temporal-term-list*>

<*nonempty-temporal-term-list*> ::=
<*temporal-term*>
| <*temporal-term*> , <*nonempty-temporal-term-list*>

The temporal terms that are produced according to the second and third production rule of <*temporal-term*> are excluded from the production of temporal formulae according to the third production rule of <*temporal-formula*>.

The production rules of <*expression*> are presented in Section 5.8.

The sets TFormula and TTerm of syntactically correct temporal formula constructs and temporal term constructs are defined by

TFormula :=
$\{\varphi \mid \varphi$ is a terminal production of <*temporal-formula*>$\}$,
TTerm := $\{\tau \mid \tau$ is a terminal production of <*temporal-term*>$\}$.

Well-formedness. The well-formedness of syntactically correct temporal formula constructs and temporal term constructs, respectively, are defined by predicates

wf: TFormula × NCxt,
wf: TTerm × NCxt.

$wf(\varphi, N)$ indicates that φ is well-formed in the name context N. $wf(\tau, N)$ is used similarly for the temporal term τ. Instead of $wf(\varphi, N)$ and $wf(\tau, N)$, we write 'φ is well-formed in N' and 'τ is well-formed in N', respectively. The well-formedness of temporal formulae is defined in terms of the well-formedness of temporal terms which in turn is defined in terms of the well-formedness of expressions (defined in Section 5.8).

Syntactic properties. The typing of temporal terms is also described by means of typing rules. They inductively define a predicate

$mtyping$: TTerm × Type × NCxt.

Instead of $mtyping(\tau, T, N)$, we write $N \vdash_{\mathrm{m}} \tau \mathbin{⨾} T$. It indicates that, in the name context N, τ has minimal type T. The inductive rules used to define this predicate are written in a notation which conforms to the view of these rules as type inference rules. This notation is explained in Section 5.8. There is exactly one rule for each form of temporal term given by the production rules of <*temporal-term*>.

Meaning. The meaning of temporal formulae and temporal terms are defined by mappings

$$[\![\bullet]\!]^{\bullet}_{\bullet,\bullet,\bullet}\colon \mathsf{TFormula} \times \mathsf{Cxt} \times \mathsf{MComp} \times \mathcal{N} \times \mathsf{Term} \to \mathsf{Form},$$
$$[\![\bullet]\!]^{\bullet}_{\bullet,\bullet,\bullet}\colon \mathsf{TTerm} \times \mathsf{Cxt} \times \mathsf{MComp} \times \mathcal{N} \times \mathsf{Term} \to \mathsf{Form}\,.$$

$[\![\varphi]\!]^{C}_{c,k,y}$ expresses the fact that, in the symbol context C, the evaluation of the temporal formula φ at point k in computation c yields truth value y. $[\![\tau]\!]^{C}_{c,k,y}$ is used similarly for the temporal term τ. The meaning of temporal formulae is defined in terms of the meaning of temporal terms which in turn is defined in terms of the meaning of expressions. $[\![\varphi]\!]^{C}_{c,k,y}$ is only defined if φ is well-formed in $\overline{C}$ and $sort(y) = \underline{\mathrm{B}}$. Similarly, $[\![\tau]\!]^{C}_{c,k,y}$ is only defined if τ is well-formed in $\overline{C}$ and $sort(y) = T^{C}$, for some type T such that $type(\tau, \overline{C}) \leq^{\overline{C}} T$ or $T \leq^{\overline{C}} type(\tau, \overline{C})$. For temporal terms, the type of the yielded value need not be the expected type. In any situation where the type of the yielded value is a subtype of the type that is expected, there is an implicit conversion to that type. In the reverse case, there is an implicit conversion to the subtype. This gives rise to a proof obligation for definedness of the conversion.

The temporal formulae and temporal terms of the different forms are now treated separately.

Internal temporal formula

The evaluation of the internal temporal formula is-I yields true if there is an internal step from the current point in the computation, and false otherwise.

Structure:

is-I

Well-formedness in N:

True.

Meaning:

$$[\![\mathsf{is\text{-}I}]\!]^{C}_{c,k,y} \;:=\; \mathsf{int}_k(c) \leftrightarrow y = \mathit{tt}.$$

External temporal formula

The evaluation of the external temporal formula is-E yields true if there is an external step from the current point in the computation, and false otherwise.

Structure:

is-E

Well-formedness in N:

True.

Meaning:

$[\![\text{is-E}]\!]^{C}_{c,k,y} := \text{ext}_k(c) \leftrightarrow y = tt.$

Truth-valued temporal term

The evaluation of the truth-valued temporal term τ, which is a temporal term of type $\mathbb{B}$, as a temporal formula yields:

- the truth value that is yielded by the evaluation of τ as a temporal term, if the evaluation of τ as a temporal term can only yield one value;
- no value, otherwise.

If the temporal term τ can yield both true and false, then its evaluation as a temporal formula is undefined. In that case, the truth of τ when interpreted as a temporal formula cannot be established.

Structure:

τ

Well-formedness in N:

τ is well-formed in N,

the minimal type of τ in N is $\mathbb{B}$.

Meaning:

$[\![\tau]\!]^{C}_{\vec{s},y} := \forall y' : \underline{\text{B}}([\![\tau]\!]^{C}_{c,k,y'} \leftrightarrow y' = y)$

where

y' is a fresh value symbol such that $\tau(y') = \langle \text{obj}, \underline{\text{B}} \rangle$.

Equality temporal formula

The evaluation of the equality temporal formula $\tau_1 = \tau_2$ yields:

- true, if the evaluations of the temporal terms τ_1 and τ_2 can only yield identical values;
- false, if the evaluations of the temporal terms τ_1 and τ_2 can only yield different values;
- no value, otherwise.

Consequently, the evaluation cannot yield true if either τ_1 or τ_2 can yield more than one value. If τ_1 and τ_2 can yield more than one common value, then its evaluation is not even defined. In that case, the truth of $\tau_1 = \tau_2$ is meaningless.

Structure:

$\tau_1 = \tau_2$

Well-formedness in N:

τ_1, τ_2 are well-formed in N,

τ_1 and τ_2 are type compatible in N.

Meaning:

Let $\overline{C} \vdash_{\mathrm{m}} \tau_1 \mathbin{\mathring{:}} T_1$, $\overline{C} \vdash_{\mathrm{m}} \tau_2 \mathbin{\mathring{:}} T_2$, $lub^{\overline{C}}(T_1, T_2, T')$, $raise^{\overline{C}}(T') = T$, then:

$$
\begin{array}{l}
[\![\tau_1 = \tau_2]\!]^C_{c,k,y} := \\
\quad \forall y' : \underline{\mathrm{B}} \\
\quad (\exists x_1 : T^C, x_2 : T^C \\
\quad\; (([\![\tau_1]\!]^C_{c,k,x_1} \land [\![\tau_2]\!]^C_{c,k,x_2}) \land \\
\quad\;\; ((x_1 = x_2 \land y' = tt) \lor (x_1 \neq x_2 \land y' = f\!f))) \leftrightarrow y' = y),
\end{array}
$$

where

x_1, x_2 are fresh value symbols such that for $i = 1, 2$: $\tau(x_i) = \langle \mathsf{obj}, T^C \rangle$,
y' is a fresh value symbol such that $\tau(y') = \langle \mathsf{obj}, \underline{\mathrm{B}} \rangle$.

Chop temporal formula

The evaluation of the chop temporal formula $\varphi_1 \,\mathcal{C}\, \varphi_2$ yields:

- true, if it is possible to divide the computation at some future point into two subcomputations such that evaluation of φ_1 yields true at the current point in the first subcomputation and the evaluation of φ_2 yields true at the first point in the second subcomputation;
- true, if the computation is infinite and evaluation of φ_1 yields true at the current point in the computation;
- false, otherwise.

So the evaluation of $\varphi_1 \,\mathcal{C}\, \varphi_2$ always yields one of the truth values, even when evaluation of φ_1 can yield no value at the current point in any prefix of the computation.

Structure:

$\varphi_1 \,\mathcal{C}\, \varphi_2$

Well-formedness in N:

φ_1, φ_2 are well-formed in N.

Meaning:

$$
\begin{array}{l}
[\![\varphi_1 \,\mathcal{C}\, \varphi_2]\!]^C_{c,k,y} := \\
\quad \exists c_1 : \mathsf{Comp}\ \exists c_2 : \mathsf{Comp} \\
\quad\; (\bigvee_n (\mathrm{Prefix}_n(c, c_1) \land \mathrm{Suffix}_n(c, c_2)) \land [\![\varphi_1]\!]^C_{c_1,k,tt} \land [\![\varphi_2]\!]^C_{c_2,0,tt}) \lor \\
\quad \bigwedge_n (\mathsf{st}_n(c)\downarrow) \land [\![\varphi_1]\!]^C_{c,k,tt} \leftrightarrow \\
\quad y = tt,
\end{array}
$$

where

c_1, c_2 are fresh computation symbols.

Next temporal formula

The evaluation of the next temporal formula $\bigcirc\, \varphi$ yields:

- true, if there is a next point in the computation and evaluation of the temporal formula φ yields true at that point;
- false, otherwise.

So the evaluation of $\bigcirc\, \varphi$ always yields one of the truth values, even when evaluation of φ can yield no value at the next point.

Structure:

$\bigcirc\, \varphi$

Well-formedness in N:

φ is well-formed in N.

Meaning:

$$[\![\bigcirc\, \varphi]\!]^C_{c,k,y} \ := \ \mathsf{st}_{k+1}(c)\!\downarrow \wedge\ [\![\varphi]\!]^C_{c,k+1,tt} \leftrightarrow y = tt.$$

Until temporal formula

The evaluation of the until temporal formula $\varphi_1 \,\mathcal{U}\, \varphi_2$ yields:

- true, if evaluation of the temporal formula φ_2 yields true at the current or some future point in the computation and evaluation of the temporal formula φ_1 yields true at all points until that one;
- false, otherwise.

So the evaluation of $\varphi_1 \,\mathcal{U}\, \varphi_2$ always yields one of the truth values, even when evaluation of φ_2 can yield no value at the current and any future point.

Structure:

$\varphi_1 \,\mathcal{U}\, \varphi_2$

Well-formedness in N:

φ_1, φ_2 are well-formed in N.

Meaning:

$$[\![\varphi_1 \,\mathcal{U}\, \varphi_2]\!]^C_{c,k,y} \ :=$$

$$\bigvee\nolimits_n (\mathsf{st}_{k+n}(c)\!\downarrow \wedge\ [\![\varphi_2]\!]^C_{c,k+n,tt} \wedge \bigwedge_{m=0}^{n-1} ([\![\varphi_1]\!]^C_{c,k+m,tt})) \leftrightarrow y = tt.$$

Previous temporal formula

The evaluation of the previous temporal formula $\ominus\,\varphi$ yields:

- true, if there is a previous point in the computation and evaluation of the temporal formula φ yields true at that point;
- false otherwise.

So the evaluation of $\ominus\,\varphi$ always yields one of the truth values, even when evaluation of φ can yield no value at the previous point.

Structure:

$\ominus\,\varphi$

Well-formedness in N:

φ is well-formed in N.

Meaning:

$$\begin{array}{lll} [\![\ominus\,\varphi]\!]^{C}_{c,k,y} & := & [\![\varphi]\!]^{C}_{c,k\text{-}1,tt} \leftrightarrow y = tt \quad \text{if } k > 0 \\ & & y = f\!f \qquad\qquad\qquad\; \text{otherwise.} \end{array}$$

Since temporal formula

The evaluation of the since temporal formula $\varphi_1\ \mathcal{S}\ \varphi_2$ yields:

- true, if evaluation of the temporal formula φ_2 yields true at the current or some past point in the computation and evaluation of the temporal formula φ_1 yields true at all points since that one;
- false otherwise.

So the evaluation of $\varphi_1\ \mathcal{S}\ \varphi_2$ always yields one of the truth values, even when evaluation of φ_2 can yield no value at the current and any past point.

Structure:

$\varphi_1\ \mathcal{S}\ \varphi_2$

Well-formedness in N:

φ_1, φ_2 are well-formed in N.

Meaning:

$$[\![\varphi_1\ \mathcal{S}\ \varphi_2]\!]^{C}_{c,k,y} \;:=\; \bigvee_{l=0}^{k} ([\![\varphi_2]\!]^{C}_{c,k-l,tt} \wedge \bigwedge_{m=0}^{l-1} ([\![\varphi_1]\!]^{C}_{c,k-m,tt})) \leftrightarrow y = tt.$$

Negation temporal formula

The evaluation of the negation temporal formula $\neg\,\varphi$ yields:

- true, if evaluation of the temporal formula φ yields false;

- false, if evaluation of the temporal formula φ yields true;
- no value, otherwise.

Structure:

$\neg\,\varphi$

Well-formedness in N:

φ is well-formed in N.

Meaning:

$$[\![\neg\,\varphi]\!]^{C}_{c,k,y} := ([\![\varphi]\!]^{C}_{c,k,tt} \wedge y = f\!f) \vee ([\![\varphi]\!]^{C}_{c,k,f\!f} \wedge y = tt).$$

Disjunction temporal formula

The evaluation of the disjunction temporal formula $\varphi_1 \vee \varphi_2$ yields:

- true, if evaluation of the temporal formula φ_1 yields true or evaluation of the temporal formula φ_2 yields true;
- false, if evaluation of the temporal formula φ_1 yields false and evaluation of the temporal formula φ_2 yields false;
- no value, otherwise.

Structure:

$\varphi_1 \vee \varphi_2$

Well-formedness in N:

φ_1, φ_2 are well-formed in N.

Meaning:

$$\begin{aligned}&[\![\varphi_1 \vee \varphi_2]\!]^{C}_{c,k,y} := \\ &\qquad (([\![\varphi_1]\!]^{C}_{c,k,tt} \vee [\![\varphi_2]\!]^{C}_{c,k,tt}) \wedge y = tt) \vee \\ &\qquad (([\![\varphi_1]\!]^{C}_{c,k,f\!f} \wedge [\![\varphi_2]\!]^{C}_{c,k,f\!f}) \wedge y = f\!f).\end{aligned}$$

Exists temporal formula

The evaluation of the exists temporal formula $\exists\, x \in t \,\cdot\, \varphi$ yields:

- true, if evaluation of the temporal formula φ yields true under some assignment of a value to the value name x;
- false, if evaluation of the temporal formula φ yields false under each assignment of a value to the value name x;
- no value, otherwise.

Structure:

$\exists\, x \in t \,\cdot\, \varphi$

Well-formedness in N:

x is not defined as a value or state variable name in N,

t is defined as a type name in N,

φ is well-formed in $N \cup \{[\mathsf{val}\ \ x\colon t]\}$.

Meaning:

$$[\![\exists\, x \in t \,\cdot\, \varphi]\!]^{C}_{c,k,y} :=$$
$$(\exists x'\colon t^{C}([\![\varphi]\!]^{C\cup\{x'\}}_{c,k,tt}) \wedge y = tt) \vee (\forall x'\colon t^{C}([\![\varphi]\!]^{C\cup\{x'\}}_{c,k,ff}) \wedge y = ff),$$

where

x' is a fresh value symbols such that $\iota(x') = x$ and $\tau(x') = \langle \mathsf{obj}, t^{C}\rangle$.

Local definition temporal formula

The evaluation of the local definition temporal formula $\mathsf{let}\ x\colon t \triangleq \tau\ \mathsf{in}\ \varphi$ yields the truth value that is yielded by evaluation of the temporal formula φ when value name x is assigned a value that can be yielded by evaluation of the temporal term τ.

Structure:

$\mathsf{let}\ x\colon t \triangleq \tau\ \mathsf{in}\ \varphi$

Well-formedness in N:

x is not defined as a value or state variable name in N,

t is defined as a type name in N,

τ is well-formed in N and φ is well-formed in $N \cup \{[\mathsf{val}\ \ x\colon t]\}$,

the minimal type of τ in N is a subtype of t.

Meaning:

$$[\![\mathsf{let}\ x\colon t \triangleq \tau\ \mathsf{in}\ \varphi]\!]^{C}_{c,k,y} := \exists x'\colon t^{C}([\![\tau]\!]^{C}_{c,k,x'} \wedge [\![\varphi]\!]^{C\cup\{x'\}}_{c,k,y}),$$

where

x' is a fresh value symbol such that $\iota(x') = x$ and $\tau(x') = \langle \mathsf{obj}, t^{C}\rangle$.

Application temporal term

The evaluation of the application temporal term $f(\tau_1, \ldots, \tau_n)$ can yield any value that is the value of the function denoted by f for arguments $x_1, \ldots, x_n$ which are values that can be yielded by evaluation of the temporal terms $\tau_1, \ldots, \tau_n$, respectively. Generally, the function denoted by f depends on the types of the argument expressions.

Structure:

$f(\tau_1, \ldots, \tau_n)$

Well-formedness in N:

f is defined as a function name in N,

$\tau_1, \ldots, \tau_n$ are well-formed in N,
$f(\tau_1, \ldots, \tau_n)$ is well-typed in N.

Typing:

$$\frac{N \vdash_{\mathrm{m}} \tau_1 \mathbin{\raisebox{0pt}{$\circ\!\!\circ$}} T_1, \ldots, N \vdash_{\mathrm{m}} \tau_n \mathbin{\circ\!\circ} T_n}{N \vdash_{\mathrm{m}} f(\tau_1, \ldots, \tau_n) \mathbin{\circ\!\circ} T} \text{ if } \mathit{mtyping}^N(f, \langle T_1, \ldots, T_n \rangle, T).$$

Meaning:

Let $\overline{C} \vdash_{\mathrm{m}} \tau_1 \mathbin{\circ\!\circ} T_1, \ldots, \overline{C} \vdash_{\mathrm{m}} \tau_n \mathbin{\circ\!\circ} T_n$,
$\mathit{ftypes}^{\overline{C}}(f, \langle T_1, \ldots, T_n \rangle, \langle T_1', \ldots, T_n' \rangle)$,
$[\mathsf{func}\ f \colon T_1' \times \cdots \times T_n' \to T'] \in \overline{C}, \mathit{sort}(y) = S$, then:

$$[\![f(\tau_1, \ldots, \tau_n)]\!]^C_{c,k,y} :=$$
$$\exists x_1 \colon T_1'^C, \ldots, x_n \colon T_n'^C$$
$$(\bigwedge_{i=1}^{n} ([\![\tau_i]\!]^C_{c,k,x_i}) \wedge \mathit{cnv}^C_{T'^C \to S}(f^C_{T_1' \times \cdots \times T_n' \to T'}(x_1, \ldots, x_n)) = y),$$

where

$x_1, \ldots, x_n$ are fresh value symbols such that for all $i = 1, \ldots, n$:
$\tau(x_i) = \langle \mathsf{obj}, T_i'^C \rangle$,
y' is a fresh value symbol such that $\tau(y') = \langle \mathsf{obj}, \underline{\mathrm{B}} \rangle$.

Next temporal term

The evaluation of the next temporal term $\bigcirc\, \tau$ can yield any value that can be yielded by evaluation of the temporal term τ at the next point in the computation. In case there is no next point, evaluation can yield no value.

Structure:

$\bigcirc \tau$

Well-formedness in N:

τ is well-formed in N.

Typing:

$$\frac{N \vdash_{\mathrm{m}} \tau \mathbin{\circ\!\circ} T}{N \vdash_{\mathrm{m}} \bigcirc \tau \mathbin{\circ\!\circ} T}.$$

Meaning:

$$[\![\bigcirc\, \tau]\!]^C_{c,k,y} := \mathsf{st}_{k+1}(c){\downarrow} \wedge [\![\tau]\!]^C_{c,k+1,y}.$$

Previous temporal term

The evaluation of the previous temporal term $\ominus\, \tau$ can yield any value that can be yielded by evaluation of the temporal term τ at the previous point in the computation. In case there is no previous point, evaluation can yield no value.

Structure:

$\ominus\tau$

Well-formedness in N:

τ is well-formed in N.

Typing:

$$\frac{N \models_{\mathrm{m}} \tau \mathbin{⦂} T}{N \models_{\mathrm{m}} \ominus\tau \mathbin{⦂} T}.$$

Meaning:

$$[\![\ominus\, \tau]\!]^{C}_{c,k,y} \;:=\; \begin{array}{ll} [\![\tau]\!]^{C}_{c,k\text{-}1,y} & \text{if } k > 0 \\ \bot & \text{otherwise.} \end{array}$$

Current temporal term

The evaluation of the value temporal term e can yield any value that can be yielded by evaluation of the expression e in the state at the current point in the computation.

Structure:

e

Well-formedness in N:

e is well-formed in $\langle N, 1\rangle$.

Typing:

$$\frac{N \models_{\mathrm{m}} e \mathbin{⦂} T}{N \models_{\mathrm{m}} e \mathbin{⦂} T}.$$

Meaning:

$$[\![e]\!]^{C}_{c,k,y} \;:=\; \exists s\colon \mathsf{State}(\mathsf{st}_k(c) = s \wedge [\![e]\!]^{C}_{\langle s\rangle,y}).$$

6

Foundations of the Structuring Language

In Chapter 5, the logic MPL_ω was used as the basis for a semantics of flat VVSL. DA (Description Algebra) and $\lambda\pi$-calculus are used in Chapter 8 as the basis for a semantics of the structuring sublanguage of VVSL. The aim of this chapter is to introduce DA and $\lambda\pi$-calculus. DA is a general algebraic model of modular specification (based on MPL_ω). It has some features which are not commonly found in models proposed for modular algebraic specification. These special features make it suitable as the underlying model for modular state-based specifications. $\lambda\pi$-calculus is a variant of classical lambda calculus with parameter restrictions and a conditional β-rule. DA and $\lambda\pi$-calculus were first presented by Jonkers (1989a) and Feijs (1989), respectively.

The first section gives an overview of DA, discusses its suitability as a semantic basis for the modularization constructs of VVSL and glances at the way in which it treats name clashes. In subsequent sections, the algebra DA is defined, algebraic laws that hold for DA are presented and an abstract meaning of descriptions (the objects of interest in DA) is defined. This presentation of DA is the result of a substantial rewrite of the one in (Jonkers, 1989a). Properties, that are relevant to the use of DA for an interpretation of VVSL, are also presented. For the proofs, the reader is referred to (Jonkers, 1989a).

Thereafter, DA extended with parameters (a kind of dummy description), an implementation relation for descriptions and renaming of renamings are presented. All this is relevant to the case where descriptions may be parametrized. DA extended with parameters was treated as part of DA in the preliminary version of DA presented in (Feijs, Jonkers, Koymans and Renardel de Lavalette, 1987).

The next section gives an overview of $\lambda\pi$-calculus and discusses its suitability as a semantic basis for the parametrization constructs of VVSL. In subsequent sections, $\lambda\pi$-calculus is defined, a model of $\lambda\pi$-calculus is presented, and reduction for $\lambda\pi$-calculus is formulated. This presentation of

$\lambda\pi$-calculus is for the greater part the result of a major rewrite of the one in (Feijs, 1989). It streamlines and expands the treatment there. Properties, that are relevant to the use of $\lambda\pi$-calculus for an interpretation of VVSL, are also presented. For the proofs, the reader is referred to (Feijs, 1989).

6.1 Introduction to DA

This section gives an idea of what DA is and connects this with its role in a semantics of VVSL. Subsequent sections go into details of DA. How DA and more abstract models of modular specifications are related, is analysed in Section 9.1 by means of an extension of DA which has additional abstraction operations on descriptions. In one of those models, specification modules correspond essentially to MPL_ω theories. However, theories are presented as special kinds of descriptions, called abstract descriptions, to ease the analysis of the connections.

Overview of DA

In DA, the objects of interest are *descriptions*. A description consists of an externally visible signature, an internal signature, a set of formulae and an *origin partition*. It is essentially a presentation of a logical theory extended with an encapsulating signature and a component for dealing with name clashes in the composition of descriptions. MPL_ω, the logic that was introduced in Chapter 3, is used as the underlying logic of DA. As an abstract meaning, an MPL_ω theory can be attached to each description. Descriptions can be adapted and combined by means of operations for *renaming*, *importing*, *exporting* and *unifying*. The basic modularization concepts of decomposition and information hiding are supported by importing and exporting, respectively. Renaming provides for control of name clashes in the composition of modules. Unifying is a special operation for dealing with name clashes.

Suitability of DA

VVSL is a language for model-oriented, state-based specification. Effective separation of concerns often motivates the hiding of state variables from a module. For the adequacy of the modularization mechanism provided by VVSL for the modular structuring of specifications of many existing software systems (where a suitable modular structuring of the specification concerned requires that the same state variables are accessed by operations from several modules), it is indispensable that it permits two or more modules to have hidden state variables in common. This requires a model of specification modules which is more concrete than most models proposed for modular property-oriented, algebraic specifications, such as the ones presented in (Bergstra, Heering and Klint, 1990; Sannella and Tarlecki, 1985; Wirsing and Broy, 1989). Appropriately concrete models, e.g. the model presented in (Bergstra, 1986) and the presentation model from (Wirsing, 1986), usually treat name clashes in a way which still inhibits modules from having hidden state variables in common. DA makes it possible for modules to have hidden state variables in common. This is largely due to the way in which it treats name clashes. Nevertheless, many algebraic laws holding in the more generally accepted models also hold for DA. These laws include most laws of Module Algebra (Bergstra, Heering and Klint, 1990).

Connections with MA

DA is an algebra that is meant to be a model of modular specification suitable for state-based specifications. Module Algebra (MA) is an axiom system with algebraic axioms that hold in most models of modular specification proposed for algebraic specifications.

The operations on descriptions that have a counterpart in MA are: taking the visible signature, renaming, importing and exporting. The operation of MA for converting a signature to a module without axioms (**T**) has no counterpart in DA. Its addition to DA would be a minor enrichment. Unifying has no counterpart in MA. Its addition to MA would be a major extension.

Most axioms of MA concerning the common operations hold for DA (see Section 6.4). The axiom (E4) of MA, which postulates restricted distribution of exporting over importing, holds even unconditionally for DA. Only the axioms (R5) and (R6) of MA, which express that renamings are supposed to be of a special kind, do not hold for DA.

Name clashes in the composition of descriptions

A description can be viewed as a description of a system component which consists of named parts – modelled by sorts, functions and predicates. The presence of the name of a part in the encapsulating signature of the description indicates that the part concerned is an external part of the system component.

If the names given to parts are used to refer to them in descriptions, then there is a problem with *name clashes* in the composition of descriptions by means of importing, since there is no way to tell whether parts denoted by the same name are intended to be identical. Any solution to this problem has to make some assumptions. Commonly it is assumed that external parts denoted by the same name are identical and internal parts are never identical. By these assumptions visible names (i.e. names of external parts) are allowed to clash, while clashes of hidden names (i.e. names of internal parts) with other names are avoided by automatic renamings. As far as hidden names are concerned, this solution seems the only one which is consistent with the intention of encapsulation. However, it creates a new problem. In state-based specification, we are dealing with a state space where certain names denote variable parts of that state space. These state variables (as they are called in VVSL) should not be duplicated by automatic renamings. Duplication would make it impossible for two descriptions (and hence modules) to have hidden state variables in common.

The root of the above-mentioned problems is that the information of the identity of the definition that introduces a name has been lost where the name is used. Therefore the solution is to endow each name with an *origin* representing the identity of the definition that introduces the name. The use of combinations of a name and an origin rather than names as symbols of MPL_ω in descriptions solves the problem with name clashes in the composition of descriptions. In general, origins of names cannot simply be viewed as pointers to their definitions. This is mainly due to parametrization. Origin constants, origin variables, which can later be instantiated with fixed origins, and compound origins are needed. If, within a description, the origins of visible symbols with the same name can be unified (simultaneously for all such collections of origins), then the description is called *origin consistent.* For an origin consistent description, abstraction from the origins associated with the visible names is possible.

Note that the requirement of origin consistency does not take hidden names into account. Since the hidden names of a description may not be used outside that description, there exists no identification problem for hidden names. However, by endowing each hidden name with an appropriate origin, undesirable automatic renamings are no longer necessary and descriptions may have hidden state variables in common.

The next four sections describe DA precisely. The first of these sections introduces the notion of origin and describes the kind of symbols used in descriptions.

6.2 Symbols and origins

A description is essentially a presentation of an MPL_ω theory extended with an encapsulating signature and a component for dealing with name clashes in the composition of descriptions. In the definition of MPL_ω, only a few assumptions about symbols were made. The kind of symbols which are used in descriptions are presented below. As explained above, the symbols concerned contain origins.

We assume three disjoint countably infinite sets OCon, OVar and Ident of *origin constants*, *origin variables* and *identifiers*, respectively.

Origins

Name clashes may occur in the composition of modules. In order to solve this name clash problem in a satisfactory way, the origin of each occurrence of a name should be available.

Definition. The set Orig of *origins* is inductively defined by

$$\begin{aligned} c \in \mathsf{OCon} &\Rightarrow c \in \mathsf{Orig}, \\ x \in \mathsf{OVar} &\Rightarrow x \in \mathsf{Orig}, \\ a_1, \ldots, a_n \in \mathsf{Orig} &\Rightarrow \langle a_1, \ldots, a_n \rangle \in \mathsf{Orig}. \end{aligned}$$

A partition of Orig divides the set of all origins into disjoint non-empty sets of origins. This is used to indicate which origins are considered equal, i.e. must be unifiable.

Definition. OPar, the set of all *origin partitions*, is defined by

$$\mathsf{OPar} := \{\pi \mid \pi \text{ is a partition of } \mathsf{Orig}\}.$$

For $\pi_1, \pi_2 \in \mathsf{OPar}$, $\pi_1 \leq \pi_2$, π_1 is a *refinement* of π_2, is defined by

$$\pi_1 \leq \pi_2 \;:\Leftrightarrow\; \forall A_1 \in \pi_1 \, (\exists A_2 \in \pi_2 \, (A_1 \subseteq A_2)).$$

$\langle \mathsf{OPar}, \leq \rangle$ is a complete lattice. We write $\pi_\bot$ for the bottom of this lattice.

Definition. For $P \subseteq \mathsf{OPar}$, $\sum P$, the *sum* of the elements of P, and $\prod P$, the *product* of the elements of P, are defined by

$$\begin{aligned} \textstyle\sum P &:= \text{ the least upper bound of } P \text{ with respect to } \leq, \\ \textstyle\prod P &:= \text{ the greatest lower bound of } P \text{ with respect to } \leq. \end{aligned}$$

We write $\pi_1 + \pi_2$, where $\pi_1, \pi_2 \in \mathsf{OPar}$, for $\sum\{\pi_1, \pi_2\}$.

$\sum$ and $\prod$ are needed to define the importing operation of DA and the unifying operation of DA, respectively.

Symbols

Symbols are built from identifiers, origins and symbol types. The types of symbols are in turn built from indicators for the different kinds of types (sort, obj, func and pred) and sort symbols.

Definition. The sets Sort of *sort symbols*, Obj of *object symbols*, Func of *function symbols* and Pred of *predicate symbols* are defined by

$$\begin{aligned} \mathsf{Sort} &:= \{\langle i, a, \mathsf{sort}\rangle \mid i \in \mathsf{Ident}, a \in \mathsf{Orig}\}, \\ \mathsf{Obj} &:= \{\langle i, a, \langle \mathsf{obj}, S\rangle\rangle \mid i \in \mathsf{Ident}, a \in \mathsf{Orig}, S \in \mathsf{Sort}\}, \\ \mathsf{Func} &:= \{\, \langle i, a, \langle \mathsf{func}, S_1, \ldots, S_{n+1}\rangle\rangle \mid \\ &\qquad i \in \mathsf{Ident}, a \in \mathsf{Orig}, S_1, \ldots, S_{n+1} \in \mathsf{Sort}\}, \\ \mathsf{Pred} &:= \{\, \langle i, a, \langle \mathsf{pred}, S_1, \ldots, S_n\rangle\rangle \mid \\ &\qquad i \in \mathsf{Ident}, a \in \mathsf{Orig}, S_1, \ldots, S_n \in \mathsf{Sort}\}. \end{aligned}$$

Object symbols serve as variable symbols in MPL_ω.

Definition. The set SType of *symbol types* is inductively defined by

$$\begin{aligned}
&\mathsf{sort} \in \mathsf{SType},\\
&S \in \mathsf{Sort} \Rightarrow \langle \mathsf{obj}, S\rangle \in \mathsf{SType},\\
&S_1, \ldots, S_{n+1} \in \mathsf{Sort} \Rightarrow \langle \mathsf{func}, S_1, \ldots, S_{n+1}\rangle \in \mathsf{SType},\\
&S_1, \ldots, S_n \in \mathsf{Sort} \Rightarrow \langle \mathsf{pred}, S_1, \ldots, S_n\rangle \in \mathsf{SType}.
\end{aligned}$$

We write $t(S_1, \ldots, S_n)$ to indicate that t is a symbol type in which the sort symbols $S_1, \ldots, S_n$ occur (in that order).

Definition. The set Sym of *symbols* is defined by

$$\mathsf{Sym} := \{\langle i, a, t\rangle \mid i \in \mathsf{Ident}, a \in \mathsf{Orig}, t \in \mathsf{SType}\}.$$

We write $\iota(w)$, $\omega(w)$ and $\tau(w)$, where $w = \langle i, a, t\rangle$ is a symbol, for i, a and t, respectively.

Note that $\mathsf{Sym} = \mathsf{Sort} \cup \mathsf{Obj} \cup \mathsf{Func} \cup \mathsf{Pred}$. Symbols from Sym are interpreted as symbols in MPL_ω according to the following rules:

- each $S = \langle i, a, \mathsf{sort}\rangle$ is a sort symbol in MPL_ω,
- each $x = \langle i, a, \langle \mathsf{obj}, S\rangle\rangle$ is a variable symbol of sort S in MPL_ω,
- each $f = \langle i, a, \langle \mathsf{func}, S_1, \ldots, S_{n+1}\rangle\rangle$ is a function symbol $f\colon S_1 \times \cdots \times S_n \to S_{n+1}$ in MPL_ω,
- each $P = \langle i, a, \langle \mathsf{pred}, S_1, \ldots, S_n\rangle\rangle$ is a predicate symbol $P\colon S_1 \times \cdots \times S_n$ in MPL_ω.

If Sort, Func and Pred are used as sets of sort symbols, function symbols and predicate symbols, respectively, signatures are defined as follows.

Definition. A *symbol signature* Σ is a subset of $\mathsf{Sort} \cup \mathsf{Func} \cup \mathsf{Pred}$ such that

$$\forall w \in \Sigma\, (w = \langle i, a, t(S_1, \ldots, S_n)\rangle \Rightarrow S_1, \ldots, S_n \in \Sigma).$$

SSig, the set of all symbol signatures, is defined by

$$\mathsf{SSig} := \{\Sigma \mid \Sigma \text{ is a symbol signature }\}.$$

If symbol signatures are used as signatures, the language of a given signature is defined as follows.

Definition. For $\Sigma \in \mathsf{SSig}$, $\mathcal{L}(\Sigma)$, the *language* of Σ, is the set of MPL_ω formulae defined by

$$\mathcal{L}(\Sigma) := \{\varphi \mid \varphi \text{ is a formula of } \mathrm{MPL}_\omega(\Sigma)\}.$$

For a set of formulae Φ from the language of Σ, the theory presented by Φ consists of all formulae that Φ entails according to the proof system of $\mathrm{MPL}_\omega(\Sigma)$.

Definition. For $\Sigma \in \mathsf{SSig}$ and a set of formulae $\Phi \subseteq \mathcal{L}(\Sigma)$, $Th(\Sigma, \Phi)$, the *theory* of Φ, is the set of MPL_ω formulae defined by

$$Th(\Sigma, \Phi) := \{\varphi \in \mathcal{L}(\Sigma) \mid \Phi \vdash \varphi\}.$$

The notion of symbol defined above as well as the related notions defined in this section are basic to DA. The domains and operations of DA presented in the next section require understanding of these notions.

6.3 Domains and operations of DA

DA has four domains: a domain of names, a domain of renamings, a domain of signatures and a domain of descriptions. These domains and the operations of DA on them are introduced in this section.

Names

Symbols are considered to have the same name if they are the same except for the origins occurring in them. This means roughly that, for function and predicate symbols, their type is considered to be a part of the name. Symbols with the same name are called name equivalent.

Definition. The *name equivalence* relation $\equiv$ on Sym is inductively defined by

$$S_1 \equiv S_1', \ldots, S_n \equiv S_n' \;\Rightarrow\; \langle i, a, t(S_1, \ldots, S_n)\rangle \equiv \langle i, a', t(S_1', \ldots, S_n')\rangle.$$

A *name* is an equivalence class of the name equivalence relation $\equiv$ on Sym. We write $\overline{w}$, where $w \in \mathsf{Sym}$, for the name with representative w. We write $\overline{W}$, where $W \subseteq \mathsf{Sym}$, for the set of names $\{\overline{w} \mid w \in W\}$.

The names of DA are very similar to the typed names of VVSL. All representatives of a name are symbols with the same identifier and the same kind of type. Their types need not be the same, but the corresponding sort symbols in their types are representatives of the same name. The set of all names is one of the domains of DA.

Definition. Nam, the set of all sort, function and predicate names, is defined by

$$\mathsf{Nam} := \{\overline{w} \mid w \in \mathsf{Sort} \cup \mathsf{Func} \cup \mathsf{Pred}\}.$$

For a set of symbols W, there is a corresponding origin partition indicating that the origins of symbols in W with the same name are considered equal.

Definition. For a set of symbols W, $\pi_\omega(W)$, the *origin partition* of W, is defined by

$$\begin{array}{l}\pi_\omega(W) := \\ \quad \prod\{\pi \in \mathsf{OPar} \mid \\ \qquad \forall w_1, w_2 \in W\,(\overline{w_1} = \overline{w_2} \;\Rightarrow\; \exists A \in \pi\,(\omega(w_1) \in A, \omega(w_2) \in A))\}.\end{array}$$

So π_ω is the most refined origin partition such that symbols with the same name are in the same element of the partition. It is used to define the unifying operation on descriptions.

Next, renamings and related operations are introduced. This includes an operation for the renaming of names. Thereafter, signatures and related operations are introduced. This includes an operation for deleting names from signatures.

Renamings

A renaming is a total mapping from symbols to symbols that maps symbols with the same name to symbols with the same name, leaves the origins of symbols unaffected and changes the types of symbols consistently.

Definition. A *renaming* is a mapping $\rho\colon \mathsf{Sym} \to \mathsf{Sym}$ such that

$$\begin{aligned}
&w \equiv w' \;\Rightarrow\; \rho(w) \equiv \rho(w'),\\
&\omega(\rho(w)) = \omega(w),\\
&\tau(w) = t(S_1, \ldots, S_n) \;\Rightarrow\; \tau(\rho(w)) = t(\rho(S_1), \ldots, \rho(S_n)).
\end{aligned}$$

The set of all renamings is another domain of DA.

Definition. Ren, the set of all renamings, is defined by

$$\mathsf{Ren} := \{\rho\colon \mathsf{Sym} \to \mathsf{Sym} \mid \rho \text{ is a renaming }\}.$$

It is assumed that renamings are extended to MPL_ω formulae in the usual homomorphic way. Renaming of a MPL_ω formula may involve renaming of variable symbols (not necessarily bound) occurring in the formula. However, in DA a renaming can only be applied (by means of renaming operations) such that renamed variable symbols are only affected in the usual way, viz. their sorts are changed according to the renaming. So renaming does not really lead to a kind of α-conversion.

The set of all names of symbols that are changed by a renaming is considered to be the domain of the renaming. The range of a renaming is viewed likewise.

Definition. For a renaming ρ, $dom(\rho)$ and $rng(\rho)$, the *domain* and *range* of ρ, are defined by

$$\begin{aligned}
dom(\rho) &:= \overline{\{w \in \mathsf{Sym} \mid \rho(w) \neq w\}},\\
rng(\rho) &:= \overline{\{\rho(w) \in \mathsf{Sym} \mid \rho(w) \neq w\}}.
\end{aligned}$$

Injectivity of renamings is defined with respect to a given set of names.

Definition. For a renaming ρ and a set of names N, $inj(\rho, N)$, ρ is *injective* on N, is defined by

$$\begin{aligned}
&inj(\rho, N) \;:\Leftrightarrow\\
&\quad \forall w_1, w_2 \in \mathsf{Sym}\,(\overline{w_1}, \overline{w_2} \in N \Rightarrow (\rho(w_1) = \rho(w_2) \;\Rightarrow\; w_1 = w_2)).
\end{aligned}$$

We write $inj(\rho, W)$, where $\rho \in \mathsf{Ren}$ and $W \subseteq \mathsf{Sym}$, instead of $inj(\rho, \overline{W})$.

The operations of DA include a renaming operation on names. Renaming on names amounts to application of a renaming to a representative of a name. It follows immediately from the definition of renamings that the particular choice of representative is irrelevant.

Definition. The *renaming* operation $\bullet\colon \mathsf{Ren} \times \mathsf{Nam} \to \mathsf{Nam}$ on names is defined by

$$\rho \bullet \overline{w} \ := \ \overline{\rho(w)} \quad (\overline{w} \in \mathsf{Nam}).$$

The operations of DA also include a composition operation on renamings. It is the usual functional composition.

Definition. The *composition* operation $\circ\colon \mathsf{Ren} \times \mathsf{Ren} \to \mathsf{Ren}$ on renamings is defined by

$$(\rho_1 \circ \rho_2)(w) \ := \ \rho_1(\rho_2(w)).$$

Neither operation is used for providing the modularization constructs of VVSL with a semantics. They are not left out because they may be needed for the modularization constructs of other specification languages. The exclusion of such operations in this chapter could be mistaken for a lack of generality.

Next, signatures and related operations are introduced. This includes an operation for the renaming of signatures. Thereafter, descriptions and related operations are introduced. This includes an operation for the renaming of descriptions.

Signatures

Name signatures result from forgetting about the origins in symbol signatures. The set of all name signatures is still another domain of DA.

Definition. Sig, the set of all *name signatures*, is defined by

$$\mathsf{Sig} \ := \ \{\overline{\Sigma} \mid \Sigma \in \mathsf{SSig}\}.$$

The operations of DA include four operations on name signatures: renaming, union, intersection and deletion. Renaming on name signatures amounts to application of a renaming to representatives of the names in a name signature.

Definition. The *renaming* operation $\bullet\colon \mathsf{Ren} \times \mathsf{Sig} \to \mathsf{Sig}$ on name signatures is defined by

$$\rho \bullet \overline{\Sigma} \ := \ \overline{\rho(\Sigma)} \quad (\overline{\Sigma} \in \mathsf{Sig}).$$

Union and intersection of signatures is just set union and set intersection.

Definition. The *union* operation $+\colon \mathsf{Sig} \times \mathsf{Sig} \to \mathsf{Sig}$ and the *intersection* operation $\Box\colon \mathsf{Sig} \times \mathsf{Sig} \to \mathsf{Sig}$ on name signatures are defined by

$$\Sigma_1 + \Sigma_2 \ := \ \Sigma_1 \cup \Sigma_2,$$

$$\Sigma_1 \Box \Sigma_2 \ := \ \Sigma_1 \cap \Sigma_2.$$

Deletion of names from signatures is not just a simple case of set difference.

Definition. The *deletion* operation Δ: $\mathsf{Nam} \times \mathsf{Sig} \to \mathsf{Sig}$ on name signatures is defined by

$$u \,\Delta\, \Sigma \;:=\; \bigcup\{\Sigma' \in \mathsf{Sig} \mid \Sigma' \subseteq \Sigma \wedge u \notin \Sigma'\}.$$

The deletion operation is not used for providing the modularization constructs of VVSL with a semantics.

Next descriptions and related operations are introduced. This includes operations for taking the signature of descriptions and for restricting the signature of descriptions.

Descriptions

A description can be viewed as a presentation of an MPL_ω theory, together with an encapsulating signature for supporting the concept of information hiding and an origin partition indicating which origins of the symbols used in the description are considered equal. The set of all descriptions is the primary domain of DA.

Definition. Des, the set of all *descriptions*, is defined by

$$\begin{array}{l}\mathsf{Des} \;:= \\ \quad \{\langle \Sigma, \Gamma, \Phi, \pi\rangle \mid \Sigma \in \mathsf{SSig}, \Gamma \in \mathsf{SSig}, \Sigma \subseteq \Gamma, \Phi \subseteq \mathcal{L}(\Gamma), \pi \in \mathsf{OPar}\}.\end{array}$$

We write Σ_X, Γ_X, Φ_X and π_X, where $X = \langle \Sigma, \Gamma, \Phi, \pi\rangle$ is a description, for Σ ,Γ, Φ and π, respectively.

The operations of DA include six operations on descriptions: taking the signature, renaming, importing, exporting, unifying and an auxiliary operation 'π'. Taking the signature of a description yields the name signature that consists precisely of the visible names of the description.

Definition. The *signature* operation $\mathbf{\Sigma}$: $\mathsf{Des} \to \mathsf{Sig}$ on descriptions is defined by

$$\mathbf{\Sigma}(X) \;:=\; \overline{\Sigma_X}.$$

The names of symbols in a description can be changed by applying a renaming to the description.

Definition. The *renaming* operation $\bullet$: $\mathsf{Ren} \times \mathsf{Des} \to \mathsf{Des}$ on descriptions is defined by

$$\rho \bullet X \;:=\; \langle \rho(\Sigma_X), \rho(\Gamma_X), \rho(\Phi_X), \pi_X\rangle.$$

Two descriptions can be combined into a new one by means of importing.

Definition. The *importing* operation $+$: $\mathsf{Des} \times \mathsf{Des} \to \mathsf{Des}$ on descriptions is defined by

$$X_1 + X_2 \;:=\; \langle \Sigma_{X_1} \cup \Sigma_{X_2}, \Gamma_{X_1} \cup \Gamma_{X_2}, \Phi_{X_1} \cup \Phi_{X_2}, \pi_{X_1} + \pi_{X_2}\rangle.$$

The visible signature of a description can be restricted by means of exporting.

Definition. The *exporting* operation $\Box\colon \mathsf{Sig} \times \mathsf{Des} \to \mathsf{Des}$ on descriptions is defined by

$$\Sigma \Box X \ := \ \langle \{w \in \Sigma_X \mid \overline{w} \in \Sigma\}, \Gamma_X, \Phi_X, \pi_X \rangle.$$

Unifying enforces the origins of symbols in the externally visible signature of a description with the same name to be considered equal.

Definition. The *unifying* operation $\mu\colon \mathsf{Des} \to \mathsf{Des}$ on descriptions is defined by

$$\mu(X) \ := \ \langle \Sigma_X, \Gamma_X, \Phi_X, \pi_X + \pi_\omega(\Sigma_X) \rangle.$$

The unifying operation is not used for providing the modularization constructs of VVSL with a semantics. However, it plays an important part in attaching, as an abstract meaning, an MPL_ω theory to each description. The following operation is an auxiliary operation. It throws away everything but the origin partition of a description. This operation is mainly used in formulating algebraic laws relating renaming and exporting to unifying.

Definition. The operation $\pi\colon \mathsf{Des} \to \mathsf{Des}$ on descriptions is defined by

$$\pi(X) \ := \ \langle \{\}, \{\}, \{\}, \pi_X \rangle.$$

Refinement ($\leq$) on origin partitions can be extended to descriptions in a natural way.

Definition. For $X_1, X_2 \in \mathsf{Des}$, $X_1 \leq X_2$, is defined by

$$X_1 \leq X_2 \ :\Leftrightarrow \ \Sigma_{X_1} \subseteq \Sigma_{X_2} \wedge \Gamma_{X_1} \subseteq \Gamma_{X_2} \wedge \Phi_{X_1} \subseteq \Phi_{X_2} \wedge \pi_{X_1} \leq \pi_{X_2}.$$

$\langle \mathsf{Des}, \leq \rangle$ is a complete lattice.

Definition. For $\mathcal{X} \subseteq \mathsf{Des}$, $\sum \mathcal{X}$, the *sum* of the elements of $\mathcal{X}$, is defined by

$$\textstyle\sum \mathcal{X} \ := \ \text{the least upperbound of } \mathcal{X} \text{ with respect to } \leq.$$

Obviously, importing can be uniquely characterized by means of $\sum$:

$$X_1 + X_2 = \textstyle\sum \{X_1, X_2\}.$$

The next section recounts the domains and operations of DA and presents a number of algebraic laws that hold for DA.

6.4 Description Algebra

Description Algebra is the heterogeneous algebra consisting of the following domains, constants and operations:

$$
\begin{array}{lll}
\text{Domains:} & \mathsf{Nam} & \\
& \mathsf{Ren} & \\
& \mathsf{Sig} & \\
& \mathsf{Des} & \\
\\
\text{Constants:} & u & : \mathsf{Nam} \quad (u \in \mathsf{Nam}) \\
& \rho & : \mathsf{Ren} \quad (\rho \in \mathsf{Ren}) \\
& \Sigma & : \mathsf{Sig} \quad (\Sigma \in \mathsf{Sig}) \\
& X & : \mathsf{Des} \quad (X \in \mathsf{Des}) \\
\\
\text{Operations:} & \bullet & : \mathsf{Ren} \times \mathsf{Nam} \to \mathsf{Nam} \\
& \circ & : \mathsf{Ren} \times \mathsf{Ren} \to \mathsf{Ren} \\
\\
& \bullet & : \mathsf{Ren} \times \mathsf{Sig} \to \mathsf{Sig} \\
& + & : \mathsf{Sig} \times \mathsf{Sig} \to \mathsf{Sig} \\
& \Box & : \mathsf{Sig} \times \mathsf{Sig} \to \mathsf{Sig} \\
& \Delta & : \mathsf{Nam} \times \mathsf{Sig} \to \mathsf{Sig} \\
\\
& \mathbf{\Sigma} & : \mathsf{Des} \to \mathsf{Sig} \\
& \bullet & : \mathsf{Ren} \times \mathsf{Des} \to \mathsf{Des} \\
& + & : \mathsf{Des} \times \mathsf{Des} \to \mathsf{Des} \\
& \Box & : \mathsf{Sig} \times \mathsf{Des} \to \mathsf{Des} \\
& \mu & : \mathsf{Des} \to \mathsf{Des} \\
& \pi & : \mathsf{Des} \to \mathsf{Des}\,.
\end{array}
$$

For each domain of DA, all elements of the domain are taken as constants. No special symbols are introduced to denote these constants. They are considered to be symbols themselves.

The symbols introduced above to denote the domains, constants and operations of DA constitute the signature of DA. The terms of DA, i.e. the terms used to denote elements of the domains of DA, are constructed from the constant and operation symbols in the usual way.

The following theorem presents a number of algebraic laws that hold for DA. The laws followed by ** are also axioms of MA (Bergstra, Heering and Klint, 1990). The laws followed by * are similar to axioms of MA. The remaining laws are laws concerning the unifying operation of DA and the auxiliary operation 'π', neither of which has a counterpart in MA.

Theorem. The following algebraic laws are satisfied by Description Algebra:

$$
\begin{array}{lll}
\mathbf{\Sigma}(\rho \bullet X) = \rho \bullet \mathbf{\Sigma}(X) & \text{(S1)} & ** \\
\mathbf{\Sigma}(X_1 + X_2) = \mathbf{\Sigma}(X_1) + \mathbf{\Sigma}(X_2) & \text{(S2)} & ** \\
\mathbf{\Sigma}(\Sigma \square X) = \Sigma \square \mathbf{\Sigma}(X) & \text{(S3)} & ** \\
\mathbf{\Sigma}(\mu(X)) = \mathbf{\Sigma}(X) & \text{(S4)} & \\
\mathbf{\Sigma}(\pi(X)) = \{\} & \text{(S5)} &
\end{array}
$$

$$
\begin{array}{lll}
\rho_1 \bullet (\rho_2 \bullet X) = (\rho_1 \circ \rho_2) \bullet X & \text{(R1)} & * \\
\rho \bullet (X_1 + X_2) = (\rho \bullet X_1) + (\rho \bullet X_2) & \text{(R2)} & ** \\
\rho \bullet (\Sigma \square X) = (\rho \bullet \Sigma) \square (\rho \bullet X) & \text{(R3)} & ** \\
\rho \bullet \mu(X) = (\rho \bullet X) + \pi(\mu(X)) & \text{(R4)} & \\
\rho \bullet \pi(X) = \pi(X) & \text{(R5)} &
\end{array}
$$

$$
\begin{array}{lll}
X + (\Sigma \square X) = X & \text{(I1}'\text{)} & ** \\
X_1 + X_2 = X_2 + X_1 & \text{(I2)} & ** \\
(X_1 + X_2) + X_3 = X_1 + (X_2 + X_3) & \text{(I3)} & ** \\
X + \mu(X) = \mu(X) & \text{(I4)} & \\
X + \pi(X) = X & \text{(I5)} & \\
X + \pi(\mu(X)) = \mu(X) & \text{(I6)} &
\end{array}
$$

$$
\begin{array}{lll}
\mathbf{\Sigma}(X) \square X = X & \text{(E1)} & ** \\
\Sigma \square (X_1 + X_2) = (\Sigma \square X_1) + (\Sigma \square X_2) & \text{(E2)} & * \\
\Sigma_1 \square (\Sigma_2 \square X) = (\Sigma_1 \square \Sigma_2) \square X & \text{(E3)} & ** \\
\Sigma \square \mu(X) = \mu(\Sigma \square X) + \pi(\mu(X)) & \text{(E4)} & \\
\Sigma \square \pi(X) = \pi(X) & \text{(E5)} &
\end{array}
$$

$$
\begin{array}{ll}
\mu(\rho \bullet \mu(X)) = \mu(\rho \bullet X) & \text{(M1)} \\
\mu(\mu(X_1) + X_2) = \mu(X_1 + X_2) & \text{(M2)} \\
\mu(\Sigma \square \mu(X)) = \Sigma \square \mu(X) & \text{(M3)} \\
\mu(\mu(X)) = \mu(X) & \text{(M4)} \\
\mu(\pi(X)) = \pi(X) & \text{(M5)}
\end{array}
$$

$$
\begin{array}{ll}
\pi(\rho \bullet X) = \pi(X) & \text{(P1)} \\
\pi(X_1 + X_2) = \pi(X_1) + \pi(X_2) & \text{(P2)} \\
\pi(\Sigma \square X) = \pi(X) & \text{(P3)} \\
\pi(\pi(X)) = \pi(X) & \text{(P4).}
\end{array}
$$

Proof: Straightforward from the definitions of the operations. □

The law numbering is in accordance with the one used in (Jonkers, 1989a). Law (I1) from that paper, $X + X = X$ (the idempotent law for +), is a special case of law (I1′).

It is shown in the next section how a logical theory in which names are used as symbols can be attached to each description. In Section 6.6, an implementation relation on descriptions is defined in terms of their theories.

6.5 Abstract meaning of descriptions

As an abstract meaning, an MPL_ω theory in which names are used as symbols of MPL_ω can be attached to each origin consistent description.

Informally, a description is origin consistent if the sets of origins of visible symbols with the same name are simultaneously unifiable. This is the case if there exists an instantiation of origin variables that identifies all origins in each of the elements of the corresponding partition. In this section, first instantiation of origin variables and simultaneous unifiability are made precise by defining origin substitution and unification for origin partitions. Next, origin consistency of a description and the abstract meaning of an origin consistent description are defined. Last, it is shown how a theory can also be attached to each non-origin-consistent description.

Origin substitutions

The origin variables occurring in an origin can be instantiated by applying an origin substitution to the origin.

Definition. For an origin a, the set $OV(a) \subseteq \mathsf{OVar}$, the set of origin variables occurring in a, is inductively defined by

$$OV(c) = \{\},$$
$$OV(x) = \{x\},$$
$$OV(\langle a_1, \ldots, a_n \rangle) = OV(a_1) \cup \ldots \cup OV(a_n).$$

This is extended to origin sets, origin partitions and symbols as follows:
For $A \subseteq \mathsf{Orig}$, the set $OV(A) \subseteq \mathsf{OVar}$ is defined by

$$OV(A) := \bigcup_{a \in A} OV(a).$$

For $\pi \subseteq \mathsf{OPar}$, the set $OV(\pi) \subseteq \mathsf{OVar}$ is defined by

$$OV(\pi) := \bigcup \{OV(A) \mid A \in \pi, \operatorname{card} A \neq 1\}.$$

For $w \in \mathsf{Sym}$, the set $OV(w) \subseteq \mathsf{OVar}$ is defined by

$$OV(\langle i, a, t(S_1, \ldots, S_n) \rangle) := OV(a) \cup OV(S_1) \cup \ldots \cup OV(S_n).$$

For $W \subseteq \mathsf{Sym}$, the set $OV(W) \subseteq \mathsf{OVar}$ is defined by

$$OV(W) := \bigcup_{w \in W} OV(w).$$

Definition. OSub, the set of all *origin substitutions*, is defined by

$$\mathsf{OSub} := \{\alpha \mid \alpha \colon \mathsf{OVar} \to \mathsf{Orig}\}.$$

This is extended to origins, origin partitions and symbols as follows:

Each origin substitution α is extended to a mapping $\alpha\colon \mathsf{Orig} \to \mathsf{Orig}$ by the following rules:

$$\alpha(c) = c,$$
$$\alpha(x) = \alpha(x),$$
$$\alpha(\langle a_1, \ldots, a_n\rangle) = \langle \alpha(a_1), \ldots, \alpha(a_n)\rangle.$$

Each origin substitution α is extended to a mapping $\alpha\colon \mathsf{OPar} \to \mathsf{OPar}$ by the following rule:

$$\alpha(\pi) = \prod\{\pi' \in \mathsf{OPar} \mid \forall A \in \pi\,(\exists A' \in \pi'\,(\alpha(A) \subseteq A'))\}.$$

Each origin substitution α is extended to a mapping $\alpha\colon \mathsf{Sym} \to \mathsf{Sym}$ by the following rule:

$$\alpha(\langle i, a, t(S_1, \ldots, S_n)\rangle) = \langle i, \alpha(a), t(\alpha(S_1), \ldots, \alpha(S_n))\rangle.$$

Renamings permute with origin substitutions.

Fact. For all $w \in \mathsf{Sym}$, $\alpha \in \mathsf{OSub}$, $\rho \in \mathsf{Ren}$:

$$\alpha(\rho(w)) = \rho(\alpha(w)).$$

Proof: See (Jonkers, 1989a, Lemma 3.2.2). □

It is assumed that origin substitutions on symbols are extended to MPL_ω formulae in the usual homomorphic way. Furthermore, they are extended to descriptions.

Definition. Each origin substitution α is extended to a mapping $\alpha\colon \mathsf{Des} \to \mathsf{Des}$ by the following rule:

$$\alpha(X) = \langle \alpha(\Sigma_X), \alpha(\Gamma_X), \alpha(\Phi_X), \alpha(\pi_X)\rangle.$$

The set of all origin variables that are changed by an origin substitution (from OSub) is considered to be its domain.

Definition. For an origin substitution $\alpha \in \mathsf{OSub}$, $dom(\alpha)$, the *domain* of α, is defined by

$$dom(\alpha) := \{x \in \mathsf{OVar} \mid \alpha(x) \neq x\}.$$

Unification for origin partitions

The origin partition of a description declares certain origins to be equal (usually the origins of symbols in the externally visible signature with the same name). The elements of the origin partition, i.e. sets of origins declared to be equal, should be simultaneously unifiable. This unification for origin partitions is made precise below.

Definition. For $\pi \in \mathsf{OPar}$, $\mathcal{U}_P(\pi)$, the set of all *P-unifiers* of π, is the set of origin substitutions defined by

$$\mathcal{U}_P(\pi) := \{\alpha \in \mathsf{OSub} \mid \forall A \in \pi\,(\exists a \in \mathsf{Orig}\,(\alpha(A) = \{a\}))\}.$$

π is called *P-unifiable* iff

$$\mathcal{U}_P(\pi) \neq \{\}.$$

P-unifiable origin partitions have a most general P-unifier.

Definition. For $\alpha_1, \alpha_2 \in \mathsf{OSub}$, $\alpha_1 \leq \alpha_2$, α_1 is an *instantiation* of α_2, is defined by

$$\alpha_1 \leq \alpha_2 \;:\Leftrightarrow\; \exists \beta \in \mathsf{OSub}\,(\forall x \in \mathsf{OVar}\,(\alpha_1(x) = \beta(\alpha_2(x)))).$$

Fact. If $\pi \in \mathsf{OPar}$ is P-unifiable, then $\mathcal{U}_P(\pi)$ has a maximum with respect to $\leq$.

Proof: See (Jonkers, 1989a, Theorem 2.4.7). □

Definition. For a P-unifiable origin partition π, μ_π, the *most general P-unifier* of π, is the maximum of $\mathcal{U}_P(\pi)$ with respect to $\leq$.

It is assumed that $\mu_\pi(x) = x$ for all $x \in \mathsf{OVar} - OV(\pi)$.

Because of the extensions defined for origin substitutions, the most general unifier of an origin partition can be applied to symbols and formulae. This is used below to define the most general unifier of descriptions.

Origin independent meaning of descriptions

First, origin consistency is defined by extending P-unifiability to descriptions. Thereafter, the notion of a most general unifier is extended correspondingly (for origin consistent descriptions).

Definition. For $X \in \mathsf{Des}$, $\mathcal{U}_D(X)$, the set of all *unifiers* of X, is the set of origin substitutions defined by

$$\mathcal{U}_D(X) \;:=\; \mathcal{U}_P(\pi_{\mu(X)}).$$

X is called *origin consistent* iff

$$\mathcal{U}_D(X) \neq \{\}.$$

Definition. For an origin consistent description X, μ_X, the *most general unifier* of X, is defined by

$$\mu_X \;:=\; \mu_{\pi_{\mu(X)}}.$$

A theory can be attached to each origin consistent description X as follows. First of all, apply μ_X, i.e. the most general unifier of the description, to its components. Thus, symbols from the externally visible signature with the same name will be actually identified. Secondly, take the theory of the set of formulae $\mu_X(\Phi_X)$ (which are from the language of the internal signature $\mu_X(\Gamma_X)$) and restrict this theory to the language of the externally visible signature $\mu_X(\Sigma_X)$. Thus, a theory will be obtained which is the set of all the visible consequences of the axioms $\mu_X(\Phi_X)$.

Definition. For an origin consistent description X, $Th_S(X)$, the *symbol theory* of X, is defined by

$$Th_S(X) \ := \ \mathcal{L}(\mu_X(\Sigma_X)) \cap Th(\mu_X(\Gamma_X), \mu_X(\Phi_X)).$$

For an origin consistent description there is a one-to-one correspondence between the visible names and the visible symbols. Hence abstraction from the origins of the visible symbols is possible. It requires names to be interpreted as symbols in MPL_ω.

Names are interpreted as symbols in MPL_ω according to the following rules:

- each $\overline{S} = \overline{\langle i, a, \mathsf{sort}\rangle}$ is a sort symbol in MPL_ω,
- each $\overline{x} = \overline{\langle i, a, \langle \mathsf{obj}, S\rangle\rangle}$ is a variable symbol of sort $\overline{S}$ in MPL_ω,
- each $\overline{f} = \overline{\langle i, a, \langle \mathsf{func}, S_1, \ldots, S_{n+1}\rangle\rangle}$ is a function symbol $\overline{f}\colon \overline{S_1} \times \cdots \times \overline{S_n} \to \overline{S_{n+1}}$ in MPL_ω,
- each $\overline{P} = \overline{\langle i, a, \langle \mathsf{pred}, S_1, \ldots, S_n\rangle\rangle}$ is a predicate symbol $\overline{P}\colon \overline{S_1} \times \cdots \times \overline{S_n}$ in MPL_ω.

If name signatures are used as signatures, the language of a given name signature is defined as follows.

Definition. For $\Sigma \in \mathsf{Sig}$, $\mathcal{L}(\Sigma)$, the *language* of Σ, is the set of MPL_ω formulae defined by

$$\mathcal{L}(\Sigma) \ := \ \{\varphi \mid \varphi \text{ is a formula of } \mathrm{MPL}_\omega(\Sigma)\}.$$

For a set of formulae Φ from the language of Σ, the theory presented by Φ consists of all formulae that Φ entails according to the proof system of $\mathrm{MPL}_\omega(\Sigma)$.

Definition. For $\Sigma \in \mathsf{Sig}$ and a set of formulae $\Phi \subseteq \mathcal{L}(\Sigma)$, $Th(\Sigma, \Phi)$, the *theory* of Φ, is the set of MPL_ω formulae defined by

$$Th(\Sigma, \Phi) \ := \ \{\varphi \in \mathcal{L}(\Sigma) \mid \Phi \vdash \varphi\}.$$

Definition. If $\Sigma \in \mathsf{SSig}$, then the formulae from $\mathcal{L}(\Sigma)$ are called *symbol* formulae. If $\Sigma \in \mathsf{Sig}$, then the formulae from $\mathcal{L}(\Sigma)$ are called *name* formulae. We write $\overline{\varphi}$, where φ is a symbol formula, for the name formula obtained by replacing the occurrences of symbols w in φ by their name $\overline{w}$ and we write $\overline{\Phi}$, where Φ is a set of symbol formulae, for the set of name formulae $\{\overline{\varphi} \mid \varphi \in \Phi\}$. For an origin consistent description X, $Th(X)$, the *theory* of X, is defined by

$$Th(X) \ := \ \overline{Th_S(X)}.$$

Non-origin-consistent descriptions

In Section 6.6, a notion of implementation for descriptions is introduced. It is defined in terms of theories of descriptions. Because the implementation relation on descriptions should be reflexive, the theory of an arbitrary description should be defined. The definition of the theory of a non-origin-consistent description is suggested by a characterization of the theory of an origin consistent description.

Fact. If X is an origin consistent description, then

$$Th(X) = \bigcup\{Th(X') \mid X' \leq X,\ X' \text{ origin consistent}\}.$$

Proof: See (Jonkers, 1989a, Lemma 3.6.5). □

Definition. For a non-origin-consistent description X, $Th(X)$ is defined by

$$Th(X) \ := \ \bigcup\{Th(X') \mid X' \leq X,\ X' \text{ origin consistent}\}.$$

As mentioned before, the theory of a non-origin-consistent description is defined for technical reasons. It is not intended to give an abstract meaning to non-origin-consistent descriptions. It seems more appropriate to consider non-origin-consistent descriptions meaningless.

How descriptions and their theories are related is further analysed in Chapter 9. In the next section, additions to DA are treated which are relevant to the case where descriptions may be parametrized. This includes an implementation relation on descriptions which is described in terms of their theories.

6.6 DA with parameters

Additional domains and operations

$\lambda\pi$-calculus (described in Sections 6.7 to 6.13) is the basis for the semantics of the parametrization constructs of VVSL. $\lambda\pi$-calculus supports descriptions which are parametrized over entire descriptions (rather than over names, signatures, etc.). However, when a parametrized description is instantiated for a given description, the origins of certain visible symbols of the latter should be substituted for the corresponding origin variables in the parametrized description. This is achieved by the origin substitution operation α defined in this section. This operation requires a dummy description, called a parameter. Only the externally visible signature of a parameter is relevant. The origin of any symbol from this signature is either an origin variable or contains no origin variables. Besides there are no two symbols with the same origin variable as their origins.

Definition. A *parameter signature* is a signature $\Sigma \in \mathsf{SSig}$ such that

$$\forall w \in \Sigma\,(\omega(w) \in \mathsf{OVar} \vee OV(w) = \{\,\}),$$
$$\forall w, w' \in \Sigma\,(\omega(w) \in \mathsf{OVar} \wedge \omega(w) = \omega(w') \ \Rightarrow\ w = w').$$

Par, the set of *parameters*, is defined by

$$\mathsf{Par} \ := \ \{\langle \Sigma, \Sigma, \{\,\}, \pi_\perp \rangle \mid \Sigma \text{ is a parameter signature}\}.$$

For $P \in \mathsf{Par}$, P is called *origin unique* iff

$$\forall w, w' \in \Sigma_P\,(\omega(w) \in \mathsf{OVar} \wedge w \equiv w' \;\Rightarrow\; \omega(w) = \omega(w')).$$

The operations on parameters include the trivial embedding from parameters to descriptions as an auxiliary operation. This operation is used in formulating an algebraic law concerning origin substitution. It is also used in defining the other operations on parameters.

Definition. The *embedding* operation $\delta\colon \mathsf{Par} \rightarrow \mathsf{Des}$ on parameters is defined by

$$\delta(P) \;:=\; P.$$

So embedding is the inclusion function from Par to Des. When a parametrized description is instantiated for a given description, the origins of certain visible symbols of the latter can be substituted for the corresponding origin variables in the parametrized description by means of origin substitution.

Definition. The *origin substitution* operation $\alpha\colon \mathsf{Par} \times \mathsf{Des} \times \mathsf{Des} \rightarrow \mathsf{Des}$ is defined by

$$\begin{array}{l}\alpha(P, X_1, X_2) \;:= \\ \quad \sum\{\beta(X_2) \mid \beta \in \mathsf{OSub} \wedge dom(\beta) \subseteq OV(\Sigma_{X'}) \wedge \beta(\Sigma_{X'}) \subseteq \Sigma_{X_1}\}, \\ \text{where } X' = \mathbf{\Sigma}(X_1) \,\square\, \delta(P).\end{array}$$

$\sum \mathcal{X}$ is the least upper bound of $\mathcal{X}$ in the complete lattice $\langle \mathsf{Des}, \leq \rangle$ (see Section 6.3).

Roughly speaking, $\alpha(P, X_1, X_2)$ replaces everywhere in the description X_2 the origin variables of the parameter P by the corresponding origins of the description X_1. Because symbols of X_1 with the same name may have different origins (even in the case that X_1 is origin consistent), there may be several corresponding origins. Therefore, the actual definition of origin substitution is more involved. The origin substitution takes place such that the 'origin non-uniqueness' which prevails in X_1 is inherited by the result. The names of symbols in a parameter can be changed by applying a renaming.

Definition. The *renaming* operation $\bullet\colon \mathsf{Ren} \times \mathsf{Par} \rightarrow \mathsf{Par}$ on parameters is defined by

$$\rho \bullet P \;:=\; \rho \bullet \delta(P).$$

Description Algebra with Parameters (DA_α) is the heterogeneous algebra, which is obtained from DA (Section 6.4) by the following additions:

$$
\begin{array}{llcl}
\text{Domains:} & \mathsf{Par} & & \\
\text{Constants:} & P & : & \mathsf{Par} \quad (P \in \mathsf{Par}) \\
\text{Operations:} & \bullet & : & \mathsf{Ren} \times \mathsf{Par} \to \mathsf{Par} \\
 & \alpha & : & \mathsf{Par} \times \mathsf{Des} \times \mathsf{Des} \to \mathsf{Des} \\
 & \delta & : & \mathsf{Par} \to \mathsf{Des}\,.
\end{array}
$$

The following theorem presents a number of algebraic laws concerning the substitution operation that hold for DA with parameters. These laws have no counterpart in MA.

Theorem. The following algebraic laws are satisfied by Description Algebra with Parameters:

$$
\begin{array}{ll}
\mathbf{\Sigma}(\alpha(P, X_1, X_2)) = \mathbf{\Sigma}(X_2) & \text{(S6)} \\
\alpha(P, X_1, \rho \bullet X_2) = \rho \bullet \alpha(P, X_1, X_2) & \text{(R6)} \\
\alpha(P, X_1, X_2 + X_3) = \alpha(P, X_1, X_2) + \alpha(P, X_1, X_3) & \text{(A2)} \\
\alpha(P, X_1, \Sigma \,\Box\, X_2) = \Sigma \,\Box\, \alpha(P, X_1, X_2) & \text{(E6)} \\
\alpha(P, \delta(P), X) = X & \text{(A1)}.
\end{array}
$$

Proof: Straightforward from the definitions of the operations. □

The (seemingly strange) law numbering is in accordance with the one used in (Feijs, Jonkers, Koymans and Renardel de Lavalette, 1987), where the laws given in Section 6.4 are presented together with the ones given above.

Renaming of renamings

A last operation that is defined on renamings is a partial operation which is not part of DA_α. It is a renaming operation on renamings. A renaming of a renaming only exists under a renameability condition given below. This operation is needed for the generalization of renaming to parametrized descriptions in Chapter 7.

Definition. For $\rho_1, \rho_2 \in \mathsf{Ren}$, ρ_2 is called *renameable* by ρ_1 iff

$$\forall w, w' \in \mathsf{Sym}\, (\rho_1(w) \equiv \rho_1(w') \;\Rightarrow\; \rho_1(\rho_2(w)) \equiv \rho_1(\rho_2(w'))).$$

Definition. The partial operation $\cdot : \mathsf{Ren} \times \mathsf{Ren} \rightarrow \mathsf{Ren}$ is inductively defined by

$$\begin{array}{l}\text{if } \rho_2 \text{ is renameable by } \rho_1\text{, then:}\\ w \in \rho_1(\mathsf{Sym}) \wedge w = \rho_1(w') \;\Rightarrow\; (\rho_1 \cdot \rho_2)(w) = \rho_1(\rho_2(w')),\\ w \notin \rho_1(\mathsf{Sym}) \;\Rightarrow\\ \quad \iota((\rho_1 \cdot \rho_2)(w)) = \iota(w) \wedge\\ \quad \omega((\rho_1 \cdot \rho_2)(w)) = \omega(w) \wedge\\ \quad (\tau(w) = t(S_1, \ldots, S_n) \;\Rightarrow\\ \qquad \tau((\rho_1 \cdot \rho_2)(w)) = t((\rho_1 \cdot \rho_2)(S_1), \ldots, (\rho_1 \cdot \rho_2)(S_n))).\end{array}$$

Implementation relations

In the case that Description Algebra is used to provide the modularization constructs of a particular specification language with a semantics, a subalgebra of DA_α is usually needed. Therefore, a notion of an implementation relation is presented, which is defined with respect to the domains of a subalgebra of DA_α. It is defined in terms of theories of descriptions.

Definition. Let $N \subseteq \mathsf{Nam}$, $R \subseteq \mathsf{Ren}$, $S \subseteq \mathsf{Sig}$, $D \subseteq \mathsf{Des}$, and $P \subseteq \mathsf{Par}$ be the domains of a subalgebra of DA_α. Then for $X_1, X_2 \in D$, $X_1 \sqsubseteq X_2$, X_1 is an *implementation* of X_2, is defined by

$$X_1 \sqsubseteq X_2 \;:\Leftrightarrow\; \mathbf{\Sigma}(X_1) \supseteq \mathbf{\Sigma}(X_2) \wedge \mathit{Th}(X_1) \supseteq \mathit{Th}(X_2).$$

The relation $\sqsubseteq$ on D is called the *implementation relation* of the subalgebra of DA_α.

The relation $\sqsubseteq$ is a pre-order and the operation $\mathbf{\Sigma}$ is monotonic with respect to $\sqsubseteq$ (and $\supseteq$).

Fact. For every subalgebra $\mathbf{D}$, its implementation relation $\sqsubseteq$ has the following properties:

$$\begin{array}{l} X \sqsubseteq X,\\ X_1 \sqsubseteq X_2 \wedge X_2 \sqsubseteq X_3 \;\Rightarrow\; X_1 \sqsubseteq X_3,\\ X_1 \sqsubseteq X_2 \;\Rightarrow\; \mathbf{\Sigma}(X_1) \supseteq \mathbf{\Sigma}(X_2).\end{array}$$

Proof: Straightforward from the definitions of the implementation relation and the operation $\mathbf{\Sigma}$. □

The auxiliary operation π is also monotonic with respect to the relation $\sqsubseteq$. Monotonicity does not generally hold for the other operations. Restriction to origin consistent descriptions is sufficient for monotonicity of $\Box$ and μ. Further restrictions are required for the operations $\bullet$, $+$ and α.

Des has $\langle \{\}, \{\}, \{\}, \pi_\perp \rangle$ as maximal element with respect to the implementation relation of DA_α itself. For an arbitrary subalgebra of DA_α, it does not generally hold that its domain of descriptions has a maximal element with respect to its implementation relation.

Here ends the presentation of DA. The remainder of this chapter is concerned with $\lambda\pi$-calculus.

6.7 Introduction to $\lambda\pi$-calculus

This section gives an idea of what $\lambda\pi$-calculus is and connects this with its role in a semantics of VVSL. Subsequent sections go into details of $\lambda\pi$-calculus.

Overview of $\lambda\pi$-calculus

In $\lambda\pi$-calculus, lambda terms have unique types. Types are interpreted as non-empty domains of values or functions. The types are used to exclude the formation of problematic lambda terms, like terms expressing self-application of a function.

Lambda abstractions have parameter restrictions in $\lambda\pi$-calculus. More precisely, instead of lambda terms of the form $(\lambda x.M)$, there are lambda terms of the form $(\lambda x \sqsubseteq L.M)$ (where both L and M are lambda terms). Herein L is called a parameter restriction. The intended meaning is the function that maps x to M, provided that x and L are in the relation $\sqsubseteq$, and is undefined otherwise. This is reflected in the rule (π) of $\lambda\pi$-calculus, which is a conditional version of the rule (β) of classical lambda calculus.

$\lambda\pi$-calculus is put 'on top' of an algebraic system with pre-order, i.e. a heterogeneous algebra together with a pre-order on one of its domains, such as DA together with the implementation relation on the domain of descriptions.

Suitability of $\lambda\pi$-calculus

For the adequacy of the parametrization mechanism provided by VVSL for practical applications, it is highly desirable that it permits requirements to be put on the actual parameters to which parametrized modules may be applied. This is supported by the parameter restriction feature of $\lambda\pi$-calculus. Moreover, it does so without imposing essential deviations from classical typed lambda calculus. Reduction for $\lambda\pi$-calculus resembles reduction for classical typed lambda calculus. The Church-Rosser property is not invalidated by addition of parameter restrictions and the strong normalization property is inherited from typed lambda calculus. This means that reduction of lambda terms always leads in finitely many steps to a unique normal form (up to renaming of bound variables).

Connections with other approaches to parametrization

$\lambda\pi$-calculus is a variant of typed lambda calculus with parameter restriction.

A lambda calculus based approach is used to provide for a parametrization mechanism in various existing languages for structured specifications, e.g. ASL (Wirsing, 1986). The parametrization mechanism of ASL is also based on a variant of typed lambda calculus with parameter restriction. Because the parameters of parametrized modules are not limited to modules, parameter restriction is not treated as uniformly as in $\lambda\pi$-calculus. A lambda calculus based approach to parametrization is also pursued in theoretical work presented by Sannella and Tarlecki (1988), but only a very simple kind of parameter restriction is envisaged, viz. parameter signature restrictions.

In (Burstall and Goguen, 1980) an approach to parametrization is used for Clear, where parametrized modules are viewed as morphisms in the category of 'based theories'. However, the definition of application given by Sannella (1984) seems close to a set-theoretic construction that models a variant of β-conversion. A category-theoretic approach to parametrization is also used for ACT ONE (Ehrig, Feys and Hansen, 1983).

The next five sections describe $\lambda\pi$-calculus precisely. The first of these sections introduces the systems on top of which $\lambda\pi$-calculus can be put.

6.8 Algebraic systems for $\lambda\pi$-calculus

There is an instance of $\lambda\pi$-calculus for every algebraic system with pre-order. DA together with the implementation relation on the domain of descriptions introduced in Section 6.6 is an algebraic system with pre-order. An algebraic system with pre-order is roughly a heterogeneous algebra together with a pre-order on one of its domains. The algebra may be heterogeneous, which means that it may have 'secondary domains' (such as domains of signatures, renamings, etc. in the case of DA). For a given algebraic system with pre-order, say $\mathcal{A}$, the terms of the $\lambda\pi$-calculus are called the terms of $\lambda\pi$ for $\mathcal{A}$ or the terms of $\lambda\pi[\mathcal{A}]$. The corresponding rules are analogously called the rules of $\lambda\pi[\mathcal{A}]$.

Definition. A *heterogeneous algebra* $\mathbf{A}$ is a triple

$$\langle\langle A_\kappa\rangle_{\kappa\in K}, \langle C_c\rangle_{c\in\Gamma}, \langle F_f\rangle_{f\in\Omega}\rangle,$$

where

1. K, Γ and Ω are disjoint index sets;
2. for every $\kappa \in K$: A_κ is a non-empty set, called a *domain* of $\mathbf{A}$;
3. for every $c \in \Gamma$: C_c is an element of A_κ, for some $\kappa \in K$, called a *constant* of $\mathbf{A}$;

4. for every $f \in \Omega$: F_f is a total function $F_f: A_{\kappa_1} \times \cdots \times A_{\kappa_n} \to A_{\kappa_{n+1}}$, for some $\kappa_1, \ldots, \kappa_{n+1} \in K$ $(n \geq 0)$, called an *operation* of $\mathbf{A}$.

An *algebraic system with pre-order* $\mathcal{A}$ is a quadruple

$$\langle\langle A_\kappa\rangle_{\kappa\in K}, \langle C_c\rangle_{c\in\Gamma}, \langle F_f\rangle_{f\in\Omega}, R\rangle,$$

where

1. $\langle\langle A_\kappa\rangle_{\kappa\in K}, \langle C_c\rangle_{c\in\Gamma}, \langle F_f\rangle_{f\in\Omega}\rangle$ is a heterogeneous algebra with $0 \in K$;
2. $\langle A_0, R\rangle$ is a pre-ordered class with a maximal element.

The pre-ordered domain A_0 is called the *domain of interest* of $\mathcal{A}$. The other domains are called *secondary domains*. We write $\kappa^{\mathcal{A}}$ for A_κ $(\kappa \in K)$, $c^{\mathcal{A}}$ for C_c $(c \in \Gamma)$, $f^{\mathcal{A}}$ for F_f $(f \in \Omega)$, and $R^{\mathcal{A}}$ for R. We also write $K^{\mathcal{A}}$, $\Gamma^{\mathcal{A}}$ and $\Omega^{\mathcal{A}}$, for K, Γ and Ω, respectively. However, these notations are used without superscripts when it is clear from context or unimportant which algebraic system is meant.

Thus, a heterogeneous algebra and a pre-order on one of its domains induce an algebraic system with pre-order in a trivial way if the domain has a maximal element with respect to the pre-order. In Chapter 7, MDA, a subalgebra of DA, is introduced. MDA together with the restriction of the implementation relation associated with DA to the restricted domain of descriptions induces an algebraic system with pre-order. A generalization of the instance of $\lambda\pi$-calculus for this algebraic system with pre-order is used to provide the modularization and parametrization constructs of VVSL with a semantics in Chapter 8.

The restriction above to a single domain of interest is not fundamental, but generalization leads to loss of uniformity in the treatment of parameter restriction in $\lambda\pi$-calculus.

We have to distinguish between the elements of the domains of an algebraic system with pre-order and the terms denoting them. For the sake of simplicity, the index sets are considered to be sets of symbols.

Definition. The *signature* of an algebraic system with pre-order $\mathcal{A}$, written $\mathrm{Sig}(\mathcal{A})$, is defined by

$$\mathrm{Sig}(\mathcal{A}) := \langle K^{\mathcal{A}}, \Gamma^{\mathcal{A}}, \Omega^{\mathcal{A}}, \sqsubseteq\rangle.$$

The $\kappa \in K^{\mathcal{A}}$ are *basic types* or *sort symbols*, the $c \in \Gamma^{\mathcal{A}}$ are *constant symbols*, the $f \in \Omega^{\mathcal{A}}$ are *function symbols* and $\sqsubseteq$ is a *predicate symbol* (denoting $R^{\mathcal{A}}$). We write $c: \kappa$ to indicate that $c^{\mathcal{A}} \in \kappa^{\mathcal{A}}$. We write $f: \kappa_1 \times \cdots \times \kappa_n \to \kappa_{n+1}$ to indicate that $f^{\mathcal{A}}: {\kappa_1}^{\mathcal{A}} \times \cdots \times {\kappa_n}^{\mathcal{A}} \to {\kappa_{n+1}}^{\mathcal{A}}$.

Conventionally, we use the same notation for the constant symbols and the elements of domains. Because terms can contain symbols only, this cannot cause any confusion.

We assume a set $LVAR_0$ of *variable symbols* standing for arbitrary elements of the domain of interest $0^{\mathcal{A}}$. Furthermore, it is assumed that $\Gamma \cup \Omega$ and $LVAR_0$ are two disjoint sets.

Given Sig($\mathcal{A}$) and $LVAR_0$, *terms* denoting elements of the domains $\kappa^{\mathcal{A}}$ can be constructed as usual (for secondary domains, only closed terms can be constructed). These terms are not formally defined here. They coincide with the flat terms which are defined as terms of $\lambda\pi[\mathcal{A}]$ of a special kind in Section 6.10. It is assumed that *evaluation* of terms is defined as usual.

From terms L and M denoting elements of the same domain $\kappa^{\mathcal{A}}$ ($\kappa \in K$), atomic formulae of the form $L = M$ can be constructed and from terms L and M denoting elements of the domain of interest $0^{\mathcal{A}}$, atomic formulae of the form $L \sqsubseteq M$ can be constructed. Non-atomic *formulae* can be constructed from atomic formulae as usual. These formulae are not formally defined here. The atomic formulae coincide with the flat-term formulae which are defined as formulae constructed from terms of $\lambda\pi[\mathcal{A}]$ in Section 6.10. It is assumed that *validity* of formulae is defined as usual (with $=$ corresponding to real equality and $\sqsubseteq$ corresponding to $R^{\mathcal{A}}$).

The next section introduces two notions of type and gives the assumptions which are made about variable symbols for $\lambda\pi$-calculus.

6.9 Typed variable symbols for $\lambda\pi[\mathcal{A}]$

The terms of $\lambda\pi[\mathcal{A}]$ are constructed with constant and function symbols from Sig($\mathcal{A}$) and lambda variable symbols. The formation rules for the terms of $\lambda\pi[\mathcal{A}]$ take the types of constituent terms into account. The types concerned are basic types and higher types.

Definition. HType, the set of *higher types*, is inductively defined by

1. 0 is a higher type;

2. if σ, τ are higher types, then $(\sigma \to \tau)$ is a higher type.

Type[$\mathcal{A}$], the set of *types* for $\mathcal{A}$, is defined by

$$\mathsf{Type}[\mathcal{A}] \; := \; K^{\mathcal{A}} \cup \mathsf{HType}\,.$$

The elements of $K^{\mathcal{A}}$ were already called *basic types*. The type 0, which is both a basic type and a higher type, is called the *ground type* of the higher types. We write $(\sigma_1, \ldots, \sigma_n \to \tau)$ for $(\sigma_1 \to (\cdots \to (\sigma_n \to \tau)\cdots))$.

We assume a set $LVAR$ of *lambda variable symbols*. Every $x \in LVAR$ has a *type* τ ($\tau \in$ HType). It is assumed that $LVAR_0$ is the set of all lambda variable symbols of type 0. Furthermore, it is assumed that $\Gamma \cup \Omega$ and $LVAR$ are two disjoint sets. In Sections 6.10 to 6.12, we write $x \equiv y$, where x and y are lambda variable symbols, to indicate that x and y are identical lambda variable symbols.

The terms and rules of $\lambda\pi[\mathcal{A}]$ are defined in Sections 6.10 and 6.11, respectively.

6.10 Terms of $\lambda\pi[\mathcal{A}]$

The terms of $\lambda\pi[\mathcal{A}]$ are also called lambda terms. They are constructed according to the formation rules which are given below.

Definition. The *lambda terms* of $\lambda\pi[\mathcal{A}]$, denoted by $\mathbf{\Lambda}[\mathcal{A}]$, are inductively defined by the following formation rules:

1. variable symbols of type τ are lambda terms of type τ, for any $\tau \in \mathsf{HType}$;
2. if $c \in \Gamma$, $c\colon \kappa$, then c is a lambda term of type κ;
3. if $f \in \Omega$, $f\colon \kappa_1 \times \cdots \times \kappa_n \to \kappa_{n+1}$, and $L_1, \ldots, L_n$ are a lambda term of type $\kappa_1, \ldots, \kappa_n$, respectively, then $f(L_1, \ldots, L_n)$ is a lambda term of type κ_{n+1};
4. if L and M are lambda terms of types $(\sigma \to \tau)$ and σ, respectively, then (LM) is a lambda term of type τ;
5. if L and M are lambda terms of types σ and τ, respectively, and x is a variable symbol of type σ that does not occur in L, then $(\lambda x \sqsubseteq L.M)$ is a lambda term of type $(\sigma \to \tau)$.

α-congruent lambda terms are identified – this obviates the need to build renaming of bound variables into the calculus. We write *ltype*(L), where L is a lambda term, for the type of L.

We shall henceforth use (with or without subscripts):

κ to stand for an arbitrary basic type from $K^{\mathcal{A}}$,
c to stand for an arbitrary constant symbol from $\Gamma^{\mathcal{A}}$,
f to stand for an arbitrary function symbol from $\Omega^{\mathcal{A}}$,
σ and τ to stand for arbitrary types for $\mathcal{A}$,
x, y and z to stand for arbitrary lambda variable symbols (of appropriate type),
L, M and N to stand for arbitrary lambda terms of $\lambda\pi[\mathcal{A}]$.

The next thing is to define free variables of lambda terms and substitution.

Free variables

Informally, a variable x occurs free in a lambda term if it occurs outside a subterm of the form $\lambda x \sqsubseteq M.N$.

Definition. The free variables of lambda terms are given by a function *free*, which is inductively defined by

$$\begin{aligned}
\mathit{free}(x) &= \{x\},\\
\mathit{free}(c) &= \{\},\\
\mathit{free}(f(L_1, \ldots, L_n)) &= \mathit{free}(L_1) \cup \ldots \cup \mathit{free}(L_n),\\
\mathit{free}(LM) &= \mathit{free}(L) \cup \mathit{free}(M),\\
\mathit{free}(\lambda x \sqsubseteq L.M) &= \mathit{free}(L) \cup (\mathit{free}(M) - \{x\}).
\end{aligned}$$

So *free*(L) is the set of variable symbols occurring free in lambda term L. A variable symbol x is called *free in* L if $x \in$ *free*(L). A term L of $\lambda\pi[\mathcal{A}]$ is a *closed* term iff *free*$(L) = \{\,\}$.

The notion of a free occurrence of a variable in a lambda term is used in connection with substitution and derivations.

Substitution

Substitution is basic for derivations in $\lambda\pi$-calculus.

Definition. Let y be a variable symbol and let M be a lambda term of the same type. Then $[y := M]$ is called a *substitution*. A substitution $[y := M]$ denotes a function on lambda terms that is inductively defined by

$$\begin{array}{lcll}
[y := M]x & = & M & \text{if } x \equiv y, \\
 & & x & \text{if } x \not\equiv y, \\
[y := M]c & = & c, & \\
[y := M]f(L_1, \ldots, L_m) & = & f([y := M]L_1, \ldots, [y := M]L_m), & \\
[y := M](L_1 L_2) & = & (([y := M]L_1)([y := M]L_2)), & \\
[y := M](\lambda x \sqsubseteq L_1.L_2) & = & & \\
\multicolumn{3}{l}{\quad (\lambda x \sqsubseteq L_1.L_2)} & \text{if } x \equiv y, \\
\multicolumn{3}{l}{\quad (\lambda z \sqsubseteq [y := M]L_1.[y := M]([x := z]L_2))} & \text{if } x \not\equiv y \text{ and } x \text{ free in } M \\
 & & & \quad (z \text{ not in } L_1, L_2 \text{ or } M), \\
\multicolumn{3}{l}{\quad (\lambda x \sqsubseteq [y := M]L_1.[y := M]L_2)} & \text{otherwise.}
\end{array}$$

So $[y := M]L$ is the result of the replacement of the lambda term M for the free occurrences of the variable symbol y in L, avoiding free variables in M becoming bound by means of renaming bound variables.

The derivation system presented in the next section requires understanding of the substitution of a variable.

Flat terms

Flat terms are defined below. They are exactly the terms of $\lambda\pi[\mathcal{A}]$ that can be evaluated in $\mathcal{A}$.

Definition. A *flat term* is a lambda term L of a basic type that contains only subterms of basic types. We write $L^{\mathcal{A}}$, where L is a closed flat term, for the evaluation of L in $\mathcal{A}$.

Obviously, flat terms can be interpreted in $\mathcal{A}$: they are terms denoting elements of the domains $\kappa^{\mathcal{A}}$ $(\kappa \in K)$. In Section 6.8, it was assumed that their evaluation in $\mathcal{A}$ is defined as usual.

The formulae of $\lambda\pi[\mathcal{A}]$ defined in the next section include formulae which are constructed from flat terms.

Definition. A *flat-term formula* is an expression of the form $L \sqsubseteq M$ or $L = M$ where L and M are flat terms. We write $\mathcal{A} \models \varphi$, where φ is a closed flat-term formula, to indicate that φ is valid in $\mathcal{A}$.

Obviously, flat-term formulae can also be interpreted in $\mathcal{A}$: $=$ corresponds to real equality and $\sqsubseteq$ corresponds to $R^{\mathcal{A}}$. In Section 6.8, it was assumed that their validity in $\mathcal{A}$ is defined as usual.

In $\lambda\pi[\mathcal{A}]$, closed flat-term formulae valid in $\mathcal{A}$ can always be derived, as is expressed by the rule ($\models_2$) of the derivation system presented in the next section.

6.11 Rules of $\lambda\pi[\mathcal{A}]$

$\lambda\pi[\mathcal{A}]$ is formulated as a derivation system for statements of the form $\Gamma \vdash \varphi$, where

- φ is a formula of the form $L = M$ or $L \sqsubseteq M$, where L and M are lambda terms of the same type;
- Γ is a finite set of assumptions, each of the form $[\varphi']$, where φ' is a formula of one of the above-mentioned forms.

These statements are called sequents. Intuitively, a sequent $\Gamma \vdash \varphi$ indicates that the formulae in the set of assumptions Γ entail the formula φ. Sequents are derived by means of the derivation rules given below. They make it possible to compare not only terms that can be interpreted in $\mathcal{A}$, but also to compare (in a syntactic way) terms that can only be interpreted in extensions of $\mathcal{A}$ with function domains. First the definitions are given which concern the formulae of $\lambda\pi[\mathcal{A}]$ and the sequents that may be derived.

Formulae are constructed from lambda terms according to the formation rules which are given below.

Definition. The *formulae* of $\lambda\pi[\mathcal{A}]$ are defined by the following formation rules:

1. if L and M are lambda terms of the same type σ and σ is a higher type, then $L \sqsubseteq M$ is a formula;
2. if L and M are lambda terms of the same type σ, then $L = M$ is a formula.

free is extended to formulae by the following rules:

$$\begin{aligned} \mathit{free}(L_1 \sqsubseteq L_2) &= \mathit{free}(L_1) \cup \mathit{free}(L_2), \\ \mathit{free}(L_1 = L_2) &= \mathit{free}(L_1) \cup \mathit{free}(L_2). \end{aligned}$$

A variable symbol x is called *free in* φ if $x \in \mathit{free}(\varphi)$. A formula φ of $\lambda\pi[\mathcal{A}]$ is a *closed* formula iff $\mathit{free}(\varphi) = \{\}$.

Each substitution $[y := M]$ is extended to formulae by the following rules:

$$\begin{aligned} [y := M](L_1 \sqsubseteq L_2) &= [y := M]L_1 \sqsubseteq [y := M]L_2, \\ [y := M](L_1 = L_2) &= [y := M]L_1 = [y := M]L_2. \end{aligned}$$

The derivation system of $\lambda\pi[\mathcal{A}]$ is a derivation system for sequents in Gentzen-style.

Definition. An *assumption* is an expression of the form $[\varphi]$, where φ is a formula. A *context* is a finite set of assumptions. Instead of $\Gamma \cup \{[\varphi]\}$ we write $\Gamma, [\varphi]$. We write $x \notin \Gamma$ to indicate that x is not free in φ for all $[\varphi] \in \Gamma$. A *sequent* is an expression of the form $\Gamma \vdash \varphi$, where Γ is a context and φ is a formula.

We shall henceforth use (with or without subscript):

φ and φ' to stand for arbitrary formulae,
Γ and Γ' to stand for arbitrary contexts.

Furthermore, for $f\colon \kappa_1 \times \cdots \times \kappa_n \to 0$ and i $(1 \leq i \leq n)$ such that $\kappa_i = 0$, we shall use $f(\ldots, M_i, \ldots)$ to stand, in rule $(\models_1)$, for an arbitrary lambda term of the form

$$f(L_1, \ldots, L_{i-1}, M_i, L_{i+1}, \ldots, L_n).$$

In the rule $(\models_1)$, we write '$\mathcal{A} \models f$ monotonic' for validity, in $\mathcal{A}$, of the formula

$$\bigwedge_{i=1}^{n} \varphi_i \to f(x_1, \ldots, x_n) \sqsubseteq f(y_1, \ldots, y_n),$$

where φ_i is $x_i \sqsubseteq y_i$ if $\kappa_i = 0$ and φ_i is $x_i = y_i$ otherwise, assuming that $f\colon \kappa_1 \times \cdots \times \kappa_n \to 0$.

Definition. The *derivation system* of $\lambda\pi[\mathcal{A}]$ is defined by the following derivation rules:

$(\models_1)$ $$\frac{\Gamma \vdash L_i \sqsubseteq M_i}{\Gamma \vdash f(\ldots, L_i, \ldots) \sqsubseteq f(\ldots, M_i, \ldots)} \text{ if } \mathcal{A} \models f \text{ monotonic}$$

$(\models_2)$ $$\frac{}{\Gamma \vdash \varphi} \text{ if } \mathcal{A} \models \varphi \quad (\varphi \text{ closed})$$

(cxt) $$\frac{}{\Gamma, [\varphi] \vdash \varphi}$$

$(\text{refl}_=)$ $$\frac{}{\Gamma \vdash L = L}$$

(subst) $$\frac{\Gamma \vdash [y := L]\varphi \quad \Gamma \vdash L = M}{\Gamma \vdash [y := M]\varphi}$$

(refl) $$\frac{}{\Gamma \vdash L \sqsubseteq L}$$

(trans) $$\frac{\Gamma \vdash L_1 \sqsubseteq L_2 \quad \Gamma \vdash L_2 \sqsubseteq L_3}{\Gamma \vdash L_1 \sqsubseteq L_3}$$

(appl) $$\frac{\Gamma \vdash L_1 \sqsubseteq L_2}{\Gamma \vdash (L_1 M) \sqsubseteq (L_2 M)}$$

(λI_1) $$\frac{\Gamma, [x \sqsubseteq L] \vdash M_1 \sqsubseteq M_2}{\Gamma \vdash (\lambda x \sqsubseteq L.M_1) \sqsubseteq (\lambda x \sqsubseteq L.M_2)} \text{ if } x \notin \Gamma$$

(λI_2) $$\frac{\Gamma \vdash L_1 \sqsubseteq L_2}{\Gamma \vdash (\lambda x \sqsubseteq L_2.M) \sqsubseteq (\lambda x \sqsubseteq L_1.M)}$$

(λI_3) $$\frac{\Gamma, [x \sqsubseteq L] \vdash M_1 = M_2}{\Gamma \vdash (\lambda x \sqsubseteq L.M_1) = (\lambda x \sqsubseteq L.M_2)} \text{ if } x \notin \Gamma$$

(π) $$\frac{\Gamma \vdash L_2 \sqsubseteq L_1}{\Gamma \vdash (\lambda x \sqsubseteq L_1.M)L_2 = [x := L_2]M}$$

Definition. A sequent $\Gamma \vdash \varphi$ is *derivable* if it is the conclusion of an instance of one of the derivation rules, all premises (none, for the cases of ($\models_2$), (cxt), (refl$_=$) and (refl)) are derivable, and all side-conditions are satisfied (for the cases of ($\models_1$), ($\models_2$), (λI_1) and (λI_3)). We write $\lambda\pi[\mathcal{A}]\colon \Gamma \vdash \varphi$ (and sometimes just $\Gamma \vdash \varphi$) to indicate that $\Gamma \vdash \varphi$ is derivable.

The rule ($\models_1$) is a monotonicity rule for the monotonic functions of the algebraic system with pre-order $\mathcal{A}$. Thus, for each monotonic function of $\mathcal{A}$, its monotonicity can be used in the calculus. The rule ($\models_2$) expresses that closed flat-term formulae (i.e. closed atomic formulae which have been constructed from terms of $\mathcal{A}$) valid in $\mathcal{A}$ can be derived in any context. The rule (cxt) expresses that assumptions from a context can be derived in that context.

The rules (refl$_=$) and (subst) are the usual rules for $=$. The rules (refl) and (trans) are a reflexivity rule and a transitivity rule for the pre-order $\sqsubseteq$.

Each lambda term of the form $(\lambda x \sqsubseteq L.M)$ can be viewed as a function with a restriction on its argument: the argument must be an 'implementation' of L. The rule (appl) expresses that application is monotonic with respect to $\sqsubseteq$ in its first argument. This rule reflects the intuition that if one function implements another function then for any argument the result of the one function implements the result of the other function. The rules (λI_1) and (λI_2) express that abstraction is monotonic with respect to $\sqsubseteq$ in its second argument and anti-monotonic in its first argument. The rule (λI_3) expresses that abstraction is monotonic with respect to $=$ in its second argument. Because an assumption $[x \sqsubseteq L]$ is discharged, this rule is not redundant. The rule (λI_1) reflects the intuition that for two functions with the same argument restriction, the one function implements the other function if for every acceptable argument the result of the one function implements the result of the other function. The rule (λI_2) reflects the intuition that for two functions with the same function body and with comparable argument restrictions, the function with the 'weakest' restriction implements the other function. The rule (λI_3) reflects the intuition that for two functions with the same argument restriction, the one function equals the other function if for every acceptable argument the result of the one function equals the result of the other function. The rule (π) is a conditional version of the rule (β) of classical lambda calculus. The 'condition' reflects the intuition that the result of a function is undefined for every argument that does not meet the argument restriction.

The types of terms should not be confused with the parameter restrictions associated with lambda abstractions. Types are used in the definition of lambda terms; their purpose being to exclude meaningless lambda terms. On the other hand, parameter restrictions play a role in the calculus. Their purpose is to restrict the applicability of the rule (β) of classical lambda calculus.

The model presented in the next section can be viewed as a justification of the derivation rules given above.

6.12 Model construction for $\lambda\pi[\mathcal{A}]$

By constructing the model $\mathcal{A}^+$, the intuition, that a lambda term of the form $(\lambda x \sqsubseteq L.M)$ denotes a function, can be made precise.

The model $\mathcal{A}^+$ is obtained below as an extension of the underlying algebraic system with pre-order $\mathcal{A}$ ($\mathcal{A} = \langle\langle A_\kappa\rangle_{\kappa\in K}, \langle C_c\rangle_{c\in\Gamma}, \langle F_f\rangle_{f\in\Omega}, R\rangle$, see Section 6.8). The model $\mathcal{A}^+$ has, in addition to domains A_κ^+ for the basic types κ (including the higher type 0) that are just the domains $\kappa^{\mathcal{A}}$ of $\mathcal{A}$, function domains $A_{\sigma\to\tau}^+ = A_\sigma^+ \to A_\tau^+$ for the higher types $\sigma \to \tau$. The model $\mathcal{A}^+$ has also, in addition to the pre-order $\sqsubseteq_0$ on A_0^+ that is just the pre-order R on the domain A_0, pre-orders $\sqsubseteq_{\sigma\to\tau}$ on $A_{\sigma\to\tau}^+$ for the higher types $\sigma \to \tau$. Every pre-order $\sqsubseteq_\tau$ is defined such that A_τ^+ contains a maximal element $*_\tau$ with respect to $\sqsubseteq_\tau$. This element corresponds to the terms of type τ that cannot be contracted due to the premise of the rule (π), i.e. the 'undefined' terms. Besides, the model $\mathcal{A}^+$ has the constants $c^{\mathcal{A}}$ and operations $f^{\mathcal{A}}$ of $\mathcal{A}$ (which are related to the domains A_κ^+ for the basic types κ only).

Definition. The *model* $\mathcal{A}^+$ is defined by

$$\mathcal{A}^+ := \langle\langle A_\sigma^+\rangle_{\sigma\in\mathsf{Type}[\mathcal{A}]}, \langle C_c\rangle_{c\in\Gamma}, \langle F_f\rangle_{f\in\Omega}, \langle\sqsubseteq_\tau\rangle_{\tau\in\mathsf{HType}}\rangle,$$

where A_σ^+ and $\sqsubseteq_\tau \subseteq A_\tau^+ \times A_\tau^+$ are defined by

$$\begin{array}{lll} A_\kappa^+ & := A_\kappa & \text{for } \kappa \in K, \\ A_{\sigma\to\tau}^+ & := A_\sigma^+ \to A_\tau^+ & \text{for } \sigma, \tau \in \mathsf{HType}, \end{array}$$

$$\begin{array}{lll} a \sqsubseteq_0 b & :\Leftrightarrow aRb, & \\ f \sqsubseteq_{\sigma\to\tau} g & :\Leftrightarrow \forall x \in A^+_\sigma\,(f(x) \sqsubseteq_\tau g(x)) & \text{for } \sigma,\tau \in \mathsf{HType}. \end{array}$$

We write $*_\tau$ for the maximal element of A^+_τ with respect to $\sqsubseteq_\tau$. The subscripts of $\sqsubseteq$ and $*$ are dropped when it is clear from context which type is meant.

The restriction on $\mathcal{A}$ that the pre-ordered class $\langle A_0, R\rangle$ must have a maximal element may be relaxed. When there is no maximal element, we can always add $*_0$ as a fresh element, and define $A^+_0 := A_0 \cup \{*_0\}$ and $a \sqsubseteq_0 b :\Leftrightarrow aRb \vee b = *_0$. This would not work properly if rule ($\models_2$) was not restricted to closed formulae, because for formulae with free variables generally validity in $\mathcal{A}$ does not coincide with validity in what is obtained by adding a fresh element to A_0.

The interpretation of terms of $\lambda\pi[\mathcal{A}]$ in the model $\mathcal{A}^+$ is given below with respect to an assignment in this model.

Definition. An *assignment* in the model $\mathcal{A}^+$ is mapping $\eta\colon LVAR \to \bigcup\{A^+_\tau \mid \tau \in \mathsf{HType}\}$ such that $\eta(x) \in A^+_\tau$ if x is a variable of type τ. For every assignment η, variable symbol x of type τ and element $a \in A^+_\tau$, we write $\eta(x \to a)$ for the assignment η' such that $\eta'(y) = \eta(y)$ if $y \not\equiv x$ and $\eta'(x) = a$.

The interpretation of lambda terms in the model $\mathcal{A}^+$ is given by a function mapping lambda term L of type σ and assignment η to the element of A^+_σ that is the value of L in $\mathcal{A}^+$ under assignment η. Similarly, the interpretation of formulae is given by a function mapping formula φ and assignment η to the truth value of φ in $\mathcal{A}^+$ under assignment η. We write $[\![L]\!]^{\mathcal{A}^+}_\eta$ and $[\![\varphi]\!]^{\mathcal{A}^+}_\eta$ for these interpretations. The superscripts are omitted when it is clear from the context which model is meant.

Definition. The *interpretation* functions for terms and formulae are inductively defined by

$$\begin{array}{ll} [\![x]\!]_\eta & = \eta(x), \\ [\![c]\!]_\eta & = c, \\ [\![f(L_1,\ldots,L_n)]\!]_\eta & = f([\![L_1]\!]_\eta,\ldots,[\![L_n]\!]_\eta) \\ [\![(LM)]\!]_\eta & = [\![L]\!]_\eta([\![M]\!]_\eta), \\ [\![(\lambda x \sqsubseteq L.M)]\!]_\eta & = \end{array}$$

the unique $f\colon A^+_{ltype(L)} \to A^+_{ltype(M)}$ *such that for all* $a \in A^+_{ltype(L)}$:

$$f(a) = \begin{array}{ll} [\![M]\!]_{\eta(x\to a)} & \text{if } a \sqsubseteq [\![L]\!]_\eta, \\ *_{ltype(M)} & \text{otherwise,} \end{array}$$

$$\begin{array}{lll} [\![(L \sqsubseteq M)]\!]_\eta & = \mathsf{T} & \text{if } [\![L]\!]_\eta \sqsubseteq [\![M]\!]_\eta, \\ & \ \mathsf{F} & \text{otherwise,} \\ [\![(L = M)]\!]_\eta & = \mathsf{T} & \text{if } [\![L]\!]_\eta = [\![M]\!]_\eta, \\ & \ \mathsf{F} & \text{otherwise.} \end{array}$$

We write $\mathcal{A}^+ \models \varphi[\eta]$ for $[\![\varphi]\!]_\eta = \mathsf{T}$.

Theorem. $\lambda\pi$-calculus has the following soundness property:

if $\lambda\pi[\mathcal{A}]: \Gamma \vdash \varphi$, then for all assignments η:
$\mathcal{A}^+ \models \varphi'[\eta]$ for all $[\varphi'] \in \Gamma \;\Rightarrow\; \mathcal{A}^+ \models \varphi[\eta]$.

Proof: This soundness property is proved for the case that there are no secondary domains in (Feijs, 1989, Theorem 3.5.3). That proof extends directly to the general case. □

In the next section, it is shown how terms of $\lambda\pi$-calculus can be reduced.

6.13 Reduction for $\lambda\pi$-calculus

In $\lambda\pi$-calculus, terms can be reduced with respect to a context in a meaning preserving way to a form not containing subterms of the form $(\lambda x \sqsubseteq L_1.M)L_2$, where L_1 and L_2 are such that $L_2 \sqsubseteq L_1$ in that context. Such subterms are contracted corresponding to the rule (π).

Reduction for $\lambda\pi$-calculus is similar to reduction for classical lambda calculus. The main difference is that it is defined with respect to a context Γ. As indicated above, not every lambda term of the form $(\lambda x \sqsubseteq L_1.M)L_2$ can be contracted. Whether this is the case, depends upon the context. One-step reduction is tantamount to contraction of a subterm. Reduction is the reflexive and transitive closure of one-step reduction.

Definition. The *one-step reduction* relation $\rightarrow$ and the *reduction* relation $\twoheadrightarrow$ on lambda terms are inductively defined by

$$
\begin{array}{ll}
\Gamma \vdash L_2 \sqsubseteq L_1 & \Rightarrow \Gamma \vdash (\lambda x \sqsubseteq L_1.M)L_2 \rightarrow [x := L_2]M, \\
\Gamma \vdash M_i \rightarrow N_i & \Rightarrow \Gamma \vdash f(L_1,\ldots,M_i,\ldots,L_n) \rightarrow \\
& \qquad\qquad f(L_1,\ldots,N_i,\ldots,L_n), \\
\Gamma \vdash M \rightarrow N & \Rightarrow \Gamma \vdash (LM) \rightarrow (LN), \\
\Gamma \vdash M \rightarrow N & \Rightarrow \Gamma \vdash (ML) \rightarrow (NL), \\
\Gamma \vdash M \rightarrow N & \Rightarrow \Gamma \vdash (\lambda x \sqsubseteq M.L) \rightarrow (\lambda x \sqsubseteq N.L), \\
\Gamma, [x \sqsubseteq L] \vdash M \rightarrow N, x \notin \Gamma & \Rightarrow \Gamma \vdash (\lambda x \sqsubseteq L.M) \rightarrow (\lambda x \sqsubseteq L.N), \\
\\
\Gamma \vdash M \rightarrow N & \Rightarrow \Gamma \vdash M \twoheadrightarrow N, \\
\Gamma \vdash M \twoheadrightarrow M, & \\
\Gamma \vdash L \twoheadrightarrow M, \Gamma \vdash M \twoheadrightarrow N & \Rightarrow \Gamma \vdash L \twoheadrightarrow N.
\end{array}
$$

One-step reduction and reduction convert lambda terms without changing their meaning.

Fact.

$$\Gamma \vdash M \rightarrow N \Rightarrow \Gamma \vdash M = N,$$
$$\Gamma \vdash M \twoheadrightarrow N \Rightarrow \Gamma \vdash M = N.$$

Proof: By induction over the definition of $\rightarrow$ and the definition of $\twoheadrightarrow$, respectively. □

The following two theorems present the properties of reduction for $\lambda\pi$-calculus which guarantee that reduction always leads in finitely many steps to a unique fully reduced form.

Theorem. $\lambda\pi$-calculus has the diamond property, i.e.:
if $\Gamma \vdash L \twoheadrightarrow M_1$ and $\Gamma \vdash L \twoheadrightarrow M_2$,
then $\Gamma \vdash M_1 \twoheadrightarrow N$ and $\Gamma \vdash M_2 \twoheadrightarrow N$ for some lambda term N from $\mathbf{\Lambda}[\mathcal{A}]$.

Proof: As for the case that there are no secondary domains, see (Feijs, 1989, Theorem 3.8.1). □

The diamond property is also known as the Church-Rosser property and confluence.

Definition. For a lambda term M from $\mathbf{\Lambda}[\mathcal{A}]$, an *infinite reduction path* of M is an infinite sequence $\Gamma \vdash M \to L_0 \to L_1 \to \cdots$ such that

$$\Gamma \vdash M \to L_0 \text{ and for every } i \in \mathcal{N},\ \Gamma \vdash L_i \to L_{i+1}.$$

M is called *strongly normalizing*, written $\mathrm{SN}(M)$, iff there does not exist an infinite reduction path of M.

Theorem. In $\lambda\pi$-calculus every term is strongly normalizing:
$\mathrm{SN}(M)$, for all lambda terms M from $\mathbf{\Lambda}[\mathcal{A}]$.

Proof: As for the case that there are no secondary domains, see (Feijs, 1989, Theorem 3.9.7). □

In the proof given in (Feijs, 1989), the strong normalization property for $\lambda\pi$-calculus follows from the strong normalization property for $\lambda\beta$-calculus. $\lambda\beta$-calculus for $\mathcal{A}$, $\lambda\beta[\mathcal{A}]$, is the calculus with the terms and rules of $\lambda\pi[\mathcal{A}]$ except that the rule (π) has been replaced by the rule (β):

$$(\beta) \qquad \frac{}{\Gamma \vdash (\lambda x \sqsubseteq L_1.M)L_2 = [x := L_2]M}.$$

Reduction for $\lambda\beta[\mathcal{A}]$ is likewise obtained by replacing the first rule of the inductive definition of $\to$ by the following unconditional rule:

$$\Gamma \vdash (\lambda x \sqsubseteq L_1.M)L_2 \to [x := L_2]M.$$

Reduction for $\lambda\beta[\mathcal{A}]$ will be referred to as *unconditional* reduction and reduction for $\lambda\pi[\mathcal{A}]$ will be referred to as *conditional* reduction. $\lambda\beta$-calculus has the diamond property as well. The proof for $\lambda\pi$-calculus reduces directly to $\lambda\beta$-calculus.

It follows immediately from the previous two theorems that reduction always leads in finitely many steps to a unique normal form.

Definition. A lambda term M from $\mathbf{\Lambda}[\mathcal{A}]$ is a *normal form* (with respect to conditional reduction) iff there exists no lambda term N from $\mathbf{\Lambda}[\mathcal{A}]$ with $M \to N$ (where $\to$ is the one-step reduction relation of conditional reduction).

Fact. In $\lambda\pi$-calculus, every term reduces to a unique normal form.
Proof: A direct consequence of the diamond property and the strong normalization property. □

We write $red_\pi(M)$, where M is a lambda term from $\mathbf{\Lambda}[\mathcal{A}]$, for the unique normal form to which M reduces using conditional reduction.

Normal form with respect to unconditional reduction is defined as for conditional reduction, but with $\rightarrow$ referring to the one-step reduction relation of unconditional reduction. Obviously in $\lambda\beta$-calculus, every term reduces to a unique normal form as well. We write $red_\beta(M)$, where M is a lambda term from $\mathbf{\Lambda}[\mathcal{A}]$, for the unique normal form to which M reduces using unconditional reduction.

7

Specialization and Generalization for VVSL

In Chapter 6 DA and $\lambda\pi$-calculus were introduced. The semantics of the structuring language presented in Chapter 8 describes the meaning of constructs in the structuring language in terms of terms from $\lambda\pi^{++}[\mathcal{M}]$, which is roughly an instance of $\lambda\pi$-calculus for a subalgebra of DA extended with higher-order generalizations of the operations of this algebra. The relevant subalgebra of DA, MDA,* the relevant instance of $\lambda\pi$-calculus, $\lambda\pi[\mathcal{M}]$, and the relevant higher-order generalizations thereof are all presented in this chapter.

The mathematical framework for the semantics of specification languages presented in Chapters 3 and 6 usually needs specialization and sometimes generalization to fit a particular specification language. This chapter shows the specialization and generalization needed for VVSL.

First, MDA (Module Description Algebra) is presented. This includes a precise description of the specific symbols and signatures used for the semantics of flat VVSL, the language for writing the building blocks of modularly structured VVSL specifications. Thereafter, $\lambda\pi[\mathcal{M}]$ (module description calculus) and $\lambda\pi^{++}[\mathcal{M}]$ (extended module description calculus) are presented. $\lambda\pi[\mathcal{M}]$ is obtained by putting $\lambda\pi$-calculus on top of MDA. $\lambda\pi^{++}[\mathcal{M}]$ is obtained by extending $\lambda\pi[\mathcal{M}]$ with higher-order generalizations of renaming, importing and exporting. Finally, the semantic domains for the interpretation of the structuring sublanguage of VVSL are defined. The main semantic domain consists of the terms of $\lambda\pi^{++}[\mathcal{M}]$. The material on MDA, which is presented in Section 7.1, makes more precise what was treated informally in Section 4.1.

* Strictly speaking, MDA is a reduct of a subalgebra of DA_α (DA extended with parameters, see Section 6.6).

7.1 MDA and MSA

For the semantics of VVSL, there are restrictions on the ways in which symbols may be built from identifiers, origins and symbol types. Not all symbols from Sym can be used. Amongst the symbols used in the semantics of VVSL, symbols corresponding to user-defined names, symbols corresponding to pre-defined names, symbols corresponding to constructed types and special symbols (not corresponding to either user-defined names, pre-defined names or constructed types) must be distinguished. This leads to VVSL specific restrictions on symbols, symbol signatures and renamings.

One of the special symbols is a special sort symbol for the state space. It allows, for example, function symbols which correspond to names of state variables. Amongst the special symbols are also function symbols which are used for implicit conversion from subtype to type and vice versa.

Module symbols, signatures and renamings

The VVSL specific kinds of symbols, symbol signatures and renamings are now defined.

We assume three disjoint countably infinite subsets of Ident: the set UIdent of *user-defined* names, the set PIdent of *pre-defined* names and the set CIdent of *constructed type* names. In other words, we assume that we can distinguish identifiers usable as user-defined names, identifiers usable as pre-defined names and identifiers usable as names of constructed types.

Symbols corresponding to user-defined or pre-defined names are symbols with an identifier that is a user-defined or pre-defined name. Other symbols cannot be referred to by name, but symbols corresponding to constructed types can be referred to by type.

Definition. The sets NIdent of user-defined and pre-defined names, and MIdent extending NIdent with constructed type names are defined by

$$\begin{aligned} \mathsf{NIdent} &:= \mathsf{UIdent} \cup \mathsf{PIdent}, \\ \mathsf{MIdent} &:= \mathsf{NIdent} \cup \mathsf{CIdent}. \end{aligned}$$

Having introduced NIdent and MIdent, the symbols corresponding to types (including user-defined or pre-defined type names as well as constructed types) and the symbols corresponding to user-defined or pre-defined function names can be introduced.

Definition. The sets MType of *type symbols* and MFunc of *proper function symbols* are defined by

$$\begin{aligned} \mathsf{MType} &:= \{\langle i, a, \mathsf{sort}\rangle \mid i \in \mathsf{MIdent}, a \in \mathsf{Orig}\}, \\ \mathsf{MFunc} &:= \{\, \langle i, a, \langle \mathsf{func}, S_1, \ldots, S_{n+1}\rangle\rangle \mid \\ &\qquad i \in \mathsf{NIdent}, a \in \mathsf{Orig}, S_1, \ldots, S_{n+1} \in \mathsf{MType}\}. \end{aligned}$$

The indication proper is used to distinguish function symbols that correspond to user-defined or pre-defined names of functions.

Sort symbols for the state space and the computation space allow function symbols and predicate symbols which correspond to names of state variables and operations. The identifiers of the sort symbols for the state space and the computation space as well as various associated function and predicate symbols are not a user-defined, pre-defined or constructed type name.

Definition. State and Comp are special sort symbols, called *state sort symbol* and *computation sort symbol*, respectively, such that

$$\begin{array}{lll} \iota(\mathsf{State}) \notin \mathsf{MIdent}, & \omega(\mathsf{State}) = \langle\rangle, & \tau(\mathsf{State}) = \mathsf{sort}, \\ \iota(\mathsf{Comp}) \notin \mathsf{MIdent}, & \omega(\mathsf{Comp}) = \langle\rangle, & \tau(\mathsf{Comp}) = \mathsf{sort}, \\ \mathsf{State} \not\equiv \mathsf{Comp}\,. & & \end{array}$$

s0 is a special constant symbol, called *initial state symbol*, such that

$$\iota(\mathsf{s0}) \notin \mathsf{MIdent}, \quad \omega(\mathsf{s0}) = \langle\rangle, \quad \tau(\mathsf{s0}) = \langle \mathsf{func}, \mathsf{State}\rangle.$$

st_n, int_n and ext_n (for all $n < \omega$) are special function and predicate symbols, called *state selection function symbols*, *internal transition predicate symbols* and *external transition predicate symbols*, respectively, such that

$$\begin{array}{lll} \iota(\mathsf{st}_n) \notin \mathsf{MIdent}, & \omega(\mathsf{st}_n) = \langle\rangle, & \tau(\mathsf{st}_n) = \langle \mathsf{func}, \mathsf{Comp}, \mathsf{State}\rangle, \\ \iota(\mathsf{int}_n) \notin \mathsf{MIdent}, & \omega(\mathsf{int}_n) = \langle\rangle, & \tau(\mathsf{int}_n) = \langle \mathsf{pred}, \mathsf{Comp}\rangle, \\ \iota(\mathsf{ext}_n) \notin \mathsf{MIdent}, & \omega(\mathsf{ext}_n) = \langle\rangle, & \tau(\mathsf{ext}_n) = \langle \mathsf{pred}, \mathsf{Comp}\rangle, \\ \multicolumn{3}{l}{\text{for all } m < \omega\text{: } \mathsf{int}_n \not\equiv \mathsf{ext}_m,} \\ \multicolumn{3}{l}{\text{for all } m < \omega\text{: } n \neq m \;\Rightarrow\; \mathsf{st}_n \not\equiv \mathsf{st}_m, \mathsf{int}_n \not\equiv \mathsf{int}_m, \mathsf{ext}_n \not\equiv \mathsf{ext}_m\,.} \end{array}$$

Σ_{Comp}, the set of basic symbols associated with the state space and the computation space, is defined by

$$\Sigma_{\mathsf{Comp}} := \{\mathsf{State}, \mathsf{Comp}\} \,\dot\cup\, \{\mathsf{s0}\} \cup \bigcup \{\{\mathsf{st}_n, \mathsf{int}_n, \mathsf{ext}_n\} \mid n < \omega\}.$$

Having introduced sort symbols for the state space and the computation space, the symbols corresponding to user-defined names of state variables and operations can also be introduced.

Definition. The sets MVar of *state variable symbols* and MOp of *operation symbols* are defined by

$$\begin{array}{lll} \mathsf{MVar} & := & \{ \langle i, a, \langle \mathsf{func}, \mathsf{State}, S\rangle\rangle \mid \\ & & \quad i \in \mathsf{UIdent}, a \in \mathsf{Orig}, S \in \mathsf{MType}\}, \\ \mathsf{MOp} & := & \{ \langle i, a, \langle \mathsf{pred}, S_1, \ldots, S_n, \mathsf{Comp}, S'_1, \ldots, S'_m\rangle\rangle \mid \\ & & \quad i \in \mathsf{UIdent}, a \in \mathsf{Orig}, S_1, \ldots, S_n, S'_1, \ldots, S'_m \in \mathsf{MType}\}. \end{array}$$

Variable symbols ranging over all values of a type (for every type), variable symbols ranging over all states and variable symbols ranging over all computations are also needed.

Definition. The sets MVal of *value symbols*, MState of *state symbols* and MComp of *computation symbols* are defined by

$$\begin{array}{ll} \mathsf{MVal} & := \{\langle i, a, \langle \mathsf{obj}, S\rangle\rangle \mid i \in \mathsf{Ident}, a \in \mathsf{Orig}, S \in \mathsf{MType}\}, \\ \mathsf{MState} & := \{\langle i, \langle\rangle, \langle \mathsf{obj}, \mathsf{State}\rangle\rangle \mid i \in \mathsf{Ident}\}, \\ \mathsf{MComp} & := \{\langle i, \langle\rangle, \langle \mathsf{obj}, \mathsf{Comp}\rangle\rangle \mid i \in \mathsf{Ident}\}. \end{array}$$

The write variables specified for an operation, indicate that the operation leaves all state variables other than the ones mentioned as write variables unmodified. This yields an instance of the frame problem. It has to be made explicit, what exactly is left unmodified. Because this may expand by module composition, it is convenient to have modification predicate symbols for every collection of write variables.

Definition. mod_l (for all $l \in \mathsf{Orig}^*$) are special symbols, called *modification predicate symbols*, such that

$$\begin{array}{l} \iota(\mathsf{mod}_l) \notin \mathsf{MIdent}, \quad \omega(\mathsf{mod}_l) = l, \quad \tau(\mathsf{mod}_l) = \langle \mathsf{pred}, \mathsf{State}, \mathsf{State}\rangle, \\ \text{for all } l' \in \mathsf{Orig}^*\colon l \neq l' \ \Rightarrow\ \mathsf{mod}_l \not\equiv \mathsf{mod}_{l'} . \end{array}$$

The set of modification predicate symbols Mod is defined by

$$\mathsf{Mod} := \{\mathsf{mod}_l \mid l \in \mathsf{Orig}^*\}.$$

Any value belonging to a type can be generated in a certain way. This gives an induction principle for the type, which has also to be made explicit. Hence, it is necessary to have generation predicate symbols for every type.

Definition. gen^S (for all $S \in \mathsf{MType}$) are special symbols, called *generation predicate symbols*, such that

$$\begin{array}{l} \iota(\mathit{gen}^S) \notin \mathsf{MIdent}, \quad \omega(\mathit{gen}^S) = \omega(S), \quad \tau(\mathit{gen}^S) = \langle \mathsf{pred}, S\rangle, \\ \text{for all } S' \in \mathsf{MType}\colon \iota(\mathit{gen}^S) = \iota(\mathit{gen}^{S'}). \end{array}$$

The set of generation predicate symbols Gen is defined by

$$\mathsf{Gen} := \{\mathit{gen}^S \mid S \in \mathsf{MType}\}.$$

A number of pairs of conversion function symbols is associated with the basic types $\mathbb{Z}$ and $\mathbb{Q}$, every basic type that is an enumerated type, and every defined type. They are special function symbols which are used for implicit conversion from subtype to type and vice versa.

Definition. $\imath_{S \to S'}$ and $\imath^{-1}_{S' \to S}$ (for $S, S' \in \mathsf{MType}$) are special symbols, called *conversion function symbols*, such that

$$\begin{array}{l} \iota(\imath_{S \to S'}) \notin \mathsf{MIdent}, \omega(\imath_{S \to S'}) = \langle \omega(S), \omega(S')\rangle, \tau(\imath_{S \to S'}) = \langle \mathsf{func}, S, S'\rangle, \\ \iota(\imath^{-1}_{S' \to S}) \notin \mathsf{MIdent}, \omega(\imath^{-1}_{S' \to S}) = \langle \omega(S), \omega(S')\rangle, \tau(\imath^{-1}_{S' \to S}) = \langle \mathsf{func}, S', S\rangle, \\ \text{for all } T, T' \in \mathsf{MType}\colon \iota(\imath_{S \to S'}) = \iota(\imath_{T \to T'}), \iota(\imath^{-1}_{S' \to S}) = \iota(\imath^{-1}_{T' \to T}), \\ \text{for all } T, T' \in \mathsf{MType}\colon \iota(\imath_{S \to S'}) \neq \iota(\imath^{-1}_{T' \to T}). \end{array}$$

The set of conversion function symbols Conv is defined by

$$\mathsf{Conv} := \bigcup \{\{\imath_{S \to S'}, \imath^{-1}_{S' \to S}\} \mid S, S' \in \mathsf{MType}\}.$$

Having introduced all symbols that may be used for the semantics of VVSL, the VVSL specific kinds of symbols, symbol signatures and renamings can be defined.

Definition. The set MSym of *module symbols* is defined by

$$\begin{aligned}\mathsf{MSym} \ := \ & \mathsf{MType} \cup \mathsf{MFunc} \cup \mathsf{MVar} \cup \mathsf{MOp} \cup \\ & \Sigma_{\mathsf{Comp}} \cup \mathsf{Mod} \cup \mathsf{Gen} \cup \mathsf{Conv} \cup \mathsf{MVal} \cup \mathsf{MState} \cup \mathsf{MComp}\,.\end{aligned}$$

Each non-empty symbol signature used in the semantics of VVSL contains the following module symbols: the symbols associated with the basic type $\mathbb{B}$, the basic symbols associated with the state space and the computation space and the modification predicate symbols.

Definition. A *module symbol signature* is a signature $\Sigma \in \mathsf{SSig}$ such that

$$\Sigma \neq \{\} \ \Rightarrow \ \{\underline{\mathrm{B}}, tt, f\!f\} \cup \Sigma_{\mathsf{Comp}} \cup \mathsf{Mod} \subseteq \Sigma \subseteq \mathsf{MSym}\,.$$

$\underline{\mathrm{B}}, tt, f\!f$ are used to denote the symbols which are associated with the basic type $\mathbb{B}$, i.e. the type denoting the set of boolean values (see also Appendix D). The *least non-empty module symbol signature* Σ_* is defined by

$$\Sigma_* \ := \ \{\underline{\mathrm{B}}, tt, f\!f\} \cup \Sigma_{\mathsf{Comp}} \cup \mathsf{Mod}\,.$$

The set MSSig of all module symbol signatures is defined by

$$\mathsf{MSSig} \ := \ \{\Sigma \mid \Sigma \text{ is a module symbol signature }\}.$$

Σ_* is included in every non-empty module symbol signature. Note that the modification predicate symbols mod_l are in every non-empty module symbol signature. Because the externally visible signature of a module description must be a module symbol signature (see next subsection), these modification predicate symbols are always among the visible ones. This prevents an anomaly in the composition of descriptions, since, irrespective of their visibility, properties about modification rights from the descriptions concerned generally give rise to new visible consequences.

Definition. A *module renaming* is a renaming $\rho \in \mathsf{Ren}$ such that

$$\begin{array}{lll}
\rho(\mathsf{State}) = \mathsf{State}, & \rho(gen^S) = gen^{\rho(S)}, & \\
\rho(\mathsf{Comp}) = \mathsf{Comp}, & \rho(\imath_{S\to S'}) = \imath_{\rho(S)\to\rho(S')}, & \\
\rho(\mathsf{s0}) = \mathsf{s0}, & \rho(\imath^{-1}_{S\to S'}) = \imath^{-1}_{\rho(S)\to\rho(S')}, & \rho(\underline{\mathrm{B}}) = \underline{\mathrm{B}}, \\
\rho(\mathsf{st}_n) = \mathsf{st}_n, & \rho(\mathsf{MType}) \subseteq \mathsf{MType}, & \rho(tt) = tt, \\
\rho(\mathsf{int}_n) = \mathsf{int}_n, & \rho(\mathsf{MFunc}) \subseteq \mathsf{MFunc}, & \rho(f\!f) = f\!f. \\
\rho(\mathsf{ext}_n) = \mathsf{ext}_n, & \rho(\mathsf{MVar}) \subseteq \mathsf{MVar}, & \\
\rho(\mathsf{mod}_l) = \mathsf{mod}_l, & \rho(\mathsf{MOp}) \subseteq \mathsf{MOp}, &
\end{array}$$

So each renaming used in the semantics of VVSL maps symbols from Σ_* to themselves.

Domains of MDA

Having introduced module symbols, module symbol signatures and module renamings, the domains of MDA can be introduced.

Definition. MNam, the set of all user-defined names for types, functions, state variables and operations, is defined by

$$\mathsf{MNam} := \{\overline{w} \in \mathsf{Nam} \mid w \in \mathsf{MType} \cup \mathsf{MFunc} \cup \mathsf{MVar} \cup \mathsf{MOp}, \iota(w) \in \mathsf{UIdent}\}.$$

MRen, the set of all *module renamings*, is defined by

$$\mathsf{MRen} := \{\rho \in \mathsf{Ren} \mid \rho \text{ is a module renaming}\}.$$

MSig, the set of all *module name signatures*, is defined by

$$\mathsf{MSig} := \{\overline{\Sigma} \in \mathsf{Sig} \mid \Sigma \in \mathsf{MSSig}\}.$$

MDes, the set of all *module descriptions*, is defined by

$$\mathsf{MDes} := \{X \in \mathsf{Des} \mid \Sigma_X \in \mathsf{MSSig}, \Gamma_X \in \mathsf{MSSig}\}.$$

MPar, the set of all *module parameters*, is defined by

$$\mathsf{MPar} := \{P \in \mathsf{Par} \mid \delta(P) \in \mathsf{MDes}\}.$$

Note that the empty symbol signature is also a module symbol signature. Thus, a set MDes is obtained, which is also closed under the auxiliary operation π.

The specialization MDA

The sets MNam, MRen, MSig, MDes and MPar are subsets of Nam, Ren, Sig, Des and Par, respectively, and they are closed under the operations of DA_α. So they determine a subalgebra of DA_α in a trivial way: MNam, MRen, MSig, MDes and MPar are its domains and the operations of DA_α restricted to these domains are its operations. This subalgebra still includes one domain and several operations that are not needed for the meaning of the modularization constructs in VVSL.

Definition. Let MDA' be the subalgebra of DA_α with domains MNam, MRen, MSig, MDes and MPar. MDA (*Module Description Algebra*) is the reduct of MDA' that is obtained by removing the domain MNam and the operations $\bullet$ on names, $\circ$ on renamings, Δ on signatures, μ and π on descriptions, and δ on parameters.

MDA consists of the following domains, constants and operations:

Domains: MRen, MSig, MDes, MPar

$$\begin{array}{llll}
\text{Constants:} & \rho & : & \mathsf{MRen} \quad (\rho \in \mathsf{MRen}) \\
& \Sigma & : & \mathsf{MSig} \quad (\Sigma \in \mathsf{MSig}) \\
& X & : & \mathsf{MDes} \quad (X \in \mathsf{MDes}) \\
& P & : & \mathsf{MPar} \quad (P \in \mathsf{MPar})
\end{array}$$

$$\begin{array}{llll}
\text{Operations:} & \bullet & : & \mathsf{MRen} \times \mathsf{MSig} \to \mathsf{MSig} \\
& + & : & \mathsf{MSig} \times \mathsf{MSig} \to \mathsf{MSig} \\
& \Box & : & \mathsf{MSig} \times \mathsf{MSig} \to \mathsf{MSig} \\
\\
& \mathbf{\Sigma} & : & \mathsf{MDes} \to \mathsf{MSig} \\
& \bullet & : & \mathsf{MRen} \times \mathsf{MDes} \to \mathsf{MDes} \\
& + & : & \mathsf{MDes} \times \mathsf{MDes} \to \mathsf{MDes} \\
& \Box & : & \mathsf{MSig} \times \mathsf{MDes} \to \mathsf{MDes} \\
\\
& \bullet & : & \mathsf{MRen} \times \mathsf{MPar} \to \mathsf{MPar} \\
& \alpha & : & \mathsf{MPar} \times \mathsf{MDes} \times \mathsf{MDes} \to \mathsf{MDes}\,.
\end{array}$$

The symbols introduced above to denote the domains, constants and operations of MDA constitute the signature of MDA. The terms of MDA, i.e. the terms used to denote elements of the domains of MDA are constructed from the constant and operation symbols in the usual way.

According to the definition of the implementation relation for subalgebras of DA_α in Section 6.6, the implementation relation of MDA′ (the subalgebra of DA_α that was used in the definition of MDA) is the restriction of the implementation relation of DA_α to MDes. This relation is a pre-order on MDes. $\langle \{\,\}, \{\,\}, \{\,\}, \pi_\bot \rangle$ is a maximal element with respect to this pre-order. MDA together with this implementation relation make up an algebraic system with pre-order which is put on top of $\lambda\pi$-calculus in Section 7.2.

The specialization MSA

It is useful to define a particular reduct of MDA, which covers only the syntactic aspects of modules, viz. their signatures. In Chapter 8, a generalized instance of $\lambda\pi$-calculus for this reduct (together with an appropriate pre-order) is used, among other things, to describe the well-formedness of constructs in the structuring language.

Definition. MSA (*Module Signature Algebra*) is the reduct of MDA, that is obtained by removing the domains MDes and MPar and every operation having MDes or MPar as one of its argument domains or its result domain. MSA consists of the following domains, constants and operations:

Domains:	MRen			
	MSig			
Constants:	ρ	:	MRen	$(\rho \in \mathsf{MRen})$
	Σ	:	MSig	$(\Sigma \in \mathsf{MSig})$
Operations:	$\bullet$	:	$\mathsf{MRen} \times \mathsf{MSig} \to \mathsf{MSig}$	
	$+$	:	$\mathsf{MSig} \times \mathsf{MSig} \to \mathsf{MSig}$	
	$\square$	:	$\mathsf{MSig} \times \mathsf{MSig} \to \mathsf{MSig}$.	

The symbols introduced above to denote the domains, constants and operations of MSA constitute the signature of MSA. The terms of MSA, i.e. the terms used to denote elements of the domains of MSA are constructed from the constant and operation symbols in the usual way.

The inverse of the set inclusion relation on $\mathcal{P}(\overline{\mathsf{MSym}})$, $\supseteq$, restricted to MSig is a pre-order on MSig. $\{\,\}$ is a maximal element with respect to this pre-order. $\supseteq$ can be viewed as a simplified version of the implementation relation. MSA together with $\supseteq$ make up another algebraic system with pre-order which is put on top of $\lambda\pi$-calculus in Section 7.2.

7.2 Instantiating $\lambda\pi$-calculus

In order to provide the structuring sublanguage of VVSL with a semantics, $\lambda\pi$-calculus is put on top of a specific algebraic system with pre-order, viz. the one induced by MDA and the implementation relation $\sqsubseteq$ on module descriptions (see Section 7.1). The $\lambda\pi$-calculus obtained in this way is denoted by $\lambda\pi[\mathcal{M}]$. In VVSL, all constituent modules of modularization constructs may be parametrized modules. This necessitates generalizations of renaming, importing and exporting which can be applied to description terms of higher types other than the ground type 0. $\lambda\pi[\mathcal{M}]$ extended with these generalizations is denoted by $\lambda\pi^{++}[\mathcal{M}]$. Both calculi are defined in this section.

It is useful to put $\lambda\pi$-calculus also on top of the algebraic system with pre-order that is induced by MSA and its associated pre-order $\supseteq$ on module name signatures (see Section 7.1). The $\lambda\pi$-calculus obtained in this way, denoted by $\lambda\pi[\mathcal{S}]$, covers only the syntactic aspects of modules. For $\lambda\pi[\mathcal{S}]$, generalizations of renaming, union and intersection which can be applied to signature terms of higher types other than 0, are likewise needed. The resulting calculus is denoted by $\lambda\pi^{++}[\mathcal{S}]$. These calculi are also defined in this section. The generalized calculus is mainly used to describe the well-formedness of constructs in the structuring language.

The instantiation $\lambda\pi[\mathcal{M}]$

$\lambda\pi[\mathcal{M}]$ is the $\lambda\pi$-calculus with MDA together with its implementation relation as underlying algebraic system with pre-order.

Definition. The algebraic system with pre-order $\mathcal{M}$ is the algebraic system with pre-order induced by MDA and the restriction of the implementation relation of DA_α to MDes. 0 is identified with MDes.

$\lambda\pi[\mathcal{M}]$ (*Module Description Calculus*) is the instance of $\lambda\pi$-calculus for $\mathcal{M}$. So MRen, MSig, MDes and MPar are the basic types of $\lambda\pi[\mathcal{M}]$.

The constant symbols and function symbols from $\mathrm{Sig}(\mathcal{M})$, i.e. the signature of MDA introduced in Section 7.1, are used as constant symbols and function symbols for the terms of $\lambda\pi[\mathcal{M}]$. Because constants are considered to be symbols themselves, this implies that the collection of constant symbols contains all elements of each of the domains of $\mathcal{M}$.

The binary function symbols $\bullet$, $+$ and $\square$ are used in infix notation.

The generalization $\lambda\pi^{++}[\mathcal{M}]$

$\mathbf{\Lambda}[\mathcal{M}]$ contains only terms of the forms

$\rho \bullet L$, $L_1 + L_2$, $\Sigma \square L$ and $\alpha(P, L_1, L_2)$,

where L, L_1 and L_2 are lambda terms from $\mathbf{\Lambda}[\mathcal{M}]$ of higher type 0. Using the intuition that terms of the form $(\lambda x \sqsubseteq L.M)$ denote functions, this means that renaming, importing, exporting and origin substitution are not generalized to (higher-order) functions on module descriptions. The generalizations are straightforward except for renaming, but unfortunately none of them can be treated as an abbreviation. They must all be treated as extensions. The intention is that, with the introduction of the extensions, renaming, importing, exporting and origin substitution become interchangeable with application. For generalized renaming, this means that it has to yield functions which when applied to *renamed* arguments deliver results as if renaming has been applied to the value of the original function for the original arguments. Unlike with the other operations, renaming does not have the suitable properties to make this derivable by a simple additional rule. The rule concerned has to be very explicit about how terms with generalized renamings are to be 'unfolded'. Following the definition of the *unfold* operation, this unfolding will be explained. Origin substitution yields the module description provided as third argument except that the origins of symbols may be different. The sole purpose of the module description provided as second argument is to provide for the origins to be substituted for certain origin variables in the third argument. Therefore, the above-mentioned interchangeability only applies to the third argument of generalized origin substitution.

Below, $\lambda\pi[\mathcal{M}]$ is extended with the generalizations of renaming, importing, exporting and origin substitution.[†] The resulting calculus is denoted by $\lambda\pi^{++}[\mathcal{M}]$.

In the construction of the terms of $\lambda\pi^{++}[\mathcal{M}]$, the following additional (higher-order) function symbols are used:

for every $\sigma \in \mathsf{HType}$, the symbol $\bullet^\sigma$;
for every $\sigma, \tau \in \mathsf{HType}$, the symbol $+^{(\sigma,\tau)}$;
for every $\sigma \in \mathsf{HType}$, the symbol $\Box^\sigma$;
for every $\sigma, \tau \in \mathsf{HType}$, the symbol $\alpha^{(\sigma,\tau)}$.

The symbols $\bullet$, $+$, $\Box$ and α are identified with $\bullet^0$, $+^{(0,0)}$, $\Box^0$ and $\alpha^{(0,0)}$, respectively. These additional symbols are used without superscripts when this causes no ambiguity.

Definition. The *lambda terms* of $\lambda\pi^{++}[\mathcal{M}]$, denoted by $\mathbf{\Lambda}^{++}[\mathcal{M}]$, are inductively defined by the formation rules for the terms of $\lambda\pi[\mathcal{M}]$ and the following additional formation rules:

6. if ρ is a lambda term of the basic type MRen and L is a lambda term of higher type σ, then $(\rho \bullet^\sigma L)$ is a lambda term of higher type σ;

7. if L_1 and L_2 are lambda terms of higher types $\sigma = \sigma_1, \ldots, \sigma_n \to 0$ and $\tau = \tau_1, \ldots, \tau_m \to 0$, respectively, then $(L_1 +^{(\sigma,\tau)} L_2)$ is a lambda term of higher type $\sigma_1, \ldots, \sigma_n, \tau_1, \ldots, \tau_m \to 0$;

8. if Σ is a lambda term of the basic type MSig and L is a lambda term of higher type σ, then $(\Sigma \Box^\sigma L)$ is a lambda term of higher type σ;

9. if P is a lambda term of the basic type MPar, and L_1 and L_2 are lambda terms of higher types σ and τ, respectively, then $\alpha^{(\sigma,\tau)}(P, L_1, L_2)$ is a lambda term of higher type τ.

We shall henceforth use (with or without subscripts):

ρ to stand for an arbitrary lambda term of the basic type MRen,
Σ to stand for an arbitrary lambda term of the basic type MSig,
P to stand for an arbitrary lambda term of the basic type MPar,
L, M and N to stand for arbitrary lambda terms of higher type (which includes the basic type MDes).

In the rule $(+_1)$, we write M_1^0 to indicate that M_1 must have higher type 0.

Definition. The *derivation system* of $\lambda\pi^{++}[\mathcal{M}]$ is defined by the deriva-

[†] In (Feijs, Jonkers, Koymans and Renardel de Lavalette, 1987, Section 4.4), class calculus, a $\lambda\pi$-calculus closely connected to $\lambda\pi[\mathcal{M}]$, is extended with similar generalizations.

tion rules of $\lambda\pi[\mathcal{M}]$ and the following additional rules:

$$(\bullet)\quad \frac{}{\Gamma \vdash L = \mathit{unfold}(L)} \qquad \frac{}{\Gamma \vdash \Sigma = \mathit{unfold}(\Sigma)}$$

$$(+_1)\quad \frac{}{\Gamma \vdash M_1^0 + (\lambda x \sqsubseteq L.M_2) = \lambda x \sqsubseteq L.(M_1 + M_2)} \text{ if } x \notin M_1$$

$$(+_2)\quad \frac{}{\Gamma \vdash (\lambda x \sqsubseteq L.M_1) + M_2 = \lambda x \sqsubseteq L.(M_1 + M_2)} \text{ if } x \notin M_2$$

$$(\Box)\quad \frac{}{\Gamma \vdash \Sigma \Box (\lambda x \sqsubseteq L.M) = \lambda x \sqsubseteq L.(\Sigma \Box M)}$$

$$(\alpha_1)\quad \frac{}{\Gamma \vdash \alpha(P, \lambda x \sqsubseteq L.M_1, M_2) = \alpha(P, [x := L]M_1, M_2)}$$

$$(\alpha_2)\quad \frac{}{\Gamma \vdash \alpha(P, M_1, \lambda x \sqsubseteq L.M_2) = \lambda x \sqsubseteq \alpha(P, M_1, L).\, \alpha(P, M_1, M_2)}$$

The operation *unfold* (on lambda terms of a higher type or the basic type MSig) and an auxiliary operation *expand* are simultaneously and inductively defined by

$$\begin{array}{ll}
\mathit{unfold}(x) & = x, \\
\mathit{unfold}(c) & = c, \\
\mathit{unfold}(LM) & = \mathit{unfold}(L)\mathit{unfold}(M), \\
\mathit{unfold}(\lambda x \sqsubseteq L.M) & = \lambda x \sqsubseteq \mathit{unfold}(L).\mathit{unfold}(M), \\
\mathit{unfold}(\rho \bullet L) & = \mathit{expand}(\rho, \mathit{unfold}(L), \{\}), \\
\mathit{unfold}(L_1 + L_2) & = \mathit{unfold}(L_1) + \mathit{unfold}(L_2), \\
\mathit{unfold}(\Sigma \Box L) & = \mathit{unfold}(\Sigma) \Box \mathit{unfold}(L), \\
\mathit{unfold}(\alpha(P, L_1, L_2) & = \alpha(P, \mathit{unfold}(L_1), \mathit{unfold}(L_2)), \\
\mathit{unfold}(\rho \bullet \Sigma) & = \mathit{expand}(\rho, \mathit{unfold}(\Sigma), \{\}), \\
\mathit{unfold}(\Sigma_1 + \Sigma_2) & = \mathit{unfold}(\Sigma_1) + \mathit{unfold}(\Sigma_2), \\
\mathit{unfold}(\Sigma_1 \Box \Sigma_2) & = \mathit{unfold}(\Sigma_1) \Box \mathit{unfold}(\Sigma_2), \\
\mathit{unfold}(\mathbf{\Sigma}(L)) & = \mathbf{\Sigma}(\mathit{unfold}(L)),
\end{array}$$

$$\begin{array}{ll}
\mathit{expand}(\rho, x, V) & = x \quad \text{if } x \in V, \\
 & \rho \bullet x \quad \text{otherwise}, \\
\mathit{expand}(\rho, c, V) & = \rho \bullet c, \\
\mathit{expand}(\rho, LM, V) & = \mathit{expand}(\rho, L, V)\mathit{expand}(\rho, M, V), \\
\mathit{expand}(\rho, \lambda x \sqsubseteq L.M, V) & = \lambda x \sqsubseteq \mathit{expand}(\rho, L, V).\mathit{expand}(\rho, M, V \cup \{x\}), \\
\mathit{expand}(\rho, \rho_1 \bullet L, V) & = (\rho \cdot \rho_1) \bullet \mathit{expand}(\rho, L, V), \\
\mathit{expand}(\rho, L_1 + L_2, V) & = \mathit{expand}(\rho, L_1, V) + \mathit{expand}(\rho, L_2, V), \\
\mathit{expand}(\rho, \Sigma \Box L, V) & = \mathit{expand}(\rho, \Sigma, V) \Box \mathit{expand}(\rho, L, V), \\
\mathit{expand}(\rho, \alpha(P, L_1, L_2, V) & = \alpha(\rho \bullet P, \mathit{expand}(\rho, L_1, V), \mathit{expand}(\rho, L_2, V)),
\end{array}$$

$$
\begin{aligned}
expand(\rho, \rho_1 \bullet \Sigma, V) &= (\rho \cdot \rho_1) \bullet expand(\rho, \Sigma, V),\\
expand(\rho, \Sigma_1 + \Sigma_2, V) &= expand(\rho, \Sigma_1, V) + expand(\rho, \Sigma_2, V),\\
expand(\rho, \Sigma_1 \,\Box\, \Sigma_2, V) &= expand(\rho, \Sigma_1, V) \,\Box\, expand(\rho, \Sigma_2, V),\\
expand(\rho, \mathbf{\Sigma}(L), V) &= \mathbf{\Sigma}(expand(\rho, L, V)).
\end{aligned}
$$

The operation *expand* is a partial operation, because the above-mentioned rules may introduce undefined module renamings $\rho \cdot \rho_1$. This is the case if ρ_1 is not renameable by ρ (see Section 6.6).

The simple rules $(+_1)$, $(+_2)$, $(\Box)$ and (α_2) are sufficient to make the intended interchangeability of importing, exporting and origin substitution with application derivable. The complex rule $(\bullet)$ is needed to make the intended interchangeability of renaming with application derivable. This rule is very explicit about how terms with generalized renamings are to be unfolded. In order to unfold a term of the form $\rho \bullet L$, all subterms of L with generalized renamings have to be unfolded first. It is important that, when L is of the form $(\lambda x \sqsubseteq L'.M')$, free occurrences of x in M' are not renamed (i.e. not replaced by the term $\rho \bullet x$). The auxiliary operations *expand* accomplish this by 'remembering' the lambda variables that may not be renamed.

The rule (α_1) expresses that the second argument of origin substitution can always be replaced by a module description. This is in accordance with the intuition that the sole purpose of the second argument of origin substitution is to provide for the origins to be substituted for certain origin variables.

Definition. By considering the rules $(\bullet)$, $(+_1)$, $(+_2)$, $(\Box)$, (α_1) and (α_2) as reduction rules, reduction for $\lambda\pi^{++}[\mathcal{M}]$ is obtained.

It will only be described informally here. As usual, one-step reduction for $\lambda\pi^{++}[\mathcal{M}]$ is tantamount to contraction of a subterm. The main difference with reduction for $\lambda\pi[\mathcal{M}]$ is that not only subterms of the form $(\lambda x \sqsubseteq L_1.M)L_2$ can be contracted. The subterms that are candidates for contraction are terms of the following forms:

$$
\begin{aligned}
&(\lambda x \sqsubseteq L_1.M)L_2,\\
&\rho \bullet L,\\
&M_1^0 + (\lambda x \sqsubseteq L.M_2),\\
&(\lambda x \sqsubseteq L.M_1) + M_2,\\
&\Sigma \,\Box\, (\lambda x \sqsubseteq L.M),\\
&\alpha(P, \lambda x \sqsubseteq L.M_1, M_2),\\
&\alpha(P, M_1, \lambda x \sqsubseteq L.M_2).
\end{aligned}
$$

Subterms of the first two forms cannot always be contracted. For terms of the first form, it depends upon the context as for $\lambda\pi[\mathcal{M}]$. Terms of the second form cannot be contracted if they are already in unfolded form, which is obvious.

Fact. In $\lambda\pi^{++}[\mathcal{M}]$, every term reduces to a unique normal form.

Proof: By showing that the diamond property and the strong normalization property hold. This is shown in a similar way as for generalized class calculus, see (Feijs, Jonkers, Koymans and Renardel de Lavalette, 1987, Theorems 4.4.8.1 and 4.4.9.4), using that the following holds:

$$\Gamma \vdash M \to N \;\Rightarrow\; \Gamma \vdash \mathit{unfold}(M) \twoheadrightarrow \mathit{unfold}(N). \qquad \square$$

Unconditional reduction for $\lambda\pi^{++}[\mathcal{M}]$, which only differs in the fact that subterms of the form $(\lambda x \sqsubseteq L_1.M)L_2$ can always be contracted, gives also unique normal forms.

The instantiation $\lambda\pi[\mathcal{S}]$

$\lambda\pi[\mathcal{S}]$ is the $\lambda\pi$-calculus with MSA together with the inverse inclusion relation on its signatures as underlying algebraic system with pre-order.

Definition. The algebraic system with pre-order $\mathcal{S}$ is the algebraic system with pre-order induced by MSA and the restriction of the inverse of the set inclusion relation on $\mathcal{P}(\overline{\mathsf{MSym}})$ to MSig. 0 is identified with MSig.

$\lambda\pi[\mathcal{S}]$ (*Module Signature Calculus*) is the instance of $\lambda\pi$-calculus for $\mathcal{S}$. So MRen and MSig are the basic types of $\lambda\pi[\mathcal{S}]$.

The constant symbols and function symbols from Sig($\mathcal{S}$), i.e. the signature of MSA introduced in Section 7.1, are used as constant symbols and function symbols for the terms of $\lambda\pi[\mathcal{S}]$. Because constants are considered to be symbols themselves, this implies that the collection of constant symbols contains all elements of each of the domains of $\mathcal{S}$.

The binary function symbols $\bullet$, $+$ and $\square$ are used in infix notation.

The generalization $\lambda\pi^{++}[\mathcal{S}]$

Below, $\lambda\pi[\mathcal{S}]$ is extended with higher-order generalizations of renaming, union and intersection of signatures. The generalizations are analogous to those for $\lambda\pi^{++}[\mathcal{M}]$. The resulting calculus is denoted by $\lambda\pi^{++}[\mathcal{S}]$.

In the construction of the terms of $\lambda\pi^{++}[\mathcal{S}]$, the following additional (higher-order) function symbols are used:

for every $\sigma \in \mathsf{HType}$, the symbol $\bullet^{\sigma}$;
for every $\sigma, \tau \in \mathsf{HType}$, the symbol $+^{(\sigma,\tau)}$;
for every $\sigma \in \mathsf{HType}$, the symbol $\square^{\sigma}$.

The symbols $\bullet$, $+$ and $\square$ are identified with $\bullet^0$, $+^{(0,0)}$ and $\square^0$, respectively. The additional symbols are used without superscripts when this causes no ambiguity.

Definition. The lambda terms of $\lambda\pi^{++}[\mathcal{S}]$, denoted by $\mathbf{\Lambda}^{++}[\mathcal{S}]$, are inductively defined by the formation rules for the terms of $\lambda\pi[\mathcal{S}]$ and the following additional formation rules:

6′. if ρ is a lambda term of the basic type MRen and Σ is a lambda term of higher type σ, then $(\rho \bullet^{\sigma} \Sigma)$ is a lambda term of higher type σ;

7′. if Σ_1 and Σ_2 are lambda terms of higher types $\sigma = \sigma_1, \ldots, \sigma_n \to 0$ and $\tau = \tau_1, \ldots, \tau_m \to 0$, respectively, then $(\Sigma_1 +^{(\sigma,\tau)} \Sigma_2)$ is a lambda term of higher type $\sigma_1, \ldots, \sigma_n, \tau_1, \ldots, \tau_m \to 0$;

8′. if Σ_1 and Σ_2 are lambda terms of higher types 0 and σ, respectively, then $(\Sigma_1 \Box^{\sigma} \Sigma_2)$ is a lambda term of higher type σ.

We shall henceforth use (with or without subscripts):

ρ to stand for an arbitrary lambda term of the basic type MRen,
Σ to stand for an arbitrary lambda term of higher type (which includes the basic type MSig).

Definition. The *derivation system* of $\lambda\pi^{++}[\mathcal{S}]$ is defined by the derivation rules of $\lambda\pi[\mathcal{S}]$ and the additional derivation rules $(\bullet)$, $(+_1)$, $(+_2)$ and $(\Box)$ of $\lambda\pi^{++}[\mathcal{M}]$, but with the place-holder L replaced by Σ, etc.

The operations *unfold* and *expand* are in this case simultaneously and inductively defined by

$$
\begin{aligned}
&\mathit{unfold}(x) &&= x,\\
&\mathit{unfold}(c) &&= c,\\
&\mathit{unfold}(\Sigma_1\Sigma_2) &&= \mathit{unfold}(\Sigma_1)\mathit{unfold}(\Sigma_2),\\
&\mathit{unfold}(\lambda x \sqsubseteq \Sigma_1.\Sigma_2) &&= \lambda x \sqsubseteq \mathit{unfold}(\Sigma_1).\mathit{unfold}(\Sigma_2),\\
&\mathit{unfold}(\rho \bullet \Sigma) &&= \mathit{expand}(\rho, \mathit{unfold}(\Sigma), \{\,\}),\\
&\mathit{unfold}(\Sigma_1 + \Sigma_2) &&= \mathit{unfold}(\Sigma_1) + \mathit{unfold}(\Sigma_2),\\
&\mathit{unfold}(\Sigma_1 \Box \Sigma_2) &&= \mathit{unfold}(\Sigma_1) \Box \mathit{unfold}(\Sigma_2),
\end{aligned}
$$

$$
\begin{aligned}
&\mathit{expand}(\rho, x, V) &&= x \quad \text{if } x \in V,\\
& &&\ \rho \bullet x \quad \text{otherwise},\\
&\mathit{expand}(\rho, c, V) &&= \rho \bullet c,\\
&\mathit{expand}(\rho, \Sigma_1\Sigma_2, V) &&= \mathit{expand}(\rho, \Sigma_1, V)\mathit{expand}(\rho, \Sigma_2, V),\\
&\mathit{expand}(\rho, \lambda x \sqsubseteq \Sigma_1.\Sigma_2, V) &&= \lambda x \sqsubseteq \mathit{expand}(\rho, \Sigma_1, V).\\
& &&\ \mathit{expand}(\rho, \Sigma_2, V \cup \{x\}),\\
&\mathit{expand}(\rho, \rho_1 \bullet \Sigma, V) &&= (\rho \cdot \rho_1) \bullet \mathit{expand}(\rho, \Sigma, V),\\
&\mathit{expand}(\rho, \Sigma_1 + \Sigma_2, V) &&= \mathit{expand}(\rho, \Sigma_1, V) + \mathit{expand}(\rho, \Sigma_2, V),\\
&\mathit{expand}(\rho, \Sigma_1 \Box \Sigma_2, V) &&= \mathit{expand}(\rho, \Sigma_1, V) \Box \mathit{expand}(\rho, \Sigma_2, V).
\end{aligned}
$$

This operation *expand* is also a partial operation: one of the rules introduces undefined module renamings $\rho \cdot \rho_1$, if ρ_1 is not renameable by ρ.

Definition. For $\Sigma \in \mathbf{\Lambda}^{++}[\mathcal{S}]$, Σ is *renameable* by ρ iff $\mathit{expand}(\rho, \Sigma, \{\,\})$ is defined.

Reduction for $\lambda\pi^{++}[\mathcal{S}]$ is similar to reduction for $\lambda\pi^{++}[\mathcal{M}]$. We only mention here that the subterms that are candidates for contraction are terms of the following forms:

$$(\lambda x \sqsubseteq \Sigma_1.\Sigma_2)\Sigma_3,$$
$$\rho \bullet \Sigma,$$
$$\Sigma_1^0 + (\lambda x \sqsubseteq \Sigma_2.\Sigma_3),$$
$$(\lambda x \sqsubseteq \Sigma_1.\Sigma_2) + \Sigma_3,$$
$$\Sigma_1 \Box (\lambda x \sqsubseteq \Sigma_2.\Sigma_3).$$

Subterms of the first two forms cannot always be contracted. For terms of the first form, it depends upon the context as for $\lambda\pi[\mathcal{S}]$. Terms of the second form cannot be contracted if they are already in unfolded form.

In $\lambda\pi^{++}[\mathcal{S}]$, every term reduces to a unique normal form. The corresponding unconditional reduction, which only differs in the fact that subterms of the form $(\lambda x \sqsubseteq \Sigma_1.\Sigma_2)\Sigma_3$ can always be contracted, also gives unique normal forms.

7.3 Semantic domains for the structuring language

The main semantic domain for the interpretation of the modularization and parametrization constructs of VVSL is a domain of description terms. A domain of signature terms is used to represent syntactic properties of the modularization and parametrization constructs.

This section starts with the definition of the set of lambda variable symbols that underlie the domain of signature terms and the domain of description terms. Thereafter, these domains are defined.

Lambda variable symbols

In the definition of $\lambda\pi$-calculus, only one assumption about lambda variable symbols is made (viz. the assumption that there are lambda variable symbols for each higher type). So lambda variable symbols may be actualized in many ways. For the use of $\lambda\pi$-calculus in the formal definition of VVSL, this is done in a way resembling the way in which the symbols of MPL_ω are actualized for the use of this logic as the underlying logic of DA in Section 6.2. Lambda variable symbols are built from user-defined names and higher types.

Definition. The set LVar of *lambda variable symbols* is defined by

$$\mathsf{LVar} := \{\langle i, \tau\rangle \mid i \in \mathsf{UIdent}, \tau \in \mathsf{HType}\}.$$

We write $\iota(x)$, where $x = \langle i, \tau\rangle$ is a lambda variable symbol, for i. Instead of $\langle i, \tau\rangle$, we write i^τ.

Symbols from LVar are interpreted as lambda variable symbols of $\lambda\pi$-calculus according to the following rule:

- each $x = i^\tau$ is a lambda variable symbol of type τ in $\lambda\pi$-calculus.

This actualization of lambda variable symbols is implicit in the definition of the domains of module signature terms and module description terms.

Domains of signature terms and description terms

Definition. The domain STerm of module *signature terms* is defined by

$$\mathsf{STerm} := \mathbf{\Lambda}^{++}[\mathcal{S}].$$

The domain DTerm of module *description terms* is defined by

$$\mathsf{DTerm} := \mathbf{\Lambda}^{++}[\mathcal{M}].$$

We write STerm_R and STerm_S for the subdomains $\{\rho \in \mathsf{STerm} \mid \mathit{ltype}(\rho) = \mathsf{MRen}\}$ and $\{\rho \in \mathsf{STerm} \mid \mathit{ltype}(\rho) \in \mathsf{HType}\}$, respectively, of STerm. We write DTerm_R, DTerm_S, and DTerm_D for the subdomains $\{\rho \in \mathsf{DTerm} \mid \mathit{ltype}(\rho) = \mathsf{MRen}\}$, $\{\rho \in \mathsf{DTerm} \mid \mathit{ltype}(\rho) = \mathsf{MSig}\}$, $\{\rho \in \mathsf{DTerm} \mid \mathit{ltype}(\rho) \in \mathsf{HType}\}$, respectively, of DTerm.

There is a mapping from description terms to signature terms corresponding to taking the signature for description terms of type MDes.

Definition. The forgetful transformation from description terms to signature terms is given by a mapping $\mathit{sterm}\colon \mathsf{DTerm} \to \mathsf{STerm}$, which is inductively defined by

$$\begin{array}{ll}
\mathit{sterm}(x) & = \mathbf{\Sigma}(x), \\
\mathit{sterm}(c) & = \begin{array}{ll} \mathbf{\Sigma}(c) & \text{if } c\colon \mathsf{MDes}, \\ c & \text{otherwise}, \end{array} \\
\mathit{sterm}(LM) & = \mathit{sterm}(L)\mathit{sterm}(M), \\
\mathit{sterm}(\lambda x \sqsubseteq L.M) & = \lambda x \sqsubseteq \mathit{sterm}(L).\mathit{sterm}(M), \\
\mathit{sterm}(\rho \bullet L) & = \rho \bullet \mathit{sterm}(L), \\
\mathit{sterm}(L_1 + L_2) & = \mathit{sterm}(L_1) + \mathit{sterm}(L_2), \\
\mathit{sterm}(\Sigma \,\square\, L) & = \mathit{sterm}(\Sigma) \,\square\, \mathit{sterm}(L), \\
\mathit{sterm}(\alpha(P, L_1, L_2)) & = \mathit{sterm}(L_2), \\
\mathit{sterm}(\rho \bullet \Sigma) & = \rho \bullet \mathit{sterm}(\Sigma), \\
\mathit{sterm}(\Sigma_1 + \Sigma_2) & = \mathit{sterm}(\Sigma_1) + \mathit{sterm}(\Sigma_2), \\
\mathit{sterm}(\Sigma_1 \,\square\, \Sigma_2) & = \mathit{sterm}(\Sigma_1) \,\square\, \mathit{sterm}(\Sigma_2), \\
\mathit{sterm}(\mathbf{\Sigma}(L)) & = \mathit{sterm}(L).
\end{array}$$

Obviously, $\mathit{red}_\beta(\mathbf{\Sigma}(L)) = \mathit{red}_\beta(\mathit{sterm}(L))$ if $\mathit{ltype}(L) = 0$.

8

Definition of the Structuring Language

This chapter contains a formal semantics for the structuring sublanguage of VVSL. This language consists of modularization constructs and parametrization constructs. The semantics presented describes the meaning of constructs in the language in terms of terms from $\lambda\pi^{++}[\mathcal{M}]$, which is roughly an instance of $\lambda\pi$-calculus for a subalgebra of DA extended with higher-order generalizations of the operations of this algebra. DA and $\lambda\pi$-calculus were introduced in Chapter 6. DA is a general algebraic model of modular specification and $\lambda\pi$-calculus is a variant of classical typed lambda calculus. The relevant subalgebra of DA, MDA, the relevant instance of $\lambda\pi$-calculus, $\lambda\pi[\mathcal{M}]$, and the relevant higher-order generalizations thereof were all introduced in Chapter 7. The presentation in this chapter illustrates an approach to give a formal semantics for a language for modular structuring of specifications. The semantics presented describes the meaning of modularly structured VVSL specifications as lambda terms denoting essentially presentations of logical theories about what is described in them or (higher-order) functions on such theory presentations.

Chapter 5 contains a logic-based semantics for flat VVSL by which the meaning of constructs in flat VVSL is described in terms of formulae from the language of MPL_ω. The semantics for the structuring language of VVSL presented in this chapter, which describes the meaning of the modularization and parametrization constructs complementing flat VVSL, is built on top of the logic-based semantics for flat VVSL. The building blocks of the terms of $\lambda\pi^{++}[\mathcal{M}]$ are the constants of MDA and these constants are essentially presentations of theories by sets of formulae of MPL_ω.

It is worth noticing again that many laws commonly holding in models proposed for modularly structured algebraic specification also hold in DA, the model used, together with $\lambda\pi$-calculus, as the basis for the presented semantics. Nevertheless, DA has some special features, which are not found in those models, making it more suitable as the underlying model for modularizing model-oriented, state-based specifications. In $\lambda\pi$-calculus, no essential deviations from classical typed lambda calculus are imposed: $\lambda\pi$-calculus has parameter restrictions in lambda abstractions and consequently a conditional version of the rule (β). This extension permits us to put requirements on the actual parameters to which parametrized modules may be applied.

The illustrated approach is applicable to any structuring language for model-oriented specifications. The only prerequisite is a logic-based semantics for the flat specification language concerned. Other proposed approaches commonly have the same prerequisite, but notwithstanding formal semantics for flat model-oriented specification languages are generally not logic-based. For example, the formal semantics of VDM-SL presented in the draft ISO standard is not logic-based. However, the logic-based semantics of flat VVSL presented in Chapter 5 includes a logic-based semantics for most of VDM-SL. Note that modularization and parametrization are not incorporated in the standardized version of VDM-SL; the mathematical foundations of the proposals could not be completed satisfactorily.

Note that as a result of the approach applied in this book features of flat VVSL can be understood without any understanding of the modularization and parametrization features of VVSL, the modularization features of VVSL can be understood without any understanding of the features of flat VVSL and the parametrization features of VVSL, etc. Indeed, the high degree of orthogonality is perhaps more relevant than the particular ingredients used. It supports the development of proof rules which allow theorems to be proved about a module from theorems about the modules from which it has been constructed. This is further discussed in Section 9.2. Such proof rules naturally suggest general proof strategies which exploit the modular structure of specifications, which matters to the issue of formal correctness proofs of design steps (i.e. verified design). Besides, they enable compositional development of theories about modules, which seems essential to the issue of module reusability. The proof rules concerned can be devised without understanding the features of flat VVSL. If efficiency is an issue, it seems rarely possible to maintain the modular structure of a specification in the ultimate software system – see also (Fitzgerald and Jones, 1990). This justifies the supply of conversion rules which allow us to transform a specification to another specification with a different modular structure in a meaning preserving way. Such conversion rules can also be devised without understanding the features of flat VVSL. Of course, all this is also relevant to other model-oriented specification languages.

The meaning of constructs in the structuring language is only defined for well-formed language constructs. Both the well-formedness and meaning of a construct generally depend on the name introducing constructs in the scope in which it occurs. In the case of the modularization and parametrization constructs of VVSL, the constructs concerned comprise definitions introducing names for types, functions, state variables and operations as well as constructs introducing names for modules (abstractions and local definitions). So it does not suffice to use the contexts introduced in Chapter 5 for modelling the scope. For modelling the scope with respect to names for modules, other contexts are needed. They are introduced before the actual presentation of the syntax and semantics begins. In later sections, the well-formedness and meaning of constructs in the structuring sublanguage of VVSL is described with respect to a context modelling the scope in relation to names for types, functions, state variables and operations as well as a context modelling the scope in relation to names for modules.

There is a section that deals with the syntax and semantics of complete modularly structured specifications and a section that deals with the modularization and parametrization constructs. Each section starts with an overview of the constructs concerned, a presentation of their syntax and some general remarks regarding their well-formedness, syntactic properties and meaning. Following this introduction, there are separate subsections on the constructs of the various forms that are distinguished by the production rules given in the syntax presentation concerned. In fact, only a kernel of the structuring sublanguage of VVSL is defined in this chapter: the remainder is introduced as abbreviations in Appendix E.

8.1 Contexts

The well-formedness and meaning of a construct from flat VVSL generally depends on its name context and symbol context, respectively. Name contexts and symbol contexts were introduced in Section 5.1, together with predicates and mappings on them which are relevant to the well-formedness and meaning of constructs in flat VVSL. Name contexts and symbol contexts, as well as some of these predicates and mappings, are also relevant to the well-formedness and meaning of modularization and parametrization constructs, but they are not sufficient. This section introduces two additional notions of context which are needed for the well-formedness and meaning of the modularization and parametrization constructs in addition to the above-mentioned ones. Predicates and mappings, which are used to describe the context dependent aspects of the well-formedness, syntactic properties and meaning of the modularization and parametrization constructs, are also defined.

In the structuring sublanguage of VVSL, abstraction modules and local definition modules introduce names for modules. Such a name introducing construct introduces a name for a possibly parametrized module description; the constructs within which the name is visible constitute the scope of the construct. For this name, there must be a corresponding lambda variable symbol in $\lambda\pi^{++}[\mathcal{M}]$. The corresponding lambda variable symbol is obtained by combining the name and the type of the lambda variable symbol. Both the well-formedness and meaning of a modularization or parametrization construct depend on the symbols corresponding to the names of modules that occur in the construct as well as the terms associated with them (see below). A prerequisite for well-formedness is that that these names have been introduced by constructs in the scope in which the modularization or parametrization construct occurs.

The context of a modularization or parametrization construct consists of all lambda variable symbols corresponding to names introduced by name introducing constructs in the scope in which the construct occurs, each one together with the term it is associated with: the parameter restriction for restricted parameters of abstraction modules and the abbreviated term for module bindings of local definition modules. This provides all details about the names of modules occurring in the construct on which its well-formedness and meaning depends.

In fact, we distinguish between two different kinds of lambda variable contexts: those where the lambda variable symbols are coupled with description terms, called description contexts, and those where they are coupled with signature terms, called signature contexts. This is not essential, but it avoids blurring the distinction between well-formedness and meaning. For well-formedness, the signature contexts suffice.

Definition. The sets SCxt of *signature contexts* and DCxt of *description contexts* are defined by

$$\begin{aligned}\mathsf{SCxt} \;:=\; & \{\, \langle\langle x_1, \Sigma_1\rangle, \ldots, \langle x_n, \Sigma_n\rangle\rangle \in \mathsf{LVar} \times \mathsf{STerm}_S)^* \mid \\ & \bigwedge_{j=1}^{n} (\mathit{ltype}(x_j) = \mathit{ltype}(L_j)) \wedge \bigwedge_{j=1}^{n} (\bigwedge_{k=j+1}^{n} (\iota(x_j) \neq \iota(x_k)))\}, \\ \mathsf{DCxt} \;:=\; & \{\, \langle\langle x_1, L_1\rangle, \ldots, \langle x_n, L_n\rangle\rangle \in (\mathsf{LVar} \times \mathsf{DTerm}_D)^* \mid \\ & \bigwedge_{j=1}^{n} (\mathit{ltype}(x_j) = \mathit{ltype}(L_j)) \wedge \bigwedge_{j=1}^{n} (\bigwedge_{k=j+1}^{n} (\iota(x_j) \neq \iota(x_k)))\}.\end{aligned}$$

The requirement expressed by $\bigwedge_{j=1}^{n} (\bigwedge_{k=j+1}^{n} (\iota(x_j) \neq \iota(x_k)))$, enforces that there is at most one lambda variable symbol corresponding to each name. Note that signature and description contexts are sequences (in contrast with sets). Sequences are used to preserve the introduction order of lambda variable symbols. Thus, substitutions can be applied in the right order when free variables are removed from a term (in order to determine by syntactic manipulation properties which it represents).

The reconstruction of the signature context of a construct from its description context is straightforward. It is needed to describe the meaning of import module constructs.

Definition. The mapping $\mathit{scxt}\colon \mathsf{DCxt} \to \mathsf{SCxt}$ is defined by

$$\mathit{scxt}(\langle\langle x_1, L_1\rangle, \ldots, \langle x_n, L_n\rangle\rangle) \;:=\; \langle\langle x_1, \mathit{sterm}(L_1)\rangle, \ldots, \langle x_n, \mathit{sterm}(L_n)\rangle\rangle$$

(the mapping *sterm*: DTerm $\to$ STerm was introduced in Section 7.3). We write $\overline{\Gamma}$ for $scxt(\Gamma)$.

An identifier used as a name for a module description is called visible in its signature context if it is part of a lambda variable symbol being found in that context. This property is defined for signature contexts only, because it is only needed to define well-formedness.

Definition. The predicate *visible*: UIdent $\times$ SCxt is defined by

$$visible(i, \langle\langle x_1, \Sigma_1\rangle, \ldots, \langle x_n, \Sigma_n\rangle\rangle) :\Leftrightarrow \bigvee_{j=1}^{n} (i = \iota(x_j)).$$

In the description of the well-formedness of constructs, we write 'x is visible in Δ' instead of $visible(x, \Delta)$

$visible(i, \Delta)$ indicates that i is the name of a module description for which there is a corresponding lambda variable symbol in the context Δ.

Partial mappings, which give the lambda variable symbol corresponding to an identifier in a signature context and in a description context, are defined below. These mappings are only defined if the identifier is visible in the context. This condition is met by all well-formed modularization and parametrization constructs. These mappings are used to describe the syntactic properties and meaning of modularization and parametrization constructs.

Definition. The mapping *lvar*: UIdent $\times$ SCxt $\to$ LVar and the mapping *lvar*: UIdent $\times$ DCxt $\to$ LVar are inductively defined by

$$\begin{array}{lll} x \in dom(\Delta) \wedge i = \iota(x) & \Rightarrow & lvar(i, \Delta) = x, \\ x \in dom(\Gamma) \wedge i = \iota(x) & \Rightarrow & lvar(i, \Gamma) = x, \end{array}$$

where $dom(\Delta)$ and $dom(\Gamma)$ are defined by

$$\begin{array}{ll} dom(\langle\langle x_1, \Sigma_1\rangle, \ldots, \langle x_n, \Sigma_n\rangle\rangle) & := \{x_1, \ldots, x_n\}, \\ dom(\langle\langle x_1, L_1\rangle, \ldots, \langle x_n, L_n\rangle\rangle) & := \{x_1, \ldots, x_n\}. \end{array}$$

We write m^{Δ} and m^{Γ} for $lvar(m, \Delta)$ and $lvar(m, \Gamma)$, respectively.

$lvar(i, \Delta)$ and $lvar(i, \Gamma)$ are the lambda variable symbols corresponding to the identifier i in the signature context Δ and the description context Γ, respectively.

Module name signatures and name contexts are closely connected. The construction of a name context from a signature term and a signature context is defined below. First two auxiliary mappings are introduced. The following partial mapping is used to reduce a given signature term to its normal form. A signature context is needed to remove the free variables from the signature term concerned before its reduction. More precisely, the mapping gives the closed flat signature term corresponding to a signature term of type 0 in a given signature context where all the free lambda variables of the term are visible.

Definition. The auxiliary mapping *flatten*: $\mathsf{STerm}_S \times \mathsf{SCxt} \rightarrow \mathsf{STerm}_S$ is inductively defined by

$$\begin{aligned}&\Delta = \langle\langle x_1, \Sigma_1\rangle, \ldots, \langle x_n, \Sigma_n\rangle\rangle \wedge \\ &\mathit{free}(\Sigma) \subseteq \{x_1, \ldots, x_n\} \wedge \mathit{ltype}(\Sigma) = 0 \Rightarrow \\ &\quad \mathit{flatten}(\Sigma, \Delta) = \mathit{red}_\beta([x_1 := \Sigma_1] \ldots [x_n := \Sigma_n]\Sigma).\end{aligned}$$

$\mathit{flatten}(\Sigma, \Delta)$ is the closed flat signature term representing the module name signature consisting of those names for which it can be determined 'statically' that they belong to the module name signature represented by the signature term Σ, given the signature context Δ.

The following partial mapping is used to get the module name signature represented by a closed flat signature term.

Definition. The auxiliary mapping *sig*: $\mathsf{STerm}_S \rightarrow \mathsf{MSig}$ is inductively defined by

$$\Sigma \text{ is flat } \wedge \mathit{free}(\Sigma) = \{\,\} \Rightarrow \mathit{sig}(\Sigma) = \Sigma^{\mathcal{S}}.$$

So $\mathit{sig}(\Sigma)$ is the module name signature to which the closed flat signature term Σ evaluates in the algebraic system with pre-order $\mathcal{S}$.

The construction of a name context from a signature term and a signature context is now defined. This mapping is used to describe the well-formedness and meaning of import module constructs.

Definition. The mapping *ncxt*: $\mathsf{STerm}_S \times \mathsf{SCxt} \rightarrow \mathsf{NCxt}$ is defined by

$$\begin{aligned}&\mathit{ncxt}(\Sigma, \Delta) := \\ &\quad \{\overline{w} \in \mathsf{MNam} \mid \overline{w} \in \mathit{sig}(\mathit{flatten}(\Sigma, \Delta))\} \cup \quad \text{if } \mathit{ltype}(\Sigma) = 0, \\ &\quad \{\langle \overline{S}, \overline{S'}\rangle \mid \overline{\imath_{S \rightarrow S'}} \in \mathit{sig}(\mathit{flatten}(\Sigma, \Delta))\} \\ &\quad \{\,\} \quad \text{otherwise.}\end{aligned}$$

Instead of $\mathit{ncxt}(\Sigma, \Delta)$, we write $\mathit{ncxt}^{\Delta}(\Sigma)$.

$\mathit{ncxt}(\Sigma, \Delta)$ is the name context (from which the module name signature can be reconstructed) that consists of those names for which it can be determined statically that they belong to the module name signature represented by the signature term Σ, given the signature context Δ.

The symbols used to denote values of enumerated types and 'option' values require special treatment, for symbols with the same name must always be identical. The following mapping gives the corresponding name context of basic modules. It is used in the description of the meaning of basic modules.

Definition. The mapping *atdefs*: $\mathsf{BasicModule} \rightarrow \mathsf{NCxt}$ is defined by

$$\begin{aligned}\mathit{atdefs}(B) := \; &\{[\mathsf{func}\ a\colon \rightarrow \{\, a_1 , \ldots , a_n \,\}] \in \{\!\![B]\!\!\} \mid \\ &\quad a_1, \ldots, a_n \in \mathsf{UIdent}, a \in \{a_1, \ldots, a_n\}\} \cup \\ &\{[\mathsf{func}\ \mathsf{nil}\colon \rightarrow t] \in \{\!\![B]\!\!\} \mid t \in \mathsf{UIdent}\}.\end{aligned}$$

$\mathit{atdefs}(B)$ is the name context that corresponds to the atom names and nil's associated with the basic module B.

In an import module, the importing module may use visible names of the imported module without introducing them. This forces the gathering of the imported name context of the basic modules. The following mapping is used for this purpose.

Definition. The mapping *imp*: BasicModule $\rightarrow$ NCxt is defined by

$$\begin{array}{l} imp(B) \ := \\ \quad \text{is the least name context } N \text{ such that } B \text{ is well-formed in } \{\![B]\!\} \cup N \end{array}$$

(the predicate *wf*: BasicModule $\times$ NCxt, notation: 'B is well-formed in N', and the mapping $\{\![\bullet]\!\}$: BasicModule $\rightarrow$ NCxt were defined in Section 5.5).

$imp(B)$ is the name context that corresponds to the names used but not introduced in basic module B.

Given the imported context of a basic module (determined by means of *imp*), the following can be fixed: the symbols corresponding to user-defined names, the symbols corresponding to pre-defined names, the conversion function symbols corresponding to subtype relationships declared by type definitions (both the 'externally visible' and the 'internal' ones), and the generation predicate symbols corresponding to user-defined type names as well as basic and constructed types used to define them.

Definition. The five auxiliary mappings *usym*, *psym*, *ecsym*, *icsym* and *gsym*: Cxt $\rightarrow$ $\mathcal{P}$(MSym) are defined by

$$\begin{array}{lll} usym(C) & := & symbols(C), \\ psym(C) & := & symbols(predefs(C)), \\ ecsym(C) & := & \bigcup\{\, \{\imath_{S\to S'}, \imath^{-1}_{S'\to S}\} \mid \\ & & \quad \langle S, S'\rangle \in sdcls(C), S, S' \in usym(C)\}, \\ icsym(C) & := & \bigcup\{\, \{\imath_{S\to S'}, \imath^{-1}_{S'\to S}\} \mid \\ & & \quad \langle S, S'\rangle \in sdcls(C \cup predefs(C))\}, \\ gsym(C) & := & \\ \multicolumn{3}{l}{\quad \{gen^S \mid S \in (usym(C) \cap \mathsf{MType}) \cup bctypes(C \cup predefs(C))\}} \end{array}$$

(the mappings *bctypes*: Cxt $\rightarrow$ $\mathcal{P}$(MType) and *predefs*: Cxt $\rightarrow$ Cxt, were defined in Section 5.1).

usym is for the symbols corresponding to user-defined names, *psym* is for the symbols corresponding to pre-defined names, *ecsym* is for the externally visible conversion function symbols, *icsym* is for the internal conversion function symbols, *gsym* is for the generation predicate symbols.

Having introduced mappings which give the sets of symbols of various kinds corresponding to a context, mappings which give the externally visible signature corresponding to a context and the internal signature corresponding to a context, respectively, can easily be defined. These mappings are used to describe the meaning of basic modules.

Definition. The mappings *extsig*: Cxt $\rightarrow$ MSSig and *intsig*: Cxt $\rightarrow$ MSSig are defined by

$extsig(C)$:=
 the least module name signature $\Sigma \in \mathsf{MSig}$ such that
 $usym(C) \cup ecsym(C) \subseteq \Sigma \cup \mathsf{MVal}$,

$intsig(C)$:=
 the least module name signature $\Sigma \in \mathsf{MSig}$ such that
 $usym(C) \cup psym(C) \cup icsym(C) \cup gsym(C) \subseteq \Sigma \cup \mathsf{MVal}$.

$extsig(C)$ is the externally visible signature corresponding to a context where we have symbols as given by C. $intsig(C)$ is the internal signature corresponding to a context where we have symbols as given by C.

In the semantics of the structuring sublanguage of VVSL, the context dependence of the meaning of basic modules is modelled by means of the origin substitution operation α of DA_α (see Section 6.6). A module parameter and a module description are used as the first and second argument of α. It is mainly the externally visible signature of the module parameter and the module description concerned that matters. Symbol contexts might be regarded as representations of these signatures. However, the requirements that apply to symbol contexts have to be relaxed in the case of the externally visible signature of the module description. The origin uniqueness requirement is too restrictive for the current purpose in the presence of parametrization. Therefore, the proto-contexts which were introduced in Chapter 5 are used instead.

Definition. The set PCxt of all proto-contexts is defined by

$$\mathsf{PCxt} := \{C \subseteq \mathsf{NSym} \cup \mathsf{SDcl} \mid C \text{ is a proto-context}\}.$$

Because a special kind of signature is required for module parameters, a special kind of symbol context is used as well. A parameter context is a symbol context in which the origin of each symbol is either an origin variable or $\langle\rangle$ and the origins of each two distinct symbols are not the same unless they are $\langle\rangle$.

Definition. A *parameter context* is a symbol context $C \in \mathsf{Cxt}$ such that

$$\forall w \in symbols(C)\,(\omega(w) \in \mathsf{OVar} \vee \omega(w) = \langle\rangle),$$
$$\forall w, w' \in symbols(C)\,(\omega(w) \in \mathsf{OVar} \wedge \omega(w) = \omega(w') \;\Rightarrow\; w = w').$$

The set QCxt of all parameter contexts is defined by

$$\mathsf{QCxt} := \{C \in \mathsf{Cxt} \mid C \text{ is a parameter context}\}.$$

Module descriptions are constructed from proto-contexts like the trivial embedding from module symbol signatures to module descriptions. Module parameters are constructed from parameter contexts in exactly the same way. The following mappings are used for this in the description of the meaning of basic modules.

Definition. The mappings des: $\mathsf{PCxt} \to \mathsf{MDes}$ and par: $\mathsf{QCxt} \to \mathsf{MPar}$ are defined by

$$des(C) := \langle \Sigma', \Sigma', \{\}, \pi_\perp \rangle,$$
$$par(C) := \langle \Sigma', \Sigma', \{\}, \pi_\perp \rangle,$$

where Σ' is the least module symbol signature Σ such that $symbols(C) \subseteq \Sigma \cup \mathsf{MVal}$.

$des(C)$ is the module description corresponding to the proto-context C. $par(C)$ is the module parameter corresponding to the parameter context C.

8.2 Typed names

Typed names are subconstructs of renamings and signatures in the structuring sublanguage of VVSL. The name from MNam (the subset of Nam relevant to VVSL, see Section 7.1) corresponding to a typed name is given by the mapping *name* defined below. This mapping is a degenerate case of a meaning function. It is used to describe the syntactic properties and meaning of renaming constructs and signature constructs.

Definition. The mapping $name$: $\mathsf{TypedName} \to \mathsf{MNam}$ is inductively defined by

$$\iota(w) = t \land \tau(w) = \mathsf{sort} \;\Rightarrow\; name(t) = \overline{w},$$

$$name(t) = \overline{S} \land \iota(w) = v \land \tau(w) = \langle \mathsf{func}, \mathsf{State}, S \rangle \;\Rightarrow\; name(v\colon t) = \overline{w},$$

$$\bigwedge_{k=1}^{n+1} (name(t_k) = \overline{S_k}) \land \iota(w) = f \land \tau(w) = \langle \mathsf{func}, S_1, \ldots, S_n, S_{n+1} \rangle \;\Rightarrow\; name(f\colon t_1 \times \cdots \times t_n \to t_{n+1}) = \overline{w},$$

$$\bigwedge_{k=1}^{n} (name(t_k) = \overline{S_k}) \land \bigwedge_{k=1}^{m} (name(t'_k) = \overline{S'_k}) \land \iota(w) = op \land \tau(w) = \langle \mathsf{pred}, S_1, \ldots, S_n, \mathsf{Comp}, S'_1, \ldots, S'_m \rangle \;\Rightarrow\; name(op\colon t_1 \times \cdots \times t_n \Rightarrow t'_1 \times \cdots \times t'_m) = \overline{w}.$$

$name(u)$ is the name from MNam corresponding to the typed name u.

The typed names of VVSL are similar to the names from MNam. For user-defined names, there is a unique correspondence between typed names and names from MNam. In Chapter 5, names from MNam are also used for the pre-defined names that are associated with the basic types and constructed types that are used for type definition. For these names from MNam there is no corresponding typed name in VVSL. This is not by accident. Inside a basic module, pre-defined names can, in many respects, be treated just as user-defined names. However, the defining type for a user-defined type name is never available outside the module in which it is defined: only user-defined names may be renamed or exported.

8.3 Organization of the definition

The remarks made in Section 5.4 also apply to the definition of the structuring sublanguage.

The variables used in this case range over the terminal productions of fixed nonterminals as follows (subscripts and primes are not shown):

Z	*<specification-document>*
M	*<module>*
R	*<renaming>*
S	*<signature>*
u	*<typed-name>*
i	*<name>*
B	*<basic-module>*
m	*<module-name>*

There are no production rules given for the nonterminal *<module-name>*. They are supposed to produce *identifiers*, which are considered to be terminals.

8.4 Specification documents

Specification documents are modules that are intended for the specification of complete systems (in contrast with system components). They are considered to be complete specifications in full VVSL. This language can be viewed as being composed of five sublanguages: one for *modules*, one for *definitions*, one for *types*, one for *expressions* and *logical expressions*, and one for *temporal formulae*. Their hierarchical structure is indicated by the following:

- Specification documents are modules regarded as complete specifications.
- Modules (Section 8.5) are constructed from basic modules and *names*; basic modules are roughly collections of definitions.
- Definitions are constructed from types, expressions and logical expressions, temporal formulae, and names.
- Types are constructed from names only.
- Expressions are constructed from logical expressions, names and *numbers*, and logical expressions are constructed from expressions and names.
- Temporal formulae are also constructed from expressions and names.

The remainder of this section and the next section deal with the syntax and semantics of specification documents and modules, respectively. The other sublanguages are described in Chapter 5.

To introduce specification documents in broad outline, the following suffices. A specification document is generally a modularly structured specification, but it may also be a flat specification (i.e. basic module). Anyhow, a specification document is just a module that has been designated as a complete specification. So, in principle, any module could serve as an example. Examples which are meant to illustrate a good choice of modular structure to achieve the goals of modular structuring are given in Chapters 11 to 13.

Syntax

Specification documents are the terminal productions of the nonterminal *<specification-document>*. Specification documents must be considered to be the sentences of VVSL, i.e. *<specification-document>* is the start symbol of the grammar for VVSL.

<specification-document> ::=
  system is *<module>*

The production rules of *<module>* are presented in Section 8.5.

The set SpecDocument of syntactically correct specification document constructs is defined by

$$\mathsf{SpecDocument} := \{Z \mid Z \text{ is a terminal production of } \textit{<specification-document>}\}.$$

Well-formedness. The well-formedness of syntactically correct specification document constructs is defined by a predicate

$$wf\colon \mathsf{SpecDocument}\,.$$

$wf(Z)$ indicates that Z is well-formed. Instead of $wf(Z)$, we write 'Z is well-formed'. The well-formedness of specification documents is defined in terms of the well-formedness of modules (defined in Section 8.5).

Meaning. The meaning of specification documents is defined by a mapping

$$[\![\bullet]\!]\colon \mathsf{SpecDocument} \to \mathsf{DTerm}_D\,.$$

$[\![Z]\!]$ is the description term representing the meaning of the specification document Z. $[\![Z]\!]$ is only defined if Z is well-formed. The meaning of specification documents is defined in terms of the meaning of modules (defined in Section 8.5).

Below specification documents are precisely described.

Specification document

There is no essential difference between the module M and the specification document system is M, but a specification document is intended for the specification of a complete 'system'. The intended global nature of specification documents is reflected in their meaning, which does not depend upon a context.

Structure:

system is M

Well-formedness:

M is well-formed in $\langle\{\}, \langle\rangle\rangle$.

Meaning:

$[\![\text{system is } M]\!] := [\![M]\!]^{\{\}}_{\langle\rangle}$.

8.5 The module sublanguage

The previous section dealt with the syntax and semantics of specification documents. Specification documents are just modules. They are built from basic modules using modularization and parametrization constructs. This section deals with the syntax and semantics of modules. An overview of modular structuring of specifications in VVSL was given in Section 2.2. A short example was also given in that section. Chapters 11 to 13 contain long examples of modular structuring in VVSL.

Syntax

Modules are the terminal productions of *<module>*. *Renamings* and *signatures* are the terminal productions of *<renaming>* and *<signature>*, respectively.

<module> ::=
  <basic-module>
  | rename *<renaming>* in *<module>*
  | import *<module>* into *<module>*
  | export *<signature>* from *<module>*
  | abstract *<restricted-parameter-list>* of *<module>*
  | apply *<module>* to *<module-list>*
  | let *<module-binding>* in *<module>*
  | *<module-name>*

<renaming> ::=
<atomic-renaming>
| *<atomic-renaming>* , *<renaming>*

<atomic-renaming> ::=
<typed-name> $\mapsto$ *<name>*

<signature> ::=
<typed-names>
| signature *<module>*
| add *<signature>* to *<signature>*

<typed-names> ::=
<typed-name>
| *<typed-name>* , *<typed-names>*

<typed-name> ::=
<type-name>
| *<variable-name>* : *<type-name>*
| *<function-name>* : *<type-name-list>* $\rightarrow$ *<type-name>*
| *<operation-name>* : *<type-name-list>* $\Rightarrow$ *<type-name-list>*

<type-name-list> ::=
<empty>
| *<nonempty-type-name-list>*

<nonempty-type-name-list> ::=
<type-name>
| *<type-name>* $\times$ *<nonempty-type-name-list>*

<name> ::=
<type-name>
| *<variable-name>*
| *<function-name>*
| *<operation-name>*

<restricted-parameter-list> ::=
<restricted-parameter>
| *<restricted-parameter>* , *<restricted-parameter-list>*

<restricted-parameter> ::=
<module-name> : *<module>*

<module-list> ::=
  <module>
  | *<module>* , *<module-list>*

<module-binding> ::=
  <module-name> $\triangleq$ *<module>*

The single production rule of *<basic-module>* is presented in Section 5.5.

The sets Module, Renaming and Signature of syntactically correct module constructs, renaming constructs and signature constructs, respectively, are defined by

$$\begin{aligned}
\mathsf{Module} &:= \{M \mid M \text{ is a terminal production of } \textit{<module>}\},\\
\mathsf{Renaming} &:= \{R \mid R \text{ is a terminal production of } \textit{<renaming>}\},\\
\mathsf{Signature} &:= \{S \mid S \text{ is a terminal production of } \textit{<signature>}\}.
\end{aligned}$$

The set TypedName of syntactically correct typed name constructs is defined by

$$\mathsf{TypedName} := \{u \mid u \text{ is a terminal production of } \textit{<typed-name>}\}.$$

Well-formedness. The well-formedness of syntactically correct module constructs is defined by a predicate

$$wf\colon \mathsf{Module} \times \mathsf{NCxt} \times \mathsf{SCxt}\,.$$

$wf(M, N, \Delta)$ indicates that M is well-formed in the name context N and the signature context Δ. Instead of $wf(M, N, \Delta)$, we write 'M is well-formed in $\langle N, \Delta\rangle$'. The well-formedness of modules is defined in terms of the well-formedness of renamings and signatures and the well-formedness of basic modules in flat VVSL (defined in Section 5.5).

The well-formedness of syntactically correct renaming constructs is defined by a predicate

$$wf\colon \mathsf{Renaming}\,.$$

$wf(R)$ indicates that R is well-formed. Instead of $wf(R)$, we write 'R is well-formed'.

The well-formedness of syntactically correct signature constructs is defined by a predicate

$$wf\colon \mathsf{Signature} \times \mathsf{SCxt}\,.$$

$wf(S, \Delta)$ indicates that S is well-formed in the signature context Δ. Instead of $wf(S, \Delta)$, we write 'S is well-formed in Δ'. The well-formedness of signatures is defined in terms of the well-formedness of modules.

Syntactic properties. The signature term associated with modules is defined by a mapping

$$\langle\!\langle\bullet\rangle\!\rangle_\bullet : \mathsf{Module} \times \mathsf{SCxt} \rightarrow \mathsf{STerm}_S \,.$$

$\langle\!\langle M\rangle\!\rangle_\Delta$ is a signature term representing the externally visible signature of the module M in the signature context Δ. The signature terms for modules is defined in terms of the signature terms for renamings and signatures.

The signature term associated with renamings is defined by a mapping

$$\langle\!\langle\bullet\rangle\!\rangle : \mathsf{Renaming} \rightarrow \mathsf{STerm}_R \,.$$

$\langle\!\langle R\rangle\!\rangle$ is a signature term representing the renaming R.

The signature term associated with signatures is defined by a mapping

$$\langle\!\langle\bullet\rangle\!\rangle_\bullet : \mathsf{Signature} \times \mathsf{SCxt} \rightarrow \mathsf{STerm}_S \,.$$

$\langle\!\langle S\rangle\!\rangle_\Delta$ is a signature term representing the signature S in the signature context Δ. The signature terms for signatures is defined in terms of the signature terms for modules.

Meaning. The meaning of modules is defined by a mapping

$$[\![\bullet]\!]_\bullet^\bullet : \mathsf{Module} \times \mathsf{PCxt} \times \mathsf{DCxt} \rightarrow \mathsf{DTerm}_D \,.$$

$[\![M]\!]_\Gamma^C$ is the description term representing the meaning of the module M in the proto-context C and the description context Γ. $[\![M]\!]_\Gamma^C$ is only defined if M is well-formed in $\langle\overline{C}, \overline{\Gamma}\rangle$. The meaning of modules is defined in terms of the meaning of renamings and signatures and the meaning of basic modules in flat VVSL (defined in Section 5.5).

The meaning of renamings is defined by a mapping

$$[\![\bullet]\!] : \mathsf{Renaming} \rightarrow \mathsf{DTerm}_R \,.$$

$[\![R]\!]$ is the description term representing the meaning of the renaming R. $[\![R]\!]$ is only defined if R is well-formed.

The meaning of signatures is defined by a mapping

$$[\![\bullet]\!]_\bullet : \mathsf{Signature} \times \mathsf{DCxt} \rightarrow \mathsf{DTerm}_S \,.$$

$[\![S]\!]_\Gamma$ is the description term representing the meaning of the signature S in the description context Γ. $[\![S]\!]_\Gamma$ is only defined if S is well-formed in $\overline{\Gamma}$. The meaning of signatures is defined in terms of the meaning of modules.

The modules, renamings and signatures of the different forms are now treated separately.

Basic module

The basic module B is a basic building block of modules. Its visible names are the names introduced by the definitions which constitute the basic module. There are no hidden names. Its formulae represent the properties characterizing what is denoted by these names according to their definitions.

If B occurs as an importing module, then the names from the imported module, that are used but not introduced in B, are treated as if they are introduced in B by a free definition. This means that the origins associated with these names are not fixed at all inside B.

In the case of names for values of enumerated types and the name nil for the option value, the value denoted by the same name is considered identical in all modules. This means that the origins associated with these names are fixed throughout the specification document concerned.

Structure:

B

Well-formedness in $\langle N, \Delta\rangle$:

B is well-formed in N.

Signature:

$\langle\!\!\{B\}\!\!\rangle_\Delta$:=

the least module name signature $\Sigma \in \mathsf{MSig}$ such that

$$\overline{w} \in \mathit{names}(\{\![B]\!\} \cup \mathit{imp}(B)) \;\Rightarrow\; \overline{w} \in \Sigma,$$

$$\langle \overline{S}, \overline{S'}\rangle \in \mathit{sdcls}(\{\![B]\!\} \cup \mathit{imp}(B)) \wedge \overline{S}, \overline{S'} \in \Sigma \;\Rightarrow\; \overline{\imath_{S\to S'}}, \overline{\imath^{-1}_{S'\to S}} \in \Sigma.$$

Meaning:

$[\![B]\!]^C_\Gamma$:=

$$\alpha(\mathit{par}(C_p), \mathit{des}(C_d), \langle \mathit{extsig}(C'), \mathit{intsig}(C'), [\![B]\!]^{C'}, \pi_\omega(\Sigma_{\mathit{des}(C_d)})\rangle),$$

where

C_p is a fresh parameter context such that $\overline{C_p} = \{\![B]\!\} \cup \mathit{imp}(B)$,
C_d is the greatest subset of C such that $\overline{C_d} = \overline{C_p}$,
C' is a symbol context such that

$$\overline{C'} = \overline{C_p},$$

$$w, w' \in \mathit{symbols}(C') \;\Rightarrow\; (\omega(w) = \omega(w') \wedge \omega(w) \neq \langle\rangle \;\Rightarrow\; w = w'),$$

$$\overline{w} \in \mathit{atdefs}(B) \;\Rightarrow\; \langle \iota(w), \langle\rangle, \tau(w)\rangle \in C',$$

$$\overline{w} \in \{\![B]\!\}_{\mathsf{free}} \;\Rightarrow\; \exists x \in \mathsf{OVar}\,(\langle \iota(w), x, \tau(w)\rangle \in C'),$$

$$\overline{w} \in \mathit{imp}(B) \;\Rightarrow\; \exists x \in \mathsf{OVar}\,(\langle \iota(w), x, \tau(w)\rangle \in C_p \cap C'),$$

$$\overline{w} \in \{\![B]\!\} - (\mathit{atdefs}(B) \cup \{\![B]\!\}_{\mathsf{free}}) \;\Rightarrow\; \exists c \in \mathsf{OCon}\,(\langle \iota(w), \langle c, x_1, \ldots, x_m\rangle, \tau(w)\rangle \in C'),$$

$$\{x_1, \ldots, x_m\} = \{x \in \mathsf{OVar} \mid \exists \overline{w} \in \{\![B]\!\}_{\mathsf{free}} \cup \mathit{imp}(B)\,(\langle \iota(w), x, \tau(w)\rangle \in C')\}.$$

Renaming module

The renaming module rename R in M has the same meaning as the module M, except that the names have been changed. The visible names of the module M are renamed according to the renaming R and all occurrences of these names in the formulae of the module M are replaced by the new names for them.

Structure:

rename R in M

Well-formedness in $\langle N, \Delta \rangle$:

R is well-formed,

M is well-formed in $\langle \{\}, \Delta \rangle$,

$\langle\!| M |\!\rangle_\Delta$ is renameable by $\langle\!| R |\!\rangle$.

Signature:

$\langle\!| \text{rename } R \text{ in } M |\!\rangle_\Delta := \langle\!| R |\!\rangle \bullet \langle\!| M |\!\rangle_\Delta$.

Meaning:

$[\![\text{rename } R \text{ in } M]\!]^C_\Gamma := [\![R]\!] \bullet [\![M]\!]^{\{\}}_\Gamma$.

Import module

The import module import M_1 into M_2 combines the two modules M_1 and M_2. The visible names and formulae of the 'imported' module M_1 are added to those of the 'importing' module M_2. It is assumed that all visible names of M_1 which are used but not defined in M_2, are implicitly introduced in M_2 by a free definition.

Structure:

import M_1 into M_2

Well-formedness in $\langle N, \Delta \rangle$:

M_1 is well-formed in $\langle N, \Delta \rangle$,

M_2 is well-formed in $\langle N \cup ncxt^\Delta(\langle\!| M_1 |\!\rangle_\Delta), \Delta \rangle$.

Signature:

$\langle\!| \text{import } M_1 \text{ into } M_2 |\!\rangle_\Delta := \langle\!| M_1 |\!\rangle_\Delta + \langle\!| M_2 |\!\rangle_\Delta$.

Meaning:

$[\![\text{import } M_1 \text{ into } M_2]\!]^C_\Gamma := [\![M_1]\!]^C_\Gamma + \alpha(par(C'), [\![M_1]\!]^C_\Gamma, [\![M_2]\!]^{C \cup C'}_\Gamma)$,

where

C' is a fresh parameter context such that $\overline{C'} = ncxt^{\overline{\Gamma}}(\langle\!| M_1 |\!\rangle_{\overline{\Gamma}})$.

Export module

The export module export S from M restricts the visible names of module M to those which are also in the signature S. The visible names of the 'exporting' module M are intersected with the names of the 'exported' signature S. The formulae remain the formulae of the exporting module M.

Structure:

export S from M

Well-formedness in $\langle N, \Delta\rangle$:

S is well-formed in Δ,

M is well-formed in $\langle N, \Delta\rangle$.

Signature:

$\{\!|\text{export } S \text{ from } M|\!\}_\Delta := \{\!|S|\!\}_\Delta \sqcap \{\!|M|\!\}_\Delta.$

Meaning:

$[\![\text{export } S \text{ from } M]\!]_\Gamma^C := [\![S]\!]_\Gamma \sqcap [\![M]\!]_\Gamma^C.$

Abstraction module

The abstraction module abstract $m_1 \colon M_1, \ldots, m_n \colon M_n$ of M parametrizes the module M. The intended meaning is the function that maps modules $m_1, \ldots, m_n$ to module M, provided that the visible names of m_i and the properties represented by the formulae of m_i include those of the 'parameter restriction' module M_i $(1 \leq i \leq n)$, and is undefined otherwise.

Structure:

abstract $m_1 \colon M_1, \ldots, m_n \colon M_n$ of M

Well-formedness in $\langle N, \Delta\rangle$:

$m_1, \ldots, m_n$ are distinct identifiers,

$m_1, \ldots, m_n$ are not visible in Δ,

$M_1, \ldots, M_n$ are well-formed in $\langle \{\}, \Delta\rangle$,

M is well-formed in $\langle N, \Delta'\rangle$,

where

$\Delta' = \Delta + \langle\langle m_1^{\tau_1}, \{\!|M_1|\!\}_\Delta\rangle, \ldots, \langle m_n^{\tau_n}, \{\!|M_n|\!\}_\Delta\rangle\rangle,$
$\tau_i = \mathit{ltype}(\{\!|M_i|\!\}_\Delta) \quad (1 \leq i \leq n).$

Signature:

$\{\!|\text{abstract } m_1 \colon M_1, \ldots, m_n \colon M_n \text{ of } M|\!\}_\Delta :=$
$(\lambda m_1^{\tau_1} \sqsubseteq \{\!|M_1|\!\}_\Delta. \cdots (\lambda m_n^{\tau_n} \sqsubseteq \{\!|M_n|\!\}_\Delta. \{\!|M|\!\}_{\Delta+\Delta'}) \cdots),$

where

$\Delta' = \Delta + \langle\langle m_1^{\tau_1}, \{\!\!\{M_1\}\!\!\}_\Delta\rangle, \ldots, \langle m_n^{\tau_n}, \{\!\!\{M_n\}\!\!\}_\Delta\rangle\rangle$,
$\tau_i = ltype(\{\!\!\{M_i\}\!\!\}_\Delta) \quad (1 \leq i \leq n)$.

Meaning:

$[\![\textsf{abstract } m_1\colon M_1, \ldots, m_n\colon M_n \textsf{ of } M]\!]_\Gamma^C :=$
$(\lambda m_1^{\tau_1} \sqsubseteq [\![M_1]\!]_\Gamma^{\{\}}. \cdots (\lambda m_n^{\tau_n} \sqsubseteq [\![M_n]\!]_\Gamma^{\{\}}. [\![M]\!]_{\Gamma+\Gamma'}^C) \cdots)$,

where

$\Gamma' = \Gamma + \langle\langle m_1^{\tau_1}, [\![M_1]\!]_\Gamma^{\{\}}\rangle, \ldots, \langle m_n^{\tau_n}, [\![M_n]\!]_\Gamma^{\{\}}\rangle\rangle$,
$\tau_i = ltype([\![M_i]\!]_\Gamma^{\{\}}) \quad (1 \leq i \leq n)$.

Application module

The application module apply M to $M_1, \ldots, M_n$ instantiates the parametrized module M. The intended meaning is the value of the function M for arguments $M_1, \ldots, M_n$.

Structure:

apply M to $M_1, \ldots, M_n$

Well-formedness in $\langle N, \Delta\rangle$:

$M_1, \ldots, M_n, M$ are well-formed in $\langle N, \Delta\rangle$,

there are higher types $\sigma_1, \ldots, \sigma_n, \tau$ such that
$ltype(\{\!\!\{M_i\}\!\!\}_\Delta) = \sigma_i$ for $i = 1, \ldots, n$, and
$ltype(\{\!\!\{M\}\!\!\}_\Delta) = \sigma_1, \ldots, \sigma_n \to \tau$.

Signature:

$\{\!\!\{\textsf{apply } M \textsf{ to } M_1, \ldots, M_n\}\!\!\}_\Delta := (\cdots(\{\!\!\{M\}\!\!\}_\Delta \{\!\!\{M_1\}\!\!\}_\Delta) \cdots \{\!\!\{M_n\}\!\!\}_\Delta)$.

Meaning:

$[\![\textsf{apply } M \textsf{ to } M_1, \ldots, M_n]\!]_\Gamma^C := (\cdots([\![M]\!]_\Gamma^C [\![M_1]\!]_\Gamma^C) \cdots [\![M_n]\!]_\Gamma^C)$.

Local definition module

The local definition module let $m \triangleq M_1$ in M_2 introduces the name m as an abbreviation of the module M_1 to be used in the module M_2.

Structure:

let $m \triangleq M_1$ in M_2

Well-formedness in $\langle N, \Delta\rangle$:

m is not visible in Δ,

M_1 is well-formed in $\langle\{\}, \Delta\rangle$,

M_2 is well-formed in $\langle N, \Delta'\rangle$,

where

$\Delta' = \Delta + \langle\langle m^\tau, \{\!\!\{M_1\}\!\!\}_\Delta\rangle\rangle$, $\tau = ltype(\{\!\!\{M_1\}\!\!\}_\Delta)$.

Signature:

$\{\!\!\{\text{let } m \triangleq M_1 \text{ in } M_2\}\!\!\}_\Delta := [m^\tau := \{\!\!\{M_1\}\!\!\}_\Delta]\{\!\!\{M_2\}\!\!\}_{\Delta'}$,

where

$\Delta' = \Delta + \langle\langle m^\tau, \{\!\!\{M_1\}\!\!\}_\Delta\rangle\rangle$, $\tau = ltype(\{\!\!\{M_1\}\!\!\}_\Delta)$.

Meaning:

$[\![\text{let } m \triangleq M_1 \text{ in } M_2]\!]_\Gamma^C := [m^\tau := [\![M_1]\!]_\Gamma^{\{\}}][\![M_2]\!]_{\Gamma'}^C$,

where

$\Gamma' = \Gamma + \langle\langle m^\tau, [\![M_1]\!]_\Gamma^{\{\}}\rangle\rangle$, $\tau = ltype([\![M_1]\!]_\Gamma^{\{\}})$.

Reference module

The reference module m is what the module name m stands for.

What the module name stands for is known if m acts as an abbreviation of some module and is unknown if m acts as a formal parameter.

Structure:

m

Well-formedness in $\langle N, \Delta\rangle$:

m is visible in Δ.

Signature:

$\{\!\!\{m\}\!\!\}_\Delta := m^\Delta$.

Meaning:

$[\![m]\!]_\Gamma^C := m^\Gamma$.

Renaming

The renaming $u_1 \mapsto i_1, \ldots, u_n \mapsto i_n$ is roughly a type preserving mapping which associates with the enumerated 'old' names the corresponding 'new' names. Due to the possibility of 'identifier overloading', the old names must be accompanied with their types. The renaming behaves like an identity mapping for names that are not enumerated.

A renaming is used in renaming modules only.

Structure:

$u_1 \mapsto i_1, \ldots, u_n \mapsto i_n$

Well-formedness:

$u_1, \ldots, u_n$ are distinct typed names.

Signature:

$\{\!\!\{u_1 \mapsto i_1, \ldots, u_n \mapsto i_n\}\!\!\} :=$

the unique $\rho \in \mathsf{MRen}$ such that for all $w \in \mathsf{MSym}$:

$w \in name(u_k) \Rightarrow \iota(\rho(w)) = i_k \ (k = 1, \ldots, n),$
$w \notin \bigcup_{k=1}^{n} name(u_k) \Rightarrow \iota(\rho(w)) = \iota(w).$

Meaning:

$[\![u_1 \mapsto i_1, \ldots, u_n \mapsto i_n]\!] :=$
the unique $\rho \in \mathsf{MRen}$ such that for all $w \in \mathsf{MSym}$:
$w \in name(u_k) \Rightarrow \iota(\rho(w)) = i_k \ (k = 1, \ldots, n),$
$w \notin \bigcup_{k=1}^{n} name(u_k) \Rightarrow \iota(\rho(w)) = \iota(w).$

Enumeration signature

The enumeration signature $u_1, \ldots, u_n$ is roughly the set of enumerated names, which are accompanied with their types because of the possibility of identifier overloading.

Like the other signature constructs, an enumeration signature is used in export modules only. The subtype relationships in force in the exporting module remain in force if the types concerned are in the exported signature. This requires that the associated conversion function names (which are not available as pre-defined names) must be exported implicitly.

Structure:

$u_1, \ldots, u_n$

Well-formedness in Δ:

True.

Signature:

$\langle\!| u_1, \ldots, u_n |\!\rangle_\Delta :=$
the least module name signature $\Sigma \in \mathsf{MSig}$ such that:
$\bigcup_{k=1}^{n} name(u_k) \subseteq \Sigma,$
$\overline{S}, \overline{S'} \in \Sigma \cap \overline{\mathsf{MType}} \Rightarrow \overline{\imath_{S \to S'}}, \overline{\imath_{S' \to S}^{-1}} \in \Sigma.$

Meaning:

$[\![u_1, \ldots, u_n]\!]_\Gamma :=$
the least module name signature $\Sigma \in \mathsf{MSig}$ such that:
$\bigcup_{k=1}^{n} name(u_k) \subseteq \Sigma,$
$\overline{S}, \overline{S'} \in \Sigma \cap \overline{\mathsf{MType}} \Rightarrow \overline{\imath_{S \to S'}}, \overline{\imath_{S' \to S}^{-1}} \in \Sigma.$

Union signature

The union signature $\mathsf{add}\ S_1\ \mathsf{to}\ S_2$ is the set-theoretic union of the signatures S_1 and S_2.

Structure:

$\mathsf{add}\ S_1\ \mathsf{to}\ S_2$

Well-formedness in Δ:

S_1, S_2 are well-formed in Δ.

Signature:

$\langle\!|\mathsf{add}\ S_1\ \mathsf{to}\ S_2|\!\rangle_\Delta \ := \ \langle\!|S_1|\!\rangle_\Delta + \langle\!|S_2|\!\rangle_\Delta.$

Meaning:

$[\![\mathsf{add}\ S_1\ \mathsf{to}\ S_2]\!]_\Gamma \ := \ [\![S_1]\!]_\Gamma + [\![S_2]\!]_\Gamma.$

Module signature

The module signature signature M is the signature consisting of the visible names of the module M.

Structure:

signature M

Well-formedness in Δ:

M is well-formed in $\langle\{\}, \Delta\rangle$,

$ltype(\langle\!|M|\!\rangle_\Delta) = 0.$

Signature:

$\langle\!|\mathsf{signature}\ M|\!\rangle_\Delta \ := \ \langle\!|M|\!\rangle_\Delta.$

Meaning:

$[\![\mathsf{signature}\ M]\!]_\Gamma \ := \ \mathbf{\Sigma}([\![M]\!]_\Gamma^{\{\}}).$

9

Discussion

In this chapter some points are discussed which were raised by the material in preceding chapters, but for which space could not be found there.

The first section analyses how DA, used in Chapter 8 as the basis for the semantics of the structuring sublanguage of VVSL, and two more abstract models of modular specifications are related. This is analysed by means of an extension of DA which has additional abstraction operations on descriptions. In one of the models concerned, specification modules correspond essentially to MPL_ω theories. In the other model, they correspond to module objects (Bergstra, 1986), which are less abstract than theories.

The formal semantics for VVSL presented in Chapters 5 and 8 opens up the possibility of constructing formal proofs to justify claims concerning specifications written in VVSL. The next section is concerned with proof rules for VVSL. The principal proof rules are presented and their connection with the formal semantics for VVSL is described informally and in broad outline. They include proof rules for a typed first-order temporal logic which extends LPF and proof rules which are needed to construct proofs of facts about modules.

The last section demonstrates the generality of the logic-based approach to semantics which is applied to VVSL in Chapter 5. This is done by applying it to a language whose constructs are common control constructs of imperative programming languages. They include parallel composition and await constructs. The language is a simplified version of an extension of VVSL which is needed to be able to specify operations explicitly by a defining program.

9.1 DA and more abstract models

The mapping from origin consistent descriptions to their theories can be split into three mappings which treat 'origin consistency enforcement', 'symbol identification' and 'hidden symbol abstraction', respectively.

The first mapping, when applied to origin consistent descriptions, yields 'origin consistency enforcing' descriptions. Origin consistency enforcing descriptions are roughly descriptions with an origin partition which declares the origins of symbols in the externally visible signature with the same name to be equal. The second mapping, when applied to origin consistent descriptions, yields 'semi-abstract' descriptions. In semi-abstract descriptions, symbols from the externally visible signature with the same name must have the same origin (the origin partitions of semi-abstract descriptions are dummy components). Semi-abstract descriptions correspond to Bergstra's module objects (Bergstra, 1986). The third mapping, when applied to origin consistent descriptions, yields 'abstract' descriptions. Abstract descriptions are essentially logical theories.

The first mapping corresponds to the operation μ of DA. The second and third mapping correspond to the new operations 'identifying' (ν) and 'abstracting' (γ) of DA$^+$ (Extended Description Algebra).

DA$^+$ is an extension of DA. The extension consists of the addition of two operations which are only defined for origin consistent descriptions: ν and γ. These operations are meant for abstracting from the origins of externally visible names and for abstracting from the names that are not externally visible. By means of these operations, each origin consistent description can be adapted in such a way that the resulting description is essentially the theory of the description. Thus, the theory of an origin consistent description can be obtained within DA$^+$.

In this section, first the additional operations of DA$^+$ are defined. Next, each of the above-mentioned kinds of descriptions is defined (together with specializations of the operations of DA on descriptions for that kind) and analysed. The operations $\mathbf{\Sigma}$ and π are not taken into account.

Additional operations on descriptions

The operations of DA$^+$ include all operations of DA and two additional operations on descriptions: identifying and abstracting. These additional operations are partial functions. In other words, DA$^+$ is a partial heterogeneous algebra.

Externally visible symbols in an origin consistent description with the same name can be made equal, according to the origin partition of the description, by means of identifying.

Definition. The partial *identifying* operation $\nu\colon \mathsf{Des} \to \mathsf{Des}$ on descriptions is defined by

$$\nu(X) := \begin{cases} \langle \mu_X(\Sigma_X), \mu_X(\Gamma_X), \mu_X(\Phi_X), \pi_\perp \rangle & \text{if } X \text{ origin consistent,} \\ \text{undefined} & \text{otherwise.} \end{cases}$$

$\pi_\perp$ is the bottom of the complete lattice $\langle \mathsf{OPar}, \leq \rangle$ (see Section 6.2).

Symbols in an origin consistent description which are not externally visible, i.e. hidden symbols, can be forgotten about by means of abstracting.

Definition. The partial *abstracting* operation $\gamma\colon \mathsf{Des} \to \mathsf{Des}$ on descriptions is defined by

$$\gamma(X) := \begin{cases} \langle \Sigma_{X'}, \Sigma_{X'}, \mathcal{L}(\Sigma_{X'}) \cap Th(\Gamma_{X'}, \Phi_{X'}), \pi_\perp \rangle & \text{if } X \text{ origin consistent,} \\ \text{undefined} & \text{otherwise,} \end{cases}$$

where $X' = \nu(X)$.

Extended Description Algebra (DA$^+$) is the partial heterogeneous algebra, which is obtained from DA (Section 6.4) by the following additions:

$$\text{Operations:} \quad \begin{array}{lcl} \nu & : & \mathsf{Des} \to \mathsf{Des} \\ \gamma & : & \mathsf{Des} \to \mathsf{Des}\,. \end{array}$$

In the remainder of this section, we write $X = Y$, where X and Y are terms of DA$^+$ for denoting descriptions, to indicate that the descriptions denoted X and Y are both defined and equal.

Total variants of the operations ν and γ are conceivable. However, using the bottom or top of the complete lattice $\langle \mathsf{Des}, \leq \rangle$ as 'the undefined description' is not very satisfactory since importing is not strict with respect to bottom and exporting is not strict with respect to top. On the other hand, using a new element added to the domain of descriptions as the undefined description would lead to a non-conservative extension of DA. Besides, the partial operations ν and γ are only undefined for descriptions that should be considered meaningless, i.e. non-origin-consistent descriptions. Moreover, these operations are not needed for the interpretation of the VVSL modularization constructs. This means that the partial operations are appropriate for analysis while their total variants cause anomalies.

Origin consistency enforcing descriptions

The origin partition of a description declares certain origins to be equal. No restrictions are imposed on the origin partition of a description. For an origin consistency enforcing description, the origin partition must at least declare the origins of symbols in the externally visible signature with the same name to be equal.

Definition. For $X \in \mathsf{Des}$, X is called *origin consistency enforcing* iff

$$\pi_\omega(\Sigma_X) \leq \pi_X\,.$$

The unifying operation $\mu\colon \mathsf{Des} \to \mathsf{Des}$ of DA, yields origin consistency enforcing descriptions.

Definition. The operations $\bullet_\mu : \mathsf{Ren} \times \mathsf{Des} \to \mathsf{Des}$, $+_\mu : \mathsf{Des} \times \mathsf{Des} \to \mathsf{Des}$ and $\Box_\mu : \mathsf{Sig} \times \mathsf{Des} \to \mathsf{Des}$ are defined by

$$\begin{aligned} \rho \bullet_\mu X &:= \mu(\rho \bullet X), \\ X +_\mu Y &:= \mu(X + Y), \\ \Sigma \Box_\mu X &:= \mu(\Sigma \Box X). \end{aligned}$$

An operation $\mu_\mu : \mathsf{Des} \to \mathsf{Des}$ is not defined, since $\mu(\mu(X)) = \mu(X)$.

These derived operations of DA are defined for all descriptions. Their restrictions to origin consistency enforcing descriptions are interesting. Together with the set of origin consistency enforcing descriptions, these restricted operations constitute an 'algebra of origin consistency enforcing descriptions' within DA. The operation μ of DA can be regarded as a function from the objects of DA to the objects of this algebra of origin consistency enforcing descriptions. If exporting is restricted to signatures that do not hide symbols with the same name but different origins, then μ is a homomorphism with respect to renaming, importing and exporting.

Fact. For descriptions X and Y:

$$\begin{aligned} &\mu(\rho \bullet X) = \rho \bullet_\mu \mu(X), \\ &\mu(X + Y) = \mu(X) +_\mu \mu(Y), \\ &\mu(\Sigma \Box X) = \Sigma \Box_\mu \mu(X) \qquad \text{if } \forall v, w \in \Sigma_X \\ &\qquad\qquad (\overline{v} = \overline{w} \wedge \overline{v} \notin \Sigma \Rightarrow \omega(v) = \omega(w)). \end{aligned}$$

Proof: The first and second property follow immediately from the laws (M1) and (M2) of DA (Section 6.4). The third property is a direct consequence of the law (M3) of DA and the definition of the operation μ. $\Box$

Origins, which are declared to be equal (e.g. to enforce origin consistency), may be different. In pure DA, there is no operation for identifying origins that are declared to be equal, but such an operation (ν) was introduced earlier in this section. With that operation origins that are declared to be equal will be made the same, provided that there are no origin consistency violations. The condition of the third property only expresses that possible origin consistency violations should not be hidden. The condition is *not* automatically met by descriptions yielded by interpretation of the modularization constructs of VVSL. The condition does not seem to be restrictive in practice.

Semi-abstract descriptions

The origin partition of a description declares certain origins to be equal. The intention is that origins that are declared to be equal should be identified. After actual identification, the origin partition goes out of use. Apart from the restriction that the externally visible signature must be a subsignature of the internal signature, no restrictions are imposed on the externally visible signature of a description. In a semi-abstract description, symbols in the externally visible signature with the same name must have the same origin and the origin partition must not declare origins to be equal.

Definition. For $X \in \mathsf{Des}$, X is called *semi-abstract* iff

$$\forall v, w \in \Sigma_X \, (\overline{v} = \overline{w} \;\Rightarrow\; \omega(v) = \omega(w)),$$
$$\pi_X = \pi_\perp .$$

The operations $\bullet$, $\Box$, $+$ and μ, applied to semi-abstract descriptions, always yield $\pi_\perp$ as origin partition. In other words, the origin partition of a semi-abstract description is a dummy component; exactly as intended. Semi-abstract descriptions are origin consistent descriptions whose origin partitions are irrelevant. They correspond to Bergstra's module objects (Bergstra, 1986).

The operation $\nu\colon \mathsf{Des} \to \mathsf{Des}$, when applied to origin consistent descriptions, yields semi-abstract descriptions.

Definition. The partial operations $\bullet_\nu\colon \mathsf{Ren} \times \mathsf{Des} \to \mathsf{Des}$, $+_\nu\colon \mathsf{Des} \times \mathsf{Des} \to \mathsf{Des}$, $\Box_\nu\colon \mathsf{Sig} \times \mathsf{Des} \to \mathsf{Des}$ and $\mu_\nu\colon \mathsf{Des} \to \mathsf{Des}$ are defined by

$$\begin{aligned}
\rho \bullet_\nu X &:= \nu(\rho \bullet X),\\
X +_\nu Y &:= \nu(X + Y),\\
\Sigma \Box_\nu X &:= \nu(\Sigma \Box X),\\
\mu_\nu(X) &:= \nu(\mu(X)).
\end{aligned}$$

These derived operations of DA$^+$ are not defined for all descriptions. Their restrictions to semi-abstract descriptions are interesting. Together with the set of semi-abstract descriptions, these restricted operations constitute an 'algebra of semi-abstract descriptions' within DA$^+$. Note that the objects of DA and the ones of DA$^+$ are the same. The operation ν can be viewed as a function from the objects of DA to the objects of the algebra of semi-abstract descriptions. Moreover, its restriction to origin consistency enforcing descriptions can be viewed as a function from the objects of the algebra of origin consistency enforcing descriptions to the objects of the algebra of semi-abstract descriptions. If importing is restricted to pairs of descriptions with origin partitions that do not identify more than the origin partition of the union of externally visible symbols, then ν is a homomorphism with respect to renaming, importing, exporting and unifying, for origin consistency enforcing descriptions.

Fact. For origin consistency enforcing descriptions X and Y:

$$\begin{aligned}
&\nu(\rho \bullet X) = \rho \bullet_\nu \nu(X),\\
&\nu(X + Y) = \nu(X) +_\nu \nu(Y) \quad \text{if} \quad \pi_X \le \pi_\omega(\Sigma_X \cup \Sigma_Y) \wedge\\
&\qquad\qquad\qquad\qquad\qquad\qquad\quad\; \pi_Y \le \pi_\omega(\Sigma_X \cup \Sigma_Y),\\
&\nu(\Sigma \Box X) = \Sigma \Box_\nu \nu(X),\\
&\nu(\mu(X)) = \mu_\nu(\nu(X)).
\end{aligned}$$

Proof: The first property follows immediately from the fact that renaming permutes with origin substitution (Section 6.5). The third and fourth property are direct consequences of the definitions of the operations involved. For the proof of the second property, it suffices to show that

$$\mu_\omega(\Sigma_X \cup \Sigma_Y) = \mu_\omega(\mu_\omega(\Sigma_X) \cup \mu_\omega(\Sigma_Y))$$
$$\text{where } \mu_\omega(\Sigma) = \mu_{\pi_\omega(\Sigma)}(\Sigma),$$

which is straightforward from the definitions of π_ω and μ_π. □

The condition of the second property expresses that only origins associated with the two descriptions concerned should be declared to be equal in either one. This condition is automatically met by descriptions $\mu(X)$, for descriptions X yielded by interpretation of modularization constructs of VVSL.

The application of the composition of μ and ν to an origin consistent description yields a result which is half-way between the description and the theory of the description.

Abstract descriptions

The formulae of a description present the properties characterizing the sets, functions and relations which may be associated with the symbols introduced in the internal signature. The formulae constitute a collection of properties from which the others can be derived. Apart from the restriction that the formulae must be MPL_ω formulae whose signature is a subsignature of the internal signature, no restrictions are imposed on the formulae of a description. The externally visible signature declares certain symbols from the internal signature to be externally visible. The intention is that the other symbols from the internal signature as well as the properties characterizing the sets, functions and relations which may be associated with these symbols should be hidden from the outside. These sets, functions and relations are considered to be of an auxiliary nature. Apart from the restriction that the externally visible signature must be a subsignature of the internal signature, no restrictions are imposed on the externally visible signature of a description. In an abstract description, the externally visible signature must declare all symbols from the internal signature to be externally visible, symbols in the externally visible signature with the same name must have the same origin, the formulae must include all derivable properties (thus abstracting from the presentation of these properties), and the origin partition must not declare origins to be equal.

Definition. For $X \in \mathsf{Des}$, X is called *abstract* iff

$$\begin{aligned}
&\forall v, w \in \Sigma_X\,(\overline{v} = \overline{w} \;\Rightarrow\; \omega(v) = \omega(w)),\\
&\Gamma_X = \Sigma_X,\\
&\Phi_X = Th(\Sigma_X, \Phi_X),\\
&\pi_X = \pi_\perp\,.
\end{aligned}$$

The formulae of an abstract description constitute an MPL_ω theory. Given these formulae, the externally visible signature, the internal signature and the origin partition can be reconstructed. In other words, these components are superfluous for an abstract description; an abstract description is a theory in disguise. It is considered convenient to treat theories as descriptions of a special kind.

The operation $\gamma\colon \mathsf{Des} \to \mathsf{Des}$, when applied to origin consistent descriptions, yields abstract descriptions.

Definition. The partial operations $\bullet_\gamma\colon \mathsf{Ren} \times \mathsf{Des} \to \mathsf{Des}$, $+_\gamma\colon \mathsf{Des} \times \mathsf{Des} \to \mathsf{Des}$, $\Box_\gamma\colon \mathsf{Sig} \times \mathsf{Des} \to \mathsf{Des}$ and $\mu_\gamma\colon \mathsf{Des} \times \mathsf{Des}$ are defined by

$$\begin{aligned}
\rho \bullet_\gamma X &:= \gamma(\rho \bullet X),\\
X +_\gamma Y &:= \gamma(X + Y),\\
\Sigma \Box_\gamma X &:= \gamma(\Sigma \Box X),\\
\mu_\gamma(X) &:= \gamma(\mu(X)).
\end{aligned}$$

Like the operations $\bullet_\nu$, $+_\nu$, $\Box_\nu$ and μ_ν, these derived operations are not defined for all descriptions. Their restrictions to abstract descriptions are interesting. Together with the set of abstract descriptions, these restricted operations constitute an 'algebra of abstract descriptions' within DA^+. The objects of DA and the ones of DA^+ are the same. The operation γ can be considered to be a function from the objects of DA to the objects of the algebra of abstract descriptions. Besides, its restriction to semi-abstract descriptions can be considered to be a function from the objects of the algebra of semi-abstract descriptions to the objects of the algebra of abstract descriptions. If renaming is restricted to renamings that map symbols with different names to symbols with different names and importing is restricted to pairs of descriptions such that symbols occurring in the formulae of both descriptions are externally visible in both descriptions, then γ is a homomorphism with respect to renaming, importing, exporting and unifying, for semi-abstract descriptions.

Fact. For semi-abstract descriptions X and Y:

$$\begin{aligned}
&\gamma(\rho \bullet X) = \rho \bullet_\gamma \gamma(X) && \text{if } inj(\rho, \Sigma_X \cup sig(\Phi_X)),\\
&\gamma(X + Y) = \gamma(X) +_\gamma \gamma(Y) && \text{if } sig(\Phi_X) \cap sig(\Phi_Y) \subseteq \Sigma_X \cap \Sigma_Y,\\
&\gamma(\Sigma \Box X) = \Sigma \Box_\gamma \gamma(X),\\
&\gamma(\mu(X)) = \mu_\gamma(\gamma(X)).
\end{aligned}$$

Proof: The operations $\bullet_\gamma$, $+_\gamma$ and $\Box_\gamma$ on abstract descriptions correspond closely to the operators $\bullet$, $+$ and $\Box$ of MA (Bergstra, Heering and Klint,

1990), respectively. It is also easy to devise operations $\mathbf{\Sigma}_\gamma$ and $\mathbf{T}_\gamma$ corresponding to $\mathbf{\Sigma}$ and $\mathbf{T}$ of MA, leading to a model of the axioms of MA except axioms (R4), (R5) and (R6). However, it is obvious that the following variants of (R4) and (R6) hold:

$$\begin{aligned}
&\mathit{inj}(\rho, \Sigma \cup \mathbf{\Sigma}(X)) \Rightarrow \\
&\qquad\qquad \rho \bullet (\Sigma \,\Box\, X) = (\rho \bullet \Sigma) \,\Box\, (\rho \bullet X) \quad (\text{R4}^*) \\
&(\mathit{dom}(\rho) \cup \mathit{rng}(\rho)) \cap \Sigma = \{\,\} \wedge \mathit{inj}(\rho, \mathbf{\Sigma}(X)) \Rightarrow \\
&\qquad\qquad \Sigma \,\Box\, X = \Sigma \,\Box\, (\rho \bullet X) \quad (\text{R6}^*)
\end{aligned}$$

The differences with (R4) and (R6) are consequences of the restriction in MA to 'atomic renamings'. Atomic renamings are bijective and permutative renamings of a restricted kind.

For any semi-abstract description X, we have $\gamma(X) = \Sigma_X \,\Box\, (\mathbf{T}(\Gamma_X) + \Phi_X) = \Sigma_X \,\Box\, \Phi_X$ by axioms (C4) and (E3) of MA. The first property now follows immediately from axiom (R4*). Proof of the second property is straightforward from axioms (E1), (E2) and (E4) of MA. The third property follows immediately from axiom (E2) of MA. The fourth property is a direct consequence of the definition of μ and γ. □

This proof shows a strong connection between DA and MA. The proof amounts to viewing the restriction of γ to semi-abstract descriptions as a function from module objects to theories. A model of the axioms of MA based on theories (Bergstra, Heering and Klint, 1990) as well as models based on module objects (Bergstra, 1986) have been explored.

The condition of the second property and the weaker condition of axiom (E4) of MA are strongly related. The former condition is equivalent to

$$\begin{aligned}
&\mathit{sig}(\Phi_X) \cap \mathit{sig}(\Phi_Y) \subseteq \Sigma_X \cup \Sigma_Y \wedge \\
&\mathit{sig}(\Phi_X) \cap \Sigma_Y \subseteq \Sigma_X \wedge \mathit{sig}(\Phi_Y) \cap \Sigma_X \subseteq \Sigma_Y\,.
\end{aligned}$$

The first conjunct is due to the application of axiom (E4) of MA. The other two conjuncts are necessary conditions.

The condition of the second property is *not* automatically met by descriptions $\nu(\mu(X))$, for descriptions X yielded by translation of modularization constructs of VVSL. The condition seems to be restrictive in practice. For example, this condition is not met if the same hidden state variable is accessed by operations from modules that are combined by means of importing (see also Section 6.1).

The application of the composition of μ, ν and γ to an origin consistent description yields a result which is essentially the theory of the description.

Fact. For an origin consistent description X:

$$\gamma(\nu(\mu(X))) = \langle \mathit{sig}(\mathit{Th}_S(X)), \mathit{sig}(\mathit{Th}_S(X)), \mathit{Th}_S(X), \pi_\perp \rangle.$$

Proof: Follows immediately from the definitions of μ, ν and γ.

Summary of analysis

In this section, the connections between DA and two more abstract models of specification modules are analysed. In the most abstract model, specification modules correspond essentially to MPL_ω theories. In the other model, they correspond essentially to module objects (Bergstra, 1986). However, module objects and theories are presented as special kinds of descriptions, called semi-abstract descriptions and abstract descriptions, respectively, to ease the analysis of the connections between the models.
The results of the analysis can be summarized as follows:

- The mapping which assigns to each origin consistent description its abstraction to a module object can be proven to be a homomorphism under mild restrictions on the use of importing and exporting.
- The mapping which assigns to each origin consistent description its abstraction to a theory can be proven to be a homomorphism under a mild restriction on the use of renaming, the above-mentioned restrictions on the use of importing and exporting, and an additional restriction on the use of importing which is generally severe for state-based specification.

Of course, these mappings can always be used to provide the modularization constructs of VVSL with a more abstract semantics than the compositional semantics defined in Chapter 8. However, the results show that, generally, such a semantics is not compositional.

9.2 Proof rules for VVSL

The formal semantics for VVSL presented in Chapters 5 and 8 opens up the possibility of formal reasoning about specifications written in VVSL. This section introduces the principal proof rules for VVSL. It begins by presenting proof rules for a typed version of LPF and additional rules for conditional expressions and explicit function definitions. These rules are basic to formal reasoning about VVSL specifications. Thereafter, proof rules are given which are needed to construct proofs of temporal properties. Finally, special proof rules are introduced which allow facts about a module to be inherited from its constituent modules. The connection between the proof rules and the formal semantics for VVSL is described in broad outline.

The basis of formal reasoning

The logical expressions of VVSL are considered to be formulae of a typed version of LPF. The proof system of the monotone part of this logic is used in formal reasoning about VVSL specifications. Extensions are needed for the basic and constructed types, for recursively defined functions, etc.

There are also non-monotone connectives in LPF which make it an expressively complete three-valued logic. However, these connectives are neither needed for specifying software systems nor for reasoning about specifications.

The proof system of the monotone part of the typed version of LPF is defined by the following axiom schemas and rules of inference:

Logical Axioms.

$$(\top) \quad \vdash \top$$

$$(\bot) \quad \bot \vdash$$

$$(\text{taut}) \quad E \vdash E$$

$$(\text{contr}) \quad E, \neg E \vdash$$

Non-logical Axioms.

$$(\text{eqv}) \quad \vdash (\forall x \in T \cdot x = x) \wedge (\forall x \in T, y \in T, z \in T \cdot x = y \wedge x = z \to y = z)$$

$$(\text{sub}) \quad e_1 = e_2, [x := e_1]E \vdash [x := e_2]E$$

$$(\text{var}) \quad \vdash x = x$$

$$(\text{strict}_1) \quad e_1 = e_2 \vdash e_1 = e_1 \wedge e_2 = e_2$$

$$(\text{strict}_2) \quad \neg(e_1 = e_2) \vdash e_1 = e_1 \wedge e_2 = e_2$$

$$(\text{comp}) \quad e_1 = e_1, e_2 = e_2 \vdash e_1 = e_2, \neg(e_1 = e_2)$$

Rules of Inference.

$$(\neg\neg L) \quad \frac{\Gamma, E \vdash \Delta}{\Gamma, \neg\neg E \vdash \Delta}$$

$$(\neg\neg R) \quad \frac{\Gamma \vdash \Delta, E}{\Gamma \vdash \Delta, \neg\neg E}$$

$$(\wedge L) \quad \frac{\Gamma, E_i \vdash \Delta}{\Gamma, E_1 \wedge E_2 \vdash \Delta} \text{ for } i = 1, 2$$

$$(\wedge R) \quad \frac{\Gamma \vdash \Delta, E_1 \quad \Gamma \vdash \Delta, E_2}{\Gamma \vdash \Delta, E_1 \wedge E_2}$$

$$(\neg\wedge L) \quad \frac{\Gamma, \neg E_1 \vdash \Delta \quad \Gamma, \neg E_2 \vdash \Delta}{\Gamma, \neg(E_1 \wedge E_2) \vdash \Delta}$$

$$(\neg\wedge R) \quad \frac{\Gamma \vdash \Delta, \neg E_i}{\Gamma \vdash \Delta, \neg(E_1 \wedge E_2)} \text{ for } i = 1, 2$$

$$(\forall L) \quad \frac{\Gamma \vdash \Delta, e \in T \quad \Gamma, [x := e]E \vdash \Delta}{\Gamma, \forall x \in T \cdot E \vdash \Delta}$$

$$(\forall R) \quad \frac{\Gamma \vdash \Delta, E}{\Gamma \vdash \Delta, \forall x \in T \cdot E} \; x \text{ not free in } \Gamma \cup \Delta$$

$$(\neg\forall L) \quad \frac{\Gamma, \neg E \vdash \Delta}{\Gamma, \neg\forall x \in T \cdot E \vdash \Delta} \; x \text{ not free in } \Gamma \cup \Delta$$

$$(\neg\forall R) \quad \frac{\Gamma \vdash \Delta, e \in T \quad \Gamma \vdash \Delta, \neg[x := e]E}{\Gamma \vdash \Delta, \neg\forall x \in T \cdot E}$$

$$(\text{cut}) \quad \frac{\Gamma \vdash \Delta, E \quad \Gamma', E \vdash \Delta'}{\Gamma, \Gamma' \vdash \Delta, \Delta'}$$

$$(\text{weak}) \quad \frac{\Gamma \vdash \Delta}{\Gamma, \Gamma' \vdash \Delta, \Delta'}$$

$e \in T$ is used as an abbreviation of the formula $\exists x \in T \cdot x = e$.

Negation, disjunction and existential quantification were taken as basic in the logical expression sublanguage of VVSL presented in Section 5.8. In order to make comparison with the proof system of MPL_ω (presented in Section 3.4) easier, negation, conjunction and universal quantification are taken as basic in the proof system presented above. Conjunction and universal quantification are introduced as abbreviations in Appendix E in the usual way. For comparison with MPL_ω, the rules are moreover given as inference rules of a sequent calculus for classical deduction in Gentzen's style. The rules given by Jones (1990) are for natural deduction. Natural deduction proofs are generally more comprehensive but more difficult to construct.

Adding the axiom schema $\vdash E, \neg E$, corresponding to the law of the excluded middle, would make the above collection of axiom schemas and inference rules a complete proof system for classical many-sorted first-order logic with equality. Because this law does not hold, the rules $(\neg L)$ and $(\neg R)$ are replaced by the axiom schema (contr) and the special rules concerning negation for negation, conjunction and universal quantification. The axiom schema (var) expresses that free variables always denote. The additional axiom schemas for equality are due to the extension of equality to the three-valued case. The axiom schema (strict_1) is similar to the axiom schema $(=\downarrow)$ of MPL_ω. The usual rules for universal quantification are slightly adapted, because bound variables always denote. The adapted rules also differ from the corresponding rules of MPL_ω, because, unlike in MPL_ω, free variables always denote in LPF.

The formulae of LPF are mapped to formulae of MPL_ω by the logic-based semantics presented in Chapter 5. This translation can be extended to sequents such that what can be proved in LPF remains the same after translation. This implies that the axiom schemas and inference rules of LPF become derived ones of MPL_ω after translation. See also (Middelburg and Renardel de Lavalette, 1991). So the logic-based semantics for VVSL justifies the axiom schemas and inference rules of LPF.

Jones (1990) informally explains how a recursive definition of a partial function can be rendered into inference rules. The inference rules concerned resemble the appropriate rules of an inductive definition of the function (for partial functions, such rules usually need to be of a particular form). Given the recursive definition, the inference rules can also be regarded as derived rules of the above version of LPF extended with the following additional inference rules for conditional expressions and explicit function definitions:

$$(\mathsf{if}) \qquad \frac{\vdash e_1 \in T \quad \vdash E}{\vdash \mathsf{if}\ E\ \mathsf{then}\ e_1\ \mathsf{else}\ e_2 = e_1} \qquad \frac{\vdash e_2 \in T \quad \vdash \neg E}{\vdash \mathsf{if}\ E\ \mathsf{then}\ e_1\ \mathsf{else}\ e_2 = e_2}$$

$$(f\text{-form}) \qquad \frac{\vdash x_1 \in T_1 \quad \ldots \quad \vdash x_n \in T_n \quad \vdash E}{\vdash f(x_1, \ldots, x_n) \in T}$$

$$(f\text{-def}) \qquad \frac{\vdash x_1 \in T_1 \quad \ldots \quad \vdash x_n \in T_n \quad \vdash E \quad \vdash e \in T}{\vdash f(x_1, \ldots, x_n) = e}$$

if f is defined by $f(x_1\colon T_1, \ldots, x_n\colon T_n)T\ \mathsf{pre}\ E \triangleq e$.

Because the inference rules do not cover the 'leastness' of recursively defined functions, they are not sufficient to prove all properties that hold for those functions. Their undefinedness properties cannot be proved.

Just like formulae of LPF, conditional expressions and recursive function definitions are mapped to formulae of MPL_ω by the logic-based semantics presented in Chapter 5. The rules (if), (f-form) and (f-def) become derived rules of MPL_ω after translation. So the logic-based semantics for VVSL justifies these additional rules as well. Consequently, it also justifies the generation of rules from recursive function definitions according to (Jones, 1990).

Other additional rules needed for formal reasoning about VVSL specifications, such as the rules given in (Jones, 1990) for proofs about basic and constructed types can be justified in the same vein. In general, the justifications are straightforward. In the author's opinion, the justifications would be more difficult in case the semantics would describe the meaning of specifications in terms of the models that satisfy them.

Temporal reasoning

The temporal formulae of VVSL are the formulae of a typed first-order temporal logic which extends the typed version of LPF discussed just now.

This temporal logic includes temporal operators referring to the future and temporal operators referring to the past. Its proof system is obtained by adapting and extending the proof system of the typed version of LPF.

The adaptation consists of a common restriction on the axiom schema (sub) and the rules ($\forall L$) and ($\neg\,\forall R$). The restriction is that the substitution of the term concerned for the free occurrences of x does not introduce new occurrences of state variables in the scope of a temporal operator.

Axiom schemas and rules of inference for the future temporal operators $\bigcirc$ and $\mathcal{U}$ are:

$$\vdash \bigcirc\varphi \Rightarrow \underline{\bigcirc}\varphi$$

$$\vdash \underline{\bigcirc}(\varphi_1 \Rightarrow \varphi_2) \Rightarrow (\underline{\bigcirc}\varphi_1 \Rightarrow \underline{\bigcirc}\varphi_2)$$

$$\vdash \Box(\varphi_1 \Rightarrow \varphi_2) \Rightarrow (\Box\varphi_1 \Rightarrow \Box\varphi_2)$$

$$\vdash \Box\varphi \Rightarrow \underline{\bigcirc}\varphi$$

$$\vdash \Box(\varphi \Rightarrow \underline{\bigcirc}\varphi) \Rightarrow (\varphi \Rightarrow \Box\varphi)$$

$$\vdash \varphi_1 \,\mathcal{U}\, \varphi_2 \Leftrightarrow \varphi_2 \vee (\varphi_1 \wedge \bigcirc(\varphi_1 \,\mathcal{U}\, \varphi_2))$$

$$\vdash \varphi_1 \,\mathcal{U}\, \varphi_2 \Rightarrow \Diamond\varphi_2$$

$$\vdash (\forall x \in T \cdot \bigcirc\varphi) \Leftrightarrow (\bigcirc\forall x \in T \cdot \varphi)$$

$$\vdash (\exists x \in T \cdot \varphi_1 \,\mathcal{U}\, \varphi_2) \Rightarrow ((\exists x \in T \cdot \varphi_1) \,\mathcal{U}\, \varphi_2) \quad \text{if } x \text{ not free in } \varphi_2$$

$$\vdash (\exists x \in T \cdot \varphi_1 \,\mathcal{U}\, \varphi_2) \Leftrightarrow (\varphi_1 \,\mathcal{U}\, (\exists x \in T \cdot \varphi_2)) \quad \text{if } x \text{ not free in } \varphi_1$$

$$\frac{\vdash \varphi}{\vdash \Box\varphi}$$

$\underline{\bigcirc}\varphi$ is used as an abbreviation of $\neg\bigcirc\neg\,\varphi$,
$\Diamond\varphi$ is used as an abbreviation of $\mathsf{true}\,\mathcal{U}\,\varphi$,
$\Box\varphi$ is used as an abbreviation of $\neg\Diamond\neg\,\varphi$.

The conjecture is that adding the axiom schemas $\vdash \bigcirc\varphi \vee \neg\bigcirc\varphi$ and $\vdash \varphi_1 \,\mathcal{U}\, \varphi_2 \vee \neg(\varphi_1 \,\mathcal{U}\, \varphi_2)$, expressing that the temporal operators $\bigcirc$ and $\mathcal{U}$ are always defined, leads to completeness for these future temporal operators.

Temporal operators referring to the past obviate the need to introduce auxiliary state variables acting as history variables.

Axiom schemas and rules of inference for the past temporal operators $\ominus$ and $\mathcal{S}$ are:

$$\vdash \ominus\varphi \Rightarrow \underline{\ominus}\varphi$$

$$\vdash \underline{\ominus}(\varphi_1 \Rightarrow \varphi_2) \Rightarrow (\underline{\ominus}\varphi_1 \Rightarrow \underline{\ominus}\varphi_2)$$

$$\vdash \boxminus(\varphi_1 \Rightarrow \varphi_2) \Rightarrow (\boxminus\varphi_1 \Rightarrow \boxminus\varphi_2)$$

$$\vdash \boxminus\varphi \;\Rightarrow\; \underline{\ominus}\varphi$$

$$\vdash \boxminus(\varphi \;\Rightarrow\; \underline{\ominus}\varphi) \;\Rightarrow\; (\varphi \;\Rightarrow\; \boxminus\varphi)$$

$$\vdash \varphi_1 \,\mathcal{S}\, \varphi_2 \;\Leftrightarrow\; \varphi_2 \vee (\varphi_1 \wedge \ominus(\varphi_1 \,\mathcal{S}\, \varphi_2))$$

$$\vdash \diamondminus\underline{\ominus}\mathsf{false}$$

$$\vdash (\forall x \in T \cdot \ominus\varphi) \;\Leftrightarrow\; (\ominus\forall x \in T \cdot \varphi)$$

$$\vdash (\exists x \in T \cdot \varphi_1 \,\mathcal{S}\, \varphi_2) \;\Rightarrow\; ((\exists x \in T \cdot \varphi_1) \,\mathcal{S}\, \varphi_2) \quad \text{if } x \text{ not free in } \varphi_2$$

$$\vdash (\exists x \in T \cdot \varphi_1 \,\mathcal{S}\, \varphi_2) \;\Leftrightarrow\; (\varphi_1 \,\mathcal{S}\, (\exists x \in T \cdot \varphi_2)) \quad \text{if } x \text{ not free in } \varphi_1$$

$$\frac{\vdash \varphi}{\vdash \boxminus\varphi}$$

$\underline{\ominus}\varphi$ is used as an abbreviation of $\neg\ominus\neg\varphi$,
$\diamondminus\varphi$ is used as an abbreviation of $\mathsf{true}\,\mathcal{S}\,\varphi$,
$\boxminus\varphi$ is used as an abbreviation of $\neg\diamondminus\neg\varphi$.

Note the duality between past and future. The only asymmetry is due to the fact that, unlike the future, the past is always bounded. The following axiom schemas relate past and future:

$$\varphi \vdash \underline{\bigcirc}\ominus\varphi$$

$$\varphi \vdash \underline{\ominus}\bigcirc\varphi$$

The conjecture is that adding axiom schemas expressing that the temporal operators $\ominus$ and $\mathcal{S}$ are always defined leads to completeness for these past temporal operators as well.

An additional chop operator obviates the need to introduce auxiliary state variables acting as control variables.

Axiom schemas and rules of inference for the chop temporal operator $\mathcal{C}$ are:

$$\vdash (\varphi_1 \,\mathcal{C}\, \varphi_2) \,\mathcal{C}\, \varphi_3 \;\Leftrightarrow\; \varphi_1 \,\mathcal{C}\, (\varphi_2 \,\mathcal{C}\, \varphi_3)$$

$$\vdash (\varphi_1 \vee \varphi_2) \,\mathcal{C}\, \varphi_3 \;\Rightarrow\; \varphi_1 \,\mathcal{C}\, \varphi_3 \vee \varphi_2 \,\mathcal{C}\, \varphi_3$$

$$\vdash \varphi_1 \,\mathcal{C}\, (\varphi_2 \vee \varphi_3) \;\Rightarrow\; \varphi_1 \,\mathcal{C}\, \varphi_2 \vee \varphi_1 \,\mathcal{C}\, \varphi_3$$

$$\vdash \varphi_1 \,\mathcal{C}\, \varphi_2 \;\Rightarrow\; \varphi_1 \quad \text{if no temporal operator in } \varphi_1$$

$$\vdash (\underline{\bigcirc}\mathsf{false}) \,\mathcal{C}\, \varphi \;\Leftrightarrow\; \varphi \quad \text{if no past temporal operator in } \varphi$$

$$\vdash (\bigcirc\varphi_1) \,\mathcal{C}\, \varphi_2 \;\Rightarrow\; \bigcirc(\varphi_1 \,\mathcal{C}\, \varphi_2)$$

$$\vdash (\exists x \in T \cdot \varphi_1 \,\mathcal{C}\, \varphi_2) \;\Leftrightarrow\; ((\exists x \in T \cdot \varphi_1) \,\mathcal{C}\, \varphi_2) \quad \text{if } x \text{ not free in } \varphi_2$$

$$\vdash (\exists x \in T \cdot \varphi_1 \,\mathcal{C}\, \varphi_2) \;\Leftrightarrow\; (\varphi_1 \,\mathcal{C}\, (\exists x \in T \cdot \varphi_2)) \quad \text{if } x \text{ not free in } \varphi_1$$

$$\frac{\vdash \varphi_1 \;\Rightarrow\; \varphi_1' \qquad \vdash \varphi_2 \;\Rightarrow\; \varphi_2'}{\vdash \varphi_1 \,\mathcal{C}\, \varphi_2 \;\Rightarrow\; \varphi_1' \,\mathcal{C}\, \varphi_2'}$$

Adding an axiom schema expressing that the temporal operator $\mathcal{C}$ is always defined appears to be insufficient for completeness.

The temporal operators $\bigcirc$ and $\ominus$ are available on terms as well. Their use generally reduces the need for existential quantification.

Axiom schemas for the temporal operator $\bigcirc$ on terms are:

$$\vdash \bigcirc x = x$$

$$f(\bigcirc t_1, \ldots, \bigcirc t_n) = t \vdash \bigcirc f(t_1, \ldots, t_n) = t$$

$$\bigcirc f(t_1, \ldots, t_n) = t \vdash f(\bigcirc t_1, \ldots, \bigcirc t_n) = t$$

$$P(\bigcirc t_1, \ldots, \bigcirc t_n) \vdash \bigcirc P(t_1, \ldots, t_n)$$

$$\vdash \bigcirc P(t_1, \ldots, t_n) \;\Rightarrow\; P(\bigcirc t_1, \ldots, \bigcirc t_n)$$

$$\bigcirc t_1 = \bigcirc t_2 \vdash \bigcirc(t_1 = t_2)$$

$$\vdash \bigcirc(t_1 = t_2) \;\Rightarrow\; \bigcirc t_1 = \bigcirc t_2$$

Axiom schemas for the temporal operator $\ominus$ on terms are obtained by replacing $\ominus$ for $\bigcirc$ in the axiom schemas for the temporal operator $\bigcirc$ on terms.

Temporal formulae of VVSL are mapped to formulae of MPL_ω by the logic-based semantics in Chapter 5. It is straightforward to prove that the above axiom schemas and rules are sound by showing that they become derived ones of MPL_ω after translation.

As far as the propositional part of this temporal logic is concerned, the axiom schemas and rules presented here are similar to the ones in (Lichtenstein, Pnueli and Zuck, 1985) and (Rosner and Pnueli, 1986).

Structured proofs

For proofs of theorems about modules, special inference rules are needed which allow theorems about a module to be inherited from its constituent modules. For example:

$$\frac{\mathit{thm}\ \mathbf{in}\ M}{\mathit{thm}\ \mathbf{in}\ \mathsf{import}\ M\ \mathsf{into}\ M'}\quad \text{if the common state variables on which } \mathit{thm} \text{ depends are visible in } M \text{ and } M'$$

$$\frac{\mathit{thm}\ \mathbf{in}\ M}{\mathit{thm}\ \mathbf{in}\ \mathsf{export}\ \Sigma\ \mathsf{from}\ M}\quad \text{if } \mathit{sig}(\mathit{thm}) \subseteq \Sigma \text{ and hidden names are origin unique}$$

$$\frac{\mathit{thm}\ \mathbf{in}\ M}{\rho(\mathit{thm})\ \mathbf{in}\ \mathsf{rename}\ \rho\ \mathsf{in}\ M}\quad \text{if } \rho \text{ is injective}$$

where *thm* stands for an arbitrary sequent.

The restrictions on these rules are stated informally above but can be made mathematically precise. The intended meaning of $\Gamma \vdash \Delta$ **in** M is that one of the formulae in Δ logically follows from the formulae in Γ and the theory of the description corresponding to the module M. It is easy to prove that the rules are sound. They are strongly related to the results concerning the connections between DA and more abstract models of modular specification given in Section 9.1. Only the restriction on the first rule requires some understanding of the features of flat VVSL.

9.3 Logic-based semantics of an imperative language

The logic-based approach to semantics which is applied to VVSL in Chapter 5 is applied to another language in this section. Its purpose is to demonstrate the generality of the approach. The constructs of the language concerned are the control constructs usually found in imperative programming languages. The language is a simplified version of an extension of VVSL which is needed to be able to specify operations explicitly by a defining program. The simplified version is not adequate for operations that yield result values. It includes the following:

skip	skip
$v := e$	assignment
call $op(e_1, \ldots, e_n)$	call
$S_1; S_2$	sequential composition
if E then S_1 else S_2	conditional
while E do S	while loop
$S_1 \| S_2$	parallel composition
await E do S	await
$\langle S \rangle$	atomic

So the typical control constructs for sequential programming are available as well as powerful constructs for parallel programming with shared-variables. Await statements are used for synchronization between subprograms that are executed in parallel. Atomic statements are used to make a subprogram insensitive to interference.

More on states and computations

Some abbreviations of terms and formulae of MPL_ω are introduced which are used below to describe the meaning of the control constructs. All of them are concerned with states and computations.

The first two abbreviations are perfectly simple.

$$\begin{aligned}\mathrm{ini}(c) &:= \mathsf{st}_0(c)\\ \mathrm{fin}(c) &:= \iota s\colon \mathsf{State}(\textstyle\bigvee_n(\neg(\mathsf{st}_{n+1}(c){\downarrow}) \wedge \mathsf{st}_n(c) = s))\end{aligned}$$

$\mathrm{ini}(c)$ and $\mathrm{fin}(c)$ are terms denoting the initial state and the final state, respectively, of computation c.

State changes caused by the execution of a statement and external state changes may often be alternated. The next two abbreviations are used to delimit the possible alternation.

$$\text{is-skip}(c) \;:=\; \bigvee_n(\neg(\mathsf{st}_{n+1}(c)\downarrow) \wedge \bigwedge_{m=0}^{n} (\mathsf{ext}_m(c)))$$

is-skip(c) is a formula stating that c is a finite computation with external steps only.

$$\begin{array}{l}\text{atomic}(c) \;:= \\ \quad (\mathsf{st}_1(c)\downarrow \to \mathsf{int}_0(c) \wedge \neg(\mathsf{st}_2(c)\downarrow)) \vee \bigwedge_n(\mathsf{st}_n(c) = \mathsf{st}_{n+1}(c) \wedge \mathsf{int}_n(c))\end{array}$$

atomic(c) is a formula stating that c is a computation with zero, one or infinitely many internal steps and no external steps.

The following two abbreviations are only used to describe the meaning of assigment statements.

$$\text{mod-only}(s_1, s_2, v) \;:=\; \mathsf{mod}_{\langle\omega(v)\rangle}(s_1, s_2)$$

mod-only(s_1, s_2, v) is a formula stating that state variables other than v are not modified if the state changes from s_1 to s_2.

$$\text{no-trans}(c) \;:=\; \neg(\mathsf{st}_1(c)\downarrow)$$

no-trans(c) is a formula stating that there are no state transitions in computation c.

The next two abbreviations are basic to the description of sequential composition and parallel composition, respectively.

$$\begin{array}{l}\text{Concat}(c_1, c_2, c) \;:= \\ \quad \bigvee_n(\text{Prefix}_n(c, c_1) \wedge \text{Suffix}_n(c, c_2)) \vee (\bigwedge_n(\mathsf{st}_n(c_1)\downarrow) \wedge c = c_1)\end{array}$$

Concat(c_1, c_2, c) is a formula stating that computation c_1 followed by computation c_2 yields computation c. Note that c equals c_1 if c_1 is an infinite computation.

$$\begin{array}{l}\text{Conjoin}(c_1, c_2, c) \;:= \\ \quad \bigwedge_n(\mathsf{st}_n(c) \simeq \mathsf{st}_n(c_1) \wedge \mathsf{st}_n(c) \simeq \mathsf{st}_n(c_2) \wedge \\ \qquad\quad ((\mathsf{int}_n(c) \wedge ((\mathsf{int}_n(c_1) \wedge \mathsf{ext}_n(c_2)) \vee (\mathsf{ext}_n(c_1) \wedge \mathsf{int}_n(c_2)))) \vee \\ \qquad\quad\; (\mathsf{ext}_n(c) \wedge (\mathsf{ext}_n(c_1) \wedge \mathsf{ext}_n(c_2))) \vee \\ \qquad\quad\; \neg(\mathsf{st}_{n+1}(c)\downarrow)))\end{array}$$

Conjoin(c_1, c_2, c) is a formula stating that computation c_1 intertwined with computation c_2 yields computation c.

The execution of while loops may give rise to no state change for an infinitely long time. The next abbreviation is used to exhibit this.

$$\text{Stutter}(c_1, c_2) \;:=\; \text{no-trans}(c_1) \wedge \bigwedge_n(\mathsf{st}_n(c_2) = \mathsf{st}_0(c_1) \wedge \mathsf{int}_n(c_2))$$

Stutter(c_1, c_2) is a formula stating that adding infinitely many internal identity steps to a computation c_1 without any step yields computation c_2.

The following abbreviation is used to make the execution of statements insensitive to interference. It is needed for await statements and atomic statements.

$$
\begin{aligned}
&\text{Flatten}(c_1, c_2) := \\
&\quad \textstyle\bigwedge_n (\mathsf{st}_{n+1}(c_1)\!\downarrow\; \rightarrow \mathsf{int}_n(c_1)) \wedge \text{atomic}(c_2) \wedge \\
&\quad \text{ini}(c_1) = \text{ini}(c_2) \wedge (\text{fin}(c_1) = \text{fin}(c_2) \vee \textstyle\bigwedge_n (\mathsf{st}_n(c_1)\!\downarrow\; \wedge\; \mathsf{st}_n(c_2)\!\downarrow))
\end{aligned}
$$

Flatten(c_1, c_2) is a formula stating that removal of intermediate steps from a computation c_1 with internal steps only yields computation c_2.

The meaning of the control constructs is now described using the abbreviations just introduced. Expression evaluation is assumed to be deterministic.

Skip

Execution of skip does not cause any state change and terminates successfully.

$$
[\![\mathsf{skip}]\!]_c^C \;:=\; \text{is-skip}(c)
$$

Assignment

The execution of $v := e$ normally causes a state change in which the state variable v gets the value of the expression e in the state directly before the change and terminates immediately thereafter. In this case, only the state variable v is modified. The execution may also terminate without any state change in a state in which the values of v and e are the same.

$$
\begin{aligned}
&\text{Let } [\mathsf{var}\ v \colon T] \in \overline{C}, \text{ then:} \\
&[\![v := e]\!]_c^C \;:= \\
&\exists c_1 \colon \mathsf{Comp}, c_2 \colon \mathsf{Comp}, s_1 \colon \mathsf{State}, s_2 \colon \mathsf{State} \\
&\quad (\text{Concat}(c_1, c_2, c) \wedge \text{is-skip}(c_1) \wedge \text{atomic}(c_2) \wedge \\
&\quad\ \text{ini}(c_2) = s_1 \wedge \text{fin}(c_2) = s_2 \wedge \text{mod-only}(s_1, s_2, v_T^C) \wedge \\
&\quad\ \exists y \colon T^C([\![e]\!]_{\langle s_1 \rangle, y}^C \wedge [\![v]\!]_{\langle s_2 \rangle, y}^C \wedge ([\![v]\!]_{\langle s_1 \rangle, y}^C \rightarrow \text{no-trans}(c_2))))
\end{aligned}
$$

Note that an assignment is not visible as a step in computations if it does not give rise to a state change.

Call

The execution of call $op(e_1, \ldots, e_n)$ causes a succession of state changes that the operation op may perform according to its definition in case its arguments are the values of the expressions $e_1, \ldots, e_n$.

Let $[\mathsf{op}\ op\colon T_1 \times \cdots \times T_n \Rightarrow] \in \overline{C}$, then:

$$\begin{array}{l}
[\![\mathsf{call}\ op(e_1, \ldots, e_n)]\!]_c^C \ := \\
\exists c_1\colon \mathsf{Comp},\, c_2\colon \mathsf{Comp},\, s\colon \mathsf{State} \\
\quad (\mathrm{Concat}(c_1, c_2, c) \land \text{is-skip}(c_1) \land \mathrm{ini}(c_2) = s \land \\
\quad \exists x_1\colon T_1^C, \ldots, x_n\colon T_n^C(\bigwedge_{i=1}^{n}([\![e_i]\!]_{\langle s\rangle, x_i}^C) \land op_{T_1 \times \cdots \times T_n \Rightarrow}^C(x_1, \ldots, x_n, c_2)))
\end{array}$$

Sequential composition

The execution of $S_1; S_2$ causes the succession of state changes caused by the execution of S_1 immediately followed by the succession of state changes caused by the execution of S_2 provided that the execution of S_1 terminates.

$$[\![S_1; S_2]\!]_c^C \ := \ \exists c_1\colon \mathsf{Comp},\, c_2\colon \mathsf{Comp}(\mathrm{Concat}(c_1, c_2, c) \land [\![S_1]\!]_{c_1}^C \land [\![S_2]\!]_{c_2}^C)$$

Conditional

The execution of if E then S_1 else S_2 causes the succession of state changes caused by the execution of S_1 if the value of the logical expression E is initially true and causes the succession of state changes caused by the execution of S_2 if the value of logical expression E is initially false.

$$\begin{array}{l}
[\![\mathsf{if}\ E\ \mathsf{then}\ S_1\ \mathsf{else}\ S_2]\!]_c^C \ := \\
\exists c_1\colon \mathsf{Comp},\, c_2\colon \mathsf{Comp},\, s\colon \mathsf{State} \\
\quad (\mathrm{Concat}(c_1, c_2, c) \land \text{is-skip}(c_1) \land \mathrm{ini}(c_2) = s \land \\
\quad (([\![E]\!]_{\langle s\rangle, tt}^C \land [\![S_1]\!]_{c_2}^C) \lor ([\![E]\!]_{\langle s\rangle, ff}^C \land [\![S_2]\!]_{c_2}^C)))
\end{array}$$

Note that a condition test is not visible as a step in computations – just like an assignment that does not give rise to a state change.

While loop

The execution of while E do S causes the succession of state changes caused by the repeated execution of S while E is true at the start of its execution.

$$\begin{array}{l}
[\![\mathsf{while}\ E\ \mathsf{do}\ S]\!]_c^C \ := \\
\mathrm{Iter}(c) \land \forall s\colon \mathsf{State}(\mathrm{fin}(c) = s \rightarrow [\![E]\!]_{\langle s\rangle, ff}^C) \lor \\
\bigwedge_n(\exists c'\colon \mathsf{Comp}(\bigvee_m(\mathrm{Prefix}_{n+m}(c, c')) \land \mathrm{Iter}(c')))
\end{array}$$

where Iter is

$$\begin{array}{l}
\delta iter. \\
\forall c_1\colon \mathsf{Comp}, c_2\colon \mathsf{Comp}, c_3\colon \mathsf{Comp}, c_4\colon \mathsf{Comp}, c_5\colon \mathsf{Comp}, s\colon \mathsf{State} \\
\quad ((\text{is-skip}(c_1) \rightarrow iter(c_1)) \wedge \\
\quad\; (\text{Concat}(c_1, c_4, c_5) \wedge \text{Concat}(c_2, c_3, c_4) \wedge \text{ini}(c_2) = s \wedge \\
\quad\;\; iter(c_1) \wedge [\![E]\!]^C_{\langle s\rangle, tt} \wedge [\![S]\!]^C_{c_2} \wedge (\text{is-skip}(c_3) \vee \text{Stutter}(c_2, c_3)) \rightarrow \\
\quad\;\; iter(c_5)))
\end{array}$$

The execution does not terminate if the condition test never fails. Note that, if the execution does not cause any state change for an infinitely long time, the iterations concerned are made visible as steps.

Parallel composition

The execution of $S_1 \| S_2$ causes the succession of state changes caused by the execution of S_1 intertwined with the succession of state changes caused by the execution of S_2.

$$\begin{array}{l}
[\![S_1 \| S_2]\!]^C_c \;:= \\
\exists c_1\colon \mathsf{Comp}, c_2\colon \mathsf{Comp} \\
\quad (\text{Conjoin}(c_1, c_2, c) \wedge \\
\quad\; \exists c'\colon \mathsf{Comp}, c''\colon \mathsf{Comp}(\text{Concat}(c', c'', c_1) \wedge [\![S_1]\!]^C_{c'} \wedge \text{is-skip}(c'')) \wedge \\
\quad\; \exists c'\colon \mathsf{Comp}, c''\colon \mathsf{Comp}(\text{Concat}(c', c'', c_2) \wedge [\![S_2]\!]^C_{c'} \wedge \text{is-skip}(c'')))
\end{array}$$

The termination of the intertwined executions is possibly delayed in order to achieve simultaneous termination.

Await

The execution of $\mathsf{await}\ E\ \mathsf{do}\ S$ waits until E is true and causes immediately thereafter the succession of state changes caused by the execution of S without any interference.

$$\begin{array}{l}
[\![\mathsf{await}\ E\ \mathsf{do}\ S]\!]^C_c \;:= \\
\exists c_1\colon \mathsf{Comp}, c_2\colon \mathsf{Comp}, s\colon \mathsf{State} \\
\quad (\text{Concat}(c_1, c_2, c) \wedge \text{is-skip}(c_1) \wedge \text{atomic}(c_2) \wedge \text{ini}(c_2) = s \wedge \\
\quad\; [\![E]\!]^C_{\langle s\rangle, tt} \wedge \exists c'\colon \mathsf{Comp}(\text{Flatten}(c', c_2) \wedge [\![S]\!]^C_{c'}))
\end{array}$$

In the case that the execution of S does not terminate, this is visible as an infinite sequence of internal steps without state changes.

Atomic

The execution of $\langle S\rangle$ causes the succession of state changes caused by the execution of S but without any interference.

$$[\![\langle S\rangle]\!]^C_c \;:=\; \exists c'\colon \mathsf{Comp}(\text{Flatten}(c', c) \wedge [\![S]\!]^C_{c'})$$

An await statement $\mathsf{await\ true\ do}\ S$ is semantically equivalent to $\mathsf{skip};\ \langle S\rangle$.

Decomposition rules

For the restriction of the language to the constructs for sequential programming, it is easy to prove that the decomposition rules for operations given in (Jones, 1990) are consistent with the semantics given above.

For the full programming language, these rules have to be generalized to assertions with inter-conditions. For example, the decomposition rule for sequential composition becomes:

$$\frac{\{E_1\}S[\varphi]\{E_1' \wedge E_2\} \quad \{E_1'\}S'[\varphi']\{E_2'\}}{\{E_1\}S;S'[\varphi \mathrel{C} \varphi']\{E_2 \mid E_2'\}}$$

Some rules get rather complex. They can be simplified if the form of the inter-conditions is restricted to, for example, the form corresponding to rely- and guarantee-condition pairs.

10

Introduction to Case Studies

The remaining chapters are concerned with two case studies in VVSL. They are meant to clarify the extent to which the specification of software systems can be improved by the extensions of VDM-SL for modular structuring and specifying interference of operations. Both case studies are related to 'Relational DataBase Management Systems' (RDBMSs). They are case studies for demonstrating the practical usefulness of the above-mentioned extensions. Relational database management systems are sufficiently familiar to most people involved in the construction of software systems to allow them to concentrate on the formal specification tasks rather than on the examples used for them. The case studies are also interesting because the specifications yielded by them give comprehensive pictures of (1) the relational approach to databases and (2) transaction management in database systems, which are mathematically precise and modularly structured as well. Such descriptions are still rare.

The first case study deals with the underlying concepts of relational database management systems and the operations for data manipulation and data definition which can be performed by such systems. An attempt is made to give a full picture of the relational approach. The concepts concerned include many of the basic concepts of the 'Relational Data Model' (RDM), which was introduced by Codd (1970). They include the concepts which are considered fundamental in (Brodie and Schmidt, 1981). The operations concerned make up an external RDBMS interface: the operations are available directly to the users of the RDBMS. The interface is abstract in the sense that it does not deal with details of actual interfaces like concrete syntax of operations, their embedding in a host language, concrete representation of the data objects yielded by query operations, etc. The modular structure of the specification yielded by this case study isolates the description of the RDM concepts from the description of the external RDBMS interface. This means that large parts of the specification can be re-used in specifications of other possible external RDBMS interfaces and even various internal RDBMS interfaces.

The second case study deals with the underlying concepts and operations of systems for handling concurrent access to a relational database by multiple transactions. The specification yielded by this case study provides for a way of looking at 'Transaction Management' (TM) in database systems. The concepts concerned are concepts associated with the following facets of transaction management in database systems: concurrency control for databases (Eswaran, Gray, Lorie and Traiger, 1976; Rosenkrantz, Stearns and Lewis, 1978; Kung and Papadimitriou, 1983) and in-progress transaction backup (Gray, 1978; Gray et al., 1981; Haerder and Reuter, 1983). It does not cover the low-level concepts that are needed for particular solutions of transaction management problems, e.g. locking protocols for solving concurrency control problems – see (Bernstein and Goodman, 1981) for a survey – and log protocols for solving transaction backup problems are not described. The operations concerned make up an internal RDBMS interface: the operations are not available directly to the users of the RDBMS. In any existing RDBMS, the execution of the high-level data manipulation operations of its external interface gives rise to the execution of lower-level access handling operations of an internal interface which is comparable to the described internal interface.

It was argued in Chapter 1 that a precise specification is the right starting-point for the development of a satisfactory software system. This carries over to theoretical development of solutions for idealizations of common problems in software systems of a certain kind – such as locking protocols for concurrency control problems in database systems. Here, a formal specification of the idealization of such a problem provides a reference point against which the correctness of the proposed solutions can be established and the confidence in the pertinence of the idealization to the actual problems can be increased. The usual absence of such specifications in the area of transaction management in database systems – as well as in many other areas – is reflected by the difficulties in relating the different solutions to seemingly the same problem. A specification like the one given in Chapter 13 was already needed before the early work concerning locking protocols for solving database concurrency control problems and log protocols for solving transaction backup problems (such as the work presented in (Eswaran, Gray, Lorie and Traiger, 1976; Gray, Lorie, Putzolu and Traiger, 1976; Gray, 1978) was carried out. Actually, the specification was largely acquired by seeking the unmentioned assumptions about the problem(s) to be solved in the presentations of that work.

In the remainder of this chapter general remarks are made about the case studies worked out in Chapters 11 to 13. This includes remarks about the scope of the formal specifications, summaries of formalized concepts, short overviews of the interfaces and outlines of the specifications. This introduction is meant to excite interest in the later chapters and to make them more comprehensible. It is possible to understand the material in these chapters without reading the remainder of this chapter. However, the material is better understood with an picture of what is formally described and how the descriptions concerned are organized.

Neither this chapter nor the later chapters are intended to be used in becoming familiar with the relational approach to databases or transaction management in database systems. For that purpose, it is better to study a textbook such as (Ullman, 1988).

10.1 Scope of the specifications

RDM concepts and an external RDBMS interface

A formal definition of RDM concepts necessarily has to be selective. Some RDM concepts have several definitions based on different views of the concept. The most striking example is the basic concept of a relation: there exists a 'set-of-sequences' view and a 'set-of-maps' view of relations. Furthermore, in several areas there is a multitude of closely related concepts. One such area is the area of dependencies: there are functional dependencies, multi-valued dependencies, join dependencies, implied dependencies, transitive dependencies, mutual dependencies, extended transitive dependencies, embedded implicational dependencies, etc. Both in cases of different views of concepts and in cases of multitudes of closely related concepts, choices have been made. The generality of the definition, its ability to fit a coherent collection of concepts and its practical relevance have been taken into account. Naturally the choices also reflect the taste and biases of the author.

Another problem one encounters in formalizing RDM concepts is that some concepts of practical relevance have imprecise definitions. An example is the definition of inclusion dependency for the general case (involving one or more attributes), which is imprecise in both (Fagin, 1981) and (Fagin and Vardi, 1986). As is often the case, the concept seems so straightforward that inaccuracies in its definition only show up if one tries to formalize it. In such cases, attempts have been made to find out the intentions in order to acquire the exact details in a faithful manner. As a matter of course, concepts that are both imprecisely defined and not very relevant have been dropped.

Concerning the concept of a relation, the set-of-maps view has been chosen. It can be regarded as a generalization of the set-of-sequence view and it is the basis of most experimental and commercially available RDBMSs, e.g. PRTV (Todd, 1976), QBE (Zloof, 1977), INGRES (Stonebraker, Wong, Kreps and Held, 1976; Stonebraker, 1980) and the RDBMSs providing SQL (Astrahan et al., 1976; Chamberlin et al., 1981). Moreover, it turns out not to hinder a coherent collection of RDM concepts. Originally, relations were viewed as sets of sequences (Codd, 1970). The consequences of choosing one view over the other are illustrated by Bjørner (1982).

With respect to the concept of a relation schema, the view has been taken that it should define not only the attributes of the relations which are considered to be its instances, but also the domains of these attributes and the sets of attributes which form a key. However it should not define more than this. One reason for this choice is that it corresponds roughly to what is offered most commonly in existing RDBMSs. Another reason is that many proposed definitions of a relation schema are based on concepts which are not generally accepted as RDM concepts. These concepts are usually related to attempts to extend the RDM to capture more meaning (Codd, 1979). In the presented formalization, domain dependencies and key dependencies are the only ones that are supported by the relation schema. The concept of a domain dependency generalizes in a purely relational way the semantic idea of entity integrity advocated by Codd (1979) and Date (1986). Other dependencies are also considered to be of practical interest, but mainly for database design. For this reason several of them, including the well-known functional dependencies and multi-valued dependencies, are treated separately (but connected with the concept of a relation schema).

Remarks, which are similar to those made above, apply to the concept of a database schema. In the presented formalization, inclusion dependencies are the only additional ones that are supported by the database schema. The concept of an inclusion dependency generalizes in a purely relational way the semantic idea of referential integrity advocated by Codd (1979) and Date (1986).

One usually distinguishes two kinds of notation for querying relational databases: algebraic notation and logical notation. One abstract language of the former kind called relational algebra has been proposed by Codd (1972) and two abstract languages of the latter kind, called tuple relational calculus and domain relational calculus have been proposed by Codd (1972) and Lacroix and Pirotte (1977), respectively. These abstract languages are equivalent in expressive power. See, for example, (Ullman, 1988). Query languages of existing RDBMSs often resemble one of these abstract languages. For example, ISBL (PRTV) resembles relational algebra, QUEL (INGRES) resembles tuple relational calculus and Query-by-Example (QBE) resembles domain relational calculus. The influential SQL (Chamberlin et al., 1976) resembles relational algebra for simple queries and resembles tuple relational calculus for more complex queries. For the description of an external RDBMS interface a choice from the abstract languages has been made in favour of relational algebra. The main reason for this choice is that it gives rise to an abstract interface which can be concisely defined in terms of the formalized RDM concepts and illustrates most of them. This yields an interface that supports the RDM concepts directly. Such an external interface is sometimes even considered to be a part of the RDM, for example, in (Brodie and Schmidt, 1981). Its specification is not meant to provide the sole starting-point for the design of concrete ones which are convenient for the user, because it is somewhat extreme with respect to queries.

TM concepts and an internal RDBMS interface

The description of an internal RDBMS interface covers concepts associated with concurrency control for databases and in-progress transaction backup. Some formalized concepts are precisely defined instances of concepts which are widely used in this area but which are usually only vaguely described. Even nameless concepts described by expressions like 'the dynamic syntactic information about the transactions issuing access requests' had to be formalized. Other formalized concepts are generalizations of concepts which are mostly used in theoretical work on transaction management but which are often not very useful in practice. For example, many concepts are based on assumptions that preclude dynamic creation of transactions. However, as in existing systems, the internal RDBMS interface described later on provides for dynamic transaction creation. Moreover, some formalized concepts are abstractions of concepts which are used in this area, since the original concepts were too concrete to underlie the formalized interface.

Concerning concurrency control, the view has been taken that the interface should completely hide the mechanism used for scheduling the access requests issued on behalf of various transactions. For example, the interface should not include operations for locking. This view corresponds to 'concurrency transparency', which is mentioned as one of the types of transparency that transactions should provide, for example, in (Traiger, Gray, Galtieri and Lindsay, 1982). The main reason for this choice is that it leads to an interface which reflects the essential characteristics of concurrency control for databases instead of the details of a particular mechanism supporting it. Such an interface seems more suitable to provide for a way of looking at transaction management. Another reason for this choice is that it gives rise to an interface which, as far as concurrency control is concerned, can be defined in terms of a small collection of underlying concepts that are both simple and general.

One usually distinguishes two purposes of transaction-oriented database recovery: in-progress transaction backup and crash recovery. See, for example, (Gray, 1978). In-progress transaction backup is needed in order to be able to undo the updates of the database made by a particular transaction in the event that the transaction cannot complete due to an error which allows its abortion in a controlled manner. Crash recovery is needed in order to be able to undo the updates made by any transaction that was incomplete at the time of a crash (i.e. an error which does not allow its abortion in a controlled manner) and to redo the updates made by any completed transaction whose effects were lost due to the crash. A choice has been made not to take crash recovery into account. A useful treatment of crash recovery would require a multitude of low-level concepts to be formalized.

A system for handling concurrent access to a relational database may handle access to either single tuples of stored relations, subsets of stored relations or entire stored relations. For the description given a choice from these 'units of access' has been made in favour of subsets of stored relations. The main reason for this choice is that access to subsets of stored relations is a generalization of the other cases. Moreover, the distinction between access to single tuples and access to subsets of stored relations is blurred in comparable internal interfaces of existing RDBMSs by the provision of 'scans' – also called cursors; see, for example, (Gray, 1987).

The above-mentioned choices determine the scope of the specification given in Chapter 13. For example, concepts underlying particular concurrency control mechanisms and concepts underlying crash recovery are not covered. It builds on the formalization of RDM concepts given in Chapter 11. This means that the definitions are couched in terms of the RDM. This restricts the scope of the formalization slightly. The definitions seem to carry over to other data models without many problems.

10.2 Subject matter of the specifications

The first specification makes precise many of the basic concepts of the relational data model and describes an external RDBMS interface. The second specification makes precise many concepts associated with transaction management in database systems and describes an internal RDBMS interface.

Summary of the formalized RDM concepts

The principal formalized *structure* concepts are tuple, relation, database, tuple structure, relation schema and database schema. The concepts relation and relation schema are connected through a predicate 'is valid instance of' on relations and relation schemas. The concepts database and database schema are connected analogously.

The principal formalized *manipulation* concepts are the usual ones connected with relations: union, intersection, difference, product, projection, selection, renaming, joining and division of relations. Concepts concerning the manipulation of relations in databases and relation schemas in database schemas are formalized as well.

The general *integrity* concepts connected with relations and databases, relation constraint and database constraint, are also formalized. The formalized specializations of these concepts are functional dependency, multivalued dependency, join dependency, domain dependency, key dependency and inclusion dependency. The concepts relation schema and relation constraint are connected through a predicate 'in domain-key normal form with respect to' on relation schemas and collections of relation constraints. The concepts database schema and database constraint are connected analogously. Domain-key normal form is the only formalized normal form.

The formalized concepts include the concepts which are considered fundamental in (Brodie and Schmidt, 1981). The remaining formalized concepts are mainly integrity concepts. Concepts concerning aspects of a DBMS that are not specifically associated with the RDM (e.g. views and authorization, transactions) are not included.

Overview of the external RDBMS interface

The formalized external interface consists of two parts: a data manipulation interface and a data definition interface. The data manipulation interface comprises an operation for selecting a relation that is derived from the ones stored in the current database and operations for altering one of the relations stored in the current database by insertion, deletion or replacement. The data definition interface comprises operations for changing the current database schema by addition and removal of relation schemas.

The main arguments of the data manipulation operations are queries, i.e. expressions denoting relations. These queries resemble expressions from relational algebra. The description of queries makes precise their abstract syntax, their well-formedness and their evaluation in a database. Both well-formedness and evaluation are defined with respect to a given database schema. Evaluation of queries yields relations. So well-formedness and evaluation of queries connect queries to relations, databases and database schemas. This means that the description of queries illustrates many of the formalized RDM concepts.

Given the description of queries, the definition of the data manipulation operations is straightforward. A large part of the description of the data manipulation interface relates to the well-formedness of queries. This is not exceptional. Well-formedness (also called 'context conditions' and 'static semantics') tends not to be defined in a concise way for any language even if it is well thought out with respect to semantics.

The main arguments of the data definition operations are declarations. Declarations are syntactic objects corresponding to relation schemas. The description of declarations makes precise their abstract syntax, their well-formedness and their evaluation. Different from the well-formedness of queries, the well-formedness of declarations is entirely straightforward.

Summary of the formalized TM concepts

The formalized *concurrency control* concepts include: access and access table. The concept of an access was originally defined in connection with the idea of predicate locks (Eswaran, Gray, Lorie and Traiger, 1976). The concept of an access table makes precise what is informally described as 'dynamic syntactic information about a transaction system' in (Kung and Papadimitriou, 1983). The formalized concepts also include operators for creating, updating and destroying the access information about a single transaction. The concepts of access and access table are connected through predicates 'conflicts' and 'deadlock liable' on accesses and access tables.

The formalized *transaction backup* concepts include: transition record, transition log and log table. The concept of a transition record generalized what is used in, for example, System R (Gray et al., 1981) to record the differences occurring when changes are made to a tuple of some stored relation. The concept of a log table is based on the informal concept of a system log described in (Gray, 1978). The formalized concepts also include operators for creating, updating and destroying transition logs in log tables, and an operator for undoing changes made to stored relations according to transition logs.

Together with the description of RDM concepts in Chapter 11, this description of concurrency control and transaction backup concepts provides all of the concepts that are needed to understand the internal RDBMS interface which is described in Chapter 13.

Overview of the internal RDBMS interface

The formalized internal interface comprises operations for starting and stopping a transaction, operations for accessing a subset of one of the stored relations to read it or to overwrite it, and operations for creating and destroying stored relations.

The main arguments of these operations are simple formulae for stating the properties of tuples. The description of simple formulae makes precise their abstract syntax, their well-formedness and their evaluation.

Most of the operations can be regarded as requests on behalf of some transaction to perform an action on a subset of a stored relation. Transactions are the units of consistency: it is assumed that each action which is performed on behalf of a transaction may violate database consistency, but that each transaction, when executed alone, preserves database consistency. Interleaved performance of actions requested by several transactions is provided in such a manner that each transaction sees a consistent database and produces a consistent database. When a transaction issues a request, it is never made to wait for ever for the grant of the request. An issued request is rejected immediately if the request would cause deadlock. Other reasons why a transaction might wait for ever are prevented from occurring by the way of granting requests. One of the operations stops an transaction after undoing all changes made to the database so far. This is usually needed if an issued request is rejected.

The external RDBMS interface which is described in Chapter 12 does not deal with concurrency at all. This is in accordance with the view that it should appear to any user of the RDBMS as if each operation is executed in isolation. The internal RDBMS interface which is described in Chapter 13 deals with concurrency. Access handling requests issued on behalf of several data manipulation operations are executed in an interleaved way by which it appears as if each of them is executed in isolation. This can be used for an implementation of the RDBMS with concurrent execution of data manipulation operations in a multi-user environment.

10.3 Related work

Date's definition of the RDM (Date, 1986, Chapter 7), called 'A Formal Definition of the Relational Model', is a semi-formal* mixture of syntactic and semantic aspects, static and dynamic aspects, etc., which provides for a restricted picture of the relational approach. For example, it covers only a very restricted 'name-based' variant of relational algebra and it does not cover 'dynamic' data definition. The first case study in this book tries to give a well-structured formal description of many of the basic RDM concepts, which provides for a full picture of the relational approach.

In (Tompa, 1980), an algebra of quotient relations, is formally defined using an algebraic specification technique. It endows relational algebra with explicit set-processing capabilities which are closely connected with the GROUP BY clause of SQL (Chamberlin et al., 1976). The concept of a quotient relation, which is relevant to efficient implementation of query evaluation and for the support of 'views', is not treated in Chapter 11.

An RDBMS with a layered architecture, in which an external, conceptual and internal level are distinguished, is formally described in (Neuhold and Olnhoff, 1980) using the VDM specification language described in (Jones, 1982) and known as META-IV. It covers some general aspects of a DBMS, i.e. aspects that are not particularly relational in nature. These aspects are not covered in this book.

In (Brodie and Schmidt, 1981), a start is made with a formal definition of the RDM using META-IV in behalf of a 'Relational Standard'. Using META-IV, Bjørner (1982) focusses on query languages resembling relational algebra and tuple relational calculus. Both have influenced the descriptions in Chapters 11 and 13.

Usual set theoretic notation is the basis of a formalization of basic con-

* A BNF-like syntax notation and English text is used.

cepts of a data model by Niemi and Järvelin (1984). The data model concerned is called the RDM by the authors. However, the concepts deviate rather a lot from the usual RDM concepts since the separation between instances (objects) and schemas (meta-objects) is avoided, e.g. a structure concept such as tuple or relation is defined so that it contains a description of its structure. In the description in Chapter 11, we try not to deviate so much.

The ideas, which are elaborated in the presented description of an internal RDBMS interface, were mainly developed by abstraction and combination of many useful ideas that have been developed in the area of concurrency control. The latter ideas are usually associated with particular (kinds of) concurrency control mechanisms. Amongst the ideas that have been most influential are the ideas of 'two-phase' locking and 'predicate locks' which are introduced in (Eswaran, Gray, Lorie and Traiger, 1976), the ideas of 'strict' and 'superstrict' concurrency control which are introduced in (Rosenkrantz, Stearns and Lewis, 1978), and the idea of 'optimal schedulers' (for available information) which is introduced in (Kung and Papadimitriou, 1983). However, none of these ideas themselves are directly formalized. Influential ideas in the area of transaction backup are mainly the ideas described in (Gray, 1978) and partly in (Gray et al., 1981); notably the idea that should be called 'logical transition logging' according to the classification of log data presented in (Haerder and Reuter, 1983).

The ideas of two-phase locking and predicate locks are treated formally in (Eswaran, Gray, Lorie and Traiger, 1976). Usual set theoretic notation is used as the basis of the formalization in that paper. Other early work in this area is often informal or semi-formal. For example, useful ideas about granularity of locks are introduced and elaborated informally in (Gray, Lorie, Putzolu and Traiger, 1976). In (Schlageter, 1978) only a few concepts are formalized – perhaps it is due to this lack of formality that several results are in error. A good example of a formal presentation is (Bernstein, Shipman and Wong, 1979). Herein several concurrency control mechanisms and properties of schedules are defined and analysed in a formal manner, but under several simplifying assumptions. Therefore, it has not influenced the description in Chapter 13.

10.4 Outline of the first specification

Structure

The choice of modular structure was mainly governed by the criteria mentioned in Section 2.2. If the reader wants to understand the formalized concepts of the RDM and the external RDBMS interface in detail, he or she can study the modules in the next two chapters in the order in which they appear. For a global understanding, he or she may find it better to read them in reverse order.

The modules in Chapter 11 are modules containing definitions of underlying concepts of RDBMSs and the modules in Chapter 12 are modules containing definitions concerning the states of an RDBMS and the operations of the external RDBMS interface. The latter modules are composed of the former modules.

In Chapter 12 the modules **SELECTION_WFF**, **QUERY** and **DECLARATION** only contain definitions of types and functions, while **DBMS_STATE**, **MANIPULATION** and **DEFINITION** only contain definitions of state variables and operations. This means that the state independent aspects of the external RDBMS interface and the state dependent ones are separated.

RDM concepts

In Chapter 11, many of the basic RDM concepts are defined. In the definitions concerned, *relation names*, *attributes* and *values* are regarded as primitive concepts about which it suffices to make a few assumptions. The modules **REL_NM**, **ATTRIBUTE** and **VALUE** contain the assumptions concerned. Relation names and attributes have no a priori properties. For values, it is assumed that any finite set of values constitutes a domain. Of course, relation names and attributes are usually identifiers and values are usually numbers from some finite range of integers and strings over a finite alphabet up to some finite length. However, because the definitions of RDM concepts do not rely on any property of relation names and attributes and rely on only a few properties of values, we do not commit ourselves to a particular choice of relation names, attributes and values.

Attribute sets and attribute bijections (one-to-one maps between attribute sets) are jointly used in various modules, e.g. as arguments of functions on tuples, relations, etc. The relevant definitions are collected in the module **ATTR_SUPPL**. The closely related key sets (sets of attribute sets) are mainly used in other modules, e.g. as components of relation schemas. The relevant definitions are collected in the module **KEY_SUPPL**.

In the module **TUPLE**, tuples are defined as maps from attributes to values. Tuples can be viewed as records, with the attributes corresponding to fields. Tuple predicates are defined as maps from tuples to truth values. A tuple predicate is used to select tuples from some relation.

In the module **RELATION**, relations are defined as sets of tuples. All tuples from a relation must have the same attributes, i.e. they must have the same domain. Relations can be viewed as files of records with the same fields. Relations together with the functions defined in this module for constructing new relations from old ones constitute a version of *relational algebra* (Codd, 1972). These functions comprises traditional set operators and special relational operators.

In the module **RELATION_EXTENSION**, some additional functions for constructing a new relation from old ones are defined in terms of the primitive ones defined in the module **RELATION**.

In the module **DATABASE**, databases are defined as maps from relation names to relations. Informally, it is a collection of uniquely named relations. Databases together with the functions defined in this module for constructing them constitute an algebra of databases, in the same vein as relational algebra is an algebra of relations.

In the module **TUPLE_STRUCT**, tuple structures are defined as maps from attributes to domains. Tuple structures can be viewed as record types, with the attributes and domains corresponding to fields and types of the fields, respectively. A tuple structure is used to present structural constraints on the tuples of some relation.

In the module **REL_SCHEMA**, relation schemas are defined as composite values with a tuple structure and a set of keys as components. A relation schema is used to present intra-relational constraints which must be obeyed by some named relation. Its tuple structure presents the structural constraints on the tuples of the relation and each of the keys presents a uniqueness constraint on the relation. The relations that obey the constraints presented by a given relation schema are its valid instances.

In the module **DB_SCHEMA**, database schemas are defined as composite values with a map from relation names to relation schemas and a set of inclusions as components. A database schema is used to present intra-relational constraints on the named relations of some database, in the form of relation schemas, as well as inter-relational constraints on the database, in the form of inclusions. Each of the inclusions presents an inclusion constraint between two named relations in the database. The databases that obey the constraints presented by a given database schema are its valid instances.

In the module **REL_CONSTRAINT**, relation constraints are defined as maps from relations to truth values. Intra-relational constraints, such as the well-known functional dependencies and multi-valued dependencies, are special kinds of relation constraints. Domain dependencies and key dependencies are the only two kinds of intra-relational constraints that can be presented in relation schemas as defined in the module **REL_SCHEMA**. Domain-key normal form is introduced to connect relation schemas with relation constraints.

In the module **DB_CONSTRAINT**, database constraints are defined as maps from databases to truth values. Inclusion dependencies are a special kind of database constraints. It is the only kind of inter-relational constraint that can be presented in database schemas as defined in **DB_SCHEMA**. The intra-relational constraints which are treated as special kinds of relation constraints in the module **REL_CONSTRAINT** are lifted to database constraints. Domain-key normal form is lifted to connect database schemas with database constraints.

The external RDBMS interface

In Chapter 12, an external RDBMS interface is described. In the definitions, *value constants* and *domain constructions* are also regarded as primitive concepts. Value constants and domain constructions are used as syntactic objects denoting values and domains, respectively. The definitions only rely on the existence of evaluation functions for value constants and domain constructions.

The module **VALUE_CONST** is based on the assumptions with respect to values from the module **VALUE**. In this module it is assumed that there is a type *Value_const* and a total evaluation function *value* on value constants yielding values.

The module **DOMAIN_CONST** is based on the assumptions with respect to values from the module **VALUE**. In this module it is assumed that there is a type *Domain_const* and a total evaluation function *domain* on domain constructions yielding domains.

In the module **SELECTION_WFF**, selection formulae are defined as composite values of several kinds. Selection formulae are simple formulae for stating properties of tuples. They should be considered to be abstract syntactic objects since they do not deal with concrete representation details. A selection formula is used as a constituent of queries in which a relation is expressed as a selection from another one. The well-formedness and evaluation of selection formulae are also defined.

In the module **QUERY**, queries are defined as composite values of several kinds. Queries can be viewed as expressions denoting relations. Like selection formulae, they should be considered to be abstract syntactic objects. Queries are used as arguments of data manipulation operations. Their well-formedness and evaluation are also defined.

In the module **DECLARATION**, declarations are defined as composite values. Declarations can be viewed as expressions denoting relation schemas. Like selection formulae and queries, they should be considered to be abstract syntactic objects. Declarations are used as arguments of data definition operations. Their well-formedness and evaluation are also defined.

In the module **DBMS_STATE**, a varying database and a varying database schema are defined as state variables. They can be viewed as taking at any point in time the current database value and the current database schema value, respectively. Together they constitute the changing state of a database management system. The intention that the current database schema always applies to the current database, is made precise with a state invariant.

In the module **MANIPULATION**, an operation for the selection of a relation that is derived from the ones stored in the current database and three operations for altering one of the relations stored in the current database (by insertion, deletion and replacement) are defined as operations. Together they constitute the data manipulation interface of a database management system.

In the module **DEFINITION**, three operations for altering the current database schema are defined as operations. Together they constitute the data definition interface of a database management system.

In the system module (system), the relevant definitions from the previous modules are combined and what constitutes the external RDBMS interface is specified by making only the names of these concepts visible.

10.5 Outline of the second specification

Structure

The structure of the second specification is similar to the structure of the first one. Again, if the reader wants to understand the formalized TM concepts and the internal RDBMS interface in detail, he or she can study the modules in Chapter 13 in the order in which they appear. But for a global understanding, he or she may find it better to read them in reverse order. The reused part from Chapter 11 is not really repeated in the second specification.

In Chapter 13 the modules **SIMPLE_WFF**, ..., **LOG_TABLE** only contain definitions of types and functions. The modules **AH_STATE** and **ACCESS_HANDLING** only contain definitions of state variables and operations (except the definition of the type *Status* which is used by most operations to return an indication of success or failure). This means that the state independent aspects of the internal RDBMS interface and the state dependent ones are separated.

TM concepts and the internal RDBMS interface

In Chapter 13, an internal RDBMS interface is described. In the definitions, *transaction names* are also regarded to be primitive. Transaction names are usually identifiers.

In the module **TRANS_NM** it is assumed that there is a type *Trans_nm* with no a priori properties.

The modules **ATTR_SUPPL**, ..., **DB_SCHEMA** contain the required definitions of RDM concepts. These modules were outlined before.

In the module **SIMPLE_WFF**, simple formulae are defined as composite values of several kinds. Simple formulae and selection formulae (defined in the module **SELECTION_WFF**) are almost the same. Simple formulae are used as arguments of access handling operations. Their well-formedness and evaluation are also defined.

In the module **ACCESS**, accesses are defined as composite values with an access mode (READ, WRITE, CREATE or DESTROY), a relation name and a simple formula as components. An access is used to present syntactic properties of an access request issued by some transaction. These properties are made use of to grant the request concerned amongst requests issued by other transactions in a consistency preserving order. One access is in conflict with another one if the effects of the requested actions possibly interfere according to the syntactic properties concerned.

In the module **ACCESS_TABLE**, access tables are defined as maps from transaction names to access records (composite values with two sets of accesses as components). An access table is used to present, for each active transaction, the syntactic properties of its previously granted requests and its currently waiting request (only when it is currently waiting). All this is made use of to grant the waiting and coming requests of the active transactions in a consistency preserving order. For a given transaction, an access is in conflict with an access table if the effect of the requested action possibly interferes with the effect of one of the actions that was previously requested by another active transaction. A conflicting request is not granted immediately; it becomes a waiting request which eventually will be granted or it is rejected immediately. The latter will happen when it would otherwise be waiting for itself indirectly, i.e. the access is liable for deadlock.

In the module **TRANSITION_RECORD**, transition records are defined as composite values with a transition mode (NORMAL, INIT, FINAL), a relation name and two relations as components. A transition record reflects the effect of a write action on some stored relation by recording the differences that occur when the stored relation is changed by performing the write action on it. It provides all the details of its effect that are required to undo the effect.

In the module **TRANSITION_LOG**, transition logs are defined as sequences of transition records. A transition log is used to record the effects of all write actions on stored relations which have been performed on request of some transaction, in the order in which they have taken place. The transition log of a transaction provides all the details that are required to undo its cumulative effect.

In the module **LOG_TABLE**, log tables are defined as maps from transaction names to transition logs. A log table is used to record the effects of all write actions on stored relations which have been performed on the request of active transactions, in the order in which they have taken place and aggregated by transaction. The log table provides all the details that are required to abort any of the active transactions in a controlled manner.

In the module **AH_STATE**, a varying database, a varying database schema, a varying access table and a varying log table are defined as state variables. They can be viewed as taking at any point in time the current database value, the current database schema value, the current access table value and the current log table value, respectively. Together they constitute the changing state of the access handler.

In the module **ACCESS_HANDLING**, the operations which constitute the internal RDBMS interface are defined as operations. The definition of these operations is quite straightforward but far from concise. A large part is related to the characterization of all possible ways in which they may be scheduled.

In the system module (system), the relevant definitions from the previous modules are combined and what constitutes the internal RDBMS interface is specified by making only the names of these concepts visible.

Miscellaneous

In the specifications, the universe of values for the attributes of tuples is not fixed, but restricted to be finite. By this restriction, the specifications could be founded on a simple algebraic theory of finite sets and maps instead of a strong variety of set theory like Zermelo-Fraenkel set theory. In particular, various concepts could be defined as finite maps instead of general functions. Thus, higher-order functions have been avoided. Assuming an infinite universe of values, as is done sometimes in theoretical work, is quite unrealistic. In reality, every RDBMS supports only a finite universe of values. Values are usually numbers from some finite range of integers and strings over a finite alphabet up to some finite length. Therefore, the restriction to a finite universe of values is not considered to be a loss.

It often occurs that a function is a generalization of another function. In these cases, the same name is used for both functions, unless the usual names for them are different. This causes no problems in VVSL, since overloading of function names is allowed. For the reader, it means that sometimes he may have to look back a few lines to fix the function concerned exactly. Instead, long compound names could be used. It is doubtful whether that would enhance comprehension of the specification.

11

Formalization of RDM Concepts

This chapter is the first of two chapters in which the first case study in VVSL is presented. This case study deals with the underlying concepts of relational database management systems and the operations for data manipulation and data definition which can be performed by such systems. The underlying concepts are described in this chapter and the operations are described in Chapter 12. The second case study is presented in Chapter 13. The current chapter contains the part of the specification yielded by the first case study that is re-used in the second case study. The purpose of the first case study is to demonstrate the practical usefulness of the extensions of VDM-SL for modular structuring.

The concepts described in this chapter include many of the basic concepts of the RDM. The RDM is the way of looking at data which underlies any RDBMS. The relevant concepts cover data *structure*, data *manipulation* and data *integrity* aspects.

The description of RDM concepts in this chapter has the following key features: (1) it gives a full picture of the RDM, (2) it is mathematically precise and (3) it is modularly structured. Descriptions having features (1) and (2) are not of frequent occurrence; those having in addition feature (3) are really rare. It is worth noting that the use of VVSL is not needed for the features (1) and (2): the notation employed is mostly fairly standard mathematical notation. However, notation for modular structuring is really a deviation from ordinary mathematical practice. Besides, the descriptions given in Chapters 12 and 13, which build upon the description in the current chapter, employ special notation which makes it easier to describe software systems in terms of operations which interrogate and/or modify a state.

The main criteria for the choice of modular structure mentioned in Section 2.2 were: the simplicity of the separate modules, the intuitive clarity of the modular structure and the suitability of the separate modules for re-use. In this connection, it is worth noting the following about the description in this chapter. An important indication for the simplicity of the separate modules is the ease with which theories about them can be developed. It is obvious that it must be relatively easy to develop theories about most of the modules that constitute the description of RDM concepts in this chapter. It is difficult to assess whether the clearness of the modular structure chosen in this chapter might be improved. In any case, it is clear that the chosen modular structuring aids a global understanding. Each of the modules describes concepts of great generality and wide applicability. Many modules are first used in the description of an external RDBMS interface in Chapter 12 and later re-used in the description of an internal RDBMS interface in Chapter 13.

The description of RDM concepts begins with the presentation of three parameter modules which are used to make precise what assumptions are made. Subsequently, there are separate sections on the modules which constitute the description of RDM concepts. Each module is preceded by an explanation of what the module concerned is about.

A reader who is unfamiliar with the relational approach to databases should first study a textbook such as (Ullman, 1988) to acquire an intuitive understanding of what is described formally in this chapter and Chapter 12.

11.1 Assumptions

Later on modules are presented in which tuples, relations, relational databases and other RDM concepts are defined. Tuples are defined in terms of attributes and values, relations are defined in terms of tuples, databases are defined in terms of relation names and relations, etc. Both relation names and attributes are usually identifiers. Values are usually numbers from some finite range of integers and strings over a finite alphabet up to some finite length. However, in the definitions concerned relation names, attributes and values are regarded as primitive objects about which it suffices to make a few assumptions.

The modules **REL_NM**, **ATTRIBUTE** and **VALUE** contain the assumptions concerned. For relation names and attributes, it suffices to assume that there are types *Rel_nm* and *Attribute*, respectively, with no a priori properties. For values, it does not suffice to assume that there is a type *Value*. It is in addition assumed that any finite set of values constitutes a domain for which membership can be tested and cardinality can be computed and also that there is a fixed domain *all*. These additional assumptions are needed to describe tuples and tuple structures (the latter present structural constraints on tuples) and they are consequently used in the modules **TUPLE** and **TUPLE_STRUCT**. The last of the abovementioned assumptions is connected with the need for a domain that can serve as a finite universe of values. Furthermore, it is assumed that there is a fixed ordering relation *lt* on values. This assumption is needed to describe the meaning of the selection formulae that are used in queries for selection of tuples from relations and it is used in the module **SELECTION_WFF**. That module is a part of the description of an external RDBMS interface in Chapter 12.

Most later modules are parametrized. **REL_NM**, **ATTRIBUTE** and **VALUE** are used as parameter restriction modules for the parameters of those modules. In this way, it is made precise that they are based on the above-mentioned assumptions about relation names, attributes and values.

```
component

REL_NM is
  module
    types
    Rel_nm free
  end

ATTRIBUTE is
  module
    types
    Attribute free
  end

VALUE is
  module
    types
    Value free

    Domain = Value-set

    functions
    member(v: Value, d: Domain)𝔹
     ≜  v ∈ d

    card(d: Domain)ℕ
     ≜  card d

    all()Domain free
     post  true

    lt(v1: Value, v2: Value)b: 𝔹 free
     pre   false
     post  true
  end
```

It should be remarked that relation names and attributes are used both as abstract syntactic objects and as semantic objects. That is, RDM concepts such as relation, which are semantic in nature, are defined in terms of them and syntactic concepts of the external RDBMS interface such as query are also defined in terms of them. This mix-up of syntax and semantics can be circumvented by 'copying' the objects involved and connecting these copies to their originals by a bijection. Here it is preferred to keep the minor mix-up, since copying is not felt to result in a real gain.

Value in the sense of the RDM should not be confused with value in the sense of VVSL. Only the elements of the assumed type *Value* are values in the sense of the RDM. In Chapters 11 to 13, value is mainly used in the sense of the RDM. Where it is used in the sense of VVSL and confusion may occur, it is explicitly mentioned that it is used in the other sense.

11.2 Attribute sets, etc.

Attribute sets are just sets of attributes and *attribute bijections* are bijections between attribute sets. Attribute sets and attribute bijections are jointly used in various modules, e.g. as arguments of functions on tuples, relations, etc. Therefore, the definitions concerned are collected in a general module which is imported into these modules.

The module **ATTR_SUPPL** contains the definitions concerning attribute sets and attribute bijections. As a matter of course, this module is based on assumptions contained in the module **ATTRIBUTE**. Therefore, the parameter module **X**, which actualizes the assumptions, is imported.

The only constant (i.e. nullary functions) for attribute sets is *empty*, the empty attribute set. The following functions on attribute sets are defined: *singleton* (converts an attribute to an attribute set), *union* (combines two attribute sets), *difference* (removes from an attribute set attributes that are members of another attribute set), *member* (checks whether an attribute is in an attribute set or not), *included* (checks whether an attribute set is a subset of another attribute set or not), and *disjoint* (checks whether two attribute sets are disjoint or not). All these function are total functions.

There are no constants for attribute bijections. The following functions on attribute bijections are defined: *singleton* (converts an attribute-attribute pair to an attribute bijection), *merge* (joins two attribute bijections with disjoint domains), *inverse* (inverts an attribute bijection), $attrs_1$ (extracts the domain of an attribute bijection), $attrs_2$ (extracts the range of an attribute bijection) and *rename* (renames an attribute according to an attribute bijection). Most of these function are total functions.

All of the functions defined in the module **ATTR_SUPPL** correspond to basic operators on sets and maps as is clear from their simple explicit definitions.

The constructor functions *empty*, *singleton* and *union* for attribute sets and the constructor functions *singleton* and *merge* for attribute bijections are made available because attribute sets and attribute bijections are not only used as semantic objects but also as abstract syntactic objects, just like attributes. The remaining constructor functions, *difference* for attribute sets and *inverse* for attribute bijections, are used in the module **RELATION_EXTENSION** to define some well-known functions on relations in terms of the primitive ones defined in the module **RELATION**. The non-constructor functions for attribute sets and attribute bijections are frequently used in other modules, starting with the module **TUPLE**.

ATTR_SUPPL is
abstract
X: **ATTRIBUTE**
of

import
X
into

module
types

$Attr\_set \;=\; Attribute\text{-set}$

$Attr\_bij \;=\; Attribute \overset{m}{\longleftrightarrow} Attribute$

functions

$empty()Attr\_set$
$\triangleq \; \{\,\}$

$singleton(a\colon Attribute)Attr\_set$
$\triangleq \; \{a\}$

$union(as_1\colon Attr\_set, as_2\colon Attr\_set)Attr\_set$
$\triangleq \; as_1 \cup as_2$

$difference(as_1\colon Attr\_set, as_2\colon Attr\_set)Attr\_set$
$\triangleq \; as_1 - as_2$

$member(a\colon Attribute, as\colon Attr\_set)\mathbb{B}$
$\triangleq \; a \in as$

$included(as_1\colon Attr\_set, as_2\colon Attr\_set)\mathbb{B}$
$\triangleq \; as_1 \subseteq as_2$

$disjoint(as_1\colon Attr\_set, as_2\colon Attr\_set)\mathbb{B}$
$\triangleq \; as_1 \cap as_2 = \{\,\}$

$singleton(a_1\colon Attribute, a_2\colon Attribute)Attr\_bij$
$\triangleq \; \{a_1 \mapsto a_2\}$

$merge(ab_1\colon Attr\_bij, ab_2\colon Attr\_bij) Attr\_bij$
pre $disjoint(attrs_1(ab_1), attrs_1(ab_2)) \wedge$
$disjoint(attrs_2(ab_1), attrs_2(ab_2))$
$\triangleq$ $ab_1 \cup ab_2$

$inverse(ab\colon Attr\_bij) Attr\_bij$
$\triangleq$ $\{ rename(a, ab) \mapsto a \mid$
$a \in Attribute \; ; \; member(a, attrs_1(ab))\}$

$attrs_1(ab\colon Attr\_bij) Attr\_set$
$\triangleq$ dom ab

$attrs_2(ab\colon Attr\_bij) Attr\_set$
$\triangleq$ rng ab

$rename(a\colon Attribute, ab\colon Attr\_bij) Attribute$
pre $member(a, attrs_1(ab))$
$\triangleq$ $ab(a)$

end

Note that the above-mentioned functions to generate attribute sets and attribute bijections (the constructor functions) and to analyse them (the non-constructor functions) are the only ones that can be used outside the module **ATTR_SUPPL**. That is, their representation by sets and maps are not available outside this module.

Key sets are just sets of attribute sets. The attribute sets concerned are called keys.

The module **KEY_SUPPL** contains definitions concerning key sets. The module is based on definitions contained in the parametrized module **ATTR_SUPPL**. Consequently, the appropriate application of this module is imported.

The only constant for key sets is *empty*, the empty key set. The following functions on key sets are defined: *singleton* (converts a key to a key set), *union* (combines two key sets) and *member* (checks whether a key is in a key set or not). All these function are total functions.

All of the functions defined in the module **KEY_SUPPL** correspond to basic operators on sets as well.

The constructor functions *empty*, *singleton* and *union* for key sets are also made available because key sets are not only used as semantic objects but also as abstract syntactic objects. The functions on key sets are mainly used in the modules **REL_SCHEMA** and **REL_CONSTRAINT** to define the functions *is_valid_instance* (which connects relations and relation schemas) and *dom_key_normal_form* (which connects relation schemas and relation constraints).

KEY_SUPPL is
abstract
X: **ATTRIBUTE**
of

import
apply **ATTR_SUPPL** to **X**
into

module
types
$Key\_set = Attr\_set\text{-set}$

functions
$empty()Key\_set$
$\triangleq \{\}$

$singleton(as: Attr\_set)Key\_set$
$\triangleq \{as\}$

$union(ass_1: Key\_set, ass_2: Key\_set)Key\_set$
$\triangleq ass_1 \cup ass_2$

$member(as: Attr\_set, ass: Key\_set)\mathbb{B}$
$\triangleq as \in ass$
end

The next four sections present modules in which tuples, relations, databases and functions to manipulate them are defined. Both attribute sets and attribute bijections are used as arguments of functions on tuples and relations. Key sets are used later in connection with schemas and constraints which are treated in subsequent sections.

11.3 Tuples

Tuples are maps from attributes to values with a non-empty domain. The values associated with the attributes concerned have to be elements of *all* (so *all* plays the role of a finite universe of values). The domain of a tuple is called its attribute set. Tuples can be thought of as records, with the attributes corresponding to fields.

The module **TUPLE** contains the definitions concerning tuples. This module is based on assumptions contained in the modules **ATTRIBUTE** and **VALUE** as well as definitions contained in the parametrized module **ATTR_SUPPL**. Therefore, **X** and **Y**, which actualize the assumptions, and the appropriate application of the module **ATTR_SUPPL** are imported.

There are no constants for tuples. The following functions on tuples are defined: *singleton* (converts an attribute-value pair to a tuple), *merge* (joins two tuples with disjoint attribute sets), *restrict* (restricts a tuple to a subset of its attribute set), *rename* (renames the attributes of a tuple), *attrs* (extracts the attribute set of a tuple) and *value* (looks up the value of an attribute in a tuple). Most of these functions are partial functions.

Tuple predicates are maps from tuples to truth values. The attribute sets of the tuples concerned have to be the same. A tuple predicate holds for a given tuple if the map concerned associates with the tuple the truth value true. The tuple predicate is only defined for tuples that are in the domain of the map. A tuple predicate is like a property that tuples can have.

The following functions on tuple predicates are defined: *holds* (checks whether a tuple predicate holds for a tuple or not) and *defined* (checks whether a tuple predicate is defined for a tuple or not).

Most of the functions defined in the module **TUPLE** correspond to basic operators on maps as is clear from their simple explicit definitions. The function *rename* is defined by means of map comprehension.

In the module **RELATION**, relations are defined in terms of tuples. The functions defined in the module **TUPLE** are used in that module to define functions to manipulate relations. They are also used in the module **SELECTION_WFF** (which is a part of the description of an external RDBMS interface given in Chapter 12) to define the evaluation of selection formulae. For that latter module, relations do not matter. That is why the definitions concerning tuples and the definitions concerning relations are in separate modules. Nothing defined in the module **TUPLE** is regarded as being of an auxiliary nature. This means that nothing is hidden by means of exporting.

TUPLE is
  abstract
    X: **ATTRIBUTE**,
    Y: **VALUE**
  of

  import
    X
    Y
    apply **ATTR_SUPPL** to **X**
  into

  module
    types
    $Tuple \; = \; Attribute \xrightarrow{m} Value$
    where $\mathsf{inv}(t) \triangleq$
      $\mathsf{dom}\, t \neq \{\,\} \wedge \forall a \in Attribute \cdot a \in \mathsf{dom}\, t \;\Rightarrow\; member(t(a), all)$

$$Tuple\_predicate = Tuple \xrightarrow{m} \mathbb{B}$$

where $\mathsf{inv}(tp) \triangleq$
$\forall t_1 \in Tuple, t_2 \in Tuple \cdot$
$t_1 \in \mathsf{dom}\ tp \wedge t_2 \in \mathsf{dom}\ tp \ \Rightarrow\ attrs(t_1) = attrs(t_2)$

functions

% constructor functions
$singleton(a\colon Attribute, v\colon Value)\, Tuple$
$\triangleq\ \{a \mapsto v\}$

$merge(t_1\colon Tuple, t_2\colon Tuple)\, Tuple$
pre $disjoint(attrs(t_1), attrs(t_2))$
$\triangleq\ t_1 \cup t_2$

$restrict(t\colon Tuple, as\colon Attr\_set)\, Tuple$
pre $included(as, attrs(t))$
$\triangleq\ as \lhd t$

$rename(t\colon Tuple, ab\colon Attr\_bij)\, Tuple$
pre $attrs(t) = attrs_1(ab)$
$\triangleq\ \{\, rename(a, ab) \mapsto value(t, a) \mid$
$a \in Attribute\ ;\ member(a, attrs(t))\}$

% non-constructor functions
$holds(tp\colon Tuple\_predicate, t\colon Tuple)\mathbb{B}$
pre $defined(tp, t)$
$\triangleq\ tp(t)$

$defined(tp\colon Tuple\_predicate, t\colon Tuple)\mathbb{B}$
$\triangleq\ t \in \mathsf{dom}\ tp$

$attrs(t\colon Tuple)\, Attr\_set$
$\triangleq\ \mathsf{dom}\ t$

$value(t\colon Tuple, a\colon Attribute)\, Value$
pre $member(a, attrs(t))$
$\triangleq\ t(a)$

end

It is worth noting that the importing of **X** is superfluous here. apply **ATTR_SUPPL** to **X** includes **X** as a result of importing. Such superfluous importing is not left undone, because the result would be a loss of clarity.

The restriction to a finite universe of values for the attributes of tuples allows extensive use of maps in formalizing RDM concepts. Assumptions made about values in the module **VALUE** are used in the module **TUPLE** to enforce this restriction.

Tuples are defined as maps from attributes to values. It is not uncommon to define tuples as sequences of values, which is in accordance with Codd's original definition in (Codd, 1970). The consequences of choosing one definition over the other are illustrated in (Bjørner, 1982). In (Ullman, 1988), it is suggested that converting between the two viewpoints is always obvious, but this suggestion detracts from the contrasting consequences.

11.4 Relations

Relations are sets of tuples with the same attribute set. This common attribute set of the tuples of a relation is called the attribute set of the relation. A relation can be thought of as a file of records with the same fields.

The module **RELATION** contains the definitions concerning relations. This module is based on definitions contained in the parametrized module **TUPLE**. So the appropriate application of this module is imported.

The only constant is *empty*, the empty relation. The following functions on relations are defined: *singleton* (converts a tuple to a relation), *union* (combines two relations with a common attribute set), *difference* (removes from a relation tuples that are member of another relation with the same attribute set), *product* (joins the tuples of two relations with disjoint attribute sets), *projection* (restricts the tuples of a relation to a subset of its attribute set), *selection* (selects the tuples of a relation for which a tuple predicate holds), *rename* (renames the attributes of the tuples in a relation), *attrs* (extracts the attribute set of a relation), *values* (looks up the values of an attribute in the tuples of a relation) and *member* (checks whether a tuple is in a relation or not). All except the last three functions are constructor functions for relations.

Roughly speaking, relations together with the constructor functions defined for them constitute a version of *relational algebra*. These functions comprise traditional set operators (*empty*, *union*, *difference*), modified slightly since relations are not arbitrary sets, and special relational operators (*product*, *projection*, *selection* and *rename*).

The functions *union* and *difference* on two relations are normal set union and set difference on relations with the same attribute set. If they do not have the same attribute set, then the set union or set difference does not yield a relation as a result. The special relational operators are all defined, by means of set comprehension, in terms of functions on tuples defined in the module **TUPLE**. For example, *projection* of a relation to an attribute set is defined as the set that is obtained as follows: *restrict* each *member* of the relation to the attribute set.

The non-constructor functions *attrs* and *values* have been implicitly defined with pre- and post-conditions. *attrs* maps relations to their attribute sets. The post-condition characterizes the result uniquely because the tuples of a relation have a common attribute set. *values* maps a relation and one of its attributes to the domain consisting of all values associated with the attribute concerned in tuples of the relation. In this case, the assumptions made about values and domains are insufficient for an explicit definition.

In the module **DATABASE**, databases are defined in terms of relation names and relations. The constructor functions on relations are used in the module **QUERY** (which is a part of the description of an external RDBMS interface given in Chapter 12) to define the evaluation of relational database queries. The non-constructor functions are used in the module **REL_SCHEMA** to define a function *is_valid_instance* through which relations and relation schemas are connected. They are also used in the module **REL_CONSTRAINT** to define several special kinds of relation constraints such as functional dependencies and join dependencies.

Nothing defined in this module is hidden by means of exporting.

RELATION is
  abstract
    X: **ATTRIBUTE**,
    Y: **VALUE**
  of

  import
    apply **TUPLE** to **X**, **Y**
  into

  module
    types
    $Relation \; = \; Tuple\text{-set}$
    where $\mathrm{inv}(r) \triangleq$
      $\forall t_1 \in Tuple, t_2 \in Tuple \cdot$
        $t_1 \in r \wedge t_2 \in r \;\Rightarrow\; attrs(t_1) = attrs(t_2)$

    functions
    % constructor functions
    $empty()Relation$
      $\triangleq \;\; \{\}$

    $singleton(t\colon Tuple)Relation$
      $\triangleq \;\; \{t\}$

    $union(r_1\colon Relation, r_2\colon Relation)Relation$
      pre $\;r_1 \neq empty \wedge r_2 \neq empty \;\Rightarrow\; attrs(r_1) = attrs(r_2)$
      $\triangleq \;\; r_1 \cup r_2$

$difference(r_1\colon Relation, r_2\colon Relation)Relation$
pre $r_1 \neq empty \wedge r_2 \neq empty \;\Rightarrow\; attrs(r_1) = attrs(r_2)$
$\triangleq$ $r_1 - r_2$

$product(r_1\colon Relation, r_2\colon Relation)Relation$
pre $r_1 \neq empty \wedge r_2 \neq empty \;\Rightarrow\; disjoint(attrs(r_1), attrs(r_2))$
$\triangleq$ $\{\, merge(t_1, t_2) \mid$
$t_1 \in Tuple, t_2 \in Tuple \;;\; member(t_1, r_1) \wedge member(t_2, r_2)\}$

$projection(r\colon Relation, as\colon Attr\_set)Relation$
pre $r \neq empty \;\Rightarrow\; included(as, attrs(r))$
$\triangleq$ $\{restrict(t, as) \mid t \in Tuple \;;\; member(t, r)\}$

$selection(r\colon Relation, tp\colon Tuple\_predicate)Relation$
pre $\forall t \in Tuple \cdot member(t, r) \;\Rightarrow\; defined(tp, t)$
$\triangleq$ $\{t \mid t \in Tuple \;;\; member(t, r) \wedge holds(tp, t)\}$

$rename(r\colon Relation, ab\colon Attr\_bij)Relation$
pre $r \neq empty \;\Rightarrow\; attrs(r) = attrs_1(ab)$
$\triangleq$ $\{rename(t, ab) \mid t \in Tuple \;;\; member(t, r)\}$

% non-constructor functions
$attrs(r\colon Relation)as\colon Attr\_set$
pre $r \neq empty$
post $\exists t \in Tuple \cdot member(t, r) \wedge attrs(t) = as$

$values(r\colon Relation, a\colon Attribute)d\colon Domain$
pre $r \neq empty \wedge member(a, attrs(r))$
post $\forall v \in Value \cdot$
$member(v, d) \;\Leftrightarrow$
$\exists t \in Tuple \cdot member(t, r) \wedge value(t, a) = v$

$member(t\colon Tuple, r\colon Relation)\mathbb{B}$
$\triangleq$ $t \in r$

end

Relational algebra as originally defined by Codd in (Codd, 1972) reflects the set-of-sequences view of relations. Besides, it contains additional functions which can be defined in terms of the others. They include the functions *intersection*, *equi_join* and *division* defined later in the module **RELATION_EXTENSION**. A renaming function as present in our version is not found in the original one, since it does not make much sense in the set-of-sequences view.

The functions on relations underlying the query language ISBL of the PRTV (Todd, 1976) resemble the constructor functions for relations defined here.

A relation can be perceived as a table. In that case the tuples are called rows and the attributes are called column names. However, note that such a table is an unordered collection of rows. Moreover, the order of the columns does not matter.

Perceiving relations as tables the above-mentioned functions on relations can also be informally explained as follows:

- *empty* creates an empty table, that is, a table with no rows.
- *singleton* creates a table with one given row only.
- *union* adds to a given table the rows in another one, forming a new table with more rows. In the case that the resulting table contains some rows that are identical, all but one of them are discarded. Both tables must have the same column names.
- *difference* removes from a given table the rows that are also in another one, forming a new table with fewer rows. Both tables must have the same column names.
- *product* puts each row in a given table and each row in another one together, forming a new table with one row for each combination of rows from the old ones. The tables must have no column name in common.
- *projection* selects certain columns in a given table, forming a new table with fewer columns. A collection of column names is given to indicate the columns to be selected. In the case that the resulting table contains some rows that are identical, all but one of them are discarded.
- *selection* selects certain rows in a given table, forming a new table with fewer rows. A property of rows is given to indicate the rows to be selected. A selection property may be, for example, that one or more entries have a specific value.
- *rename* changes the names of the columns in a given table, leaving everything else the same. A correspondence between old column names and new column names is given to indicate the name change.

It is usual to explain relational concepts in terms of tables. However such explanations normally do not mention details such as how identical rows are treated in building new tables from existing ones.

11.5 Additional functions on relations

The module **RELATION_EXTENSION** contains the definitions of some additional functions on relations. They are defined in terms of the functions on relations defined in the module **RELATION**. That is, the module is based on definitions contained in the parametrized module **RELATION**. So the appropriate application of this module is imported.

The functions concerned are *intersection* (takes the common tuples of two relations), *equi_join* (joins the tuples of two relations with disjoint attribute sets that have the same value for connected attributes), and *division* (divides a relation by another non-empty relation). *division* is so-named because $division(product(r_1, r_2), r_2, ab) = r_1$ if ab is the identity on the attributes of r_2. *intersection* of two relations is defined in terms of *difference*, as for sets. *equi_join* of two relations is defined in terms of *product* and *selection*. *division* of a relation by another relation is defined in terms of *difference*, *product*, *projection* and *rename*.

The tuple predicate *tp* used in the definition of *equi_join* is such that it holds only for the tuples from the product for which the values of attributes associated with each other by the given attribute bijection are the same. *tp* is uniquely characterized by the logical expression following s.t. θ-join (where θ is $<$, $\leq$, $\neq$, $\geq$ or $>$ instead of $=$), natural join and semijoin can be defined in terms of the functions on relations defined in the module **RELATION** as well.

Division as defined here is a straightforward generalization of the usual one. It does not require relations with common attributes as operands. Therefore the function *inverse* on attribute bijections, defined in the module **ATTR_SUPPL**, is needed in the definition of *division*.

RELATION_EXTENSION is
abstract
  X: **ATTRIBUTE**,
  Y: **VALUE**
of

import
  apply **RELATION** to **X**, **Y**
into

module
  functions

  $intersection(r_1\colon Relation, r_2\colon Relation) Relation$
   pre $r_1 \neq empty \wedge r_2 \neq empty \;\Rightarrow\; attrs(r_1) = attrs(r_2)$
   $\triangleq$ $difference(r_1, difference(r_1, r_2))$

  $equi\_join(r_1\colon Relation, r_2\colon Relation, ab\colon Attr\_bij) Relation$
   pre $r_1 \neq empty \wedge r_2 \neq empty \;\Rightarrow$
     $disjoint(attrs(r_1), attrs(r_2)) \wedge$
     $included(attrs_1(ab), attrs(r_1)) \wedge$
     $included(attrs_2(ab), attrs(r_2))$
   $\triangleq$ $selection(product(r_1, r_2), tp)$
     where

tp: *Tuple_predicate* is s.t.
$\forall t \in Tuple \cdot$
$(defined(tp, t) \Leftrightarrow$
$attrs(t) = union(attrs(r_1), attrs(r_2))) \wedge$
$(holds(tp, t) \Leftrightarrow$
$\forall a \in Attribute \cdot$
$member(a, attrs_1(ab)) \Rightarrow$
$value(t, a) = value(t, rename(a, ab)))$

$division(r_1: Relation, r_2: Relation, ab: Attr\_bij) Relation$
pre $r_2 \neq empty \wedge$
$(r_1 \neq empty \Rightarrow$
$included(attrs_1(ab), attrs(r_1)) \wedge$
$included(attrs_2(ab), attrs(r_2)))$
$\triangleq$ if $r_1 = empty$
then $empty$
else $difference(projection(r_1, as'),$
$projection(difference(r', r_1), as'))$
where
r': *Relation* $\triangleq$
$product(projection(r_1, as'),$
$projection(rename(r_2, ab'), as)),$
$as: Attr\_set \triangleq attrs_1(ab),$
$as': Attr\_set \triangleq difference(attrs(r_1), as),$
$ab': Attr\_bij \triangleq inverse(ab)$
end

Joining the tuples of relations is important in practice. Division, generalized or not, is considered esoteric. Its main use has been in Codd's proof of the relational completeness of relational algebra in (Codd, 1972).

None of the functions defined in this module is used in another one. The module is added to illustrate that some well-known functions on relations can be defined in terms of the 'primitive' ones defined in the module **RELATION**.

11.6 Databases

Databases are just maps from relation names to relations. This makes the intuition of a collection of uniquely named tables precise. The domain of a database is called its relation name set. A relation name is in use by a database if it is in the relation name set of the database.

The module **DATABASE** contains the definitions concerning databases. This module is based on assumptions contained in the module **REL_NM** and definitions contained in the parametrized module **RELATION**. Therefore, **X**, which actualizes the assumptions, and the appropriate application of the module **RELATION** are imported.

The only constant is *empty_database*, the empty database. The following functions on databases are defined: *create* (adds a new named relation to a database; the new relation is empty), *destroy* (removes a named relation from a database), *update* (replaces a named relation in a database), *rel_nms* (extracts the relation name set of a database), *in_use* (checks whether a relation name is in use by a database or not) and *relation* (looks up a named relation in a database). The first three functions are constructor functions for databases.

Most of the functions defined in the module **DATABASE** correspond to basic operators on maps as is clear from their simple explicit definitions.

The constructor functions on databases are used in the modules **DBMS_STATE**, **DEFINITION** and **MANIPULATION** (which are parts of the description of an external RDBMS interface given in Chapter 12) to define the initial state of an RDBMS and the operations which make up an external RDBMS interface. The non-constructor functions are used in the modules **DB_SCHEMA** to define a function *is_valid_instance* through which databases and database schemas are connected. They are also used in the module **DB_CONSTRAINT** to define a special kind of database constraint called inclusion dependency.

DATABASE is
  abstract
    X: **REL_NM**,
    Y: **ATTRIBUTE**,
    Z: **VALUE**
  of

  import
    X
    apply **RELATION** to **Y**, **Z**
  into

  module
    types

$$Database = Rel\_nm \xrightarrow{m} Relation$$

$$Rel\_nms = Rel\_nm\text{-set}$$

    functions

    % constructor functions
    empty_database() *Database*
    $\triangleq$ { }

$create(db\colon Database, rnm\colon Rel\_nm)Database$
pre $\neg\, in\_use(db, rnm)$
$\triangleq$ $db \cup \{rnm \mapsto empty\}$

$destroy(db\colon Database, rnm\colon Rel\_nm)Database$
pre $in\_use(db, rnm)$
$\triangleq$ $rnm \lhd db$

$update(db\colon Database, rnm\colon Rel\_nm, r\colon Relation)Database$
pre $in\_use(db, rnm)$
$\triangleq$ $db \dagger \{rnm \mapsto r\}$

% non-constructor functions
$rel\_nms(db\colon Database)Rel\_nms$
$\triangleq$ dom db

$in\_use(db\colon Database, rnm\colon Rel\_nm)\mathbb{B}$
$\triangleq$ $rnm \in rel\_nms(db)$

$relation(db\colon Database, rnm\colon Rel\_nm)Relation$
pre $in\_use(db, rnm)$
$\triangleq$ $db(rnm)$

end

The table view of relations is usually also applied to databases. Perceiving databases as collections of uniquely named tables the constructor functions on databases can also be informally explained as follows:

- *empty* creates a database with no tables.
- *create* adds to a given database an empty table with a given table name, forming a new database with more tables. The old database must have no table with the given name.
- *destroy* removes from a given database the table with a given table name, forming a new database with fewer tables. The old database must have a table with the given name.
- *update* replaces in a given database the table with a given table name by another given table, forming a new database with the same number of tables but with a new table assigned to one of its table names. The old database must have a table with the given name.

In Chapter 12, databases are used as values that a time-varying object (state variable in VVSL terminology) can take. Not uncommonly, this time-varying object is also called database. Therefore, where confusion may occur, the name *database value* will be used in the explanation instead of database to refer to the concept defined in the module **DATABASE**.

The next three sections present modules in which tuple structures, relation schemas and database schemas are defined. They are used to present constraints on tuples, relations and databases, respectively. Constraints on relations and databases are further treated in subsequent sections.

11.7 Tuple structures

Tuple structures are maps from attributes to domains. The domains associated with the attributes concerned have to be subsets of *all* and have a cardinality greater than 1. The domain of a tuple structure is called its attribute set. A tuple structure can be thought of as a record type, with the attributes corresponding to fields and the domains corresponding to the types of the fields. So a tuple structure is a kind of meta-object. It presents structural constraints on the tuples of a relation as follows: for each tuple of the relation, the attribute set has to be the same as the attribute set of the tuple structure and the value associated with each of these attributes has to be an element of the corresponding domain.

The module **TUPLE_STRUCT** contains the definitions concerning tuple structures. This module is based on assumptions contained in the modules **ATTRIBUTE** and **VALUE** as well as definitions contained in the parametrized module **ATTR_SUPPL**. Therefore, **X** and **Y**, which actualize the assumptions, and the appropriate application of the module **ATTR_SUPPL** are imported.

The only constant is *empty*, the empty tuple structure. The following functions are defined on tuple structures: *singleton* (converts an attribute-domain pair to a tuple structure), *merge* (joins two tuple structures with disjoint attribute sets), *restrict* (restricts a tuple structure to a subset of its attribute set), *rename* (renames the attributes of a tuple structure), *attrs* (extracts the attribute set of a tuple structure) and *domain* (looks up the domain of an attribute in a tuple structure).

Each of the functions on tuples that were defined in the module **TUPLE** has a counterpart on tuple structures. Like most of the functions on tuples that were defined in that module, most of the functions on tuple structures defined in the module **TUPLE_STRUCT** correspond to basic operators on maps. Like the function *rename* on tuples, the function *rename* on tuple structures is defined by means of map comprehension.

Tuple structures with an empty attribute set are, unlike tuples with an empty attribute set, not excluded. Such empty tuple structures are not used to present structural constraints on the tuples of some relations. An empty tuple structure is used in well-formedness checking of queries (as defined in the module **QUERY**) to indicate that a useful tuple structure could not be extracted for the query being checked.

In the module **REL_SCHEMA**, relation schemas are defined in terms of tuple structures and key sets. The non-constructor functions defined in the module **TUPLE_STRUCT** are used in that module to define the function *is_valid_instance* which connects relations and relation schemas. These functions are also used in the modules **SELECTION_WFF** and **QUERY** to define the well-formedness of the selection formulae and queries. In the latter module, the constant *empty* and the constructor functions *restrict* and *rename* are used as well.

```
TUPLE_STRUCT is
  abstract
    X: ATTRIBUTE,
    Y: VALUE
  of

  import
    X
    Y
    apply ATTR_SUPPL to X
  into

  module
    types
    Tuple_struct  =  Attribute -m-> Domain
    where inv(tstr) ≜
     ∀a ∈ Attribute ·
       a ∈ dom tstr  ⇒
       card (tstr(a)) ≥ 2∧
       ∀v ∈ Value  ·  member(v, tstr(a))  ⇒  member(v, all)

    functions
    % constructor functions
    empty() Tuple_struct
     ≜  {}

    singleton(a: Attribute, d: Domain) Tuple_struct
     ≜  {a ↦ d}

    merge(tstr1: Tuple_struct, tstr2: Tuple_struct) Tuple_struct
     pre   disjoint(attrs(tstr1), attrs(tstr2))
     ≜     tstr1 ∪ tstr2

    restrict(tstr: Tuple_struct, as: Attr_set) Tuple_struct
     ≜   as ◁ tstr

    rename(tstr: Tuple_struct, ab: Attr_bij) Tuple_struct
     pre   attrs(tstr) = attrs1(ab)
     ≜     { rename(a, ab) ↦ domain(tstr, a) |
             a ∈ Attribute ; member(a, attrs(tstr))}
```

```
% non-constructor functions
attrs(tstr: Tuple_struct)Attr_set
  ≜ dom tstr

domain(tstr: Tuple_struct, a: Attribute)Domain
  pre  member(a, attrs(tstr))
  ≜    tstr(a)
end
```

As pointed out by Fagin (1981), tuple structures with domains that violate the restriction that the cardinality must be greater than 1 are unreasonable. Besides, this cardinality restriction allows that some well-known normal forms (Ullman, 1988), such as Boyce-Codd normal form, fourth normal form and projection-join normal form, are simply connected to the domain-key normal form described in the module **RELATION-CONSTRAINT**. Assumptions made about values in the module **VALUE** are used in the module **TUPLE_STRUCT** to enforce this restriction.

11.8 Relation schemas

Relation schemas are composite values with a non-empty tuple structure and a key set as components. The keys have to be subsets of the attribute set of the tuple structure concerned. The attribute set of the tuple structure of a relation schema is called its attribute set. A relation schema is a kind of meta-object connected with relations, like a tuple structure is a kind of meta-object connected with tuples. It presents intra-relational constraints on a relation in a database. Its tuple structure presents the structural constraints on the tuples of the relation. Each of the keys presents a uniqueness constraint on the relation as follows: no two distinct tuples of the relation may have the same value for each of the attributes from the key. The relations that obey the constraints presented by a given relation schema are its valid instances.

The module **REL_SCHEMA** contains the definitions concerning relation schemas. This module is based on definitions contained in the parametrized modules **KEY_SUPPL**, **TUPLE_STRUCT** and **RELATION**. Consequently, the appropriate applications of these modules are imported.

The principal function defined in this module is *is_valid_instance*. This function checks whether a relation is a valid instance of a relation schema or not. Its definition is not short, but it describes the constraints presented by relation schemas in plain terms. Furthermore, the functions *attrs* and *domain* are lifted from tuple structures to relation schemas.

The constructor function *mk-Rel_schema* for creating relation schemas and the selector functions *struct* and *keys* for selecting the components of relation schemas are implicitly defined in the definition of the type *Rel_schema*.

In the module **DB_SCHEMA**, database schemas are defined in terms of relation names, relation schemas and attribute bijections. The functions defined in the module **REL_SCHEMA** are used in that module to define the function *is_valid_instance* which connects databases and database schemas. The functions *attrs* and *domain* are also used in the module **REL_CONSTRAINT** to define the function *dom_key_normal_form* which connects relation schemas and relation constraints.

REL_SCHEMA is
abstract
X: **ATTRIBUTE**,
Y: **VALUE**
of

import
apply **KEY_SUPPL** to **X**
apply **TUPLE_STRUCT** to **X**, **Y**
apply **RELATION** to **X**, **Y**
into

module
types

$Rel\_schema :: struct\colon Tuple\_struct \;\; keys\colon Key\_set$

where $\mathsf{inv}(rsch) \triangleq$
$attrs(struct(rsch)) \neq empty \land$
$\forall as \in Attr\_set \cdot$
$member(as, keys(rsch)) \Rightarrow$
$included(as, attrs(struct(rsch)))$

functions

% non-constructor functions
$is\_valid\_instance(r\colon Relation, rsch\colon Rel\_schema)\mathbb{B}$
$\triangleq \;\; r \neq empty \Rightarrow$
$attrs(r) = attrs(rsch) \land$
$(\forall a \in Attribute, v \in Value \cdot$
$member(a, attrs(r)) \land member(v, values(r, a)) \Rightarrow$
$member(v, domain(rsch, a))) \land$
$(\forall as \in Attr\_set, t_1 \in Tuple, t_2 \in Tuple \cdot$
$member(as, keys(rsch)) \land$
$member(t_1, r) \land member(t_2, r) \Rightarrow$
$(restrict(t_1, as) = restrict(t_2, as) \Rightarrow t_1 = t_2))$

$attrs(rsch\colon Rel\_schema)Attr\_set$
$\triangleq \;\; attrs(struct(rsch))$

```
domain(rsch: Rel_schema, a: Attribute)Domain
  pre member(a, attrs(rsch))
  ≜   domain(struct(rsch), a)
end
```

A relation schema is often defined to be simply an attribute set; e.g. in (Ullman, 1988; Fagin and Vardi, 1986). In (Fagin, 1981), it is defined to be a composite value with an attribute set and a set of relation constraints (defined in the module **REL_CONSTRAINT**) as components. These concepts of a relation schema are regarded as extremes. Here, a concept of a relation schema which is similar to the one envisaged in (Brodie and Schmidt, 1981) is formalized. It is between the two extremes.

11.9 Database schemas

Database schemas are composite values with a map from relation names to relation schemas, called a database structure, and a set of inclusions as components. The inclusions are composite values with two relation names and an attribute bijection as components. The use of relation names and attributes in each inclusion has to fit in with the database structure concerned. The domain of the database structure of a database schema is called its relation name set. A relation name is in use by a database schema if it is in the relation name set of the database structure. Database schemas are used as semantic counterparts of database descriptions. A database schema presents intra-relational constraints on the named relations in a database as well as inter-relational constraints on the database. Relation schemas are used to present the intra-relational constraints and inclusions are used to present the inter-relational constraints. Each of the inclusions presents an inclusion constraint between two named relations as follows: for each tuple in the first one, there must be a tuple in the second one with the same values for certain attributes. The databases that obey the constraints presented by a given database schema are its valid instances.

The module **DB_SCHEMA** contains the definitions concerning database schemas. This module is based on assumptions contained in the module **REL_NM** and definitions contained in the parametrized modules **ATTR_SUPPL**, **REL_SCHEMA** and **DATABASE**. So **X**, which actualizes the assumptions, and the appropriate applications of the above-mentioned parametrized modules are imported.

A principal function defined in this module is *is_valid_instance*. This function checks whether a database is a valid instance of a database schema or not. Just like the definition of the corresponding function in the module **REL_SCHEMA**, its definition is not short, but it reflects the constraints presented by database schemas in plain terms. For database schemas, the only constant is *empty_schema*, the empty database schema. The following functions on databases schemas are defined as well: *create* (adds a new named relation schema to a database schema), *destroy* (removes a named relation schema from a database schema), *constrain* (adds an inclusion to a database schema), *rel_nms* (extracts the relation name set of a database schema), *in_use* (checks whether a relation name is in use by a database schema or not) and *attrs* (looks up the attribute set of a named relation schema in a database schema), *struct* (looks up the tuple structure of a named relation schema in a database schema), *applicable* (checks whether the use of relation names and attributes in an inclusion fits in with a database schema or not). The first three functions are constructor functions for database schemas.

Most of the functions on databases that were defined in the module **DATABASE** have a counterpart on database schemas. *destroy* on database schemas is not as simple as *destroy* on databases: inclusions referring to the named relation schema that is removed are also removed.

The constructor function *mk-Db_schema* for creating database schemas and the selector functions *struct* and *inclusions* for selecting the components of database schemas are implicitly defined in the definition of the type *Db_schema*.

Most of the functions defined in this module are used in the modules **DEFINITION** and **MANIPULATION** to define operations which make up an external RDBMS interface. The non-constructor functions are also used in the module **QUERY** to define the well-formedness and evaluation of queries. Furthermore, they are used in the module **DB_CONSTRAINT** to define the function *dom_key_normal_form* which connects database schemas and database constraints.

```
DB_SCHEMA is
  abstract
    X: REL_NM,
    Y: ATTRIBUTE,
    Z: VALUE
  of

  import
    X
    apply ATTR_SUPPL to Y
    apply REL_SCHEMA to Y, Z
    apply DATABASE to X, Y, Z
  into

  module
    types
    Db_schema :: struct: Database_struct  inclusions: Inclusions
```

where $\mathsf{inv}(dbsch) \triangleq$
$\quad \forall incl \in Inclusion \cdot$
$\quad\quad incl \in inclusions(dbsch) \Rightarrow$
$\quad\quad \mathsf{let}$
$\quad\quad mk\text{-}Inclusion(rnm_1, rnm_2, ab) \triangleq incl$
$\quad\quad \mathsf{in}$
$\quad\quad rnm_1 \in \mathsf{dom}\, struct(dbsch) \wedge$
$\quad\quad included(attrs_1(ab), attrs(struct(dbsch)(rnm_1))) \wedge$
$\quad\quad rnm_2 \in \mathsf{dom}\, struct(dbsch) \wedge$
$\quad\quad included(attrs_2(ab), attrs(struct(dbsch)(rnm_2))) \wedge$
$\quad\quad \forall a \in Attribute \cdot$
$\quad\quad\quad member(a, attrs_1(ab)) \Rightarrow$
$\quad\quad\quad domain(struct(dbsch)(rnm_1), a)$
$\quad\quad\quad\; = domain(struct(dbsch)(rnm_2), rename(a, ab))$

$Database\_struct = Rel\_nm \xrightarrow{m} Rel\_schema$

$Inclusions = Inclusion\text{-}\mathsf{set}$

$Inclusion :: Rel\_nm \;\; Rel\_nm \;\; Attr\_bij$

functions

% constructor functions
$empty\_schema()\, Db\_schema$
$\triangleq \quad mk\text{-}Db\_schema(\{\,\}, \{\,\})$

$create(dbsch\colon Db\_schema, rnm\colon Rel\_nm, rsch\colon Rel\_schema)\, Db\_schema$
$\quad \mathsf{pre} \quad \neg\, in\_use(dbsch, rnm)$
$\triangleq \quad \mathsf{let}$
$\quad\quad dbstr'\colon Database\_struct \triangleq struct(dbsch) \cup \{rnm \mapsto rsch\},$
$\quad\quad incls\colon Inclusions \triangleq inclusions(dbsch)$
$\quad\quad \mathsf{in}$
$\quad\quad mk\text{-}Db\_schema(dbstr', incls)$

$destroy(dbsch\colon Db\_schema, rnm\colon Rel\_nm)\, Db\_schema$
$\quad \mathsf{pre} \quad in\_use(dbsch, rnm)$
$\triangleq \quad \mathsf{let}$
$\quad\quad dbstr'\colon Database\_struct \triangleq rnm \ntriangleleft struct(dbsch),$
$\quad\quad incls'\colon Inclusions \triangleq$
$\quad\quad\quad \{\, mk\text{-}Inclusion(rnm_1, rnm_2, ab) \mid$
$\quad\quad\quad\quad rnm_1 \in Rel\_nm, rnm_2 \in Rel\_nm, ab \in Attr\_bij\;;$
$\quad\quad\quad\quad mk\text{-}Inclusion(rnm_1, rnm_2, ab) \in inclusions(dbsch) \wedge$
$\quad\quad\quad\quad rnm_1 \neq rnm \wedge rnm_2 \neq rnm\}$
$\quad\quad \mathsf{in}$
$\quad\quad mk\text{-}Db\_schema(dbstr', incls')$

$constrain(dbsch: Db\_schema, incl: Inclusion)Db\_schema$
pre $applicable(incl, dbsch)$
$\triangleq$ let
$dbstr: Database\_struct \triangleq struct(dbsch),$
$incls': Inclusions \triangleq inclusions(dbsch) \cup \{incl\}$
in
$mk\text{-}Db\_schema(dbstr, incls')$

% non-constructor functions
$is\_valid\_instance(db: Database, dbsch: Db\_schema)\mathbb{B}$
$\triangleq$ $(struct(dbsch) = \{\,\} \wedge db = empty\_database) \vee$
$(struct(dbsch) \neq \{\,\} \wedge rel\_nms(db) = rel\_nms(dbsch) \wedge$
$(\forall rnm \in Rel\_nm \cdot$
$in\_use(db, rnm) \Rightarrow$
$is\_valid\_instance(relation(db, rnm), struct(dbsch)(rnm))) \wedge$
$(\forall incl \in Inclusion \cdot$
$incl \in inclusions(dbsch) \Rightarrow$
let
$mk\text{-}Inclusion(rnm_1, rnm_2, ab) \triangleq incl$
in
let
$r_1: Relation \triangleq projection(relation(db, rnm_1), attrs_1(ab)),$
$r_2: Relation \triangleq projection(relation(db, rnm_2), attrs_2(ab))$
in
$included(rename(r_1, ab), r_2)))$

$rel\_nms(dbsch: Db\_schema)Rel\_nms$
$\triangleq$ dom $struct(dbsch)$

$in\_use(dbsch: Db\_schema, rnm: Rel\_nm)\mathbb{B}$
$\triangleq$ $rnm \in rel\_nms(dbsch)$

$attrs(dbsch: Db\_schema, rnm: Rel\_nm)Attr\_set$
pre $in\_use(dbsch, rnm)$
$\triangleq$ $attrs(struct(dbsch)(rnm))$

$struct(dbsch: Db\_schema, rnm: Rel\_nm)Tuple\_struct$
pre $in\_use(dbsch, rnm)$
$\triangleq$ $struct(struct(dbsch)(rnm))$

$applicable(incl\colon Inclusion, dbsch\colon Db\_schema)\mathbb{B}$
$\triangleq$ let
  $mk\text{-}Inclusion(rnm_1, rnm_2, ab) \triangleq incl$
  in
  $in\_use(dbsch, rnm_1) \wedge in\_use(dbsch, rnm_2) \wedge$
  $included(attrs_1(ab), attrs(dbsch, rnm_1)) \wedge$
  $included(attrs_2(ab), attrs(dbsch, rnm_2)) \wedge$
  $\forall a \in Attribute \cdot$
    $member(a, attrs_1(ab)) \Rightarrow$
    $domain(struct(dbsch, rnm_1), a)$
      $= domain(struct(dbsch, rnm_2), rename(a, ab))$
end

A database schema is often defined to be simply a set of relation schemas, e.g. in (Ullman, 1988; Fagin and Vardi, 1986). In (Fagin, 1981), it is defined to be a composite value with a set of relation schemas and a set of database constraints (defined in the module **DB_CONSTRAINT**) as components. These concepts of a database schema are regarded as extremes. Here, a concept of a database schema which is similar to the one envisaged in (Brodie and Schmidt, 1981) is formalized. It is between the two extremes.

In Chapter 12, database schemas (like databases) are used as values that a time-varying object can take. Not uncommonly, this time-varying object is also called database schema. Therefore, where confusion may occur, the name *database schema value* will be used in the explanation instead of database schema to refer to the concept defined in this section.

The next two sections present modules in which relation constraints and database constraints are defined. These constraints are mainly of practical interest for database design. The modules concerned are not imported into any other module.

11.10 Relation constraints

Relation constraints are maps from relations to truth values. The attribute sets of all relations concerned have to be the same. A relation constraint holds for a relation if the map concerned associates with the relation the truth value true. The relation constraint is only defined for relations that are in the domain of the map. A relation constraint is like a property that relations can have.

The module **REL_CONSTRAINT** contains the definitions concerning relation constraints. This module is based on definitions contained in the parametrized modules **RELATION** and **REL_SCHEMA**. Therefore, the appropriate applications of these modules are imported.

Dependencies, which are of practical interest for database design, are shown to be special kinds of relation constraints (this section winds up with an informal explanation of the dependencies concerned). The functions *func_dep*, *join_dep* and *dom_dep* express functional dependencies, join dependencies and domain dependencies, respectively, as relation constraints. It is also shown that key dependencies and multi-valued dependencies are actually special cases of functional dependencies and join dependencies, respectively. The functions *key_dep* and *multi_val_dep* express key dependencies and multi-valued dependencies as relation constraints. They are defined in terms of *fun_dep* and *join_dep*.

Relation constraints are intra-relational. Only two special kinds of such constraints can be presented in a relation schema, namely domain dependencies and key dependencies. Domain-key normal form, originally defined by Fagin (1981), is introduced to connect relation schemas with relation constraints. The function *dom_key_normal_form* checks whether a relation schema is in domain-key normal form with respect to a set of relation constraints. That is the case if each of the relation constraints is a consequence of the domain dependencies and key dependencies presented by the relation schema.

The following functions on relation constraints are also defined: *holds* (checks whether a relation constraint holds for a relation or not), *defined* (checks whether a relation constraint is defined for a relation or not), *consequence* (checks whether a relation constraint is a consequence of a set of relation constraints or not), *dom_deps* (extracts the domain dependencies presented in a relation schema), *key_deps* (extracts the key dependencies presented in a relation schema) and *attrs* (computes the common attribute set of the relations for which a relation constraint is defined).

The functions defined in this module are only used in the module **DB_CONSTRAINT**. The modules **REL_CONSTRAINT** and **DB_CONSTRAINT** are added to connect the concepts of a relation schema and a database schema from the module **REL_SCHEMA** and **DB_SCHEMA**, respectively, with some well-known concepts concerning relational database design.

REL_CONSTRAINT is
  abstract
    X: **ATTRIBUTE**,
    Y: **VALUE**
  of

  import
    apply **RELATION** to **X**, **Y**
    apply **REL_SCHEMA** to **X**, **Y**
  into

  module
    types
    $Rel\_constraint = Relation \xrightarrow{m} \mathbb{B}$

where inv$(rc) \triangleq$
$\forall r_1 \in Relation, r_2 \in Relation \cdot$
$r_1 \in \mathsf{dom}\ rc \wedge r_2 \in \mathsf{dom}\ rc \Rightarrow attrs(r_1) = attrs(r_2)$

$Rel\_constraint\_set = Rel\_constraint\text{-}\mathsf{set}$

functions

$fun\_dep(as_1{:}\ Attr\_set, as_2{:}\ Attr\_set, c{:}\ Attr\_set) rc{:}\ Rel\_constraint$
pre $included(as_1, c) \wedge included(as_2, c)$
post $\forall r \in Relation \cdot$
$(defined(rc, r) \Leftrightarrow attrs(r) = c) \wedge$
$(holds(rc, r) \Leftrightarrow$
$\forall t \in Tuple, t' \in Tuple \cdot$
$member(t, r) \wedge member(t', r) \Rightarrow$
$(restrict(t, as_1) = restrict(t', as_1) \Rightarrow$
$restrict(t, as_2) = restrict(t', as_2)))$

$join\_dep(ass{:}\ Key\_set, c{:}\ Attr\_set) rc{:}\ Rel\_constraint$
pre $(\forall as \in Attr\_set \cdot member(as, ass) \Rightarrow included(as, c)) \wedge$
$(\forall a \in Attribute \cdot$
$member(a, c) \Rightarrow$
$\exists as' \in Attr\_set \cdot member(as', ass) \wedge member(a, as'))$
post $\forall r \in Relation \cdot$
$(defined(rc, r) \Leftrightarrow attrs(r) = c) \wedge$
$(holds(rc, r) \Leftrightarrow$
$\forall t \in Tuple \cdot$
$attrs(t) = c \Rightarrow$
$((\forall as \in Attr\_set \cdot$
$member(as, ass) \Rightarrow$
$\exists t' \in Tuple \cdot$
$member(t', r) \wedge restrict(t', as) = restrict(t, as)) \Rightarrow$
$member(t, r)))$

$dom\_dep(a{:}\ Attribute, d{:}\ Domain, c{:}\ Attr\_set) rc{:}\ Rel\_constraint$
pre $member(a, c)$
post $\forall r \in Relation \cdot$
$(defined(rc, r) \Leftrightarrow attrs(r) = c) \wedge$
$(holds(rc, r) \Leftrightarrow$
$\forall v \in Value \cdot member(v, values(r, a)) \Rightarrow member(v, d))$

$key\_dep(as{:}\ Attr\_set, c{:}\ Attr\_set) Rel\_constraint$
pre $included(as, c)$
$\triangleq$ $fun\_dep(as, difference(c, as), c)$

$multi\_val\_dep(as_1{:}\ Attr\_set, as_2{:}\ Attr\_set, c{:}\ Attr\_set)rc{:}\ Rel\_constraint$
pre $included(as_1, c) \land included(as_2, c)$
$\triangleq$ $join\_dep(union(ass, ass'), c)$
where
$ass{:}\ Key\_set \triangleq singleton(union(as_1, as_2)),$
$ass'{:}\ Key\_set \triangleq$
$singleton(union(as_1, difference(c, union(as_1, as_2))))$

$holds(rc{:}\ Rel\_constraint, r{:}\ Relation)\mathbb{B}$
pre $defined(rc, r)$
$\triangleq$ $rc(r)$

$defined(rc{:}\ Rel\_constraint, r{:}\ Relation)\mathbb{B}$
$\triangleq$ $r \in \mathsf{dom}\ rc$

$consequence(rcs{:}\ Rel\_constraint\_set, rc{:}\ Rel\_constraint, c{:}\ Attr\_set)\mathbb{B}$
pre $(\forall rc' \in Rel\_constraint \cdot$
$member(rc', rcs) \Rightarrow attrs(rc') = c) \land$
$attrs(rc) = c$
$\triangleq$ $\forall r \in Relation \cdot$
$attrs(r) = c \Rightarrow$
$((\forall rc' \in Rel\_constraint \cdot$
$member(rc', rcs) \Rightarrow holds(rc', r)) \Rightarrow holds(rc, r))$

$dom\_key\_normal\_form(rsch{:}\ Rel\_schema, rcs{:}\ Rel\_constraint\_set)\mathbb{B}$
pre $\forall rc \in Rel\_constraint \cdot$
$member(rc, rcs) \Rightarrow attrs(rc) = attrs(rsch)$
$\triangleq$ $\forall rc \in Rel\_constraint \cdot$
$member(rc, rcs) \Rightarrow$
$consequence(dom\_key\_deps(rsch), rc, attrs(rsch))$

$dom\_key\_deps(rsch{:}\ Rel\_schema)rcs{:}\ Rel\_constraint\_set$
post $\forall rc \in Rel\_constraint \cdot$
$member(rc, rcs) \Leftrightarrow$
$member(rc, dom\_deps(rsch)) \lor member(rc, key\_deps(rsch))$

$dom\_deps(rsch{:}\ Rel\_schema)rcs{:}\ Rel\_constraint\_set$
post $\forall rc \in Rel\_constraint \cdot$
$member(rc, rcs) \Leftrightarrow$
$\exists a \in Attribute \cdot$
$member(a, attrs(rsch)) \land$
$rc = dom\_dep(a, domain(rsch, a), attrs(rsch))$

$key\_deps(rsch{:}\ Rel\_schema)rcs{:}\ Rel\_constraint\_set$
post $\forall rc \in Rel\_constraint \cdot$
$member(rc, rcs) \Leftrightarrow$
$\exists as \in Attr\_set \cdot$
$member(as, keys(rsch)) \land$
$rc = key\_dep(as, attrs(rsch))$

$attrs(rc\colon Rel\_constraint)as\colon Attr\_set$
pre $\mathsf{dom}\ rc \neq \{\}$
post $\exists r \in Relation \cdot r \in \mathsf{dom}\ rc \wedge attrs(r) = as$

$member(rc\colon Rel\_constraint, rcs\colon Rel\_constraint\_set)\mathbb{B}$
$\triangleq$ $rc \in rcs$
end

Contrary to the usual definition of join dependency, the (equivalent) definition in this module is not in terms of joins and projections; the definition is 'operator free'.

Because of the restriction that the cardinality of domains must be greater than 1 (see the module **TUPLE-STRUCTURE**), Boyce-Codd normal form and fourth normal form (Ullman, 1988) are implied by domain-key normal form; projection-join normal form is implied by domain-key normal form under some mild conditions.

The dependencies defined in the module **REL_CONSTRAINT** can be informally explained as follows:

- A functional dependency $fun\_dep(as_1, as_2, as)$ is a constraint on relations with attribute set as which holds for such a relation if each two tuples in the relation that agree on the attributes as_1 also agree on the attributes as_2.
- A join dependency $join\_dep(\{as_1, \ldots, as_n\}, as)$ is a constraint on relations with attribute set as which holds for such a relation if the relation contains each tuple t for which there are tuples $t_1, \ldots, t_n$ in the relation such that t and t_1 agree on the attributes as_1, t and t_2 agree on the attributes as_2, $\ldots$, t and t_n agree on the attributes as_n.
- A domain dependency $dom\_dep(a, d, as)$ is a constraint on relations with attribute set as which holds for such a relation if each tuple in the relation has a value associated with the attribute a that is a member of the domain d.
- A key dependency $key\_dep(as', as)$ is a constraint on relations with attribute set as which holds for such a relation if no two tuples in the relation agree on the attributes as'.
- A multi-valued dependency $multi\_val\_dep(as_1, as_2, as)$ is a constraint on relations with attribute set as which holds for such a relation if the relation contains each two tuples t_1 and t_2 that can be obtained from two tuples t_1' and t_2' in the relation that agree on the attributes as_1 by exchanging the values associated with the attributes as_2.

11.11 Database constraints

Database constraints are maps from databases to truth values. The relation name sets of all databases concerned have to be the same and, for each of the relation names, the attribute sets of the associated relations have to be the same. A database constraint holds for a database if this map associates with the database the truth value true. The database constraint is only defined for databases that are in the domain of the map. A database constraint is like a property that databases can have.

The module **DB_CONSTRAINT** contains the definitions concerning database constraints. This module is based on definitions contained in the parametrized modules **DATABASE**, **DB_SCHEMA** and **REL_CONSTRAINT**. Consequently, the appropriate applications of these modules are imported.

Database constraints can be intra-relational or inter-relational. Only one special kind of inter-relational constraints can be presented in a database schema, namely inclusion dependencies. They are shown to be database constraints of a special kind. The function *incl_dep* express inclusion dependencies as database constraints. The functions *func_dep*, *join_dep*, *dom_dep*, *key_dep* and *multi_val_dep* now express functional dependencies, join dependencies, domain dependencies, key dependencies and multivalued dependencies, respectively, as database constraints. Domain-key normal form is also lifted to connect database schemas with database constraints. The function *dom_key_normal_form* checks whether a database schema is in domain-key normal form with respect to a set of database constraints. That is the case if each of the database constraints is a consequence of the domain dependencies, key dependencies and inclusion dependencies presented by the database schema.

The following functions on database constraints are also defined: *holds* (checks whether a database constraint holds for a database or not), *defined* (checks whether a database constraint is defined for a database or not), *consequence* (checks whether a database constraint is a consequence of a set of database constraints or not), *dom_deps* (extracts the domain dependencies presented in a database schema), *key_deps* (extracts the key dependencies presented in a database schema) and *incl_deps* (extracts the inclusion dependencies presented in a database schema).

Catalogs are maps from relation names to attribute sets. The notion of a catalog is of an auxiliary nature. It provides the context in which dependencies occur. The catalog of a database presents its relation name set and the attribute sets of the relations associated with each of the relation names concerned. The use of catalogs can be circumvented by introducing the requirement that attributes must be unique within a database. However, this requirement would complicate the definitions in various preceding modules very much. There are functions *catalog* to compute the catalogs corresponding to databases, database schemas and database constraints. In the latter two cases the common catalog of the valid instances and the common catalog of the databases for which the constraint is defined, respectively, is taken.

None of the functions defined in this module is used in another one. The module is added to connect the concept of a database schema from the module **DB_SCHEMA** with some well-known concepts concerning relational database design.

DB_CONSTRAINT is
abstract
X: **REL_NM**,
Y: **ATTRIBUTE**,
Z: **VALUE**
of

import
apply **DATABASE** to **X**, **Y**, **Z**
apply **DB_SCHEMA** to **X**, **Y**, **Z**
apply **REL_CONSTRAINT** to **Y**, **Z**
into

module
types

$$Db\_constraint \;=\; Database \xrightarrow{m} \mathbb{B}$$

where inv(dbc) $\triangleq$
$\forall db_1 \in Database, db_2 \in Database \cdot$
$db_1 \in \mathsf{dom}\ dbc \wedge db_2 \in \mathsf{dom}\ dbc \;\Rightarrow\; catalog(db_1) = catalog(db_2)$

$$Db\_constraint\_set \;=\; Db\_constraint\text{-}\mathsf{set}$$

$$Catalog \;=\; Rel\_nm \xrightarrow{m} Attr\_set$$

functions

$incl\_dep(\, rnm_1\colon Rel\_nm, rnm_2\colon Rel\_nm, ab\colon Attr\_bij, c\colon Catalog)$
$dbc\colon Db\_constraint$
pre $rnm_1 \in \mathsf{dom}\ c \wedge rnm_2 \in \mathsf{dom}\ c \wedge$
$included(attrs_1(ab), c(rnm_1)) \wedge included(attrs_2(ab), c(rnm_2))$
post $\forall db \in Database \cdot$
$(defined(dbc, db) \;\Leftrightarrow\; catalog(db) = c) \wedge$
$(holds(dbc, db) \;\Leftrightarrow$
$\forall t_1 \in Tuple \cdot$
$member(t_1, relation(db, rnm_1)) \;\Rightarrow$
$\exists t_2 \in Tuple \cdot$
$member(t_2, relation(db, rnm_2)) \wedge$
$rename(restrict(t_1, attrs_1(ab)), ab)$
$= restrict(t_2, attrs_2(ab)))$

$fun\_dep(\,rnm\colon Rel\_nm,\ as_1\colon Attr\_set,\ as_2\colon Attr\_set,\ c\colon Catalog)$
$\quad dbc\colon Db\_constraint$
pre $rnm \in \mathsf{dom}\ c \wedge$
$\quad included(as_1, c(rnm)) \wedge included(as_2, c(rnm))$
post $\forall db \in Database \cdot$
$\quad (defined(dbc, db) \Leftrightarrow catalog(db) = c) \wedge$
$\quad (holds(dbc, db) \Leftrightarrow$
$\quad\quad fun\_dep(as_1, as_2, c(rnm))(relation(db, rnm)))$

$join\_dep(rnm\colon Rel\_nm,\ ass\colon Key\_set,\ c\colon Catalog)\,dbc\colon Db\_constraint$
pre $rnm \in \mathsf{dom}\ c \wedge$
$\quad (\forall as \in Attr\_set \cdot$
$\quad\quad member(as, ass) \Rightarrow included(as, c(rnm))) \wedge$
$\quad (\forall a \in Attribute \cdot$
$\quad\quad member(a, c(rnm)) \Rightarrow$
$\quad\quad \exists as' \in Attr\_set \cdot member(as', ass) \wedge member(a, as'))$
post $\forall db \in Database \cdot$
$\quad (defined(dbc, db) \Leftrightarrow catalog(db) = c) \wedge$
$\quad (holds(dbc, db) \Leftrightarrow$
$\quad\quad join\_dep(ass, c(rnm))(relation(db, rnm)))$

$dom\_dep(\,rnm\colon Rel\_nm,\ a\colon Attribute,\ d\colon Domain,\ c\colon Catalog)$
$\quad dbc\colon Db\_constraint$
pre $rnm \in \mathsf{dom}\ c \wedge member(a, c(rnm))$
post $\forall db \in Database \cdot$
$\quad (defined(dbc, db) \Leftrightarrow catalog(db) = c) \wedge$
$\quad (holds(dbc, db) \Leftrightarrow$
$\quad\quad dom\_dep(a, d, c(rnm))(relation(db, rnm)))$

$key\_dep(rnm\colon Rel\_nm,\ as\colon Attr\_set,\ c\colon Catalog)\,dbc\colon Db\_constraint$
pre $rnm \in \mathsf{dom}\ c \wedge included(as, c(rnm))$
post $\forall db \in Database \cdot$
$\quad (defined(dbc, db) \Leftrightarrow catalog(db) = c) \wedge$
$\quad (holds(dbc, db) \Leftrightarrow$
$\quad\quad key\_dep(as, c(rnm))(relation(db, rnm)))$

$multi\_val\_dep(\,rnm\colon Rel\_nm,\ as_1\colon Attr\_set,\ as_2\colon Attr\_set,\ c\colon Catalog)$
$\quad dbc\colon Db\_constraint$
pre $rnm \in \mathsf{dom}\ c \wedge$
$\quad included(as_1, c(rnm)) \wedge included(as_2, c(rnm))$
post $\forall db \in Database \cdot$
$\quad (defined(dbc, db) \Leftrightarrow catalog(db) = c) \wedge$
$\quad (holds(dbc, db) \Leftrightarrow$
$\quad\quad multi\_val\_dep(as_1, as_2, c(rnm))(relation(db, rnm)))$

$holds(dbc\colon Db\_constraint,\ db\colon Database)\mathbb{B}$
pre $defined(dbc, db)$
$\triangleq \quad dbc(db)$

$defined(dbc\colon Db\_constraint,\ db\colon Database)\mathbb{B}$
$\triangleq\quad db \in \mathsf{dom}\ dbc$

$consequence(dbcs\colon Db\_constraint\_set,\ dbc\colon Db\_constraint,\ c\colon Catalog)\mathbb{B}$
pre $(\forall dbc' \in Db\_constraint \cdot$
$\quad member(dbc', dbcs) \Rightarrow catalog(dbc') = c)\wedge$
$catalog(dbc) = c$
$\triangleq\quad \forall db \in Database \cdot$
$\quad catalog(db) = c \Rightarrow$
$\quad ((\forall dbc' \in Db\_constraint \cdot$
$\qquad member(dbc', dbcs) \Rightarrow holds(dbc', db)) \Rightarrow holds(dbc, db))$

$dom\_key\_normal\_form(dbsch\colon Db\_schema,\ dbcs\colon Db\_constraint\_set)\mathbb{B}$
pre $\forall dbc \in Db\_constraint \cdot$
$\quad member(dbc, dbcs) \Rightarrow catalog(dbc) = catalog(dbsch)$
$\triangleq\quad \forall dbc \in Db\_constraint \cdot$
$\quad member(dbc, dbcs) \Rightarrow$
$\quad consequence(dom\_key\_incl\_deps(dbsch), dbc, catalog(dbsch))$

$dom\_key\_incl\_deps(dbsch\colon Db\_schema)dbcs\colon Db\_constraint\_set$
post $\forall dbc \in Db\_constraint \cdot$
$\quad member(dbc, dbcs) \Leftrightarrow$
$\quad member(dbc, dom\_deps(dbsch)) \vee$
$\quad member(dbc, key\_deps(dbsch)) \vee$
$\quad member(dbc, incl\_deps(dbsch))$

$dom\_deps(dbsch\colon Db\_schema)dbcs\colon Db\_constraint\_set$
post $\forall dbc \in Db\_constraint \cdot$
$\quad member(dbc, dbcs) \Leftrightarrow$
$\quad \exists rnm \in Rel\_nm,\ a \in Attribute \cdot$
$\qquad in\_use(dbsch, rnm) \wedge member(a, attrs(dbsch, rnm))\wedge$
$\qquad dbc = dom\_dep(rnm, a, domain(struct(dbsch, rnm), a),$
$\qquad\qquad catalog(dbsch))$

$key\_deps(dbsch\colon Db\_schema)dbcs\colon Db\_constraint\_set$
post $\forall dbc \in Db\_constraint \cdot$
$\quad member(dbc, dbcs) \Leftrightarrow$
$\quad \exists rnm \in Rel\_nm,\ as \in Attr\_set \cdot$
$\qquad in\_use(dbsch, rnm)\wedge$
$\qquad member(as, keys(struct(dbsch, rnm)))\wedge$
$\qquad dbc = key\_dep(rnm, as, catalog(dbsch))$

$incl\_deps(dbsch: Db\_schema)dbcs: Db\_constraint\_set$
post $\forall dbc \in Db\_constraint \cdot$
$member(dbc, dbcs) \Leftrightarrow$
$\exists\, rnm_1 \in Rel\_nm, rnm_2 \in Rel\_nm, ab \in Attr\_bij \cdot$
$in\_use(dbsch, rnm_1) \wedge in\_use(dbsch, rnm_2) \wedge$
$member(attrs_1(ab), attrs(dbsch, rnm_1)) \wedge$
$member(attrs_2(ab), attrs(dbsch, rnm_2)) \wedge$
$member(mk\text{-}Inclusion(rnm_1, rnm_2, ab), inclusions(dbsch)) \wedge$
$dbc = incl\_dep(rnm_1, rnm_2, ab, catalog(dbsch))$

$member(dbc: Db\_constraint, dbcs: Db\_constraint\_set)\mathbb{B}$
$\triangleq$ $dbc \in dbcs$

$catalog(db: Database)c: Catalog$
post $rel\_nms(db) = \mathsf{dom}\ c \wedge$
$\forall rnm \in Rel\_nm \cdot$
$in\_use(db, rnm) \Rightarrow attrs(relation(db, rnm)) = c(rnm)$

$catalog(dbsch: Db\_schema)c: Catalog$
post $rel\_nms(dbsch) = \mathsf{dom}\ c \wedge$
$\forall rnm \in Rel\_nm \cdot$
$in\_use(dbsch, rnm) \Rightarrow attrs(dbsch, rnm) = c(rnm)$

$catalog(dbc: Db\_constraint)c: Catalog$
pre $\mathsf{dom}\ dbc \neq \{\,\}$
post $\exists db \in Database \cdot defined(dbc, db) \wedge catalog(db) = c$
end

In this module, the concept of an inclusion dependency is formalized. This requires that we make precise which attribute of the one relation corresponds to which attribute of the other relation. The author could not find definitions elsewhere that were accurate at this point.

Inclusion dependencies can be informally explained as follows. An inclusion dependency $incl\_dep(rnm_1, rnm_2, ab, c)$ is a constraint on databases with catalog c which holds for such a database if for each tuple t in the relation rnm_1 there is a tuple t' in the relation rnm_2 such that t and t' agree on the attributes associated with each other by means of the attribute bijection ab.

The module **DB_CONSTRAINT** is the last module that contains definitions concerning RDM concepts. Most of the modules presented in this chapter are imported into modules presented in Chapters 12 and 13. In these chapters, descriptions of an external RDBMS interface and an internal RDBMS interface, respectively, are given.

12

An External RDBMS Interface

This chapter is the second of two chapters in which the first case study in VVSL is presented. This case study deals with the underlying concepts of relational database management systems and the operations for data manipulation and data definition which can be performed by such systems. The underlying concepts are described in Chapter 11 and the operations are described in this chapter. The purpose of the first case study is to demonstrate the practical usefulness of the extensions of VDM-SL for modular structuring.

The concepts described in the previous chapter include many of the basic concepts of the RDM. The relevant concepts cover data structure, data manipulation and data integrity aspects. An RDBMS is a system that supports the storage of data objects structured according to the structure concepts of the RDM, the querying and updating of the stored data objects according to the manipulation concepts of the RDM, and the control of the integrity of the stored data objects according to the integrity concepts of the RDM. Operations which can be performed by such a system are described in the current chapter. The operations concerned make up an external interface of an RDBMS: the operations are available directly to the users of the system. The interface is abstract in the sense that it does not deal with details of concrete interfaces like concrete syntax of operations, their embedding in a host language, concrete representation of the data objects yielded by query operations, etc.

The description of RDM concepts in the previous chapter together with the description of operations which can be performed by an RDBMS in this chapter give a representative picture of the relational approach to databases. As for the RDM concepts, the description in this chapter is mathematically precise and modularly structured. In contrast with the description of RDM concepts, more than standard mathematical notation is needed. Special notation for describing software systems in terms of the operations that they can perform is now needed.

In connection with the criteria for the choice of modular structure mentioned in Section 2.2, it is worth noting the following about the description in this chapter. The separate modules of the description of an external RDBMS interface in this chapter are relatively simple, considering everything. For example, well-formedness of queries is not really simple but this is not exceptional for the context-sensitivity involved. A positive effect with regard to the simplicity of the separate modules is attained by isolating state dependent aspects in three modules. It is difficult to assess whether the clearness of the modular structure chosen in this chapter might be improved. As for the RDM concepts, it is clear that the chosen modular structuring aids a global understanding. Most of the modules describe concepts of great generality and wide applicability.

The description of an external RDBMS interface begins with the presentation of two parameter modules which are used in addition to the ones presented in Chapter 11. Subsequently, there are separate sections on the modules which constitute the description of an external RDBMS interface. Each module is preceded by an explanation of what the module concerned is about.

A reader who is unfamiliar with the relational approach to databases should first study a textbook such as (Ullman, 1988) to acquire an intuitive understanding of what is described formally in Chapter 11 and this chapter.

12.1 More assumptions

Later on modules are presented in which selection formulae, queries, relation declarations and other concepts concerning the external RDBMS interface are defined. Selection formulae are defined in terms of attributes and value constants, queries are defined in terms of relation names, attributes, value constants and selection formulae, declarations are defined in terms of attributes and domain constructions, etc. Value constants and domain constructions are meant to be syntactic objects denoting values and domains, respectively. Value constants and domain constructions are regarded as primitive objects about which it suffices to make a few assumptions, just like relation names, attributes and values.

The modules **VAL_CONST** and **DOMAIN_CONST** contain the assumptions concerned. It does not suffice to assume that there are types *Val_const* and *Domain_const*, respectively. It is in addition assumed that there is a total evaluation function *value* for value constants yielding values that are elements of *all* and a total evaluation function *domain* for domain constructions yielding domains that are subsets of *all*. This means that both modules are based on assumptions contained in the module **VALUE**. Therefore, the parameter module **X**, which actualizes the assumptions, is imported into both modules. The additional assumptions about value constants and domain constructions are needed to describe the evaluation of selection formulae, queries and declarations (the last denote relation schemas) and they are consequently used in the modules **SELECTION_WFF**, **QUERY** and **DECLARATION**.

Most later modules are parametrized modules. In addition to the modules **REL_NM**, **ATTRIBUTE** and **VALUE**, the modules **VAL_CONST** and **DOMAIN_CONST** are used as parameter restriction modules for the parameters of those modules. In this way, it is made precise that they are based on the above-mentioned assumptions about value constants and domain constructions.

```
VAL_CONST is
  abstract
    X: VALUE
  of

  import
    X
  into

  module
    types
    Val_const free

    functions
    value(Val_const)v: Value free
      pre   true
      post  member(v, all)
  end

DOMAIN_CONST is
  abstract
    X: VALUE
  of

  import
    X
  into

  module
    types
    Domain_const free

    functions
    domain(Domain_const)d: Domain free
      pre   true
      post  ∀v ∈ Value · member(v, d) ⇒ member(v, all)
  end
```

The next three sections present modules in which selection formulae, queries, declarations and functions concerning their well-formedness and evaluation are defined. The modules combined describe the state independent aspects of the external RDBMS interface. The state dependent aspects are treated in subsequent sections.

12.2 Selection formula

Selection formulae are composite values of several kinds. Selection formulae are just simple formulae for stating properties of tuples. They denote tuple predicates. However, they are abstract syntactic objects since they do not deal with concrete representation details like the concrete symbols used to represent operators, delimiter symbols and operator priorities to handle syntactic ambiguities, etc. A selection formula is used as constituent of queries in which a relation is described as a selection from another one.

The module **SELECTION_WFF** contains the definitions concerning selection formulae. This module is based on assumptions contained in the modules **ATTRIBUTE** and **VAL_CONST** as well as definitions contained in the parametrized modules **TUPLE** and **TUPLE_STRUCT**. Therefore, **X** and **Z**, which actualize the assumptions, and the appropriate applications of the above-mentioned parametrized modules are imported.

The principal functions defined in this module are *is_wf* and *predicate*. *is_wf* checks whether a selection formula is well-formed or not and *predicate* evaluates a selection formula (yielding a tuple predicate). As usual, evaluation is only defined for well-formed syntactic objects. Both well-formedness and evaluation are defined with respect to a given non-empty tuple structure.

There are five kinds of selection formulae: equalities, less-than-inequalities, greater-than-inequalities, negations and disjunctions. Selection formulae of the first three kinds, which are called atomic selection formulae, are composite values with an attribute and a value expression as components. Value expressions are variables and constants, which are composite values with an attribute and a value constant, respectively, as sole component. Negations and disjunctions are composite values with one selection formula and two selection formulae, respectively, as components.

The constructor functions *mk-Eq*, *mk-Less*, *mk-Greater*, *mk-Negation* and *mk-Disjunction* for creating formulae of the different kinds are implicitly defined and so are the constructor functions *mk-Variable* and *mk-Constant* for creating value expressions.

The module **SELECTION_WFF** exports these constructor functions, the well-formedness function *is_wf* for selection formulae and the evaluation function *predicate* for selection formulae. Note that the argument types and result types of exported functions are always implicitly exported if it is not done explicitly.

The exported functions *is_wf* and *predicate* are used in the module **QUERY** to define the well-formedness and evaluation of queries. The constructor functions must be made available to allow for creating selection formulae, which are constituents of selection queries. The remaining functions, *conforms* and *value*, are regarded as being of an auxiliary nature.

The module **SELECTION_WFF** is a higher-order parametrized module: applying it to modules corresponding to a particular choice of attributes and values yields another parametrized module. The latter module can be applied to any module corresponding to a particular choice of value constants for the relevant choice of values. This dependence of choices is made precise in the parameter restriction module for **Z**, which could not be done by means of first-order parametrization.

```
SELECTION_WFF is
  abstract
    X: ATTRIBUTE,
    Y: VALUE
  of

  abstract
    Z: apply VAL_CONST to Y
  of

  export
    mk-Eq: Attribute × Val_expression → Eq,
    mk-Less: Attribute × Val_expression → Less,
    mk-Greater: Attribute × Val_expression → Greater,
    mk-Negation: Selection_wff → Negation,
    mk-Disjunction: Selection_wff × Selection_wff → Disjunction,
    mk-Variable: Attribute → Variable,
    mk-Constant: Val_const → Constant,
    is_wf: Selection_wff × Tuple_struct → 𝔹,
    predicate: Selection_wff × Tuple_struct → Tuple_predicate
  from

  import
    X
    Z
    apply TUPLE to X, Y
    apply TUPLE_STRUCT to X, Y
  into

  module
    types
    Selection_wff = Eq | Less | Greater | Negation | Disjunction
```

$Eq :: Attribute\ Val\_expression$
$Less :: Attribute\ Val\_expression$
$Greater :: Attribute\ Val\_expression$
$Negation :: Selection\_wff$
$Disjunction :: Selection\_wff\ Selection\_wff$

$Val\_expression = Variable \mid Constant$

$Variable :: Attribute$
$Constant :: Val\_const$

functions

% well-formedness

```
is_wf(sf: Selection_wff, tstr: Tuple_struct)𝔹
 pre  attrs(tstr) ≠ empty
 △    cases sf of
        mk-Eq(a, ve) →
          member(a, attrs(tstr))∧
          conforms(ve, tstr, domain(tstr, a))
        mk-Less(a, ve) →
          member(a, attrs(tstr))∧
          conforms(ve, tstr, domain(tstr, a))
        mk-Greater(a, ve) →
          member(a, attrs(tstr))∧
          conforms(ve, tstr, domain(tstr, a))
        mk-Negation(sf) →
          is_wf(sf, tstr)
        mk-Disjunction(sf1, sf2) →
          is_wf(sf1, tstr) ∧ is_wf(sf2, tstr)
      end

conforms(ve: Val_expression, tstr: Tuple_struct, d: Domain)𝔹
 △  cases ve of
      mk-Variable(a) →
        member(a, attrs(tstr)) ∧ domain(tstr, a) = d
      mk-Constant(vc) →
        member(value(vc), d)
    end
```

```
% evaluation
predicate(sf: Selection_wff, tstr: Tuple_struct)tp: Tuple_predicate
 pre   attrs(tstr) ≠ empty ∧ is_wf(sf, tstr)
 post  ∀t ∈ Tuple ·
         (defined(tp, t) ⇔
          attrs(t) = attrs(tstr)∧
          ∀a ∈ Attribute ·
            member(a, attrs(t)) ⇒
            member(value(t, a), domain(tstr, a)))∧
         (holds(tp, t) ⇔
          cases sf of
            mk-Eq(a, ve) →
               value(t, a) = value(t, ve)
            mk-Less(a, ve) →
               lt(value(t, a), value(t, ve))
            mk-Greater(a, ve) →
               lt(value(t, ve), value(t, a))
            mk-Negation(sf) →
               ¬ predicate(sf, tstr)(t)
            mk-Disjunction(sf1, sf2) →
               predicate(sf1, tstr)(t) ∨ predicate(sf2, tstr)(t)
          end)

value(t: Tuple, ve: Val_expression) Value
 △  cases ve of
      mk-Variable(a) → value(t, a)
      mk-Constant(vc) → value(vc)
    end
end
```

The assumption made about values in the module **VALUE** concerning the function *lt* is needed in the module **SELECTION_WFF** to evaluate the less-than-inequalities and greater-than-inequalities.

12.3 Query

Queries are composite values of several kinds. A query can be thought of as an expression that denotes a relation. Just like selection formulae, queries are abstract syntactic objects. Queries are used as arguments of data manipulation operations.

The module **QUERY** contains the definitions concerning queries. This module is based on assumptions contained in the modules **REL_NM**, **ATTRIBUTE** and **VAL_CONST** as well as definitions contained in the parametrized modules **SELECTION_WFF**, **RELATION**, **DATABASE** and **DB_SCHEMA**. Therefore, **X**, **Y** and **U**, which actualize the assumptions, and the appropriate applications of the above-mentioned parametrized modules are imported.

The principal functions defined in this module are *is_wf* and *eval*. *is_wf* checks whether a query is well-formed or not and *eval* evaluates a query in a database (yielding a relation). As usual, evaluation is only defined for well-formed syntactic objects. Both well-formedness and evaluation are defined with respect to a given database schema.

There are eight kinds of queries: references, singletons, unions, differences, products, projections, selections and renamings. References are composite values with a relation name as sole component. Singletons are composite values with a tuple constant, which is a finite map from attributes to value constants, as sole component. Unions, differences and products are composite values with two queries as components. Projections are composite values with a query and an attribute set as components. Selections are composite values with a query and a selection formula as components. Renamings are composite values with a query and an attribute bijection as components.

The constructor functions *mk-Ref*, *mk-Singleton*, ..., *mk-Renaming* for creating queries of the different kinds are implicitly defined. The following constructor functions for tuple constants are also defined: *singleton* (converts an attribute-value-constant pair to a tuple constant) and *merge* (joins two tuple constants with disjoint attribute sets).

The module **QUERY** exports these constructor functions as well as the ones for selection formulae and value expressions (from the imported module **SELECTION_WFF**), the well-formedness function *is_wf* for queries and the evaluation function *eval* for queries.

Most of the exported functions are used later in the module **MANIPULATION** to define the data manipulation operations of the external RDBMS interface. The constructor functions must be made available to allow for creating queries, which are the main arguments of data manipulation operations. The hidden functions, such as *conforms* and *struct*, are regarded as being of an auxiliary nature.

The tuple structure of the relation denoted by a query is of utmost importance in establishing its well-formedness. In general, context information is required for extracting this tuple structure. This complexity is due to the singleton queries, which denote relations that consist of only one tuple. The problem is that relation names, referring to relation schemas from which the tuple structure can be derived, never occur in a singleton query. This problem can be circumvented by adding to singleton queries a syntactic object denoting its tuple structure. This solution, which is used by Date in his definition of the RDM, is considered to deviate too much from the nature of queries.

The function *struct* extracts the tuple structure of a given query according to a certain database schema. If the query is not well-formed but all relation names occurring in it refer to relation schemas in the database schema, then *struct* still yields a tuple structure. The reason is that the well-formedness of the query can only be fully established if its tuple structure is known. So to avoid circularities, the extracted tuple structure is based on some assumptions about the well-formedness of the query. These assumptions are checked when the extracted tuple structure is used to establish the well-formedness by means of the function *conforms*. It may also be the case that *struct* yields an empty tuple structure. An empty tuple structure seems useless, since tuples with an empty domain are excluded (in the module **TUPLE**). However, the empty tuple structure is used here to indicate that a useful tuple structure could not be extracted, due to lack of context information.

QUERY is
abstract
  X: **REL_NM**,
  Y: **ATTRIBUTE**,
  Z: **VALUE**
of

abstract
  U: apply **VAL_CONST** to **Z**
of

export
  mk-Ref: *Rel_nm* $\rightarrow$ *Ref*,
  mk-Singleton: *Tuple_const* $\rightarrow$ *Singleton*,
  mk-Union: *Query* $\times$ *Query* $\rightarrow$ *Union*,
  mk-Difference: *Query* $\times$ *Query* $\rightarrow$ *Difference*,
  mk-Product: *Query* $\times$ *Query* $\rightarrow$ *Product*,
  mk-Projection: *Query* $\times$ *Attr_set* $\rightarrow$ *Projection*,
  mk-Selection: *Query* $\times$ *Selection_wff* $\rightarrow$ *Selection*,
  mk-Renaming: *Query* $\times$ *Attr_bij* $\rightarrow$ *Renaming*,

  mk-Eq: *Attribute* $\times$ *Val_expression* $\rightarrow$ *Eq*,
  mk-Less: *Attribute* $\times$ *Val_expression* $\rightarrow$ *Less*,
  mk-Greater: *Attribute* $\times$ *Val_expression* $\rightarrow$ *Greater*,
  mk-Negation: *Selection_wff* $\rightarrow$ *Negation*,
  mk-Disjunction: *Selection_wff* $\times$ *Selection_wff* $\rightarrow$ *Disjunction*,

  mk-Variable: *Attribute* $\rightarrow$ *Variable*,
  mk-Constant: *Val_const* $\rightarrow$ *Constant*,

  singleton: *Attribute* $\times$ *Val_const* $\rightarrow$ *Tuple_const*,
  merge: *Tuple_const* $\times$ *Tuple_const* $\rightarrow$ *Tuple_const*,

is_wf: $Query \times Db\_schema \rightarrow \mathbb{B}$,
$eval$: $Query \times Db\_schema \times Database \rightarrow Relation$
from

import
X
Y
U
apply apply **SELECTION_WFF** to **Y**, **Z** to **U**
apply **RELATION** to **Y**, **Z**
apply **DATABASE** to **X**, **Y**, **Z**
apply **DB_SCHEMA** to **X**, **Y**, **Z**
into

module
types

$Query = Ref \mid Singleton \mid Union \mid Difference \mid$
$\quad Product \mid Projection \mid Selection \mid Renaming$

$Ref :: Rel\_nm$
$Singleton :: Tuple\_const$
$Union :: Query\ Query$
$Difference :: Query\ Query$
$Product :: Query\ Query$
$Projection :: Query\ Attr\_set$
$Selection :: Query\ Selection\_wff$
$Renaming :: Query\ Attr\_bij$

$Tuple\_const = Attribute \xrightarrow{m} Val\_const$

functions

% constructor functions
$singleton(a: Attribute, vc: Val\_const)\, Tuple\_const$
$\triangleq \{a \mapsto vc\}$

$merge(tc_1: Tuple\_const, tc_2: Tuple\_const)\, Tuple\_const$
pre $disjoint(attrs(tc_1), attrs(tc_2))$
$\triangleq tc_1 \cup tc_2$

% well-formedness
$is\_wf(q: Query, dbsch: Db\_schema)\mathbb{B}$
$\triangleq ok\_references(q, dbsch) \wedge$
$\quad conforms(q, dbsch, struct(q, dbsch))$

```
ok_references(q: Query, dbsch: Db_schema)𝔹
△  cases q of
     mk-Ref(rnm) →
       in_use(dbsch, rnm)
     mk-Singleton(tc) →
       true
     mk-Union(q1, q2) →
       ok_references(q1, dbsch) ∧ ok_references(q2, dbsch)
     mk-Difference(q1, q2) →
       ok_references(q1, dbsch) ∧ ok_references(q2, dbsch)
     mk-Product(q1, q2) →
       ok_references(q1, dbsch) ∧ ok_references(q2, dbsch)
     mk-Projection(q, as) →
       ok_references(q, dbsch)
     mk-Selection(q, sf) →
       ok_references(q, dbsch)
     mk-Renaming(q, ab) →
       ok_references(q, dbsch)
   end
```

$conforms(q{:}\ Query, dbsch{:}\ Db\_schema, tstr{:}\ Tuple\_struct)\mathbb{B}$

$\triangleq$ cases q of

$\quad mk\text{-}Ref(rnm) \rightarrow$

$\quad\quad$ true

$\quad mk\text{-}Singleton(tc) \rightarrow$

$\quad\quad tstr \neq empty \wedge attrs(tstr) = attrs(tc) \wedge$

$\quad\quad \forall a \in Attribute \cdot$

$\quad\quad\quad member(a, attrs(tc)) \Rightarrow$

$\quad\quad\quad member(value(tc, a), domain(tstr, a))$

$\quad mk\text{-}Union(q_1, q_2) \rightarrow$

$\quad\quad conforms(q_1, dbsch, tstr) \wedge conforms(q_2, dbsch, tstr) \wedge$

$\quad\quad (struct(q_1, dbsch) = tstr \vee struct(q_1, dbsch) = empty) \wedge$

$\quad\quad (struct(q_2, dbsch) = tstr \vee struct(q_2, dbsch) = empty)$

$\quad mk\text{-}Difference(q_1, q_2) \rightarrow$

$\quad\quad conforms(q_1, dbsch, tstr) \wedge conforms(q_2, dbsch, tstr) \wedge$

$\quad\quad (struct(q_1, dbsch) = tstr \vee struct(q_1, dbsch) = empty) \wedge$

$\quad\quad (struct(q_2, dbsch) = tstr \vee struct(q_2, dbsch) = empty)$

$\quad mk\text{-}Product(q_1, q_2) \rightarrow$

$\quad\quad conforms(q_1, dbsch, restrict(tstr, attrs(q_1, dbsch))) \wedge$

$\quad\quad conforms(q_2, dbsch, restrict(tstr, attrs(q_2, dbsch))) \wedge$

$\quad\quad disjoint(attrs(q_1, dbsch), attrs(q_2, dbsch))$

$\quad mk\text{-}Projection(q, as) \rightarrow$

$\quad\quad conforms(q, dbsch, struct(q, dbsch)) \wedge$

$\quad\quad included(as, attrs(q, dbsch))$

$\quad mk\text{-}Selection(q, sf) \rightarrow$

$\quad\quad conforms(q, dbsch, tstr) \wedge is\_wf(sf, tstr)$

$\quad mk\text{-}Renaming(q, ab) \rightarrow$

$\quad\quad conforms(q, dbsch, rename(tstr, inverse(ab))) \wedge$

$\quad\quad attrs(q, dbsch) = attrs_1(ab)$

end

$struct(q: Query, dbsch: Db\_schema)tstr: Tuple\_struct$
pre $ok\_references(q, dbsch)$
post cases q of
$mk\text{-}Ref(rnm) \rightarrow$
$tstr = struct(dbsch, rnm)$
$mk\text{-}Singleton(tc) \rightarrow$
$tstr = empty$
$mk\text{-}Union(q_1, q_2) \rightarrow$
$(struct(q_1, dbsch) = tstr \vee struct(q_2, dbsch) = tstr) \wedge$
$(tstr = empty \Rightarrow$
$struct(q_1, dbsch) = empty \wedge$
$struct(q_2, dbsch) = empty)$
$mk\text{-}Difference(q_1, q_2) \rightarrow$
$(struct(q_1, dbsch) = tstr \vee struct(q_2, dbsch) = tstr) \wedge$
$(tstr = empty \Rightarrow$
$struct(q_1, dbsch) = empty \wedge$
$struct(q_2, dbsch) = empty)$
$mk\text{-}Product(q_1, q_2) \rightarrow$
$(attrs(tstr) = attrs(mk\text{-}Product(q_1, q_2), dbsch) \wedge$
$struct(q_1, dbsch) = restrict(tstr, attrs(q_1, dbsch)) \wedge$
$struct(q_2, dbsch) = restrict(tstr, attrs(q_2, dbsch))) \vee$
$(tstr = empty \wedge$
$(struct(q_1, dbsch) = empty \vee$
$struct(q_2, dbsch) = empty))$
$mk\text{-}Projection(q, as) \rightarrow$
$tstr = restrict(struct(q, dbsch), as)$
$mk\text{-}Selection(q, sf) \rightarrow$
$tstr = struct(q, dbsch)$
$mk\text{-}Renaming(q, ab) \rightarrow$
$tstr = rename(struct(q, dbsch), ab)$
end

$attrs(q\colon Query, dbsch\colon Db\_schema)\, as\colon Attr\_set$
pre $ok\_references(q, dbsch)$
post cases q of
  $mk\text{-}Ref(rnm) \rightarrow$
    $as = attrs(dbsch, rnm)$
  $mk\text{-}Singleton(tc) \rightarrow$
    $as = attrs(tc)$
  $mk\text{-}Union(q_1, q_2) \rightarrow$
    $attrs(q_1, dbsch) = as \vee attrs(q_2, dbsch) = as$
  $mk\text{-}Difference(q_1, q_2) \rightarrow$
    $attrs(q_1, dbsch) = as \vee attrs(q_2, dbsch) = as$
  $mk\text{-}Product(q_1, q_2) \rightarrow$
    $\forall a \in Attribute \cdot$
     $member(a, as) \Leftrightarrow$
     $member(a, attrs(q_1, dbsch)) \vee$
     $member(a, attrs(q_2, dbsch))$
  $mk\text{-}Projection(q, as') \rightarrow$
    $as = as'$
  $mk\text{-}Selection(q, sf) \rightarrow$
    $as = attrs(q, dbsch)$
  $mk\text{-}Renaming(q, ab) \rightarrow$
    $as = attrs_2(ab)$
  end

```
% evaluation
eval(q: Query, dbsch: Db_schema, db: Database)Relation
  pre  is_wf(q, dbsch) ∧ is_valid_instance(db, dbsch)
  △    cases q of
         mk-Ref(rnm) →
           relation(db, rnm)
         mk-Singleton(tc) →
           singleton(tuple(tc))
         mk-Union(q1, q2) →
           union(eval(q1 dbsch, db), eval(q2, dbsch, db))
         mk-Difference(q1, q2) →
           difference(eval(q1, dbsch, db), eval(q2, dbsch, db))
         mk-Product(q1, q2) →
           product(eval(q1, dbsch, db), eval(q2, dbsch, db))
         mk-Projection(q, as) →
           projection(eval(q, dbsch, db), as)
         mk-Selection(q, sf) →
           selection( eval(q, dbsch, db),
                      predicate(sf, struct(q, dbsch)))
         mk-Renaming(q, ab) →
           rename(eval(q, dbsch, db), ab)
       end

tuple(tc: Tuple_const)t: Tuple
  post attrs(t) = attrs(tc)∧
       ∀a ∈ Attribute ·
         member(a, attrs(t)) ⇒ value(t, a) = value(tc, a)

attrs(tc: Tuple_const)Attr_set
  △  dom tc

value(tc: Tuple_const, a: Attribute)Value
  pre  member(a, attrs(tc))
  △    value(tc(a))
end
```

A large part of this module is concerned with well-formedness of queries and only a small part with evaluation of queries. Moreover, the part that is concerned with well-formedness is relatively complex. This is not exceptional. For query evaluation, extensive use is made of what is defined in the modules concerning RDM concepts (Chapter 11), as for well-formedness of queries no 'foundation' is available. In general, well-formedness tends not to be defined in a concise way for any language.

12.4 Declaration

Declarations are just composite values with a structure description, which is a finite map from attributes to domain constructions, and a key set as components. The domain of the structure description is called its attribute set. A declaration can be thought of as an expression that denotes a relation schema. Just like selection formulae and queries, declarations are abstract syntactic objects. Declarations are the main arguments of data definition operations.

The module **DECLARATION** contains the definitions concerning declarations. This module is based on assumptions contained in the modules **ATTRIBUTE** and **DOMAIN_CONST** as well as definitions contained in the parametrized modules **KEY_SUPPL** and **REL_SCHEMA**. Therefore, **X** and **Z**, which actualize the assumptions, and the appropriate applications of the above-mentioned parametrized modules are imported.

The principal functions defined in this module are *is_wf* and *schema*. *is_wf* checks whether a declaration is well-formed or not and *schema* evaluates a declaration (yielding a relation schema). As usual, evaluation is only defined for well-formed syntactic objects.

The constructor function *mk-Declaration* for creating declarations is implicitly defined. The following constructor functions for structure descriptions are also defined: *singleton* (converts an attribute-domain-construction pair to a structure description) and *merge* (joins two structure descriptions with disjoint attribute sets).

The module **DECLARATION** exports these constructor functions as well as the well-formedness function *is_wf* for declarations and the evaluation function *schema* for declarations.

Most of the exported functions are used in the module **DEFINITION** to define the data definition operations of the external RDBMS interface. The constructor functions must be made available to allow for creating declarations, which are the main arguments of data definition operations. The hidden functions are regarded as being of an auxiliary nature.

```
DECLARATION is
  abstract
    X: ATTRIBUTE,
    Y: VALUE
  of

  abstract
    Z: apply DOMAIN_CONST to Y
  of
```

export
$mk\text{-}Declaration$: $Structure\_descr \times Key\_set \rightarrow Declaration$,
$singleton$: $Attribute \times Domain\_const \rightarrow Structure\_descr$,
$merge$: $Structure\_descr \times Structure\_descr \rightarrow Structure\_descr$,
is_wf: $Declaration \rightarrow \mathbb{B}$,
$schema$: $Declaration \rightarrow Rel\_schema$
from

import
X
Z
apply **KEY_SUPPL** to **X**
apply **REL_SCHEMA** to **X**, **Y**
into

module
types
$Declaration :: Structure\_descr\ Key\_set$

$Structure\_descr = Attribute \xrightarrow{m} Domain\_const$

functions
% constructor functions
$singleton(a: Attribute, dc: Domain\_const) Structure\_descr$
$\triangleq \{a \mapsto dc\}$

$merge(sd_1: Structure\_descr, sd_2: Structure\_descr) Structure\_descr$
pre $disjoint(\mathsf{dom}\ sd_1, \mathsf{dom}\ sd_2)$
$\triangleq sd_1 \cup sd_2$

% well-formedness
$is\_wf(decl: Declaration)\mathbb{B}$
$\triangleq$ let
$mk\text{-}Declaration(sd, ks) \triangleq decl$
in
$\mathsf{dom}\ sd \neq empty \wedge$
$\forall as \in Attr\_set \cdot member(as, ks) \Rightarrow included(as, \mathsf{dom}\ sd)$

```
% evaluation
schema(decl: Declaration)rsch: Rel_schema
 pre   is_wf(decl)
 post  let
         mk-Declaration(sd, ks) ≜ decl
       in
         attrs(rsch) = dom sd ∧ keys(rsch) = ks∧
         ∀a ∈ Attribute ·
           member(a, attrs(rsch)) ⇒
           domain(rsch, a) = domain(sd(a))
end
```

The next three sections present modules in which the states of an RDBMS and the data manipulation and data definition operations which interrogate and modify them are defined. The modules combined describe the state dependent aspects of the external RDBMS interface.

12.5 DBMS state

The module **DBMS_STATE** contains the definitions concerning the changing state of a database management system. This module is based on definitions contained in the modules **DATABASE** and **DB_SCHEMA**. So the appropriate applications of these modules are imported.

No types and functions are defined. The concepts of a varying database and a varying database schema are made precise with the state variables *curr_database* and *curr_dbschema*. These state variables can be thought of as taking at any point in time the current database value and the current database schema value, respectively. Together they constitute the changing state of a database management system. The intention that the current database and the current database schema are initially empty is made precise with an initial condition and the intention that the current database schema always applies to the current database, is made precise with a state invariant.

The state variables *curr_dbschema* and *curr_database* are used in the module **MANIPULATION** as well as the module **DEFINITION** to define the operations which make up the external RDBMS interface. So these modules have state variables in common.

```
DBMS_STATE is
  abstract
    X: REL_NM,
    Y: ATTRIBUTE,
    Z: VALUE
  of
```

```
import
  apply DATABASE to X, Y, Z
  apply DB_SCHEMA to X, Y, Z
into

module
  state
  curr_dbschema: Db_schema

  curr_database: Database

   inv   is_valid_instance(curr_database, curr_dbschema)
   init  curr_dbschema = empty_schema ∧
         curr_database = empty_database
end
```

12.6 Manipulation

The module **MANIPULATION** contains the definitions concerning the data manipulation operations which can be performed by a database management system. This module is based on assumptions contained in the module **REL_NM** and definitions contained in the parametrized modules **RELATION**, **QUERY** and **DBMS_STATE**. Therefore, **X**, which actualizes the assumptions, and the appropriate applications of the abovementioned parametrized modules are imported.

The states of the database management system, with the components *curr_dbschema* and *curr_database*, were already defined in the imported module **DBMS_STATE**. The operations defined in the current module are *SELECT* (for selection of a relation that is derived from the ones stored in the current database), *INSERT*, *DELETE* and *REPLACE* (for alteration of one of the relations stored in the current database). Together they constitute the data manipulation interface of a database management system. All operations interrogate the current database schema but do not modify it. The first operation interrogates the current database but does not modify it. The other ones also modify the current database, unless the modified database would no longer be a valid instance of the current database schema.

SELECT evaluates a query in the current database (according to the current database schema), yields the relation obtained as result and does not change the state. *INSERT* evaluates a query in the current database (according to the current database schema) and adds the tuples of the relation obtained to a named relation in the current database. *DELETE* evaluates a query in the current database (according to the current database schema) and removes the tuples of the relation obtained from a named relation in the current database. *REPLACE* evaluates a query in the current database (according to the current database schema), removes the tuples of the relation obtained from a named relation in the current database, evaluates another query in the intermediate database (according to the current database schema) and adds the tuples of the relation obtained to the named relation in the intermediate database.

The operation *SELECT* must be executed successfully if the query concerned is well-formed with respect to the current database schema. Each of the other operations must be executed successfully if the relation name concerned fits in with the queries concerned (only one for *INSERT* and *DELETE*), the relation name is in use by the current database and the queries are well-formed with respect to the current database schema.

The module **MANIPULATION** exports the data manipulation operations *SELECT*, *INSERT*, *DELETE* and *REPLACE*. All types and functions that were exported from the imported modules are hidden, except the types *Rel_nm*, *Relation* and *Query* which are implicitly exported. The state variables *curr_dbschema* and *curr_database*, which were exported from the imported module **DBMS_STATE**, are also hidden. Interrogating or modifying them can only be done by means of the operations made available by the interface. This is in accordance with the viewpoint that only the effect of updates on subsequent queries really matters.

```
MANIPULATION is
  abstract
    X: REL_NM,
    Y: ATTRIBUTE,
    Z: VALUE
  of

  abstract
    U: apply VAL_CONST to Z
  of

  export
    SELECT: Query ⇒ Relation,
    INSERT: Rel_nm × Query ⇒,
    DELETE: Rel_nm × Query ⇒,
    REPLACE: Rel_nm × Query × Query ⇒
  from

  import
    X
    apply RELATION to Y, Z
    apply apply QUERY to X, Y, Z to U
    apply DBMS_STATE to X, Y, Z
  into
```

```
module
  operations
  SELECT(q: Query)r: Relation
   ext   rd curr_dbschema: Db_schema,
         rd curr_database: Database
   pre   is_wf(q, curr_dbschema)
   post  r = eval(q, curr_dbschema, curr_database)

  INSERT(rnm: Rel_nm, q: Query)
   ext   rd curr_dbschema: Db_schema,
         wr curr_database: Database
   pre   is_wf(mk-Union(mk-Ref(rnm), q), curr_dbschema)
   post  let
         dbsch: Db_schema △ curr_dbschema↼,
         db: Database △ curr_database↼,
         r: Relation △
           eval(mk-Union(mk-Ref(rnm), q), dbsch, db),
         db′: Database △ update(db, rnm, r)
         in
         curr_database
           = if is_valid_instance(db′, dbsch) then db′ else db

  DELETE(rnm: Rel_nm, q: Query)
   ext   rd curr_dbschema: Db_schema,
         wr curr_database: Database
   pre   is_wf(mk-Difference(mk-Ref(rnm), q), curr_dbschema)
   post  let
         dbsch: Db_schema △ curr_dbschema↼,
         db: Database △ curr_database↼,
         r: Relation △
           eval(mk-Difference(mk-Ref(rnm), q), dbsch, db),
         db′: Database △ update(db, rnm, r)
         in
         curr_database
           = if is_valid_instance(db′, dbsch) then db′ else db
```

$REPLACE(rnm: Rel\_nm, q_1: Query, q_2: Query)$
ext rd $curr\_dbschema: Db\_schema$,
wr $curr\_database: Database$
pre $is\_wf(mk\text{-}Difference(mk\text{-}Ref(rnm), q_1), curr\_dbschema) \wedge$
$is\_wf(mk\text{-}Union(mk\text{-}Ref(rnm), q_2), curr\_dbschema)$
post let
$dbsch: Db\_schema \triangleq \overleftarrow{curr\_dbschema}$,
$db: Database \triangleq \overleftarrow{curr\_database}$,
$r: Relation \triangleq$
$eval(mk\text{-}Difference(mk\text{-}Ref(rnm), q_1), dbsch, db)$,
$db': Database \triangleq update(db, rnm, r)$,
$r': Relation \triangleq$
$eval(mk\text{-}Union(mk\text{-}Ref(rnm), q_2), dbsch, db')$,
$db'': Database \triangleq update(db', rnm, r')$
in
$curr\_database$
$=$ if $is\_valid\_instance(db'', dbsch)$ then db'' else db
end

The operation *REPLACE* is defined in a rather indirect way to suggest that replacement is like deletion followed by insertion. However, $REPLACE(rnm, q_1, q_2)$ does not always have the same effect as $DELETE(rnm, q_1)$ followed by $INSERT(rnm, q_2)$. In the latter case there may be no deletion to avoid an invalid intermediate instance of the current database schema.

The collection of data manipulation operations defined in this module, which reflects roughly what is offered in each of the existing RDBMSs, is certainly not minimal. For example, the modifications that can be made by means of the operations *INSERT*, *DELETE* and *REPLACE*, can also be made by means of a single 'relational assignment' operation such as in (Date, 1986, Chapter 7).

12.7 Definition

The module **DEFINITION** contains the definitions concerning the data definition operations which can be performed by a database management system. This module is based on assumptions contained in the module **REL_NM** and definitions contained in the parametrized modules **DECLARATION** and **DBMS_STATE**. Therefore, **X**, which actualizes the assumptions, and the appropriate applications of the above-mentioned parametrized modules are imported.

The states of the database management system, with the components *curr_dbschema* and *curr_database*, were already defined in the imported module **DBMS_STATE**. The operations defined in the current module are *CREATE*, *DESTROY* and *CONSTRAIN* (mainly for alteration of the current database schema). Together they constitute the data definition interface of a database management system. All operations interrogate the current database schema as well as the current database. The first two operations also modify both of them, unless the modified database would no longer be a valid instance of the modified database schema. The last operation only modifies the current database schema, unless the current database would no longer be a valid instance of the modified database schema.

CREATE evaluates a declaration, adds the relation schema obtained under a given relation name to the current database schema and adds an empty relation under the same name to the current database. *DESTROY* removes the relation schema under a given relation name (and the inclusions referring to it) from the current database schema and removes the relation under the same name from the current database. *CONSTRAIN* adds an inclusion constraint to the current database schema.

CREATE must be executed successfully if the relation name concerned is not in use by the current database schema and the declaration concerned is well-formed. *DESTROY* must be executed successfully if the relation name concerned is in use by the current database schema. *CONSTRAIN* must be executed successfully if the inclusion concerned is applicable to the current database schema.

The module **DEFINITION** exports the data definition operations *CREATE*, *DESTROY* and *CONSTRAIN*. All types and functions that were exported from the imported modules are hidden, except the types *Rel_nm*, *Inclusion* and *Declaration* which are implicitly exported. The state variables *curr_dbschema* and *curr_database*, which were exported from the imported module **DBMS_STATE**, are also hidden. Interrogating or modifying them can only be done by means of the operations made available by the interface.

```
DEFINITION is
  abstract
    X: REL_NM,
    Y: ATTRIBUTE,
    Z: VALUE
  of

  abstract
    U: apply DOMAIN_CONST to Z
  of
```

export
  $CREATE$: $Rel\_nm \times Declaration \Rightarrow$,
  $DESTROY$: $Rel\_nm \Rightarrow$,
  $CONSTRAIN$: $Inclusion \Rightarrow$
from

import
  X
  apply apply **DECLARATION** to **Y**, **Z** to **U**
  apply **DBMS_STATE** to **X**, **Y**, **Z**
into

module
  operations

  $CREATE(rnm\colon Rel\_nm,\ decl\colon Declaration)$
  ext wr $curr\_dbschema\colon Db\_schema$,
      wr $curr\_database\colon Database$
  pre $\neg\, in\_use(curr\_dbschema, rnm) \wedge is\_wf(decl)$
  post let
      $dbsch\colon Db\_schema \triangleq \overleftarrow{curr\_dbschema}$,
      $db\colon Database \triangleq \overleftarrow{curr\_database}$,
      $rsch\colon Rel\_schema \triangleq schema(decl)$,
      $dbsch'\colon Db\_schema \triangleq create(dbsch, rnm, rsch)$,
      $db'\colon Database \triangleq create(db, rnm)$
      in
      $curr\_database$
       $=$ if $is\_valid\_instance(db', dbsch')$ then db' else $db \wedge$
      $curr\_dbschema$
       $=$ if $is\_valid\_instance(db', dbsch')$ then $dbsch'$ else $dbsch$

$DESTROY(rnm\colon Rel\_nm)$
ext wr $curr\_dbschema\colon Db\_schema$,
wr $curr\_database\colon Database$
pre $in\_use(curr\_dbschema, rnm)$
post let
$dbsch\colon Db\_schema \triangleq \overleftarrow{curr\_dbschema}$,
$db\colon Database \triangleq \overleftarrow{curr\_database}$,
$dbsch'\colon Db\_schema \triangleq destroy(dbsch, rnm)$,
$db'\colon Database \triangleq destroy(db, rnm)$
in
$curr\_database$
$= \text{if } is\_valid\_instance(db', dbsch') \text{ then } db' \text{ else } db \wedge$
$curr\_dbschema$
$= \text{if } is\_valid\_instance(db', dbsch') \text{ then } dbsch' \text{ else } dbsch$

$CONSTRAIN(incl\colon Inclusion)$
ext wr $curr\_dbschema\colon Db\_schema$,
rd $curr\_database\colon Database$
pre $applicable(incl, curr\_dbschema)$
post let
$dbsch\colon Db\_schema \triangleq \overleftarrow{curr\_dbschema}$,
$db\colon Database \triangleq \overleftarrow{curr\_database}$,
$dbsch'\colon Db\_schema \triangleq constrain(dbsch, incl)$
in
$curr\_dbschema$
$= \text{if } is\_valid\_instance(db, dbsch') \text{ then } dbsch' \text{ else } dbsch$

end

Many existing RDBMSs offer a more powerful collection of data definition operations. The rather restricted power offered by the operations defined in this module is intentional. It is the opinion of the author that modification of a relation schema or a database schema conflicts with the usual intuition about schemas. Therefore we have tried to maintain their static character as far as possible without making them impractical. For example, the addition of new relation schemas and the removal of existing ones is supported, but the addition of new attributes to an existing relation schema is not supported.

12.8 System

The former modules combined cover all things relevant to the external RDBMS interface. Therefore, the system module contains no definitions. No new concepts are defined. Instead the relevant definitions from the previous modules are combined and it is specified what, from the defined concepts, constitutes the external RDBMS interface by making only the names of these concepts visible.

The system module exports the constructor functions which are required for creating all queries, declarations and inclusions, the data manipulation operations and the data definition operations.

```
system is
  abstract
    X: REL_NM,
    Y: ATTRIBUTE,
    Z: VALUE
  of

  abstract
    U: apply VAL_CONST to Z,
    V: apply DOMAIN_CONST to Z
  of

  export
    mk-Ref: Rel_nm → Ref,
    mk-Singleton: Tuple_const → Singleton,
    mk-Union: Query × Query → Union,
    mk-Difference: Query × Query → Difference,
    mk-Product: Query × Query → Product,
    mk-Projection: Query × Attr_set → Projection,
    mk-Selection: Query × Selection_wff → Selection,
    mk-Renaming: Query × Attr_bij → Renaming,
    mk-Eq: Attribute × Val_expression → Eq,
    mk-Less: Attribute × Val_expression → Less,
    mk-Greater: Attribute × Val_expression → Greater,
    mk-Negation: Selection_wff → Negation,
    mk-Disjunction: Selection_wff × Selection_wff → Disjunction,
    mk-Variable: Attribute → Variable,
    mk-Constant: Val_const → Constant,
    mk-Declaration: Structure_descr × Key_set → Declaration,
    mk-Inclusion: Rel_nm × Rel_nm × Key_bij → Inclusion,
    singleton: Attribute × Val_const → Tuple_const,
    merge: Tuple_const × Tuple_const → Tuple_const,
    singleton: Attribute × Domain_const → Structure_descr,
    merge: Structure_descr × Structure_descr → Structure_descr,
    singleton: Attribute → Attr_set,
    union: Attr_set × Attr_set → Attr_set,
```

$singleton$: $Attribute \times Attribute \rightarrow Attr\_bij$,
$merge$: $Attr\_bij \times Attr\_bij \rightarrow Attr\_bij$,

$empty$: $\rightarrow Key\_set$,
$singleton$: $Attr\_set \rightarrow Key\_set$,
$union$: $Key\_set \times Key\_set \rightarrow Key\_set$,

$SELECT$: $Query \Rightarrow Relation$,
$INSERT$: $Rel\_nm \times Query \Rightarrow$,
$DELETE$: $Rel\_nm \times Query \Rightarrow$,
$REPLACE$: $Rel\_nm \times Query \times Query \Rightarrow$,
$CREATE$: $Rel\_nm \times Declaration \Rightarrow$,
$DESTROY$: $Rel\_nm \Rightarrow$,
$CONSTRAIN$: $Inclusion \Rightarrow$

from

import
X
apply **RELATION** to **Y**, **Z**
apply apply **QUERY** to **X**, **Y**, **Z** to **U**
apply apply **DECLARATION** to **Y**, **Z** to **V**
apply apply **MANIPULATION** to **X**, **Y**, **Z** to **U**
apply apply **DEFINITION** to **X**, **Y**, **Z** to **V**
into

module
end

It is worth noting that the modules **MANIPULATION** and **DEFINITION**, which are combined in the complete specification, have hidden state variables in common, viz. *curr_dbschema* and *curr_database*. Although data manipulation operations and data definition operations are only loosely connected, operations of both kinds interrogate or modify both state variables.

13

An Internal RDBMS Interface

In this chapter, the second case study in VVSL is presented. This case study deals with the underlying concepts and operations of systems for handling concurrent access to a relational database by multiple transactions. The main purpose of the second case study is to demonstrate the practical usefulness of the extensions of VDM-SL for specifying operations which interfere through shared state components, but it demonstrates the practical usefulness of the extensions for modular structuring as well.

The operations described in this chapter make up a hypothetical internal interface of an RDBMS: the operations are not made available directly to the users of the RDBMS. This interface, which handles concurrent access to stored relations by multiple transactions, is meant to provide for a way of looking at transaction management in database systems. The underlying concepts are concepts associated with *concurrency control* and *in-progress transaction backup* aspects of transaction management. Most of the operations can be regarded as requests on behalf of some transaction to perform an action on a subset of a stored relation.

Transactions are the units of consistency. It is assumed that each action which is performed on behalf of a transaction may violate database consistency, but that each transaction, when executed alone, preserves database consistency. An 'Access Handler' (AH), which supports the internal RDBMS interface defined in this chapter, provides for interleaved performance of actions requested by several transactions in such a manner that each transaction sees a consistent database and produces a consistent database. In this case, it is said that the requests are granted in a consistency preserving order. The AH does so on the ground of the above-mentioned assumptions; it does not know what the consistency requirements are. When a transaction issues a request, it is never made to wait for ever for the granting of the request. Deadlock is one possible reason why a transaction might wait for ever. The AH will reject an issued request immediately, if the request would cause deadlock. Other reasons, e.g. livelock, are prevented from occurring by the way of granting requests. If a request is rejected, then the transaction concerned usually has to stop after undoing all changes made to the database so far. One of the operations provides for this rollback of transactions.

The description of underlying concepts of access handlers and operations which can be performed by such systems in this chapter gives a detailed picture of transaction management in database systems. Like the descriptions in the previous two chapters, the description in this chapter is mathematically precise and modularly structured. In contrast with the description of RDM concepts, more than standard mathematical notation is needed. As for the external RDBMS interface, special notation for describing software systems in terms of the operations that they can perform is needed. For the internal RDBMS interface, this includes notation for describing the possible effects of performing interleaved operations which relate to interference through shared state components. This notation was not needed for the external RDBMS interface. It is also worth noting that in the current description existing modules (modules from Chapter 11 used in Chapter 12) have been re-used.

In the remainder of this chapter, first the re-used modules are mentioned. Subsequently, there are separate sections on the other modules. Each module is preceded by an explanation of what the module concerned is about.

A reader who is unfamiliar with the relational approach to databases or transaction management in database systems should first study a textbook such as (Ullman, 1988) to acquire an intuitive understanding of what is described formally in this chapter.

13.1 RDM concepts

In Chapter 11 many of the basic concepts of the RDM were defined. The relevant concepts cover the data structure, data manipulation and data integrity aspects of the RDM. The description given in this chapter builds upon the description of RDM concepts in Chapter 11. That description of RDM concepts should be repeated here. For practical reasons, only the names of the relevant modules are given. The reader is asked to imagine that it is repeated completely. For short informal explanations of what these modules are about, see Section 10.4.

component

REL_NM is . . .

ATTRIBUTE is . . .

VALUE is . . .

ATTR_SUPPL is . . .

TUPLE is ...

RELATION is ...

DATABASE is ...

TUPLE_STRUCT is ...

REL_SCHEMA is ...

DB_SCHEMA is ...

VAL_CONST is ...

13.2 More assumptions

Later on modules are presented in which simple formulae, accesses, access tables and other concepts concerning the internal RDBMS interface are defined. Simple formulae are defined in terms of attributes and value constants, accesses are defined in terms of relation names and simple formulae, access tables are defined in terms of transaction names and accesses, etc. Transaction names are regarded as primitive objects about which it suffices to make a few assumptions, in the same way as relation names, attributes, values and values constants. Transaction names are usually identifiers.

The module **TRANS_NM** contains the assumptions concerned. For transaction names it suffices to assume that there is a type *Trans_nm* with no a priori properties.

Most modules in this chapter are parametrized ones. In addition to the modules **REL_NM**, **ATTRIBUTE**, **VALUE** and **VAL_CONST**, the module **TRANS_NM** is used as parameter restriction modules for the parameters of those modules. In this way, it is made precise that they are based on the above-mentioned assumptions about transaction names.

TRANS_NM is
module
types
Trans_nm free
end

The next three sections present modules in which simple formulae, accesses and access tables are defined. These modules describe the concepts according to which the internal RDBMS interface handles concurrent access to stored relations by multiple transactions. The operations relating to this are completed with an operation to stop a transaction that is in progress after undoing its changes made to the database so far. The concepts according to which provision is made for the in-progress transaction backup are treated in subsequent sections.

13.3 Simple formula

Simple formulae are composite values of several kinds. Simple formulae are very simple formulae for stating properties of tuples. They denote tuple predicates. However, they are abstract syntactic objects since they do not deal with concrete representation details. A simple formula is used as a constituent of accesses, which present requests to perform a read or write action on a subset of a stored relation.

The module **SIMPLE_WFF** contains the definitions concerning simple formulae. This module is based on assumptions contained in the modules **ATTRIBUTE** and **VAL_CONST** as well as definitions contained in the parametrized modules **TUPLE** and **TUPLE_STRUCT**. Therefore, **X** and **Z**, which actualize the assumptions, and the appropriate applications of the above-mentioned parametrized modules are imported.

The principal functions defined in this module are *is_wf* and *predicate*. *is_wf* checks whether a simple formula is well-formed or not and *predicate* evaluates a simple formula (yielding a tuple predicate). As usual, evaluation is only defined for well-formed syntactic objects. Both well-formedness and evaluation are defined with respect to a given non-empty tuple structure.

There are six kinds of simple formulae: boolean literals, equalities, less-than-inequalities, greater-than-inequalities, negations and disjunctions. Simple formulae of the first kind are composite values with a truth value as sole component. Simple formulae of the next three kinds are composite values with an attribute and a value constant as components. Simple formulae of the first four kinds are called atomic simple formulae. Negations and disjunctions are composite values with one simple formula and two simple formulae, respectively, as components.

The constructor functions *mk-Bool_lit*, *mk-Eq*, *mk-Less*, *mk-Greater*, *mk-Negation* and *mk-Disjunction* for creating formulae of the different kinds are implicitly defined.

The module **SIMPLE_WFF** exports these constructor functions, the well-formedness function *is_wf* for simple formulae and the evaluation function *predicate* for simple formulae.

The exported functions *is_wf* and *predicate* are used in the module **ACCESS** to define functions on accesses. The constructor functions must be made available to allow for creating simple formulae, which are constituents of accesses.

```
SIMPLE_WFF is
  abstract
    X: ATTRIBUTE,
    Y: VALUE
  of
```

abstract
  Z: apply **VAL_CONST** to **Y**
of

export
  $mk\text{-}Bool\_lit: \mathbb{B} \rightarrow Bool\_lit,$
  $mk\text{-}Eq: Attribute \times Val\_const \rightarrow Eq,$
  $mk\text{-}Less: Attribute \times Val\_const \rightarrow Less,$
  $mk\text{-}Greater: Attribute \times Val\_const \rightarrow Greater,$
  $mk\text{-}Negation: Simple\_wff \rightarrow Negation,$
  $mk\text{-}Disjunction: Simple\_wff \times Simple\_wff \rightarrow Disjunction,$
  $is\_wf: Simple\_wff \times Tuple\_struct \rightarrow \mathbb{B},$
  $predicate: Simple\_wff \times Tuple\_struct \rightarrow Tuple\_predicate$
from

import
  X
  Z
  apply **TUPLE** to **X**, **Y**
  apply **TUPLE_STRUCT** to **X**, **Y**
into

module
  types
  $Simple\_wff =$
    $Bool\_lit \mid Eq \mid Less \mid Greater \mid Negation \mid Disjunction$

  $Bool\_lit :: \mathbb{B}$
  $Eq :: Attribute \; Val\_const$
  $Less :: Attribute \; Val\_const$
  $Greater :: Attribute \; Val\_const$
  $Negation :: Simple\_wff$
  $Disjunction :: Simple\_wff \; Simple\_wff$

functions

% well-formedness

$is\_wf(sf: Simple\_wff, tstr: Tuple\_struct)\mathbb{B}$

pre $attrs(tstr) \neq empty$

$\triangleq$ cases sf of

$mk\text{-}Bool\_lit(b) \rightarrow$

true

$mk\text{-}Eq(a, vc) \rightarrow$

$member(a, attrs(tstr)) \wedge$

$member(value(vc), domain(tstr, a))$

$mk\text{-}Less(a, vc) \rightarrow$

$member(a, attrs(tstr)) \wedge$

$member(value(vc), domain(tstr, a))$

$mk\text{-}Greater(a, vc) \rightarrow$

$member(a, attrs(tstr)) \wedge$

$member(value(vc), domain(tstr, a))$

$mk\text{-}Negation(sf) \rightarrow$

$is\_wf(sf, tstr)$

$mk\text{-}Disjunction(sf_1, sf_2) \rightarrow$

$is\_wf(sf_1, tstr) \wedge is\_wf(sf_2, tstr)$

end

```
% evaluation
predicate(sf: Simple_wff, tstr: Tuple_struct)tp: Tuple_predicate
  pre   attrs(tstr) ≠ empty ∧ is_wf(sf, tstr)
  post  ∀t ∈ Tuple ·
          (defined(tp, t) ⇔
           attrs(t) = attrs(tstr)∧
           ∀a ∈ Attribute ·
            member(a, attrs(t)) ⇒
            member(value(t, a), domain(tstr, a)))∧
          (holds(tp, t) ⇔
           cases sf of
            mk-Bool_lit(b) →
              b
            mk-Eq(a, vc) →
              value(t, a) = value(vc)
            mk-Less(a, vc) →
              lt(value(t, a), value(vc))
            mk-Greater(a, vc) →
              lt(value(vc), value(t, a))
            mk-Negation(sf) →
              ¬ predicate(sf, tstr)(t)
            mk-Disjunction(sf1, sf2) →
              predicate(sf1, tstr)(t) ∨ predicate(sf2, tstr)(t)
           end)
end
```

The simple formulae defined in the module **SIMPLE_WFF** and the selection formulae defined in the module **SELECTION_WFF** are almost the same. An atomic simple formula is a boolean literal or an atomic selection formula with a value constant as the right-hand side. The right-hand side of an atomic selection formula may also be an attribute. This is the main difference. Firthermore, the boolean literals are no selection formulae.

13.4 Access

Accesses are composite values with an access mode (READ, WRITE, CREATE or DESTROY), a relation name and a simple formula as components. The simple formula concerned has to be the boolean literal denoting truth if the access mode is CREATE or DESTROY. An access can be thought of as an abstraction of a request to perform an action on a subset of some stored relation. An access presents syntactic properties of an access request issued by some transaction. It captures all the details of the request that can be used to grant this request amongst requests issued by other transactions in a consistency preserving order. Two accesses are in conflict if it cannot be determined from the syntactic properties concerned whether the requested actions will not interfere. That is, their access modes are not both read mode, their relation names are the same and the tuples referred to by their simple formulae overlap. The tuples concerned are determined with respect to a given database schema. Thus, tuples are included irrespective of their presence in the stored relation concerned.

The module **ACCESS** contains the definitions concerning accesses. This module is based on assumptions contained in the module **REL_NM** and definitions contained in the parametrized modules **SIMPLE_WFF**, **RELATION** and **DB_SCHEMA**. Therefore, **X**, which actualizes the assumptions, and the appropriate applications of the above-mentioned parametrized modules are imported.

The principal functions defined in this module are *tuples* and *conflicts*. *tuples* determines the set of all tuples referred to by an access according to a database schema and *conflicts* checks whether two accesses are in conflict according to a database schema or not. The functions *compatible*, which is also defined in this module, checks whether an access is consistent with a database schema or not.

The constructor function *mk-Access* for creating accesses and the selector functions *am*, *rnm* and *sf* for selecting the components of accesses are implicitly defined.

The functions *conflicts* and *compatible* are used in the module **ACCESS_TABLE** to define functions to manipulate access tables. The functions *tuples* and *mk-Access* are used in the module **ACCESS_HANDLING** to define the operations which make up the internal RDBMS interface.

```
ACCESS is
  abstract
    X: REL_NM,
    Y: ATTRIBUTE,
    Z: VALUE
  of

  abstract
    U: apply VAL_CONST to Z
  of

  import
    X
    apply apply SIMPLE_WFF to Y, Z to U
    apply RELATION to Y, Z
    apply DB_SCHEMA to X, Y, Z
  into
```

```
module
  types
  Access :: am: Access_mode  rnm: Rel_nm  sf: Simple_wff
  where inv(acc) ≜
    am(acc) = CREATE ∨ am(acc) = DESTROY  ⇒
    sf(acc) = mk-Bool_lit(true)

  Access_mode  =  {READ, WRITE, CREATE, DESTROY}

  functions

  % non-constructor functions
  tuples(dbsch: Db_schema, acc: Access)r: Relation
    pre   compatible(acc, dbsch)
    post  let
            tp: Tuple_predicate ≜
              predicate(sf(acc), struct(dbsch, rnm(acc)))
          in
          ∀t ∈ Tuple ·
            member(t, r)  ⇔  defined(tp, t) ∧ holds(tp, t)

  conflicts(acc1: Access, acc2: Access, dbsch: Db_schema)𝔹
    pre  compatible(acc1, dbsch) ∧ compatible(acc2, dbsch)
    ≜    let
         tp1: Tuple_predicate ≜
           predicate(sf(acc1), struct(dbsch, rnm(acc1))),
         tp2: Tuple_predicate ≜
           predicate(sf(acc2), struct(dbsch, rnm(acc2)))
         in
         ¬ (am(acc1) = READ ∧ am(acc2) = READ)∧
         rnm(acc1) = rnm(acc2)∧
         ∃t ∈ Tuple  ·  defined(tp1, t) ∧ holds(tp1, t) ∧ holds(tp2, t)

  compatible(acc: Access, dbsch: Db_schema)𝔹
    ≜  in_use(dbsch, rnm(acc))∧
         is_wf(sf(acc), struct(dbsch, rnm(acc)))
end
```

The definitions show that subsets of stored relations have been chosen as the units of access. The concept of an access was originally defined in connection with the idea of predicate locks by Eswaran, Gray, Lorie and Traiger (1976). Although locks are not defined here, the concept of an access is still regarded as being useful. It facilitates the description of what is required of a scheduler for access requests issued on behalf of multiple transactions.

13.5 Access table

Access tables are maps from transaction names to access records. The access records are composite values with two disjoint sets of accesses as components. The domain of an access table is called its transaction name set. A transaction name is in use by an access table if it is in the transaction name set of the access table. An access record with two empty sets of accesses as components is called an empty access record. An access table can be thought of as an abstraction of the state of a collection of transactions whose actions are performed in an interleaved fashion. An access table presents, for each active transaction, the syntactic properties of its previously granted requests and, in case it is currently waiting, its currently waiting request. That is, the sets of accesses from the access records present the set of previously granted requests and the set of currently waiting requests of the transactions concerned. Thus, it captures all the details of the active transactions that can be used to grant waiting requests and coming requests of the active transactions in a consistency preserving order.

For a given transaction, an access is in conflict with an access table if it cannot be determined from the syntactic properties concerned whether the requested action will not interfere with the actions that were previously requested by another active transaction. That is, the access is in conflict with an access from the access record associated with another transaction. A conflicting request is not granted immediately; it becomes a waiting request which eventually will be granted or it is rejected immediately. A conflicting request will be rejected if it would otherwise be waiting for itself indirectly; in which case it is called liable for deadlock. For example, the request issued by the transaction is currently granted to another transaction which is already waiting because of a conflict with a request currently granted to the issuing transaction.

The module **ACCESS_TABLE** contains the definitions concerning access tables. This module is based on assumptions contained in the module **TRANS_NM** and definitions contained in the parametrized module **ACCESS**. Therefore, **U**, which actualizes the assumptions, and the appropriate application of the module **ACCESS** are imported.

The principal functions defined in this module are *conflicts* and *deadlock_liable*. *conflicts* checks whether, for a given transaction, an access is in conflict with an access table according to a database schema or not and *deadlock_liable* checks whether, for a given transaction, an access is liable for deadlock with an access table according to a database schema or not. For access tables, the only constant is *empty_acctbl*, the empty access table. The following functions on access tables are defined as well: *create* (adds an access record for a new transaction to an access table; the new access record is empty), *destroy* (removes the access record of a transaction from an access table), *add_to_grants* (adds an access to the granted accesses of a transaction in an access table), *add_to_waits* (adds an access to the waiting accesses of a transaction in an access table), *in_use* (checks whether a transaction name is in use by an access table or not), *granted* (looks up the granted accesses of a transaction in an access table), *waiting* (looks up the waiting accesses of a transaction in an access table) and *compatible* (checks whether an access table is consistent with a database schema or not). The first four functions are constructor functions for access tables.

The constructor function *mk-Access_record* for creating access records and the selector functions *grants* and *waits* for selecting the components of access records are implicitly defined.

The above-mentioned functions are used in the modules **AH_STATE** and **ACCESS_HANDLING** to define the states of an access handler and the operations which make up an internal RDBMS interface.

The function *add_to_grants* is defined such that the access, which is added to the grants of some access record, is also removed from the waits of this access record (if present). There is no function available for removing the access from the waits without adding it to the grants. This is in accordance with the intuitive idea that a waiting request should eventually be granted.

The function *add_to_waits* is defined such that it does not add an access to the waits of some access record if it is already one of the grants of this access record. This is essentially a special provision for transactions which inadvertently issue the same request more than once.

```
ACCESS_TABLE is
  abstract
    X: REL_NM,
    Y: ATTRIBUTE,
    Z: VALUE,
    U: TRANS_NM
  of

  abstract
    V: apply VAL_CONST to Z
  of

  import
    U
    apply apply ACCESS to X, Y, Z to V
  into

  module
    types
    Access_table = Trans_nm -m-> Access_record
```

$Access\_record :: grants: Access\_set \;\; waits: Access\_set$
where $\text{inv}(ar) \triangleq grants(ar) \cap waits(ar) = \{\}$

$Access\_set = Access\text{-set}$

functions

% constructor functions
$empty\_acctbl()Access\_table$
$\triangleq \{\}$

$create(acctbl: Access\_table, tnm: Trans\_nm)Access\_table$
pre $\neg\, in\_use(acctbl, tnm)$
$\triangleq \quad acctbl \cup \{tnm \mapsto mk\text{-}Access\_record(\{\}, \{\})\}$

$destroy(acctbl: Access\_table, tnm: Trans\_nm)Access\_table$
pre $in\_use(acctbl, tnm)$
$\triangleq \quad \{tnm\} \ntriangleleft acctbl$

$add\_to\_grants(acctbl: Access\_table, tnm: Trans\_nm, acc: Access)$
$\quad Access\_table$
pre $in\_use(acctbl, tnm)$
$\triangleq$ let
$\quad gaccs: Access\_set \triangleq grants(acctbl(tnm)),$
$\quad waccs: Access\_set \triangleq waits(acctbl(tnm))$
in
$acctbl\dagger$
$\{tnm \mapsto mk\text{-}Access\_record(gaccs \cup \{acc\}, waccs - \{acc\})\}$

$add\_to\_waits(acctbl: Access\_table, tnm: Trans\_nm, acc: Access)$
$\quad Access\_table$
pre $in\_use(acctbl, tnm)$
$\triangleq$ let
$\quad gaccs: Access\_set \triangleq grants(acctbl(tnm)),$
$\quad waccs: Access\_set \triangleq waits(acctbl(tnm))$
in
$acctbl\dagger$
$\{tnm \mapsto mk\text{-}Access\_record(gaccs, waccs \cup (\{acc\} - gaccs))\}$

% non-constructor functions
$conflicts(tnm: Trans\_nm, acc: Access,$
$\quad acctbl: Access\_table, dbsch: Db\_schema)\mathbb{B}$
pre $compatible(acc, dbsch) \wedge compatible(acctbl, dbsch)$
$\triangleq \quad \exists tnm' \in Trans\_nm \;, acc' \in Access \cdot$
$\quad tnm \neq tnm' \wedge in\_use(acctbl, tnm') \wedge$
$\quad requested(tnm', acc', acctbl) \wedge conflicts(acc, acc', dbsch)$

$deadlock\_liable(\ tnm\colon Trans\_nm,\ acc\colon Access,$
$\quad acctbl\colon Access\_table,\ dbsch\colon Db\_schema)\mathbb{B}$
pre $in\_use(acctbl, tnm) \wedge$
$compatible(acc, dbsch) \wedge compatible(acctbl, dbsch)$
$\triangleq$ $conflicts(tnm, acc, acctbl, dbsch) \wedge$
$waits\_for(tnm, tnm, add\_to\_waits(acctbl, tnm, acc), dbsch)$

$waits\_for(\ tnm_1\colon Trans\_nm,\ tnm_2\colon Trans\_nm,$
$\quad acctbl\colon Access\_table,\ dbsch\colon Db\_schema)\mathbb{B}$
pre $in\_use(acctbl, tnm_1) \wedge in\_use(acctbl, tnm_2) \wedge$
$compatible(acctbl, dbsch)$
$\triangleq$ $waits\_dir\_for(tnm_1, tnm_2, acctbl, dbsch) \vee$
$\exists tnm' \in Trans\_nm \cdot$
$in\_use(acctbl, tnm') \wedge$
$waits\_dir\_for(tnm_1, tnm', acctbl, dbsch) \wedge$
$waits\_for(tnm', tnm_2, acctbl, dbsch)$

$waits\_dir\_for(\ tnm_1\colon Trans\_nm,\ tnm_2\colon Trans\_nm,$
$\quad acctbl\colon Access\_table,\ dbsch\colon Db\_schema)\mathbb{B}$
pre $in\_use(acctbl, tnm_1) \wedge in\_use(acctbl, tnm_2) \wedge$
$compatible(acctbl, dbsch)$
$\triangleq$ $tnm_1 \neq tnm_2 \wedge$
$\exists acc_1 \in Access\ ,\ acc_2 \in Access \cdot$
$waiting(tnm_1, acc_1, acctbl) \wedge granted(tnm_2, acc_2, acctbl) \wedge$
$conflicts(acc_1, acc_2, dbsch)$

$in\_use(acctbl\colon Access\_table,\ tnm\colon Trans\_nm)\mathbb{B}$
$\triangleq$ $tnm \in \text{dom}\ acctbl$

$granted(tnm\colon Trans\_nm,\ acc\colon Access,\ acctbl\colon Access\_table)\mathbb{B}$
pre $in\_use(acctbl, tnm)$
$\triangleq$ $acc \in grants(acctbl(tnm))$

$waiting(tnm\colon Trans\_nm,\ acc\colon Access,\ acctbl\colon Access\_table)\mathbb{B}$
pre $in\_use(acctbl, tnm)$
$\triangleq$ $acc \in waits(acctbl(tnm))$

$requested(tnm\colon Trans\_nm,\ acc\colon Access,\ acctbl\colon Access\_table)\mathbb{B}$
pre $in\_use(acctbl, tnm)$
$\triangleq$ $granted(tnm, acc, acctbl) \vee waiting(tnm, acc, acctbl)$

$compatible(acctbl\colon Access\_table,\ dbsch\colon Db\_schema)\mathbb{B}$
$\triangleq$ $\forall tnm \in Trans\_nm\ ,\ acc \in Access \cdot$
$in\_use(acctbl, tnm) \wedge requested(tnm, acc, acctbl) \Rightarrow$
$compatible(acc, dbsch)$

end

Roughly speaking, the concept of an access table is a formalized instance of what is described as 'dynamic syntactic information' (about a transaction system) in (Kung and Papadimitriou, 1983). There is also a strong connection between the idea of 'superstrict' concurrency control from (Rosenkrantz, Stearn and Lewis, 1978) and the function conflicts on accesses and access tables.

The next three sections present modules in which transition records, transition logs and log tables are defined. These modules describe the concepts according to which the internal RDBMS interface makes provision for in-progress transaction backup. Together with the modules presented in the previous three sections, they describe the state independent aspects of the internal RDBMS interface. The state dependent aspects are treated in subsequent sections.

13.6 Transition record

Transition records are composite values with a transition mode (NORMAL, INIT or FINAL), a relation name and two relations, called deletion relation and insertion relation, as components. The attribute sets of the deletion and insertion relation have to be the same. Besides, both relations have to be empty if the transition mode is INIT and the insertion relation is empty if the transition mode is FINAL. A transition record is meant to reflect the effect of a write action on some stored relation. It is used to record the differences occurring when the stored relation is changed by performing the write action on it. That is, the deletion relation is intended for the tuples that were deleted and the insertion relation is intended for the tuples that were inserted. Thus, it can provide all the details that are required to undo the effect.

The module **TRANSITION_RECORD** contains the definitions concerning transition records. This module is based on assumptions contained in the module **REL_NM** and definitions contained in the parametrized modules **RELATION** and **DATABASE**. Therefore, **X**, which actualizes the assumptions, and the appropriate application of the above-mentioned parametrized modules are imported.

The principal function defined in this module is *undo*. This function normally replaces the relation referred to by a transition record in a database as follows: first it deletes the tuples of the insertion relation concerned from the named relation and after that it inserts the tuples of the deletion relation concerned into the named relation. Herewith, the effect of the recorded update is only undone if the deletion relation and insertion relation do not contain tuples which were superfluous at the time of update (because they were not relevant to the relation concerned). The function *weaken* removes such superfluous tuples. In addition to the functions *undo* and *weaken*, the following functions on transition records are defined: *weaker* (checks whether a transition record is the result of removing the tuples that would be superfluous for some relation from another transition record or not) and *applicable* (checks whether the use of transition modes and relation names in a transition record fits in with a database or not).

The constructor function *mk-Transition_record* for creating transition records and the selector functions *trm*, *rnm*, *del* and *ins* for selecting the components of transition records are implicitly defined.

The functions *undo* and *applicable* are used in the module **TRANSITION_LOG** to define functions on transition logs. The functions *weaken*, *weaker* and *mk-Transition_record* are used in the module **ACCESS_HANDLING** to define operations which make up an internal RDBMS interface.

TRANSITION_RECORD is
abstract
  X: **REL_NM**,
  Y: **ATTRIBUTE**,
  Z: **VALUE**
of

import
  X
  apply **RELATION** to **Y**, **Z**
  apply **DATABASE** to **X**, **Y**, **Z**
into

module
  types
  Transition_record ::
    trm: *Transition_mode* *rnm*: *Rel_nm* *del*: *Relation* *ins*: *Relation*
  where inv(tr) $\triangleq$

$$(del(tr) \neq empty \wedge ins(tr) \neq empty \Rightarrow attrs(del(tr)) = attrs(ins(tr))) \wedge$$
$$(trm(tr) = \mathsf{INIT} \Rightarrow del(tr) = empty \wedge ins(tr) = empty) \wedge$$
$$(trm(tr) = \mathsf{FINAL} \Rightarrow ins(tr) = empty)$$

$$Transition\_mode = \{\mathsf{NORMAL}, \mathsf{INIT}, \mathsf{FINAL}\}$$

functions

% non-constructor functions

$undo(db\colon Database, tr\colon Transition\_record) Database$
pre $applicable(tr, db)$
$\triangleq$ let
$mk\text{-}Transition\_record(m, nm, r', r'') \triangleq tr$
in
if $m = \mathsf{NORMAL}$
then
$update(db, nm, union(difference(relation(db, nm), r''), r'))$
else
if $m = \mathsf{INIT}$
then $destroy(db, nm)$
else $update(create(db, nm), nm, r')$

$weaken(tr\colon Transition\_record, r\colon Relation) Transition\_record$
pre $applicable(tr, r)$
$\triangleq$ $mk\text{-}Transition\_record(trm(tr), rnm(tr), r', r'')$
where
$r'\colon Relation \triangleq difference(del(tr), difference(del(tr), r)),$
$r''\colon Relation \triangleq difference(ins(tr), difference(r, del(tr)))$

$weaker(tr_1\colon Transition\_record, tr_2\colon Transition\_record)\mathbb{B}$
$\triangleq$ $\exists r \in Relation \cdot applicable(tr_2, r) \wedge tr_1 = weaken(tr_2, r)$

$applicable(tr\colon Transition\_record, db\colon Database)\mathbb{B}$
$\triangleq$ $(in\_use(db, rnm(tr)) \Rightarrow$
$applicable(tr, relation(db, rnm(tr)))) \wedge$
$(in\_use(db, rnm(tr)) \Leftrightarrow trm(tr) \neq \mathsf{FINAL})$

$applicable(tr\colon Transition\_record, r\colon Relation)\mathbb{B}$
$\triangleq$ $(r \neq empty \wedge del(tr) \neq empty \Rightarrow$
$attrs(r) = attrs(del(tr))) \wedge$
$(r \neq empty \wedge ins(tr) \neq empty \Rightarrow$
$attrs(r) = attrs(ins(tr)))$

end

In existing RDBMSs, e.g. in System R (Gray et al., 1981), a transition record is used to record the differences occurring when a tuple of some stored relation is changed. Because subsets of stored relations have been chosen as the unit of access, here a generalized concept of transition record is formalized.

13.7 Transition log

Transition logs are just sequences of transition records. A transition log is intended as a history of some transaction. It is meant to reflect the effects of all write actions on stored relations which have been performed on the request of the transaction, in the order in which these effects have taken place. The transition log of a transaction can provide all the details that are required to undo the cumulative effect of the transaction.

The module **TRANSITION_LOG** contains the definitions concerning transition logs. This module is based on definitions contained in the parametrized module **TRANSITION_RECORD**. So the appropriate application of this module is imported.

The principal function defined in this module is *undo*. It successively undoes, in reverse order, the effects of the changes made in a database which are reflected in the transition records of a transition log. For transition logs, the only constant is *empty*, the empty transition log. The following functions on transition logs are defined as well: *add* (appends a transition record to a transition log) and *applicable* (checks whether all transition records of a transition log fit in with a database or not).

All functions are used in the modules **LOG_TABLE** to define functions on log tables. The functions *add* and *applicable* are also used in the modules **AH_STATE** and **ACCESS_HANDLING** to define the states of an access handler and the operations which make up an internal RDBMS interface.

TRANSITION_LOG is
  abstract
    X: **REL_NM**,
    Y: **ATTRIBUTE**,
    Z: **VALUE**
  of

  import
    apply **TRANSITION_RECORD** to **X**, **Y**, **Z**
  into

  module
    types
    Transition_log = *Transition_record**

    functions
    % constructor functions
    empty() *Transition_log*
      $\triangleq$ []

$add(trlog\colon Transition\_log, tr\colon Transition\_record)\,Transition\_log$
$\triangleq$ $trlog \curvearrowright [tr]$

% non-constructor functions
$undo(db\colon Database, trlog\colon Transition\_log)\,Database$
pre $applicable(trlog, db)$
$\triangleq$ if len $trlog = 0$ then db else $undo(undo(db, \mathsf{tl}\ trlog), \mathsf{hd}\ trlog)$

$applicable(trlog\colon Transition\_log, db\colon Database)\mathbb{B}$
$\triangleq$ $\forall i \in \mathbb{N} \cdot 1 \leq i \wedge i \leq \mathsf{len}\ trlog \Rightarrow applicable(trlog(i), db)$

end

13.8 Log table

Log tables are just maps from transaction names to transition logs. The domain of a log table is called its transaction name set. A transaction name is in use by a log table if it is in the transaction name set of the log table. A log table is intended as a collection of transaction histories, one for each transaction from a collection of transactions whose actions are performed in an interleaved fashion. It is meant to reflect the effects of all write actions on stored relations which have been performed on the request of active transactions, in the order in which these effects have taken place and which are aggregated by the transactions. It can provide all the details that are required to abort any of the active transactions.

The module **LOG_TABLE** contains the definitions concerning log tables. This module is based on assumptions contained in the module **TRANS_NM** and definitions contained in the parametrized module **TRANSITION_LOG**. Therefore, **U**, which actualizes the assumptions, and the appropriate application of the module **TRANSITION_LOG** are imported.

The principal function defined in this module is *rollback*. It successively undoes, in reverse order, the effects of the changes made in a database which are reflected in the transition records of the transition log associated with a transaction name in a log table. For log tables, the only constant is *empty_logtbl*, the empty log table. The following functions on log tables are defined as well: *create* (adds a transition log for a new transaction to a log table; the new transition log is empty), *destroy* (removes the transition log of a transaction from a log table), *add* (adds a transition record to the transition log of a transaction in a log table), *in_use* (checks whether a transaction name is in use by a log table) and *log* (looks up the transition log of a transaction in a log table).

The functions defined in this module are used in the modules **AH_STATE** and **ACCESS_HANDLING** to define the states of an access handler and the operations which make up an internal RDBMS interface.

LOG_TABLE is
abstract
X: **REL_NM**,
Y: **ATTRIBUTE**,
Z: **VALUE**,
U: **TRANS_NM**
of

import
U
apply **TRANSITION_LOG** to **X**, **Y**, **Z**
into

module
types

$Log\_table = Trans\_nm \xrightarrow{m} Transition\_log$

functions

% constructor functions
$empty\_logtbl()Log\_table$
$\triangleq \{\}$

$create(logtbl\colon Log\_table, tnm\colon Trans\_nm)Log\_table$
pre $\neg in\_use(logtbl, tnm)$
$\triangleq$ $logtbl \cup \{tnm \mapsto empty\}$

$destroy(logtbl\colon Log\_table, tnm\colon Trans\_nm)Log\_table$
pre $in\_use(logtbl, tnm)$
$\triangleq$ $\{tnm\} \ntriangleleft logtbl$

$add(logtbl\colon Log\_table, tnm\colon Trans\_nm, tr\colon Transition\_record)$
Log_table
pre $in\_use(logtbl, tnm)$
$\triangleq$ $logtbl \dagger \{tnm \mapsto add(log(logtbl, tnm), tr)\}$

% non-constructor functions
$rollback(db\colon Database, tnm\colon Trans\_nm, logtbl\colon Log\_table)$
$Database$
pre $in\_use(logtbl, tnm) \wedge applicable(log(logtbl, tnm), db)$
$\triangleq$ $undo(db, log(logtbl, tnm))$

$in\_use(logtbl\colon Log\_table, tnm\colon Trans\_nm)\mathbb{B}$
$\triangleq$ $tnm \in \mathrm{dom}\ logtbl$

log(*logtbl*: *Log_table*, *tnm*: *Trans_nm*) *Transition_log*
  pre *in_use*(*logtbl*, *tnm*)
  $\triangleq$ *logtbl*(*tnm*)
end

The formalized concept of a log table is based on the informal concept of a system log described in (Gray, 1978). This formalized instance does not support crash recovery.

The next two sections present modules in which the states of an AH and the operations which interrogate and modify them are defined. The modules combined describe the state dependent aspects of the internal RDBMS interface.

13.9 AH state

The module **AH_STATE** contains the definitions concerning the changing state of an access handler. This module is based on definitions contained in the modules **DATABASE**, **DB_SCHEMA**, **ACCESS_TABLE** and **LOG_TABLE**. So the appropriate applications of these modules are imported.

No types and functions are defined. The concepts of a varying log table, a varying access table, a varying database schema and a varying database are made precise with the state variables *curr_logtable*, *curr_acctable*, *curr_dbschema* and *curr_database*. These state variables can be thought of as taking at any point in time the current log table value, the current access table value, etc. Together they constitute the changing state of an access handler.

The intention that all state variables are initially empty is made precise with an initial condition. The following intention is made precise with the state invariant:

1. the transaction name sets of the current log table and the current access table are the same,
2. all transition logs of the current log table are applicable to the current database,
3. the current access table is compatible with the current database schema,
4. the relation name set of the current database is included in the relation name set of the current database schema.

The following intention is made precise with the dynamic constraint: for each transaction that is active both before and after the last state change,

1. the collection of accesses granted to the transaction according to the current access table is preserved over the last change or has accesses added to it and

2. the transition log of the transaction in the current log table is preserved over the last change or has a transition record added to it.

The state variables *curr_logtable*, *curr_acctable*, *curr_dbschema* and *curr_database* are used in the module **ACCESS_HANDLING** to define operations which make up an internal RDBMS interface.

```
AH_STATE is
  abstract
    X: REL_NM,
    Y: ATTRIBUTE,
    Z: VALUE,
    U: TRANS_NM
  of

  abstract
    V: apply VAL_CONST to Z
  of

  import
    apply DATABASE to X, Y, Z
    apply DB_SCHEMA to X, Y, Z
    apply apply ACCESS_TABLE to X, Y, Z, U to V
    apply LOG_TABLE to X, Y, Z, U
  into

  module
    state
    curr_logtable: Log_table

    curr_acctable: Access_table

    curr_dbschema: Db_schema

    curr_database: Database

     inv  (∀tnm ∈ Trans_nm ·
             in_use(curr_logtable, tnm) ⇔
             in_use(curr_acctable, tnm))∧
          (∀tnm ∈ Trans_nm ·
             in_use(curr_logtable, tnm) ⇒
             applicable(log(curr_logtable, tnm), curr_database))∧
          compatible(curr_acctable, curr_dbschema)∧
          (∀rnm ∈ Rel_nm ·
             in_use(curr_database, rnm) ⇒
             in_use(curr_dbschema, rnm))
```

init $curr\_logtable = empty\_logtbl \wedge$
$curr\_acctable = empty\_acctbl \wedge$
$curr\_dbschema = empty\_schema \wedge$
$curr\_database = empty\_database$

dyn $\forall tnm \in Trans\_nm \cdot$
$\ominus in\_use(curr\_acctable, tnm) \wedge$
$in\_use(curr\_acctable, tnm) \Rightarrow$
$(\forall acc \in Access \cdot$
$\ominus granted(tnm, acc, curr\_acctable) \Rightarrow$
$granted(tnm, acc, curr\_acctable)) \wedge$
$(log(curr\_logtable, tnm) = log(\ominus curr\_logtable, tnm) \vee$
$\exists tr \in Transition\_record \cdot$
$log(curr\_logtable, tnm)$
$= add(log(\ominus curr\_logtable, tnm), tr))$

end

One of the design objectives for the temporal sublanguage of VVSL was the objective to obviate the need to introduce auxiliary state variables acting as history variables, control variables or scheduling variables. The state variables *curr_acctable* and *curr_logtable* resemble auxiliary ones acting as history variables. This is not a weakness of the temporal language. The necessity of auxiliary state variables has its origin in the fact that the operations which constitute the internal RDBMS interface support concurrent execution of higher-level operations. This brings about that the relevant history goes beyond the starting states of the individual operation executions.

13.10 Access handling

The module **ACCESS_HANDLING** contains the definitions concerning the operations which can be performed by an access handler. This module is based on assumptions contained in the module **REL_NM** and **TRANS_NM** as well as definitions contained in the parametrized modules **RELATION**, **SIMPLE_WFF** and **AH_STATE**. Therefore, **X** and **U**, which actualize the assumptions, and the appropriate applications of the above-mentioned parametrized modules are imported.

The states of the access handler, with the components *curr_logtable*, *curr_acctable*, *curr_dbschema* and *curr_database*, were already defined in the imported module **AH_STATE**. The operations defined in the current module are *START*, *COMMIT*, *ABORT* (for starting and stopping a transaction), *SELECT*, *INSERT*, *DELETE* (for access to a subset of one of the relations stored in the current database to read or to overwrite it), *CREATE* and *DESTROY* (for access to the current database to create a stored relation or to destroy it). Together they constitute an internal interface of a database management system. All operations interrogate and modify the current log table and the current access table, except the operation *SELECT* which never interrogates or modifies the current log table. The first three operations do not interrogate or modify other state variables, except *ABORT* which also interrogates and modifies the current database. The other ones interrogate the current database schema and the current database. They also modify the current database, except the operation *SELECT* which never modifies the current database. Only the first three operations are insensitive to interference by concurrently executed operations through shared state variables.

START adds an empty access record for a new transaction to the current access table, adds an empty transition log for it to the current log table and yields a fresh name for the transaction as a result. *COMMIT* removes the access record for a named transaction from the current access table and removes its transition log from the current log table. *ABORT* undoes the effects of all changes made by a named transaction on the current database, removes the access record for that transaction from the current access table and removes its transition log from the current log table.

Immediately before *SELECT* terminates, it selects the tuples of a named relation in the current database that have the property stated in a simple formula and yields the tuples obtained as a relation and GRANTED as status if the read access needed for this has been granted. Immediately before *INSERT* terminates, it adds all tuples determined by a simple formula (according to the current database schema) to a named relation in the current database, appends a transition record reflecting this to the transition log for the transaction concerned in the current log table and yields GRANTED as status if the write access needed for this has been granted. Immediately before *DELETE* terminates, it removes all tuples determined by a simple formula (according to the current database schema) from a named relation in the current database, appends a transition record reflecting this to the transition log for the transaction concerned in the current log table and yields GRANTED as status if the write access needed for this has been granted.

Immediately before *CREATE* terminates, it adds a new named relation to the current database, appends a transition record reflecting this to the transition log for the transaction concerned in the current log table and yields GRANTED as status if the create access needed for this has been granted. Immediately before *DESTROY* terminates, it removes a named relation from the current database, appends a transition record reflecting this to the transition log for the transaction concerned in the current log table and yields GRANTED as status if the destroy access needed for this has been granted.

The operations *SELECT*, *INSERT*, *DELETE*, *CREATE* and *DESTROY* are sensitive to interference and therefore they need additional explanation. During execution of each of these operations the following occurs:

1.(a) Eventually the access needed will not conflict with other granted and waiting accesses according to the current access table. The next state is the final state and is reached by an internal step which changes the current database and the current log table as described above (except for the operation *SELECT*) and also changes the current access table by adding the relevant access to the granted accesses of the transaction concerned. In this case, GRANTED will be the status.

(b) Until then all steps were external, except the initial step which only changes (if it is not also the final step) the current access table by adding the relevant access to the waiting accesses of the transaction concerned.

2. Initially the access needed is liable for deadlock according to the current access table and the initial state is also the final state (i.e. nothing is changed). In this case, REJECTED will be the status.

So each of these operations waits until the access needed does not conflict with other granted and waiting accesses or rejects it immediately. An access is rejected if it would otherwise be waiting for itself indirectly. In the inter-conditions given for the operations, the first disjunct corresponds to 1 and the second disjunct corresponds to 2. In the first disjunct, the second argument of the temporal operator $\mathcal{U}$ corresponds to (a) and the first one corresponds to (b).

Except for *CREATE*, the operations must be executed successfully if initially the transaction name concerned is in use, the relation name concerned is in use and the simple formula is well-formed (all if present). *CREATE* must be executed successfully if initially the transaction name concerned is in use and the relation name concerned is not in use.

The module **ACCESS_HANDLING** exports the access handling operations *START*, *COMMIT*, *ABORT*, *SELECT*, *INSERT*, *DELETE*, *CREATE* and *DESTROY*. All types and functions that were exported from the imported modules are hidden, except the types *Rel_nm*, *Trans_nm*, *Relation*, *Simple_wff* and *Status* which are implicitly exported. The state variables which were exported from the imported module **AH_STATE**, are also hidden.

```
ACCESS_HANDLING is
  abstract
    X: REL_NM,
    Y: ATTRIBUTE,
    Z: VALUE,
    U: TRANS_NM
  of
```

abstract
  V: apply **VAL_CONST** to **Z**
of

export
  $START\colon \Rightarrow Trans\_nm,$
  $COMMIT\colon Trans\_nm \Rightarrow,$
  $ABORT\colon Trans\_nm \Rightarrow,$
  $SELECT\colon$
    $Trans\_nm \times Rel\_nm \times Simple\_wff \Rightarrow Relation \times Status,$
  $INSERT\colon Trans\_nm \times Rel\_nm \times Simple\_wff \Rightarrow Status,$
  $DELETE\colon Trans\_nm \times Rel\_nm \times Simple\_wff \Rightarrow Status,$
  $CREATE\colon Trans\_nm \times Rel\_nm \Rightarrow Status,$
  $DESTROY\colon Trans\_nm \times Rel\_nm \Rightarrow Status$
from

import
  X
  U
  apply **RELATION** to **Y**, **Z**
  apply apply **SIMPLE_WFF** to **Y**, **Z** to **V**
  apply apply **AH_STATE** to **X**, **Y**, **Z**, **U** to **V**
into

module
  types
  $Status = \{\mathsf{GRANTED}, \mathsf{REJECTED}\}$

  operations
  $START()\, tnm\colon Trans\_nm$
   ext wr $curr\_acctable\colon Access\_table,$
        wr $curr\_logtable\colon Log\_table$
   post $\neg\, in\_use(\overleftarrow{curr\_acctable}, tnm) \wedge$
        $curr\_acctable = create(\overleftarrow{curr\_acctable}, tnm) \wedge$
        $curr\_logtable = create(\overleftarrow{curr\_logtable}, tnm)$

  $COMMIT(tnm\colon Trans\_nm)$
   ext wr $curr\_acctable\colon Access\_table,$
        wr $curr\_logtable\colon Log\_table$
   pre $in\_use(curr\_acctable, tnm)$
   post $curr\_acctable = destroy(\overleftarrow{curr\_acctable}, tnm) \wedge$
        $curr\_logtable = destroy(\overleftarrow{curr\_logtable}, tnm)$

$ABORT(tnm\colon Trans\_nm)$

ext wr $curr\_database\colon Database$,
wr $curr\_acctable\colon Access\_table$,
wr $curr\_logtable\colon Log\_table$

pre $in\_use(curr\_acctable, tnm)$

post $curr\_database = rollback(\overleftarrow{curr\_database}, tnm, curr\_logtable) \wedge$
$curr\_acctable = destroy(\overleftarrow{curr\_acctable}, tnm) \wedge$
$curr\_logtable = destroy(\overleftarrow{curr\_logtable}, tnm)$

$SELECT(\ tnm\colon Trans\_nm, rnm\colon Rel\_nm, sf\colon Simple\_wff)$
$r\colon Relation, st\colon Status$

ext rd $curr\_dbschema\colon Db\_schema$,
rd $curr\_database\colon Database$,
wr $curr\_acctable\colon Access\_table$

pre $in\text{-}use(curr\_acctable, tnm) \wedge in\_use(curr\_database, rnm) \wedge$
$is\_wf(sf, struct(curr\_dbschema, rnm))$

post let
$acc\colon Access \triangleq mk\text{-}Access(\mathsf{READ}, rnm, sf)$,
$r''\colon Relation \triangleq relation(curr\_database, rnm)$,
$tp\colon Tuple\_predicate \triangleq$
$predicate(sf, struct(curr\_dbschema, rnm))$
in
$(st = \mathsf{GRANTED} \;\Rightarrow\; r = selection(r'', tp)) \wedge$
$(st = \mathsf{GRANTED} \;\Leftrightarrow\; granted(tnm, acc, curr\_acctable))$

inter let
$acc\colon Access \triangleq mk\text{-}Access(\mathsf{READ}, rnm, sf)$
in
$((\neg \ominus \mathsf{true} \;\Rightarrow$
$\mathsf{is\text{-}I} \wedge$
$\bigcirc(\ curr\_acctable$
$= add\_to\_waits(\ominus curr\_acctable, tnm, acc))) \wedge$
$(\ominus \mathsf{true} \;\Rightarrow\; \mathsf{is\text{-}E}))\ \mathcal{U}$
$(\neg\ conflicts(tnm, acc, curr\_acctable, curr\_dbschema) \wedge \mathsf{is\text{-}I} \wedge$
$\bigcirc(\ curr\_acctable$
$= add\_to\_grants(\ominus curr\_acctable, tnm, acc) \wedge$
$st = \mathsf{GRANTED} \wedge \neg \bigcirc \mathsf{true})) \vee$
$(deadlock\_liable(tnm, acc, curr\_acctable, curr\_dbschema) \wedge$
$st = \mathsf{REJECTED} \wedge \neg \bigcirc \mathsf{true})$

$INSERT(tnm\colon Trans\_nm,\ rnm\colon Rel\_nm,\ sf\colon Simple\_wff)\,st\colon Status$

ext rd $curr\_dbschema\colon Db\_schema$,
wr $curr\_database\colon Database$,
wr $curr\_acctable\colon Access\_table$,
wr $curr\_logtable\colon Log\_table$

pre $in\text{-}use(curr\_acctable, tnm) \wedge in\_use(curr\_database, rnm) \wedge$
$is\_wf(sf, struct(curr\_dbschema, rnm))$

post let
$acc\colon Access \triangleq mk\text{-}Access(\mathsf{WRITE}, rnm, sf)$,
$r\colon Relation \triangleq tuples(curr\_dbschema, acc)$,
$r''\colon Relation \triangleq relation(curr\_database, rnm)$,
$tr\colon Transition\_record \triangleq$
$mk\_Transition\_record(\mathsf{NORMAL}, rnm, empty, r)$
in
$(st = \mathsf{GRANTED} \Rightarrow$
$(\forall t \in Tuple \cdot member(t, r) \Rightarrow member(t, r'')) \wedge$
$(\exists tr' \in Transition\_record \cdot$
$weaker(tr', tr) \wedge$
$log(curr\_logtable, tnm)$
$= add(log(\overleftarrow{curr\_logtable}, tnm), tr'))) \wedge$
$(st = \mathsf{GRANTED} \Leftrightarrow granted(tnm, acc, curr\_acctable))$

inter let
$acc\colon Access \triangleq mk\text{-}Access(\mathsf{WRITE}, rnm, sf)$
in
$((\neg \ominus \mathsf{true} \Rightarrow$
$\mathsf{is\text{-}I} \wedge$
$\bigcirc(\ curr\_database = \ominus curr\_database \wedge$
$curr\_logtable = \ominus curr\_logtable \wedge$
$curr\_acctable$
$= add\_to\_waits(\ominus curr\_acctable, tnm, acc))) \wedge$
$(\ominus \mathsf{true} \Rightarrow \mathsf{is\text{-}E}))\ \mathcal{U}$
$(\neg\, conflicts(tnm, acc, curr\_acctable, curr\_dbschema) \wedge \mathsf{is\text{-}I} \wedge$
let
$r\colon Relation \triangleq tuples(curr\_dbschema, acc)$,
$r'\colon Relation \triangleq relation(curr\_database, rnm)$,
$tr\colon Transition\_record \triangleq$
$mk\text{-}Transition\_record(\mathsf{NORMAL}, rnm, empty, r)$
in
$\bigcirc(\ curr\_database$
$= update(\ominus curr\_database, rnm, union(r', r)) \wedge$
$curr\_acctable$
$= add\_to\_grants(\ominus curr\_acctable, tnm, acc) \wedge$
$curr\_logtable$
$= add(\ominus curr\_logtable, tnm, weaken(tr, r')) \wedge$
$st = \mathsf{GRANTED} \wedge \neg \bigcirc \mathsf{true})) \vee$
$(deadlock\_liable(tnm, acc, curr\_acctable, curr\_dbschema) \wedge$
$st = \mathsf{REJECTED} \wedge \neg \bigcirc \mathsf{true})$

$DELETE(tnm{:}\ Trans\_nm, rnm{:}\ Rel\_nm, sf{:}\ Simple\_wff)st{:}\ Status$
ext rd $curr\_dbschema{:}\ Db\_schema,$
wr $curr\_database{:}\ Database,$
wr $curr\_acctable{:}\ Access\_table,$
wr $curr\_logtable{:}\ Log\_table$
pre $in\text{-}use(curr\_acctable, tnm) \wedge in\_use(curr\_database, rnm) \wedge$
$is\_wf(sf, struct(curr\_dbschema, rnm))$
post let
$acc{:}\ Access \triangleq mk\text{-}Access(\mathsf{WRITE}, rnm, sf),$
$r{:}\ Relation \triangleq tuples(curr\_dbschema, acc),$
$r''{:}\ Relation \triangleq relation(curr\_database, rnm),$
$tr{:}\ Transition\_record \triangleq$
$mk\_Transition\_record(\mathsf{NORMAL}, rnm, r, empty)$
in
$(st = \mathsf{GRANTED} \Rightarrow$
$(\forall t \in Tuple \cdot member(t, r) \Rightarrow \neg\, member(t, r'')) \wedge$
$(\exists tr' \in Transition\_record \cdot$
$weaker(tr', tr) \wedge$
$log(curr\_logtable, tnm)$
$= add(log(\overleftarrow{curr\_logtable}, tnm), tr'))) \wedge$
$(st = \mathsf{GRANTED} \Leftrightarrow granted(tnm, acc, curr\_acctable))$
inter let
$acc{:}\ Access \triangleq mk\text{-}Access(\mathsf{WRITE}, rnm, sf)$
in
$((\neg \ominus \mathsf{true} \Rightarrow$
$\mathsf{is\text{-}I} \wedge$
$\bigcirc(curr\_database = \ominus curr\_database \wedge$
$curr\_logtable = \ominus curr\_logtable \wedge$
$curr\_acctable$
$= add\_to\_waits(\ominus curr\_acctable, tnm, acc))) \wedge$
$(\ominus \mathsf{true} \Rightarrow \mathsf{is\text{-}E}))\ \mathcal{U}$
$(\neg\, conflicts(tnm, acc, curr\_acctable, curr\_dbschema) \wedge \mathsf{is\text{-}I} \wedge$
let
$r{:}\ Relation \triangleq tuples(curr\_dbschema, acc),$
$r'{:}\ Relation \triangleq relation(curr\_database, rnm),$
$tr{:}\ Transition\_record \triangleq$
$mk\text{-}Transition\_record(\mathsf{NORMAL}, rnm, r, empty)$
in
$\bigcirc(curr\_database$
$= update(\ominus curr\_database, rnm, difference(r', r)) \wedge$
$curr\_acctable$
$= add\_to\_grants(\ominus curr\_acctable, tnm, acc) \wedge$
$curr\_logtable$
$= add(\ominus curr\_logtable, tnm, weaken(tr, r')) \wedge$
$st = \mathsf{GRANTED} \wedge \neg \bigcirc \mathsf{true})) \vee$
$(deadlock\_liable(tnm, acc, curr\_acctable, curr\_dbschema) \wedge$
$st = \mathsf{REJECTED} \wedge \neg \bigcirc \mathsf{true})$

$$
\begin{array}{ll}
\multicolumn{2}{l}{CREATE(tnm\colon Trans\_nm,\ rnm\colon Rel\_nm)st\colon Status} \\
\mathsf{ext} & \mathsf{rd}\ curr\_dbschema\colon Db\_schema, \\
 & \mathsf{wr}\ curr\_database\colon Database, \\
 & \mathsf{wr}\ curr\_acctable\colon Access\_table, \\
 & \mathsf{wr}\ curr\_logtable\colon Log\_table \\
\mathsf{pre} & in\_use(curr\_acctable, tnm) \wedge \neg\, in\_use(curr\_database, rnm) \wedge \\
 & in\_use(curr\_dbschema, rnm) \\
\mathsf{post} & \mathsf{let} \\
 & acc\colon Access \triangleq mk\text{-}Access(\mathsf{CREATE}, rnm, mk\text{-}Bool\_lit(\mathsf{true})), \\
 & tr\colon Transition\_record \triangleq \\
 & \quad mk\_Transition\_record(\mathsf{INIT}, rnm, empty, empty) \\
 & \mathsf{in} \\
 & (st = \mathsf{GRANTED} \Rightarrow \\
 & \quad in\_use(curr\_database, rnm) \wedge \\
 & \quad relation(curr\_database, rnm) = empty \wedge \\
 & \quad log(curr\_logtable, tnm) = add(log(\overleftarrow{curr\_logtable}, tnm), tr)) \wedge \\
 & (st = \mathsf{GRANTED} \Leftrightarrow granted(tnm, acc, curr\_acctable)) \\
\mathsf{inter} & \mathsf{let} \\
 & acc\colon Access \triangleq mk\text{-}Access(\mathsf{CREATE}, rnm, mk\text{-}Bool\_lit(\mathsf{true})) \\
 & \mathsf{in} \\
 & ((\neg \ominus \mathsf{true} \Rightarrow \\
 & \quad \mathsf{is\text{-}I} \wedge \\
 & \quad \bigcirc(\ curr\_database = \ominus curr\_database \wedge \\
 & \qquad curr\_logtable = \ominus curr\_logtable \wedge \\
 & \qquad curr\_acctable \\
 & \qquad\quad = add\_to\_waits(\ominus curr\_acctable, tnm, acc))) \wedge \\
 & \quad (\ominus \mathsf{true} \Rightarrow \mathsf{is\text{-}E}))\ \mathcal{U} \\
 & (\neg\, conflicts(tnm, acc, curr\_acctable, curr\_dbschema) \wedge \mathsf{is\text{-}I} \wedge \\
 & \quad \mathsf{let} \\
 & \quad tr\colon Transition\_record \triangleq \\
 & \qquad mk\text{-}Transition\_record(\mathsf{INIT}, rnm, empty, empty) \\
 & \quad \mathsf{in} \\
 & \quad \bigcirc(\ curr\_database = create(\ominus curr\_database, rnm) \wedge \\
 & \qquad curr\_acctable \\
 & \qquad\quad = add\_to\_grants(\ominus curr\_acctable, tnm, acc) \wedge \\
 & \qquad curr\_logtable = add(\ominus curr\_logtable, tnm, tr) \wedge \\
 & \qquad st = \mathsf{GRANTED} \wedge \neg \bigcirc \mathsf{true})) \vee \\
 & (deadlock\_liable(tnm, acc, curr\_acctable, curr\_dbschema) \wedge \\
 & \quad st = \mathsf{REJECTED} \wedge \neg \bigcirc \mathsf{true})
\end{array}
$$

```
DESTROY(tnm: Trans_nm, rnm: Rel_nm)st: Status
 ext    rd curr_dbschema: Db_schema,
        wr curr_database: Database,
        wr curr_acctable: Access_table,
        wr curr_logtable: Log_table
 pre    in_use(curr_acctable, tnm) ∧ in_use(curr_database, rnm)
 post   let
        acc: Access ≜ mk-Access(DESTROY, rnm, mk-Bool_lit(true)),
        r: Relation ≜ tuples(curr_dbschema, acc),
        tr: Transition_record ≜
          mk_Transition_record(FINAL, rnm, r, empty)
        in
        (st = GRANTED ⇒
          (¬ in_use(curr_database, rnm))∧
          (∃tr′ ∈ Transition_record ·
             weaker(tr′, tr)∧
             log(curr_logtable, tnm)
               = add(log(↼curr_logtable, tnm), tr′)))∧
        (st = GRANTED ⇔ granted(tnm, acc, curr_acctable))
 inter  let
        acc: Access ≜ mk-Access(DESTROY, rnm, mk-Bool_lit(true))
        in
        ((¬ ⊖true ⇒
           is-I ∧
           ○( curr_database = ⊖curr_database∧
                curr_logtable = ⊖curr_logtable∧
                curr_acctable
                  = add_to_waits(⊖curr_acctable, tnm, acc)))∧
          (⊖true ⇒ is-E)) 𝒰
        (¬ conflicts(tnm, acc, curr_acctable, curr_dbschema) ∧ is-I ∧
          let
          r′: Relation ≜ relation(curr_database, rnm),
          tr′: Transition_record ≜
            mk-Transition_record(FINAL, rnm, r′, empty)
          in
          ○( curr_database = destroy(⊖curr_database, rnm)∧
               curr_acctable
                 = add_to_grants(⊖curr_acctable, tnm, acc)∧
               curr_logtable = add(⊖curr_logtable, tnm, tr′)∧
               st = GRANTED ∧ ¬ ○true)) ∨
        (deadlock_liable(tnm, acc, curr_acctable, curr_dbschema)∧
          st = REJECTED ∧ ¬ ○true)
end
```

The inter-conditions have a common pattern, which is also illustrated by the common explanation given above. This seems the usual experience. However, the common pattern(s) differ from system to system.

13.11 System

The former modules combined cover everything relevant to the internal RDBMS interface. Therefore, the system module contains no definitions. No new concepts are defined. Instead the relevant definitions from the previous modules are combined and it is specified what from the defined concepts constitutes the internal RDBMS interface by making only the names of these concepts visible.

The system module exports the constructor functions which are required for creating all simple formulae and the access handling operations. The state variables are not exported, since the idea is that interrogating or modifying them should only be done by means of the operations made available by the interface.

```
system is
  abstract
    X: REL_NM,
    Y: ATTRIBUTE,
    Z: VALUE,
    U: TRANS_NM
  of

  abstract
    V: apply VAL_CONST to Z
  of

  export
    mk-Bool_lit: 𝔹 → Bool_lit,
    mk-Eq: Attribute × Val_const → Eq,
    mk-Less: Attribute × Val_const → Less,
    mk-Negation: Simple_wff → Negation,
    mk-Disjunction: Simple_wff × Simple_wff → Disjunction,
    START: ⇒ Trans_nm,
    COMMIT: Trans_nm ⇒,
    ABORT: Trans_nm ⇒,
    SELECT:
      Trans_nm × Rel_nm × Simple_wff ⇒ Relation × Status,
    INSERT: Trans_nm × Rel_nm × Simple_wff ⇒ Status,
    DELETE: Trans_nm × Rel_nm × Simple_wff ⇒ Status,
    CREATE: Trans_nm × Rel_nm ⇒ Status,
    DESTROY: Trans_nm × Rel_nm ⇒ Status
  from
```

```
import
  X
  V
  apply RELATION to Y, Z
  apply apply SIMPLE_WFF to Y, Z to V
  apply apply ACCESS_HANDLING to X, Y, Z, U to V
into

module
end
```

A

Glossary of Mathematical Notation

The glossary of mathematical notation consists of two parts. Appendix A.1 provides a glossary of the general mathematical notation used in this book. This is a glossary of familiar notation of classical first-order logic (L) and general set theory. Appendix A.2 provides a glossary of special notation concerning the ingredients of the mathematical basis for the semantics of VVSL.

A.1 General mathematical notation

Naming conventions for meta-variables
x stands for a variable symbol of L
τ, τ' stand for terms of L
ψ, ψ' stand for formulae of L
$a, a', a_1, \ldots$ stand for terms denoting sets (regarded as elements)
$A, A', A_1, \ldots$ stand for terms denoting sets

$\tau = \tau'$	equality
$\neg\,\psi$	negation
$\psi \land \psi'$	conjunction
$\psi \lor \psi'$	disjunction
$\psi \;\Rightarrow\; \psi'$	logical implication
$\psi \;\Leftrightarrow\; \psi'$	logical equivalence
$\forall x\ (\psi)$	universal quantification
$\exists x\ (\psi)$	existential quantification

The logical connectives are given in decreasing order of priority.

$a \in A$	set membership
$A \subseteq A'$, $A' \supseteq A$	set inclusion
$\{a_1, \ldots, a_n\}$	set enumeration
$\{x \mid \psi\}$	set comprehension
$\{\}$	empty set
$\mathcal{P}(A)$	power set
$A \cup A'$	set union
$\bigcup A$	generalized set union
$A \cap A'$	set intersection
$\bigcap A$	generalized set intersection
$A - A'$	set difference
$\langle a_1, \ldots, a_n \rangle$	tuple
$A_1 \times \cdots \times A_n$	cartesian product
$\mathcal{N}$	natural numbers
$\mathrm{card}\, A$	cardinality
$P: A_1 \times \cdots \times A_n$	P is a relation on $A_1, \ldots, A_n$
$f: A \to A'$	f is a function from A to A'
$f(a)$	value of function
$f(A)$	image under function
$\langle A_i \rangle_{i \in I}$	indexed family
A^*	set of sequences
$\tau \ := \ \tau'$	definitional equality
$\psi \ :\Leftrightarrow \ \psi'$	definitional equivalence

A.2 Special mathematical notation

Naming conventions for meta-variables

x stands for a variable symbol of MPL_ω
S stands for a sort symbol of MPL_ω
t, t' stand for terms of MPL_ω
$A, A', A_1, \ldots$ stand for formulae of MPL_ω
u stands for a term of DA denoting a name
ρ, ρ' stand for terms of DA denoting renamings
Σ, Σ' stand for terms of DA denoting signatures
X, X' stand for terms of DA denoting descriptions
P stands for a term of DA denoting a parameter
z stands for a lambda variable symbol of $\lambda\pi$-calculus
L, M stand for lambda terms of $\lambda\pi$-calculus

MPL_ω

$t = t'$	equality
$t{\downarrow}$	definedness
$\top$	truth
$\bot$	falsity
$\neg A$	negation
$A \wedge A'$	conjunction
$A \vee A'$	disjunction
$A \rightarrow A'$	logical implication
$A \leftrightarrow A'$	logical equivalence
$\bigwedge_n A_n$	countably infinite conjunction
$\bigvee_n A_n$	countably infinite disjunction
$\forall x{:}\, S\ (A)$	universal quantification
$\exists x{:}\, S\ (A)$	existential quantification

The logical connectives are given in decreasing order of priority.

Description Algebra

$\rho \bullet u$	name renaming
$\rho \circ \rho'$	renaming composition
$\rho \bullet \Sigma$	signature renaming
$\Sigma + \Sigma'$	signature union
$\Sigma \ \Box\ \Sigma'$	signature intersection
$u \ \Delta\ \Sigma$	signature deletion
$\mathbf{\Sigma}(X)$	taking the signature
$\rho \bullet X$	renaming
$X + X'$	importing
$\Sigma \ \Box\ X$	exporting
$\mu(X)$	unifying
$\delta(P)$	parameter embedding
$\alpha(P, X, X')$	origin substitution
$\rho \bullet P$	parameter renaming

$\lambda\pi$-calculus

$(L\, M)$	application
$(\lambda z \sqsubseteq L.M)$	lambda abstraction with parameter restriction

B

Glossary of VVSL Notation

The glossary of VVSL notation consists of three parts. Appendix B.1 provides a glossary of the original VDM notation incorporated in VVSL. Appendices B.2 and B.3 provide a glossary of the additional notation for specifying interfering operations and a glossary of the additional notation for modular structuring of specifications, respectively.

Naming conventions for meta-variables
$x, x', x_1, x'_1, \ldots$ stand for value names
$t, t', \ldots, t_1, t'_1, \ldots, \ldots$ stand for type names
$e, e', e_1, e'_1, \ldots$ stand for expressions
E, E' stand for logical expressions
i, i' stand for arithmetic expressions
$\mathcal{L}, \mathcal{L}'$ stand for expressions of sequence type
$\mathcal{S}, \mathcal{S}'$ stand for expressions of set type
$\mathcal{M}, \mathcal{M}'$ stand for expressions of map type
$\mathcal{C}$ stands for an expression of composite type
$a_1, \ldots$ stand for atom names
c stands for a (composite) type constructor name
T stands for a type
$v, v', v_1, v'_1, \ldots$ stand for state variable names
$f, s_1, \ldots$ stand for function names
P stands for a truth-valued function name
op stands for an operation name
$\tau, \tau', \tau_1, \ldots$ stand for temporal terms
φ, φ' stand for temporal formulae
$m, m_1, \ldots$ stand for module names
$M, M_1, \ldots$ stand for modules
$S, S_1, \ldots$ stand for signatures
R stands for a renaming
$u, u_1, \ldots$ stand for typed names

mk-c is the function name that is obtained by prefixing the string *mk-* to the type constructor name denoted by the meta-variable c.

B.1 Flat VVSL, VDM notation

General

$f(e_1, \ldots, e_n)$	function application
$\mathsf{if}\ E\ \mathsf{then}\ e\ \mathsf{else}\ e'$	conditional
$\mathsf{let}\ x_1 \colon t_1 \triangleq e_1, \ldots, x_n \colon t_n \triangleq e_n\ \mathsf{in}\ e$	local definition
$\mathsf{let}\ x_1 \colon t_1, \ldots, x_n \colon t_n\ \mathsf{be\ s.t.}\ E\ \mathsf{in}\ e$	choice

Logic

$\mathbb{B}$	truth values
$\neg E$	negation
$E \wedge E'$	conjunction
$E \vee E'$	disjunction
$E \Rightarrow E'$	implication
$E \Leftrightarrow E'$	equivalence
$\forall x \in t \cdot E$	universal quantification
$\exists x \in t \cdot E$	existential quantification
$\exists ! x \in t \cdot E$	unique existential quantification
$e = e'$	equality

The logical connectives are given in decreasing order of priority. The scope of the quantifiers extends as far as possible to the right.

Arithmetic

$\mathbb{N}$	natural numbers
$\mathbb{Z}$	integers
$\mathbb{Q}$	rational numbers
$i + i'$	addition
$i - i'$	subtraction
$i * i'$	multiplication
$i \,/\, i'$	division
$\vdots$	$\vdots$
$i < i'$	less-than comparison

Atoms

$\{ a_1, \ldots, a_n \}$	enumerated type
a_i	atom

Sequences

t^*	sequence type construction
$[\,]$	empty sequence
$[e_1, \ldots, e_n]$	sequence enumeration
$\mathsf{hd}\,\mathcal{L}$	sequence head
$\mathsf{tl}\,\mathcal{L}$	sequence tail
$\mathcal{L}(i)$	sequence indexing
$\mathsf{len}\,\mathcal{L}$	length of sequence
$\mathcal{L} \frown \mathcal{L}'$	concatenation
$\mathsf{conc}\,\mathcal{L}$	distributed concatenation

Sets

t-set	set type construction
$\{\,\}$	empty set
$\{e_1, \ldots, e_n\}$	set enumeration
$\{e \mid x_1 \in t_1, \ldots, x_n \in t_n \,;\, E\}$	set comprehension
$\{i \,..\, i'\}$	integer range
$e \in \mathcal{S}$	set membership
$\mathcal{S} \subseteq \mathcal{S}'$	set inclusion
$\mathsf{card}\,\mathcal{S}$	cardinality of set
$\mathcal{S} \cup \mathcal{S}'$	set union
$\mathcal{S} \cap \mathcal{S}'$	set intersection
$\mathcal{S} - \mathcal{S}'$	set difference
$\bigcup \mathcal{S}$	distributed union

Maps

$t \xrightarrow{m} t'$	map type construction
$t \xleftrightarrow{m} t'$	one-one map type construction
$\{\,\}$	empty map
$\{e_1 \mapsto e'_1, \ldots, e_n \mapsto e'_n\}$	map enumeration
$\{e \mapsto e' \mid x_1 \in t_1, \ldots, x_n \in t_n \,;\, E\}$	map comprehension
$\mathsf{dom}\,\mathcal{M}$	domain of map
$\mathsf{rng}\,\mathcal{M}$	range of map
$\mathcal{M}(e)$	map application
$\mathcal{M} \dagger \mathcal{M}'$	map overwrite
$\mathcal{M} \cup \mathcal{M}'$	map merge
$\mathcal{S} \lhd \mathcal{M}$	domain restriction
$\mathcal{S} \mathrel{\lhd\!\!\!-} \mathcal{M}$	domain deletion

Composite values

compose c of $s_1\colon t_1 \ \ldots \ s_n\colon t_n$	composite type construction
$mk\text{-}c(e_1,\ldots,e_n)$	composite value construction
$s_i(\mathcal{C})$	component selection
let $mk\text{-}c(x_1,\ldots,x_n) \triangleq \mathcal{C}$ in e	local definition & decomposition
cases e of $mk\text{-}t_1(x_{1_1},\ldots,x_{1_{m_1}}) \rightarrow e_1$ $\vdots$ $mk\text{-}t_n(x_{n_1},\ldots,x_{n_{m_n}}) \rightarrow e_n$ end	case distinction & decomposition

Definitions

$t = T$ where inv$(x) \triangleq E$	type definition (subtype)
$t :: s_1\colon t_1 \ \ldots \ s_n\colon t_n$ where inv$(x) \triangleq E$	type definition (subtype of composite type)
$t = t_1 \mid \cdots \mid t_n$	type definition (union)
$t = [t_1 \mid \cdots \mid t_n]$	type definition (union with nil)
$f(x_1\colon t_1,\ldots,x_n\colon t_n)\ t_{n+1}$ pre E $\triangleq e$	function definition (explicit)
$f(x_1\colon t_1,\ldots,x_n\colon t_n)\ x_{n+1}\colon t_{n+1}$ pre E post E'	function definition (implicit)
$v\colon t$	state variable definition
$op(x_1\colon t_1,\ldots,x_n\colon t_n)\ y_1\colon t'_1,\ldots,y_m\colon t'_m$ ext rd $v_1\colon t''_1,\ldots,$ rd $v_k\colon t''_k,$ wr $v'_1\colon t'''_1,\ldots,$ wr $v'_l\colon t'''_l$ pre E post E' inter φ	operation definition (absent for atomic operations)

v	current contents (in all conditions of operation def's)
$\overleftarrow{v}$	old contents (in post-conditions of operation def's only)

B.2 Flat VVSL, temporal logic notation

Temporal terms

$f(\tau_1, \ldots, \tau_n)$	temporal function application
$\bigcirc \tau$	next value
$\ominus \tau$	previous value

Temporal formulae

is-I	internal transition proposition
is-E	external transition proposition
$P(\tau_1, \ldots, \tau_n)$	temporal predicate application
$\varphi \mathcal{C} \varphi'$	chop
$\bigcirc \varphi$	next
$\square \varphi$	henceforth
$\diamond \varphi$	eventually
$\varphi \mathcal{U} \varphi'$	until
$\ominus \varphi$	previous
$\boxminus \varphi$	always in the past
$\diamondminus \varphi$	sometime in the past
$\varphi \mathcal{S} \varphi'$	since
$\tau = \tau'$	equality
let $x_1 \colon t_1 \triangleq \tau_1, \ldots, x_n \colon t_n \triangleq \tau_n$ in φ	local definition

B.3 Structuring sublanguage

Modules

module $\mathcal{T}\ \mathcal{V}\ \mathcal{F}\ \mathcal{O}$ end	basic module *
import $M_1 \ldots M_n$ into M	import
export S from M	export
rename R in M	rename
abstract $m_1 \colon M_1, \ldots, m_n \colon M_n$ of M	module abstraction
apply M to $M_1, \ldots, M_n$	module application
let $m_1 \triangleq M_1, \ldots, m_n \triangleq M_n$ in M	local module definition

* $\mathcal{T}$, $\mathcal{V}$, $\mathcal{F}$ and $\mathcal{O}$ stand for the collections of type definitions, state variable definitions (possibly with associated state invariant, initial condition, and dynamic constraint), function definitions and operation definitions, respectively.

Signatures

$u_1, \ldots, u_n$	signature enumeration
add S_1 to S_2	signature union
signature M	module signature

Renamings

$u_1 \mapsto i_1, \ldots, u_n \mapsto i_n$	renaming †

Typed names

t	typed type name
$v\colon t$	typed state variable name
$f\colon t_1 \times \cdots \times t_n \rightarrow t_{n+1}$	typed function name
$op\colon t_1 \times \cdots \times t_n \Rightarrow t'_1 \times \cdots \times t'_m$	typed operation name

Specification document

component m_1 is $M_1, \ldots, m_n$ is M_n system is M	specification document

† Here, $i_1, \ldots, i_n$ stand for identifiers.

C

Summary of Notation for Semantics, etc.

The summary of the notation used in this book for the description of the well-formedness, syntactic properties and meaning of constructs in VVSL consists of three parts. Appendix C.1 explains the notation used when applying well-formedness predicates, semantic functions, etc. A summary of the notation connected with context dependent aspects of well-formedness and meaning is given in Appendix C.2 and a summary of the notation connected with MPL_ω, DA and $\lambda\pi$-calculus is given in Appendix C.3.

C.1 Semantic functions, etc.

The notation used when applying well-formedness predicates, semantic functions, etc. is explained below. The notation concerned is introduced in Sections 5.5 to 5.9 (flat VVSL) and 8.4 and 8.5 (structuring language).

Flat VVSL

Basic modules

'B is well-formed in N' indicates that the basic module B is well-formed in a context with names and subtype declarations as given by N;

$\{\!\![B]\!\!\}$ is the set of all names and subtype declarations introduced by the definitions of the basic module B;

$\{\!\![B]\!\!\}_{\mathsf{free}}$ is the set of all free names introduced by the definitions of the basic module B;

$[\![B]\!]^C$ is the set of formulae corresponding to the basic module B in a context with symbols as given by C.

The definition sublanguage

'D is well-formed in N' indicates that the definition D is well-formed in a context with names and subtype declarations as given by N;

$\{\![D]\!\}$ is the set of all names and subtype declarations introduced by the definition D;

$[\![D]\!]^C$ is the set of formulae corresponding to the definition D in a context with symbols as given by C.

The type sublanguage

'T is well-formed in N' indicates that the type T is well-formed in a context with names and subtype declarations as given by N;

$\{\![T]\!\}$ is the set of all names introduced by the type T;

$[\![T]\!]^C$ is the set of formulae corresponding to the type T in a context with symbols as given by C.

The expression sublanguage

'e (or E) is well-formed in $\langle N, k\rangle$' indicates that the expression e (or the logical expression E) is well-formed in a context with names and subtype declarations as given by N and k ($k \in \{0, 1, 2\}$) states to refer to;

'$N \models_{\mathrm{m}} e \mathrel{⨾} T$' indicates that, in the name context N, e has minimal type T;

$[\![e]\!]^C_{\vec{s},y}$ (or $[\![E]\!]^C_{\vec{s},y}$) is a formula expressing that, in a context with symbols as given by C, the evaluation of the expression e (or the logical expression E) in state(s) $\vec{s}$ yields value (or truth value) y ($\vec{s} = \langle s_1, \ldots, s_n\rangle$, with $n \in \{0, 1, 2\}$).

The temporal formula sublanguage

'φ (or τ) is well-formed in N' indicates that the temporal formula φ (or the temporal term τ) is well-formed in a context with names and subtype declarations as given by N;

'$N \models_{\mathrm{m}} \tau \mathrel{⨾} T$' indicates that, in the name context N, τ has minimal type T;

$[\![\varphi]\!]^C_{c,k,y}$ (or $[\![\tau]\!]^C_{c,k,y}$) is a formula expressing that, in a context with symbols as given by C, the evaluation of the temporal formula φ (or the temporal term τ) at point k in computation c yields value y.

Structuring language

Specification document

'Z is well-formed' indicates that the specification document Z is well-formed;

$[\![Z]\!]$ is a description term representing the meaning of the specification document Z.

The module sublanguage

'M is well-formed in $\langle N, \Delta\rangle$' indicates that the module M is well-formed in a context with names and subtype declarations as given by N and lambda variables as given by Δ;

'R is well-formed' indicates that the renaming R is well-formed;

'S is well-formed in Δ' indicates that the signature S is well-formed in a context with lambda variables as given by Δ;

$\langle\!|M|\!\rangle_\Delta$ is a signature term representing the externally visible signature of the module M in a context with lambda variables as given by Δ;

$\langle\!|R|\!\rangle$ is a signature term representing the renaming R;

$\langle\!|S|\!\rangle_\Delta$ is a signature term representing the signature S in a context with lambda variables as given by Δ;

$[\![M]\!]^C_\Gamma$ is a description term representing the meaning of the module M in a context with symbols as given by C and lambda variables (with associated description terms) as given by Γ;

$[\![R]\!]$ is a description term representing the meaning of the renaming R;

$[\![S]\!]_\Gamma$ is a description term representing the meaning of the signature S in a context with lambda variables (with associated description terms) as given by Γ.

C.2 Contexts, typing, etc.

A summary of the notation connected with context dependent aspects of well-formedness and meaning is given below. The notation concerned is introduced in Sections 5.1 (name and symbol contexts), 5.2 (contexts and typing) and 8.1 (signature and description contexts).

Name and symbol contexts

$\mathit{symbols}(C)$ is the set of all symbols in the symbol context C;

$\mathit{sdcls}(C)$ is the set of all subtype declarations in the symbol context C;

$\overline{C}$ is the name context obtained from the symbol context C by forgetting about origins;

$\mathit{names}(N)$ is the set of all names in the name context N;

$\mathit{sdcls}(N)$ is the set of all subtype declarations in the name context N;

[type T] is the name (equivalence class) of the symbol corresponding to the type T;

[func $f\colon T_1 \times \cdots \times T_n \rightarrow T$] is the name (equivalence class) of the symbol corresponding to the identifier f if it is meant to refer to a function with argument types $T_1, \ldots, T_n$ and result type T;

[var v: T] is the name (equivalence class) of the symbol corresponding to the identifier v if it is meant to refer to a state variable of type T;

[op op: $T_1 \times \cdots \times T_n \Rightarrow T'_1 \times \cdots \times T'_m$] is the name (equivalence class) of the symbol corresponding to the identifier op if it is meant to refer to an operation with argument types $T_1, \ldots, T_n$ and result types $T'_1, \ldots, T'_m$;

[val x: T] is the name (equivalence class) of the symbol corresponding to the identifier x if it is meant to refer to a value of type T;

$[T \leq T']$ indicates that the type T is defined as a subtype of the type T';

$nonvars(N)$ is the name context N without names for state variables;

'i is defined as a ... name in N' indicates that the identifier i can be used to refer to a ... in the context with names as given by N;

$T_1 \leq^N T_2$ indicates that T_1 is a subtype of T_2 in the context with subtype declarations as given by N;

t^C (or T^C) is the symbol of symbol type sort corresponding to the type name t (or the type T) in a context with symbols as given by C;

$f^C_{T_1 \times \cdots \times T_n \to T}$ is the symbol of symbol type $\langle \mathsf{func}, T_1^C, \ldots, T_n^C, T^C \rangle$ corresponding to the function name f in a context with symbols as given by C;

v^C_T is the symbol of symbol type $\langle \mathsf{func}, \mathsf{State}, T^C \rangle$ corresponding to the state variable name v in a context with symbols as given by C;

$op^C_{T_1 \times \cdots \times T_n \Rightarrow T'_1 \times \cdots \times T'_m}$ is the symbol of symbol type $\langle \mathsf{pred}, T_1^C, \ldots, T_n^C, \mathsf{Comp}, T_1'^C, \ldots, T_m'^C \rangle$ corresponding to the operation name op in a context with symbols as given by C;

x^C_T is the symbol of symbol type $\langle \mathsf{obj}, T^C \rangle$ corresponding to the value name x in a context with symbols as given by C;

$cnv^C_{S_1 \to S_2}(t)$ is the conversion of the term t from sort S_1 to sort S_2 in a context with subtype declarations as given by C;

$cnvax^C$ is the formula characterizing type conversions in a context with subtype declarations as given by C.

Contexts and typing

$lub^N(\{T_1, \ldots, T_n\}, T)$ indicates that T is the least type having $T_1, \ldots, T_n$ as subtypes in a context with subtype declarations as given by N;

$lower^N(T)$ is the least subtype of the type T that is comparable with all subtypes of T in a context with subtype declarations as given by N;

$raise^N(T)$ is the greatest type with T as subtype that is comparable with all types with T as subtype in a context with subtype declarations as given by N;

mtyping$^N(x, T)$ (or *mtyping*$^N(v, T)$) indicates that, in a context with names and subtype declarations as given by N, T is the minimal type for the value name x (or state variable name v);

ftypes$^N(f, \langle T_1, \ldots, T_n\rangle, \langle T'_1, \ldots, T'_n\rangle)$ indicates that, in a context with names and subtype declarations as given by N, $T'_1, \ldots, T'_n$ are the expected types of the arguments of the function corresponding to the function name f that fits minimal types $T_1, \ldots, T_n$ for the argument expressions;

mtyping$^N(f, \langle T_1, \ldots, T_n\rangle, T)$ indicates that, in a context with names and subtype declarations as given by N, T is the minimal type of application expressions of the form $f(e_1, \ldots, e_n)$ where the argument expressions $e_1, \ldots, e_n$ have minimal types $T_1, \ldots, T_n$;

'e is well-typed in N' indicates that the expression e has a minimal type in a context with names and subtype declarations as given by N;

'e_1 and e_2 are type compatible in N' indicates that, in a context with names and subtype declarations as given by N, the minimal types of the expressions e_1 and e_2 have a least upper bound;

'the minimal type of e in N' is the minimal type of e in a context with names and subtype declarations as given by N.

Signature and description contexts

$\overline{\Gamma}$ is the signature context corresponding to the description context Γ;

'm is visible in Δ' indicates that there is a lambda variable symbol corresponding to the module name m in the signature context Δ;

m^Δ (or m^Γ) is the lambda variable symbol corresponding to the module name m in a signature (or description) context with lambda variables as given by Δ (or Γ);

ncxt$^\Delta(\Sigma)$ is the name context corresponding to the module name signature that is the best statically determinable approximation of the module name signature represented by signature term Σ, given the signature context Δ;

atdefs(B) is the name context corresponding to the atom names and nil's introduced in the basic module B;

imp(B) is the name context corresponding to the names used but not introduced in basic module B;

extsig(C) is the externally visible signature corresponding to a context where we have symbols as given by C;

intsig(C) is the internal signature corresponding to a context where we have symbols as given by C;

des(C) is the module description corresponding to the symbol context C;

$par(C)$ is the module parameter corresponding to the parameter context C;

$name(u)$ is the name from MNam corresponding to the typed (VVSL) name u.

C.3 Basis for the semantics

A summary of the notation connected with MPL_ω, DA and $\lambda\pi$-calculus is given below. The notation concerned is introduced in Sections 3.3, 4.2 and 4.5 (MPL_ω), 6.2 and 6.3 (DA), 6.10 and 7.3 ($\lambda\pi$-calculus).

MPL_ω

$sort(t)$ is the sort of the term t;

$\boldsymbol{\mu}(\Gamma)$ is the set of formulae obtained by replacing the set of all simultaneous inductive definition rules contained in Γ by the corresponding set of formulae;

Compax is a formula characterizing computations;

Varmod(v) is a formula expressing that state variable v can only be modified by operations with a modification right for v;

Modcomp(R, W, c) is a formula expressing that c is a computation of an operation which interrogates the state variables $R \cup W$, but with modification rights for the state variables W only;

$\mathrm{Prefix}_k(c, c')$ is a formula expressing that the computation c' is the prefix of the computation c ending with the $(k+1)$-th state of c;

$\mathrm{Suffix}_k(c, c')$ is a formula expressing that the computation c' is the suffix of the computation c starting at the $(k+1)$-th state of c;

$axioms(S)$ is the set of defining formulae of all symbols associated with the basic or constructed type corresponding to the type symbol S.

DA

$\iota(w)$, $\omega(w)$ and $\tau(w)$ are the identifier, origin and symbol type, respectively, of symbol w;

$\overline{w}$ is the name (equivalence class) with representative w;

$\pi_\omega(W)$ is the origin partition indicating that the origins of the symbols in W with the same name are considered equal;

Σ_X is the externally visible signature of description X;

$\lambda\pi$-calculus

ltype(L) is the type of the lambda term L;

m^τ is the lambda variable symbol of type τ with module name m.

D

Basic and Constructed Types

The types of VVSL correspond to sort symbols of MPL_ω. In Section 4.5 it was explained that there are additional symbols associated with basic and constructed types that have identifiers that are available to the specifier, either directly as a pre-defined name or indirectly by a type. In this appendix, the available symbols associated with basic and constructed types and the defining axioms of all symbols associated with these types are defined. *asymbols*(S) is the set of all available symbols associated with the basic or constructed type corresponding to the type symbol S and *axioms*(S) is the set of defining axioms for all symbols associated with that type.

We use the notations $\underline{\mathrm{B}}$, $\underline{\mathrm{N}}$, $\underline{\mathrm{Z}}$, $\underline{\mathrm{Q}}$, $\underline{\mathrm{E}}(A)$ (for any $A \subseteq \mathsf{UIdent}$ and finite), $\underline{\mathrm{L}}(S_1)$, $\underline{\mathrm{F}}(S_1)$, $\underline{\mathrm{M}}(S_1, S_2)$ and $\underline{\mathrm{C}}_c(S_1, \ldots, S_n)$ (for any $c \in \mathsf{UIdent}$), where $S_1, \ldots, S_n$ are type symbols, to denote type symbols for basic and constructed types. It is assumed that the denoted type symbols are such that for all $\beta, \beta' \in \{\underline{\mathrm{B}}, \underline{\mathrm{N}}, \underline{\mathrm{Z}}, \underline{\mathrm{Q}}\}$:

$$\iota(\beta) \in \mathsf{PIdent}, \omega(\beta) = \langle\rangle, \beta \equiv \beta' \Leftrightarrow \beta = \beta',$$

for all $A \subseteq \mathsf{UIdent}$ and finite:

$$\iota(\underline{\mathrm{E}}(A)) \in \mathsf{CIdent}, \omega(\underline{\mathrm{E}}(A)) = \langle\rangle, \underline{\mathrm{E}}(A) \equiv \underline{\mathrm{E}}(A') \Leftrightarrow A = A',$$

for all $\gamma, \gamma' \in \{\mathbf{L}, \mathbf{F}, \mathbf{M}\} \cup \{\mathbf{C}_c \mid c \in \mathsf{UIdent}\}$:

$$\iota(\gamma(S_1, \ldots, S_n)) \in \mathsf{CIdent}, \omega(\gamma(S_1, \ldots, S_n)) = \langle \omega(S_1), \ldots, \omega(S_n) \rangle,$$
$$\gamma(S_1, \ldots, S_n) \equiv \gamma'(S'_1, \ldots, S'_{n'}) \Leftrightarrow \gamma = \gamma' \wedge n = n' \wedge \bigwedge_{k=1}^{n} (S_k \equiv S'_k).$$

Furthermore, we use the notation f^S (for any a sequence of characters f), where S is a type symbol, to denote function symbols associated with basic or constructed types. It is assumed that the denoted function symbols are such that

$$\iota(f^S) \in \mathsf{PIdent}, \omega(f^S) = \omega(S), f^S \equiv f'^{S'} \Leftrightarrow f = f' \wedge S \equiv S'.$$

In the defining axioms of the symbols concerned, the superscripts are dropped when this causes no ambiguity.

The sequences of characters are sometimes of the form $\sigma_0 \bullet \sigma_1 \cdots \sigma_{n-1} \bullet \sigma_n$, where each σ_i is a sequence of characters not containing $\bullet$. In such cases, we write in the defining axioms $\sigma_0\, t_1\, \sigma_1 \cdots \sigma_{n-1}\, t_n\, \sigma_n$, where each t_i is a term of MPL_ω, instead of $\sigma_0 \bullet \sigma_1 \cdots \sigma_{n-1} \bullet \sigma_n(t_1, \ldots, t_n)$.

In the case of unary function symbols and binary function symbols, prefix notation and infix notation, respectively, are freely used.

The above-mentioned notations are used in Chapter 5 as well to denote the symbols concerned.

D.1 Boolean type

Symbols:

$asymbols(\underline{\mathrm{B}}) := \{\underline{\mathrm{B}}, tt, ff\}$.

Axioms:

$axioms(\underline{\mathrm{B}}) := \{\varphi_0, \ldots, \varphi_3\}$,

where:

$\varphi_0 = tt\!\downarrow \wedge\, ff\!\downarrow$,

$\varphi_1 = gen \overset{\mathrm{I}}{:=} gen(tt) \wedge gen(ff)$,

$\varphi_2 = \forall y\colon \underline{\mathrm{B}}(gen(y))$,

$\varphi_3 = tt \neq ff$,

and

y is a value symbol such that $\tau(y) = \langle \mathsf{obj}, \underline{\mathrm{B}} \rangle$.

Intuition:

The type symbol $\underline{\mathrm{B}}$ denotes a domain of exactly two elements: the boolean values ('true' and 'false'). One of these elements is denoted by the function symbol tt and the other is denoted by the function symbol ff.

D.2 Natural type

Symbols:

$asymbols(\underline{\mathrm{N}}) :=$
$asymbols(\underline{\mathrm{B}}) \cup$
$\{\underline{\mathrm{N}}, 0^{\underline{\mathrm{N}}}, succ^{\underline{\mathrm{N}}}, pred^{\underline{\mathrm{N}}}, +^{\underline{\mathrm{N}}}, -^{\underline{\mathrm{N}}}, *^{\underline{\mathrm{N}}}, /^{\underline{\mathrm{N}}}, \bullet\bullet^{\underline{\mathrm{N}}}, <^{\underline{\mathrm{N}}}, \leq^{\underline{\mathrm{N}}}, >^{\underline{\mathrm{N}}}, \geq^{\underline{\mathrm{N}}}\}$.

Axioms:

$axioms(\underline{\mathrm{N}}) := axioms(\underline{\mathrm{B}}) \cup \{\varphi_0, \ldots, \varphi_{13}\}$,

where:

$\varphi_0 = 0\!\downarrow \wedge\, \forall y_1\colon \underline{\mathrm{N}}(succ(y_1)\!\downarrow)$

$$
\begin{aligned}
\varphi_1 = \;& gen :\stackrel{\mathrm{I}}{=} gen(0) \wedge \forall y_1 : \underline{\mathrm{N}}(gen(y_1) \rightarrow gen(succ(y_1))),\\
\varphi_2 = \;& \forall y_1 : \underline{\mathrm{N}}(gen(y_1)),\\
\varphi_3 = \;& \forall y_1 : \underline{\mathrm{N}}(succ(y_1) \neq 0) \wedge\\
& \forall y_1 : \underline{\mathrm{N}}, y_2 : \underline{\mathrm{N}}(succ(y_1) = succ(y_2) \rightarrow y_1 = y_2),\\
\varphi_4 = \;& pred :\stackrel{\mathrm{I}}{=} \forall y_1 : \underline{\mathrm{N}}(pred(succ(y_1)) = y_1),\\
\varphi_5 = \;& + :\stackrel{\mathrm{I}}{=} \forall y_1 : \underline{\mathrm{N}}, y_2 : \underline{\mathrm{N}}, y_3 : \underline{\mathrm{N}}\\
& \quad (y_1 + 0 = y_1 \wedge\\
& \quad\; (y_1 + y_2 = y_3 \rightarrow y_1 + succ(y_2) = succ(y_3))),\\
\varphi_6 = \;& - :\stackrel{\mathrm{I}}{=} \forall y_1 : \underline{\mathrm{N}}, y_2 : \underline{\mathrm{N}}, y_3 : \underline{\mathrm{N}}\\
& \quad (y_1 - 0 = y_1 \wedge\\
& \quad\; (y_1 - y_2 = y_3 \rightarrow y_1 - succ(y_2) = pred(y_3))),\\
\varphi_7 = \;& * :\stackrel{\mathrm{I}}{=} \forall y_1 : \underline{\mathrm{N}}, y_2 : \underline{\mathrm{N}}, y_3 : \underline{\mathrm{N}}\\
& \quad (y_1 * 0 = 0 \wedge (y_1 * y_2 = y_3 \rightarrow y_1 * succ(y_2) = y_1 + y_3)),\\
\varphi_8 = \;& / :\stackrel{\mathrm{I}}{=} \forall y_1 : \underline{\mathrm{N}}, y_2 : \underline{\mathrm{N}}, y_3 : \underline{\mathrm{N}}, y_4 : \underline{\mathrm{N}}\\
& \quad (y_1 = (y_2 * y_3) + y_4 \wedge y_4 < y_2 = tt \rightarrow y_1 / y_2 = y_3),\\
\varphi_9 = \;& {\bullet}^{\bullet} :\stackrel{\mathrm{I}}{=} \forall y_1 : \underline{\mathrm{N}}, y_2 : \underline{\mathrm{N}}, y_3 : \underline{\mathrm{N}}\\
& \quad (y_1^0 = succ(0) \wedge (y_1^{y_2} = y_3 \rightarrow y_1^{succ(y_2)} = y_1 * y_3)),\\
\varphi_{10} = \;& < :\stackrel{\mathrm{I}}{=} \forall y_1 : \underline{\mathrm{N}}, y_2 : \underline{\mathrm{N}}, b : \underline{\mathrm{B}}\\
& \quad (y_1 < 0 = f\!f \wedge 0 < succ(y_2) = tt \wedge\\
& \quad\; (y_1 < y_2 = b \rightarrow succ(y_1) < succ(y_2) = b)),\\
\varphi_{11} = \;& \leq :\stackrel{\mathrm{I}}{=} \forall y_1 : \underline{\mathrm{N}}, y_2 : \underline{\mathrm{N}}, b : \underline{\mathrm{B}}\\
& \quad (succ(y_1) \leq 0 = f\!f \wedge 0 \leq y_2 = tt \wedge\\
& \quad\; (y_1 \leq y_2 = b \rightarrow succ(y_1) \leq succ(y_2) = b)),\\
\varphi_{12} = \;& \forall y_1 : \underline{\mathrm{N}}, y_2 : \underline{\mathrm{N}}(y_1 > y_2 = y_2 < y_1),\\
\varphi_{13} = \;& \forall y_1 : \underline{\mathrm{N}}, y_2 : \underline{\mathrm{N}}(y_1 \geq y_2 = y_2 \leq y_1),
\end{aligned}
$$

and

$y_1, \ldots, y_4$ are distinct value symbols such that for all $i = 1, \ldots, 4$: $\tau(y_i) = \langle \mathsf{obj}, \underline{\mathrm{N}} \rangle$,
b is a value symbol such that $\tau(b) = \langle \mathsf{obj}, \underline{\mathrm{B}} \rangle$.

Intuition:

The type symbol $\underline{\mathrm{N}}$ denotes the domain of natural numbers. They are generated by the functions denoted by the function symbols $0^{\underline{\mathrm{N}}}$ ('zero') and $succ^{\underline{\mathrm{N}}}$ ('successor').

D.3 Integer type

Symbols:

$asymbols(\underline{\mathrm{Z}}) :=$
$\quad asymbols(\underline{\mathrm{N}}) \cup$

$\{\underline{\mathrm{Z}}, \ominus^{\underline{\mathrm{Z}}}, 0^{\underline{\mathrm{Z}}}, succ^{\underline{\mathrm{Z}}}, pred^{\underline{\mathrm{Z}}}, -\bullet^{\underline{\mathrm{Z}}}, +^{\underline{\mathrm{Z}}}, -^{\underline{\mathrm{Z}}},$
$*^{\underline{\mathrm{Z}}}, /^{\underline{\mathrm{Z}}}, \bullet^{\bullet\underline{\mathrm{Z}}}, |\bullet|^{\underline{\mathrm{Z}}}, <^{\underline{\mathrm{Z}}}, \leq^{\underline{\mathrm{Z}}}, >^{\underline{\mathrm{Z}}}, \geq^{\underline{\mathrm{Z}}}\}.$

Axioms:

$axioms(\underline{\mathrm{Z}}) := axioms(\underline{\mathrm{N}}) \cup \{\varphi_0, \ldots, \varphi_{19}\},$

where:

$$
\begin{aligned}
\varphi_0 = {} & \forall x_1{:}\,\underline{\mathrm{N}}, x_2{:}\,\underline{\mathrm{N}}((x_1 \ominus x_2)\downarrow),\\
\varphi_1 = {} & gen \overset{\mathrm{I}}{:=} \forall x_1{:}\,\underline{\mathrm{N}}, x_2{:}\,\underline{\mathrm{N}}(gen(x_1 \ominus x_2)),\\
\varphi_2 = {} & \forall y_1{:}\,\underline{\mathrm{Z}}(gen(y_1)),\\
\varphi_3 = {} & \forall x_1{:}\,\underline{\mathrm{N}}, x_2{:}\,\underline{\mathrm{N}}, x_3{:}\,\underline{\mathrm{N}}, x_4{:}\,\underline{\mathrm{N}}\\
& \quad (x_1 \ominus x_2 = x_3 \ominus x_4 \leftrightarrow x_1 + x_4 = x_3 + x_2),\\
\varphi_4 = {} & 0 \overset{\mathrm{I}}{:=} 0 = 0 \ominus 0,\\
\varphi_5 = {} & succ \overset{\mathrm{I}}{:=} \forall x_1{:}\,\underline{\mathrm{N}}, x_2{:}\,\underline{\mathrm{N}}(succ(x_1 \ominus x_2) = succ(x_1) \ominus x_2),\\
\varphi_6 = {} & pred \overset{\mathrm{I}}{:=} \forall x_1{:}\,\underline{\mathrm{N}}, x_2{:}\,\underline{\mathrm{N}}(pred(x_1 \ominus x_2) = x_1 \ominus succ(x_2)),\\
\varphi_7 = {} & -\bullet \overset{\mathrm{I}}{:=} \forall x_1{:}\,\underline{\mathrm{N}}, x_2{:}\,\underline{\mathrm{N}}(-(x_1 \ominus x_2) = x_2 \ominus x_1),\\
\varphi_8 = {} & + \overset{\mathrm{I}}{:=} \forall x_1{:}\,\underline{\mathrm{N}}, x_2{:}\,\underline{\mathrm{N}}, x_3{:}\,\underline{\mathrm{N}}, x_4{:}\,\underline{\mathrm{N}}\\
& \quad ((x_1 \ominus x_2) + (x_3 \ominus x_4) = (x_1 + x_3) \ominus (x_2 + x_4)),\\
\varphi_9 = {} & - \overset{\mathrm{I}}{:=} \forall x_1{:}\,\underline{\mathrm{N}}, x_2{:}\,\underline{\mathrm{N}}, x_3{:}\,\underline{\mathrm{N}}, x_4{:}\,\underline{\mathrm{N}}\\
& \quad ((x_1 \ominus x_2) - (x_3 \ominus x_4) = (x_1 + x_4) \ominus (x_2 + x_3)),\\
\varphi_{10} = {} & * \overset{\mathrm{I}}{:=} \forall x_1{:}\,\underline{\mathrm{N}}, x_2{:}\,\underline{\mathrm{N}}, x_3{:}\,\underline{\mathrm{N}}, x_4{:}\,\underline{\mathrm{N}}\\
& \quad ((x_1 \ominus x_2) * (x_3 \ominus x_4) =\\
& \quad\quad ((x_1 * x_3) + (x_2 * x_4)) \ominus ((x_1 * x_4) + (x_2 * x_3))),\\
\varphi_{11} = {} & / \overset{\mathrm{I}}{:=} \forall y_1{:}\,\underline{\mathrm{Z}}, y_2{:}\,\underline{\mathrm{Z}}, y_3{:}\,\underline{\mathrm{Z}}, y_4{:}\,\underline{\mathrm{Z}}\\
& \quad (y_1 = (y_2 * y_3) + y_4 \wedge\\
& \quad 0 \leq y_4 = tt \wedge y_4 < y_2 = tt \rightarrow y_1/y_2 = y_3),\\
\varphi_{12} = {} & \bullet^{\bullet} \overset{\mathrm{I}}{:=} \forall y_1{:}\,\underline{\mathrm{Z}}, y_2{:}\,\underline{\mathrm{Z}}, x_1{:}\,\underline{\mathrm{N}}\\
& \quad (y_1^0 = succ(0) \wedge (y_1^{x_1} = y_2 \rightarrow y_1^{succ(x_1)} = y_1 * y_2)),\\
\varphi_{13} = {} & |\bullet| \overset{\mathrm{I}}{:=} \forall x_1{:}\,\underline{\mathrm{N}}(|x_1 \ominus 0| = x_1 \ominus 0 \wedge |0 \ominus x_1| = x_1 \ominus 0),\\
\varphi_{14} = {} & < \overset{\mathrm{I}}{:=} \forall x_1{:}\,\underline{\mathrm{N}}, x_2{:}\,\underline{\mathrm{N}}, x_3{:}\,\underline{\mathrm{N}}, x_4{:}\,\underline{\mathrm{N}}, b{:}\,\underline{\mathrm{B}}\\
& \quad ((x_1 + x_4) < (x_3 + x_2) = b \rightarrow\\
& \quad (x_1 \ominus x_2) < (x_3 \ominus x_4) = b),\\
\varphi_{15} = {} & \leq \overset{\mathrm{I}}{:=} \forall x_1{:}\,\underline{\mathrm{N}}, x_2{:}\,\underline{\mathrm{N}}, x_3{:}\,\underline{\mathrm{N}}, x_4{:}\,\underline{\mathrm{N}}, b{:}\,\underline{\mathrm{B}}\\
& \quad ((x_1 + x_4) \leq (x_3 + x_2) = b \rightarrow\\
& \quad (x_1 \ominus x_2) \leq (x_3 \ominus x_4) = b),\\
\varphi_{16} = {} & \forall y_1{:}\,\underline{\mathrm{Z}}, y_2{:}\,\underline{\mathrm{Z}}(y_1 > y_2 = y_2 < y_1),\\
\varphi_{17} = {} & \forall y_1{:}\,\underline{\mathrm{Z}}, y_2{:}\,\underline{\mathrm{Z}}(y_1 \geq y_2 = y_2 \leq y_1),\\
\varphi_{18} = {} & \imath_{\underline{\mathrm{N}}\rightarrow\underline{\mathrm{Z}}} \overset{\mathrm{I}}{:=} \forall x_1{:}\,\underline{\mathrm{N}}(\imath_{\underline{\mathrm{N}}\rightarrow\underline{\mathrm{Z}}}(x_1) = x_1 \ominus 0),\\
\varphi_{19} = {} & \imath^{-1}_{\underline{\mathrm{Z}}\rightarrow\underline{\mathrm{N}}} \overset{\mathrm{I}}{:=} \forall x_1{:}\,\underline{\mathrm{N}}(\imath^{-1}_{\underline{\mathrm{Z}}\rightarrow\underline{\mathrm{N}}}(x_1 \ominus 0) = x_1),
\end{aligned}
$$

and

$x_1, \ldots, x_4$ are distinct value symbols such that for all $i = 1, \ldots, 4$: $\tau(x_i) = \langle \mathsf{obj}, \underline{\mathrm{N}} \rangle$,
$y_1, \ldots, y_4$ are distinct value symbols such that for all $i = 1, \ldots, 4$: $\tau(y_i) = \langle \mathsf{obj}, \underline{\mathrm{Z}} \rangle$,
b is a value symbol such that $\tau(b) = \langle \mathsf{obj}, \underline{\mathrm{B}} \rangle$.

Intuition:

The type symbol $\underline{\mathrm{Z}}$ denotes the domain of integers. They are generated from the natural numbers by the function denoted by the function symbol $\ominus^{\underline{\mathrm{Z}}}$ ('difference').

D.4 Rational type

Symbols:

$$\begin{aligned}&\mathit{asymbols}(\underline{\mathrm{Q}}) := \\ &\quad \mathit{asymbols}(\underline{\mathrm{Z}}) \cup \\ &\quad \{\underline{\mathrm{Q}}, \oslash^{\underline{\mathrm{Q}}}, 0^{\underline{\mathrm{Q}}}, -\bullet^{\underline{\mathrm{Q}}}, \bullet^{-1\underline{\mathrm{Q}}}, +^{\underline{\mathrm{Q}}}, -^{\underline{\mathrm{Q}}}, \\ &\quad\ *^{\underline{\mathrm{Q}}}, /^{\underline{\mathrm{Q}}}, \bullet^{\bullet\underline{\mathrm{Q}}}, |\bullet|^{\underline{\mathrm{Q}}}, <^{\underline{\mathrm{Q}}}, \leq^{\underline{\mathrm{Q}}}, >^{\underline{\mathrm{Q}}}, \geq^{\underline{\mathrm{Q}}}\}.\end{aligned}$$

Axioms:

$\mathit{axioms}(\underline{\mathrm{Q}}) := \mathit{axioms}(\underline{\mathrm{Z}}) \cup \{\varphi_0, \ldots, \varphi_{18}\}$,

where:

$$\begin{aligned}
\varphi_0 &= \forall x_1{:}\,\underline{\mathrm{Z}}, x_2{:}\,\underline{\mathrm{Z}}(x_2 \neq 0 \to (x_1 \oslash x_2){\downarrow}), \\
\varphi_1 &= \mathit{gen} :\overset{\mathrm{I}}{=} \forall x_1{:}\,\underline{\mathrm{Z}}, x_2{:}\,\underline{\mathrm{Z}}(x_2 \neq 0 \to \mathit{gen}(x_1 \oslash x_2)), \\
\varphi_2 &= \forall y_1{:}\,\underline{\mathrm{Q}}(\mathit{gen}(y_1)), \\
\varphi_3 &= \forall x_1{:}\,\underline{\mathrm{Z}}, x_2{:}\,\underline{\mathrm{Z}}, x_3{:}\,\underline{\mathrm{Z}}, x_4{:}\,\underline{\mathrm{Z}} \\
&\qquad (x_2 \neq 0 \land x_4 \neq 0 \to (x_1 \oslash x_2 = x_3 \oslash x_4 \leftrightarrow x_1 * x_4 = x_3 * x_2)), \\
\varphi_4 &= 0 :\overset{\mathrm{I}}{=} 0 = 0 \oslash \mathit{succ}(0), \\
\varphi_5 &= -\bullet :\overset{\mathrm{I}}{=} \forall x_1{:}\,\underline{\mathrm{Z}}, x_2{:}\,\underline{\mathrm{Z}}(x_2 \neq 0 \to -(x_1 \oslash x_2) = (-x_1) \oslash x_2), \\
\varphi_6 &= \bullet^{-1} :\overset{\mathrm{I}}{=} \forall x_1{:}\,\underline{\mathrm{Z}}, x_2{:}\,\underline{\mathrm{Z}}(x_1 \neq 0 \land x_2 \neq 0 \to (x_1 \oslash x_2)^{-1} = x_2 \oslash x_1), \\
\varphi_7 &= + :\overset{\mathrm{I}}{=} \ \forall x_1{:}\,\underline{\mathrm{Z}}, x_2{:}\,\underline{\mathrm{Z}}, x_3{:}\,\underline{\mathrm{Z}}, x_4{:}\,\underline{\mathrm{Z}} \\
&\qquad (x_2 \neq 0 \land x_4 \neq 0 \to \\
&\qquad\quad (x_1 \oslash x_2) + (x_3 \oslash x_4) \\
&\qquad\quad = ((x_1 * x_4) + (x_2 * x_3)) \oslash (x_2 * x_4)), \\
\varphi_8 &= - :\overset{\mathrm{I}}{=} \ \forall x_1{:}\,\underline{\mathrm{Z}}, x_2{:}\,\underline{\mathrm{Z}}, x_3{:}\,\underline{\mathrm{Z}}, x_4{:}\,\underline{\mathrm{Z}} \\
&\qquad (x_2 \neq 0 \land x_4 \neq 0 \to \\
&\qquad\quad (x_1 \oslash x_2) - (x_3 \oslash x_4) \\
&\qquad\quad = ((x_1 * x_4) - (x_2 * x_3)) \oslash (x_2 * x_4)), \\
\varphi_9 &= * :\overset{\mathrm{I}}{=} \ \forall x_1{:}\,\underline{\mathrm{Z}}, x_2{:}\,\underline{\mathrm{Z}}, x_3{:}\,\underline{\mathrm{Z}}, x_4{:}\,\underline{\mathrm{Z}} \\
&\qquad (x_2 \neq 0 \land x_4 \neq 0 \to \\
&\qquad\quad (x_1 \oslash x_2) * (x_3 \oslash x_4) = (x_1 * x_3) \oslash (x_2 * x_4)),
\end{aligned}$$

$$\varphi_{10} = \; / \overset{\mathrm{I}}{:=} \; \forall x_1{:}\,\underline{\mathrm{Z}}, x_2{:}\,\underline{\mathrm{Z}}, x_3{:}\,\underline{\mathrm{Z}}, x_4{:}\,\underline{\mathrm{Z}} \; (x_2 \neq 0 \wedge x_3 \neq 0 \wedge x_4 \neq 0 \rightarrow (x_1 \oslash x_2)/(x_3 \oslash x_4) = (x_1 * x_4) \oslash (x_2 * x_3)),$$

$$\varphi_{11} = \; \bullet^{\bullet} \overset{\mathrm{I}}{:=} \; \forall y_1{:}\,\underline{\mathrm{Q}}, y_2{:}\,\underline{\mathrm{Q}}, z{:}\,\underline{\mathrm{N}} \; (y_1^0 = \mathit{succ}(0) \oslash \mathit{succ}(0) \wedge (y_1^{z-0} = y_2 \rightarrow y_1^{\mathit{succ}(z)-0} = y_1 * y_2) \wedge (y_1 \neq 0 \wedge y_1^{z-0} = y_2 \rightarrow y_1^{0-z} = y_2^{-1})),$$

$$\varphi_{12} = \; |\bullet| \overset{\mathrm{I}}{:=} \; \forall x_1{:}\,\underline{\mathrm{N}}, x_2{:}\,\underline{\mathrm{N}} \; (x_2 \neq 0 \rightarrow |(x_1 \ominus 0) \oslash (x_2 \ominus 0)| = (x_1 \ominus 0) \oslash (x_2 \ominus 0) \wedge |(0 \ominus x_1) \oslash (x_2 \ominus 0)| = (x_1 \ominus 0) \oslash (x_2 \ominus 0)),$$

$$\varphi_{13} = \; < \overset{\mathrm{I}}{:=} \; \forall x_1{:}\,\underline{\mathrm{Z}}, x_2{:}\,\underline{\mathrm{Z}}, x_3{:}\,\underline{\mathrm{Z}}, x_4{:}\,\underline{\mathrm{Z}}, b{:}\,\underline{\mathrm{B}} \; (x_2 > 0 = \mathit{tt} \wedge x_4 > 0 = \mathit{tt} \rightarrow ((x_1 * x_4) < (x_3 * x_2) = b \rightarrow (x_1 \oslash x_2) < (x_3 \oslash x_4) = b)),$$

$$\varphi_{14} = \; \leq \overset{\mathrm{I}}{:=} \; \forall x_1{:}\,\underline{\mathrm{Z}}, x_2{:}\,\underline{\mathrm{Z}}, x_3{:}\,\underline{\mathrm{Z}}, x_4{:}\,\underline{\mathrm{Z}}, b{:}\,\underline{\mathrm{B}} \; (x_2 > 0 = \mathit{tt} \wedge x_4 > 0 = \mathit{tt} \rightarrow ((x_1 * x_4) \leq (x_3 * x_2) = b \rightarrow (x_1 \oslash x_2) \leq (x_3 \oslash x_4) = b)),$$

$$\varphi_{15} = \; \forall y_1{:}\,\underline{\mathrm{Q}}, y_2{:}\,\underline{\mathrm{Q}}(y_1 > y_2 = y_2 < y_1),$$

$$\varphi_{16} = \; \forall y_1{:}\,\underline{\mathrm{Q}}, y_2{:}\,\underline{\mathrm{Q}}(y_1 \geq y_2 = y_2 \leq y_1),$$

$$\varphi_{17} = \; \imath_{\underline{\mathrm{Z}} \rightarrow \underline{\mathrm{Q}}} \overset{\mathrm{I}}{:=} \forall x_1{:}\,\underline{\mathrm{Z}}(\imath_{\underline{\mathrm{Z}} \rightarrow \underline{\mathrm{Q}}}(x_1) = x_1 \oslash \mathit{succ}(0)),$$

$$\varphi_{18} = \; \imath^{-1}_{\underline{\mathrm{Q}} \rightarrow \underline{\mathrm{Z}}} \overset{\mathrm{I}}{:=} \forall x_1{:}\,\underline{\mathrm{Z}}(\imath^{-1}_{\underline{\mathrm{Q}} \rightarrow \underline{\mathrm{Z}}}(x_1 \oslash \mathit{succ}(0)) = x_1),$$

and

$x_1, \ldots, x_4$ are distinct value symbols such that for all $i = 1, \ldots, 4$: $\tau(x_i) = \langle \mathsf{obj}, \underline{\mathrm{Z}} \rangle$,
y_1, y_2 are distinct value symbols such that for $i = 1, 2$: $\tau(y_i) = \langle \mathsf{obj}, \underline{\mathrm{Q}} \rangle$,
z is a value symbol such that $\tau(z) = \langle \mathsf{obj}, \underline{\mathrm{N}} \rangle$,
b is a value symbol such that $\tau(b) = \langle \mathsf{obj}, \underline{\mathrm{B}} \rangle$.

Intuition:

The type symbol $\underline{\mathrm{Q}}$ denotes the domain of rational numbers. They are generated from the integers by the function denoted by the function symbol $\oslash^{\underline{\mathrm{Q}}}$ ('fraction').

D.5 Enumerated type

Symbols:

$\mathit{asymbols}(\underline{\mathrm{E}}(A)) := \{\underline{\mathrm{E}}(A)\}$.

Axioms:

$axioms(\underline{E}(A)) := \{\varphi_0, \ldots, \varphi_3\} \cup \bigcup\{\{\phi_{A'}, \psi_{A'}\} \mid A' \subseteq A\}$,

where:

$$\varphi_0 = \bigwedge_{a \in A} (\mathit{at}_a\downarrow),$$

$$\varphi_1 = \mathit{gen} :\overset{\mathrm{I}}{=} \bigwedge_{a \in A} (\mathit{gen}(\mathit{at}_a)),$$

$$\varphi_2 = \forall y{:}\, \underline{E}(A)(\mathit{gen}(y)),$$

$$\varphi_3 = \bigwedge_{a \in A} (\bigwedge_{a' \in A - \{a\}} (\mathit{at}_a \neq \mathit{at}_{a'})),$$

$$\phi_{A'} = \imath_{\underline{E}(A') \to \underline{E}(A)} :\overset{\mathrm{I}}{=} \bigwedge_{a \in A'} (\imath_{\underline{E}(A') \to \underline{E}(A)}(\mathit{at}_a) = \mathit{at}_a),$$

$$\psi_{A'} = \imath^{-1}_{\underline{E}(A) \to \underline{E}(A')} :\overset{\mathrm{I}}{=} \bigwedge_{a \in A'} (\imath^{-1}_{\underline{E}(A) \to \underline{E}(A')}(\mathit{at}_a) = \mathit{at}_a),$$

and

at_a $(a \in A)$ is the function symbol such that $\iota(\mathit{at}_a) = a$, $\omega(\mathit{at}_a) = \omega(\underline{E}(A))$ and $\tau(\mathit{at}_a) = \langle \mathsf{func}, \underline{E}(A) \rangle$,
y is a value symbol such that $\tau(y) = \langle \mathsf{obj}, \underline{E}(A) \rangle$.

Intuition:

The type symbol $\underline{E}(A)$ denotes a domain of card A elements. These elements are denoted by the function symbols at_a $(a \in A)$.

D.6 Sequence type

Symbols:

$asymbols(\underline{L}(S)) :=$ *
$asymbols(\underline{N}) \cup basymbols(\underline{L}(S)) \cup basymbols(\underline{L}(\underline{L}(S))) \cup \{\mathsf{conc}^{\underline{L}(S)}\}$,

$basymbols(\underline{L}(S)) :=$
$\{\underline{L}(S), \varnothing^{\underline{L}(S)}, \oplus^{\underline{L}(S)}, \mathsf{hd}^{\underline{L}(S)}, \mathsf{tl}^{\underline{L}(S)}, \frown^{\underline{L}(S)}, \mathsf{len}^{\underline{L}(S)}, \bullet(\bullet)^{\underline{L}(S)}, [\bullet]^{\underline{L}(S)}\}$.

Axioms:

$axioms(\underline{L}(S)) :=$
$axioms(\underline{N}) \cup baxioms(\underline{L}(S)) \cup baxioms(\underline{L}(\underline{L}(S))) \cup \{\varphi\}$,

$baxioms(\underline{L}(S)) := \{\varphi_0, \ldots, \varphi_9\}$,

where:

$$\varphi_0 = \varnothing\downarrow \wedge \forall x_1{:}\, S, y_1{:}\, \underline{L}(S)((x_1 \oplus y_1)\downarrow),$$

* The symbols associated with (the sequence type corresponding to) $\underline{L}(S)$ include most symbols associated with $\underline{L}(\underline{L}(S))$, but no symbol associated with $\underline{L}(\underline{L}(\underline{L}(S)))$.

$$\begin{aligned}
\varphi_1 = {} & gen :\stackrel{\mathrm{I}}{=} gen(\emptyset) \wedge \forall x_1 : S, y_1 : \underline{\mathrm{L}}(S)(gen(y_1) \to gen(x_1 \oplus y_1)), \\
\varphi_2 = {} & \forall y_1 : \underline{\mathrm{L}}(S)(gen(y_1)), \\
\varphi_3 = {} & \forall x_1 : S, y_1 : \underline{\mathrm{L}}(S)(x_1 \oplus y_1 \neq \emptyset) \wedge \\
& \forall x_1 : S, x_2 : S, y_1 : \underline{\mathrm{L}}(S), y_2 : \underline{\mathrm{L}}(S) \\
& \quad (x_1 \oplus y_1 = x_2 \oplus y_2 \to x_1 = x_2 \wedge y_1 = y_2), \\
\varphi_4 = {} & \mathsf{hd} :\stackrel{\mathrm{I}}{=} \forall x_1 : S, y_1 : \underline{\mathrm{L}}(S)(\mathsf{hd}\,(x_1 \oplus y_1) = x_1), \\
\varphi_5 = {} & \mathsf{tl} :\stackrel{\mathrm{I}}{=} \forall x_1 : S, y_1 : \underline{\mathrm{L}}(S)(\mathsf{tl}\,(x_1 \oplus y_1) = y_1), \\
\varphi_6 = {} & \frown :\stackrel{\mathrm{I}}{=} \forall x_1 : S, y_1 : \underline{\mathrm{L}}(S), y_2 : \underline{\mathrm{L}}(S), y_3 : \underline{\mathrm{L}}(S) \\
& \quad (\emptyset \frown y_2 = y_2 \wedge \\
& \quad (y_1 \frown y_2 = y_3 \to (x_1 \oplus y_1) \frown y_2 = x_1 \oplus y_3)), \\
\varphi_7 = {} & \mathsf{len} :\stackrel{\mathrm{I}}{=} \forall x_1 : S, y_1 : \underline{\mathrm{L}}(S), n : \underline{\mathrm{N}} \\
& \quad (\mathsf{len}\,\emptyset = 0 \wedge (\mathsf{len}\,y_1 = n \to \mathsf{len}\,(x_1 \oplus y_1) = succ(n))), \\
\varphi_8 = {} & \bullet(\bullet) :\stackrel{\mathrm{I}}{=} \forall x_1 : S, x_2 : S, y_1 : \underline{\mathrm{L}}(S), n : \underline{\mathrm{N}} \\
& \quad ((x_1 \oplus \emptyset)(succ(0)) = x_1 \wedge \\
& \quad (y_1(n) = x_2 \to (x_1 \oplus y_1)(succ(n)) = x_2)), \\
\varphi_9 = {} & \forall x_1 : S([x_1] = x_1 \oplus \emptyset), \\
\varphi = {} & \mathsf{conc} :\stackrel{\mathrm{I}}{=} \forall y_1 : \underline{\mathrm{L}}(S), y_2 : \underline{\mathrm{L}}(S), z : \underline{\mathrm{L}}(\underline{\mathrm{L}}(S)) \\
& \quad (\mathsf{conc}\;\emptyset = \emptyset \wedge \\
& \quad (\mathsf{conc}\;z = y_2 \to \mathsf{conc}\;(y_1 \oplus z) = y_1 \frown y_2)),
\end{aligned}$$

and

x_1, x_2 are distinct value symbols such that for $i = 1, 2$: $\tau(x_i) = \langle \mathsf{obj}, S \rangle$,
y_1, y_2, y_3 are distinct value symbols such that for all $i = 1, 2, 3$: $\tau(y_i) = \langle \mathsf{obj}, \underline{\mathrm{L}}(S) \rangle$,
z is a value symbol such that $\tau(z) = \langle \mathsf{obj}, \underline{\mathrm{L}}(\underline{\mathrm{L}}(S)) \rangle$,
n is a value symbol such that $\tau(n) = \langle \mathsf{obj}, \underline{\mathrm{N}} \rangle$.

Intuition:

The type symbol $\underline{\mathrm{L}}(S)$ denotes the domain of all finite sequences with elements from the domain denoted by the type symbol S. These sequences are generated from the values from the element domain by the functions denoted by the function symbols $\emptyset^{\underline{\mathrm{L}}(S)}$ ('empty sequence') and $\oplus^{\underline{\mathrm{L}}(S)}$ ('insertion').

D.7 Set type

Symbols:

$asymbols(\underline{\mathrm{F}}(S)) :=$ †
$asymbols(\underline{\mathrm{B}}) \cup asymbols(\underline{\mathrm{N}}) \cup basymbols(\underline{\mathrm{F}}(S)) \cup basymbols(\underline{\mathrm{F}}(\underline{\mathrm{F}}(S))) \cup \{\bigcup^{\underline{\mathrm{F}}(S)}\}$,

† The symbols associated with (the set type corresponding to) $\underline{\mathrm{F}}(S)$ include most symbols associated with $\underline{\mathrm{F}}(\underline{\mathrm{F}}(S))$, but no symbol associated with $\underline{\mathrm{F}}(\underline{\mathrm{F}}(\underline{\mathrm{F}}(S)))$.

$$basymbols(\underline{F}(S)) :=$$
$$\{\underline{F}(S), \emptyset^{\underline{F}(S)}, \oplus^{\underline{F}(S)}, \in^{\underline{F}(S)}, \cup^{\underline{F}(S)}, \cap^{\underline{F}(S)}, -^{\underline{F}(S)}, \subseteq^{\underline{F}(S)}, \mathsf{card}^{\underline{F}(S)}, \{\bullet\}^{\underline{F}(S)}\}.$$

Axioms:

$$axioms(\underline{F}(S)) := axioms(\underline{B}) \cup axioms(\underline{N}) \cup baxioms(\underline{F}(S)) \cup baxioms(\underline{F}(\underline{F}(S))) \cup \{\varphi\},$$

$$baxioms(\underline{F}(S)) := \{\varphi_0, \ldots, \varphi_{10}\},$$

where:

$$\varphi_0 = \emptyset{\downarrow} \wedge \forall x_1 : S, y_1 : \underline{F}(S)((x_1 \oplus y_1){\downarrow}),$$

$$\varphi_1 = \mathit{gen} :\overset{\mathrm{I}}{=} \mathit{gen}(\emptyset) \wedge \forall x_1 : S, y_1 : \underline{F}(S)(\mathit{gen}(y_1) \rightarrow \mathit{gen}(x_1 \oplus y_1)),$$

$$\varphi_2 = \forall y_1 : \underline{F}(S)(\mathit{gen}(y_1)),$$

$$\varphi_3 = \in :\overset{\mathrm{I}}{=} \forall x_1 : S, x_2 : S, y_1 : \underline{F}(S), b : \underline{B}\ (x_1 \in \emptyset = \mathit{ff} \wedge x_1 \in (x_1 \oplus y_1) = \mathit{tt} \wedge (x_1 \in y_1 = b \wedge x_1 \neq x_2 \rightarrow x_1 \in (x_2 \oplus y_1) = b)),$$

$$\varphi_4 = \forall y_1 : \underline{F}(S), y_2 : \underline{F}(S)\ (\forall x_1 : S(x_1 \in y_1 = \mathit{tt} \leftrightarrow x_1 \in y_2 = \mathit{tt}) \rightarrow y_1 = y_2),$$

$$\varphi_5 = \cup :\overset{\mathrm{I}}{=} \forall x_1 : S, y_1 : \underline{F}(S), y_2 : \underline{F}(S), y_3 : \underline{F}(S)\ (\emptyset \cup y_2 = y_2 \wedge (y_1 \cup y_2 = y_3 \rightarrow (x_1 \oplus y_1) \cup y_2 = x_1 \oplus y_3)),$$

$$\varphi_6 = \cap :\overset{\mathrm{I}}{=} \forall x_1 : S, y_1 : \underline{F}(S), y_2 : \underline{F}(S), y_3 : \underline{F}(S)\ (\emptyset \cap y_2 = \emptyset \wedge (y_1 \cap y_2 = y_3 \rightarrow (x_1 \in y_2 = \mathit{tt} \rightarrow (x_1 \oplus y_1) \cap y_2 = x_1 \oplus y_3) \wedge (x_1 \in y_2 = \mathit{ff} \rightarrow (x_1 \oplus y_1) \cap y_2 = y_3))),$$

$$\varphi_7 = - :\overset{\mathrm{I}}{=} \forall x_1 : S, y_1 : \underline{F}(S), y_2 : \underline{F}(S), y_3 : \underline{F}(S)\ (\emptyset - y_2 = \emptyset \wedge (y_1 - y_2 = y_3 \rightarrow (x_1 \in y_2 = \mathit{ff} \rightarrow (x_1 \oplus y_1) - y_2 = x_1 \oplus y_3) \wedge (x_1 \in y_2 = \mathit{tt} \rightarrow (x_1 \oplus y_1) - y_2 = y_3))),$$

$$\varphi_8 = \subseteq :\overset{\mathrm{I}}{=} \forall y_1 : \underline{F}(S), y_2 : \underline{F}(S)\ ((y_1 \cup y_2 = y_1 \rightarrow y_1 \subseteq y_2 = \mathit{tt}) \wedge (y_1 \cup y_2 \neq y_1 \rightarrow y_1 \subseteq y_2 = \mathit{ff})),$$

$$\varphi_9 = \mathsf{card} :\overset{\mathrm{I}}{=} \forall x_1 : S, y_1 : \underline{F}(S), n : \underline{N}\ (\mathsf{card}\,\emptyset = 0 \wedge (\mathsf{card}\,y_1 = n \wedge x_1 \in y_1 = \mathit{ff} \rightarrow \mathsf{card}\,(x_1 \oplus y_1) = \mathit{succ}(n))),$$

$$\varphi_{10} = \forall x_1 : S(\{x_1\} = x_1 \oplus \emptyset),$$

$$\varphi = \bigcup :\overset{\mathrm{I}}{=} \forall y_1 : \underline{F}(S), y_2 : \underline{F}(S), z : \underline{F}(\underline{F}(S))\ (\bigcup \emptyset = \emptyset \wedge (\bigcup z = y_2 \rightarrow \bigcup (y_1 \oplus z) = y_1 \cup y_2)),$$

and

x_1, x_2 are distinct value symbols such that for $i = 1,2$: $\tau(x_i) = \langle \mathsf{obj}, S\rangle$,
y_1, y_2, y_3 are distinct value symbols such that for all $i = 1,2,3$:
$\tau(y_i) = \langle \mathsf{obj}, \underline{\mathrm{F}}(S)\rangle$,
z is a value symbol such that $\tau(z) = \langle \mathsf{obj}, \underline{\mathrm{F}}(\underline{\mathrm{F}}(S))\rangle$,
n is a value symbol such that $\tau(n) = \langle \mathsf{obj}, \underline{\mathrm{N}}\rangle$,
b is a value symbol such that $\tau(b) = \langle \mathsf{obj}, \underline{\mathrm{B}}\rangle$.

Intuition:

The type symbol $\underline{\mathrm{F}}(S)$ denotes the domain of all finite sets with elements from the domain denoted by the type symbol S. These sets are generated from the values from the element domain by the functions denoted by the function symbols $\emptyset^{\underline{\mathrm{F}}(S)}$ ('empty set') and $\oplus^{\underline{\mathrm{F}}(S)}$ ('insertion').

D.8 Map type

Symbols:

$$
\begin{aligned}
&\mathit{asymbols}(\underline{\mathrm{M}}(S,S')) := \\
&\quad \mathit{asymbols}(\underline{\mathrm{F}}(S)) \cup \mathit{asymbols}(\underline{\mathrm{F}}(S')) \cup \\
&\quad \{\underline{\mathrm{M}}(S,S'), \emptyset^{\underline{\mathrm{M}}(S,S')}, \{\bullet \mapsto \bullet\} \oplus \bullet^{\underline{\mathrm{M}}(S,S')}, \mathsf{dom}^{\underline{\mathrm{M}}(S,S')}, \bullet(\bullet)^{\underline{\mathrm{M}}(S,S')}, \\
&\quad\ \dagger^{\underline{\mathrm{M}}(S,S')}, \cup^{\underline{\mathrm{M}}(S,S')}, \lhd^{\underline{\mathrm{M}}(S,S')}, ⩤^{\underline{\mathrm{M}}(S,S')}, \mathsf{rng}^{\underline{\mathrm{M}}(S,S')}, \{\bullet \mapsto \bullet\}^{\underline{\mathrm{M}}(S,S')}\}.
\end{aligned}
$$

Axioms:

$\mathit{axioms}(\underline{\mathrm{M}}(S,S')) := \mathit{axioms}(\underline{\mathrm{F}}(S)) \cup \mathit{axioms}(\underline{\mathrm{F}}(S')) \cup \{\varphi_0, \ldots, \varphi_{11}\}$,

where:

$$
\begin{aligned}
\varphi_0 = {} & \emptyset\!\downarrow \wedge\, \forall x_1{:}\, S, x_1'{:}\, S', y_1{:}\, \underline{\mathrm{M}}(S,S')((\{x_1 \mapsto x_1'\} \oplus y_1)\!\downarrow), \\
\varphi_1 = {} & \mathit{gen} \overset{\mathrm{I}}{:=} \mathit{gen}(\emptyset) \wedge \\
& \qquad \forall x_1{:}\, S, x_1'{:}\, S', y_1{:}\, \underline{\mathrm{M}}(S,S') \\
& \qquad (\mathit{gen}(y_1) \rightarrow \mathit{gen}(\{x_1 \mapsto x_1'\} \oplus y_1)), \\
\varphi_2 = {} & \forall y_1{:}\, \underline{\mathrm{M}}(S,S')(\mathit{gen}(y_1)), \\
\varphi_3 = {} & \mathsf{dom} \overset{\mathrm{I}}{:=} \forall x_1{:}\, S, x_1'{:}\, S', y_1{:}\, \underline{\mathrm{M}}(S,S'), z{:}\, \underline{\mathrm{F}}(S) \\
& \qquad (\mathsf{dom}\, \emptyset = \emptyset \wedge \\
& \qquad\ (\mathsf{dom}\, y_1 = z \rightarrow \mathsf{dom}\,(\{x_1 \mapsto x_1'\} \oplus y_1) = x_1 \oplus z)), \\
\varphi_4 = {} & \bullet(\bullet) \overset{\mathrm{I}}{:=} \forall x_1{:}\, S, x_2{:}\, S, x_1'{:}\, S', x_2'{:}\, S', y_1{:}\, \underline{\mathrm{M}}(S,S') \\
& \qquad ((\{x_1 \mapsto x_1'\} \oplus y_1)(x_1) = x_1' \wedge \\
& \qquad (y_1(x_1) = x_1' \wedge x_1 \neq x_2 \rightarrow \\
& \qquad\ (\{x_2 \mapsto x_2'\} \oplus y_1)(x_1) = x_1')), \\
\varphi_5 = {} & \forall y_1{:}\, \underline{\mathrm{M}}(S,S'), y_2{:}\, \underline{\mathrm{M}}(S,S') \\
& (\mathsf{dom}\, y_1 = \mathsf{dom}\, y_2 \wedge \\
& \ \forall x_1{:}\, S(x_1 \in \mathsf{dom}\, y_1 = \mathit{tt} \rightarrow y_1(x_1) = y_2(x_1)) \rightarrow \\
& \ y_1 = y_2),
\end{aligned}
$$

$$\begin{aligned}
\varphi_6 = \ & \dagger :\overset{\mathrm{I}}{=} \ \forall x_1{:}\, S, x_1'{:}\, S', y_1{:}\, \underline{\mathrm{M}}(S,S'), y_2{:}\, \underline{\mathrm{M}}(S,S'), y_3{:}\, \underline{\mathrm{M}}(S,S') \\
& \quad (y_2 \dagger \emptyset = y_2 \wedge \\
& \quad\ (y_1 \dagger y_2 = y_3 \rightarrow \\
& \quad\quad y_1 \dagger (\{x_1 \mapsto x_1'\} \oplus y_2) = \{x_1 \mapsto x_1'\} \oplus y_3)), \\
\varphi_7 = \ & \cup :\overset{\mathrm{I}}{=} \ \forall x_1{:}\, S, x_1'{:}\, S', y_1{:}\, \underline{\mathrm{M}}(S,S'), y_2{:}\, \underline{\mathrm{M}}(S,S'), y_3{:}\, \underline{\mathrm{M}}(S,S') \\
& \quad (\emptyset \cup y_2 = y_2 \wedge \\
& \quad\ (y_1 \cup y_2 = y_3 \wedge x_1 \in \mathsf{dom}\, y_3 = \mathit{ff} \rightarrow \\
& \quad\quad (\{x_1 \mapsto x_1'\} \oplus y_1) \cup y_2 = \{x_1 \mapsto x_1'\} \oplus y_3)), \\
\varphi_8 = \ & \lhd :\overset{\mathrm{I}}{=} \ \forall x_1{:}\, S, x_1'{:}\, S', z{:}\, \underline{\mathrm{F}}(S), y_1{:}\, \underline{\mathrm{M}}(S,S'), y_2{:}\, \underline{\mathrm{M}}(S,S') \\
& \quad (z \lhd \emptyset = \emptyset \wedge \\
& \quad\ (z \lhd y_1 = y_2 \rightarrow \\
& \quad\quad (x_1 \in z = \mathit{tt} \rightarrow \\
& \quad\quad\ z \lhd (\{x_1 \mapsto x_1'\} \oplus y_1) = \{x_1 \mapsto x_1'\} \oplus y_2) \wedge \\
& \quad\quad (x_1 \in z = \mathit{ff} \rightarrow z \lhd (\{x_1 \mapsto x_1'\} \oplus y_1) = y_2))), \\
\varphi_9 = \ & \ntriangleleft :\overset{\mathrm{I}}{=} \ \forall x_1{:}\, S, x_1'{:}\, S', z{:}\, \underline{\mathrm{F}}(S), y_1{:}\, \underline{\mathrm{M}}(S,S'), y_2{:}\, \underline{\mathrm{M}}(S,S') \\
& \quad (z \ntriangleleft \emptyset = \emptyset \wedge \\
& \quad\ (z \ntriangleleft y_1 = y_2 \rightarrow \\
& \quad\quad (x_1 \in z = \mathit{ff} \rightarrow \\
& \quad\quad\ z \ntriangleleft (\{x_1 \mapsto x_1'\} \oplus y_1) = \{x_1 \mapsto x_1'\} \oplus y_2) \wedge \\
& \quad\quad (x_1 \in z = \mathit{tt} \rightarrow z \ntriangleleft (\{x_1 \mapsto x_1'\} \oplus y_1) = y_2))), \\
\varphi_{10} = \ & \mathsf{rng} :\overset{\mathrm{I}}{=} \ \forall x_1{:}\, S, x_1'{:}\, S', y_1{:}\, \underline{\mathrm{M}}(S,S'), z'{:}\, \underline{\mathrm{F}}(S') \\
& \quad (\mathsf{rng}\, \emptyset = \emptyset \wedge \\
& \quad\ (\mathsf{rng}\, y_1 = z' \rightarrow \\
& \quad\quad (x_1 \in \mathsf{dom}\, y_1 = \mathit{ff} \rightarrow \\
& \quad\quad\ \mathsf{rng}\, (\{x_1 \mapsto x_1'\} \oplus y_1) = \{x_1'\} \cup z') \wedge \\
& \quad\quad (x_1 \in \mathsf{dom}\, y_1 = \mathit{tt} \rightarrow \\
& \quad\quad\ \mathsf{rng}\, (\{x_1 \mapsto x_1'\} \oplus y_1) = \{x_1'\} \cup (z' - \{y_1(x_1)\})))), \\
\varphi_{11} = \ & \forall x_1{:}\, S, x_1'{:}\, S' (\{x_1 \mapsto x_1'\} = \{x_1 \mapsto x_1'\} \oplus \emptyset),
\end{aligned}$$

and

x_1, x_2 are distinct value symbols such that for $i = 1, 2$: $\tau(x_i) = \langle \mathsf{obj}, S \rangle$,
x_1', x_2' are distinct value symbols such that for $i = 1, 2$: $\tau(x_i') = \langle \mathsf{obj}, S' \rangle$,
y_1, y_2, y_3 are distinct value symbols such that for all $i = 1, 2, 3$: $\tau(y_i) = \langle \mathsf{obj}, \underline{\mathrm{M}}(S, S') \rangle$,
z is a value symbol such that $\tau(z) = \langle \mathsf{obj}, \underline{\mathrm{F}}(S) \rangle$,
z' is a value symbol such that $\tau(z') = \langle \mathsf{obj}, \underline{\mathrm{F}}(S') \rangle$.

Intuition:

The type symbol $\underline{\mathrm{M}}(S, S')$ denotes the domain of all finite maps with domain elements from the domain denoted by the type symbol S and range elements from the domain denoted by the type symbol S'. These maps are generated from the values from the domain element domain and the range element domain by the functions denoted by the function symbols $\varnothing^{\underline{\mathrm{M}}(S,S')}$ ('empty map') and $\oplus^{\underline{\mathrm{M}}(S,S')}$ ('insertion').

D.9 Composite type

Symbols:

$asymbols(\underline{\mathrm{C}}_c(S_1,\dots,S_n)) :=$
$\{\underline{\mathrm{C}}_c(S_1,\dots,S_n)\} \cup \{sel_i^{\underline{\mathrm{C}}_c(S_1,\dots,S_n)} \mid 1 \le i \le n\}.$

Axioms:

$axioms(\underline{\mathrm{C}}_c(S_1,\dots,S_n)) := \{\varphi_0,\dots,\varphi_3\} \cup \{\psi_i \mid 1 \le i \le n\},$

where:

$$
\begin{aligned}
\varphi_0 = {} & \forall x_1{:}\,S_1,\dots,x_n{:}\,S_n(mk(x_1,\dots,x_n)\downarrow),\\
\varphi_1 = {} & gen :\stackrel{\mathrm{I}}{=} \forall x_1{:}\,S_1,\dots,x_n{:}\,S_n(gen(mk(x_1,\dots,x_n))),\\
\varphi_2 = {} & \forall y{:}\,\underline{\mathrm{C}}_c(S_1,\dots,S_n)(gen(y)),\\
\varphi_3 = {} & \forall x_1{:}\,S_1, x_1'{:}\,S_1,\dots,x_n{:}\,S_n, x_n'{:}\,S_n\\
& \quad (mk(x_1,\dots,x_n) = mk(x_1',\dots,x_n') \rightarrow x_1 = x_1' \wedge \dots \wedge x_n = x_n'),\\
\psi_i = {} & sel_i :\stackrel{\mathrm{I}}{=} \forall x_1{:}\,S_1,\dots,x_n{:}\,S_n(sel_i(mk(x_1,\dots,x_n)) = x_i),
\end{aligned}
$$

and

mk is the unique function symbol such that $\iota(mk) = mk(c)$, $\omega(mk) = \omega(\underline{\mathrm{C}}_c(S_1,\dots,S_n))$ and $\tau(mk) = \langle \mathsf{func}, S_1,\dots,S_n,\underline{\mathrm{C}}_c(S_1,\dots,S_n)\rangle$,
$x_1, x_1',\dots,x_n,x_n'$ are distinct value symbols such that for all $i = 1,\dots,n$: $\tau(x_i) = \tau(x_i') = \langle \mathsf{obj}, S_i\rangle$,
y is a value symbol such that $\tau(y) = \langle \mathsf{obj}, \underline{\mathrm{C}}_c(S_1,\dots,S_n)\rangle$.

Intuition:

The type symbol $\underline{\mathrm{C}}_c(S_1,\dots,S_n)$ denotes the domain of all composite values with n components, one from each of the domains denoted by the type symbols $S_1,\dots,S_n$, which are generated by the function mk.

D.10 Nil

Below, the nil constant symbols are introduced.

A *nil* function symbol is associated with each type defined as a union extended with an option value. It is the constant symbol which corresponds to the pre-defined name that is used to denote the option value.

For $S \in \mathsf{MType}$, nil^S is a function symbol such that

$\iota(nil^S) \in \mathsf{PIdent}, \quad \omega(nil^S) = \langle\rangle, \quad \tau(nil^S) = \langle \mathsf{func}, S\rangle,$
for all $f \in \mathsf{MFunc}{:}\, \forall T\ (nil^T \neq f) \Rightarrow \iota(nil^S) \neq \iota(f).$

E

Abbreviations

Only a kernel of VVSL is defined in Chapters 5 and 8. In this appendix, the remainder is introduced by abbreviations.

Type definition

The following abbreviation is used for defining map types if the maps must be one-to-one:

$$
\begin{array}{l}
t = t_1 \stackrel{m}{\longleftrightarrow} t_2 \ \textsf{where inv}(x) \triangleq E \ := \\
\quad t = t_1 \stackrel{m}{\longrightarrow} t_2 \\
\quad \textsf{where inv}(x) \triangleq (\forall y \in t_1, y' \in t_1 \ \cdot \ x(y) = x(y') \ \Rightarrow \ y = y') \wedge E.
\end{array}
$$

The following abbreviation is used for defining composite types:

$$
\begin{array}{l}
t \ :: \ s_1 \colon t_1 \ \ldots \ s_n \colon t_n \ \textsf{where inv}(x) \triangleq E \ := \\
\quad t = \textsf{compose}\ t \ \textsf{of}\ s_1 \colon t_1 \ \ldots \ s_n \colon t_n \ \textsf{where inv}(x) \triangleq E.
\end{array}
$$

Local definition

The following abbreviation is used for nested local definitions:

$$
\begin{array}{l}
\textsf{let}\ x_1 \colon t_1 \triangleq e_1, \ldots, x_n \colon t_n \triangleq e_n \ \textsf{in}\ e \ := \\
\quad \textsf{let}\ x_{k(1)} \colon t_{k(1)} \triangleq e_{k(1)} \ \textsf{in} \ \ldots \ \textsf{let}\ x_{k(n)} \colon t_{k(n)} \triangleq e_{k(n)} \ \textsf{in}\ e
\end{array}
$$

where k is some bijection on $\{1, \ldots, n\}$ such that if $x_{k(i)}$ occurs in $e_{k(j)}$ then $i < j$.

The following abbreviation introduces an alternative notation for local definitions:

$$
\begin{array}{l}
e \ \textsf{where}\ x_1 \colon t_1 \triangleq e_1, \ldots, x_n \colon t_n \triangleq e_n \ := \\
\quad \textsf{let}\ x_1 \colon t_1 \triangleq e_1, \ldots, x_n \colon t_n \triangleq e_n \ \textsf{in}\ e.
\end{array}
$$

Choice

The following abbreviation introduces an alternative notation for choices:

$$e \text{ where } x_1 : t_1, \ldots, x_n : t_n \text{ is s.t. } E \ := \\ \text{let } x_1 : t_1, \ldots, x_n : t_n \text{ be s.t. } E \text{ in } e.$$

The following abbreviation is used if a choice expression is used to decompose a composite value:

$$\text{let } mk\text{-}c(x_1, \ldots, x_n) \triangleq e_1 \text{ in } e_2 \ := \\ \text{let } x_1 : t_1, \ldots, x_n : t_n \text{ be s.t. } mk\text{-}c(x_1, \ldots, x_n) = e_1 \text{ in } e_2.$$

Conditional

The following abbreviation is for combined case distinction and decomposition:

$$\begin{array}{l}
\text{cases } e \text{ of} \\
\quad mk\text{-}t_1(x_{1_1}, \ldots, x_{1_{m_1}}) \quad \rightarrow e_1 \\
\quad \vdots \\
\quad mk\text{-}t_n(x_{n_1}, \ldots, x_{n_{m_n}}) \quad \rightarrow e_n \\
\text{end} \\
:= \\
\text{if } \exists y \in t_1 \cdot y = e \\
\text{then let } mk\text{-}t_1(x_{1_1}, \ldots, x_{1_{m_1}}) \triangleq e \text{ in } e_1 \\
\text{else} \\
\quad \vdots \\
\text{if } \exists y \in t_{n-1} \cdot y = e \\
\text{then let } mk\text{-}t_{n-1}(x_{n-1_1}, \ldots, x_{n-1_{m_{n-1}}}) \triangleq e \text{ in } e_{n-1} \\
\text{else let } mk\text{-}t_n(x_{n_1}, \ldots, x_{n_{m_n}}) \triangleq e \text{ in } e_n
\end{array}$$

(y is a fresh value name).

Set comprehension

An integer range is defined as an abbreviation of a set comprehension:

$$\{e_1 \,..\, e_2\} \ := \{y \mid y \in \mathbb{Z};\ e_1 \leq y \wedge y \leq e_2\}$$

(y is a fresh value name).

Logical expressions

Familiar logical notation is introduced by abbreviations:

$$
\begin{array}{lll}
E_1 \wedge E_2 & := & \neg(\neg E_1 \vee \neg E_2), \\
E_1 \Rightarrow E_2 & := & \neg E_1 \vee E_2, \\
E_1 \Leftrightarrow E_2 & := & (E_1 \Rightarrow E_2) \wedge (E_2 \Rightarrow E_1), \\
\forall x \in t \cdot E & := & \neg(\exists x \in t \cdot \neg E), \\
\exists! x \in t \cdot E & := & \exists y \in t \cdot (\forall x \in t \cdot (E \Leftrightarrow x = y)), \\
\exists x_1 \in t_1, \ldots, x_n \in t_n \cdot E & := & \exists x_1 \in t_1 \cdot (\cdots (\exists x_n \in t_n \cdot E) \cdots), \\
\forall x_1 \in t_1, \ldots, x_n \in t_n \cdot E & := & \forall x_1 \in t_1 \cdot (\cdots (\forall x_n \in t_n \cdot E) \cdots)
\end{array}
$$

(y is a fresh value name).

Less familiar logical notation is also introduced by abbreviations:

$$
\begin{array}{lll}
e \in t & := & \exists y \in t \cdot y = e, \\
\exists mk\text{-}c(x_1, \ldots, x_n) \in t \cdot E & := & \exists y \in t \cdot \mathsf{let}\ mk\text{-}c(x_1, \ldots, x_n) \triangleq y\ \mathsf{in}\ E, \\
\forall mk\text{-}c(x_1, \ldots, x_n) \in t \cdot E & := & \forall y \in t \cdot \mathsf{let}\ mk\text{-}c(x_1, \ldots, x_n) \triangleq y\ \mathsf{in}\ E
\end{array}
$$

(y is a fresh value name).

Temporal formulae

Familiar temporal logic notation is introduced by abbreviations:

$$
\begin{array}{lll}
\Diamond \varphi & := & \mathsf{true}\ \mathcal{U}\ \varphi, \\
\Box \varphi & := & \neg(\Diamond \neg \varphi), \\
\ominus \varphi & := & \mathsf{true}\ \mathcal{S}\ \varphi, \\
\boxminus \varphi & := & \neg(\ominus \neg \varphi).
\end{array}
$$

Modules

The following abbreviation is used for nested imports:

$\mathsf{import}\ M_1\ \ldots\ M_n\ \mathsf{into}\ M\ :=\ \mathsf{import}\ M_1\ \mathsf{into}\ \ldots\ \mathsf{import}\ M_n\ \mathsf{into}\ M.$

The following abbreviation is used for nested local module definitions:

$\mathsf{let}\ m_1 \triangleq M_1, \ldots, m_n \triangleq M_n\ \mathsf{in}\ M\ :=$
$\quad \mathsf{let}\ m_{k(1)} \triangleq M_{k(i)}\ \mathsf{in}\ \ldots\ \mathsf{let}\ m_{k(n)} \triangleq M_{k(n)}\ \mathsf{in}\ M$

where k is some bijection on $\{1, \ldots, n\}$ such that if $m_{k(i)}$ occurs in $M_{k(j)}$ then $i < j$.

The following abbreviation is used for union of module signatures:

$\mathsf{signature}\ M_1, \ldots, M_n\ :=$
$\quad \mathsf{add\ signature}\ M_1\ \mathsf{to}\ \ldots\ \mathsf{add\ signature}\ M_{n-1}\ \mathsf{to\ signature}\ M_n.$

Specification document

The following abbreviation is used for a specification document that is a local definition module (possibly nested):

$$\textsf{component } m_1 \textsf{ is } M_1 \ \ldots \ m_n \textsf{ is } M_n \textsf{ system is } M \ := \\ \textsf{system is let } m_1 \triangleq M_1, \ldots, m_n \triangleq M_n \textsf{ in } M.$$

Miscellaneous

For reasons of readability, the following abbreviations are described as notational conventions.

Suppression of conditions in definitions

The following conditions can be suppressed:

- a type invariant where $\mathsf{inv}(x) \triangleq \mathsf{true}$,
- a state invariant inv true,
- an initial condition init true,
- a dynamic constraint dyn true,
- a pre-condition pre true,
- an inter-condition inter $\bigcirc\mathsf{true} \Rightarrow (\mathsf{is\text{-}I} \wedge \bigcirc\neg\bigcirc\mathsf{true})$.

Pre-, post- and mixfix notation for function application

The usual notational conventions for application of nullary functions (omitting parentheses), unary functions (prefix notation) and binary functions (infix notation) can also be used. Mixfix notation can be used as well. Names of the form $\sigma_0 \bullet \sigma_1 \cdots \sigma_{n-1} \bullet \sigma_n$, where each σ_i is a sequence of characters not containing $\bullet$, is used for n-ary functions to indicate suitable mixfix notation:

$$\sigma_0\ e_1\ \sigma_1 \cdots \sigma_{n-1}\ e_n\ \sigma_n \text{ stands for } \sigma_0 \bullet \sigma_1 \cdots \sigma_{n-1} \bullet \sigma_n(e_1, \ldots, e_n).$$

References

Astrahan, M.M. *et al.* (1976) System R: A relational approach to data management. *ACM Transactions on Database Systems*, **1(2)**, 97–137.

Barringer, H., Cheng, H. and Jones, C.B. (1984) A logic covering undefinedness in program proofs. *Acta Informatica*, **21**, 251–269.

Barringer, H. and Kuiper, R. (1985) Hierarchical development of concurrent systems in a temporal logic framework, in *Seminar on Concurrency* (eds Brookes, S.D., Roscoe, A.W. and Winskel, G.), LNCS 197, Springer-Verlag, pp. 35–61.

Bergstra, J.A. (1986) Module algebra for relational specifications. Technical Report LGPS 16, University of Utrecht, Logic Group.

Bergstra, J.A., Heering, J. and Klint, P. (1989) *Algebraic Specification*, ACM Press Frontier Series, Addison-Wesley.

Bergstra, J.A., Heering, J. and Klint, P. (1990) Module algebra. *Journal of the ACM*, **37(2)**, 335–372.

Bernstein, P.A. and Goodman, N. (1981) Concurrency control in distributed database systems. *ACM Computing Surveys*, **13(2)**, 186–221.

Bernstein, P.A., Shipman, D.W. and Wong, W.S. (1979) Formal aspects of serializability in database concurrency control. *IEEE Transactions on Software Engineering*, **5(3)**, 203–216.

Bjørner, D. (1982) Formalization of data models, in *Formal Specification and Software Development* (eds Bjørner, D. and Jones, C.B.), Prentice Hall, Chapter 12.

Brodie, M.L. and Schmidt, J.W. (1981) Final Report of the ANSI/X3/SPARC DBS-SG Relational Database Task Group. Doc. No. SPARC-81-690.

Burstall, R.M. and Goguen, J.A. (1980) The semantics of Clear, a specification language, in *Abstract Software Specifications* (ed Bjørner, D.), LNCS 86, Springer-Verlag, pp. 292–332.

Burstall, R.M. and Goguen, J.A. (1981) An informal introduction to specifications using Clear, in *The Correctness Problem in Computer Science* (eds Boyer, R. and Moore, J.), Academic Press, Chapter 4.

Chamberlin, D.D. *et al.* (1976) SEQUEL 2: A unified approach to data definition, manipulation and control. *IBM Journal of Research and Development*, **20(6)**, 560–575.

Chamberlin, D.D. *et al.* (1981) A history and evaluation of System R. *Communications of the ACM*, **24(10)**, 632–646.

Cheng, J.H. (1986) A Logic for Partial Functions. Technical Report UMCS-86-7-1, University of Manchester, Department of Computer Science.

Codd, E.F. (1970) A relational model for large shared data banks. *Communications of the ACM*, **13(6)**, 377–387.

Codd, E.F. (1972) Relational completeness of data base sublanguages, in *Data Base Systems* (ed Rustin, R.), Prentice Hall, pp. 65–98.

Codd, E.F. (1979) Extending the data base relational model to capture more meaning. *ACM Transactions on Database Systems*, **4(4)**, 397–434.

Date, C.J. (1986) *Relational Database: Selected Writings*, Addison-Wesley.

Ehrig, H., Feys, W. and Hansen, H. (1983) ACT ONE: An algebraic specification language with two levels of semantics. Bericht Nr. 83-03, Technical University of Berlin, Department of Computer Science.

Eswaran, K.P., Gray, J.N., Lorie, R.A. and Traiger, I.L. (1976) The notion of consistency and predicate locks in a database system. *Communications of the ACM*, **19(11)**, 624–633.

Fagin, R. (1981) A normal form for relational databases that is based on domains and keys. *ACM Transactions on Database Systems*, **6(3)**, 387–415.

Fagin, R. and Vardi, M.Y. (1986) The theory of data dependencies – a survey, in *Mathematics of Information Processing* (eds Anshel, M. and Gewirtz, W.), Symposia in Applied Mathematics 34, pp. 19–72.

Feijs, L.M.G. (1989) The calculus $\lambda\pi$, in *Algebraic Methods: Theory, Tools and Applications* (eds Wirsing, M. and Bergstra, J.A.), LNCS 394, Springer-Verlag, pp. 307–328.

Feijs, L.M.G. and Jonkers, H.B.M. (1992) *Formal Specification and Design*, Cambridge Tracts in Theoretical Computer Science, Cambridge University Press.

Feijs, L.M.G., Jonkers, H.B.M., Koymans, C.P.J. and Renardel de Lavalette, G.R. (1987) Formal definition of the design language COLD-K. Technical Report METEOR/t7/PRLE/7, METEOR.

Fisher, M.D. (1987) Temporal logics for abstract semantics. Technical Report UMCS-87-12-4, University of Manchester, Department of Computer Science.

Fitzgerald, J.S. and Jones, C.B. (1990) Modularizing the formal description of a database system, in *VDM '90* (eds Bjørner, D., Hoare, C.A.R. and Langmaack, H.), LNCS 428, Springer-Verlag, pp. 189–210.

Goguen, J.A. and Meseguer, J. (1987) Order-sorted algebra solves the constructor-selector, multiple representation and coercion problems, in *Proceedings Logic in Computer Science 1987*, Computer Society Press of the IEEE, pp. 18–29.

Gordon, M.J.C., Milner, R. and Wadsworth, C. (1979) *Edinburgh LCF*, LNCS 78, Springer-Verlag.

Gray, J.N. (1978) Notes on database operating systems, in *Operating Systems: An Advanced Course* (eds Bayer, R., Graham, R.M. and Seegmüller, G.), LNCS 60, Springer-Verlag, pp. 393–481.

Gray, J.N. *et al.* (1981) The recovery manager of the System R database manager. *ACM Computing Surveys*, **13(2)**, 223–242.

Gray, J.N., Lorie, R.A., Putzolu, G.R. and Traiger, I.L. (1976) Granularity of locks and degrees of consistency in a shared data base, in *Modelling in Data Base Management Systems* (ed Nijssen, G.M.), North-Holland, pp. 365–394.

Guttag, J.V. and Horning, J.J. (1986) Report on the Larch shared language. *Science of Computer Programming*, **6**, 103–134.

Haerder, T. and Reuter, A. (1983) Principles of transaction-oriented database recovery. *ACM Computing Surveys*, **15(4)**, 287–317.

Hale, R. and Moskowski, B. (1987) Parallel programming in temporal logic, in *Proceedings PARLE*, Volume II (eds de Bakker, J.W., Nijman, A.J. and Treleaven, P.C.), LNCS 259, Springer-Verlag, pp. 277–296.

Jones, C.B. (1982) The Meta-Language, in *Formal Specification and Software Development* (eds Bjørner, D. and Jones, C.B.), Prentice Hall, Chapter 2.

Jones, C.B. (1983) Specification and design of (parallel) programs, in *IFIP '83* (ed Mason, R.E.A.), North-Holland, pp. 321–332.

Jones, C.B. (1990) *Systematic Software Development Using VDM*, 2nd edn, Prentice Hall.

Jones, C.B., Jones, K.D., Lindsay, P.A. and Moore, R. (1991) *mural – A Formal Development Support System*, Springer-Verlag.

Jones, C.B. and Shaw, R.C.F. (1990) *Case Studies in Systematic Software Development*, Prentice Hall.

Jonkers, H.B.M. (1989a) Description algebra, in *Algebraic Methods: Theory, Tools and Applications* (eds Wirsing, M. and Bergstra, J.A.), LNCS 394, Springer-Verlag, pp. 283–305.

Jonkers, H.B.M. (1989b) An introduction to COLD-K, in *Algebraic Methods: Theory, Tools and Applications* (eds Wirsing, M. and Bergstra, J.A.), LNCS 394, Springer-Verlag, pp. 139–205.

Karp, C. (1964) *Languages with Expressions of Infinite Length*, North-Holland.

Keisler, H.J. (1971) *Model Theory for Infinitary Logic*, North-Holland.

Kleene, S.C. (1952) *Introduction to Metamathematics*, North-Holland.

Koymans, C.P.J. and Renardel de Lavalette, G.R. (1989) The logic MPL_ω, in *Algebraic Methods: Theory, Tools and Applications* (eds Wirsing, M. and Bergstra, J.A.), LNCS 394, Springer-Verlag, pp. 247–282.

Kung, H.T. and Papadimitriou, C.H. (1983) An optimality theory of concurrency control for databases. *Acta Informatica*, **19**, 1–11.

Lacroix, M. and Pirotte, A. (1977) Domain oriented relational languages, in *Proceedings of Third International Conference on Very Large Data Bases.*

Lichtenstein, O., Pnueli, A. and Zuck, L. (1985) The glory of the past, in *Proceedings Logics of Programs 1985* (ed Parikh, R.), LNCS 193, Springer-Verlag, pp. 196–218.

Middelburg, C.A. (1988) The VIP VDM specification language, in *VDM '88* (eds Bloomfield, R., Marshall, L. and Jones, R.), LNCS 328, Springer-Verlag, pp. 187–201.

Middelburg, C.A. (1990) *Syntax and Semantics of VVSL – A Language for Structured VDM Specifications.* PhD thesis, University of Amsterdam. Available from PTT Research, Leidschendam, The Netherlands.

Middelburg, C.A. (1992a) Modular structuring of VDM specifications in VVSL. *Formal Aspects of Computing*, **4(1)**, 13–47.

Middelburg, C.A. (1992b) Specification of interfering programs based on inter-conditions. *Software Engineering Journal*, **7(3)**, 205–217.

Middelburg, C.A. and Renardel de Lavalette, G.R. (1991) LPF and MPL_ω – a logical comparison of VDM-SL and COLD-K, in *VDM '91*, Volume 1 (eds Prehn, S. and Toetenel, W.J.), LNCS 551, Springer-Verlag, pp. 279–308.

Neuhold, E. and Olnhoff, Th. (1980) The Vienna Development Method (VDM) and its use for the specification of a relational data base management system, in *IFIP'80* (ed Lavington, S.H.), North-Holland.

Niemi, T. and Järvelin, K. (1984) A straigthforward formalization of the relational model. *ACM SIGMOD RECORD*, **14(1)**, 15–38.

Oliver, H.E. (1988) *Formal Specification Methods for Reusable Software Components*. PhD thesis, University College of Wales, Aberystwyth.

Renardel de Lavalette, G.R. (1989) COLD-K^2, the static kernel of COLD-K. Report RP/mod-89/8, SERC, Utrecht, The Netherlands.

Reynolds, J.C. (1985) Three approaches to type structure, in *Mathematical Foundations of Software Development* (eds Ehrig, H., Floyd, C., Nivat, M. and Thatcher, J.), LNCS 185, Springer-Verlag, pp. 97–138.

Rosenkrantz, D.J., Stearns, R.E. and Lewis II, P.M. (1978) System level concurrency control for distributed database systems. *ACM Transactions on Database Systems*, **3(2)**, 178–198.

Rosner, R. and Pnueli, A. (1986) A choppy logic, in *Proceedings Logic in Computer Science 1986*, Computer Society Press of the IEEE, pp. 306–313.

Sannella, D. (1984) A set-theoretic semantics for Clear. *Acta Informatica*, **21**, 443–472.

Sannella, D. and Tarlecki, A. (1985) Building specifications in an arbitrary institution, in *Proceedings Symposium on Semantics of Data Types* (eds Kahn, G., MacQueen, D.B. and Plotkin, G.), LNCS 173, Springer-Verlag, pp. 337–356.

Sannella, D. and Tarlecki, A. (1988) Towards formal development of programs from algebraic specifications: Implementations revisited. *Acta Informatica*, **25**, 233–281.

Schlageter, G. (1978) Process synchronization in database systems. *ACM Transactions on Database Systems*, **3(3)**, 248–271.

Spivey, J.M. (1988) *Understanding Z*, Cambridge Tracts in Theoretical Computer Science 3, Cambridge University Press.

Stølen, K. (1991) Development of parallel programs on shared data-structures. Technical Report UMCS-91-1-1, University of Manchester, Department of Computer Science.

Stonebraker, M. (1980) Retrospection on a database system. *ACM Transactions on Database Systems*, **5(2)**, 225–240.

Stonebraker, M., Wong, E., Kreps, P. and Held, G. (1976) The design and implementation of INGRES. *ACM Transactions on Database Systems*, **1(3)**, 189–222.

Todd, S.J.P. (1976) The Peterlee Relational Test Vehicle – a system overview. *IBM Systems Journal*, **15(4)**, 285–308.

Tompa, F.W. (1980) A practical example of the specification of abstract data types. *Acta Informatica*, **13**, 205–224.

Traiger, I.L., Gray, J.N., Galtieri, C.A. and Lindsay, B.G. (1982) Transactions and consistency in distributed database systems. *ACM Transactions on Database*

Systems, **7(3)**, 323–342.

Turner, W.S. *et al.* (1987) *System Development Methodology*, North-Holland.

Ullman, J.D. (1988) *Principles of Database and Knowledge-base Systems*, Volume I, Computer Science Press.

VIP Project Team (1987) VDM extensions: Initial report. Document VIP.T.E.4.1, VIP.

VIP Project Team (1988a) Kernel interface: Final specification. Document VIP.T.E.8.2, VIP. Available from PTT Research, Leidschendam, The Netherlands.

VIP Project Team (1988b) Man machine interface: Final specification. Document VIP.T.E.8.3, VIP. Available from PTT Research, Leidschendam, The Netherlands.

Wirsing, M. (1986) Structured algebraic specifications: A kernel language. *Theoretical Computer Science*, **42(2)**, 123–249.

Wirsing, M. (1990) Algebraic specification, in *Handbook of Theoretical Computer Science*, Volume B (ed van Leeuwen, J.), Elsevier, Chapter 13.

Wirsing, M. and Broy, M. (1989) A modular framework for specification and implementation, in *Proceedings TAPSOFT '89*, Volume 1 (eds Diaz, J. and Orejas, F.), LNCS 351, Springer-Verlag, pp. 42–73.

Zloof, M.M. (1977) Query-by-Example: A data base language. *IBM Systems Journal*, **16(4)**, 324–343.

Index